IN THE HANDS OF STRANGERS

. . . . . .

IN THE HANDS OF STRANGERS

READINGS ON FOREIGN
· · · · · · *and* · · · · ·
DOMESTIC SLAVE TRADING
· · · · · · *and the* · · · · ·
CRISIS OF THE UNION

ROBERT EDGAR CONRAD

THE PENNSYLVANIA STATE UNIVERSITY PRESS | UNIVERSITY PARK, PENNSYLVANIA

Library of Congress Cataloging-in-Publication Data

In the hands of strangers : readings on foreign and domestic slave trading and the crisis of the
Union / [edited by] Robert Edgar Conrad.
      p.   cm.
    Includes bibliographical references and index.
    ISBN 0-271-02089-X (cloth : alk. paper)
    1. Slave trade—United States—History—Sources.   2. Slave trade—History—
Sources.   3. Slavery—United States—History—Sources.   4. Slaves—United States—
Social conditions—Sources.   5. Antislavery movements—United States—History—
19th century—Sources.   6. United States—History—Civil War, 1861–1865—Causes—
Sources.   I. Conrad, Robert Edgar, 1928–

E441.I49 2001
973.04'96—dc21   00-032669

It is the policy of The Pennsylvania State University Press to use acid-free paper for the first
printing of all clothbound books. Publications on uncoated stock satisfy the minimum
requirements of American National Standard for Information Sciences—Permanence of
Paper for Printed Library Materials, ANSI Z39.48–1992.

CONTENTS

ILLUSTRATIONS

PREFACE

This book is a three-part collection of documents concerning matters of fundamental importance to the history of the United States. The emphasis throughout is on the problem of slavery as it was understood and revealed by persons of many backgrounds and opinions, which, taken together, should help students and general readers better understand American slavery and its legacies, which affect us profoundly even today. An essay intended to provide basic historical information on the topics discussed precedes each of the three parts of the book, and brief explanatory comments introduce each document or group of documents. Finally, illustrations reinforce the messages contained in some of the writings.

The documents concentrate generally on the cruelty and humiliation associated with the buying and selling of human beings, a remarkable type of behavior that has existed for millennia. What is it about slave trading, what is it about calamitous African voyages, family separations, compulsory overland migrations, the forced propagation of human beings, the kidnapping and enslavement of free people, and the legal seizure and imprisonment of free blacks and their forced sale when unable to pay the costs of their detention that make these issues so worthy of being heard and understood by a broad public? My personal answer is that the people who endured these experiences (or feared them throughout their lives) were often severely damaged, even demoralized by their experiences, and so we need to know as much as possible about such events that we may better understand ourselves and who and what we are and have been as a people.

The readings in Part One deal mainly with two separate phases of the African slave trade, that is, the legal traffic prior to January 1, 1808, when importing slaves into what is now the United States was prohibited; and the smuggling of Africans into the United States and other countries after that date, which, despite its illegality, continued at varying levels of intensity until the Civil War. Among the topics in this section are an account of the Portuguese beginnings of the Atlantic slave trade in the fifteenth century which encapsulates some of the harsher characteristics of slave trading as it existed over many centuries. Included are accounts of later voyages to

Africa to obtain slaves at coastal depots and in the domains of African chiefs, the processes that slave traders used to acquire slaves, and the extraordinary hardships endured by captives on Atlantic voyages. They include a seventeenth-century denunciation of slave trading by Dutch émigrés in Pennsylvania, a clever justification of the African slave trade by a writer who stood to prosper greatly from the business, and a slave merchant's assessments of the market for Africans in colonial Charleston. Among the topics dealt with are the alleged tolerance of illegal slave trading by the U.S. government, British and American involvement in illegal slave trading to Brazil in the 1840s, a slave revolt at sea on an American ship bound for that South American country, and finally, an account of slave trading in the African kingdom of Dahomey in the mid-nineteenth century, which along with several other documents in this section, displays the widespread and indispensable participation of Africans in the capture and sale of slaves (see especially Docs. 1.5 and 1.16).

Part Two contains readings centered on the internal slave trade of the United States, a particularly repugnant feature of slavery, and for blacks, a dreaded process that resulted in the compulsory movement of probably more than a million persons to distant locations in the American South during a period of some seventy years (from the Revolution to the Civil War). Sold by their masters and often separated forever from family and friends, shipped on coastal vessels from east-coast ports to major Gulf-coast destinations, or made to march overland, often in chains, from slave-selling to slave-buying states, or shipped down the nation's major rivers, black people endured terrible suffering and endless degradation. Perhaps most revealing in this regard is the testimony of slaves and ex-slaves on a multitude of unforgettable experiences that took place in the course of lives marked by want and hardship (see especially Docs. 2.20 and 2.22). Other topics dealt with in this section are slavery and opposition to slavery in the District of Columbia, slave auctions, the breakup of families, legal and illegal enslavement of free persons, racist oppression in the northern states, the controversial issue of slave breeding (or if preferred, slave rearing), and finally, examples of literary responses to slavery including poetry, prose, and song.

Part Three is made up of documents intended to give readers a deeper understanding of North-South conflicts and crises centered on the issue of slavery, beginning in the early years of the American Republic and leading perhaps inevitably to the shattering of the Union and the end of legal servitude in the United States. The readings in this part include such topics as late-eighteenth-century congressional debates on whether or not slavery and the African slave trade were to continue, a journalistic dispute between

North and South on the issues of legal and illegal slave trading in the two sections of the country, the movement, begun in 1816, to "colonize" free blacks in Africa (or in other faraway locations), the spread of American slavery into Texas leading to an expansionist war with Mexico, actions calculated not only to spread slavery into huge territories of the North American continent but also to win for the South increased economic and political power within the Union. They include the opinions of clergymen and others (northern and southern), who in defense of the "peculiar institution," insisted that enslavement of black people was ordained by God's commandments, by the patriarchs of the Old Testament, and even by Christ and his apostles (see Docs. 3.10 and 3.15).

Other selections in Part Three are concerned with such topics as racism, North and South, the notorious Fugitive Slave Law of 1850, which strengthened the antislavery cause, the bitter struggle between slavery and freedom in Kansas in the 1850s, the Dred Scott Decision of 1857 of Supreme Court Justice Roger Taney, who among his other errors, denied that free black people had been or could ever become citizens of the United States. They include southern attempts in the 1850s to reopen and even legalize the African slave trade, the widespread flight of runaway slaves through northern lines to freedom that began in the opening weeks of the Civil War and was a factor in the winning of that war. Other selections reveal that many white Americans, faced with the prospect of coexisting with a multitude of ex-slaves, deemed it advantageous to "colonize" them in distant parts of the world (see Docs. 3.23 and 3.24). The final selection in Part Three (Doc. 3.26) is a response to such opinions by the black abolitionist, Frederick Douglass, and so this document echoes the general theme of the book: that is, the steadfast predilection of white people, northerners and southerners alike, to *ship, transport, barter, sell, lease, drive, hire, steal, rent, transfer, exchange* and *colonize* black people. "What shall be done with the blacks?" Douglass asks: "Our answer is do nothing with them. They have been undone by your doings, and all they now ask, and really have need of at your hands, is just to let them alone." "The negro," he continues, "should have been let alone in Africa—let alone when the pirates and robbers offered him for sale in our Christian slave markets, let alone by courts, judges, politicians, legislators, and slave-drivers. Let the American people, who have thus far only kept the colored race staggering between partial philanthropy and cruel force, be induced to try what virtue there is in justice."

I wish to thank the following persons and institutions for granting me permission to publish copyrighted materials: Simon and Schuster for use of a selection from Henry Steele Commager's *Documents of American History* (my Doc. 1.3); the University of South Carolina Press for allowing me to use letters from Philip M. Hamer's *The Papers of Henry Laurens,* vols. 1 and 2 (Doc. 1.6); Garland Publishing for extracts from Joseph Story's *A Charge Delivered to the Grand Jury of the Circuit Court of the United States,* in Paul Finkelman's *The African Slave Trade and American Courts: The Pamphlet Literature,* series 5, vol. 1, pp. 21–29 (Doc. 1.12); the University of Alabama Press for use of an extract from James Benson Seller's *Slavery in Alabama* (Tuscaloosa, Alabama, 1950), pp. 152–53; Cambridge University Press for the use of a selection from Ira Berlin's *Freedom: A Documentary History of Emancipation, 1861–1867,* vol. 1, series 1: *The Destruction of Slavery,* pp. 88–90; the Colonial Williamsburg Foundation for allowing me to use a primitive painting depicting a coffle of slaves being taken from Virginia to Tennessee; the Virginia Historical Society of Richmond, Virginia, for letting me use an illustration called *The Parting "Buy Us Too,"* depicting a family separation. I also wish to thank Dennis P. Mroczkowsk and David L. Johnson of the Casemate Museum, Fort Monroe, Virginia, for a portrayal of the start of a "general strike" among slaves early in the Civil War, and Elizabeth Rumics of the Oberlin College Library for an illustration of a coffle of slaves passing the Capitol Building in Washington, D.C.; the University of North Carolina Press for allowing me to reproduce slave-trade advertisements from J. Winston Coleman's *Slavery Times in Old Kentucky;* and finally I am particularly thankful to the University of Pittsburgh Library System's Special Collections for reproducing illustrations from *Harper's Weekly* and *Harper's New Monthly Magazine.*

I also wish to thank Seymour Drescher and Douglas Egerton for their valuable advice and my wife Ursula for her many suggestions and her help with the illustrations. I am also much indebted to the University Centers for International and Latin American Studies at the University of Pittsburgh for my ongoing appointment over the years as a Center Associate, which gave me full access to university libraries and other facilities. Notable in this regard is the rich African-American Collection at Pittsburgh's Hillman Library without which my research and writing would have been far more difficult. Finally, I thank the National Endowment for the Humanities, an independent federal agency, for a grant received in 1989–91 that helped me to increase my knowledge of the history of American slavery.

The documents in this book are generally given verbatim, but minor changes were essential at times for the sake of clarity or to make archaic language more comprehensible to modern readers. Repetitious or irrelevant

Preface

material has been removed at times, and such deletions are indicated by el-lipses. Footnotes in documents are normally as they were in the originals. Notes in my own introductions and explanatory observations preceding documents generally take the form of ordinary footnotes, but clarifications or other kinds of information are at times contained within documents in brackets. More detailed notes within documents that provide comments or useful information take the form of ordinary footnotes, but are distin-guished from the authors' notes by the word "Editor."

. . . . . .

If any one thing in my experience, more than another, served to deepen my conviction of the infernal character of slavery, and to fill me with unutterable loathing of slaveholders, it was their base ingratitude to my poor old grandmother. She had served my old master faithfully from youth to old age. She had been the source of all his wealth; she had peopled his plantation with slaves; she had become a great grandmother in his service. She had rocked him in infancy, attended him in childhood, served him through life, and at his death wiped from his icy brow the cold death-sweat, and closed his eyes forever. She was nevertheless left a slave—a slave for life—a slave in the hands of strangers; and in their hands she saw her children, her grandchildren, and her great-grandchildren, divided, like so many sheep, without being gratified with the small privilege of a single word, as to their or her own destiny.

—FREDERICK DOUGLASS

The African Slave Trade, Legal and Illegal

The complex system of labor recruitment that carried Africans to the islands and mainlands of tropical America was already well established in 1619 when John Rolfe of the new colony of Jamestown recorded in his journal that "about the last of August came a Dutch man of warre that sold us twenty negars." Thus was chronicled a late and essentially minor incident in the widespread dissemination of slavery in the Western Hemisphere. Those twenty Africans mentioned by Rolfe were in fact not even the first to reach Virginia. A document from a Virginia archive, recently rediscovered, reveals that fifteen black men and seventeen black women resided in the colony as early as March of that same year, and might have been there for years.[1] Regardless, however, which group of Africans first arrived in Virginia, human servitude had existed for thousands of years and was in the midst of an era of change and expansion. Slavery had been practiced among the Hebrews, Egyptians, and Babylonians, as revealed in the first five books of the Bible; in Mycenaean Greece as early as the second millennium B.C.; and in Ancient Rome, Carthage, Byzantium, sub-Saharan Africa, the Islamic world, India and the far East, medieval and modern Europe, and the New World colonies of Portugal and Spain and would soon draw Holland, France, England, Denmark and other nations fully into its orbit.[2] By then, in fact, Portugal's huge colony of Brazil was already a genuine slave society

---

1. Johannes Menne Postma, *The Dutch in the Atlantic Slave Trade, 1600–1815* (Cambridge: Cambridge University Press, 1990), p. 12. For the earlier data on Africans in Virginia, see Karen Ordahl Kupperman, *Virginia Magazine of History and Biography* 104, no. 1 (1996): 104–6; for the actual document, see David R. Ransome, ed., *The Ferrar Papers, 1590–1790* (microfilm, 14 reels; Wakefield, Yorkshire, England, 1992), reel 1, p. 159. Of course slaves arrived in Spanish Florida even earlier.

2. For the varied and complex nature of slavery and other forms of human bondage, see M. L. Bush, ed., *Serfdom and Slavery: Studies in Legal Bondage* (London: Addison Wesley Longman, 1996);

with tens of thousands of slaves producing an abundance of sugar and other products for European markets.[3]

Slavery was the cornerstone of the economy of Ancient Rome, but the slavery that existed there for many centuries was itself based on ancient antecedents. Medieval Europe, in turn, inherited much from Rome, serving as a thousand-year-old link between the age of Roman laws and customs and the epoch of Atlantic exploration, which began in the fifteenth century and took the Portuguese into tropical Africa and the Atlantic islands of Madeira, the Azores, São Tomé, and other conquests and discoveries, all of which served as veritable stepping-stones to the islands and continents of the Americas. By the mid-fifteenth century Portuguese caravels were transporting slaves directly from Africa for delivery to home markets and for sale in other parts of Europe (see Doc. 1.1). Not long after, Europeans were scrambling ashore in the newly discovered islands and continents of the Americas where they quickly turned for forced labor to Native American populations, who themselves had been practitioners of forced labor: the Tupí, Guaraní, and other coastal tribes of Brazil, the Taínos and the Caribs of Hispaniola, Cuba, Puerto Rico and nearby continents, and the highly developed mainland peoples of Mexico and Central and South America.[4] Native populations quickly succumbed, however, to harsh conditions and the diseases brought across the Atlantic, to which they possessed little resistance. As a result, Spanish colonists and policymakers soon found pretexts for transporting Africans to the colonies to perform the hard labor that natives often seemed unable to perform on a permanent basis. This "casually committed atrocity," in the words of historian Leslie B. Rout, began with the granting of slave-trade monopolies called *asientos,* giving individuals (often favorites at court) the right to introduce a certain number of Africans into the colonies over specified periods of time.[5] Despite the fraud and incompetence associated with *asientos,* which irregularly supplied Spanish colonies until the late eighteenth century, Spain's possessions

William D. Phillips, Jr., *Slavery from Roman Times to the Early Transatlantic Trade* (Minneapolis: University of Minnesota Press, 1985); and Robin Blackburn, *The Making of New World Slavery: 1502 to the Present Day* (London: Verso, 1997).

3. See, for example, Stuart B. Schwartz, *Sugar Plantations in the Formation of Brazilian Society: Bahia, 1550–1835* (New York: Cambridge University Press, 1985).

4. For *encomiendas, repartimientos, mitas,* and other forms of compulsory labor in Spanish America, see C. H. Haring, *The Spanish Empire in America* (New York: Harcourt, Brace & World, 1963).

5. Leslie B. Rout, Jr., *The African Experience in Spanish America: 1502 to the Present Day* (New York: Cambridge University Press, 1976), pp. 22–25.

in the Americas are said to have received more than 1,500,000 Africans over three and a half centuries.[6]

In the sixteenth century, then, the Portuguese and Spaniards were the Europeans most involved with slavery, the first as procurers of slaves mainly for use in Brazil, the latter as recipients of slaves brought to the colonies through *asientos* or other means. In that century French and English adventurers such as John Hawkins, Sir Francis Drake, and Sir Walter Raleigh ventured into the trade, but Holland became the first non-Iberian country to do so on a comparatively large scale.[7] Linked dynastically to both Spain and Portugal, the Dutch had grown wise over the years in the ways of trade and enterprise in east Asia and the Americas, playing significant roles in Brazilian sugar production, capturing Portuguese possessions in Ceylon and the East Indies, setting up colonies in Surinam and fur-trading stations in the Hudson River Valley, a slave-holding possession which took on considerable importance before its conquest by the English in 1664.[8] By 1621, if not sooner, the Dutch had entered the slave trade on the African coast, and remarkably, in 1630, under the aegis of the Dutch West India Company, they seized a rich sugar-producing region in northeastern Brazil which they held for more than thirty years. This triumph was followed by the capture of Elmina, a major Portuguese slave-trading bastion on the Gold Coast, along with other "factories" or trading posts in west Africa, including for a time even the major Portuguese colony of Angola.[9]

In 1654 the Portuguese, with the help of their black and Indian retainers, drove the Dutch from Brazil after a prolonged military struggle. But Holland possessed other valuable colonies in the Caribbean and northern South America—notably Curaçao, St. Eustatius in the Leeward islands, and Surinam, a sugar-producing colony worked by slaves—all of which were used as depots for a traffic in African slaves largely intended for Spanish America.[10] Applying their considerable experience in the sugar industry, the Dutch brought both slaves and technical know-how to the Caribbean, contributing significantly

6. Philip D. Curtin, *The Atlantic Slave Trade, A Census* (Madison: University of Wisconsin Press, 1969), p. 268.

7. Blackburn, *The Making of New World Slavery*, pp. 139–42, 219–20.

8. Edgar J. McManus, *A History of Negro Slavery in New York* (Syracuse: Syracuse University Press, 1966), pp. 1–22.

9. C. R. Boxer, *The Dutch in Brazil, 1624–1654* (Oxford: Clarendon Press, 1957), pp. 5, 20–21, 84; Postma, *The Dutch in the Atlantic Slave Trade*, pp. 56–78; P. C. Emmer, "The Dutch and the Making of the Second Atlantic System," in Barbara L. Solow, ed., *Slavery and the Rise of the Atlantic System* (Cambridge: Cambridge University Press, 1991), p. 83; James A. Rawley, *The Transatlantic Slave Trade* (New York: W. W. Norton, 1981), pp. 32–33.

10. Postma, *The Dutch in the Atlantic Slave Trade*, pp. 168–200.

to a transformation of the precariously held British and French colonies. In 1645, for example, 18,300 white male property owners inhabited the island of Barbados along with 5,680 slaves, and the principal crop was tobacco. Thirty-five years later that same island contained 37,000 slaves, most of them Africans, and the tobacco farms had given way to 350 sugar estates producing 8,000 tons of sugar per year.[11] In that same period Britain and France both seriously entered the trade to supply their possessions with workers, which in England's case, of course, included such colonies as Virginia, Maryland, North and South Carolina, and Georgia after 1750.[12] Thus it may be said that through the agency of the Portuguese, the Dutch, and the British, the contagion of slavery found its way to the British colonies of North America, which in time would become the largest concentration of slaves in the Americas.

How many slaves entered what is now the United States? In his pioneering study of the volume of the international slave trade, Philip Curtin estimated that 1,401,300 slaves were imported into British Caribbean possessions over two centuries, and that 399,000 slaves entered what is now the United States. However, a group of historians, including Curtin himself, has recently estimated the number of Africans brought into what is now the United States at more than 600,000 during the century and a half from 1620 to 1870, including 51,000 Africans allegedly introduced illegally after abolition of the traffic in 1808.[13] Finally another historian, David Richardson, recently put the number of slaves shipped from Africa to all the Americas from 1500 to 1867 at perhaps as many as twelve million persons, many of whom died at sea.[14] The exact number, of course, will never be known.

Some comments on the documents in this section may be helpful. Document 1.1 is a classic account of Portuguese raids carried out in the fifteenth century against inhabitants of several small islands off Africa's northwest coast (probably modern Mauritania), an event which seems to epitomize the nature of the slave trade over the centuries. Documents 1.2, 1.5, and 1.11

---

11. Herbert S. Klein, *African Slavery in Latin America and the Caribbean* (New York: Oxford University Press, 1986), pp. 45–53; Blackburn, *The Making of New World Slavery,* p. 230.

12. For the British ban on importation of slaves into Georgia and the later beginnings of slavery in that colony, see Harold D. Wax, "Georgia and the Negro before the American Revolution," *The Georgia Historical Quarterly* 51, no. 1 (March 1967): 63–77.

13. Curtin, *The Atlantic Slave Trade,* p. 268; Randall M. Miller and John David Smith, *Dictionary of Afro-American Slavery* (Westport, Conn.: Praeger, 1997), p. 678. Relatively few slaves entered what is now the United States because on the whole, a relatively higher standard of living there enabled more slaves to survive and reproduce. This demographic anomaly was all but unique in the Americas.

14. "Volume of Trade," in Seymour Drescher and Stanley L. Engerman, eds., *A Historical Guide to World Slavery* (New York: Oxford University Press, 1998), pp. 385–89.

are all personal accounts by slave traders of their experiences in the traffic, revealing its egregious effects upon both slaves and crews. Document 1.3 is a protest against "traffic in men-body" (the buying and selling of human beings) submitted by a group of Mennonites of Germantown, Pennsylvania, in 1688. Document 1.4 is a London merchant's detailed instructions to a subordinate slave trader concerning a prospective voyage to Guinea, conveying a considerable body of information about how slaves and other African "commodities" might best be acquired. The sixth set of documents (1.6) consists of letters from a slave-trading entrepreneur of Charleston, South Carolina, informing his clients of regional market conditions for slaves, and Document 1.7 is a highly critical account of British slave-trading practices in a period of increasing antislavery sentiment in Great Britain. Document 1.8 includes descriptions of slaves lodged aboard a slave ship and Document 1.9 contains news items from the *Charleston Courier* complaining of deceased Africans—men and women—found floating in Charleston harbor, evidently thrown into the bay to avoid the costs of burial. Document 1.10 contains denunciations of the brutal but legal African slave trade to South Carolina in its final years (1804–7). Document 1.11 is an autobiographical account of a slave trader allegedly involved in the Atlantic traffic for fifty years during which he was active in Africa, Brazil, Cuba, the United States, and the Bay Islands near the Honduran coast, among other places. Documents 1.12 and 1.13 are strongly worded criticisms by a prominent American judge and a well-known abolitionist of the illegal African slave trade to the United States after 1808 and the alleged reluctance of the American government to suppress that trade. The items in Document 1.14 reveal an extensive involvement of both Britishers and American citizens in the exceptionally large Brazilian slave trade of the 1840s, and Document 1.15 contains a British sailor's sworn testimony about a violent slave revolt at sea on an American ship, and the harsh punishment inflicted upon the rebels by members of the Brazilian crew. Finally, Document 1.16 is an account of slave trading in the African kingdom of Dahomey and an unsuccessful British effort to persuade King Ghezo of that country to replace the traffic in human beings with such agricultural commodities as cotton, coffee, and palm oil.

1.1. The Beginnings of the Portuguese-African Slave Trade in the Fifteenth Century

The following excerpt from the chronicle of African discovery and conquest completed in the mid-fifteenth century by the Portuguese historian,

Gomes Eannes de Azurara, is probably the first and certainly one of the best descriptions of the onset of the Portuguese-African slave trade in the fifteenth century, which led less than two centuries later to the beginnings of African slavery in the newly established British colonies of North America. Azurara's account reveals that while early Portuguese slave traders were motivated in part by a desire to serve God and the kingdom of Portugal, their alleged higher intentions did not prevent them from using unscrupulous methods in the capture of Africans, or from later treating them with the brutality that became characteristic of the international and internal slave trades of many countries, including the United States. As Azurara writes, for example, the captured "Moors" reached Portugal in poor condition, and little regard was shown for their personal feelings when, in the presence of Prince Henry the Navigator, they were divided among their new owners and made to go their separate ways. Similarly, although the Prince is described as pleased by the slaves' supposed opportunity to save their souls in a Christian land, his quick division of the forty-six persons who made up his royal share appears to have been carried out with little regard for any hope the newly enslaved people might have had to remain with friends and loved ones, as would so often be the case centuries later in the United States and other New World countries.

SOURCE: *Chronica do descobrimento e conquista de Guiné, escrita por mandada de Elrei D. Affonso V, sob a direcção scientifica e segundo as instrucções do Illustre D. Henrique pelo chronista Gomes Eannes de Azurara* (Paris: J. P. Aillaud, 1841), pp. 103–35.

Since Prince [Henry the Navigator] was normally to be found in the Kingdom of the Algarve after his return from Tangier because of the town he was having built there, and since the prisoners whom [his captains] brought back were landed at Lagos [the town where Henry established his headquarters], it was the people of this place who first persuaded the Prince to grant them permission to go to that land from which the Moorish captives came. . . .

The most important captain was Lançarote, and the second Gil Eannes, who, as we have written, was the first to round Cape Bojador. . . . Setting out on their voyage, they arrived at the Island of Herons [Ilha das Garças] on the Eve of Corpus Christi, where they rested for a time, living mainly from the many young birds they found there, since it was the breeding season. . . .

And so these two captains [Martim Vicente and Gil Vasquez] made preparations, and they took five boats manned by thirty men, six in each boat, and set out at about sunset. Rowing the entire night, they arrived about daybreak at the island they were looking for. And when they recognized it by signs the Moors had mentioned, they rowed for a while close to the shore until, as it was getting light, they reached a Moorish village near the beach where all the island's inhabitants were gathered together. Seeing this, our men stopped for a time to discuss what they should do. . . . And after giving their opinions, they looked toward the village where they saw that the Moors, with their women and children, were leaving their houses as fast as they could, for they had seen their enemies. The latter, crying the names of St. James, St. George, and Portugal, attacked them, killing and seizing as many as they could. There you could have seen mothers forsaking their children, husbands abandoning their wives, each person trying to escape as best he could. And some drowned themselves in the water; others tried to hide in their huts; others, hoping they would escape, hid their children among the sea grasses where they were later discovered. And in the end our Lord God, who rewards every good deed, decided that, for their labors undertaken in His service, they should gain a victory over their enemies on that day, and a reward and payment for all their efforts and expenses. For on that day they captured 165 [Moors], including men, women, and children, not counting those who died or were killed. When the battle was over they praised God for the great favor He had shown them, in wishing to grant them such a victory, and with so little harm to themselves. After their captives had been put in their boats, with others securely tied up on land, since the boats were small and could not hold so many people, they ordered a man to go as far as he could along the coast to see if he could sight the caravels. He set out at once, and, going more than a league from where the others were waiting, he saw the caravels arriving, because, as he had promised, Lançarote had sailed at dawn.

And when Lançarote, with those squires and highborn men who accompanied him, heard of the good fortune which God had granted to that handful of men who had gone to the island, and saw that they had accomplished such a great deal, it pleasing God to bring the affair to such a conclusion, they were all very happy, praising God for wishing to aid those few Christians in this manner. . . .

On the next day, which was a Friday, they prepared their boats, since the caravels had to remain where they were, and loaded into them all the supplies needed for two days only, since they did not intend to stay away from their ships any longer than that. Some thirty men departed in the boats, namely Lançarote and the other captains of the caravels, and with them squires and highborn men who were there. And they took with them two of those Moors whom they had captured, because they had told them that on the island of Tiger, which was five leagues distant, there was a Moorish village of about 150 persons. And as soon as it was morning, they set out, all very devoutly commending themselves to God, and asking His help in guiding them so that He might be served and His Holy Catholic Faith exalted. And they rowed until they reached the said island of Tiger; and as soon as they had leaped upon the shore the Moor who was with them led them to a village, where all the Moors, or at least most of those on the island, had earlier assembled . . .; and Lançarote, with fourteen or fifteen men, went toward the place where the Moor led them. And walking half a league . . . they saw nine Moors, both men and women, with ten or twelve asses loaded with turtles, who hoped to cross over to the island of Tiger, which would be a league from there, it being possible to cross from one island to the other on foot. And as soon as they saw them, they pursued them, and, offering no effective defense, they were all captured except one, who fled to inform the others in the village. And as soon as they had captured them, they sent them to the place where Gil Eannes was, Lançarote ordering him to place a guard over the Moors, and then to set out after them, using all the men he had, because he believed that they would find someone to fight with.

And as soon as the captives reached them, they bound them securely and put them in the boats, and leaving one man with them, they set out at once behind Lançarote, following constantly in his footsteps until they reached the place where Lançarote and his followers were. After capturing the Moors whom they had sent to the boats, they followed the Moors to a village that its inhabitants had abandoned, having been warned by the Moor who had escaped when the others were taken prisoner.

And then they saw all the people of the island on a smaller island where they had gone in their canoes; and the Christians could not reach them except by swimming, nor did they dare to retreat for fear of encouraging their enemies, who were much more numerous than they were. And thus they remained until all the other men had reached them; and seeing that even when they were all together they could not do them any harm, because of the water that lay between them, they decided to return to their boats which were a good two leagues away.

And, upon their return, they entered the village and searched everything to see if they might find something in the houses. And, while searching, they found seven or eight Moorish women, whom they took with them, thanking God for their good fortune, which they had received through His grace; and thus they returned to their boats, which they reached at about sunset, and they rested and enjoyed themselves that night like men who had toiled hard throughout the day. . . .

The needs of the night forced them to spend it mainly in sleep, but their minds were so fixed upon the tasks that lay before them that they could think of nothing else. And so they discussed what they would do the next day, and, after hearing many arguments they decided to go in their boats to attack the settlement before daybreak. . . . Having reached this decision, they set out in the dark, rowing their boats along the shore. And as the sun began to rise, they landed and attacked the village, but found no one in it, because the Moors, having seen their enemies leaving, had returned to the village, but, not wanting to sleep in it, they had gone to stay a league away near a crossing point by which they went over to Tiger. And when the Christians recognized that they could find nothing in the village, they returned to their boats and coasted along that island on the other side of Tiger, and they sent fifteen men overland to see if they could find any Moors or any trace of them. And on their way they saw the Moors fleeing as fast as they could, for they had already observed them, and then all our men leaped out on land and began to pursue them. They were not able to reach the men, but they took seventeen or eighteen of the women and small children who could not run so fast. And one of the boats, in which Joham Bernaldez was traveling, one of the smallest, went along the coast of the island; and the men in the boat saw some twenty canoes which were moving toward Tiger, in which Moors of both sexes were traveling, both adults and children, four or five in each boat. And they were very pleased when they first saw this, but later greatly saddened. Their pleasure came from seeing the profit and honor that lay before them, which was their reason for going there; their sadness came when they recognized that their boat was so small that they could put only a very few aboard. And with their few oars, they pursued them as well as they could, until they were among the canoes; and, stirred by pity, even though the people in the canoes were heathens, they wished to kill very few of them. However, there is no reason not to believe that many of them, who in their terror abandoned the boats, did not perish in the sea.

And some of them were on the left and some on the right, and, going in among them, they selected the smallest, because this way they could load more into their boats, of which they took fourteen, so that those who were captured in those days, not including some who died, totaled forty-eight. . . .

The caravels arrived at Lagos, from where they had set out, enjoying fine weather on the voyage, since fortune was no less generous in the mild-ness of the weather than it had been to them in the taking of their prizes. And from Lagos the news reached the Prince. . . . And the next day, Lançarote, as the man who had the main responsibility, said to the Prince: "Sir! Your Grace knows full well that you must accept the fifth of these Moors, and of everything which we took in that land, where you sent us in the service of God and yourself. And now these Moors, because of the long time we have been at sea, and because of the obvious sorrow in their hearts at finding themselves far from their birthplace and held in captivity, with-out possessing any knowledge of what their future will be; as well as be-cause they are not used to sailing on ships; for all these reasons they are in a rather poor condition and sickly; and so it seems to me that it will be useful for you to order them removed from the caravels in the morning and taken to that field that lies outside the city gate, and there divided up into five parts, according to custom, and that Your Grace should go there and select one of the parts which best suits you." The Prince said that he was well pleased, and very early the next day Lançarote ordered the masters of the caravels to bring them outside and to take them to that field, where they were to be divided up, as stated before; but, before doing anything else, they took the best of the Moors as an offering to the church of that place, and another little one who later became a friar of St. Francis they sent to São Vicente do Cabo, where he always lived as a Catholic Christian, with-out any knowledge or feeling for any other law but the holy and true doc-trine, in which all Christians await our salvation. And the Moors of that conquest numbered 235.

On the next day . . . the seamen began to prepare their boats very early in the morning, because of the heat, and to bring out those captives so that they could be transferred as ordered. And the latter, placed together in that field, were a marvelous thing to behold, because among them there were some who were reasonably white, handsome and genteel; others not so white, who were like mulattoes; others as black as Ethiopians, so deformed both in their faces and bodies, that it seemed to those who guarded them that they were gazing upon images of the lowest hemisphere. But what human heart, no matter how hard, would not be stabbed by pious feelings when gazing upon such a company of people? For some had their heads held low and their faces bathed in tears, as they looked upon one another. Others were moaning most bitterly, gazing toward heaven, fixing their eyes upon it, as if they were asking for help from the father of nature. Others struck their faces with the palms of their hands, throwing themselves pros-trate upon the ground; others performed their lamentations in the form of a chant, according to the custom of their country, and, although our people could not understand the words of their language, they were fully appropriate to the level of their sorrow. But to increase their suffering even more, those responsible for dividing them up arrived on the scene and began to separate one from another, in order to make an equal division of the fifths; from which arose the need to separate children from their parents, wives from their husbands, and brothers from their brothers. Neither friendship nor kinship was respected, but instead each one fell where fortune placed him! Oh powerful destiny, doing and undoing with your turning wheels, arranging the things of this world as you please! do you even disclose to those miserable people some knowledge of what is to become of them, so that they may receive some consolation in the midst of their tremendous sorrow? And you who labor so hard to divide them up, look with pity upon so much misery, and see how they cling to each other, so that you can hardly separate them! Who could accomplish that division without the greatest toil; because as soon as they had put the children in one place, seeing their parents in another, they rose up energetically and went over to them; mothers clasped their other children in their arms, and threw themselves face down upon the ground with them, receiving blows with little regard for their own flesh, if only they might not be parted from them!

And so with great effort they finished the dividing up, because, aside from the trouble they had with the captives, the field was quite full of people, both from the town and from the surrounding villages and districts, who for that day were taking time off from their work, which was the source of their earnings, for the sole purpose of observing this novelty. And seeing these things, while some wept, others took part in the separating, and they made such a commotion that they greatly confused those who were in charge of dividing them up.

The Prince was there mounted upon a powerful horse, accompanied by his retinue, distributing his favors, like a man who wished to derive little material advantage from his share; for of the forty-six souls who belonged to his fifth, he quickly divided them up among the rest, since his main source of wealth lay in his own purpose; for he reflected with great pleasure upon the salvation of those souls that before were lost.

1.2. The Disastrous Voyage of the *Hannibal* (1693–1694)

After their first highly successful shipment of slaves from west Africa to Portugal in 1444 (see Doc. 1.1), the Portuguese continued to explore the

African coast, reaching Guinea in 1448, passing the mouth of the Niger by 1471, and constructing the first of many forts in Africa. With this early start and the sanction of the Catholic Church, Portugal dominated much of the slave trade for nearly two hundred years, continuing to supply slaves to Brazil until the 1850s. Early in the seventeenth century, however, the Dutch emerged as ambitious empire builders in Africa, the East Indies, Surinam, and briefly in Brazil, and major competitors to the Portuguese in the slave trade. In the sixteenth century the English also experimented with slave trading, though with little success. With the onset, however, of a sugar industry in Barbados and growing labor demands in North America, the British Royal African Company, a joint stock corporation, was created in 1672 to monopolize the traffic. This company is said to have built seventeen forts or factories in Africa, dispatched 500 ships to that continent, and bought 125,000 slaves in less than fifty years. Of these, one in five allegedly died on voyages to the West Indies, and 100,000 were sold to West Indian planters.[15]

The following is an abbreviated account of a Company voyage written by Thomas Phillips, commander of the ship *Hannibal,* one of a fleet of six ships that sailed in a convoy for the African coast. Phillips describes, among other details, a "factory" at Whydah where slaves were purchased, the bargaining for slaves with the king of Whydah and other sellers, the physical inspections of potential purchases, slave branding, the feeding process at sea, and procedures intended to prevent slave revolts and to reduce mortality. Phillips ended his narrative with a report of disastrous epidemics at sea, notably the "white flux" and small pox, which on a voyage of a little more than two months killed fourteen crewmen and 320 slaves, among 692 put aboard ship, a loss of over forty-six percent.

SOURCE: Elizabeth Donnan, ed., *Documents Illustrative of the History of the Slave Trade to America* (Washington, D.C.: Carnegie Institution of Washington, 1930), vol. 1, *1441–1700,* pp. 392–93, 396–403, 406–10.

Being entr'd into [the service of the Royal African Company] on a trading voyage to Guiney, for elephants teeth, gold, and Negro slaves; and having the needful cargoes on board, wherewith to purchase them, as well as supplies of merchandize, stores, etc., for the company's castles and factories; my business being compleated at London, I took boat for Gravesend the fifth of September in the evening and got on board about eleven at night. . . .

15. See Blackburn, *The Making of New World Slavery,* pp. 250–56.

May the 19th. Steering along shore within three leagues, with fine easy gale, we spy'd a canoe making off towards us, whereupon we lay by and staid for her; when she came aboard the master of her brought in three women and four children to sell, but they ask'd very dear for them, and they were almost dead for want of victuals, looking like meer skeletons, and so weak that they could not stand, so that they were not worth buying; he promis'd to procure us 2 or 300 slaves if we would anchor, come ashore, and stay three or four days, but judging what the others might be, by the sample he brought us, and being loth to venture ashore upon his bare word, where we did not use to trade, and had no factory, we sent him away, and pursu'd our voyage; besides that we were upon the Alampo coast, which negroes are esteem'd the worst and most washy of any that are brought to the West-Indies, and yield the least price; why I know not, for they seem as well limb'd and lusty as any other negroes, and the only difference I perceiv'd in them, was, that they are not so black as the others, and are all circumcis'd, which no negroes else upon the whole coast (as I observ'd) are: The negroes most in demand at Barbadoes, are the gold coast, or, as they call them, Cormantines, which will yield 3 or 4£ a head more than the Whidaws, or, as they call them, Papa [Popo] negroes; but these are preferred before the Alampo, which are counted the worst of all. . . .

May the 21st. This morning I went ashore at Whidaw, accompany'd by my doctor and purser, Mr. Clay, the present Capt. of the *East-India Merchant,* his doctor and purser, and about a dozen of our seamen for our guard, arm'd, in order here to reside till we could purchase 1300 negro slaves, which was the number we both wanted, to compleat 700 for the *Hannibal,* and 650 for the *East-India Merchant,* according to our agreement in our charter-parties with the royal African company; in procuring which quantity of slaves we spent about nine weeks. . . .

Our factory built by Capt. Sir John Wiburne's brother, stands low near the marshes, which renders it a very unhealthy place to live in; the white men the African company send there, seldom returning to tell their tale: 'tis compass'd round with a mud-wall, about six foot high, and on the south-side is the gate; within is a large yard, a mud thatch'd house, where the factor lives, with the white men; also a store-house, a trunk [storage prison] for slaves, and a place where they bury their dead white men, call'd very improperly, the hog-yard; there is also a good forge, and some other small houses. . . . And here I must observe that the rainy season begins about the middle of May, and ends the beginning of August, in which space it was my misfortune to be there, which created sicknesses among my negroes aboard, it being noted for the most malignant season by the blacks themselves, who while the rain lasts will hardly be prevail'd upon to stir out of their huts. . . .

The factory prov'd beneficial to us in another kind; for after we had procur'd a parcel of slaves, and sent them down to the sea-side to be carry'd off, it sometimes proved bad weather, and so great a sea, that the canoes could not come ashore to fetch them, so that they returned to the factory, where they were secured and provided for till good weather presented, and then were near to embrace the opportunity, we sometimes shipping off a hundred of both sexes at a time.

The factor, Mr. Peirson, was a brisk man, and had good interest with the king, and credit with the subjects, who knowing their tempers, which is very dastard, had good skill in treating them both civil and rough, as occasion requir'd; most of his slaves belonging to the factory, being gold coast negroes, who are very bold, brave, and sensible, ten of which would beat the best forty men the king of Whidaw had in his kingdom; besides their true love, respect and fidelity to their master, for whose interest or person they will most freely expose their own lives. . . .

As soon as the king understood of our landing, he sent two of his cappasheirs, or noblemen ["caboceer": from Portuguese, *caboceiro,* a headman of a West African village or tribe] to compliment us at our factory, where we design'd to continue, that night, and pay our devoirs to his majesty next day, which we signify'd to them, and they, by a foot-express, to their monarch; whereupon he sent two more of his grandees to invite us there that night, saying he waited for us, and that all former captains used to attend him the first night: whereupon being unwilling to infringe the custom, or give his majesty any offence, we took our hammocks, and Mr. Peirson, myself, Capt. Clay, our surgeons, pursers, and about 12 men, arm'd for our guard, were carry'd to the king's town, which contains about 50 houses. . . .

We returned him thanks by his interpreter, and assur'd him how great affection our masters, the royal African company of England, bore to him, for his civility and fair and just dealings with their captains; and that notwithstanding there were many other places, more plenty of negro slaves that begg'd their custom, yet they had rejected all the advantageous offers made them out of their good will to him, and therefore had sent us to trade with him, to supply his country with necessaries, and that we hop'd he would endeavour to continue their favour by his kind usage and fair dealing with us in our trade, that we may have our slaves with all expedition, which was the making of our voyage; that he would oblige his cappasheirs to do us justice, and not impose upon us in their prices; all which we should faithfully relate to our masters, the royal African company, when we came to England. He answer'd that the African company was a very good brave man; that he lov'd him; that we should be fairly dealt with, and not impos'd upon. But he did not prove as good as his word; nor indeed (tho' his cappasheirs shew him so much respect) dare he do any thing but what they please. . . . [S]o after having examin'd us about our cargoe, what sort of goods we had, and what quantity of slaves we wanted, etc., we took our leaves, and return'd to the factory, having promised to come in the morning to make our palavera, or agreement with him about prices, how much of each of our goods for a slave. According to promise we attended his majesty with samples of our goods, and made our agreement about the prices, tho' not without difficulty; he and his cappasheirs exacted very high. . . . [T]hen the bell was order'd to go about to give notice to all people to bring their slaves to the trunk to sell us: this bell is a hollow piece of iron in shape of a sugar loaf, the cavity of which could contain about 50 lb. of cowries [shells used as currency]: this a man carry'd about and beat with a stick, which made a small dead sound. . . .

Capt. Clay and I had agreed to go to the trunk to buy the slaves by turns, each his day, that we might have no distraction or disagreement in our trade, which often happens when there are here more ships than one, and the commanders can't set their horses together, and go hand in hand in their traffick, whereby they have a check upon the blacks, whereas their disagreements create animosities, underminings, and out-bidding each other, whereby they enhance the prices to their general loss and detriment, the blacks well knowing how to make the best use of such opportunities, and as we found make it their business, and endeavour to create and foment misunderstandings and jealousies between commanders, it turning to their great account in the disposal of their slaves.

When we were at the trunk, the king's slaves, if he had any, were the first offer'd to sale, which the cappasheirs would be very urgent with us to buy, and would in a manner force us to it ere they would shew us any other, saying they were the Reys Cosa [the king's property], and we must not refuse them, tho' as I observed they were generally the worst slaves in the trunk, and we paid more for them than any others, which we could not remedy, it being one of his majesty's prerogatives: then the cappasheirs each brought out his slaves according to his degree and quality, the greatest first, etc. and our surgeon examin'd them well in all kinds, to see that they were sound wind and limb, making them jump, stretch out their arms swiftly, looking in their mouths to judge of their age; for the cappasheirs are so cunning, that they shave them all close before we see them, so that let them be never so old we can see no grey hairs in their heads or beards; and then having liquor'd them well and sleek with palm oil, 'tis no easy matter to know an old one from a middle-aged one, but by the teeths decay; but our greatest care of all is to buy none that are pox'd, lest they should infect the rest aboard. . . .

When we had selected from the rest such as we liked, we agreed on what goods to pay for them, the prices being already stated before the king, how much of each sort of merchandize we were to give for a man, woman, and child, which gave us much ease, and saved abundance of disputes and wranglings, and gave the owner a note, signifying our agreement of the sorts of goods; upon delivery of which the next day he receive'd them; then we mark'd the slaves we had bought in the breast, or shoulder, with a hot iron, having the letter of the ship's name on it, the place being before anointed with a little palm oil, which caus'd but little pain, the mark being usually well in four or five days, appearing very plain and white after.

When we had purchased to the number of 50 or 60 we would send them aboard, there being a cappasheir, intitled the captain of the slaves, whose care it was to secure them to the water-side, and see them all off; and if in carrying to the marine any were lost, he was bound to make them good, to us, the captain of the trunk being oblig'd to do the like, if any ran away while under his care, for after we buy them we give him charge of them all till the captain of the slaves comes to carry them away: These are two officers appointed by the king for this purpose, to each of which every ship pays the value of a slave in what goods they like best for their trouble, when they have done trading; and indeed they discharg'd their duty to us very faithfully, we not having lost one slave thro' their neglect in 1300 we bought here. . . .

When our slaves were come to the seaside, our canoes were ready to carry them off to the longboat, if the sea permitted, and she convey'd them aboard ship, where the men were all put in irons, two of them shackled together, to prevent their mutiny, or swimming ashore.

The negroes are so wilful and loth to leave their own country that they often leap'd out of the canoes, boat and ship, into the sea, and kept under water till they were drowned, to avoid being taken up and saved by our boats, which pursued them; they having a more dreadful apprehension of Barbadoes than we can have of hell, tho' in reality they live much better there than in their own country: but home is home, etc.: we have likewise seen divers of them eaten by the sharks, of which a prodigious number kept about the ships in this place, and I have been told will follow her hence to Barbadoes, for the dead negroes that are thrown over-board in the passage. . . . We had about 12 negroes did wilfully drown themselves, and others starv'd themselves to death; for tis their belief that when they die they return home to their own country and friends again.

I have been inform'd that some commanders cut off the legs and arms of the most wilful, to terrify the rest, for they believe if they lose a member, they cannot return home again: I was advis'd by some of my officers to do the same, but I could not be perswaded to entertain the least thought of it, much less put in practice such barbarity and cruelty to poor creatures, who, excepting their want of christianity and true religion (their misfortune more than fault) are as much the works of God's hands, and no doubt as dear to him as ourselves; nor can I imagine why they should be despis'd for their colour, being what they cannot help, and the effect of the climate it has pleas'd God to appoint them. I can't think there is any intrinsick value in one colour more than another, nor that white is better than black, only we think so because we are so, and are prone to judge favourable in our own case, as well as the blacks, who in odium of the colour, say, the devil is white, and so paint him. . . .

When our slaves are aboard we shackle the men two and two, while we lie in port, and in sight of their own country, for 'tis then they attempt to make their escape, and mutiny; to prevent which we always keep centinels upon the hatchways, and have a chest full of small arms, ready loaden and prim'd, constantly lying at hand upon the quarter-deck, together with some granada shells; and two of our quarter-deck guns, pointing on the deck thence, and two more out of the steerage, the door of which is always kept shut, and well barr'd; they are fed twice a day, at 10 in the morning, and 4 in the evening, which is the time they are aptest to mutiny, being all upon deck; therefore all that time, what of our men are not employ'd in distributing their victuals to them, and settling them, stand to their arms; and some with lighted matches at the great guns that yaun upon them, loaden with partridge, till they have done and gone down to their kennels between decks. Their chief diet is call'd dabbadabb, being Indian corn ground as small as oat-meal, in iron mills. which we carry for that purpose; and after mix'd with water, and boiled well in a large copper furnace, till 'tis as thick as a pudding, about a peckful of which in vessels, call'd crews, is allow'd to 10 men, with a little salt, malagetta, and palm oil, to relish; they are divided into messes of ten each for the easier and better order in serving them: Three days a week they have horse-beans boil'd for their dinner and supper, great quantities of which the African company do send aboard us for that purpose; these beans the negroes extremely love and desire, beating their breast, eating them, and crying Pram! Pram! which is Very good! they are indeed the best diet for them, having a binding quality, and consequently good to prevent the flux, which is the inveterate distemper that most affects them, and ruins our voyages by their mortality: The men are all fed upon the main deck and forecastle, that we may have them all under command of our arms from the quarter-deck, in case of any disturbance; the women eat upon the quarter-deck with us, and the boys and girls upon the poop; after they are once divided into messes, and appointed their places, they will readily run there in good order of themselves afterwards; when they have eaten their victuals clean up, (which we force them to do for to thrive the better) they are order'd down between decks, and every one as he passes has a pint of water to drink after his meat, which is serv'd them by the cooper out of a large tub. . . .

When we come to sea we let them all out of irons, they never attempting then to rebel, considering that should they kill or master us, they could not tell how to manage the ship, or must trust us, who would carry them where we pleas'd; therefore the only danger is while we are in sight of their own country, which they are loth to part with; but once out of sight out of mind: I never heard that they mutiny'd in any ships of consequence, that had a good number of men, and the least care; but in small tools where they had but few men, and those negligent or drunk, then they surpriz'd and butcher'd them, cut the cables, and let the vessel drive ashore, and every one shift for himself. . . . We often at sea in the evenings would let the slaves come up into the sun to air themselves, and make them jump and dance for an hour or two to our bag-pipes, harp, and fiddle, by which exercise to preserve them in health; but notwithstanding all our endeavour, 'twas my hard fortune to have great sickness and mortality among them. . . .

We spent in our passage from St. Thomas [São Thomé] to Barbadoes two months eleven days, from the 25th of August to the 4th of November following: in which time there happen'd much sickness and mortality among my poor men and negroes, that of the first we buried 14, and of the last 320, which was a great detriment to our voyage, the Royal African Company losing ten pounds by every slave that died, and the owners of the ship ten pounds ten shillings, being the freight agreed on to be paid them by the charter-party for every negroe deliver'd alive ashore to the African company's agents at Barbadoes; whereby the loss in all amounted to near 6560 pounds sterling. The distemper which my men as well as the blacks mostly die of, was the white flux, which was so violent and inveterate, that no medicine would in the least check it; so that when any of our men were seiz'd with it, we esteem'd him a dead man, as he generally proved. I cannot imagine what should cause it in them so suddenly, they being free from it till about a week after we left the island of St. Thomas. And next to the malignity of the climate, I can attribute it to nothing else but the unpurg'd black sugar, and raw unwholesome rum they bought there, of which they drank in punch to great excess, and which it was not in my power to hinder, having chastis'd several of them, and flung over-board what rum and sugar I could find. . . .

The negroes are so incident to the small-pox, that few ships that carry them escape without it, and sometimes it makes vast havock and destruction among them: but tho' we had 100 at a time sick of it, and that it went thro' the ship, yet we lost not above a dozen by it. All the assistance we gave the diseased was only as much water as they desir'd to drink, and some palm-oil to anoint their sores, and they would generally recover without any other helps but what kind nature gave them.

One thing is very surprizing in this distemper among the blacks, that tho' it immediately infects those of their own colour, yet it will never seize a white man; for I had several white men and boys aboard that had never had that distemper, and were constantly among the blacks that were sick of it, yet none of them in the least catch'd it, tho' it be the very same malady in its effects, as well as symptoms, among the blacks, as among us in England, beginning with the pain in the head, back, shivering, vomiting, fever, etc. But what the small-pox spar'd, the flux swept off, to our great regret, after all our pains and care to give them their messes in due order and season, keeping their lodgings as clean and sweet as possible, and enduring so much misery and stench so long among a parcel of creatures nastier than swine; and after all our expectations to be defeated by their mortality. No gold-finders can endure so much noisome slavery, as they do who carry negroes; for those have some respite and satisfaction, but we endure twice the misery; and yet by their mortality our voyages are ruin'd, and we pine and fret our selves to death, to think that we should undergo so much misery, and take so much pains to so little purpose.

I deliver'd alive at Barbadoes to the company's factor 372, which being sold, came out at about nineteen pounds per head one with another. . . .

1.3. "That Men Should Be Handelled So in Pennsylvania." An Early Mennonite Protest Against Slavery and the Slave Trade (1688)

About five years before the sailing of the *Hannibal* (see Doc. 1.2) and more than seventy years after the first known arrival of black slaves in the English colonies of North America, a group of Mennonites of Germantown, Pennsylvania, prepared a protest against slavery at one of their monthly meetings. This message, signed by four members of the Mennonite community and said to be the first known statement of its kind in the colonies, was composed in a style suggesting that the author wrote it in his second language, his first being almost certainly Dutch. Though he and his fellow Mennonites might have learned a good deal about slave trading in their homeland before journeying to Pennsylvania, their message resembles that of countless other protests against slavery which were to appear over the next two centuries. Like other protesters, too, this group of Mennonites specifically chose to question what they called "the traffic of men-body," the buying and selling of human beings.

SOURCE: Henry Steele Commager, ed., *Documents of American History*, 7th ed. (New York: Appleton-Century-Crofts, 1963), pp. 37–38.

This is to the monthly meeting held at Richard Worrell's:

These are the reasons why we are against the traffic of men-body, as followeth: Is there any that would be done or handled at this manner? viz., to be sold or made a slave for all the time of his life? How fearful and faint-hearted are many at sea, when they see a strange vessel, being afraid it should be a Turk, and they should be taken, and sold for slaves into Turkey. Now, what is *this* better done, than Turks do? Yea, rather it is worse for them, which say they are Christians; for we hear that the most part of such negers are brought hither against their will and consent, and that many of them are stolen. Now, though they are black, we cannot conceive there is more liberty to have them slaves, as it is to have other white ones. There is a saying, that we should do to all men like as we will be done ourselves; making no difference of what generation, descent, or colour they are. And those who steal or rob men, and those who buy or purchase them, are they not all alike? Here is liberty of conscience, which is right and reasonable; here ought to be likewise liberty of the body, except of evil-doers, which is another case. But to bring men hither, or to rob and sell them against their will, we stand against. In Europe there are many oppressed for conscience-sake; and here there are those oppressed which are of a black colour. And we who know that men must not commit adultery—some do commit adultery *in* others, separating wives from their husbands, and giving them to others; and some sell the children of these poor creatures to other men. Ah! do consider well this thing, you who do it, if you would be done at this manner—and if it is done according to Christianity! You surpass Holland and Germany in this thing. This makes an ill report in all those countries of Europe, where they hear of [it], that the Quakers do here handel men as they handel there the cattle. And for that reason some have no mind or inclination to come hither. And who shall maintain this your cause, or plead for it? Truly, we cannot do so, except you shall inform us better hereof, viz.: that Christians have liberty to practice these things. Pray, what thing in the world can be done worse towards us, than if men should rob or steal us away, and sell us for slaves to strange countries; separating husbands from their wives and children. Being now this is not done in the manner we would be done at; therefore we contradict, and are against this traffic of men-body. And we who profess that it is not lawful to steal, must, likewise, avoid to purchase such things as are stolen, but rather help to stop this robbing and stealing, if possible. And such men ought to be delivered out of the hands of the robbers, and set free as in Europe. Then is Pennsylvania to have a good report, instead, it hath now a bad one, for this sake, in other countries; Especially whereas the Europeans are desirous to know in what manner *the Quakers* do rule in *their* province; and most of them do look upon us with an envious eye. But if this is done well, what shall we say is done evil?

If once these slaves (which they say are so wicked and stubborn men,) should join themselves—fight for their freedom, and handel their masters and mistresses, as they did handel them before; will these masters and mistresses take the sword at hand and war against these poor slaves, like, as we are able to believe, some will not refuse to do? Or, have these poor negers not as much right to fight for their freedom, as you have to keep them slaves?

Now consider well this thing, if it is good or bad. And in case you find it to be good to handel these blacks in that manner, we desire and require you hereby lovingly, that you may inform us herein, which at this time never was done, viz., that Christians have such a liberty to do so. To the end we shall be satisfied on this point, and satisfy likewise our good friends and acquaintances in our native country, to whom it is a terror, or fearful thing, that men should be handelled so in Pennsylvania.

This is from our meeting at Germantown, held ye 18th of the 2d month, 1688, to be delivered to the monthly meeting at Richard Worrell's.

Garret Henderich,
Derick op de Graeff,
Francis Daniel Pastorius,
Abram op de Graeff.

1.4. A London Merchant's Instructions to a Slave Trader on a Pending
Voyage to the Guinea Coast and from There to Virginia with a
Cargo of Slaves (1700–1701)

In 1702 a legal dispute arose between a slave-trading ship's captain, James
Westmore, and Thomas Starke, a Virginia landowner and London merchant who was also deeply involved in the African traffic to Britain's North
American colonies. In this dispute the plaintiff, Captain Westmore, demanded 678 pounds from Starke, which the latter had allegedly failed to
pay. Among the matters referred to in the evidence were fifty-seven African
men, women, and children whom Westmore had "brought into York
River," Virginia, and there sold to Starke's agent, some dying soon after
landing, and ten others having been transported to Maryland.

Included in the evidence given to the court was the following letter of
instructions from Starke to Captain Westmore regarding the latter's forth-
coming voyage to the Guinea coast and the procedures he was to follow in
bartering a wide variety of slave goods for Africans and other products, notably gold dust, malaguetta pepper, and "teeth," or elephant tusks. Of particular interest are Starke's instructions regarding the stratagems Westmore
was to use to make exemplary trades, his selection of the slaves to be
bought, and their careful treatment aboard ship to avoid sickness and excessive mortality. (A considerable amount of editing, especially insertion of
commas and shortening of sentences, was necessary to make this document
reasonably understandable to modern readers. However, most of the "curious" spellings remain.)

SOURCE: Elizabeth Donnan, *Documents Illustrative of the History of the Slave
Trade to America* (Washington, D.C.: Carnegie Institution of Washington, 1935),
vol. 4, pp. 72–77.

Starke's Instructions.

[To] *James Westmore:* London, October the twenty Second one thousand
Seaven hundred.

I have enclosed an Invoyce and bill of lading for the Cargo of goods
Shipt on board your Shipp *Affrica* Gally, consigned to your selfe, as also instructions for the disposal of the same. And these are to desire you to make
your best of your way into the Downes [a popular anchorage in England]
with all speed possibly you can with safety, then with the first oppertunity
saile from thence and make the best of your way to the Grand Coast [Grain
Coast?] in Guinea and there purchase what Guinea Grain [a grain-yielding

sorghum], Teeth [elephant tusks] and Gold dust you can in a day or two or three not to exceed, as you go along the Grand Coast, and if with a day or two att Cape Coast or thereabouts to purchase what Corne you think is needfull and from thence to Cape Formoso. . . . And if you should have a good passage thither, that in probability you are [there] before the Shipp that now goes out along with you that intends for New Callebarr [Calabar], I would have you go downe a long shoare from Cape Formoso to New Callebarr, and at every opening where you may with Safety anchor and send your Boate on Shoare and trade for Negroes [and] Teeth, and, if any encouragement, you may stay a day or two att a place, especially at Tone and another place adjacent. I am informed there is plenty of slaves and Teeth and, if [you get] any encouragement, you may stay six or seaven dayes if it be in the Month of December, or the beginning of January, for, if I were not afraid of the other Shipp being before you at Callebarr, I should not desire your being there before the middle of January. If Negroes [are] present you may buy a hundred or more, as you shall see fitt before you come to Callebarr. Endeavour to buy what Teeth you cann if plenty. Buy no small ones. At all these places where you shall trade you must shew all your small Comodityes that are not Staple att New Callebarr, and ask for them more than I have barred them at, especially what they seem to fancy, and alwayes observe to persuade them to take of your Hatts, Pewter, some Clapper Bells, Round Brass Bells, Shirts, Knives, Lookinglasses, Trunks, Chaires, Tables, Flints, and some Cases of Spiritts, for they are not Staple Comodityes att New Callebarr and Bandy [Bonny?] as other goods are. What slaves you buy in them places, lett them be very likely to believe you may buy them for Eight or Nine Iron Barrs per head, but you may give to Tenn or more for very likely men. And I would have you att all these places buy what Yeames [yams] you cann, and when, please [god] you shall arrive at New Callebarr, take all care possible you cann to find out the best depth of Water over the Barr, which I am informed is to Eastward. Take time before you venture over and send out your Boats to sound all about to find out the best depth of water. . . .

[A]nd when, please God, you are gott over, saile up to the Point which is near Callebar and then anchor where you may ride open to Bandy as well as to New Callebarr (as I am informed) so that the Negroes may see you to come on board out of both places, and by that meanes you will have an oppertunity of trading from both places and agreeing with them for the purchase of your Slaves at a reasonabler rate than if you went wholly to one place, and have a quicker dispatch. The people att New Callebar are much greater than the people of Bandy, but there are more Shipps go to Bandy than new Callebarr, especially Dutch and Portuguese, the Channell being better to Bandy than to New Callebarr, so that Slaves and Teeth are dearer att Bandy than att New Callebarr, and also I am informed that there is more plenty of Slaves and Teeth at New Callebar than att Bandy.

When, please God, you arrive there, you will be sensible of the trade of each place. Therefore leave it wholly to your discretion where to cutt a trade at one or both places, and which will engage to furnish you cheapest and quickest. There cutt for the most, and if they should pretend to keep up their Slaves High, you must declare you will be gone. Formerly Men Slaves have bought for Nine and Tenn, Women for Seaven Pecys [pieces?], and girles for five and six Iron Barrs per head. But rather than lye there, if you cann have a quick dispatch, you may cutt a trade for Twelve for Men, Nine for Women, and Six or Seaven for Boys and Girles, as you shall see they reserve. The trade which you cutt with the Kings is alwayes the highest [most expensive]. Those slaves which are brought by others out of the Countrey you may buy cheaper. If they should hold upp their Slaves higher than is expected, your holding off Two or Three dayes will make them comply with you if there be no other Shipps. But if there be, you must do as well as you cann.

I have inclosed an account what Custome used to be given to the Kings to Trade. Note that Iron Barrs is the Staplest Comodity there, and you haveing great plenty of them may give Seaven or Eight Iron Barrs with other goods for a Man Slave, and for a Woman five and six Iron Barrs with other goods. There is no certainty for Boys or Girles of any sort of goods, but as you cann agree and have to spare. In Copper, for Men Three or Four Copperr Barrs. For Women two Copper Barrs, that being the next Staple Comoditye. And in other goods you must make upp the Rest of the Barrs you are to give. You may be asked for Guinea Stuffs, but you have none. You have a good quantity of Blew Callicoes, which is in great esteem there, but you cannot sell them for more than a Copper Barrs length for a Copper Barr, nor you must not sell them for less. The pewter is not soe much desired, but will goe off for Slaves with other goods. Beads, Manelices[16] Clapper Bells, and several other goods are in very good esteem and will go off with Iron and Copper for Slaves. I cannot direct you how much of each sort of all the goods you shall certainly give for a Slave, for some will have more or less of each sort. Only your Iron and Copper, them sorts, you must keep att a certainty as near as you cann for Men Slaves, but for Women, Boys and

---

16. According to Elizabeth Donnan, *manelloes* were metal rings, often mentioned in the African trade. Editor.

Girles you may lessen the Quantity of Iron and Copper and make them take more of other goods that you have most of. Always those goods that are not much desired putt off for Boys and Girles. Teeth and Yeames and all the parcells of goods that are not Staple, being not of a certain value, there you must endeavour to gett more for them than I have barred them att, but if you cannot gett so much for Hatts, Shirts, Chaires, Tables, Cases of Knives, Flints and Horse Bells and Trunks and looking glasses and Cases of Spirits, you may abate.

I doe beleive [*sic*] I have advised you the needful as to the sale of the Cargoe which, with your discretion, doubt not but you will buy your Slaves as cheape and dispose of your Cargoe as well as others have done. You have a cargoe enough to buy four hundred and fifty Slaves and above three Tunn of Teeth and some gold dust and Provision sufficient for the Slaves. Therefore . . . you will endeavour to buy all the Teeth you can refuseing none that are large. At the first of your Slaving you may venture to dispose of the value of Seaven or Eight hundred Barrs for Teeth and Mallegatoes [Mallegata or Guinea Pepper]. I would have you, if it be not loss of time, to fill the Partition of the Beane room with Mallegata and what dry Casks you have empty. You must observe that all Teeth that have any Rents Cracks or any broaken off are much less in value than if they be clear. You must not buy any Negroes that are above Thirty yeares of Age, and take perticular care that both Men and Women, Boys and Girles, be all clear of any distemper . . . or any sore upon them, always takeing the doctors advice upon every Negro that you buy so that you may buy none but what are healthy, sound and clear limbed, always keeping an account, entring every day of the Month what Negroes and quantity of Teeth, Mallegata, Yeames and Gold dust you buy, and the perticular quanityes of what goods you give in Barter for each Negroe or Negroes and for each Tooth and Teeth and each quantity of Yeames, Gold dust and Mallegata that you shall buy of any one Man att one time. And when you have bought four hundred and fifty Slaves or more and also Teeth, Gold dust and Mallegata and Provisions as much as your Cargoe will purchase, or that if it should soe happen, Contrary to expectation, that you cannot purchase above four hundred Slaves, or not so many, without tarrying a long time for them, and that per sicknesse or any other reason that you shall judge it best to Saile from thence with what you have, You must make the best of your way to Virginea and go up the Bay to the opening of Yorke River and come to anchor without the River so that you may not be obleiged to enter your Ship there and send one of your Mates with your Boate to Tyndall Point, and there he must hire a horse and ride up to Mattapony in King and Queen County and goe to Mr. Henry

Fox. And there you shall receive orders where to go with your Negroes. And in the mean time take perticular care, and also at all other times, that none of your Negroes is runn a shoare, for if any be your Ship and Cargo will be co[n]fisticated to the Government, and you and your Shipps Company to the Owners here.[17] And you must deliver to Mr. John Sheffeild to whom my order is, which you will receive from Mr. Henry Fox, all your Negroes, Teeth, Mallegata, and Gold dust for to take an account and weigh and give bills of lading for them to be delivered att London to me freight free. . . .

In case of your Mortality, which I pray God in his Mercy to prevent, as soon as you find yourselfe ill, deliver a Copy of all your Barters and disposeing of the Cargoe and goods unsold, and what Negroes, Teeth, Mallegata and Gold dust and all perticulars as above directed to your Second Mate, or any other that you cann best trust, so that nothing may be concealed from me and the owners per the Cheife Mate, or him who takes possession after you. And take care that the Boatswaine and other officers keep the Ship cleane, and them and no other of your Men abuse the Negroes, and also be sure to keep a continuall Centry to prevent your Negroes getting to your Armes or any riseing per them. Wash your decks with vinegar and smother between decks with Pitch and Tarr every other day, or as you shall see occasion, and prevent your Negroes coming up in the Night as much as you cann, for the Cold dews in the night hath been the cheife occasion of the Negroes Gripes [severe pain in the bowels]. And endeavour what you cann to make your Negroes Chearfull and pleasant, makeing them dance at the beating of your Drumm, etc. In fair weather keep them upon decks as much as you cann, giveing them dramms when occasion, and they that have the Gripes to Boyle water and thicken it with Flower and chaulk for them, and also to rellish your Beans and other food for your Negroes with some of your Beefe, as you shall see occasion, and, for change, lett them have a day in a week of Grout [a coarse meal], or more if there be enough. All this I leave to your discretion to order as you shall see fitt. Take a perticular care that your doctor and his Mate doe daily their duty in looking after their Negroes, that they want for nothing. The whole benefit of the Voyage lyes in your care in Preserving the Negroes lives. Trust not to the Account your Officers shall give you of your Provisions and Stores, but examine them yourselfe every week, and that you see your Cooper search the Water Casks every week that if any leake it may be prevented. Trust to no man,

---

17. The result perhaps of a duty of twenty shillings imposed on imported slaves in 1699. See W. E. B. Du Bois, *The Suppression of the African Slave Trade to the United States, 1638–1870* (New York: Schocken Books, 1969), p. 203. Editor.

but see that every man do his duty in his Station, and that the Steward, Boatswaine, Cooper, Carpenter and Gunner give in writeing every week what Stores [are] expended dureing the whole Voyage, and that you enter them in a Booke to be delivered to me when, please God, you returne, and that you take care your Yeames are well dryed and stowed away where they cann take no whett and not be bruised. And be sure you purchase Yeames enough early and use no Beans nor Grout nor meat while you are a Slaving, nor till after you are come away from St Tomay [São Thomé], not till your Yeames are almost spent without they will [not?] keep. These b[e]ing all at present that I cann think of, only praying to God for your health and a prosperous Voyage, I am your Friend, **Tho. Starke.**

1.5. A Professional Slave Trader Analyzes and Justifies the African Slave Trade (1734)

William Snelgrave, the son of a British slave trader, succeeded his father in the business and, despite its inherent dangers, was active for decades. The following excerpts from his book, *A New Account of Some Parts of Guinea, and the Slave Trade,* describes the various ways Africans enslaved other Africans, justifies the traffic on several grounds, estimates the number of Africans annually shipped by Europeans from the Guinea coast, and describes slave management at sea intended to increase the likelihood of getting them to their intended destination. Finally, in some detail Snelgrave describes shipboard rebellions witnessed during his long career.

SOURCE: William Snelgrave, *A New Account of Some Parts of Guinea, and the Slave Trade* (London: James, John & Paul Knapton, 1734), pp. 157–72.

As for the *Manner* how those People become Slaves; it may be reduced under these several Heads.

I. It has been the Custom among the *Negroes,* time out of Mind, and is so to this day, for them to make Slaves of all the Captives they take in War. Now, before they had an Opportunity of selling them to the white People, they were often obliged to kill great Multitudes, when they had taken more than they could well employ in their own Plantations, for fear they should rebel, and endanger their Masters Safety.

2dly. Most Crimes amongst them are punished by Mulcts and Fines; and if the Offender has not wherewithal to pay his Fine, he is sold for a Slave: this is the Practice of the inland People, as well as those of the Sea side.

3dly. Debtors who refuse to pay their Debts, or are insolvent, are likewise liable to be made Slaves; but their Friends may redeem them: And if they are not able or willing to do it, then they are generally sold for the Benefit of their Creditors. But few of these come into the hands of the *Europeans,* being kept by their Countrymen for their own use.

4thly. I have been told, That it is common for some inland People to sell their Children for Slaves, tho' they are under no Necessity for so doing; which I am inclined to believe. But I never observed, that the People near the Sea Coast practice this, unless compelled thereto by extreme Want and Famine, as the People of *Whidaw* have lately been.

Now, by these means it is that so many of the Negroes become Slaves, and more especially by being taken Captives in War. Of these the Number is so great, that I may safely affirm, without any Exaggeration, that the *Europeans* of all Nations, that trade to the Coast of *Guinea,* have, in some Years, exported at least seventy thousand. And tho' this may no doubt be thought at first hearing a prodigious Number; yet when 'tis considered how great the Extent of this Coast is, namely from *Cape Verd* to *Angola,* which is about four thousand Miles in length; and that *Polygamy* is allowed in general amongst them, by which means the Countries are full of People, I hope it will not be thought improbable that so many are yearly exported from thence.

Several Objections have often been raised against the Lawfulness of this Trade, which I shall not here undertake to refute. I shall only observe in general, That tho' to traffick in human Creatures, may at first sight appear barbarous, inhuman and unnatural; yet the Traders herein have as much to plead in their own Excuse, as can be said for some other Branches of Trade, namely the *Advantage* of it: And that not only in regard to the Merchants, but also of the Slaves themselves, as will plainly appear from these following Reasons.

First, It is evident, that abundance of Captives, taken in War, would be inhumanly destroyed, was there not an Opportunity of disposing of them to the *Europeans.* So that at least many Lives are saved, and great Numbers of useful Persons kept in being.

Secondly, When they are carried to the Plantations, they generally live much better there, than they ever did in their own Country; for as the Planters pay a great price for them, 'tis their interest to take care of them.

Thirdly, By this means the *English* Plantations have been so much improved, that 'tis almost incredible, what great Advantages have accrued to the Nation thereby; especially to the *Sugar Islands,* which lying in a Climate near as hot as the Coast of *Guinea,* the *Negroes* are fitter to cultivate the Lands there, than white People.

Then as to the Criminals amongst the *Negroes,* they are by this means effectually transported, never to return again; a Benefit which we very much want here.

In a word, from this Trade proceed Benefits, far outweighing all, either real or pretended Mischiefs and Inconveniences. And, let the worst that can be said of it, it will be found, like all other earthly Advantages, tempered with a mixture of Good and Evil.

I come now to give an Account of the Mutinies that have happened on board the Ships where I have been.

These Mutinies are generally occasioned by the Sailors ill usage of these poor People, when on board the Ships wherein they are transported to our Plantations. Wherever therefore I have commanded it has been my principal Care, to have the *Negroes* on board my Ship kindly used; and I have always strictly charged my white People to treat them with Humanity and Tenderness: In which I have usually found my Account, both in keeping them from mutinying, and preserving them in health.

And whereas it may seem strange to those that are unaquainted with the method of managing them, how we can carry so many hundreds together in a small Ship, and keep them in order; I shall just mention what is generally practised. When we purchase grown People, I acquaint them by the Interpreter, "That, now they are become my Property, I think fit to let them know what they are bought for, that they may be easy in their Minds: (For these poor People are generally under terrible Apprehensions upon their being bought by white Men, many being afraid that we design to eat them; which, I have been told, is a story much credited by the inland *Negroes;*) "So after informing them, That they are bought to till the Ground in our Country, with several other Matters; I then acquaint them, how they are to behave themselves on board, towards the white Men; that if any one abuses them, they are to complain to the Linguist, who is to inform me of it, and I will do them Justice: But if they make a Disturbance, or offer to strike a white Man, they must expect to be severely punished."

When we purchase the *Negroes,* we couple the sturdy Men together with Irons; but we suffer the Women and Children to go freely about: And soon after we have sail'd from the Coast, we undo all the Mens Irons.

They are fed twice a day, and are allowed in fair Weather to come on Deck at seven a clock in the Morning, and to remain there, if they think proper, till Sun setting. Every *Monday* Morning they are served with Pipes and Tobacco, which they are fond of. The Men *Negroes* lodge separate from the Women and Children; and the places where they all lye are cleaned every day, some white Men being appointed to see them do it. . . .

The first Mutiny I saw among the *Negroes,* happened during my first Voyage, in the year 1704. It was on board the *Eagle Galley* of *London,* commanded by my Father, with whom I was as Purser. We had bought our Negroes in the River of *Old Callabar* in the Bay of *Guinea.* At the time of their mutinying we were in that River, having four hundred of them on board, and not above ten white Men who were able to do Service: For several of our Ship's Company were dead, and many more sick; besides, two of our Boats were just then gone with twelve People on Shore to fetch Wood, which lay in sight of the Ship. All these Circumstances put the *Negroes* on consulting how to mutiny, which they did at four a clock in the Afternoon, just as they went to Supper. But as we had always carefully examined the Mens Irons, both Morning and Evening, none had got them off, which in a great measure contributed to our Preservation. Three white Men stood on the Watch with Cutlaces in their Hands. One of them who was on the Forecastle, a stout fellow, seeing some of the Men Negroes take hold of the chief Mate, in order to throw him over board, he laid on them so heartily with the flat side of his Cutlace, that they soon quitted the Mate, who escaped from them, and run on the Quarter Deck to get Arms. I was then sick with an Ague, and lying on a Couch in the great Cabbin, the Fit being just come on. However, I no sooner heard the Outcry, *That the Slaves were mutinying,* but I took two Pistols, and run on the Deck with them; where meeting with my Father and the chief Mate, I delivered a Pistol to each of them. Whereupon they went forward on the Booms, calling to the Negroe Men that were on the Forecastle; but they did not regard their Threats, being busy with the Centry, (who had disengaged the chief Mate,) and they would have certainly killed him with his own Cutlace, could they have got it from him; but they could not break the Line wherewith the Handle was fastened to his Wrist. And so, tho' they had seized him, yet they could not make use of his Cutlace. Being thus disappointed, they endeavoured to throw him overboard, but he held so fast by one of them that they could not do it. My Father seeing this stout Man in so much Danger, ventured amonst the *Negroes,* to save him; and fired his Pistol over their Heads, thinking to frighten them. But a lusty Slave struck him with a Billet so hard, that he was almost stunned. The Slave was going to repeat the Blow, when a young Lad about seventeen years old, whom we had been kind to, interposed his Arm, and received the Blow, by which his Arm-bone was fractured. At the same instant the Mate fired his Pistol, and shot the *Negroe* that had struck my Father. At the sight of this the Mutiny ceased, and all the Men-negroes on the Forecastle threw themselves flat on their Faces, crying out for Mercy.

1. "Insurrection on Board a Slave Ship." From C. B. Wadstrom, *An Essay on Colonization* (1794). From a sketch obtained by Wadstrom in Gorée in 1787. Reprint: Augustus M. Kelley (New York, 1968).

Upon examining into the matter, we found, there were not above twenty Men Slaves concerned in this Mutiny; and the two Ringleaders were missing, having, it seems, jumped overboard as soon as they found their Project defeated, and were drowned. This was all the Loss we suffered on this occasion: For the *Negroe* that was shot by the Mate, the Surgeon, beyond all Expectation, cured. And I had the good Fortune to lose my Ague, by the fright and hurry I was put into. Moreover, the young Man, who had received the Blow on his Arm to save my Father was cured by the Surgeon in our Passage to *Virginia.* At our arrival in that place we gave him his Freedom; and a worthy Gentleman, one Colonel *Carter,* took him into his Service, till be became well enough acquainted in the Country to provide for himself.

I have been several Voyages, when there has been no Attempt made by our Negroes to mutiny; which, I believe, was owing chiefly, to their being kindly used, and to my Officers Care in keeping a good Watch. But sometimes we meet with stout stubborn People amongst them, who are never to be made easy; and these are generally some of the *Cormantines,* a Nation of the *Gold Coast.* I went in the year 1721, in the *Henry of London,* a Voyage to that part of the *Coast,* and bought a good many of these People. We were obliged to secure them very well in Irons, and watch them narrowly: Yet they nevertheless mutinied, tho' they had little prospect of succeeding. I lay at that time near a place called *Mumfort* on the *Gold Coast,* having near five hundred Negroes on board, three hundred of which were Men. Our Ship's Company consisted of fifty white People, all in health: And I had very good Officers; so that I was very easy in all respects.

This Mutiny began at Midnight (the Moon then shining very bright) in this manner. Two Men that stood Centry at the Fore-hatch way, where the Men Slaves came up to go to the house of Office, permitted four to go to that place; but neglected to lay the Gratings again, as they should have done: Whereupon four more Negroes came on Deck, who had got their Irons off, and the four in the house of Office having done the same, all the eight fell on the two Centries, who immediately called out for help. The Negroes endeavoured to get their Cutlaces from them, but the Lineyards (that is the Lines by which the handles of the Cutlaces were fastened to the Mens Wrists) were so twisted in the Scuffle, that they could not get them off before we came to their Assistance. The Negroes perceiving several white Men coming towards them, with Arms in their hands, quitted the Centries, and jumped over the Ship's side into the Sea.

I being by this time come forward on the Deck, my first care was to secure the Gratings, to prevent any more Negroes from coming up; and then I ordered People to get into the Boat, and save those that had jumped overboard, which they luckily did: For they found them all clinging to the Cables the Ship was moored by.

After we had secured these People, I called the Linguists, and ordered them to bid the Men-Negroes between Decks be quiet; (for there was a great noise amongst them.) On their being silent, I asked, "What had induced them to mutiny?" They answered, "I was a great Rogue to buy them, in order to carry them away from their own Country; and that they were resolved to regain their Liberty if possible." I replied, "That they had forfeited their Freedom before I bought them, either by Crimes, or by being taken in War, according to the Customs of their Country; and they being now my Property, I was resolved to let them feel my Resentment, if they abused my Kindness: Asking at the same time, Whether they had been ill used by the white Men, or had wanted for any thing the Ship afforded?" To this they replied, "They had nothing to complain of." Then I observed to them, "That if they should gain their Point and escape to the Shore, it would be no Advantage to them, because their Countrymen would catch them, and sell them to other Ships." This served my purpose, and they seemed to be convinced of their Fault, begging, "I would forgive them, and promising for the future to be obedient, and never mutiny again, if I would not punish them this time." This I readily granted, and so they went to sleep. When Day-light came we called the Men Negroes up on deck, and examining their Irons, found them all secure. So this Affair happily ended, which I was very glad of; for these People are the stoutest and most sensible *Negroes* on the Coast: Neither are they so weak as to imagine as others do, that we buy them to eat them; being satisfied we carry them to work in our Plantations, as they do in their own Country.

However, a few days after this, we discovered they were plotting again, and preparing to mutiny. For some of the Ringleaders proposed to one of our Linguists, If he could procure them an Ax, they would cut the Cables the ship rid by in the night; and so on her driving (as they imagined) ashore, they should get out of our hands, and then would become his Servants as long as they lived.

For the better understanding of this, I must observe here that these Linguists are Natives and Freemen of the Country, whom we hire on account of their speaking good *English*, during the time we remained trading on the Coast; and they are likewise Brokers between us and the black Merchants.

This Linguist was so honest as to acquaint me with what had been proposed to him; and advised me to keep a strict Watch over the Slaves: For tho' he had represented to them the same as I had done on their mutinying before, That they would all be catch'd again, and sold to other Ships, in case they could carry their Point, and get on Shore; yet it had no effect upon them

This gave me a good deal of Uneasiness. For I knew several Voyages had proved unsuccessful by Mutinies; as they occasioned either the total loss of the Ship and the white Mens Lives; or at least by rendering it absolutely necessary to kill or wound a great number of the Slaves, in order to prevent a total Destruction. Moreover, I knew many of these Cormantine Negroes despised Punishment, and even Death itself: It having often happened at *Barbadoes* and other Islands, that on their being any ways hardly dealt with to break them of their Stubbornness in refusing to work, twenty or more have hang'd themselves at a time in a Plantation.

1.6. A Charleston Slave Trader Informs Clients of Conditions in the Market (1755–1756)

Henry Laurens, the heir to a South Carolina fortune, formed a commercial partnership in his native Charleston while still in his early twenties, soon becoming one of the leading slave dealers of that city and the owner of enormous plantations in South Carolina and Georgia, where he built elegant residences and raised indigo and rice. Late in life he was elected to the Continental Congress and after the surrender of Cornwallis at Yorktown in 1781 became a member of a five-man peace commission to Europe, which included John Adams, Benjamin Franklin, John Jay, and Thomas Jefferson. The letters included here, all directed to fellow slave traders, were written in both prosperous and difficult times, the latter the result in part of epidemics, the low prices planters were getting for their crops, a danger of war with France (the Seven Years' War), and the diminutive size of some recently imported Africans

Abolitionists often argued that buyers and sellers of slaves conducted their affairs with little more regard for their "merchandise" than dealers in horses and cattle. Laurens seems to have been this kind of trader, since, though he was steadfastly polite and solicitous to colleagues and customers, the "parcells" of Africans he sold seemed for him to constitute little more than the high road to wealth, or, in more difficult times, a source of frustration and lost opportunities.[18]

SOURCE: Philip M. Hamer, ed., *The Papers of Henry Laurens* (Columbia: University of South Carolina Press, 1968), vol. 1, pp. 254–58, 263–64, 270, 281; vol. 2, pp. 81–83.

18. For the slave trade to South Carolina in Laurens's period of activity, see Daniel L. Littlefield, "Charleston and Internal Slave Distribution," *South Carolina Historical Magazine* 87, no. 2 (April 1986): 93–105.

To Smith and Clifton, Merchants of St. Christopher Island (St. Kitts).
26th May, 1755.
Gentlemen:

We have before us your kind favour of the 2d Current per Capt. Dickinson & we wish you great success in the Mercantile business during your Copartnership. . . .

Our Common method of selling Slaves, arrive at what time they will, is for payment in January or March following. If they are a very fine parcell Purchasers often appear that will produce the ready money in order to command a preference. The engagements we enter into in the Slave Trade are these, to Load the Ship with such Produce as can be got, pay the Coast Commissions & Mens half Wages & to remit the remainder as the payments shall grow due. We sold three Cargo's last Year after the first of July & every Shilling was remitted for them by the 18th March & every preceeding Year has been much the same. All our Remittances hitherto but trifles have been Bills of Exchange at 30 or 40 days sight. An entire parcell of fine Negroes must enable us to remit quicker than we can for a Cargo which consist of a mixture of all sorts & sizes, for the ordinary & small Slaves we must sell on such Terms of payment as we can, those which are prime enable us to pick our Customers. At some times of the Year we can advance [credit] for our Friends without any inconveniency, at others when we have large orders for Produce it is very inconvenient as our Planters produce such as is fine always commands Cash down. Thus we have given you the best Account we can of our African business. If at any time you should be disposed to try it be assur'd it shall be our endeavours to give you satisfaction.

To Wells, Wharton, and Doran, Merchants of St. Christopher.
27th May 1755
Gentlemen,

Your kind favour of the 28th December now before us did not reach us till 14th March, from which time we have had no oppertunity of replying to it. We are sorry Capt. Raite in the *Earl of Radnor* brought down so sickly a Cargo that you could not Venture to Stop her at so low a limit as £21 per head, from this We conclude that she must have made the Gentlemen concern'd but a bad Voyage; are glad she did not Come here as a sickly Cargo from Callabar at that Season of the Year especially would have mov'd very heavily & very probably have been order'd a long Quarentine; had they been healthy & in good flesh we shou'd have been very glad to have seen her as there never was a better opening for a cargo of Callabar Slaves than in the Months of October & November last owing to a Number of small Indigo

Planters finding a ready sale for their Crops at 32/6 to 35/ per lb. which brought them in such large sums they were all mad for more Negroes, & gave for very ordinary Calabar Men £250 Cash; Our imports this Year hitherto have been very small. None yet sold but a few small Parcels from Barbadoes and a little Cargo of about 70 in a Sloop of Rhode Island, Capt. Godfrey, from Gambia; a few of the fine Men sold so high as £280-or £40 Sterling but our People will not Currently give that price. They seem very content to give £260 for Men & a large Number would this day sell at that rate. We have two from Africa now under Quarantine on Account of the Small Pox. One of them a Sloop of New York, Griffith, Master with about 40 Slaves from Gambia, the other the *Matilda* of Bristol from Calabar with 190, these we apprehend can't be sold this Month or two; many more Vessels are expected, but if a Warr with France should take place which we seem to be at the Eve of we presume most of them will stop in the West Indies. Such an Event would give a sudden Check to the Rice Planters but not at all to those who go upon Indigo, so that we judge we may have vend for about half the Number in time of Warr that we have in Peace, Say from 12 [hundred] to 1500 per Annum; We are Sorry Capt. Darbyshire's Tender brought no more than 60 Slaves as our Good Freind Mr. Knight promis'd himself 100 by her, but Mr. Furnell advises us from Jamaica that he made a great sale of Darbyshires Cargo, sold about 350 Slaves at upwards of £45 per head that money which we think must make up for the defficiency of the other; We were empower'd to order down here 100 of the Prime Men out of Darbyshire's Cargo, but did not chuse to do it being of Opinion we could not for those Slaves exceed the Prices at Jamaica. Our people like the Gambia and Windward coast full as well or the Angola Men such as are large. . . .

To Charles Gwynn, a Bristol Privateer and Captain of the Slave Ship *Emperor*.

12th June 1755
Sir,

We have before us your kind favour of the 3d May from Jamaica. The date would have pleas'd us much better if it had been from Rebellion Rhoad [an anchorage off Sullivans Island in Charleston Harbor]. However what can't be cur'd must be submitted to which we do on our parts as chearfully as can be expected on such an occasion & are thankfull that you are safe & that matters are no worse after such a trying Storm as you describe. To be sure if you had arriv'd about the middle of April or any time since we should have made a glorious Sale of your Cargo. Our planters are in full spirits for purchasing Slaves & have almost all the money hoarded up for that purpose. In-

The African Slave Trade, Legal and Illegal

TO BE SOLD on board the Ship *Bance-Yland*, on tuesday the 6th of *May* next, at *Asbley-Ferry*; a choice cargo of about 250 fine healthy NEGROES, just arrived from the Windward & Rice Coast. —The utmost care has already been taken, and shall be continued, to keep them free from the least danger of being infected with the SMALL-POX, no boat having been on board, and all other communication with people from *Charles-Town* prevented.

Austin, Laurens, & Appleby.

N. B. Full one Half of the above Negroes have had the SMALL-POX in their own Country.

2.
Advertisement for sale of newly arrived slaves, by Austen, Laurens, and Appleby of Charleston, South Carolina. Courtesy of Crown Publishers, New York.

digo has kept up at a most exorbitant price in England, so has Rice & in short every Article from our Colony sells mightily well at home. Our Planters in general have bent their strength to Indigo & we verily believe that many of them have planted much more than they can reap & work without an augmentation of their Slaves relying on the importation of this Summer. From hence we expect to make a fine Sale the 24th Inst. of the *Pearl's* Cargo, Capt. Jeffries. He arriv'd here the 10th Inst, with 251 pretty Slaves. We shall strain hard to get £40 Sterling per head for the best Men, 'tho we must be carefull not to break the Cord. Besides this Guinea Man here's only the *Matilda* from the Bight & a Sloop from Gambia both performing Quarentine for the small Pox. The latter indeed has gone through it. Our Accounts from Gambia are very bad, Slaves scarce, upward of 20 Sail in the River & the small pox currant among them. We believe few Slaves will come from that Quarter. Capt. Timberman has lost his Ship going over the Bar of Bonny [in the Niger River Delta near New Calabar] & we judge no other Vessell will come here from Angola. From all this we are of the opinion our importation will not be excessive & that barring a War with France the price of Slaves will hold up here thro this Summer, good prices and quick payment.

To John Knight. a Merchant, Slave Trader and a Liverpool Alderman.
26th June 1755
Sir, . . .

Capt. Bennet [of the Snow Orrel] has given us a Letter of the 15th March soon after his arrival in Gambia in which he informs us that Slaves were very scarse in the River, the number of Purchasers so great that he shall think himself very well off to get 2/3rds of his Compliment. We wish he had been with us with the number two days ago when we made Sale of the Cargo of the *Pearl,* Jeffries, of Bristol from Angola which avaraged £33.17.1 Sterling. Her Cargo was 250. We had Chaps for more than double the number could we have furnish'd them. There was in this parcell near 150 Men & large Boys, the men all to a trifle brought 270 and £280. Five of them sold so high as £290 per head, a very great price we think for Angola Slaves. Our ready money upon the Sale does not exceed £1,000 Sterling but scarsely one sold for longer Credit than January.

To Henry Weare & Co.

2d July 1755
Gentlemen,

Your favour of the 5th of April reach'd us yesterday, advising of the Receipt of Sundry Bills, to the amount of £548.11.9 1/2 Sterling the Ballance of the *Fortune's* Cargo [of 180 slaves brought from the Windward and Gold Coasts Edward Bouchier, master.] We are glad the Remittance was satisfactory, wish the Sales had been so & really had the Cargo been tolerable. We are sure it was in our power on that day to have made as good a Sale as any that preceeded it. We had as many purchasers as we could have wish'd, there were forty or fifty that came upwards of Seventy Miles distance most of which return'd without a Slave & these sort of People are the only ones to raise a Sale for if they like the Slaves they won't go back empty handed so far for 10 or £20 in the price. We had not in Capt. Jeffries Cargo the other day six Men so ordinary as the best of Capt. Bouchers. This Sale will show what might have been done with a Cargo of good Slaves. We need not tell Mr. Weare that this Cargo averages £33.17/ Sterling as we see he is concern'd in the Ship. Those per Boucher were sold every bit as well considering what a scabby Flock he brought. We sold some of those Men from 240 to £260, that we would not have insur'd to reach the Masters plantation alive for £100 per head they were so very Poor. . . .

To Law, Satterthwaite, and Jones, a Slave-Trading Company of Barbados

31st January 1756.

Gentlemen, We have now chiefly to confirm the foregoing Copy of our last and to inform you of the further progress we have made in the Sale of your Slaves which stands as below. We have two still remaining on hand, a Man & a Woman, the Man extreamly low in flesh and we fear wont bring more than £100, the Woman 'tho able, no one seems to like her so that to this day we have not had an offer for her. We had but very few come to our Sale of the 140 Slaves per the *Relief.* Indeed it unluckily happen'd that a Pereparamina [pneumonia] prevail'd at that time & does so still amongst the Slaves in many parts of the Province which sweeps off great numbers and is a great discouragement to such as would now otherways buy. We have however put off all to about ten that were able to appear in the Yard which have sold much better than we at first hoped for as they were a mighty small People such as our Planters dont at all like. We see clearly Slaves will not maintain a price with us whilst our Planters Produce continues so low and it cannot amend if we should be involved in a War. . . .

To Gidney Clarke of Barbados.

31st January 1756.
Sir: . . .

Permit us now to inform you what progress we have made in the Sale of your Slaves address'd to us which we have taken every measure in our power to put off to advantage but with poor success. Our people thought them a very indifferent parcell, that they were much too small a People for the business in this Country & on this Account many went away empty handed that would otherways have purchas'd. Another grand impediment to the Sale was a Pereparamina breaking out in many parts of the Province and sweeping off great numbers of Negroes a little before the day of Sale which prevented a great many from attending & the success of a Sale much depends on the Numbers that attend. In short every thing contributed to induce us to think we must inevitably make a very poor Sale & what added greatly to it was that we could only bring into the Yard 105, the rest that remained alive were in a bad condition with the Flux from which disorder there are dead to this time 13 & we are sorry to say several more in great danger. What we have sold at this day are 102. The Amount £21,291.10/ Currency. We have 14 more that are able to come abroad and 11 sick in the Hospital. Those which are well are a very diminutive parcell of Mortalls, Children in size but at their full growth, so that upon the whole we fear you must make a very indifferent Voyage & what will add to it is that the major part of those sold are on Credit to January next. The monstrous prices given for a few Slaves in the month of October has produced all this Evil, brought down parcell after parcell from the West Indias incessantly all this Winter, which has put it in the power of the Planter to play upon the Sellers their own Game. This we can safely assert, that yours are sold for better prices than any since they arriv'd. As proof of it we ourselves purchased four

Angola Men the prime of a parcell and not to be equald by any four of yours for £212.10/ per head & we obtain'd for some of yours £240 per head. We see clearly whilst our Planters produce continues so low they will not buy Slaves unless at a price proportionate to that of their Goods. They paid very little regard to the prospect of a War until they sensibly felt the consequences by the Sale of their Produce. . . .

1.7. "The Hardships Are Scarcely to Be Conceived." British Slave Trading in the Late Eighteenth Century

The following portrayal of the African slave trade was the result of the sudden rise of opposition to that "commerce" in Britain during and after the American war for independence. The author of this account, Alexander Falconbridge, made several voyages to Africa in the capacity of ship's surgeon, and so possessed a large stock of personal experience enabling him to offer the British public and Parliament a description, as he put it, "of the hardships which the unhappy objects of it undergo, and the cruelties they suffer, from the period of their being reduced to a state of slavery, to their being disposed of in the West India islands." The conditions Falconbridge describes were, of course, much like those experienced by slaves transported to other parts of the Americas such as Brazil, the colonies of Spain, France, Holland and Denmark, and the United States. Among the topics he discusses are the procedures used to procure slaves in the African interior, the selling of slaves on the coast, the bitter conditions at sea, and the selling of slaves in the West Indies. The latter includes so-called "scrambles," a method of sale that normally took place in a large outdoor enclosure where, without warning to the Africans within, prospective buyers rushed in upon them, brutally seizing their victims and creating confusion and terror among them.

SOURCE: Alexander Falconbridge, *An Account of the Slave Trade on the Coast of Africa* (London: J. Phillips, 1788), pp. 5, 7–25, 27–30, 33–35.

Proceedings during the Voyage . . .

The slave ships generally lie near or below the town, in Bonny River [in Nigeria in the Bight of Biafra], in seven or eight fathom water. Sometimes fifteen sail, English and French, but chiefly the former, meet here together. Soon after they cast anchor, the captains go on shore, to make known their arrival, and to inquire into the state of the trade. They likewise invite the kings of Bonny to come on board, to whom, previous to breaking bulk [unloading the cargo], they usually make presents (in that country termed *dashes)* which generally consist of pieces of cloth, cotton, chintz, silk handkerchiefs, and other India goods, and sometimes of brandy, wine, or beer.

When I was at Bonny a few years ago, it was the residence of two kings, whose names were *Norfolk* and *Peppel.* The houses of these princes were not distinguished from the cottages or huts of which the town consists, in any other manner than by being of somewhat larger dimensions, and surrounded with warehouses containing European goods, designed for the purchase of slaves. These slaves, which the kings procure in the same manner as the black traders do theirs, are sold by them to the ships. And for every negroe sold there by the traders, the kings receive a duty, which amounts to a considerable sum in the course of a year. This duty is collected by officers, stationed on board the ships, who are termed *officer boys;* a denomination which it is thought they received from the English.

The kings of Bonny are absolute, though elective. . . . Every ship on its arrival, is expected to send a present to these gentlemen, of a small quantity of bread and beef, and likewise to treat them as often as they come on board. When they do this, their approach to the ship is announced by blowing through a hollow elephant's tooth, which produces a sound resembling that of a post-horn.

After the kings have been on board, and have received the usual presents, permission is granted by them for trafficking with any of the black traders. When the royal guests return from the ships, they are saluted by the guns.

From the time of the arrival of the ships to their departure, which is usually near three months, scarce a day passes without some negroes being purchased; and carried on board, sometimes in small, sometimes in large numbers. The whole number taken on board, depends, in a great measure, on circumstances. In a voyage I once made, our stock of merchandize was exhausted in the purchase of about 380 negroes, which was expected to have procured 500. The number of English and French ships then at Bonny, had so far raised the price of negroes, as to occasion this difference.

The reverse (and a *happy* reverse I think I may call it) was known during the late war [with the American colonies]. When I was last at Bonny, I frequently made inquiries on this head, of one of the black traders, whose intelligence I believe I can depend upon. He informed me that only one ship had been there for three years during that period; and that was the *Moseley Hill,* Captain Ewing, from Leverpool [*sic*], who made an extraordinary purchase, as he found negroes remarkably cheap from the dulness of the trade. Upon further inquiring of my black acquaintance, what was the consequence of this decay of their trade, he shrugged up his shoulders, and answered, *only making us traders poorer, and obliging us to work for our maintenance.* One of these black merchants being informed, that a particular set of people, called Quakers, were for abolishing the trade, he said, *it was a very bad thing, as they should then be reduced to the same state they were in during the war, when, through poverty, they were obliged to dig the ground and plant yams.*

I was once upon the coast of Angola also, when there had not been a slave ship at the River Ambris for five years previous to our arrival, although a place to which many usually resort every year; and the failure of the trade for that period, as far as we could learn, had not any other effect, than to restore peace and confidence among the natives; which, upon the arrival of any ships, is immediately destroyed, by the inducement then held forth in the purchase of slaves. And during the suspension of trade at Bonny, as above-mentioned, none of the dreadful proceedings, which are so confidently asserted to be the natural consequence of it, were known. The reduction of the price of negroes, and the poverty of the black traders, appear to have been the only *bad* effects of the discontinuance of trade; the *good* ones were, *most probably,* the restoration of peace and confidence among the natives, and a suspension of kidnapping. . . .

The Manner in which the Slaves Are Procured.

After permission has been obtained for *breaking trade,* as it is termed, the captains go ashore from time to time to examine the negroes that are exposed to sale, and to make their purchases. The unhappy wretches thus disposed of are bought by the black traders at fairs, which are held for that purpose, at the distance of upwards of two hundred miles from the sea coast; and these fairs are said to be supplied from an interior part of the country. Many negroes, upon being questioned relative to the places of their nativity, have asserted, that they have travelled during the revolution of several moons, (their usual method of calculating time) before they have reached the places where they were purchased by the black traders. At these fairs, which are held at uncertain periods, but generally every six weeks, several thousands are frequently exposed to sale, who had been collected from all parts of the country for a very considerable distance round. While I was upon the coast, during one of the voyages I made, the black traders brought down in different canoes from twelve to fifteen hundred negroes, which had been purchased at one fair. They consisted chiefly of men and boys, the women seldom exceeding a third of the whole number. From forty to two

GANG OF CAPTIVES MET AT MBAME'S ON THEIR WAY TO TETTE.

3. "Gang of Captives Met at Mbame's on their Way to Tette." From *Harper's New Monthly Magazine,* May 1866. Courtesy of the University of Pittsburgh Library System.

hundred negroes are generally purchased at a time by the black traders, according to the opulence of the buyer; and consist of those of all ages, from a month to sixty years and upwards. Scarce any age or situation is deemed an exception, the price being proportionable. Women sometimes form a part of them, who happen to be so far advanced in their pregnancy, as to be delivered during their journey from the fairs to the coast; and I have frequently seen instances of deliveries on board ship. The slaves purchased at these fairs are only for the supply of the markets at Bonny, and Old and New Calabar.

There is great reason to believe, that most of the negroes shipped off from the coast of Africa, are *kidnapped.* But the extreme care taken by the black traders to prevent the Europeans from gaining any intelligence of their modes of proceeding; the great distance inland from whence the negroes are brought; and our ignorance of their language, (with which, very frequently, the black traders themselves are equally unacquainted) prevent our obtaining such information on this head as we could wish. I have, however, by means of occasional inquiries, made through interpreters, procured some intelligence relative to the point, and such, as I think, puts the matter beyond a doubt.

From these I shall select the following striking instances:—While I was in employ on board one of the slave ships, a negroe informed me, that being one evening invited to drink with some of the black traders, upon his going away they attempted to seize him. As he was very active, he evaded their design, and got out of their hands. He was however prevented from effecting his escape by a large dog, which laid hold of him, and compelled him to submit. These creatures are kept by many of the traders for that purpose; and being trained to the inhuman sport, they appear to be much pleased with it.

I was likewise told by a negroe woman, that as she was on her return home, one evening, from some neighbors, to whom she had been making a visit by invitation, she was kidnapped; and, notwithstanding she was big with child, sold for a slave. This transaction happened a considerable way up the country, and she had passed through the hands of several purchasers before she reached the ship. A man and his son, according to their own information, were seized by professed kidnappers, while they were planting yams, and sold for slaves. This likewise happened in the interior parts of the country, and after passing through several hands, they were purchased for the ship to which I belonged.

It frequently happens, that those who kidnap others, are themselves in their turns, seized and sold. A negro in the West-Indies informed me, that after having been employed in kidnapping others, he had experienced this reverse. And he assured me that it was a common incident among his countrymen.

Continual enmity is thus fostered among the negroes of Africa, and all social intercourse between them destroyed, which most assuredly would not be the case, had they not these opportunities of finding a ready sale for each other. . . .

Previous to my being in this employ, I entertained a belief, as many others have done, that the kings and principal men *breed* negroes for sale, as we do cattle. During the different times I was in the country, I took no little pains to satisfy myself in this particular; but notwithstanding I made many inquiries, I was not able to obtain the least intelligence of this being the case, which it is more than probable I should have done, had such a practice prevailed. All the information I could procure, confirms me in the belief, that to *kidnapping,* and to crimes, (and many of these fabricated as a pretext) the slave trade owes its chief support. . . .

The preparations made at Bonny by the black traders, upon setting out for the fairs which are held up the country, are very considerable. From twenty to thirty canoes, capable of containing thirty or forty negroes each, are assembled for this purpose; and such goods put on board them as they expect will be wanted for the purchase of the number of slaves they intend to buy. When their loading is completed, they commence their voyage, with colours flying and musick playing; and in about ten or eleven days, they generally return to Bonny with full cargoes. As soon as the canoes arrive at the trader's landing-place, the purchased negroes are cleaned and oiled with palm oil; and on the following day they are exposed for sale to the captains.

The black traders do not always purchase their slaves at the same rate. The speed with which the information of the arrival of ships upon the coast is conveyed to the fairs, considering it is the interest of the traders to keep them ignorant, is really surprising. In a very short time after any ships arrive upon the coast, especially if several make their appearance together, those who dispose of the negroes at the fairs are frequently known to increase the price of them.

These fairs are not the only means, though they are the chief, by which the black traders on the coast are supplied with negroes. Small parties of them, from five to ten, are frequently brought to the houses of the traders by those who make a practice of kidnapping; and who are constantly employed in procuring a supply, while purchasers are to be found.

When the negroes, whom the black traders have to dispose of, are shewn to the European purchasers, they first examine them relative to their age. They then minutely inspect their persons, and inquire into the state of their health; if they are afflicted with any infirmity, or are deformed, or have bad eyes or teeth; if they are lame, or weak in the joints, or distorted in the back, or of a slender make, or are narrow in the chest; in short, if they have been, or are afflicted in any manner, so as to render them incapable of much labour; if any of the foregoing defects are discovered in them, they are rejected. But if approved of, they are generally taken on board the ship the same evening. The purchaser has liberty to return on the following morning, but not afterwards, such as upon re-examination are found exceptionable.

The traders frequently beat those negroes which are objected to by the captains, and use them with great severity. It matters not whether they are refused on account of age, illness, deformity, or any other reason. At New Calabar, in particular, the traders have frequently been known to put them to death. Instances have happened at that place, that the traders, when any of their negroes have been objected to, have dropped their canoes under the stern of the vessel, and instantly beheaded them, in sight of the captain.

Upon the Windward Coast, another mode of procuring slaves is pursued; which is, by what they term *boating;* a mode that is very pernicious and destructive to the crews of the ships. The sailors, who are employed upon this trade, go in boats up the rivers, seeking for negroes, among the villages situated on the banks of them. But this method is very slow, and not always effectual. For, after being absent from the ship during a fortnight or three weeks, they sometimes return with only from eight to twelve negroes. Numbers of these are procured in consequence of alleged crimes, which, as before observed, whenever any ships are upon the coast, are more productive than at any other period. Kidnapping, however, prevails here. . . .

Treatment of the Slaves.

As soon as the wretched Africans, purchased at the fairs, fall into the hands of the black traders, they experience an earnest of those dreadful sufferings which they are doomed in future to undergo. And there is not the least room to doubt, but that even before they can reach the fairs, great numbers perish from cruel usage, want of food, travelling through inhospitable deserts, &c. They are brought from the places where they are purchased to Bonny, &c. in canoes; at the bottom of which they lie, having their hands tied with a kind of willow twigs, and a strict watch is kept over them. Their usage in other respects during the time of the passage, which generally lasts several days, is equally cruel. Their allowance of food is so scanty that it is barely sufficient to support nature. They are, besides, much exposed to the violent rains which frequently fall here, being covered only with mats that afford but a slight defence; and as there is usually water at the bottom of the canoes, from their leaking, they are scarcely ever dry.

Nor do these unhappy beings, after they become the property of the Europeans (from whom, as a more civilized people, more humanity might naturally be expected) find their situation in the least amended. Their treatment is no less rigorous. The men negroes on being brought aboard the ship are immediately fastened together, two and two, by hand-cuffs on their wrists, and by irons rivetted on their legs. They are then sent down beneath the decks, and placed in an apartment partitioned off for that purpose. The women likewise are placed in a separate apartment between decks, but without being ironed. And an adjoining room, on the same deck, is besides appointed for the boys. Thus they are all placed in different apartments.

But at the same time, they are frequently stowed so close, as to admit of no other posture than lying on their sides. Neither will the height between decks, unless directly under the grating, permit them the indulgence of an erect posture; especially where there are platforms, which is generally the case. These platforms are a kind of shelf, about eight or nine feet in breadth, extending from the side of the ship towards the centre. They are placed nearly midway between the decks, at the distance of two or three feet from each deck. Upon these the negroes are stowed in the same manner as they are on the deck underneath.

In each of the apartments are placed three or four large buckets, of a conical form, being near two feet in diameter at the bottom, and only one foot at the top, and in depth about twenty-eight inches; to which, when necessary, the negroes have recourse. It often happens that those who are placed at a distance from the buckets, in endeavouring to get to them, tumble over their companions, in consequence of their being shackled. These accidents, although unavoidable, are productive of continual quarrels, in which some of them are always bruised. In this distressed situation, unable to proceed, and prevented from getting to the tubs, they desist from the attempt; and, as the necessities of nature are not to be repelled, ease themselves as they lie. This becomes a fresh source of broils [brawls] and disturbances, and tends to render the condition of the poor captive wretches still more uncomfortable. The nuisance arising from these circumstances is not unfrequently increased by the tubs being much too small for the purpose intended, and their being usually emptied but once every day. The rule for doing this, however, varies according to the attention paid to the health and convenience of the slaves by the captain.

About eight o'clock in the morning the negroes are generally brought upon deck. Their irons being examined, a long chain, which is locked to a ring-bolt, fixed in the deck, is run through the rings of the shackles of the men, and then locked to another ring-bolt, fixed also in the deck. By this means fifty or sixty, and sometimes more, are fastened to one chain, in order to prevent them from rising, or endeavouring to escape. If the weather proves favourable, they are permitted to remain in that situation till four or five in the afternoon, when they are disengaged from the chain, and sent down.

The diet of the negroes, while on board, consists chiefly of horse-beans, boiled to the consistence of a pulp; of boiled yams and rice, and sometimes of a small quantity of beef or pork. The latter are frequently taken from the provisions laid in for the sailors. They sometimes make use of a sauce, composed of palm-oil, mixed with flour, water, and pepper, which the sailors call *flabber-sauce*. Yams are the favourite food of the Eboe, or Bight negroes, and rice or corn, of those from the Gold and Windward Coasts, each preferring the produce of their native soil. . . .

Their food is served up to them in tubs about the size of a small water bucket. They are placed round these tubs in companies of ten to each tub, out of which they feed themselves with wooden spoons. These they soon lose, and when they are not allowed others, they feed themselves with their hands. In favourable weather they are fed upon deck, but in bad weather their food is given them below. Numberless quarrels take place among them during their meals; more especially when they are put upon short allowance, which frequently happens, if the passage from the coast of Guinea to the West-India islands, proves of unusual length. In that case, the weak are obliged to be content with a very scanty portion. Their allowance of water is about half a pint each at every meal. It is handed round in a bucket, and given to each negroe in a pannekin, a small utensil with a straight handle, somewhat similar to a sauce-boat. However, when the ships approach the islands with a favourable breeze, they are no longer restricted.

Upon the negroes refusing to take sustenance, I have seen coals of fire, glowing hot, put on a shovel, and placed so near their lips, as to scorch and burn them. And this has been accompanied with threats, of forcing them to swallow the coals, if they any longer persisted in refusing to eat. These means have generally had the desired effect. I have also been credibly informed that a certain captain in the slave trade poured melted lead on such of the negroes as obstinately refused their food.

Exercise being deemed necessary for the preservation of their health, they are sometimes obliged to dance, when the weather will permit their coming on deck. If they go about it reluctantly, or do not move with agility, they are flogged; a person standing by them all the time with a cat-o'-nine-tails in his hand for that purpose. Their musick, upon these occasions, consists of a drum, sometimes with only one head; and when that is worn out, they do not scruple to make use of the bottom of one of the tubs before described. The poor wretches are frequently compelled to sing also; but when they do so, their songs are generally, as may naturally be expected, melancholy lamentations of their exile from their native country.

The women are furnished with beads for the purpose of affording them some diversion. But this end is generally defeated by the squabbles which are occasioned, in consequence of their stealing them from each other.

On board some ships, the common sailors are allowed to have intercourse with such of the black women whose consent they can procure. And some of them have been known to take the inconstancy of their paramours so much to heart, as to leap overboard and drown themselves. The officers are permitted to indulge their passions among them at pleasure, and sometimes are guilty of such brutal excesses, as disgrace human nature.

The hardships and inconveniences suffered by the negroes during the passage are scarcely to be enumerated or conceived. They are far more violently affected by the sea-sickness than the Europeans. It frequently terminates in death, especially among the women. But the exclusion of the fresh air is among the most intolerable. For the purpose of admitting this needful refreshment, most of the ships in the slave-trade are provided, between the decks, with five or six air-ports on each side of the ship, of about six inches in length, and four in breadth; in addition to which, some few ships, but not one in twenty, have what they denominate *wind-sails*. But whenever the sea is rough, and the rain heavy, it becomes necessary to shut these, and every other conveyance by which the air is admitted. The fresh air being thus excluded, the negroes' rooms very soon grow intolerably hot. The confined air, rendered noxious by the effluvia exhaled from their bodies, and by being repeatedly breathed, soon produces fevers and fluxes, which generally carries off great numbers of them.

During the voyages I made, I was frequently a witness to the fatal effects of this exclusion of the fresh air. I will give one instance, as it serves to convey some idea, though a very faint one, of the sufferings of those unhappy beings whom we wantonly drag from their native country, and doom to perpetual labour and captivity. Some wet and blowing weather having occasioned the port-holes to be shut, and the grating to be covered, fluxes and fevers among the negroes ensued. While they were in this situation, my profession requiring it, I frequently went down among them, till at length their apartments became so extremely hot as to be only sufferable for a very short time. But the excessive heat was not the only thing that rendered their situation intolerable. The deck, that is, the floor of their rooms, was so covered with the blood and mucus which had proceeded from them in consequence of the flux, that it resembled a slaughter-house. It is not in the power of the human imagination to picture to itself a situation more dreadful or disgusting. Numbers of the slaves having fainted, they were carried upon deck, where several of them died, and the rest were, with great difficulty, restored. It had nearly proved fatal to me also. The climate was too warm to admit the wearing of any clothing but a shirt, and that I had pulled off before I went down; notwithstanding which, by only continuing among them for about a quarter of an hour, I was so overcome with the heat, stench, and foul air that I had nearly fainted; and it was not without assistance, that I could get upon deck. The consequence was that I soon after fell sick of the same disorder, from which I did not recover for several months. . . .

The place allotted for the sick negroes is under the half deck, where they lie on the bare planks. By this means, those who are emaciated frequently have their skin and even their flesh entirely rubbed off by the motion of the ship, from the prominent parts of the shoulders, elbows, and hips, so as to render the bones in those parts quite bare. And some of them, by constantly lying in the blood and mucus, that had flowed from those afflicted with the flux, and which, as before observed, is generally so violent as to prevent their being kept clean, have their flesh much sooner rubbed off than those who have only to contend with the mere friction of the ship. The excruciating pain which the poor sufferers feel from being obliged to continue in such a dreadful situation, frequently for several weeks, in case they happen to live so long, is not to be conceived or described. Few, indeed, are ever able to withstand the fatal effects of it. The utmost skill of the surgeon is here ineffectual. If plaisters [plasters] be applied, they are very soon displaced by the friction of the ship; and when bandages are used, the negroes very soon take them off, and appropriate them to other purposes.

The surgeon, upon going between decks, in the morning, to examine the situation of the slaves, frequently finds several dead; and among the men, sometimes a dead and living negroe fastened by their irons together. When this is the case, they are brought upon the deck, and being laid on the grating, the living negroe is disengaged, and the dead one thrown overboard. . . .

Almost the only means by which the surgeon can render himself useful to the slaves is by seeing that their food is properly cooked and distributed among them. It is true, when they arrive near the markets for which they are destined, care is taken to polish them for sale by an application of the lunar caustic to such as are afflicted with the yaws. This, however, affords but a temporary relief, as the disease most assuredly breaks out whenever the patient is put upon a vegetable diet. . .

The loss of slaves, through mortality, arising from the causes just mentioned, are frequently very considerable. In the voyage lately referred to . . . one hundred and five, out of three hundred and eighty, died in the passage. A proportion seemingly very great, but by no means uncommon. One half, sometimes two thirds, and even beyond that, have been known to perish. . . .

As very few of the negroes can so far brook the loss of their liberty, and the hardships they endure, as to bear them with any degree of patience, they are ever upon the watch to take advantage of the least negligence in their oppressors. Insurrections are frequently the consequence; which are seldom suppressed without much bloodshed. Sometimes these are successful, and the whole ship's company is cut off. They are likewise always ready to seize every opportunity for committing some act of desperation to free themselves from their miserable state; and notwithstanding the restraints under which they are laid, they often succeed. . . .

Sale of the Slaves.

When the ships arrive in the West-Indies, (the chief mart for this inhuman merchandize), the slaves are disposed of . . . by different methods. Sometimes the mode of disposal is that of selling them by what is termed a *scramble;* and a day is soon fixed for that purpose. But previous thereto, the sick or refuse slaves, of which there are frequently many, are usually conveyed on shore and sold at a tavern by vendue or public auction. These, in general, are purchased by the Jews and surgeons, but chiefly the former, upon speculation, at so low a price as five or six dollars a head. I was informed by a mulatto woman that she purchased a sick slave at Grenada, upon speculation for the small sum of one dollar, as the poor wretch was apparently dying of the flux. It seldom happens that any, who are carried ashore in the emaciated state to which they are generally reduced by that disorder, long survive their landing. I once saw sixteen conveyed on shore and sold in the foregoing manner, the whole of whom died before I left the island, which was within a short time after. Sometimes the captains march their slaves through the town at which they intend to dispose of them; and then place them in rows where they are examined and purchased.

The mode of selling them by scramble having fallen under my observation the oftenest, I shall be more particular in describing it. Being some years ago at one of the islands in the West-Indies, I was witness to a sale by scramble, where about 250 negroes were sold. Upon this occasion all the negroes scrambled for bear an equal price; which is agreed upon between the captains and the purchasers before the sale begins.

On a day appointed, the negroes were landed and placed together in a large yard, belonging to the merchants to whom the ship was consigned. As soon as the hour agreed on arrived, the doors of the yard were suddenly thrown open, and in rushed a considerable number of purchasers with all the ferocity of brutes. Some instantly seized such of the negroes as they could conveniently lay hold of with their hands. Others, being prepared with several handkerchiefs tied together, encircled with these as many as they were able. While others, by means of a rope, effected the same purpose. It is scarcely possible to describe the confusion of which this mode of selling is productive. It likewise causes much animosity among the purchasers, who, not unfrequently upon these occasions, fall out and quarrel with each other. The poor astonished negroes were so much terrified by these proceedings that several of them, through fear, climbed over the walls of the court yard, and ran wild about the town; but were soon hunted down and retaken.

While on a former voyage from Africa to Kingston in Jamaica, I saw a sale there by scramble, on board a snow. The negroes were collected together upon the main and quarter decks, and the ship was darkened by sails suspended over them, in order to prevent the purchasers from being able to see, so as to pick or chuse. The signal being given, the buyers rushed in, as usual, to seize their prey; when the negroes appeared to be extremely terrified, and near thirty of them jumped into the sea. But they were all soon retaken, chiefly by boats from other ships.

On board a ship, lying at Port Maria, in Jamaica, I saw another scramble; in which, as usual, the poor negroes were greatly terrified. The women, in particular, clang to each other in agonies scarcely to be conceived, shrieking through excess of terror at the savage manner in which their brutal purchasers rushed upon and seized them. Though humanity, one should imagine, would dictate the captains to apprize the poor negroes of the mode by which they were to be sold, and by that means to guard them, in some degree, against the surprize and terror which must attend it, I never knew that any notice of the scramble was given to them. Nor have I any reason to think that it is done; or that this mode of sale is less frequent at this time than formerly.[19]

1.8. Africans Stowed Aboard the Slave Ship *Brooks* in the Late Eighteenth Century

The following excerpts from a pamphlet of the London Abolition Society appeared soon after publication of Alexander Falconbridge's account of the slave trade (see Doc. 1.7). Designed to inform the public of the enormous waste and brutality of the traffic and its destructive effects on African slaves and British seamen as well, the piece included illustrations of slaves aboard a slave ship called the *Brooks,* that were often reproduced, and therefore the pamphlet may be regarded as in the forefront of the emerging British antislavery movement. The broadside was reprinted by C. B. Wadstrom in his *Essay on Colonization,* published in 1794.

SOURCE: C. B. Wadstrom, *An Essay on Colonization, Particularly Applied to the Western Coast of Africa* (1794; reprint, New York: Augustus M. Kelley, 1968), unnumbered pocket insert.

19. A slave trader living in Charleston, South Carolina, in the 1760s described a scramble as follows: "Notice of the sale having been given some days before, the slaves were ranged in a close yard, a great gun fired, and buyers rushed violently in, and seized the best looking slaves, afterwards picking and culling them to their minds. They were immediately purchased and hurried out of the yard; so that, in a few hours, only the refuse slaves remained; whose health had suffered, generally, as he conceived, from crowding and confined air on board, and who afterwards sold at a great under-price." *Bridgment of the Minutes of Evidence, Taken before a Committee of the Whole House, to whom it was referred to consider the slave-trade* (London, 1790), no. 3, pp. 72–73.

The Plan and Sections annexed exhibit a slave ship with the slaves stowed. In order to give a representation of the trade . . . the *Brooks* is here described, a ship well known in the trade, and the first mentioned in the report delivered to the House of Commons by Captain Parrey, who was sent to Liverpool by Government to take the dimensions of the ships employed in the African slave trade from that port. . . .

The number of slaves which this vessel actually carried, appears from the accounts given to Captain Parrey by the slave-merchants themselves, as follows:

Men   351
Women   127   Total   609
Boys   90
Girls   41

The room allowed to each description of slaves in this plan, is:
To the men 6 feet by 1 foot 4 inches.
Women 5 feet 10 inches by 1 foot 4 inches.
Boys 5 feet by 1 foot 2 inches.
Girls 4 feet 6 inches by 1 foot.

With this allowance of room the utmost number that can be stowed in a vessel of the dimension of the *Brooks* is as follows (being the number exhibited in the plan, and is 1½ to a ton) viz.

	On the Plan	Actually Carried	
Men—on the lower deck, at CC	124	190	351
Ditto on the platform of ditto, CC DD		66	
Boys—lower deck EE	58	82	90
Ditto—platform FF	24		
Women—lower deck, GG	83		
Ditto—platform, HH	40	183	127
Women half deck, MM	36		
Platform, ditto, NN	24		
Girls—Gun room, II		27	41
General total		482	609

The principal difference is in the *men*. It must be observed, that the men from whom insurrections are to be feared, are kept continually in irons, and must be stowed in the room allotted for them, which is of a more secure construction than the rest. . . . [T]he room allowed them, instead of being 16 inches, as in the plan, was in reality only 10 inches each; but if the whole number 351 were stowed in the men's room, they had only 9 inches to lay in.

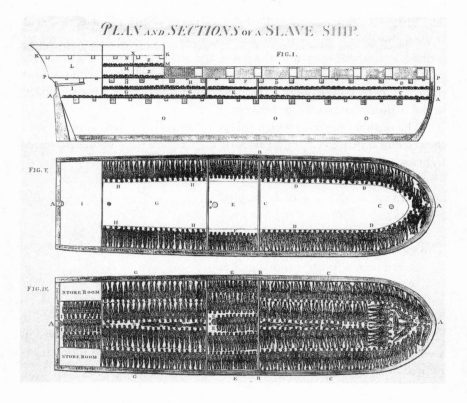

4. Printed propaganda broadside of the London Abolition Society. From C. B.
Wadstrom, *An Essay on Colonization* (1794). Reprint: Augustus M. Kelley
(New York, 1968).

The men, therefore, instead of lying on their backs, were placed, as is
usual, in full ships, on their sides, or on each other. In which last situation
they are not unfrequently found dead in the morning.

The longitudinal section, fig. I, shews the manner in which the
slaves were placed on all the decks and platforms, which is also further
illustrated by the transverse sections, fig. II and III. By which it appears,
that the height between the decks is 5 feet 8 inches, which, allowing 2
inches for the platform and its bearers, makes the height between the
decks and the platform 2 feet 9 inches; but the beams and their knees,
with the carlings [short timbers running lengthwise of a ship, beneath
transverse deck beams], taking 4 inches on an average, this space is
unequally divided, and above or under the platforms cannot be estimated
at more than 2 feet 7 inches; so that slaves cannot, when placed either

on or under the platform, relieve themselves by sitting up; the very short ones excepted, nor can *they,* except on board the larger vessels. The average of nine vessels measured by Captain Parrey, being mostly large ships, was only 5 feet 2 inches. The height of the Venus between decks was 4 feet 2 inches; of the Kitty, 4 feet 4 inches, both of which had platforms. In these smaller vessels therefore they have not 2 feet under or upon the platforms. . . .

It may be expected from this mode of packing a number of our fellow-creatures, used in their own country to a life of ease, and from the anguish of mind their situation must necessarily create, that many of them fall sick and die. Instances sometimes occur of horrible mortality. The average is not less than 1–5th, or 20 per cent. The half deck is sometimes appropriated for a sick birth; but the *men slaves* are seldom indulged with the privilege of being placed there, till there is little hope of recovery. The slaves are never allowed the least bedding, either sick or well; but are stowed on the bare boards, from the friction of which, occasioned by the motion of the ship, and their chains, they are frequently much bruised: and in some cases the flesh is rubbed off their shoulders, elbows, and hips.

It may not be improper to add a short account of the mode of securing, airing, and exercising the slaves.

The women and children are not chained, but the men are constantly chained two and two; the right leg of one to the left leg of the other, and their hands are secured in the same manner.

They are brought up on the main deck every day, about eight o'clock, and as each pair ascend, a strong chain, fastened by ring-bolts to the deck, is passed through their shackles; a precaution absolutely necessary to prevent insurrections. In this state, if the weather is favourable, they are permitted to remain about one-third of the twenty-four hours, and during this interval they are fed, and their apartment below is cleaned; but when the weather is bad, even those indulgencies cannot be granted them, and they are only permitted to come up in small companies, of about ten at a time, to be fed, where after remaining a quarter of an hour, each mess is obliged to give place to the next in rotation.

In *very* bad weather, some are unavoidably brought on deck: there being no other method of getting water, provisions, &c. out of the hold, but by removing those slaves who lie on the hatch-ways. The consequence of this violent change from their rooms, which are inconceivably hot, to the wind and rain, is their being attacked with coughs, swellings of the glands of the neck, fevers and dysenteries; which are communicated by infection to the other slaves, and also to the sailors.

The only exercise of the men-slaves is their being made to jump in their chains; and this, by the friends of the trade, is called *dancing*.

To persons unacquainted with the mode of carrying on this system of trading in human flesh, these Plans and Sections will appear rather a fiction, than a real representation of a slave ship. They will probably object, that there is no room for stowing cables, and such other utensils and stores as are usually placed between decks. In a slave ship (i. e. a full one) these articles are either deposited in the hold, or piled upon the upper deck; and from thence, in case of bad weather, or accidents, no small confusion is occasioned. It may also be said, the slaves are placed so very close, that there is not room for the surgeon to visit and assist them: the fact is, that when the surgeon goes amongst them, he picks out his way as well as he can, by stepping between their legs. He frequently finds it to be impossible to afford them that relief which a humane man (and such there are even in this trade) would willingly give them. When attacked with fluxes, their situation is scarcely to be described. . . .

Another objection which may be stated, is, that here no room is allowed for the sailors *(sic)* hammocks. In slave ships, while the slaves are on board, the sailors have no other lodging than the bare decks, or (in large ships) the tops. From this exposure, they often are wet for a long time together, the rains in those climates being frequent and extremely heavy. There is in wet weather a tarpawling placed over the gratings: if the sailors, to shelter themselves, creep under this, they are exposed to the noisome and infectious effluvia which continually exhale from the slaves below.

It appeared from the evidence given by the slave merchants last year before the House of Commons, that the employment of seamen, viz. boating up the rivers after the negroes, guarding them on board, cleansing the vessel, &c. is of a nature offensive and dangerous beyond that of seamen in other services, and that the small-pox, measles, flux, and other contagious disorders, are frequent on board these ships.

It is therefore falsely said, by the well-wishers of this trade, that the suppression of it will destroy a great nursery for seamen, and annihilate a very considerable source of commercial profit. The Rev. Mr. [Thomas] Clarkson, in his admirable treatise on the Impolicy of the Trade, has proved, from the most incontestable authority, that so far from being a nursery, it has been constantly and regularly a grave for our seamen; *for that in this traffic only, a greater proportion of men perish in* one year, *than in all the other trades of Great Britain in two years.*

Besides the time spent on the coast to complete their cargoes, which sometimes lasts several months, the slaves are from six to eight weeks on their passage from thence to the West-Indies.

Now let any person reflect on the situation of a number of these devoted people, thus managed and thus crammed together, and he must
think it dreadful, even under every favourable circumstance of a humane
captain, an able surgeon, fine weather, and a short passage. But when to a
long passage are added, inhuman treatment, scanty and bad provisions,
and rough weather, their condition is miserable beyond description. So destructive is this traffic in some circumstances, particularly in bad weather,
when the slaves are kept below, and the gratings covered with tarpawlings,
that a schooner, which carried only 140 slaves, meeting with a gale of wind
which lasted eighteen hours, no less than 50 slaves perished in that small
space of time.

As then the inhumanity of this trade must be universally admitted and
lamented, people would do well to consider, that it does not often fall to
the lot of individuals, to have an opportunity of performing so important,
a moral, and religious duty, as that of endeavouring to put an end to a practice, which may, without exaggeration, be styled one of the *greatest evils at
this day existing upon the earth.*

1.9. "Death by the Visitation of God." News Items on the African Slave
Trade from the *Charleston Courier* (April 1807)

In 1803 South Carolina revoked a state ban on the African slave trade that
had been passed into law sixteen years earlier. As a result, in the four years
prior to the *federal* prohibition of the African traffic, which took effect on
January 1, 1808, more than 39,000 Africans were listed as having entered
the state from abroad, most of these through the port of Charleston. In the
final year of the legal traffic, in fact, no less than 15,676 slaves were so registered, a volume of activity that inevitably produced a high level of mortality not only at sea but also on shipboard and ashore in the days and weeks
following the arrival of slave cargoes.[20]

This loss of life did not go unnoticed in and about the city. In 1805 the
Charleston Courier reported "several incidents . . . of dead human bodies
having been thrown into the waters of the Harbour of Charleston," as a result of which the City Council imposed a hundred-dollar fine on any person who threw a corpse into the city's rivers. As the following newspaper
reports reveal, however, despite the fine, this means of disposing of the dead

20. See Ulrich B. Phillips, *American Negro Slavery* (Baton Rouge: Louisiana State University Press,
1969), pp. 132–49.

was common in 1807 and probably remained so until the large-scale arrival of Africans at the port of Charleston ended in 1808.

SOURCE: Elizabeth Donnan, ed., *Documents Illustrative of the History of the Slave Trade to America* (Washington, D.C.: Carnegie Institution of Washington, 1935), vol. 4, pp. 526–27.

April 8, 1807.

A Jury of Inquest was held on Monday, last, on the body of a Negro Man, found floating by Benjamin Johnson's new wharf; supposed to be an African, and thrown overboard from some slave ship in the harbour, to save the expense of burial. The jury brought in a verdict, that he came to his death by the visitation of God.

A Jury of Inquest was held yesterday, on the body of an African Negro floating in Pritchard's dock. It appeared to be one thrown overboard from one of the slave ships from Africa, now in the harbour. A practice too prevalent among the captains, and disgraceful to humanity. The jury brought in a verdict, that he came to his death by the visitation of God.

April 21, 1807.

A Jury of Inquest was held on Sunday afternoon, on the body of an African negro woman, found floating near the Market dock—it appeared to the jurors, from its having on the usual dress, of a blue flannel frock, to have belonged to one of the slave ships in the harbour, and thrown into the river, to save the expense of burial; a custom too prevalent in this port with the officers of slave ships, and in itself shocking to humanity. The jury brought in a verdict, that she came to her death by the visitation of God. And the coroner begs leave to remind the seamen and petty officers of those ships, that the City Council have passed an Ordinance, prohibiting so inhuman and brutal a custom, and have offered a reward of One Hundred Dollars, to any person or persons, who will give information, so that the offender or offenders, may be prosecuted to conviction, and their names exposed to the good citizens of this state. The coroner has received information that there are at this time, the bodies of three or more of these poor wretches floating about Hog-Island, and the marshes opposite the city—the effluvia arising from which, must be very prejudicial to the health of passengers in boats, passing and repassing them daily.

April 22, 1807.

A Jury of Inquest was held yesterday, on the body of an African Negro woman, found floating at Craft's north wharf. The jury brought in a verdict, that she came to her death by the visitation of God—and supposed her to belong to some of the slave ships in this harbour, and thrown into the river, to save expense of burial.

1.10. "I Hardly Believe Myself in My Own Country." The Last Years of the Legal Slave Trade of South Carolina (1804–1807): A Glimpse at the Record

The following article, a denunciation of the South Carolina slave trade during its final phase, was published (date unknown) in *The Pennsylvania Advocate,* a journal of the city of Washington, Pennsylvania, and republished in William Lloyd Garrison's *Liberator* in 1832. The article provides an emotional glimpse into the legal slave trade of South Carolina during its last years, with an emphasis on the numbers of slaves involved and the massive mortality among imported blacks compared to death rates among whites and settled blacks, a situation reminiscent of the means of human disposal described in Document 1.9. An excerpt from a newspaper article of 1804 (following the renewal of the legal traffic on December 18, 1803), describes the sorrowful separation of three young African girls aboard a slave ship in Charleston harbor.

SOURCE: *The Liberator,* December 1, 1832.

SLAVERY RECORD.
From the Pennsylvania Advocate.
A HEAVY ACCOUNT TO SETTLE.

The people of South Carolina and Georgia, among whom, no doubt, there are some, if not many, humane persons, are to a proverb barbarous in the treatment of their slaves, as well as for slave trading. The most dreadful manglings and tortures, which I knew to be inflicted in ———, were principally perpetrated by persons from these states, especially South Carolina. May there not be, in the course of Providence, an old and very serious account to settle with these States?

There seems to be much reason and truth in the ancient adage, or proverbial maxim, *Quem deus rult perdere, prius de mentat*—those whom God wills to destruction, he first deprives of their senses; which appears to mean, that being so bereft, they may work their perdition themselves, without the shadow of a miraculous interposition. A large portion of the inhabitants of these two States seem already sufficiently maddened to leap a very dangerous precipice.

I will take leave to note a few items of the account before me, which South Carolina may possibly be compelled to settle; and in which Georgia may have had some partnership, and no small concern.

Extract of a letter from Charleston, (S.C.)

'I hardly believe myself in my own country.—Slavery I detest; and I have seen a horrid share of it. This port has for some time past, been opened for the importation of negroes. Several ships crowded with wretched victims, are now at the wharves. I have been on board of them during the hours of sale, and felt all the horrors which the abominable traffic could inspire. One scene I shall never forget: Three young girls of the same country, of the same family, who had probably never been separated, who were comparatively happy, even as slaves, while together, were brought upon deck, and one of them selected and bought by a planter. With the most piercing anguish, she received her master's habilaments, and stood ready to leave every thing dear to her. She appeared to be overloaded with horror and dismay, at the separation from her two friends. They looked wishfully at her, and she at them. At last, they threw themselves into each other's arms, and burst into the most piteous exclamations. They hung together, and sobbed and screamed, and bathed each other with their tears. At length they were torn asunder by the unfeeling whites, and the planter's purchase dragged from the ship. But at parting, one of the girls took a string of beads with an amulet from her neck, kissed it and hung it on her friend's. This was too much! I was afraid my emotions would be noticed, and I left the spot.

'The Almighty will, one day or other, revenge this inhuman outrage upon the laws of heaven.'

[Transcribed from *The Western Telegraph and Washington Advertiser,* of Monday, May 21, 1804; No. 457. Washington, Washington Co., Pennsylvania.]

In order to induce the members of the chief slaveholding states, in the convention of 1787, to accede to the plan of the federal constitution, and, of course, to save the states from perpetual disunion, irreconcilable hostility, and probably foreign domination and provincial vassalage, it was agreed, that the migration, or importation of such persons as any of the states, then existing, should think proper to admit, should not be prohibited by the Congress prior to the year 1808; that is, that the legislature of the United States for twenty years should have no power paramount to the power of the individual states, for the purpose of preventing the importation of slaves, and the continuance of the barbarous traffic in human beings; leaving the authority under the policy and humanity of the legislatures of the several states respectively. And it was further agreed and declared that no amendment made to the constitution, prior to the year 1808, should in any manner affect this inhuman, murderous and anti-christian power of slave-trading reserved to the states; and we find how barbarously it was executed, by South Carolina in particular, of which the preceding article from the Charleston letter furnishes a small but leading specimen.

During the years 1804, 1805, 1806, and 1807, as appears from Magazines, Registers, and other periodical works of the times, of authentic character, 39,310 human beings were imported, as slaves, from Africa into the city of Charleston alone. *Thirty-nine thousand three hundred and ten!* The last mentioned year, 1807, was the year immediately prior to that in which the prohibition or abolition might commence under the authority of Congress, and many were imported during that year; 9,766 arrived from the first of January to the first of November, (of course, a considerable part during the most sickly months)—1,487 during the months of August, September and October, and many of them died of dysentery and other complaints.

The number of deaths of people of color, for these three months, so far as ascertained, is stated to be 444; but it was probably much greater. If 444 died out of 1,847, in that time, how many died out of 39, 310, during the same time, after the arrival of the respective vessels, in which they were immured, in the same ratio or proportion? The answer will be eleven thousand, several hundred, and upwards. But it may be captiously said that more of those who arrived during the months of August, September, and October, died, than of those, who arrived during other months. Let this be granted, and allow six months, nine months, or a year in the calculation. Mortality to a great extent prevails among the Africans, imported as slaves, no doubt, at all seasons; and for a considerable length of time after this arrival; probably not so much from change of climate, as from their worse than savage treatment on board the *floating hells,* the slave ships. On a very moderate calculation, it may be estimated that more than TEN THOUSAND of the native children of Africa, imported as slaves during the four years mentioned, lost their lives in consequence of their importation, during the first year after their arrival at Charleston in South Carolina.

The following is a general account of deaths in Charleston, for August, 1807.

Whites	59
Negroes	40
New Negroes	116

Here the deaths of the New, or lately imported Africans, are more than double those of all the white inhabitants and colored persons, living at home, and inured to the climate and mode of life there. How immense must be the disproportion! This, however, cannot be ascertained without having a correct statement of the respective numbers of the three above classes, or denominations.

But did these ten thousand comprise all, who were murdered in the Charleston trade during the four years from 1804 to 1807, inclusive? How many lost their lives in the various attempts and stratagems to capture them? How many perished on shipboard amidst the filth, contaminating air, contagious pestilence, and putrid exhalations of the infernal holds in which they were stowed;—and were thrown into the insatiable ocean, naked, and food for the monsters of the deep? Shall we put down these also at ten thousand, or only at five thousand? Shall the whole number of victims be estimated at twenty, or only fifteen thousand? Is there any schedule or register of those, who never arrived?

I will not dare to invoke the vengeance, or *justice,* of Heaven, on the guilty heads of the murdering traffickers; but may I not ask, will there not be a day of retribution; and even in this life? Is it not insultingly challenged?

Ann of Austria, Queen of Louis XIII, was most cruelly treated by the imperious Richelieu. She said one day to the Cardinal, after some insult he had put upon her, '*Dieu ne paye pas toutes les semaines, mois enfin il paye;*'— God, sir, does not settle his accounts with mankind every week, but at last he settles them with effect.—NOBLE LADY!

Many of the friends of humanity, when considering only the cruel treatment of slaves, where slave trading with Africa has been abolished, have appealed to Heaven for the interposition of its justice. It will be seen that the extract of the Charleston letter concludes with confident assurance that 'the Almighty will one time or other revenge this inhuman outrage upon the laws of heaven.'. . .

While transcribing the foregoing, the following questions occurred to the mind of the author:

Is not the prohibition of the slave trade by the general government the real and fundamental cause of the discontents of the *nullifiers* in South Carolina, and advocates of disunion?

Does it not appear to every dispassionate and reflecting man, that these enemies to the union of our great federal republic are calling down upon their own heads, and upon their state, the most awful and *sudden* calamities?

A NATIVE PENNSYLVANIAN.

1.11. "Revelations of a Slave Smuggler" (1808–1853)

Richard Drake (also known as Phillip Drake), the British author of the following selections, was allegedly involved in the slave trade for half a century, principally as a medic, but also taking part in the shipment and sale of tens of thousands of Africans to major world markets. Among these were Brazil (to which Drake claimed to have made many voyages), Cuba, British Guiana, the United States, and the Bay Islands off the coast of Honduras.

Some writers have questioned the authenticity of parts of Drake's narrative, but have accepted other parts. For example, two reputable historians of the traffic regarded much of the book as "lurid fiction," but nevertheless quoted it extensively, arguing that Drake "was unquestionably familiar with the slave trade, especially the American end of it," and that many of his statements could be verified by independent sources.[21] Some parts of the work may have been intended to serve as antislavery propaganda, but Drake's account of a rehabilitation center for slaves newly arrived in Brazil and other Brazilian matters seems genuine, as do his reports of slave trading to and within the United States

The first excerpt from Drake's autobiographical narrative deals with the following topics, among others: his youthful involvement in the establishment of a slave depot called Rio Basso[22] to facilitate illegal British slave trading and to ship slaves to Brazil; an account of a turbulent voyage from Rio Basso to Pensacola, Florida, with nine hundred slaves, and a subsequent overland trek through the American South with a "coffle" of Africans and "native blacks" who were sold along the way; and finally, the author's impressions of slavery and the slave trade in the United States, with an emphasis on the selling of slaves.

The second excerpt contains a brief description of slave buying in Dahomey for a shipment to Brazil and a longer account of Drake's employment in Brazil in the 1840s as the supervisor of a "slave nursery" designed to restore newly imported Africans to health prior to sale. This section ends with Drake's later employment at a slave station on one of the Bay Islands

---

21. Daniel P. Mannix and Malcolm Cowley, *Black Cargoes, A History of the Atlantic Slave Trade, 1518–1865* (New York: Viking Press, 1962), pp. 203–5, 232–35.

22. Perhaps the port of Bassa Cove (some forty-five miles southeast of Monrovia, Liberia), where slave traders remained highly active at least as late as 1834 when "Bassa Land" was purchased by the governor of Liberia from King Joe Harris, "the sovereign of that fine harbor." See William Jay, *Inquiry into the Character and Tendency of the American Colonization and American Anti-Slavery Societies* (1838; reprint, New York: Negro Universities Press, 1969), pp. 56–61. Bassa Cove and nearby places called Little Bassa and Grand Bassa all appear on a map in the sixth volume of *The African Repository and Colonial Journal*, the periodical of the Colonization Society.

off the northern coast of Honduras, where he helped to prepare Africans for shipment to Texas, Florida, Cuba, and other destinations. Parts of the text were drawn from Drake's diary which he allegedly wrote over much of his life.

SOURCE: *Revelations of a Slave Smuggler: being the Autobiography of Capt. Rich'd Drake, An African Trader for Fifty Years—from 1807 to 1857; During which Period He Was Concerned in the Transportation of Half a Million Blacks from African Coasts to America. With a Preface by His Executor, Rev. Henry Byrd West, of the Protestant Home Mission* (New York: Robert M. De Witt, 1860), pp. 46–52, 96–97.

Establishment of the Slave Depot of Rio Basso, a Voyage to Florida, and a Slave-Selling Expedition through the American South.

I now quote from such portions of my journal as contain matters of interest:

Nov. 3d, 1808.—Cast anchor to-day off Cape Palmas, African coast, and shipped forty Kroo fishermen with their canoes. This part of the coast is considered to be a fine field for the traffic. My uncle [Richard Willing, who had introduced Drake to the slave trade] intends establishing a station on one of the rivers.

Nov. 6th.—We have chopped down to this place called Assinam, a couple of miles from the mouth of a river said to be populous. Our Kroomen [23] are engaged in setting up sheds, and we are to have a grand *palabra* with the natives, who have sent messengers to negotiate. The country hereabouts is ruled by a black king named Prince Vinegar. He must be a sour sort of fellow.

Nov. 8th.—Our trading post is quite a respectable place already. The river bends at this point, making a little harbor, and the shore is thick with grass down to the sandy beach, the forest behind making a semi-circle. Our Kroos got the assistance of some hundred blacks, and we have a picket fence and covered sheds, to shelter goods. Pots are boiling, hammers and saws sounding, and canoes running back and forth to the brig, which commands the whole beach with her guns. There is safe anchorage here, and the river is navigable for the brig some thirty or forty miles up, so it is said.

Nov. 9th.—. . . It is understood that we are to hold undisputed posses-

---

23. A people skillful as seamen who inhabited what is now Liberia. One of their kin groups was known as the Bassa. Editor.

sion of this part of the coast, and my uncle is to have jurisdiction from a point just above this place, to the sea, more than two miles of fine country. This jurisdiction includes the power of life and death over any negro, under the rank of prince, who may come within our domain. . . . My uncle is now known as Don Ricardo, and my name is transmogrified into Felipe. So we are called by the crew, and so we shall pass, if we chance to be over-hauled by British armed vessels, and there are several now on the coast.

Nov. 10th.—My uncle has told me his plans about future operations. The British slave trade ended in July last, but there are many British Liver-pool and Scotch vessels on the coast now, with full cargoes. Don Ricardo intends to make our new settlement a depot for these, and we shall run car-goes to the Brazils. We have landed a couple of carronades [a short iron can-non used on ships], and will soon have a respectable station.

Nov. 11th.—To-day arrived the Loango, one of my uncle's schooners, from the Congo. She is anchored off our settlement, which Don Ricardo has christened Rio Basso. In her came a Spaniard, Don Miguel Barca, a crony of my uncle, who is to be factor at this place. . . . To day King Vine-gar sent us a couple of bullocks and a milch cow.

The above extracts from my journal commence the routine life I led at Rio Basso, during five years that I remained there. The settlement grew to be one of the most thriving on the windward coast, and was the means of saving scores of British merchants from ruin, if it did no good otherwise. By means of our fast schooners, together with the Coralline and an Ameri-can built brig, just her mate, called the *Florida,* we kept up a constant tap-ping of the coast from Cape Palmas to the Rio Gambia, whence Captain Fraley's stations were still supplied with negroes. My uncle received the car-goes at Rio Basso, transhipped them to his own or other legal bottoms, and coined money by every operation. . . . Our barracoons, as the slave-pens are called, were built close to the river, and on an island about a hundred yards in the stream, thickly grown with mangrove-bushes, bamboos, and palm trees. They were constructed of cane, matted with vine, and plastered with mud, the whole strengthened by uprights and picket barriers. Into these capacious receptacles the slaves were driven on arrival, and placed in charge of gangsmen of their own color. The gangsmen superintended the head-shaving, washing, and branding, and saw that the blacks were duly se-cured every night to posts driven in the ground. The proportion of gangs-men was one to twenty slaves, and they took turns standing guard, with whips, through the nights, to keep order.

We had a quarantine hospital built on a little island farther down the river, for treatment of sick stock, and a burial place in the sand behind. I instructed a dozen intelligent blacks in the mysteries of simple drugging, cupping, and blistering, and in a short time could boast of quite a medical board. We were generally lucky with our patients, and lost a small average. Out of seventy-two thousand slaves received and transhipped from Rio Basso, in five years, we lost only eight thousand; and this included deaths by accidental drowning, suicides, and by a small pox epidemic in 1811, when our barracoons were crowded, and when we shipped thirty thousand souls to Brazil and the West Indies.

A year after the establishment of barracoons at Rio Basso, the colony of free negroes planted by the British abolitionists at Sierra Leone, near the old Portuguese factories, was taken possession of by the British government, and an English man-of-war was stationed on the coast. My uncle's policy was then found completely successful. His schooners coasted up and down, running into rivers and creeks, where English factories still kept up inland connections, and bringing down cargoes to Rio Basso under the Portuguese, Spanish, and French flags. If boarded by a British cruiser, my uncle or his captains could always show papers corresponding with the flag carried; and he was so good a linguist himself that, with his swarthy face, he could pass for any countryman besides his own. His English name [Richard Willing] was twisted into Spanish as Ricardo Villeno.

But I must hurry over this part of my life to the next voyage I made from Rio Basso to the Floridas, and its dismal records, as entered in my journal of that year:

Oct. 28, 1812.—Left Rio Basso this day in the *Boa Morte,* formerly an American trader, now owned by Don Ricardo Villeno, my respectable uncle. She is commanded by a crew of St. Domingo, Pierre Leclerc, and bound for Pensacola, in the Floridas, with a cargo of nine hundred slaves. Monsieur Leclerc is a peppery little fellow, an old slaver, and has an interest in the freight. The second officer is Diego Ramos, a Portuguese from Fayal, and we three were in the round-house, as every inch of space is occupied by the blacks, cabin and hold knocked into slave decks, and packed tight at that. The stock is healthy, however, and we look for a profitable trip.

Oct. 30.—Leclerc is reckoning up his anticipated profits, and I may as well do the same. I have one hundred prime blacks—only twenty females—all branded, in good Spanish, with my name, "Fellipe Drax," and I begin to feel the anxieties of a property owner. My little venture, at present prices, ought to bring me $8,000-a tolerable set-up, with a little stock left on hand at Rio Basso. I shall invest my profitable goods, as my uncle advises, and go back prepared to begin trade for my own profit. I can find no fault with my uncle; the Don has become rather moody of late, but he has kept his business word, and I have to thank him for a good start in the world.

Nov. 1.—Everything prosperous, only three sick cases, low fever. Quinine will make them all right, though the sharks are following us, as if they smelt sickness. Leclerc and I have had a chat to day about this African business. He says he's repugnant to it, and I confess it's not a thing I like. But, as my uncle argues, slaves must be bought and sold; somebody must do the trading; and why not make hay while the sun shines?

Nov. 2.—Pedro, my assistant, reports one of our patients blind. We had half the gangs on deck today for exercise; they danced and sung, under the driver's whip, but are far from sprightly. Captain Leclerc says he never knew such a sluggish set; yet they all appear healthy.

Nov. 3.—Bad news. We have ophthalmia among the slaves, decidedly, and spreading. Eight are reported as blind.

Nov. 4.—Captain Leclerc is sick, confined to his birth. The ophthalmia is spreading among the blacks. I have nineteen on deck, under treatment.

Nov. 7.—My God! That scourge of destruction, the smallpox, has broken out. Leclerc is down with it, and two of the crew, and I fear it is among the slaves. We are threatened with foul weather.

Nov. 14.—I make another entry into my journal. God knows whether I shall ever reach port alive. The *Boa Morte* is well named. It is a death ship, and has been feeding the sharks with corpses for seven days past. . . . Death and despair on every side. Last Tuesday the smallpox began to rage, and we hauled sixty corpses out of the hold. Diego Ramos can hardly control the crew, and we have to rely on gangs of slaves to drag the dead heaps from among the living. Captain Leclerc is out of danger, but remains blind with ophthalmia. God help us all, if this goes on.

Nov. 15.—I have got through another day and night, and am yet alive. Diego Ramos and a half dozen sailors, are all of the crew to be relied on. We stimulate the blacks with rum, in order to get their help in removing corpses; thirty negroes and two Portuguese sailors were thrown overboard to-day. I have been among the blacks in a reckless way, under the artificial excitement of laudanum and liquor, and the sights I witnessed, may I never look upon such again. This is a dreadful trade. Leclerc says it sometimes drives men crazy, and I think it is no wonder. . . .

Nov. 17.—We have had a violent storm, and the hatches are closed. The work of death goes on unseen. Captain Leclerc is better to day, and begins to see a little. God grant he may recover! Diego Ramos is still well, and so am I, after all we have gone through: but what would tempt me to pass such another ten days as the last? Not all the wealth of the Indies! Leclerc is quite serious and intends to abandon the slave traffic. He says to-day he thought it was an accursed thing; I told Diego Ramos, and he laughed, remarking that the "devil was sick, and wanted to turn monk." . . .

Nov. 19.—Thanks be to God! we are alive, on a steady sea, after experiencing a most frightful hurricane. Yesterday even Diego Ramos thought we were lost. The sun went down red, as the previous night, and Diego prophesied a continuance of the tempest, which before terrified us. The wind shifted to the west, the sky grew black as ink, and was filled with fiery appearances. The thunder roared and lightning flashed incessantly. Our ship was whirled about like a top, and driven before the gale, nearly all night, without a rag of canvas. We heard guns during the storm, but have seen no sail, though we are approaching the Mexican Gulf to-day. Captain Leclerc is on deck, very feeble, but able to see once more. Diego Ramos advises not to open the hatches till we reach port, which we hope to do by sunset, if the wind continues fair.

Nov. 20.—Anchored last night in Pensacola Bay.

The voyage of the *Boa Morte* terminated at Pensacola Bay, after we had landed our surviving negroes on one of the shallow beaches near the mouth of the Escambia River. Here, with the assistance of laborers from the neighboring town, we rigged sheds for our sick, and took measures for lime-washing and fumigating the ship. Strange as it may seem, we saved five hundred and nineteen out of nine hundred, and, much to my satisfaction, sixty-four of these had my brand, so that I was not such a loser as I expected to be.

Captain Leclerc was as good as his word. He sold the *Boa Morte* to the House of Bernard & Co., at the Matanzas [Cuba], and closed his accounts with my uncle's consignees. After settlement of all our business, I found myself entitled to $6,430, proceeds of my negroes. Diego Ramos came in for his own share of luck, as the captain presented him with fifty slaves, in testimony of his skill and services, which no doubt, saved the ship and all on board. After resting a few days at St. Augustine, where I took a final leave of Captain Leclerc, I agreed to accompany Diego on a land trip through the United States, where a *kaffle* of negroes was to precede us, for whose disposal the shrewd Portuguese had already made arrangements with my uncle's consignees.

I soon learned how readily, and at what profits the Florida negroes were sold into the neighboring American states. The *kaffle,* under charge of negro drivers, was to strike up the Escambia River, and thence cross the boundary into Georgia, where some of our wild Africans were mixed with various squads of native blacks, and driven inland, till sold off, singly or by

couples, on the road. At this period (1812) the United States had declared
the African slave trade illegal, and passed stringent laws to prevent the importation of negroes; yet the Spanish possessions were thriving on this inland exchange of negroes and mulattoes; Florida was a sort of nursery for
slave-breeders, and many American citizens grew rich by trafficking in
Guinea negroes, and smuggling them continually, in small parties, through
the Southern United States. At the time I mention, the business was a lively
one, owing to the war then going on between the States and England, and
the unsettled condition of affairs on the border.

Diego Ramos spoke English as well as I did Spanish, and we passed
very well for a couple of southern merchants. I had taken drafts on
Philadelphia for the amount of my credit with the house of Bernard & Co.,
and was able to make a show of ready money, and indulge in a little display
at our hotels. Diego, with an eye for business, looked after the sale of the
negro squads, and, through his means, he became a guest on many plantations on our line of travel. I had an opportunity of studying the practical
working of slavery in a civilized and democratic country, as I had seen it in
the huts and rice fields of the Volta and Gambia rivers and in the Brazilian
empire. I was also enabled to estimate the influence of civilization on the
Congo and the Ashantee stock after a generation or two, and compare their
condition on American plantations with their native life in African forests.
What I saw and what I thought, in my journey from Florida to Philadelphia, in 1813, may be gleaned from a few brief notes then made and copied
afterward into my journal:

I have begun to jot down my impressions of these States for future reference. Last night I passed, with Diego Ramos, at a plantation on the river,
which they call the Ockmulgee. Mr. Olds, our host, was very frank on the
subject of slave-holding, and is an opponent of the traffic, though a large
planter of cotton. He spoke of the treatment of "black boys," as they are
termed by many of his neighbors. A case had lately occurred of a "boy"
being hung up by the wrists to a tree, with a wooden rail tied to his feet, and
beaten by his master till he expired under the torture. This cruelty was perpetrated on suspicion of a petty theft, which had been committed by the
master's little son, who afterward confessed to the fact. I inquired what
punishment was inflicted on the owner, and was told that the subject had
been talked over, but no complaint made. A slave's testimony is not taken
against a white man; and any crime may be done in presence of a black, by
his master, without fear of detection. Mr. Olds called up a black fellow,
who had been in his family for fifty years, since his birth. This negro is his
master's confidential servant, and is trusted to go into the town weekly to

draw money from the bankers. He has a wife and children very faithful and industrious, and they are all emancipated by provision of our host's last will and testament, as he himself assured us. Such are the lights and shades of slavery.

In Carolina I have become acquainted with several wealthy farmers. Slave merchants drive their kaffles in gangs of ten over the highways, and have pens in the principal villages, where they hold vendues. The number of mulattoes is astonishing. I am told by residents that illicit connections between whites and negroes are much more common than formerly. I have noticed some really handsome quadroon men and women on the auction block, the latter commanding double prices; this indicates the state of morals among the white population.

Cultivation of land in the slave territory is slovenly done, compared with Brazil and Guiana. There is much waste of labor in all operations. I have seen a gang of blacks, with two oxen, engaged a whole morning in drawing a log of timber from the river, to build a house a few miles off. In Rio Basso we should have a dozen cut down and shifted by such a force in the same space of time. The slaves hereabouts are well treated and fat, though nearly naked or ragged; the men wear linsey woolsey shirts and trowsers, the women a petticoat of coarse ducking, and all go barefoot. I have seen boys and girls of fifteen on the plantations, without a stitch of covering, in full sight of their master's verandas. Licentiousness is so common in this country that no one seems to remark it.

In Virginia I found the oldest plantations, and well stocked; but the practice of intercourse between whites and negroes is ruining the slaves for usefulness. A respectable citizen of Fredericksburg, on the Rappahannock River, told me that slave-breeding is getting to be the most profitable business in this quarter. Whole farms are used as nurseries to supply the market with young mulattoes of both sexes. Irish and Scotch overseers have charge of the gangs. The fertility of the negresses in this country is almost the same as in Africa; on a farm near Alexandria, I counted thirty about to become mothers, and the huts swarmed with pickaninnies of different shades.

I heard a story yesterday concerning a slave family, which shows the effects of the system. It seems that a large owner at his death, lately liberated some thirty odd mulattoes, his own children; but his eldest son and heir, a dissipated white man, succeeded in destroying the writings, and afterward sold his dusky skinned brothers and sisters, with some of his own children, to a company of Georgia slave-dealers. One of the blacks, who had a wife and children, according to slave usage, refused to surrender their liberty, and defended his own by barring his hut and threatening the dealers with concealed firearms. An attack was made by night on the negro, and his hut fired. The slave, with two of his young sons, fought until one of the boys was shot, when the whole family were seized and driven to the river, to be put on board a Georgia sloop. At the beach this desperate fellow made fight again, and was assisted by his wife, a strong wench. The Georgia men were unable to master either, till they had beaten the woman with their muskets. The black tried to swim the river, but was shot at and drowned; and the negress was so badly injured that she is said to be quite valueless. . . .

Slave Trading in Dahomey, Employment in Brazil and at a Slave Depot in the Bay Islands off the Coast of Honduras, and the Smuggling of Africans into the United States, 1839–1853

In September, 1839, we set out for Dahomey, and in October we reached Abomey, the capital. I need not dwell on the scenes witnessed at that place. The Dahoman king collected his fetish men, and gave a great feast, it being the season of annual "customs" or slave markets. Four thousand slaves were sold to the traders, of which we bought and branded 700, and dispatched them with the kaffles to the great slaving depot of Whydah. A hundred of our purchase were Amazons, or women-soldiers of the king's guard, who had been engaged in a revolt, and were punished by being sold off. They were fine-limbed and robust females, made healthy by their exercise in military service. . . .

I left Whydah to return with our traders, in a ship which had been consigned to them from Brazil. We took a cargo of 1,000 Africans, and lost only 80 on the return voyage. My life in Africa was finished, and I was glad to be offered a permanent situation in Brazil, under the trading company which I had served as interpreter. . . .

My business in the Brazils was partially professional. A few miles from Rio, on the bay, was located a large slave-depot, and hospital ground. This was for the reception of sick and disabled negroes. It was by no means a charitable institution, however; but planned with a close eye to profit. It was owned by the joint-stock company, of which I was an employee, and my Ponta Negra friend, Don Felix, a director. This company had established agencies along the coast, at intervals, for 2,600 miles, and controlled an immense smuggling traffic in negroes. Its agents to Africa, whom I had accompanied as interpreter, made extensive arrangements whilst there with all the kings we met, for an increase of the trade, and provided also for consignments of stock from the coast. Its South American head-quarters were at Pernambuco.

My specialty, under this company, was to superintend the slave-nursery, or fattening-farm, for negroes who were not merchantable on arrival. Here they were brought in feluccas [small coastal vessels], or driven by squads, overland, to be "doctored" for the market. On arrival, they presented the most deplorable and disgusting spectacle. The greater part were living skeletons; some unable to stand; some covered with ulcers; some with cramped limbs, from packing on shipboard. They often dropped dead in the *corrals,* or yards. Others were ophthalmic, others scrofulous, and many insane. These wretches were to be "doctored," and fatted for sale, or, if that could not be done, allowed to die speedily. The majority were reduced by dysenteries, and required delicate handling, in order to save them. Very often, gangs would be brought to our pens, by outside traders, or by farmers, and offered for sale as low as five, three, and even one dollar a-piece. We lost about forty per cent., on the average, of all that came. When seasoned, we sent the survivors off in gangs to market. I might relate many horrors connected with this service, in which I continued nearly seven years, till I became sick of a fever, and was nearly dying myself. On recovering I was transferred, through the influence of Don Felix, to other masters and another establishment.

I now hurry to the conclusion of the record of my wretched life. I was verging on toward three-score, and had nothing to look back on, but disasters and crimes; nothing to hope for in the future. . . . My new location was on one of the Bay Islands, so called, near the Coast of Honduras, in the Gulf of Mexico. Here a slave-depot and farm were established, to which cargoes were brought, in American clippers, from slave settlements near Cape Mesurado,[24] in Africa. The negroes were landed, under the name of colonists; and the company had permits from Central American authorities. They had a branch farm on the Rio Grande, in Texas, which was broken up, and its stock dispersed, at the breaking out of the war between the United States and Mexico.

Our island depot was admirably suited for its purpose, being near the mainland, and with good anchorage on the ocean side. It was about seven miles long, by three in width, and well wooded [possibly Utila or Guanaja]. Our farm and nursery were in the centre, on a navigable creek. Here we received Bozal blacks [unseasoned or uninstructed slaves recently brought from Africa] of all ages, and set them at work in agricultural operations, and making goods for the African market, to exchange for their fellow-countrymen. They were taught to gabble broken Spanish and English, accustomed to discipline, and well fed and treated. I saw no misery among

24. The location of Monrovia, capital of Liberia. Editor.

these negroes, such as I had been accustomed to witness all my life; as it was our company's object to get them in prime marketable condition.

This joint-stock company was a very extensive one, and connected with leading American and Spanish mercantile houses. Our island was visited weekly, by agents from Cuba, New York, Baltimore, Philadelphia, Boston, and New Orleans. During the continuance of the Mexican war, we had 1,600 negroes in good order, and were receiving and shipping constantly. The seasoned and instructed slaves were taken to Texas or Florida, overland, and to Cuba, in sailing-boats. As no squad contained more than half a dozen, no difficulty was found in posting them to the United States, without discovery, and generally without suspicion. A single negro, sent by special agent, as far as Savannah would pay all his cost and expenses, and fifty per cent. profit in the market. . . .

The Bay Island plantation sent ventures weekly to the Florida Keys. Slaves were taken into the great American swamps, and there kept until wanted for the market. Hundreds were sold as captured runaways from the Florida wilderness. We had agents in every slave State, and our coasters were built in Maine, and came out with lumber.

I could tell curious stories, if it were worth while in my condition, of this business of smuggling Bozal negroes into the United States. It is growing more profitable every year, and if you should hang all the Yankee merchants engaged in it, hundreds would fill their places. Take the word of a dying man, there is no way the slave-trade can be stopped but by breaking up slave-holding. Whilst there is a market, there will be traders; and the entire system is a premium on wholesale robbery and murder. Men like me do its roughest work; but we are no worse than the Christian merchants whose money finds ships and freight, or the Christian planters who keep up the demand for negroes.

1.12. "Steeped Up to Their Very Mouths in This Stream of Iniquity."
Descriptions of the International Slave Trade, Legal and Illegal

The author of this selection, Joseph Story, a Harvard law professor, congressman, justice of the Supreme Court, and late in life, acting Chief Justice of the Supreme Court, was also an acknowledged opponent of slavery. In this excerpt from a speech delivered in 1820 to members of the legal profession, Story analyzes the provisions of U.S. laws intended to stop the international traffic (legally abolished in 1808), then reluctantly enumerates examples of how U.S. citizens regularly violated those laws, not only in

Africa and on the high seas, but also in Southern ports. Then in greater detail he describes the international traffic, basing his views on the abundant published records of the British Parliament and on the narratives of former slave traders and other eye witnesses.

SOURCE: Hon. Joseph Story, *A Charge Delivered to the Grand Jury of the Circuit Court of the United States, at Its First Session in Portland, for the Judicial District of Maine, May 8, 1820, and Published at the Unanimous Request of the Grand Jury and of the Bar* (Portland: A. Shirley, 1820). Republished by Paul Finkelman, *The African Slave Trade and American Courts: The Pamphlet Literature*, series 5, vol. 1 (New York; Garland Publishing, 1988), pp. 21–29.

To our country belongs the honour, as a nation, of having set the first example of prohibiting the further progress of this inhuman traffic. The Constitution of the United States, having granted to Congress the power to regulate foreign commerce, imposed a restriction for a limited period upon its rights of prohibiting the migration or importation of slaves. Nothwithstanding this, Congress, with a promptitude which does honor to their humanity and wisdom, proceeded in 1794, to pass a law to prohibit the traffic of slaves by our citizens in all cases not within the reach of the constitutional restriction; and thus cut off the whole traffic *between foreign ports*. In the year 1800 an additional law was passed to enforce the former enactments; and in the year 1807 (the epoch when the constitutional restriction was to cease, beginning with the ensuing year) a general prohibition of the traffic as well in our domestic as foreign trade was proudly incorporated into our statute book. About the same period the British Government after the most severe opposition from slave dealers and their West Indian friends, achieved a similar measure and enacted a general prohibition of the trade as well to foreign ports as to their colonies. . . .[25]

It is a most cheering circumstance that the examples of the United States and Great Britain in thus abolishing the Slave Trade have, through the strenuous exertions of the latter, been generally approved throughout the continent of Europe. The government of Great Britain has indeed employed the most indefatigable and persevering diligence to accomplish this desirable object; and treaties have been made by her with all the principal foreign powers, providing for a total abolition of the trade within a very

25. Following votes in both houses of the British Parliament, the law abolishing the British traffic was sanctioned by the king on March 25, 1807 and the trade was "utterly abolished, prohibited and declared to be unlawful" on March 1, 1808. See Michael Craton, *Sinews of Empire: A Short History of British Slavery* (New York: Anchor Books, 1974), pp. 264–65. Editor.

short period. May America not be behind her in this glorious work; but by a generous competition in virtuous deeds restore the degraded African to his natural rights, and strike his manacles from the bloody hands of his oppressors.

By our laws it is made an offence for any person to import or bring, in any manner whatsoever, into the United States, or its territories from any foreign country, any negro, mulatto, or person of color with intent to hold, sell, or dispose of him as a slave, or to be held to service or labor. It is also made an offence for any citizen or other person as master, owner, or factor, to build, fit, equip, load or otherwise prepare any vessel in any of our ports, or to cause any vessel to sail from any port whatsoever for the purpose of procuring any negro, mulatto, or person of color from any foreign country to be transported to any port or place whatsoever, to be held, sold, or disposed of, as a slave, or *to be held to service or labor*. It is also made an offence for any citizen or *other person resident within our jurisdiction* to take on board, receive or transport in any vessel from the Coast of Africa or any other foreign country, or from sea, any negro, mulatto or person of color not an inhabitant of, or held to service in the United States, for the purpose of holding, selling or disposing of such persons as a slave, or to be held to service or labour. It is also made an offence for any person within our jurisdiction to hold, purchase, sell or otherwise dispose of any negro, mulatto, or person of colour for a slave, or to be held in service or labour, who shall have been imported into the United States in violation of our laws—and in general the prohibitions in these cases extend to all persons who shall abet or aid in these illegal designs.—These offences are visited as well with severe pecuniary and personal penalties, as with the forfeiture of the vessels and their equipments, which have been employed in the furtherance of these illegal projects; and in general a moiety of the pecuniary penalties and forfeitures is given to any person who shall inform against the offenders and prosecute them to conviction. The President of the United States is also authorised to employ our armed vessels and revenue cutters to cruise on the seas for the purpose of arresting all persons and vessels engaged in this traffic in violation of our laws; and bounties, as well as a moiety of the captured property, are given to the captors to stimulate them in the discharge of their duty.

Under such circumstances it might well be supposed that the Slave Trade would in practice be extinguished; that virtuous men would by their abhorrence stay its polluted march, and wicked men would be overawed by its potent punishments. But unfortunately the case is far otherwise. We have but too many melancholy truths from unquestionable sources that it is still carried on with all the implacable ferocity and insatiable rapacity of former times. Avarice has grown more subtle in its evasions; and watches and seizes its prey with an appetite quickened rather than suppressed by its guilty vigils. American citizens are steeped up to their very mouths (I scarcely use too bold a figure) in this stream of iniquity. They throng to the Coasts of Africa under the stained flags of Spain and Portugal, sometimes selling abroad "their cargoes of despair;" and sometimes bringing them into some of our southern ports, and there under the forms of the law defeating the purposes of the law itself, and legalizing their inhuman but profitable adventures. I wish I could say that New England and New Englishmen were free from this deep pollution. But there is reason to believe that they who drive a loathsome traffic, "and buy the muscles and the bones of men," are to be found here also. It is to be hoped the number is small; but our cheeks may well burn with shame while a solitary case is permitted to go unpunished.

And, Gentlemen, how can we justify ourselves or apologize for an indifference to this subject? Our constitutions of government have declared that all men are born free and equal, and have certain unalienable rights, among which are the right of enjoying their lives, liberties and property, and of seeking and obtaining their own safety and happiness. May not the miserable African ask "Am I not a man and a brother?" We boast of our noble struggle against the encroachments of tyranny, but do we forget that it assumed the mildest form in which authority ever assailed the rights of its subjects: and yet that there are men among us who think it not wrong to condemn the shivering negro to perpetual slavery?

We believe in the Christian religion. It commands us to have good will to all men; to love our neighbors as ourselves, and to do unto all men as we would they should do unto us. It declares our accountability to the Supreme God for all our actions, and holds out to us a state of future rewards and punishments as the sanction by which our conduct is to be regulated. And yet there are men calling themselves Christians who degrade the negro by ignorance to a level with the brutes, and deprive him of all the consolations of religion. He alone of all the rational creation, they seem to think, is to be at once accountable for his actions, and yet his actions are not to be at his own disposal; but his mind, his body, and his feelings are to be sold to perpetual bondage.—To me it appears perfectly clear that the slave trade is equally repugnant to the dictates of reason and religion and is an offence equally against the laws of God and man.—Yet, strange to tell, one of the pretences upon which the modern slavery of the Africans was justified was the "duty of converting the heathen."

I have called this an *inhuman* traffic, and, gentlemen, with a view to enlist your sympathies as well as your judgments in its suppression, permit me to pass from these cold generalities to some of those details, which are the ordinary attendants upon this trade. Here indeed there is no room for the play of imagination. The records of the British Parliament present us a body of evidence on this subject, taken with the most scrupulous care while the subject of the abolition was before it; taken too from persons who had been engaged in, or eye witnesses of the trade; taken too, year after year in the presence of those whose interests or passions were most strenuously engaged to oppose it. That it was not contradicted or disproved can only be accounted for upon the ground that it was the truth and nothing but the truth.[26] What, therefore, I shall briefly state to you on this subject will be drawn principally from these records; and I am free to confess that great as was my detestation of the trade, I had no conception until I recently read an abstract of this evidence, of the vast extent of misery and cruelty occasioned by its ravages. And if, gentlemen, this detail shall awaken your minds to the absolute necessity of constant vigilance in the enforcement of the laws on this subject, we may hope that public opinion following these laws will very soon extirpate the trade among our citizens.

The number of slaves taken from Africa in 1768 amounted to one hundred and four thousand; and though the numbers somewhat fluctuated in different years afterwards, yet it is in the highest degree probable that the average, until the abolition, was not much below 100,000 a year. England alone in the year 1786 employed 130 ships, and carried off about 42,000 slaves.

The unhappy slaves have been divided into seven classes. The most considerable and that which contains at least *half* of the whole numbered transported, consists of *kidnapped people.*—This mode of procuring them includes every species of treachery and knavery. Husbands are stolen from their wives, children from their parents, and bosom friends from each other. So generally prevalent are these robberies that it is a first principle of the natives not to go unarmed while a slave ship is on the coast, for fear of being stolen. The second class of slaves, and that not *inconsiderable,* consists of those whose villages have been depopulated for obtaining them. The parties employed in these predatory expeditions go out at night, set fire to the villages, which they find, and carry off the wretched inhabitants, thus suddenly thrown into their power, as slaves. The practice is indeed so com-

---

26. Story refers to the many published volumes of Parliamentary correspondence on slavery and the slave trade, which taken together, probably comprise the most important collection of material on these subjects in existence. Editor.

mon that the remains of deserted and burnt villages are every where to be seen on the coast.

The third class of slaves consists of such persons as are said to have been convicted of crimes, and are sold on this account for the benefit of their kings; and it is not uncommon to impute crimes to them falsely, and to bring on mock trials for the purpose of bringing them within the reach of the royal traders.

The fourth class includes prisoners of war captured sometimes in ordinary wars, and sometimes in wars originated for the very purposes of slavery.

The fifth class comprehends those who are slaves by birth; and some traders on the coast make a practice of breeding them from their own slaves, for the purpose of selling them, like cattle, when they are arrived at a suitable age.—The sixth class comprehends such as have sacrificed their liberty to the spirit of gaming; and the seventh and last class of those, who being in debt, are seized according to the laws of the country, and sold to their creditors. The two last classes are very inconsiderable—and scarcely deserve mention.

Having lost their liberty in one of the ways already mentioned, the slaves are conveyed to the banks of the rivers or sea coast. Some belong to the neighborhood; others have lived in distant parts; and others are brought a thousand miles from their homes. Those who come from a distance march in droves or caufles, as they are called.[27]—They are secured from rising or running away by pieces of wood which attach the necks of two and two together—or by other pieces, which are fastened by staples to their arms.—They are made to carry their own water and provisions; and they are watched and followed by drivers, who by force compel the weak to keep up with the strong.

They are sold immediately upon their arrival on the rivers or coasts, either to land-factors, at *depots* for that purpose, or directly to the ships engaged in the trade. They are then carried in boats to the various ships whose captains have purchased them. The men are immediately confined two and two together either by the neck, leg, or arm, with fetters of solid iron.— They are then put into their apartments, the men occupying the fore part, the women the after part, and the boys the middle of the vessel. The tops of these apartments are grated for the admission of light and air; and the slaves are stowed like any other lumber, occupying only an allotted portion of room.—Many of them, while the ships are waiting for their full lading in sight of their native shore, manifest great appearance of distress and op-

27. In the United States the word was normally "coffle." Editor.

pression; and some instances have occurred where they have sought relief by suicide, and others where they have been afflicted with delirium and madness. . . .

When the number of slaves is completed, the ships begin what is called the middle passage, to transport the slaves to the colonies. The height of the apartments in the ships is different according to the size of the vessel, and is from six to three feet, so that it is impossible to stand erect in most of the vessels, and in some scarcely to sit down in the same posture. If the vessel be full, their situation is truly deplorable. In the best regulated ships, a grown person is allowed but sixteen inches in width, 32 inches in height, and five feet eleven inches in length, or to use the expressive language of a witness, not to so much room as a man has in his coffin. They are indeed so crowded below that it is almost impossible to walk through the groupes [*sic*] without treading on some of them; and if they are reluctant to get into their places they are compelled by the lash of a whip. And here their situation becomes wretched beyond description. The space between decks where they are confined becomes so hot that persons who have visited them there have found their shirts so wetted with perspiration that water might be wrung from them; and the steam from their confined bodies comes up through the grating like a furnace. The bad effects of such confinement and want of air are soon visible in the weakness and faintness which overcomes the unhappy victims. Some go down apparently well at night and are found dead in the morning. Some faint below and die of suffocation before they can be brought upon deck. As the slaves, whether well or ill, always lie upon bare planks, the motion of the ship rubs the flesh from the prominent parts of their body, and leaves their bones almost bare. The pestilential breath of so many in so confined a state renders them also very sickly and the vicissitudes of heat and cold generate a flux—when this is the case (which happens frequently) the whole place becomes covered with blood and mucus like a slaughter house; and as the slaves are fettered and wedged together, the utmost disorder arises from endeavours to relieve themselves in the necessities of nature; and the disorder is still further increased by the healthy being not unfrequently chained to the diseased, the dying, and the dead!!! When the scuttles in the ship's sides are shut in bad weather, the gratings are not sufficient for airing the room; and the slaves are then seen drawing their breath with all that anxious and laborious effort for life, which we observe in animals subjected to experiments in foul air or in an exhausted receiver of an air pump. Many of them expire in this situation crying out in their native tongues "we are dying." During the time that elapses from the slaves being put on board on the African coast to their sale in the colonies about one fourth part, or twenty-five thousand per annum are destroyed—a mortality which may be easily credited after the preceding statement.

At length the ship arrives at her destined port, and the unhappy Africans who have survived the voyage are prepared for sale. Some are consigned to Brokers who sell them for the ships at private sale. With this view they are examined by the planters, who want them for their farms, and in the selection of them, friends and relations are parted without any hesitation; and when they part with mutual embraces they are severed by a lash. Others are sold at public auctions and become the property of the highest bidder. Others are sold by what is denominated a "scramble." In this case the main and quarter decks of the ship are darkened by sails hung over them at a convenient height. The slaves are then brought out of the hold and made to stand in the darkened area. The purchasers who are furnished with long ropes rush at a given signal within the awning, and endeavour to encircle as many of them as they can. . . .

About 20,000 or one fifth part of those who are annually imported die during the "seasoning," which seasoning is said to expire when the two first years of servitude are completed. So that of the whole number about half perish within two years of their captivity. I forbear to trace the subsequent scenes of their miserable lives worn out in toils, from which they can receive no profit, and oppressed with wrongs from which they can hope for no relief.

The scenes which I have described are almost literally copied from the most authentic and unquestionable narratives published under the highest authority. They present a picture of human wretchedness and human depravity which the boldest imagination would hardly have dared to portray, and from which (one should think) the most abandoned profligate would shrink with horror. Let it be considered that this wretchedness does not arise from the awful visitations of providence in the shape of plagues, famines or earthquakes, the natural scourges of mankind; but is inflicted by man on man from the accursed love of gold. May we not justly dread the displeasure of that Almighty being, who is the common father of us all, if we do not by all means within our power endeavor to suppress such infamous cruelties. If we cannot like the good Samaritan bind up the wounds and soothe the miseries of the friendless Africans, let us not like the Levite pass with sullen indifference on the other side. What sight can be more acceptable in the eyes of heaven than that of good men struggling in the cause of oppressed humanity? What consolation can be more sweet in a dying hour than the recollection that at least one human being may have been saved from sacrifice by our vigilance in enforcing the laws?

I make no apology, Gentlemen, for having detained you so long upon this interesting subject. In vain shall we expend our wealth in missions abroad for the promotion of Christianity; in vain shall we rear at home magnificent temples to the service of the most High; if we tolerate this traffic, our charity is but a name, and our religion little more than a faint and delusive shadow.

1.13. "Every Tongue Must Be Mute." Alleged Actions of the Federal Government on Behalf of the Illegal Slave Trade

The following document is from a book by the distinguished reformer, William Jay, son of the statesman, diplomat, and jurist John Jay. The younger Jay was not only a prominent critic of slavery, but also an advocate of temperance and world peace. Author of a biography of his father, he also wrote numerous pamphlets and books on the slavery question as well as a brilliant treatise on the Mexican War demonstrating that conflict's clear relationship to the South's determined aim to expand slavery and create new markets for both the internal and external traffic.

The present selection is a sharply critical account of the U.S. government's alleged protection of both the internal slave trade and the illegal importation of African slaves after 1807, particularly into Florida, Georgia, Alabama, Louisiana, and Texas. It also strongly condemns the involvement of American ships and personnel in the traffic to Cuba and Brazil, and the government's enduring acquiescence to that trade, despite abundant federal legislation which several branches of government were obliged to respect and enforce.[28]

SOURCE: William Jay, "A View of the Action of the Federal Government, in Behalf of Slavery," in *Miscellaneous Writings on Slavery* (1853; reprint, New York: Negro Universities Press, 1958), pp. 276–82, 290–99.

The Duplicity of the Federal Government in Regard to the Suppression of the African Slave-Trade.

Whenever the opponents of abolition find it convenient to refer to the action of the Federal Government on the subject of slavery, they laud and

28. On illegal slave trading to Cuba and Brazil, see Warren Howard, *American Slavery and the Federal Law, 1837–1862* (Berkeley and Los Angeles: University of California Press, 1963); Doc. 1.13; and Robert Edgar Conrad, *World of Sorrow: The African Slave Trade to Brazil* (Baton Rouge: Louisiana State University Press, 1986), pp. 133–53.

magnify its horror of the *African* slave-trade, and exultingly point to the law of Congress, branding it with the penalties of *piracy.* And yet we are inclined to believe that the conduct of our government in relation to this very subject is one of the foulest stains attached to our national administration. Has the trade been suppressed? Has the Federal Government in good faith endeavored to suppress it? These are important questions, and we shall endeavor to solve them by an appeal to facts and official documents.

In a debate in Congress in 1819, Mr. [Henry] Middleton, of South Carolina, stated that in his opinion, 13,000 Africans were annually smuggled into the United States. Mr. [John] Wright, of Virginia, estimated the number at 15,000. . . .

On the 22nd of January, 1811, the Secretary of the Navy wrote to the commanding naval officer at Charleston:

"I hear, not without great concern, that the law prohibiting the importation of slaves has been violated in *frequent instances,* near St. Mary's [an anchorage in south Georgia on St. Mary's River], since the gun-boats have been withdrawn from that station."

On the 14th of March, 1814, the collector of Darien, Georgia, thus wrote to the Secretary of the Treasury:

"I am in possession of undoubted information that African and West Indian negroes are almost daily illicitly introduced into Georgia, for sale or settlement, or passing through it to the territories of the United States, for similar purposes. These facts are notorious, and it is not unusual to see such negroes in the streets of St. Mary's; and such too, recently captured by our vessels of war, and ordered for Savannah, were illegally bartered by *hundreds* in that city, for this bartering (or *bonding,* as it is called, but in reality *selling)* actually took place before any decision had passed by the court respecting them. I cannot but again express to you, sir, that these irregularities and mockings of the law by men who understand them, are such that it requires the immediate interposition of Congress to effect the suppression of this traffic; for as things are, should a faithful officer of the Government apprehend such negroes, to avoid the penalties imposed by the laws the proprietors disclaim them, *and some agent of the Executive demands the delivery of the same to him, who may employ them as he pleases, or effect a sale of them by way of bond for restoration of the negroes when legally called on so to do, which bond is understood to be forfeited, as the amount of the bond is so much less than the value of the property.* After much fatigue, peril, and expense, *eighty-eight* Africans are seized and brought to the surveyor at Darien; they are demanded by the Governor's agent. Notwithstanding the knowledge which his excellency had that these very Africans were some weeks within six miles of his excellency's residence, there was no effort, no stir made by him, his agents or subordinate state officers, to carry the laws into execution; but no sooner was it understood that a seizure had been effected by an officer of the United States, than a demand is made for them; and it is not difficult to perceive that the very aggressors may, by a forfeiture of the *mock bond,* be again placed in possession of the smuggled property."

In 1817, General David B. Mitchell, Governor of Georgia, resigned the Executive chair, and accepted the appointment, under the Federal Government, of Indian Agent at the Creek Agency. He was afterwards charged with being concerned, in the winter of 1817 and 1818, in the illegal importation of Africans. The documents in support of the charge, and those also which he offered to disprove it, were placed by the President in the hands of Mr. Wirt, the Attorney-General of the United States, who, on the 21st of January, 1821, made a report on the same. From this report it appears that no less than ninety-four Africans were smuggled into Georgia, and carried to Mitchell's residence. Mr. Wirt concludes his report with the expression of his conviction,

"That Gen. Mitchell is guilty of having prostituted his power as Agent for Indian Affairs at the Creek Agency, to the purpose of aiding and assisting in a conscious breach of the Act of Congress of 1807, in prohibition of the slave-trade, and this from mercenary motives [Senate Papers. 1st Session, 17th Cong., No. 93].

On the 22nd of May, 1817, the Collector at Savannah wrote to the Secretary of the Treasury:

"I have just received information from a source on which I can implicitly rely that it has already become the practice to introduce into the State of Georgia, across St. Mary's River, from Amelia Island, E. Florida, Africans who have been carried into the port of Fernandina. It is further understood that the evil will not be confined altogether to Africans, but will be extended to the worst class of *West India slaves.*"

Captain Morris, of the Navy, informed the Secretary of the Navy, 18th of June, 1817:

"Slaves are smuggled in through the numerous inlets to the westward, where *the people are but too much disposed to render every possible assistance.* Several hundred slaves are now in Galveston, and persons have gone from New Orleans to purchase them."

On the 17th of April, 1818, the Collector at New Orleans wrote to the Secretary of the Treasury:

"No efforts of the officers of the customs alone can be effectual in preventing the introduction of Africans from the westward: to put a stop to that traffic, a naval force suitable to those waters is indispensable; and vessels captured with slaves *ought not to be brought into this port, but to some other in the United States, for adjudication."*

We may learn the cause of this significant hint from a communication made the 9th of July, in the same year, to the Secretary, by the Collector at Nova Iberia [Louisiana].

"Last summer I got out State warrants, and had negroes seized to the number of eighteen, which were part of them *stolen out of the custody of the coroner;* the balance were condemned by the District Judge, and the informers received their part of the net proceeds from the State Treasurer. Five negroes that were seized about the same time were tried at Opelousas in May last, by the same judge. He decided that some Spaniards that were supposed to have set up a *sham claim,* stating that the negroes had been *stolen from them on the high seas* (!!) should have the negroes, and that the *persons who seized them should pay half the costs,* and the State of Louisiana the other. This decision had such an effect as to render it almost impossible for me to obtain any assistance in that part of the country."

The Secretary of the Treasurer, in a letter to the Speaker of the House of Representatives, 20th January, 1819, remarked:

"It is understood that proceedings have been instituted under the State authorities, which have terminated in the SALE of persons of color illegally imported into the States of Georgia and Louisiana, during the years 1817 and 1818. There is no authentic copy of the Legislatures of these States upon this subject in this department, but it is understood that in both States, Africans and other persons of color, illegally imported, are directed to be *sold for the benefit of the State."*

We have now, we think, proved from high authority that, notwithstanding the legal prohibition of the slave-trade, the people, the courts, and the executive authority in the planting States have afforded facilities for the importation of Africans. It now becomes important to inquire how far the Federal Government has enforced the penalties imposed by the Act forbidding the trade.

On the 7th of January, 1819, Joseph Nourse, Register of the Treasury, in an official document submitted to Congress, certified that there were no records in the Treasury Department of any forfeitures under the act of 1807, abolishing the slave-trade! So that notwithstanding thirteen or fifteen thousand slaves, said by Southern members of Congress to be annually smuggled into the United States—notwithstanding American citizens were declared by a Judge of the Supreme Court to be "steeped to their very mouths in this stream of iniquity," [29] *not one single forfeiture* had in eleven

29. Jay quotes Judge Joseph Story. See Doc. 1.12. Editor.

years reached the Treasury of the United States! Mr. Nourse, however, states that it was *understood* that there had been recently *two* forfeitures, one in South Carolina and the other in Alabama. Respecting the first, we have no information; of the latter, we are able to present the following extraordinary history.

The Collector at Mobile, writing Nov. 15, 1818, to the Secretary of the Treasury, remarks:

"Should West Florida be given up to the Spanish authorities, both the American and Spanish vessels, it is to be apprehended, will be employed in the importation of slaves, with an ultimate destination to this country; and even in its present situation, the greatest facilities are afforded for obtaining slaves from Havana and elsewhere through West Florida. *Three* vessels, it is true, were taken in the attempt last summer, but this was owing rather to *accident* than any well-timed arrangement to prevent the trade."

These three vessels brought in one hundred and seven slaves. By what mistake they were captured we are not informed, but another letter from the collector shows us how the "accident" was remedied.

"The vessel and cargoes and slaves have been delivered on *bonds;* the former to the owners, and the slaves to three other persons. The Grand Jury found true bills against the owners of the vessels, masters and supercargo, *all of whom have been discharged*—why or wherefore, I cannot say, except that it could *not* be for want of proof against them." . . .

We most freely acknowledge that so far as the statute book is to be received as evidence, there can be no question of the sincerity and zeal with which the Federal Government has labored to suppress the African slave-trade: but laws do not execute themselves, and we shall now appeal to the statute book, and to the minutes of Congress, to convict the government of gross hypocrisy and duplicity.

It is difficult to understand why men who are engaged in breeding slaves for the market, or why men who are employed in buying and working slaves, should have any moral or religious scruples about the African trade; and when we find political leaders professing to be ready to sacrifice the Union to secure the perpetuity of the *American* trade, we may surely be excused for doubting the sincerity of their denunciations against the foreign traffic. . . .

On the 2d of November, 1825, the Colombian Minister at Washington, in the name of his government, invited the United States to send delegates to a Congress of the South American Republics, to be held at Panama. In enumerating the topics to be discussed in the proposed Congress, he remarked:

"The consideration of means to be adopted for the entire abolition of the African slave-trade is a subject sacred to humanity, and interesting to the policy of the American States. To effect it, their energetic, general and uniform coöperation is desirable. *At the proposition of the United States,* Colombia made a convention with them on this subject, which *has not been ratified by the Government of the United States.* Would that America, which does not think politic what is unjust, might contribute in union, and with common consent, to the good of Africa!"

This document was submitted to the Senate, and on the 16th of January, 1826, a committee of the Senate made a report in relation to it, in which they observe:

"The United States have not certainly the right, and ought never to feel the inclination to dictate to others who may differ with them on this subject," (the slave-trade) "nor do the committee see the expediency of *insulting other States by ascending the moral chair,* and proclaiming from thence mere abstract principles, of the rectitude of which each nation enjoys the perfect right of deciding for itself."

The remarks made on this occasion by Mr. White, a Senator from Tennessee, are worthy of observation.

"In these new States (the South American Republics) some of them have put it down in their fundamental law, 'that whoever owns a slave shall cease to be a citizen.' Is it then fit that the United States should disturb the quiet of the *southern and western States* upon any subject connected with slavery? I think not. Can it be the desire of any prominent politician in the United States to divide us into parties upon the subject of slavery? I hope not. Let us then cease to talk about slavery in this House; let us cease to negotiate upon any subject connected with it."

We have seen most abundantly that slave-holders have no objection to talk about slavery in Congress, or to negotiate about it with foreign nations, when the object is to guard their beloved institution from danger. It is only on the abominations of the system, and the means of removing it, that every tongue must be mute, and the Federal Government passive. As that government refuses to enter into any combined efforts for the suppression of this trade, and makes none of its own, we may reasonably suppose that our citizens are *now* largely engaged in it. Let us see if this supposition accords with facts.

Present Participation of Citizens of the United States in the African Slave-trade.

In pursuance of a treaty with Spain, certain commissioners are appointed by Great Britain to reside at Havana. On the 25th of October, 1836, these commissioners wrote to their government:

"To our astonishment and regret, we have ascertained that the *Ana-conda* and *Viper,* the one on the 6th, and the other on the 10th, current, cleared out and sailed from here for the Cape de Verd Islands under the AMERICAN flag. These two vessels *arrived* at the Havana, fitted in every particular for the slave-trade, and took on board a cargo which would alone have condemned as a slaver any vessel belonging to the nations that are parties to the equipment article."

They remark that the declaration of the American President *not to make the United States a party to any convention on the subject of the slave-trade,*

"Has been the means of inducing American citizens to build and fit in their ports vessels only calculated for piracy, or the slave-trade—to enter this port, and in concert with the Havana slave-traders, to take on board a prohibited cargo, *manacles,* &c., and proceed openly to that notorious depot for this iniquitous traffic, the Cape de Verd Islands, *under shelter of the national flag;* and we may add, that while these AMERICAN SLAVERS were making their final arrangements for departure, the Havana was *visited more than once by American ships of war."*

This statement and others we are about to present to the reader explain *the practical results, and probably the secret motives* of the rejection by the Senate of the slave-trade convention with Great Britain. The commissioners proceed:

"Two AMERICAN vessels, the *Fanny Butler* and *Rosanna,* have proceeded to the Cape de Verd Islands and the coast of Africa, under the AMERICAN flag, upon the same inhuman speculation. * * * We cannot conceal our deep regret at the NEW and DREADFUL impetus imparted to the slave-trade of this island [Cuba], by the manner in which some American citizens impunibly violate every law, by embarking *openly* for the coast of Africa under the NATIONAL flag, with the *avowed* purpose of bringing slaves to this market. We are likewise assured that it is intended, by means of this *flag,* to supply slaves for the vast province of TEXAS; agents from there being in constant communication with the Havana slave merchants." [Buxton's *African Slave Trade* (1839), p. 21.]

We learn from Buxton's late work on the present state of the trade, that

"The *Venus,* said to be the sharpest clipper built vessel ever constructed at Baltimore, left that place in July, 1838, and arrived at Havana on the 4th of August following. She sailed from thence in September for Mozambique; there she took a cargo of slaves, being all this time under *the flag of the United States.* On the 7th of January, 1839, she landed 860 negroes near Havana under Portuguese *colors."* p. 23.

In certain documents, lately published by the British Parliament we have the *names of eleven* vessels, which sailed under the flag of the United States, from Havana to Africa for slaves in 1837, and of *nineteen* more, which sailed in 1838. Major McGregor, special magistrate for the Bahamas, in a letter to Mr. Buxton mentions the wreck of the schooner *Invincible,* a slaver, on the 28th of October, 1837, and adds:

"The captain's name was Potts, a native of Florida. The vessel was fitted out at Baltimore in America, and three-fourths of the crew were natives of the United States, although they pretended to be only passengers."

The major also mentions another slaver, with a cargo of 160 Africans, being wrecked on one of the islands, and says:

"This pretended Portuguese vessel was fitted out at Baltimore, United States, having been formerly a pilot boat, called the *Washington.* The super-cargo was an American citizen of Baltimore." pp. 23, 186.

Mr. Mitchell Thompson, an officer on board the British ship-of-war *Sappho,* thus wrote at Jamaica in the spring of 1839, to a gentleman from Philadelphia:

"Almost *half* the vessels employed in this trade and furnished to either the Spaniards or the Portuguese are from America, and seem to have been built at Baltimore, from which place they sail chartered for some port in Cuba with *lumber;* which lumber is converted into slave-decks on their ar-rival at the destined port. To this is now added copper, casks, and food, with the necessary slave irons; and now also is added the requisite number of Spaniards as part complement of the ship's company; *with American pa-pers and flag, they escape our cruisers, as the concession of the right of mutual search has not been made by America.*"

A recent letter from an officer of the British ship-of-war *Pelican,* pub-lished in the London papers, mentions that this ship had lately captured an AMERICAN schooner, the *Octavia* of Baltimore, with 220 slaves.

The editor of the *Baltimore Chronicle* states that Captain McDonald, of the brig *North,* just arrived from Africa, reported that the Captain of the British brig of war *Partaga* told him in conversation that they had fallen in with several vessels which had the appearance of being slavers, but having *American colors and papers* furnished by the Consul at Havana, he had to let them pass; but afterwards he fell in with them with *slaves on board,* that being proof positive of their true character.

Mr. Buchanan, Governor of Liberia, in a letter written from the colony, and published in the New York *Journal of Commerce* of July 6, 1839, says:

"Never was the AMERICAN FLAG so extensively used by those pirates upon liberty and humanity as at present. Probably THREE FOURTHS of the vessels boarded by the English cruisers and found to be slavers are PROTECTED by American PAPERS AND THE AMERICAN FLAG.

In the spring of 1839, three American slavers were captured by British cruisers, and carried into Sierra Leone. They were the Clara, Wyoming, and Eagle, and all under AMERICAN captains, and furnished with AMERICAN papers. They had no slaves on board, but were fitted up for the trade, having slave-decks, manacles, &c., &c.

At Sierra Leone it was decided that the English courts had no jurisdiction over these vessels, and of course that their capture was unauthorized. But inasmuch as the character of the vessels was obvious, and they were engaged in a trade declared piratical by the American Congress, it was deemed both prudent and friendly to send them home for trial, and they arrived at New York in June last, under the charge of a British ship-of-war. A more unwelcome present could not have been offered to the Federal Government than these three slavers. An acceptance of them would have involved various inconvenient consequences. In the first place the President [Martin Van Buren] would have been compelled, by a due regard to the feelings of his southern constituents, to inquire by what authority British officers had presumed to arrest these ships, interrupt their voyages, and transport them across the Atlantic, contrary to the known and recorded will of the Senate of the United States. This would have led to an embarrassing negotiation, and likewise to a very undesirable discussion in the newspapers, and would probably have strengthened the hostility at the North to slavery and the slave-trade. If, on the other hand, the government acquiesced in this treatment of American slavers, then our courts would be occupied in trials in which it would be impossible to avoid touching upon "the delicate subject," and men might be sentenced to the gallows, merely for buying and selling their fellow-men. It would moreover be permitting Great Britain to do without a treaty what she had entreated us to permit her to do by treaty, and which we had refused. An expedient was adopted which avoided these embarrassments. The Government, it is said, thought proper not to recognize these ships as American property, and therefore declined receiving them. By this course all public judicial investigations and disclosures were prevented; and the whole matter was hushed up as quickly as possible. The avowed reasons for this decision have not been made public.

We will now recall to the recollection of our readers the remark of the British commissioners, that "while the American slavers were making their final arrangements for departure, the Havana was visited more than once by American ships-of-war." In other words our naval officers showed no disposition to arrest such of their countrymen as were engaged in the slave-trade, and to send them home for trial and punishment. It no doubt seems very strange to foreigners that the American navy should be so exceedingly remiss in seconding the zeal of the Federal Government in suppressing the slave-trade—but it is a trite remark that foreigners cannot understand our institutions—the conduct of the navy is perfectly natural, and precisely such as might rationally be expected. We have no knowledge of any slaver having been molested by an American armed vessel for the last fifteen years. It is not necessary for our cruisers to go to Africa to capture slavers. The trade passes our very doors, and slavers are to be found by *those who look for them* off the port of Baltimore, and along the shores of Cuba and Texas.

The New York Journal of Commerce, speaking of the seizure of slavers by *British* cruisers, remarks:

"The capture of a slaver by an *American* cruiser is a thing unheard of for many years, and wholly unexpected. Scores of slave-vessels are caught every year by British cruisers, and we will not do our national vessels the injustice to suppose that they never could catch any, if they were so *disposed.*"

But why should they be "so disposed?" About one-half of our naval officers are the sons of slave-holders, and can we expect that they will voluntarily assist in bringing men to the gibbet for trading in African savages, while their own fathers are engaged in buying and selling their fellow-countrymen?

Again, pecuniary reward, professional promotion, and public applause are the chief incentive to military enterprise. Our officers have been recently taught that efforts to capture or destroy *fugitive slaves* will be liberally rewarded from the national treasury; but when have they been *paid* for capturing slavers?

It is natural that our young and ardent officers should pant for promotion, and that they should turn their anxious and expectant gaze upon the dispenser of professional favors, the SECRETARY OF THE NAVY [James Kirke Paulding]. Should they read this gentleman's work, "Slavery in the United States," they will have little hope of getting into his good graces by any exhibition of zeal against the African slave-trade. They will learn from the head of the naval department that the introduction of negro slaves into our country was in "accordance with the sanction of holy writ, as conveyed in the twenty-fifth chapter of Leviticus," p. 42; and they will be led to infer the benevolent tendency of the traffic from the following authoritative declaration of the innocency and happiness of slavery itself.

"That slavery is a great moral evil, or that its existence or continuance detracts one tittle, one *atom* from the happiness of the slaves, our own experience and observation directly contradict." p. 126.

We presume Mr. Paulding alluded to the experience and observation acquired in his intercourse with coffle-drivers during his excursion in 1816. Our officers are moreover instructed by the Secretary, that although

"The white and black races of men are probably the nearest to each other of all these varieties (animals with similar instincts), they are not homogeneous any more than the orang-outang, the ape, the baboon, and the monkey, who possibly may ere long find a new sect of philanthropists to sustain their claim to amalgamation [miscegenation]." p. 271.

But should our officers inquire how far public opinion would justify and commend them for breaking up the voyages of American merchants, seizing their vessels, and exposing their commanders and crews to an infamous death, what answer would be returned by *facts?*

The editor of the New York *Journal of Commerce* declared, in his paper of 20th June, 1835:

"We pledge ourselves to prove, to the satisfaction of the President or Secretary of War, that slave-ships have, within the past year, been actually fitted out at the port of New York."

Has the Secretary of War, the President, or any grand jury called on the editor to redeem his pledge?

The New Orleans *Courier* of May 21, 1839, after commenting on the present extent of the African slave-trade, remarks:

"If such have been the result produced by the injudicious efforts of the English philanthropists, we may well doubt the *policy* of the law of Congress which has prohibited the importation of slaves from Africa,—a policy that, by all we can learn, has no other effect than to cause the planter of Louisiana to pay to the Virginia slave-holder one thousand dollars for a negro which *now* in Cuba, and by-and-by in Texas, may be bought for half the money. It is known to those acquainted with the character of the African, that he is more patient and less unruly than the Virginia or Maryland negro—his very ignorance of many things makes him less *dangerous* in a community like ours, and his constitution is better suited to our climate. In transporting him from his own country, his position too in civilization is bettered, not worsted. The more we examine and reflect on the policy the TEXANS are likely to pursue in this matter, openly or covertly, the more we are convinced that Texas should be annexed to the Union, or else *Congress should repeal the law prohibiting the importation of slaves from Africa.* Otherwise the culture of sugar and cotton in Louisiana will suffer greatly by the cheap labor which the planters of Cuba and Texas can and will employ."

Here we find a public and cold-blooded proposal to reopen the African slave-trade. And was this proposal received with horror by the public? Alas! even the northern press has scarcely condemned it. Multitudes of our papers have not noticed it—others have republished the article without a single remark, and the "New York Express," a leading Whig and commercial journal, introduces the diabolical proposal to its readers as "The following *interesting* comments of the New Orleans *Courier.*" Openly to approve the proposal might offend some fanatical subscribers—openly to condemn it might injure the Whig party at the South.

The New York "Courier and Enquirer," another Whig and commercial journal, contained (July 27, 1839) the following editorial:

"Rio Janeiro papers have reached us to the 31st of May last. The chief information from Brazil, which they contain of *interest here,* is that of the capture of two vessels under Portuguese colors by a British ship-of-war, shortly after leaving Rio, on suspicion that they were fitted out for the slave-trade. We are not astonished that these captures should have excited much indignation to Rio. Whatever may be thought of the trade itself, *the people generally are engaged in it and interested in its success,* and it is asking a little too much of them to remain quiet while foreign vessels enter their harbor, take in provisions, remain there as long as it suits their purpose, and then sally forth, break up their enterprises, and bring back their property to be condemned under their very noses."

This appeared shortly after the three American slavers, captured by British cruisers, had been sent into New York—hence the indignation of the editor—hence the news from Rio was "of interest" in New York. It is excessively impudent in the English to take it for granted that the laws of the United States and Brazil against the trade were enacted in good faith. It matters not that Brazil had declared the trade piracy,—and that the cruisers only delivered to the Brazilian government their own pirates. The Brazilian people, like our own, are engaged in the trade and interested in its success, and it is a great outrage for foreigners to interfere! . . .

1.14. American and British Participation in the Illegal Slave Trade to Brazil in the 1840s

As Documents 1.12 and 1.13 reveal, after abolition of the African slave trade to the United States in 1808, northerners and southerners alike continued to supply African slaves to Southern farmers and planters, and this illegal traffic persisted on a reduced scale until the Civil War. More relevant, however, to the selections below was the increased involvement of American citizens in illegal slave trading to Brazil and Cuba, particularly after 1839 when Great Britain authorized its warships to seize slave vessels flying the Brazilian, Spanish, and Portuguese flags, thus making the United States the last major Western nation unwilling to permit the boarding and searching of its ships at sea. Taking advantage of the immunity from seizure provided by the American flag, U.S. citizens offered a wide variety of advantages and services to slave traders. These included swift Baltimore clippers with American crews, shipment to Africa of such necessities as water casks and food for slaves and crews, lumber for slave decks, chains and manacles, and the weapons, gunpowder, tobacco, cloth and other merchandise to be traded for slaves in Africa. After several voyages of this kind by an American ship, a final journey to Africa was normally made under the U.S. flag, after which the vessel was often transferred to a non-American crew, slaves were put aboard, and American crew members were registered as passengers for the return to Brazil.

The two letters below, sent to Washington by American ministers to Brazil in 1846 and 1850, respectively, were sharply critical of U.S. participation in the Brazilian slave trade. The first of these correspondents, Henry A. Wise,[30] emphasized the little known (but active) involvement of British subjects in that traffic, specifically the supplying of British-made products to be bartered for slaves in Africa for shipment to the Brazilian market.[31] David Tod, the second writer, whose letter was written shortly before suppression of the Brazilian slave trade, was fervent in his denunciation of U.S. participation in the traffic and deeply concerned for the "integrity of the American flag" and the "cause of humanity." (For U.S. and British participation in the Brazilian slave trade, see Robert Conrad, *World of Sorrow*, chapter 6.)

SOURCES: *An Exposition of the African Slave Trade, From the Year 1840, to 1850, Inclusive. Prepared from Official Documents, and Published by Direction of the Religious Society of Friends* . . . (Philadelphia, 1851), pp. 123–25, 128–32; *Senate Executive Documents,* 30th Congress, 1st Session, No. 28, pp. 35–40.

30. Congressman, ambassador to Brazil (1844 to 1847), and governor of Virginia from 1855 until the Civil War.

31. Historian David Eltis has calculated that "at least 90 percent of the manufactured goods used in the nineteenth-century trans-Atlantic slave trade to Brazil and Cuba came from Britain, and . . . that British credit financed half the Cuban and Brazilian slave trade." See David Murray, "Suppression of Trade," in Drescher and Engerman, *A Historical Guide to World Slavery,* p. 382. See also Conrad, *World of Sorrow*, pp. 126–33.

**The American Minister in Rio de Janeiro, Henry A. Wise,
in a Letter to the British Minister to Brazil, Mr. Hamilton,
Reveals British Involvement in the Brazilian Slave Trade,** 1846.

LEGATION UNITED STATES,

Rio de Janeiro, March 27, 1846. . . .

Sir: . . . As I have repeatedly said, there are two main foreign interests connected with the slave trade of Brazil. One is British, consisting in manufactured goods, wares, and merchandise. The other is American consisting in vessels. The goods are the very pabulum of the slave trade, its purchase money. The vessels are the carriers of *them,* as well as of the slaves. The factories on the coast are the depôts of both slaves and goods, and their harbors are the rendezvous of the vessels. . . . I cannot believe, for one moment, from what I have known of their dispositions and acts, that her Britannic Majesty's officers in Brazil, envoy, consul, commissioners, and naval commanders, all have failed to communicate true and full information on this subject to her Majesty's government. It is so palpable here, that the children and the slaves know the facts. Any candid person can attest the truth of what I have said in respect to the employment of British capital, credit, and goods in the slave trade. . . .

"Articles required for the licit and illicit traffic."

[I]n speaking of the traffic, licit or illicit, to the coast of Africa . . . I ask your excellency whether you can tell his lordship [Lord Aberdeen] what is the licit, and what is the illicit traffic, as distinguished from each other, between the coast of Africa and Brazil. *I cannot;* and, were his lordship here "four weeks" even, I would convince him that he could not distinguish the licit from the illicit traffic. The whole trade between Brazil and the African slave ports is one concatenated slave trade. The slave trade is the primary, the major, and the other is but the secondary, the minor trade, ancillary to the traffic in slaves.

Manoel Pinto da Fonseca, for example, at the head of a large company of slave dealers, employs a regular line of packets on the coasts of Brazil and Africa. He has his factories—that is, "stores," and regular depôts for goods, provisions, and slaves, both in Africa and Brazil. His head-quarters are at Rio de Janeiro. He employs a number of coasting vessels to carry to various points the requisite supplies. The coffee, rusks, crackers, farinha, black beans, jerked beef, rice, sugar, and cachaça [rum], or aguardente [brandy], are the products chiefly of Brazil. These are the chief provisions of the employees, and the slaves, and the crews of the vessels. What is not consumed by the captives themselves is necessary for the persons engaged at the slave factories, and on board the slave vessels and their tenders. Brazil has no currency to remit to Africa; and, if she had, *money* is not the medium of slave purchases in Africa. Dry goods, cotton, cloths, velvets, &c., and toys, gewgaws, beads, ornaments, and gunpowder, and muskets, and aguardente, are used as the products for purchasing slaves. A vast proportion of the dry goods, and the powder, and muskets, and a great variety of articles, under the general names of "fazendas estrangeiras" [foreign goods] or "mercadorias e varios generos" [merchandise and various commodities], are of English manufacture, and many made expressly as "panos da costa" [coast fabrics]. When the stores of provisions, goods, water casks, &c., &c., are all collected at the time and place desired, by the coasters, then vessels of a larger class are chartered, or bought to run the goods over to the factories, and to bring the slaves back. Some are bought to bring back the cargoes of slaves, and the most are chartered to carry goods over, and to be tenders to the slave vessels and the slave factories. For example, the *Agnes,* and the *Monte Video,* and the *Ganneclifft,* were nearly all three about the same time bought to carry cargoes of goods, and bring back slaves; and did each bring a cargo of slaves; and the *Sea Eagle,* and other vessels, were chartered only to take over goods and passengers, and bring back the crews of the slavers. The *Porpoise* was the tender to the *Kentucky* [see Doc. 1.15] and the *Panther,* perhaps, and I do not know how many more vessels, of late, to the *Pons.* Now, I venture to say, that the outward bound cargoes of all these vessels from Brazil were of the same general description. Look at those of the *Pons* and *Panther,* and some other vessels, which have lately made voyages, and the "despatches," of which are hereto appended. And here, I will observe, that the only mode of getting at the description of cargoes taken out hence to the slave coast is by looking at the daily reports of the *Jornal do Commercio* [a Rio newspaper], under the head of "Exportação, Embarcações, Despachadas," and "Despachos de Exportação." These show the uniform description of the cargoes to the coast, and the identity of the persons by whom they are shipped. The *Pons* was captured with 900 slaves on board of her, and her cargo out was much less suspicious, apparently, than that of the *Panther,* which vessel was captured without a slave. See the deposition of Captain Graham, . . . which states how unaccountably this vessel escaped with her slaves on board, three days in sight of a British cruiser. She was captured the 4th day out by the United States sloop of war *Yorktown.* The sloop run up the British flag, and the slaver the United States flag. I pick up a paper whilst I am writing—the *Jornal* [*do Commercio*], of the 13th instant—I find this entry:

"Africa—Bergantim Amer. Frances Ann, de 346 tons, consig: J. Birckhead: manf: 40 pipas aguardente, 1 barrica café, 10 barricas bolacha, 3 barricas arroz, 2 barricas assucar, 2 barris toucinho, e *re-exp:* 100 *barris polvora 34 volumes fazendas estrangeiras, 8 caixas espingardas e mindezas."* [32]

Such is a pretty fair specimen of the general description of these slave cargoes. Now which of the articles are licit and which are illicit? Under the laws of the United States, one is as licit as the other. They all, however, are used for the purposes and objects of the slave trade, just as much as are water pipes and shackles.

Again: all these vessels are alike permitted, with these cargoes, freely to pass and repass across the Atlantic, and to harbor on the coast of Africa, and openly and freely discharge at the slave factories. The contracts with those which are sold [provide] that as soon as they have discharged the last parcels of goods, they are to be delivered to be the carriers of the slaves; and the rest are chartered, at very high prices, to return for more goods or to transport them from one port to another in Africa, where they may be most required, taking backward and forward, all the time, the crews and agents and employees of the slave trade as passengers. And whilst carrying these goods to and fro, the vessels themselves, as well as the goods, are unmolested. If American vessels, they are preferred, because their flag does not acknowledge the right of visit and search. But to carry the passengers, goods, provisions, &c., &c., the vessels may be and are as often of other flags, such as Sardinian, (they are as often used as American), French, Portuguese, Brazilian, because, though they are of searchable flags, yet these fair cargoes of goods are called licit, and they may smile when their holds are examined, and can unload at the factory of Fonseca, consigned to his agent, Sr. Cunha, at Cabinda, in open day, with perfect impunity. . . . These licit goods, like these licit vessels, are alike on the ocean and at the factory under perfect protection, *up to the very point of time when the goods are delivered for and in consideration of the slaves directly, and when the vessels are delivered up for their shipment.* What is the difference between the British and American participation in the guilt? What is the difference in point of time of delivery, as well as moral turpitude? None. If the American flag protects the vessels up to the moment of the shipment of the slaves, so does what is erroneously termed the *licit* character of the goods protect them up to the very moment of the shipment of the purchase of the slaves. Is it worse in law or morals to furnish the means of *transportation* to the slave trade, than it is to put the very *price* of slavery in its hands? Is it not the same to allow that price to go and be deposited in its place in perfect safety, as it is to allow

---

32. Translation: "Africa, Amer. Brig: Frances Ann, of 346 tons, consig J. Birckhead: manifest: 40 cask rum, 1 barrel coffee, 10 barrels ship-biscuits, 3 barrels rice, 2 barrels sugar, 2 barrels bacon, and re-export: *100 barrels gunpowder bulk containers foreign goods, 8 crate firearms.* Editor.

the vessel to be sailed to her rendezvous of the slave market? Is the shackle which binds more a part of the trade than the piece of cotton cloth which buys the slave? His lordship would, doubtless, return the same answer to these questions which I would. The smallest articles of luxury which are sent over for the agents and employees in Africa, are part and parcels of the slave trade. Every comfort and every necessary, used by the principals and employees, enters into it as well as the slaves themselves. . . . As I said in my letter to your excellency, the very wax and ivory and gold dust, which constitute a small portion of return cargoes, is brought down on the heads of the slaves. These products are shipped in the chartered vessels, and the live stock is shipped on board the vessels sold.

But to proceed. His lordship says, "It must *sometimes happen* that British goods will be employed in the slave trade." Here is a monstrous error, most unaccountably imposed upon his lordship. "It must"—unavoidably, of course—"sometimes happen!"—now and then—not often, but rarely, and at irregular intervals, "fall out"—by accident, not design— "that British goods"—a few of them, I suppose, is meant—"will be"—*by the slave dealers who purchase them,* not by British manufacturers and merchants, is implied by the context—"employed in the slave trade!" I call upon the British authorities to undeceive her Majesty's government on this essential point of the traffic.

1st. From what I have said, the employment of British goods in the slave trade, to the vast extent of their present use and appropriation and consumption for its purposes, is not *unavoidable.* The goods may be seized in the vessels which are liable to search; they may be seized in the act of being discharged in the lighters and launches of the slave factories, and the factories themselves. They may be seized outside the marine league of Brazil wherever found. Such cargoes as I have described sold to M. P. Fonseca or Bernardino de Sá, cleared for the slave coast, are *prima facie* in Rio de Janeiro, to be employed in the slave trade.

2d. They are designed by the very British manufacturers and merchants in the capital of Great Britain herself, for the uses of the slave trade. . . .

Next: how are these British products, manufactures, and merchandise paid for in Brazil?

We have seen how little of licit imports there are from Africa, to enable the purchasers here to pay for foreign or British goods. All other imports from Africa, embracing everything except slaves, would not bear any proportion scarcely to the foreign products and merchandise re-exported to Africa. And there is no circulating medium in Brazil, which will bear taking out of the country, in payment for articles of commerce. The British man-ufacturers and merchants dare not take the slaves in exchange for the goods which purchase them. There is no such thing as cash, and there is *barter* only for coffee, sugar, rice, hides, hair, and horns.

But Great Britain almost totally excludes these slave-grown products of Brazil. The British merchants cannot send the coffee of Brazil home; they sell their goods to the Brazilian and Portuguese traders, who send nearly all of them, over and above the amount consumed in Brazil, to Africa, in ex-change for slaves. The goods are paid for in coffee here (on long credit for the piece goods, as his lordship will see by the accompanying retrospect) *and the coffee is sent to the United States,* where it is a free article. Out of 1,208,062 bags of coffee exported from Rio in 1845, 551,276 went to the United States.

As his lordship will see by the retrospect, 630,787 bags were shipped by seven houses alone; and in only two of these seven houses, Maxwell, Wright & Co., and Charles Coleman & Co., have the Americans, as far as I am in-formed, any interest.

Such is the routine of trade in the quadrangle of Great Britain, Africa, Brazil, and the United States. British merchants sell the goods here which purchase the slaves in Africa, and take coffee which finds a free market in the United States. . . .

With the highest personal and official regard, &c., &c. **HENRY A. WISE**

An American Minister in Rio Appeals to His Government for an End to U.S. Participation in the Brazilian Slave Trade, 1850.

Legation of the United States,
Rio de Janeiro, January 8, 1850.

Sir: Fifty thousand Africans are annually imported into Brazil, and sold as slaves for life. I believe one-half of this number are introduced through the facilities directly and indirectly afforded by the American flag. This belief is founded upon my familiarity with the subject, growing out of a close atten-tion to it since my arrival in Rio de Janeiro. The declaration is a humiliating one, and nothing but a desire to awaken action on the part of the legislative power of our country could induce me thus to make it. . . . The interests at stake . . . are of so high a character, the integrity of our flag and the cause of humanity being at once involved in their consideration, I cannot refrain from bringing the topic afresh to the notice of my government, in the hope that the President may esteem it of sufficient importance to be laid before Congress, and that, even at this late day, legislative action may be secured.

The following extracts from despatches of my immediate predecessors will satisfy you that I do not exaggerate the responsibility which attaches to us as a nation, in connexion with this trade.

Mr. Profitt, in his No. 9, of 27th February, 1844, wrote to Mr. [Abel Parker] Upshur [Secretary of State]:

"I regret to say this, but it is a fact not to be disguised or denied, that the Slave trade is almost entirely carried on under our flag, in American-built vessels, sold to Slave traders here, chartered for the coast of Africa, and there sold, or sold here, to be delivered on the coast. And, indeed, the scandalous traffic could not be carried to any extent, were it not for the use made of our flag, and by the facilities given by the chartering of American vessels to carry to the coast of Africa the outfit for the trade, and the materials for purchasing slaves." . . .

Mr. Wise, in his dispatch No. 12, of February 15, 1845, said to Mr. [John C.] Calhoun:

"It is not to be denied, and I boldly assert it, that the administration of the Imperial government of Brazil is forcibly constrained by its influences, and is deeply inculpated in its guilt. With that, it would at first seem, the United States have nothing to do; but an intimate and full knowledge of the subject informs us, that the only effectual mode of carrying on that trade between Africa and Brazil, at present, involves our laws and our moral responsibilities as directly and fully as it does those of this country itself. Our flag alone gives the requisite protection against the right of visit, search, and seizure; and our citizens, in all the characters of owners, consignees of agents, and of masters and crews of our vessels, are concerned in the business, and partake of the profits of the African Slave trade, to and from the ports of Brazil, as fully as the Brazilians themselves, and others in conjunction with whom they carry it on. In fact, without the aid of our own citizens and our flag, it could not be carried on with success at all."

Since the despatches were written from which the foregoing extracts have been made, no material change has taken place in the mode of conducting the Slave trade. There has been no diminution in the number of Africans imported; and the participation of American citizens in this business at the opening of the year 1850 is believed to be at least as unblushing as at any former period. The important fact is thus established, that our squadrons have failed to rescue the United States flag from the inhuman traffic, and that our existing laws upon the subject have proved signally inefficient. . . . In this unequal struggle between humanity and patriotism on the one hand, and cupidity and imaginary self-interest on the other, the influence of the United States flag is scarcely felt, except in support of the slave dealer—the seizures made by American men-of-war, weighing as nothing in the scale with the facilities which our colours afford in the transportation to Africa of slave goods, slave crews, and slave vessels. . . . It may be said, in general terms, that the entire trade carried on in American vessels between Brazil and Africa, is directly or indirectly connected with the Slave traffic. No one charters a United States vessel for Africa, and no person purchases one deliverable there, except the Slave dealer. I repeat it, the whole commerce carried on in American vessels between the two countries, is stained with the blood of the African, and is a reproach upon our national reputation. . . .

Citizens of the United States are constantly in this capital, whose only occupation is the buying of American vessels with which to supply the Slave importers. These men obtain sea-letters which entitle them to continue in use the United States flag; and it is this privilege which enables them to sell their vessels to the Slave traders, deliverable on the coast of Africa, at double, and sometimes more than double the price for which they were purchased on the preceding day. The vessels take over slave goods and slave crews, under the protection of our flag, and remain nominally American property, until a favourable opportunity occurs for receiving a cargo of slaves; and it is not unfrequently the case that our flag covers the slaver until the Africans are landed upon the coast of Brazil.

The granting of sea-letters to American purchasers in this country is one prolific source of the abuse of our flag. But under our laws and the instructions from the State Department, Consuls are obliged to grant them, when the applicants establish that they are the *bona fide* purchasers, that they are citizens of the United States, and that they do not usually reside abroad. No little of my time here has been devoted to the consideration of these applications. I have attended in person at the Consulate, and have cross-examined witnesses, and the applicants themselves; and with the exception of two or three cases, in which the usual residence abroad of the purchasers was known to the Consul and myself, the parties have never failed to swear in such manner as to entitle them to sea-letters under existing laws and instructions. It is a melancholy fact that, no matter what proofs may be exacted, the slave power will manufacture them to order. With the Slave dealers and their abettors, oaths are as the idle wind, and testimony is a fair purchasable commodity. . . .

Nearly half a century has elapsed since the Congress of the United States prohibited the introduction of Africans as slaves into our country. The wisdom and the justice of that measure are acknowledged by all classes of our citizens, regardless of their locality. The North and the South, the

East and the West, would rise as one man, to crush any attempt to open our ports to the importation of African slaves. And does it not become us, then, as a just nation, to prohibit our citizens from directly or indirectly assisting to burden another people with what we would consider a dire curse? Shall we suffer the influence of our flag to remain arrayed in opposition to the Brazilian patriots and philanthropists, who are struggling against great odds, for the suppression of the trade? Or shall we not rather, by one summary act, secure ourselves from the taint of this horrible business, that we may be enabled consistently, and with a moral power, which would be irresistible, to call upon the government of Brazil to rise in its might and crush the monster, at all hazards and at all cost.

I shall not speak of the horrors of the Slave trade, of the misery, of the wars, of the murders it occasions; neither shall I lift the veil which conceals the hellish torments of the middle passage—tortures, compared with which the most cruel death known to the law would be hailed as mercy's boon. But I do appeal to my government, as it regards the obligation devolving upon it to preserve the American escutcheon unsullied, and the duty it owes to a neighboring nation, to cut us loose from all participation in this most accursed traffic. . . . Hundreds of thousands of American bosoms would be bared to resent an insult offered to our flag by a foreign foe; and shall we hesitate to rescue that same glorious banner from the foul pollution of the Slaver's touch, when it may be done by merely lopping off a trade comparatively contemptible in extent, blood-stained in character, and in which none but outlaws and the abandoned may be presumed to participate?

I have the honour to be, very respectfully, your obedient servant,

DAVID TOD.

Hon. John M. Clayton
Secretary of State, Washington, D. C.

1.15. A Slave Revolt at Sea on an American Ship en Route from Africa to Brazil (1845)

The following sworn testimony of William Page, a British sailor, given before the U.S. consul in Rio de Janeiro, concerns the violent events that took place in 1845 aboard the U.S. slave ship *Kentucky.* Protected by the American flag, the *Kentucky* had sailed from Rio in 1844 equipped for the slave trade. Having reached the port of Inhambane in Mozambique, it acquired a Brazilian crew and a cargo of some 500 slaves, and then, with American and British crew members registered as "passengers," the ship returned to Brazil where it landed its surviving slaves. The following section of Page's testimony deals mainly with a violent slave revolt aboard the *Kentucky* and the Brazilian crew's fierce response to it, but also includes valuable details on the daily routine of an American slave ship in the final years of the international traffic.

SOURCE: *Class A. Correspondence with the British Commissioners at Sierra Leone, Havana, Rio de Janeiro, Surinam, Cape of Good Hope, Jamaica, Loanda, and Boa Vista, Relating to the Slave Trade. From January 1 to December 31, 1845, Inclusive* (London, 1846), pp. 517–18.

Deponent . . . said, that a majority of the slaves were brought on board during the night in launches, near the fort of Inhambane. There were about 500 in all that came on board. About a dozen died on the passage, and 46 men and one woman were hung and shot during the passage; and 440 or about, were landed at Cape Frio [Cabo Frio, a town northeast of Rio de Janeiro]. When the slaves came on board they were put down on the slave deck, all in irons. Across the vessel, aft, a bulkhead was run, aft of which, and in the cabin, the women, 150 to 200 in number, were put, and the men and boys forward of the bulkhead. When it was good weather, a good many of the negroes were on deck during the night and day. In stormy weather, only those that were kept at work were on deck, but all the others below. The vessel had not a full cargo. It was intended to have 700, but they could not get them. The negroes slept scattered about the slave-deck, as they chose. They were fed twice a day with beans, farina [manioc flour], rice, and dried beef, all boiled together. At the first meal they had beans, farina, and rice together, and at the second meal dried beef and farina. They eat in messes, as on board of a man-of-war, having their food in their dishes. All were provided with wooden spoons, made on board by the seamen, at Inhambane. The cooking aparatus was rigged in the galley, and so arranged and painted that it could not be discovered without coming on board. The cooking was going on all the time, excepting when near a sail, when fires were damped, and all the negroes put below.

And deponent further said, that the next day after the vessels crossed the bar on leaving Inhambane, as aforesaid, the negroes rose upon the officers and crew; a majority of the men, all of whom were in irons, got their irons off, broke through the bulkhead in the females department, and likewise into the forecastle. Upon this, the captain armed the crew with cutlasses, and got all the muskets and pistols, and loaded them, and the crew were firing down amongst the slaves for half an hour or more. In the meantime the deponent was nailing the hatches down, and used no musket or pistol; and there was no occasion, as the Brazilian sailors seemed to like the sport. In about half an hour they were subdued, and became quiet again.

The slaves were then brought on deck, eight or ten at a time, and ironed afresh. They were all re-ironed that afternoon, and put below, excepting about seven, who remained on deck. None were killed on this occasion, and but eight or ten more or less wounded. They fired with balls in the pistols and shot in the muskets. Supposes the reason none were killed is, that they had to fire through the grates of the hatches, and the slaves got out of the way as much as they could.

On the next day they were brought upon deck two or three dozens at a time, all being well ironed, and tried by Captain Fonseca and officers; and within two or three days afterwards forty-six men and one woman were hung and shot, and thrown overboard. They were ironed or chained two together, and when they were hung a rope was put round their necks, and they were drawn up to the yard-arm clear of the sail. This did not kill them, but only choked or strangled them. They were then shot in the breast, and the bodies thrown overboard. If only one or two that were ironed together were to be hung, a rope was put round his neck and he was drawn up clear of the deck, beside of the bulwarks, and his leg laid across the rail and chopped off, to save the irons and release him from his companion, who, at the same time, lifted up his leg till the other's was chopped off as aforesaid, and he released. The bleeding negro was then drawn up, shot in the breast, and thrown overboard as aforesaid. The legs of about one dozen were chopped off in this way. When the feet fell on deck, they were picked up by the Brazilian crew and thrown overboard, and sometimes at the body, while it was still living; and all kinds of sport was made of the business. When two that were chained together were both to be hung, they were hung up together by their necks, shot, and thrown overboard, irons and all. When the woman was hung up and shot, the ball did not take effect, and she was thrown overboard living, and was seen to struggle some time in the water before she sunk.

And deponent further said that, after this was over, they brought up and flogged about twenty men and six women. When they were flogged they were laid flat upon the deck, and their hands tied, and secured to one ring bolt, and their feet to another. They were then whipped by two men at a time—by the one with a stick about 2 feet long, with five or six strands of raw hide secured to the end of it (the hide was dry and hard and about 2 feet long); and by the other with a piece of the hide of a sea-horse; this was a strip about 4 feet long, from half an inch to an inch wide, as thick as one's finger or thicker, and hard as a whalebone, but more flexible. The flogging was very severe. Deponent and another Englishman on board, named Edward

Blake, were obliged to assist in the flogging, as the Brazilians got tired. Deponent flogged four, but he got clear of the hanging and shooting business. All the women that were flogged at this time died, but none of the men. Many of them, however, were sick all the passage, and were obliged to lie on their bellies during the remainder of the voyage, and some of them could hardly get on shore on arrival at Cabo Frio. The flesh of some of them where they were flogged (which was not generally on their backs, but on their posteriors) putrified and came off, in some cases 6 or 8 inches in diameter, and in places half an inch thick. Their wounds were dressed and filled up by the Contramestre [boatswain] with farina and cachaça [rum] made into a poultice, and sometimes with a salve made on board. When the farina and cachaça were applied to the poor creatures, they would shiver and tremble for half an hour, and groan and sob with the most intense agony. They were a shocking and horrible sight during the whole passage. There was no disturbance on board after this, and no flogging, excepting of the boys for stealing water, farina, and so forth, when it was not allowed them.

Deponent further said that the ages of the negroes were from nine or ten up to thirty years. They were generally healthy, as sick ones were not bought. Most of them were entirely without any article of clothes or covering, though at times they had strips of cloth around their loins, and some had handkerchiefs tied around them. The women were not so frequently naked as the men. Both the men and women frequently would get lousy, and be obliged to take off their strips of cloth to cleanse themselves. They were all brought on deck at different times during the voyage, say fifty at a time, and washed, by having water thrown over them, &c. They were washed four or five times each, and twice they had vinegar given to them to wash their mouths, and scrub their gums with brushes. In good weather the negroes themselves were obliged to sweep and wash down the slave deck every day, and thus kept it clean; but at night, and in hot weather, the hold of the deck smelt very badly. But a few of them were sick during the passage, except for those that were so badly flogged. The sick were doctored by the Contramestre, and the wounds of those that were flogged were dressed with aguardiente and farina, and a salve that was made on board.

1.16. "No Other Trade Was Known to His People." The King of Dahomey and the Slave Trade

The great importance of African participation in slave trading in their native lands is suggested by several documents in Part One. Without such involvement that traffic could hardly have thrived, and so the history of the Americas would have taken a different turn. The fact is, however, that many African monarchs and their subjects participated eagerly in the traffic. Among the states involved was the kingdom of Dahomey, a well-placed entity near the Atlantic coast that supplied many thousands of human beings to the slave markets of the Americas, a commerce that might have survived much longer but for the determination of Great Britain to replace the traffic with an agricultural economy producing such "articles of European consumption" as coffee, cotton, and palm oil.

In 1848 a British official, Brodie Cruickshank, who had spent many years in Africa, was assigned by the British government to the task of persuading King Ghezo of Dahomey to accept an annual remuneration of $2,000, in exchange for a treaty with Britain to end the kingdom's participation in the slave trade. However, as Cruickshank knew even before he met the king, the British offer was unrealistic, since each year nearly 8,000 slaves were shipped from Dahomey, and this traffic provided the king a lofty annual income of $300,000. Unable to convince the monarch that by replacing the slave trade with an agricultural economy he might enrich his people and give work to the slaves he traditionally shipped abroad, Cruickshank prepared a report to his government explaining his futile discussions with the king and proposing other ways Britain might end the Dahomey slave trade. The following excerpts from Cruickshank's report, introduced and briefly commented upon by an anonymous writer of *Chambers's Edinburgh Journal,* offers insights into slave trading and slave conditions, the advantages of the traffic to the king and his subjects, including a standing army of both men and women, and, finally, the great importance of traditional practices in Dahomey.

SOURCE: *Chambers's Edinburgh Journal,* no. 292, new Series, August 4, 1849.

The King of Dahomey and the Slave Trade

From the kingdom of Dahomey, on the western coast of Africa, the largest and most steady slave-export trade is carried on. To counteract this trade, the British government, as is well known, incurs a large annual expense, and practically fails in its object. Thus disconcerted, our government has made the attempt to persuade the king of Dahomey to abandon the trade in slaves; and the history of this attempt, drawn from a parliamentary paper [Report of 9 November, 1848, Parliamentary Papers, 1849 (Lords)] we now propose to give. The particulars are contained in a report by B. Cruickshank, Esq., respecting his mission to Dahomey.

In the Hands of Strangers

The writer of the report begins by glancing at the present state of this nefarious traffic. "For a period," says he, "extending over the last twelve years, the annual exportation of slaves from the territory of the king of Dahomey has averaged nearly 8000. In addition to this number, another thousand at least are annually brought down from the interior, and are kept in slavery in the towns and villages upon the coast, where they enjoy, when well conducted, a very considerable share of liberty, and all the necessities of life in apparent comfort and abundance; but they are subjected to exportation for acts of gross disobedience, as well as for social offences of an aggravated nature.

"It appears to be a general practice with the masters of the slaves to permit them to prosecute their own affairs, and to receive in exchange for this concession of their time a stipulated monthly sum derived from their labour; owing to this arrangement, an industrious slave is sometimes enabled to acquire his freedom by obtaining funds necessary for the purchase of two slaves, which will generally be accepted as the price of his redemption. This annual supply of 9000 slaves is chiefly, I may say entirely, derived from a systematic course of slave-hunting; for the number paid to the king by the Mahees and other tributaries, together with the criminal offenders who are exported, forms but a small item in the gross amount.

"The king generally accompanies his army to these slave hunts, which he pursues for two or three months every year. Its miserable objects are weak and detached tribes, inhabiting countries adjacent to his dominions, and at distances from his capital varying from twelve to twenty-four days' march. A battle rarely occurs, and the loss in killed in such expeditions is not so great as is generally believed in England. The ordinary plan is to send out traders to act as spies; these carry their petty merchandise into the interior towns, and make their observations upon their means of defence.

"The trader returns after the lapse of some months, guiding the king's army, and instructing the leaders how they may surround and surprise the unsuspecting inhabitants, who are often thus captured on awakening in the morning. As resistance is punished by death, they generally prefer to yield themselves prisoners, and thus the king's victories are often bloodless. It is only when African kings, of nearly equal power, are ambitious to try their strength, that those wholesale slaughters take place which only terminate in the extermination of a people. Such contests, however, are rare; the African chief having a much greater relish for an easy and unresisting prey, whom he can convert into money, than for the glory of a victory which costs him the lives of his people; so at least it is with the king of Dahomey, who often returns to his capital without the loss of a man either of his own party or that of his enemy. He has on more than one occasion been repulsed by the Akus and the people of Aberkoutah; but in these and similar cases, where the resistance is likely to be strong and determined, his troops are led away before much slaughter has been done.

"After the surrender of a town, the prisoners are presented to the king by their captors, who are rewarded by the payment of cowries, of the value of a couple of dollars for each captive, who is henceforth the king's slave; but on return to his capital after a successful enterprise, he is in the habit of distributing a number of these unfortunate creatures among his head men, and at the same time bestowing large sums as bounty to his troops. A selection is then made of a portion of the slaves, who are reserved for the king's employment; and the others are sent down to the slave merchant, who not unfrequently has already sold his goods on credit in anticipation of their arrival.

"An export duty of five dollars is paid upon each slave shipped from the king's dominions, even although the port of embarkation may not belong to him. It is a frequent practice to convey them by the lagoon either to the eastward, as Little Popo, or to westward, as Porto Nuovo, neither of which towns are in subjection to the king. He, however, has command of the lagoon leading to these places, and the duty must be paid previous to their embarkation upon it; so that from the export duty alone the king derives an annual sum of 40,000 dollars. But this is not all. The native dealer, who brings his slaves to the merchant, has also to pay duties on each slave at the different custom-house stations on their road to the barracoons. The amount paid at these stations it is more difficult to ascertain, as many of the slaves are the king's own property. A sum, however, of not less than 20,000 dollars may be set down for this item. If we estimate the annual number of the slaves sold by the king himself at 3000, and reckon them at the present price of eighty dollars, we have an additional item of 240,000 dollars; thus making in all a revenue of 300,000 dollars derived annually from the slave trade.

"But this calculation, which is a near approximation to the truth, and is under rather than above the exact amount, does not by any means convey a just impression of the advantages which the king derives from the slave trade. By the laws of his country he inherits the property of his deceased subjects; so that his head men and others who have been amassing property by this traffic, have only been acting as so many factors to the king, who receives at their death the fruits of the labour of a lifetime; a very small portion of the estate in slaves and cowries is generally returned to the natural heir, which serves as a species of capital for him to commence in like man-

ner his factorship. Under a system so calculated to induce an apathetic indifference, the king contrives by repeated marks of royal favour and by appointments to offices of trust and emolument to stimulate to industrious
exertion the principal men of his kingdom. These appointments, moreover, become hereditary, and their holders form an aristocracy with sufficient privileges to induce the ambition of entering its ranks."

In the circumstances here stated, it will not appear surprising that
Cruickshank had undertaken an impossibility. On being introduced to the
king of Dahomey, and expressing a hope that he would assent to a treaty to
extinguish the slave trade on his coast, his majesty was very much at a loss
how to reply. He was anxious to conciliate the British government; but on
the other hand, the abandonment of the slave trade was pretty nearly
equivalent to financial ruin. His majesty's excuses are admirable. 'His chiefs
had had long and serious consultations with him upon the subject, and
they had come to the conclusion that his government could not be carried
on without it. The state which he maintained was great; his army was expensive; the ceremonies and customs to be observed annually, which had
been handed down to him from his forefathers, entailed upon him a vast
outlay of money. These could not be abolished. The form of his government could not be suddenly changed without causing such a revolution as
would deprive him of his throne and precipitate his kingdom into a state of
anarchy. He was very desirous to acquire the friendship of England. He
loved and respected the English character, and nothing afforded him such
satisfaction as to see an Englishman in his country, and to do him honour.
He himself and his army were ready at all times to fight the Queen's enemies, and to do anything the English government might ask of him, but to
give up the slave trade. No other trade was known to his people. Palm-oil,
it was true, was now engaging the attention of some of them; but it was a
slow method of making money, and brought only a very small amount of
duties into his coffers. The planting of coffee and cotton had been suggested to him; but this was slower still. The trees had to grow, and he himself would probably be in his grave before he could reap any benefit from
them. And what to do in the meantime? Who would pay his troops, or buy
arms and clothing for them? Who would buy dresses for his wives? Who
would give him supplies of cowries, of rum, of powder, and of cloth to perform his annual customs? He held his power by an observance of the time-
honoured customs of his fore-fathers; and he would forfeit it, and entail
upon himself a life full of shame, and a death full of misery, if he neglected
them. It was the slave trade that made him terrible to his enemies, and
loved and honoured, and respected by his people. How could he give it up?

It had been the ruling principle of action with himself and his subjects from their earliest childhood. Their thoughts, their habits, their discipline, their mode of life, had been formed with reference to this all-engrossing occupation; even the very songs with which the mother stilled her crying infant told of triumph over foes reduced to slavery. Could he, by signing this treaty, change the sentiments of a whole people? It could not be. A long series of years was necessary to bring about such a change. He himself and his people must be made to feel the superior advantages of another traffic in an increase of riches, and of the necessaries and luxuries of life, before they could be weaned from this trade. The expenses of the English government are great; would it suddenly give up the principal sources of its revenues without some equivalent provision for defraying its expenses? He could not believe so. No more would he reduce himself to beggary. The sum offered him would not pay his expenses for a week; and even if the English government were willing to give him an annual sum equivalent to his present revenue, he would still have some difficulty in employing the energies of his people in a new direction. Under such circumstances, however, he would consider himself bound to use every exertion to meet the wishes of the English government.

"Such were the arguments which the king used in justification of his refusal to sign the treaty; and much regret did he express that the object which the English government had in view was of such vital importance to him that he could not possibly comply with its request.

"Although inwardly acknowledging the force of his objections, I did not give up the subject without endeavouring to convince him that in the course of a few years, by developing the resources of his rich and beautiful country, he would be able to increase his revenue tenfold; and that the slaves whom he now sold for exportation, if employed in the cultivation of articles of European consumption, would be far more valuable to him than they now were. I endeavoured to make him comprehend this, by informing him of the price of a slave in the Brazils, and asking him if he thought the Brazilian would give such a price for him if he did not find himself more than repaid by his labour? He believed this to be the case; but the length of time required, the whole process of an entirely new system, and want of skill among his people to conduct such operations, appear to him insurmountable difficulties. He was willing, however, to permit Englishmen to form plantations in his country, and to give instructions to his people.

"At last the king appeared anxious to escape from this harassing question; and by way of closing the interview, invited me to accompany him to witness a preview of his troops. What principally struck me upon this occasion was the animus displayed by every one present, from the king to the meanest of his people; every word of their mouths, every thought of their hearts, breathed of defiance, of battle, and slavery to their enemies: his principal captains, both male and female, expressed an anxious hope that I would remain in their country to witness their first triumph, and to behold the number of captives they would lead back to Abomey [the ancient capital of Dahomey]; and that I might be in no doubt that the general mass participated in these sentiments, such an assenting shout rent the air as must have often proclaimed the victory. A quiet smile of proud satisfaction passed across the king's face as he regarded me with a look which said, 'these are my warriors;' and when I heard the loud rattle of their arms, and saw the wild sparkle of their delighted eyes, gleaming with strong excitement, as they waved their swords and standards in the air, I fully acknowledged the force of the king's question—'Could he, by signing the treaty, change the sentiments of a whole people?' The sight which I was witnessing was to me a stronger argument than any the king had yet used; here there was no palliating, no softening down, no attempt to conceal their real sentiments under the plea of necessity for undertaking their slave-hunting wars, but a fierce, wild, and natural instinct, speaking in language that could not be misunderstood.

"At no time before my arrival in his country did I ever entertain the faintest hope of his acceding to it in good faith; and since I had ascertained at Whydah the amount of revenue derived from this trade, and had seen the rude and expensive magnificence of his state, I could not but feel that a repetition of my paltry offer of an annual subsidy of 2000 dollars would only clothe me with ridicule. I was anxious, however, to ascertain whether the king really regarded it in a merely pecuniary point of view, and would forego the trade in slaves upon finding his revenue made up from other sources. He assured me that he would; but even with this assurance, I may be allowed to doubt whether a monarch and a people of such ambitious character would cease from making war upon their neighbors." [33]

33. For a useful account of the history of Dahomey and the slave trade, see Patrick Manning, *Slavery, Colonialism and Economic Growth in Dahomey, 1640–1960* (Cambridge: Cambridge University Press, 1982), especially pp. 36–56. Editor.

PART TWO

. . . . . .

The Internal Slave Trade of the United States

. . . . . .

Internal or domestic slave trading (as distinguished from the African traffic) occurred wherever slavery existed in the Americas, but the practice was especially common in the two largest slaveholding countries of the Americas, the United States and Brazil, particularly following abrupt suspensions of the African traffic in 1808 and 1851, respectively. The ban on the importation of African slaves, long resisted by slaveowners in both countries, resulted in serious labor shortages, motivating planters and other users of slaves to turn increasingly for their labor needs to domestic slave populations. The result was a marked increase in the forced transfer of hundreds of thousands of men, women, and children, often over great distances, from less prosperous sections of the two countries to their more promising and productive agricultural regions, a practice that actually existed on a large scale for nearly forty years in Brazil and some seventy years in the United States.

A significant increase in domestic slave trading was apparent in the United States even before the end of the eighteenth century, a result in part perhaps of state bans on the importation of African slaves.[1] Already by 1798, according to a Delaware Quaker traveling through Maryland, traders were "buying Drove after Drove of the poor afflicted blacks, . . . carrying them into the Southern States for Speculation; regardless of separation of nearest Connections & natural ties." This witness was clearly shocked by what he saw, which suggests that in Delaware the overland slave trade was less vig-

---

1. In 1788 Virginia, New York, Massachusetts, Pennsylvania, and Connecticut banned the African traffic, followed by Delaware in 1789 and Georgia in 1793. North Carolina ended importations in 1794, Maryland in 1796, and in 1788 South Carolina forbade it until January 1, 1793, extended the ban in 1792 and 1796, then reopened the traffic in 1803 and kept it open until January 1, 1808. See DuBois, *The Suppression of the African Slave Trade*, pp. 71–93, 230–41, 245–46.

orous than in nearby Maryland.[2] Already in 1791, in fact, abolitionists had petitioned the Maryland state legislature to ban the exportation of slaves from the state, but in response a legislative committee argued that as long as the citizens of Maryland held slaves—"a property recognized by law and secured by the Constitution"—they could not imagine how their exportation could reasonably be prohibited.[3] Michael Tadman, a historian of the trade, calculated the existence of a substantial traffic in the final decade of the eighteenth century. In that period, he estimated, Virginia lost by interstate sale 22,767 slaves, Maryland 22,221, and Delaware 4,523, a total of 49,511 slaves, whereas Kentucky *gained* 21,636 slaves, Tennessee 6,645, Georgia 6,095, and the two Carolinas together nearly 8,106, for a total of 42,482 slaves.[4]

In fact, trading in Africans and native-born blacks was common in the colonial period, as it was almost everywhere that slavery existed. In the early years of English colonization in North America even indentured servants held for limited periods of time were "traded about as commodities"[5]; and as the native black population grew, the buying and selling of American-born slaves also increased, in part perhaps because buyers of slaves often preferred creoles to Africans. Nevertheless, in the eighteenth century, according to historian Allan Kulikoff, many native blacks of the tidewater region of Maryland and Virginia "had secured a stable family life, and few had been forced to move more than twenty miles from their birthplaces." As a result, family separations, when they occurred, were on the whole less disruptive to family relationships than they would be in the nineteenth century, since in the earlier period slaves sold or transferred to new masters often stayed near enough to relatives to maintain contacts.[6] Nevertheless, by the eighteenth-century slave auctions and sheriff sales were regular features of colonial life; and with the appearance of colonial newspapers, advertisements offering slaves for sale strongly contributed to the ease and volume of the business. The first American weekly, the *Boston News-Letter,* appeared in 1704 and almost at once began advertising the sale

2. Steven Deyle, "The Irony of Liberty: Origins of the Domestic Slave Trade," *Journal of the Early Republic* 12 (Spring 1992): 37–38.

3. Jeffrey R. Brackett, *The Negro in Maryland* (Baltimore, 1889; reprint, New York: Negro Universities Press, 1969), pp. 57–58.

4. See Michael Tadman, *Speculators and Slaves* (Madison: University of Wisconsin Press, 1989), p. 12, table 2.1.

5. See Edmund S. Morgan, *American Slavery, American Freedom: The Ordeal of Colonial Virginia* (New York: W. W. Norton, 1975), p. 296.

6. Allan Kulikoff, *Tobacco and Slaves: The Development of Southern Cultures in the Chesapeake, 1680–1800* (Chapel Hill: University of North Carolina Press, 1986), pp. 358–60; Allan Kulikoff, "Black Society and the Economics of Slavery," *Maryland Historical Society* 30, no. 2 (1975): 207–8.

of slaves, a practice imitated by most local newspapers.[7] A convincing example is Benjamin Franklin's newspaper, the *Pennsylvania Gazette,* in which Franklin advertised for sale both slaves and the unexpired time of indentured servants.[8]

The ban on the African slave trade in 1808 no doubt quickened the tempo of the internal trade. However, even earlier causes of this development were America's separation from British commerce along with the emergence in the early years of the century of two extraordinarily valuable cash crops: sugar in the newly acquired territory of Louisiana and, probably more important, a surge in upland cotton production caused by Eli Whitney's fortuitous invention of the cotton gin in 1793, both of which continued to generate huge demands for slave labor until the Civil War. Increased cotton and sugar production in developing regions accompanied by widespread soil exhaustion, agricultural decline, and poverty in such older states as Virginia and Maryland induced many slaveholders to sell some of their slaves or to migrate with their households and slaves into the Carolinas, Georgia, and other parts of the South, and as profits from cotton increased, a massive transfer of slaves carried the southern agricultural system relentlessly into such comparatively virgin regions as Alabama, Mississippi, Louisiana, Florida, Arkansas, and finally Texas, enormously swelling the slave populations of those areas between 1790 and 1860 (see Fig. 5). "The price differential told the story," the historian Winthrop Jordan wrote. "In 1797 prices for prime field hands ran about $300 in Virginia and $400 in Charleston; in 1803, over $400 in Virginia and somewhat under $600 in Charleston and Georgia; in 1808, $500 in Virginia and $550 in Charleston and Georgia."[9]

This state of affairs was well described in the 1830s by the New York abolitionist, William Jay. "Various circumstances have of late years combined to lessen the demand for slave labour in the more northern, and to increase it in the more southern and western portions of the slave region; while the enlarged consumption of sugar and cotton is enhancing the market for slaves. The most profitable employment of this species of labour is unfortunately found in those States, which, from their recent settlement, possess immense tracts which are still to be brought into cultivation, and in

7. Steven Deyle, " 'By farr the most profitable trade': Slave Trading in British Colonial America," *Slavery and Abolition: A Journal of Comparative Studies* 10, no. 2 (September 1989): 115–19.

8. Carl Van Doren, *Benjamin Franklin* (New York: Viking Press, 1938), pp. 128–29.

9. See Frederic Bancroft, *Slave Trading in the Old South* (Columbia: University of South Carolina Press, 1996), p. 12 n. 28; Winthrop D. Jordan, *White over Black: American Attitudes toward the Negro, 1550–1812* (Baltimore: Penguin Books, 1969), p. 321.

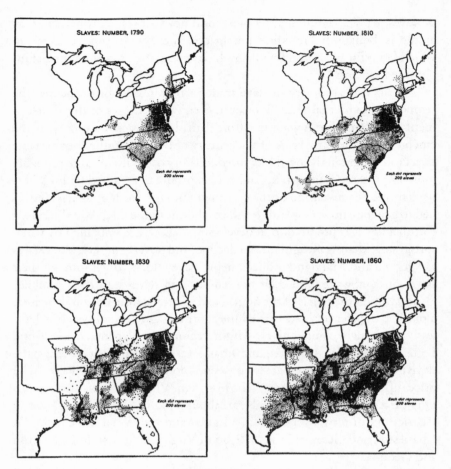

5. The Geographic Expansion of Slavery and the Growth of the Slave Population (1790–1860). From Lewis Cecil Gray, *History of Agriculture in the Southern United States to 1860,* 2 vols. (Washington, D.C.: Carnegie Institute of Washington, 1933).

which, consequently, there now is, and will long continue to be, an urgent demand for slaves." According to southern estimates, Jay added, this traffic affected more than 30,000 slaves per year, and one of its "peculiar abominations" was that, instead of dealing in family units, the market-engendered tendency of slave traders was to buy and sell the young and the very young, specifically persons of both sexes, from twelve to twenty-five years of age.[10] This grim but logical preference for youthful slaves was confirmed by Frederic Bancroft, who wrote: "The selling singly of young children pri-

10. Jay, *Inquiry,* pp. 8–9.

vately and publicly was frequent and notorious. Virtually all traders dealt in those from 10 or 12 years of age and many advertised for those from 6, 7, 8 and 9."[11]

The day-to-day operations of this traffic began as a rule in the towns and rural districts of slave-exporting areas and culminated weeks or months later far from the victims' former homes. The first step in the process was the procurement of slaves for delivery to markets in nearby towns and cities, there to be sold or auctioned off to interregional traders, who transported them overland or by sea to destinations in the lower South. The initial acquisition of slaves was the work of local traders using strategies designed to arouse the greed of prospective sellers. According to Michael Tadman, "roving speculators" toured villages and the countryside in search of opportunities to acquire slaves directly from owners or at local auctions and judicial sales, in many cases offering cash to prospective buyers to hasten the process.[12] In his study of the traffic Bancroft drew a powerful portrait of the highly motivated slave buyer always on the lookout for profitable deals, "chatting at the country stores and taverns, loitering, treating and asking questions at the barrooms, looking in at the county jails to see the latest arrivals, cordially greeting the slaveholding farmer," but never forgetting his main purpose—"to buy negroes for considerably less than the interstate traders in the District [of Columbia] would readily pay for them." A witness recalled: "So necessary is the annual decimation of slaves by sale to support these old decayed families, that it has become a settled trade for men whose occupation is to buy slaves, to travel through the 'Old Dominion,' from estate to estate. . . . Here he gets one, there another, and in a few weeks he enters Lynchburg, Alexandria or Richmond with a hundred or more. . . . As it is, slaves are raised here more as a *marketable* and money-returning commodity than for their productive labor."[13] In 1839 a pamphleteer sent Congress the following description of the type of person traders were presumably searching for: "The slaveholder of Virginia, who, seated in his old and gentlemanlike mansion, surveys the wide demèsnes, which . . . long since exhausted by slave labor, present to his eye a brown and dreary prospect, except where they have become overgrown by a miserable forest of pines. His black people have multiplied around him, and he scarcely knows how to feed them. . . . The slave jobber is prowling about the neighborhood, with his tempting offers of five hundred dollars for a lad or a girl, or one thousand dollars for an adult person. The

11. Bancroft, *Slave Trading*, p. 208.
12. Tadman, *Speculators and Slaves*, pp. 47–55.
13. Bancroft, *Slave Trading*, pp. 52, 91.

temptation soon becomes irresistible, and slave after slave supplies the southern market."[14]

Every city in the South, according to the urban historian, Richard Wade, had numerous slave depots where traders carried on their business.[15] Among the most important in the buying areas of the eastern border states were Baltimore, Richmond, Norfolk, Washington, and Alexandria, all with secondary suppliers at work in and about such towns as Lynchburg, Fredericksburg, Petersburg, and the county seats of Maryland's Eastern Shore. In the early 1830s fifteen or more "large buyers" were active in the small town of Cambridge, along with several times as many petty traders, agents, or helpers. Slave dealers were exceptionally common on the Eastern Shore, according to Bancroft, because nowhere else could they find as many slaves so cheap, and because choice young men and women bought in that part of Maryland could be sold in Mississippi or Louisiana for twice their original purchase price.[16]

Slave buyers advertised in newspapers, giving posterity insights into their aims and methods. Often employing tiny engravings of bundle-toting blacks, both male and female, to attract the public, these notices typically contained such information as the number of slaves the trader hoped to buy, the genders and ages he desired, promises of high or "the highest" prices, and such information as the preferred method of payment (normally cash); the buyer's name or firm, the hotel, tavern, or other location where he carried on his business; and sometimes the city or state where the slaves might be sent. These announcements reveal, as pointed out by William Jay and others, that the slaves in greatest demand were the young and the very young, with a general preference for males and women of reproductive age who might contribute both labor and children to the farmers and planters of slave-buying areas. Typical were the following advertisements:[17]

Cash for One Hundred Negroes,
Including both sexes, from twelve to twenty-five years of age. Persons having likely servants to dispose of, will find it to their advantage to give us a call, as we will give higher prices in cash than any other purchaser who is now in this city.

14. Quoted by David L. Lightner, "The Door to the Slave Bastille: The Abolitionist Assault upon the Interstate Slave Trade, 1833–1839," *Civil War History* 34, no. 3 (1988): 246.

15. Richard Wade, *Slavery in the Cities: The South 1820–1860* (New York: Oxford University Press, 1964), p. 198.

16. Bancroft, *Slave Trading*, pp. 29–30.

17. Jay, *Inquiry*, pp. 157–58.

We can at all times be found at Isaac Beer's tavern, a few doors below Lloyd's tavern, opposite Centre Market, Washington city. All communications promptly attended to.

September 1, 1834.   Birch & Jones

Cash for Two Hundred Negroes.

We will give cash for two hundred likely young negroes of both sexes, families included. Persons wishing to dispose of their slaves, will do well to give us a call, as we will give higher prices in cash, than any other purchasers who are now, or may hereafter come into this MARKET. All communications will meet attention. We can at all times be found at our residence on Seventh-street, immediately south of the Centre Market-house, Washington, D.C.

September 13, 1834.   Joseph W. Neal & Co.

The following assessment of the market for slave rentals and sales for 1853 appeared in a newspaper called the *Tarboro Southerner,* and was reprinted in *The Southern Argus* of Norfolk, Virginia: [18]

Hiring and Sale of Negroes, &c.

The close of one year and the beginning of another are great sources of annoyances to some and gratification to others in these parts. . . . Those who had negroes to hire, were pleased with the rapid advance in hiring as well as selling—the [annual rental] price for negro men ranging from $150 to $200, and for women, from $65 to $90. The sales generally ranged for men from $1,000 to $1,200—a likely negro man, however, a rough carpenter, aged about 23 years, brought $2,000. Young women and girls nearly grown $700 to $900.00. Corn about $1 per bushel—Fodder, 75 cents to $1 per hundred. Pork $5 to 5½, &c. *Tarboro Southerner.*

After the roving slave buyer had disposed of his collection of slaves at some nearby town or port, a new phase of the business began, this time conducted by auctioneers and inter-regional traders. Among the most important trading centers in the selling area was Washington, D.C., which was at an early stage of development when the large-scale interstate trade

---

18. *The Southern Argus* (Norfolk, Virginia), January 11, 1854. Tarboro is a town in North Carolina about one hundred miles south of Norfolk. For more newspaper advertisements for slave sales, see Docs. 2.4 and 2.21.

began. With only 1,437 resident slaves in 1810 and probably never many more than three thousand at any one time, the capital could not, on its own, supply large numbers of slaves to buying areas. Rather, its importance as a slave-trading center resulted mainly from its convenient location in the heart of the most active slave-exporting region, as well as its nearness to the Potomac River port of Alexandria, then a major commercial center accessible to ocean-going vessels and the best place, according to Bancroft, to begin both coastal and overland slave shipments.[19]

Washington's involvement in slave trafficking aroused constant disapproval until this conspicuous business was at last prohibited in the District of Columbia as part of the Compromise of 1850.[20] Most distasteful to its critics, including members of Congress, were the many manifestations of slave trading in and about the town: gangs of chained or bound slaves driven through city streets, utilization of private slave pens and public prisons for housing slaves (a common practice throughout the South), the kidnapping and selling of free people, the spectacle of public auctions, incessant slave advertising, and perhaps most offensive to sectors of the Washington public, the federal government's open sanctioning of slave trading in the city. "By authority of Congress," said the educator and congressman, Horace Mann, in a speech to the House of Representatives in 1849, "the city of Washington is the Congo of America." [21]

Slaves were sent to market in a variety of ways. They were put aboard flatboats and river steamers for transport down the Ohio, Missouri, and Mississippi Rivers, and many were conveyed in railway cars in the last years of the trade. Multitudes were forced to trek long distances overland in slave gangs or coffles (*cáfila* in Portuguese, from Arabic *qafilah,* a caravan).[22] This was the most grueling and notorious means of transporting slaves, since distances were often great, and the constant prospect of flight or rebellion required a lavish use of chains and manacles and other injurious forms of restraint. Finally, many slaves who experienced the domestic trade traveled by sea from such major east coast ports as Alexandria, Baltimore, Norfolk, Charleston, and Savannah, bound for such ports as Mobile, New Orleans, and Galveston. Some slave-trading firms owned specially con-

---

19. Bancroft, *Slave Trading,* pp. 45–66; Mary Tremain, *Slavery in the District of Columbia* (New York: Negro Universities Press, 1969). For an important article on slavery in the District of Columbia with valuable illustrations, see John Davis, "Eastman Johnson's *Negro Life at the South* and Urban Slavery in Washington, D.C.," *The Art Bulletin* 80, no. 1 (March 1998): 67–92.

20. Slavery, however, remained legal in the District of Columbia and residents could sell their slaves to other residents, or to persons removing them from the District.

21. For slavery and the slave trade in the District of Columbia, see Docs. 2.1, 2.5. 2.6, 2.13, and 3.24.

22. For slave coffles, see Docs. 1.10, 2.1–2.2, 2.8–2.10, 2.22, and 2.26.

structed ships and transported not only their own slaves but, for a charge, those of other slave traders and planters aquiring slaves in the slave-exporting region. To cite an example, on March 28, 1836, the *National Intelligencer* of Washington contained an advertisement by the major slave-trading firm of Franklin & Armfield announcing that the brig *Tribune,* Samuel C. Bush, master, would sail on the first of January, the brig *Isaac Franklin,* William Smith, master, on the fifteenth of January, and the brig *Uncas,* Nathaniel Boush, master, on the first of February; that vessels would continue sailing from Alexandria bimonthly throughout the shipping season, and that slaves intended for shipment would at any time be received for safe-keeping at twenty-five cents a day.[23] A typical ship utilized in this coastal traffic carried perhaps 150 slaves, but some as many as two hundred or more. Such overloading and the voyages to Gulf Coast ports could cause hardship, illness, and even death, though most slaves who experienced a coastal voyage reached their destinations in much better condition than slaves coming from Africa. Nevertheless, observers in the United States encountered conditions on American ships resembling those of the African trade. For example, a British traveler, Basil Hall, who in the 1820s had witnessed conditions on a slave ship at Rio de Janeiro, later described a brig docked in New Orleans after arriving from Baltimore with more than two hundred slaves. "Her decks," he wrote, "presented a scene which forcibly reminded me of Rio de Janeiro. In the one case, however, the slaves were brought from the savage regions of Africa; in the other, from the very heart of a free country. To the poor negro the distinction is probably no great matter."[24]

How many persons were affected by this traffic? In their response to *Time on the Cross,* the controversial study of slavery by Stanley Engerman and Robert Fogel, historians Herbert Gutman and Richard Sutch calculated that over a million slaves were taken across state borders between 1790 and 1860, constituting, in their opinion, one of the greatest forced migrations in history.[25] Michael Tadman also calculated the involvement of well over a million persons transferred in that same seventy-year period, including slaves transported by slave traders and those accompanying migrating masters. He thus concluded that "the domestic slave trade brought about the inter-regional transference of a very substantial proportion of the Upper South's slave population; and the extent of the domestic slave trade

23. Theodore D. Weld, *Slavery and the Internal Slave Trade in the United States* (London: Thomas Ward, 1841), pp. 207–9.

24. Basil Hall, *Travels in North America in the Years 1827 and 1828* (Edinburgh: Cadell, 1829), p. 199.

25. "The Slave Family: Protected Agent of Capitalist Masters or Victims of the Slave Trade," in Paul A. David et al., eds., *Reckoning with Slavery* (New York: Oxford University Press, 1976), p. 95.

must greatly have exceeded that of planter migration. A trade on the massive scale which has been described must have been one of the basic factors influencing the life of the ante-bellum South."[26] Elsewhere Richard Sutch calculated that in the *decade* before the Civil War more than 269,000 slaves were exported from eight selling states to six buying states, a number almost as large as William Jay's figure (based on southern estimates) of 30,000 slaves *per year* in the 1830s.[27] Such statistics would not have included, of course, the many slaves who were sold but never crossed a state line, and so these estimates, large as they are, do not tell the entire story. Finally, as the testimony of elderly ex-slaves reveals, many slaves were sold over and over again during their lives, thus experiencing numerous separations from family and friends (see Doc. 2.1). One such person was Isabella Van Waggenen, a New York slave later known as Sojourner Truth, who was sold at least five times, and whose son, Peter, though freed by New York legislation along with other slaves, was illegally sold and sent to Alabama where he was cruelly whipped before his rescue and return to the state of New York.[28]

To sum up, the domestic slave trade produced tragic results, many of which are revealed in the following documents. It broke up hundreds of thousands of families. It motivated (and caused) the kidnaping and enslavement of free people. It was a constant source of fear and anxiety to millions—not just people who experienced sale and transfer but also those who knew that at any hour this might also happen to them.[29] It encouraged prostitution and brutalized children. It disgraced the capital of the nation, where free people were confined in public jails and sold into a lifetime of slavery to pay jail fees and other minor debts (see Docs. 2.5 and 2.13). It shocked visiting foreigners. It produced the spectacle, according to Frederick Douglass, of "human flesh jobbers, armed with pistol, whip, and bowie-knife, driving a company of a hundred men, women, and children, from the Potomac to the slave market at New Orleans" (see Doc. 2.11).

26. See Tadman, *Speculators and Slaves*, chap. 2, especially table 2.1, on p. 12, and Tadman's "Slave Trading in the Ante-Bellum South: An Estimate of the Extent of the Inter-Regional Slave Trade," *American Studies* 13, no. 2 (1979): 195–220.

27. Richard Sutch, "The Breeding of Slaves for Sale and the Westward Expansion of Slavery, 1859–1860," in Stanley L. Engerman and Eugene D. Genovese, eds., *Race and Slavery in the Western Hemisphere: Quantitative Studies* (Princeton: Princeton University Press, 1975), pp. 173–98.

28. Carleton Mabee and Susan Mabee Newhouse, *Sojourner Truth: Slave, Prophet, Legend* (New York: New York Universities Press, 1993), pp. 3–21.

29. For the threat of sale as a "long term mechanism of control," the anxiety caused by such threats, responses to being sold, and efforts to relocate lost family members, see Norrece T. Jones, *Born a Child of Freedom, Yet a Slave* (Hanover, N.H.: Wesleyan University Press, 1990), pp. 37–48.

Finally, high slave prices motivated selective breeding and sexual manipulation by masters, including forced mating, the granting of rewards and advantages to prolific women, the selection of couples based on favorable physical attributes, and even the hiring of "stockmen" to improve the quality of the owner's "people."[30]

2.1. "The Speculators Have Got Us." The Evils of the Domestic Slave Trade

The following essay on the U.S. internal slave trade, published in 1834, was the work of a committee of the New England Anti-Slavery Society (later the Massachusetts Anti-Slavery Society). Its principal author, David Lee Child, was a charter member and the husband of the distinguished author and abolitionist, Lydia Maria Child (see Doc. 3.21), both of whom labored together for many years in the struggle against slavery.

Using the writings and reports of many witnesses, particularly persons associated with the famous Lane Theological Seminary in Cincinnati, David Child and his colleagues assembled a sweeping indictment of the U.S. domestic slave trade: the endless threat, faced by free blacks, of abduction into a life of bondage; the "instinctive dread" of sale, family division, unjust laws encouraging or promoting slavery and the slave trade; the legal powerlessness of blacks, slave and free; prostitution and the abuse of women; the cruelty of slave auctions; and finally, vivid accounts of the transportation of slaves on overland marches, by sea in ocean-going vessels, and by barge and riverboat to the slave-buying regions of the nation.

SOURCE: *American Anti-Slavery Reporter,* vol. 1, no. 7 (July 1834): 97–107.

Report on the Slave Trade.

The Committee on the Domestic Slave Trade of the United States ask leave respectfully to submit the following report: . . .

The domestic trade, which is now carried on in these states without an attempt to restrain it, does not differ essentially from the foreign. In its great and leading characteristics it is the same. It is commenced and attended in its progress by the same heart-breaking separations from kindred, friends and home—the same terror, anguish, and despair; it is conducted with the same violence, kidnapping and, in case of resistance or pursuit,

---

30. On this issue, see Docs. 2.18 and 2.19 and especially the testimony of former slaves in Doc. 2.20.

murder and massacre as in Africa; and it is unquestionably accompanied with more fraud than was ever perpetrated on the African coast. Your committee feel it their duty, at the risk of being thought tedious, to illustrate by facts the tremendous guilt and misery of this business.

Hezekiah Niles, Esq., editor and publisher of the *Baltimore Weekly Register,* is situated in the focus of the domestic slave trade. He has ever shown himself . . . a faithful apologist of slaveholders. His testimony, therefore, so far as it is against those persons and their agents and *protegees* (for slave traders are nothing more) is peculiarly valuable. It is the confession of the adversary. To that testimony your committee invite your attention.

In the *Register* for 1829, vol. 35, p. 4, we find the following statement, under the heading of *"Kidnapping."*

"The Winchester (Va.) Republican has an interesting narrative of a case of kidnapping in which a woman was rescued, though the wretch who sold her to a trader in human flesh escaped. Dealing in slaves has become a LARGE BUSINESS. Establishments are made at several places in *Maryland* and *Virginia,* at which they are sold like cattle. These places of deposit are strongly built and well supplied with thumb-screws and gags and ornamented with cowskins and other whips—oftentimes bloody. But the laws of these states permit the traffic and it is suffered. *All good men obey the laws!"*

Dr. Jesse Torrey, of Philadelphia, one of the earliest and therefore most meritorious laborers in the anti-slavery field, has collected a number of cases from which your committee select a few, recommending to all who hear this report to read Dr. Torrey's book.[31]

"A youth, having learned the subject on which I was occupied and being prompt to communicate whatever he might meet with relative to it, informed me, on returning from school on the evening of the 18th of December, 1815, that a black woman destined for transportation to Georgia, with a coffle about to start, attempted to escape by jumping out of the window of a garret of a three story brick tavern in F street, about daybreak in the morning, and that in the fall she had her back and both arms broken. I remarked that I did not wonder; and inquired whether it had not killed her? To which he replied, that he understood that she was dead, and that the *Georgia-men* [slave dealers] had gone off with the others. The relation of this shocking disaster excited considerable agitation in my mind, and fully confirmed the sentiments which I had already adopted and recorded of the multiplied horrors *added* to slavery when its victims are bought and sold, frequently for distant destinations, with as much indifference as four-

31. *Portraiture of Domestic Slavery in the United States* (Philadelphia: Published by the author, 1817).

footed beasts. Supposing this to be a recent occurrence, and being desirous of seeing the mangled slave before she was buried, I proceeded with haste early on the following morning in search of the house. Calling at one near where the catastrophe occurred, I was informed that it had been three weeks since it took place, and that the woman was still living. I found the house, and having obtained permission of the landlord to see her, I was conducted by a lad to her room. On entering the room, I observed her lying upon a bed on the floor, and covered with a white woollen blanket, on which were several spots of blood, which I perceived was *red,* not withstanding the *opacity* of her skin. Her countenance, though very pale from the shock she had received, appeared complacent and sympathetic.—Both arms were broken between the elbows and wrists, and had undoubtedly been well set and dressed, but from her restlessness she had displaced the bones so that they were perceptibly crooked. I have since been informed by the mayor of the city, who is a physician, and resides not far distant from the place, that he was called to visit her immediately after her fall; and found, besides her arms being broken, that the lower part of her spine was badly shattered so that it was very doubtful whether she would ever be capable of walking again, if she should survive. The lady of the mayor said she was awakened from sleep by the fall of the woman, and heard her heavy struggling groans. I inquired of her whether she was asleep when she sprang from the window? She replied, *'No: no more than I am now.'* I asked her what was the cause of her doing such a frantic act. She answered, *'They brought me away with two of my children, and would not let me see my husband. They didn't sell my husband, and I didn't want to go; I was so confused and 'istracted, that I didn't know hardly what I was about—but I didn't want to go, and I jumped out of the window;—but I am sorry now I did it. They have carried my children off with them to Carolina.'*

I was informed that the slave trader who had purchased her near Bladensburgh gave her to the landlord as a compensation for taking care of her. Thus her family was dispersed from north to south and herself nearly torn in pieces, without a shadow of hope of ever seeing or hearing from her children again. 'He that can behold this poor woman (as a respectable citizen of Washington afterwards remarked) and listen to her *unvarnished* story without a humid eye possesses a stouter heart than I do. . . .' "[32]

32. After this part of this report was read to the Convention, the Rev. Amos A. Phelps, agent of the American Anti-Slavery Society, rose and said that he had just had the privilege of seeing this woman, who still survives; that one of her arms and hands was perceptibly crooked, as Dr. Torrey described it at the time; that she had become the mother of three children by her husband, who was not sold; that her master, who gave her away as above, allured by the *children* had recently laid claim to them and their mother!

Your committee recur with a painful satisfaction to the testimony of Mr. [Henry B.] Stanton's letter. He says:—

"The slaves at the north have a kind of instinctive dread of being sold into southern slavery. They know the toil is extreme, the climate sickly, and the hope of redemption desperate. But what is more dreadful, they fear that if they are sold they will have to leave a wife, a sister or children whom they love. I hope no one will smile unbelievingly when I say, *that slaves can love.* There is no class of the community whose social affections are stronger. The above facts illustrate this truth. Mr. [Andrew] Benton [a former member of the theological department at Lane Seminary] tells me that while prosecuting his agency in Missouri, he was applied to in more than a hundred instances by slaves who were about to be sold to southern drivers, beseeching him in the most earnest manner to buy them so that they might not be driven away from their wives, their children, their brothers and their sisters. Knowing that his feelings were abhorrent to slavery, they addressed him without reserve and with an entreaty bordering on frenzy. Mr. B. related the following. He was an eye-witness. A large number of slaves were sitting near a steam-boat in St. Louis, which was to carry them down to New Orleans. Several of their relatives and acquaintances came down to the river to take leave of them. Their demonstrations of sorrow were simple but natural. They wept and embraced each other again and again. Two or three times they left their companions—would proceed a little distance from the boat, and then return to them, when the same scene would be repeated. This was kept up for more than an hour. Finally, when the boat left, they returned home, weeping and wringing their hands and making every exhibition of the most poignant grief. . . ."

One of the objections to the domestic slave trade, most grievous in its nature, though not the most extensive in its effects, is the great temptation and facility which it affords for kidnapping freemen, both in the slave and free states. Some examples will prove and illustrate this proposition.

A member of this convention [Mr. Abner Forbes, teacher of the Boston Grammar and Writing School for colored children], who formerly resided in the District of Columbia, has communicated to your committee a case which was within his own knowledge, he having interfered to prevent the unrighteous result. A drunkard and spendthrift, named Laskey, having dissipated his money, took this method to replenish his pockets. He procured a newspaper (no difficult task) containing an advertisement of a runaway slave, and presented himself before a judge of the United States Court in the District and made oath that a certain *free* colored man residing there was the slave intended by the advertisement. The accused was brought be-

KIDNAPPING.

Designed and Published by J. Torrey Jun.r Philad.a 1817.

6. "Kidnapping." From Jesse Torrey, *A Portraiture of Domestic Slavery in the United States* (Philadelphia, 1817), part 2. Reproduced by the Rare Books and Manuscript Division, Special Collections Library, Pennsylvania State University Libraries.

fore the judge, and upon the testimony of this miscreant and an accomplice, he was adjudged a slave, and was carried south, inspite of the zealous exertions of our friend. It is the opinion of the same gentleman that by a conspiracy of one or two needy and profligate men with a domestic slave trader, any free colored man in *any* state, may be, and a very considerable number annually are kidnapped *according to law!* The liberty of colored free men has not been sufficiently guarded by the laws of the United States, nor of any of the separate states; for in none, even of the free states, on the question of *liberty or slavery,* is the supposed slave allowed a trial by jury, any more than he is on the question of life and death in the slave states. New York has lately provided for such a trial where a man is claimed as a slave, but it seems to be considered very doubtful if the judicial tribunals of that state will sustain the enactment. . . .

Mr. [William] Munro and Mr. Forbes . . . concur in declaring that the practice of whites to *search* any colored persons, bond or free, male or female, whom they meet in the slave states, is universal; and indeed anyone who reflects upon the laws of those states must be aware that this right of search would necessarily result from them. This is very important in its bearing on the kidnapping branch of the domestic trade. For generally speaking a free colored man deprived of his free papers can entertain very little hope of vindicating his freedom.—Your committee are fully satisfied that, where the liberty of a slave is in question it is extremely difficult to obtain the testimony of whites to facts in favor of the slave, however clear or notorious they may be.—Mr. Forbes says that he has known white witnesses whose love of truth, justice and humanity impelled them to come forward and enabled them to defy persecution, to give their evidence amidst the hisses of the whole court-house. When it is considered that the sheriffs and constables or other persons serving subpœnas for witnesses must all be white—that the negro has very little to pay with, and can never, on the score of expense, compete with his master—that even if he should be able to bring his witnesses into court, he can seldom, from these causes, have legal counsel—and that at last he is to be judged by a slave holder—it must be seen and ackowledged that any free colored man, without his certificate in his pocket, *is a slave*—not of one man, but of every man he meets! Such are some of the consequences of substituting a bit of parchment for that great law of God that all men are free. . . .

It may be observed in general that the kidnapping of freemen is common all over this country, and prevails to an extent of which few are aware.

The following is from Mr. Stanton's letter.

"A member of this institution [Lane Seminary], recently visiting among the colored people of Cincinnati, entered a house where was a mother and her little son. The wretched appearance of the house and the extreme poverty of its inmates induced the visitor to suppose that the husband of the woman must be a drunkard. He inquired of the boy, who was two or three years old, where his father was. He replied, 'Papa stole.' The visitor seemed not to understand and, turning to the mother, said, 'What does he mean?' She then related the following circumstances. About two years ago one evening her husband was sitting in the house when two men came in and, professing great friendship, persuaded him under pretence to go on board a steamboat then lying at the dock and bound down the river. After some hesitation he consented to go. She heard nothing from him for more than a year, but supposed he had been kidnapped. Last spring, Dr. —— ——, a physician of Cincinnati, being at Natchez, Miss., saw this negro in a drove of slaves and recognized him. He ascertained from conversations with him that he had been driven about from place to place since he was decoyed from home by the slave drivers, had changed masters two or three times, and had once been lodged in jail for safe keeping where he remained some time. When Dr. ———returned to Cincinnati he saw the wife of the negro and engaged to take the necessary steps for his liberation. But soon afterwards this gentleman fell a victim to the cholera, which was then prevailing in Cincinnati. No efforts have since been made to recover this negro. No tidings have been heard from him since the return of Dr. ——— ———. He is probably now laboring on some sugar or cotton plantation in Louisiana, without the hope of escaping from slavery, although he is a free born citizen of Philadelphia.". . .

The laws of the slave states concur with private depravity to keep up this abominable trade. Their prisons, as well as that which we all pay and support in the District of Columbia, stand ever ready to fly open for the accomodation of soul-sellers and stealers and to close upon their captives. The statutes of the old slave-breeding and slave-trading southern states provide every means for rendering man-merchandizing easy and lucrative. Thus they authorize the county courts to issue, under seal, certificates of the good character of any slave about to be sold to Georgia, Louisiana, &c., which greatly enhances his merchantable value and is analogous to an invoice or bill of health in a lawful commerce. The inhuman and worse than heathen principles, universal in the slave states, that any colored man shall be taken and deemed to be a slave and shall be incompetent as a witness, whether slave or not, augment prodigiously the facility of enslaving free men. Thus any colored man may be imprisoned by any white, and if no white witness appears he must be sold to pay the advertising, jail fees, and for apprehending him. The laws in some states are so conscientious as to direct that in such cases he shall be sold only for a term of years to pay the above expenses; but all accounts of the *practise* agree that this restriction is generally nugatory. Once sold, they are taken to Georgia and other states more south, and disposed of as entire slaves, to those who know not the contrary, or disregard it if they do; and after this they must inevitably remain slaves for the residue of their lives. . . .

It is true that "free papers," as they are called, are some protection so long as they are retained, but what are they worth when every white ruffian has the RIGHT OF SEARCH, and in nine cases out of ten (we use the language of Mr. Monro) finds those papers, however carefully concealed, and tears them in pieces? . . .

There cannot be a reasonable doubt that the *American* "Middle Passage" abounds in horrors very similar to those of the African. The victims collected for the southern market are consigned to prisons attached to private establishments, or to county jails, or to the jail in the District of Columbia. There they suffer from hunger, heat and cold, in chains and in cells, which all witnesses describe as filthy and loathsome in the extreme, and even in this situation the traders still find or make occasion for using the "bloody lash."

If from these receptacles they are transported by sea, they are crowded between decks and into the hold in just such numbers as the captain pleases, and their fare is such as pleases him or the owner of them. Of course, it is not likely to be *expensive.*—The ship-room to be reserved for each slave coming from Africa was prescribed by the British Parliament long before they abolished the trade. Our Congress has found it necessary to prescribe the ship-room which captains shall reserve for *passengers* on foreign voyages to and from the United States. If these enactments were necessary, is it not probable that the unlimited liberty of crowding unreasonably and uncomfortably our coasting *slavers* is abused in nearly every voyage? . . . The ordinary cargo appears to be from one hundred and fifty to two hundred slaves. It seems to your committee that there *must* be suffering, excessive suffering from straightness of room; and we have a painful suspicion that it is much greater from this cause, and also from badness and scantiness of provision and harsh treatment on board, than is either known to us or generally suspected. No one has yet told the secrets of an *American coasting slaver.*

The following from the letter of Mr. Stanton may serve to give an inkling of what may be.

"My informant conversed with a man who accompanied a cargo of slaves from some port in Virginia round by sea to N. Orleans. He said the owners and sailors treated them most unmercifully—beating them and in some instances literally knocking them down upon the deck. They were locked up in the hold every night. Once on the passage, in consequence of alarm, they kept them in the hold the whole period of four days and nights, and none were brought on deck during that time but a few females—and they for purposes which I will not name. Mr. Editor, do the horrors of the middle passage belong exclusively to a bygone age?

"There is one feature of this nefarious traffic which no motives of delicacy can induce me to omit mentioning. . . . I allude to the fact that large numbers of female mulattoes are annually bought up and carried down to our southern cities and sold at enormous prices for the purposes of private prostitution. This is a fact of universal notoriety in the southwestern states. It is known to every soul-driver in the nation. And is it so bad that Christians may not know it and, knowing it, apply the remedy? . . ."

There is much testimony which might be heaped up on the subject of the cruelties to the droves which move to market by land. . . . On this subject Mr. Stanton says:

"The slaves are taken down in companies varying in number from 20 to 500. Men of capital are engaged in the traffic. Go into the principal towns on the Mississippi River, and you will find these negro traders in the bar-rooms, boasting of their adroitness in driving human flesh, and describing the process by which they can '*tame down*' the spirit of a *refractory* negro. Remember, by 'refractory' they mean to designate that spirit which some high-souled negro manifests when he fully recognizes the fact that God's image is stamped upon him. There are many such negroes in slavery. Their bodies may faint under the infliction of accumulated wrong, but their souls cannot be crushed. After visiting the bar-room, go into the outskirts of the town, and there you will find the slaves belonging to the drove crowded into dilapidated huts—some reveling—others apparently stupid—but others weeping over ties broken and hopes destroyed, with an agony intense, and to a free man, inconceivable. Many respectable planters in Louisiana have themselves gone into Maryland and Virginia and purchased their slaves. They think it more profitable to do so. Brother Robinson conversed with one or two of them when on their return. This shows that highly respectable men engage in this trade. But those who make it their regular employment, and thus receive the awfully significant title of '*soul drivers,*' are usually brutal, ignorant debauched men. And it is such men who exercise despotic control over thousands of down-trodden and defenceless men and women."

"The slaves which pass down to the southern market on the Mississippi River and through the interior are mostly purchased in Kentucky and Virginia. Some are bought in Tennessee. In the emigration they suffer great hardships. Those who are driven down by land travel from two hundred to a thousand miles on foot through Kentucky, Tennessee and Mississippi. They sometimes carry heavy chains the whole distance. These chains are very massive. They extend from the hands to the feet, being fastened to the wrists and ankles by an iron ring round each. When chained, every slave carries two chains—i.e. one from each hand to each foot. A wagon in which rides the 'driver,' carrying coarse provisions and a few tent coverings, generally accompanies the drove. Men, women and children, some of the latter very young, walk near the wagon; and if through fatigue or sickness they falter, the application of the whip reminds them that they are slaves. Our informant, speaking of some droves which he met, says, 'the weariness was extreme, and their dejected, despairing and woebegone countenances I shall never forget.' They encamp out nights. Their bed consists of a small blanket. Even this is frequently denied them. 'A rude tent covers them, scarcely sufficient to keep off the dew or frost, much less the rain. They frequently remain in this situation several weeks in the neighborhood of some slave trading village. The slaves are subject while on their journeys to severe sickness. On such occasions the drivers manifest anxiety lest they should lose— *their property!* But even sickness does not prevent them from hurrying their victims on to market. Sick, faint or weary, the slave knows no rest.' In the Choctaw nation my informant met a large company of these miserable beings following a wagon at some distance. From their appearance, being mostly females and children, and hence not so marketable, he supposed they must belong to some planter who was emigrating southward. He inquired if this were so and if their master was taking them home. A woman in tones of mellowed despair answered him: 'Oh, no, sir, we are not going *home!* We don't know where we are going. *The speculators have got us!* ' ". . .

The anguish, wailing and despair which are daily witnessed at the slave market are themes familiar, alas! too familiar to us all; and your committee will not now dwell upon them. The brutal examination of women which takes place is less spoken of than other particulars relating to that mighty instrument of torture, a slave auction.

On this topic your committee refer to the testimony of Mr. Robinson, a member of the Lane Seminary, a citizen of Nashville, Tennessee, where he was graduated and has resided. . . .

"The females are exposed to the same rude examinations as the men. When a large drove of slaves arrives in town for sale, placards are put up at the corners of the streets, giving notice of the place and time of sale. Often they are driven through the streets for hours together (for the purpose of exhibiting them) exposed to the jeers and insults of the speculators. About a year since Mr. Robinson saw about a hundred men, women and children exposed for sale at one time in the market place at Nashville; and while three auctioneers were striking them off, purchasers examined their limbs and bodies with inhuman roughness and unconcern. This was accompanied with profanity, indelicate allusions and boisterous laughter."

"There are planters in the northern slave states who will not sell slave families unless they can dispose of them all together. This they consider more humane—as in fact it is. But such kindnesses are of no avail after the victims come into the southern markets. If it is not just as profitable for the traders to sell them in families, they hesitate not a moment to separate husband and wife, parents and children, and dispose of them to purchasers residing in sections of the country remote from each other. When they happen to dispose of whole families to the same man, they loudly boast of it as an evidence of their humanity.". . .

It is impossible to form any satisfactory idea of the number of slaves annually sold in the United States by the regular traders. There is no other branch of commerce concerning which our government has given us no statistical information. It would be unseemly for a republican government to publish these things, but not at all for a republican people to do them.

One of your committee [Rev. Mr. Frost] has information on which we can rely that one house in the District of Columbia exported *one thousand* in the year 1833, and will export more the present year. They employ two vessels constantly. There is another house in the same District. A third, located in Georgetown has been given up; not, however, on account of the decline of the trade, for that is allowed to be increasing. The price is depressed at this moment owing to the derangement of the currency, but the trade is unquestionably brisk and profitable.

In conclusion, your committee recommend an earnest and early appeal to Congress on this subject, that a petition, setting forth the constitutional law and the practical horrors and atrocities relating to this trade be drafted under the direction of the New England Anti-Slavery Society and printed with the minutes of this convention and sent to all parts of the country and to all Anti-Slavery Societies for circulation and signatures, and they recommend the passage of the following resolve:

Resolved, As the opinion of this convention, that the domestic slave trade of the United States is equally atrocious in the sight of God with the foreign, that it equally involves the crimes of murder, kidnapping and robbery, and is equally worthy with the foreign to be denounced and treated by human laws and tribunals as piracy, and those who carry it on as enemies of the human race.

Signed,

> D. LEE CHILD,
> JOHN FROST,
> RAY POTTER,
> JESSE PUTNAM,
> JOSEPH SOUTHWICK.

2.2. "I Never Again Heard the Voice of My Poor Mother."
Incidents from the Life of Charles Ball, a Black Man

The authenticity of slave narratives has at times been questioned, and this includes *Slavery in the United States: A Narrative of the Life and Adventures of Charles Ball,* from which the following excerpts were taken. This book was published in 1837 when Ball was about fifty-four. Its writer, Thomas

Fisher, testified that Ball's chronicle was "taken from the mouth of the adventurer himself; and if the copy does not retain the identical words of the original, the sense and import, at least, are faithfully preserved." Elsewhere Fisher admitted that some anecdotes in the book were "not obtained from Ball, but rather from other creditable sources," but that "all the facts which relate personally to the fugitive, were received from his own lips."

Some scholars have expressed doubt regarding the genuineness of the book, but others such as Gilbert Osofsky, E. Franklin Frazier, and John W. Blassingame have accepted it as genuine. The most positive statement is Blassingame's, who wrote: "The first exposé [of a fraudulent work] was of the narrative of James Williams, which Alabama whites proved was an outright fraud. The only other antebellum attack on a narrative was that of the autobiography of Charles Ball. In Ball's case, however, the charges cannot be substantiated. A comparison of the narrative with antebellum gazetteers, travel accounts, manuscript census returns, and histories of South Carolina show that Ball accurately described people, places, rivers, flora and fauna, and agricultural practices in the state. Since the only narrative included in U. B. Phillips's justly acclaimed *Plantation and Frontier Documents* was that of Charles Ball, it may have been more reliable than the antebellum critics were willing to concede."[33] Thus the following account of the buying and selling of Charles Ball and the family separations he experienced may reasonably be looked upon as genuine.

SOURCE: *Slavery in the United States: A Narrative of the Life and Adventures of Charles Ball, A Black Man* (1837; reprint, New York: Negro Universities Press, 1969), pp. 15–39.

Narrative of the Adventures of Charles Ball

My grandfather was brought from Africa, and sold as a slave in Calvert county, in Maryland, about the year 1730. I never understood the name of the ship in which he was imported, nor the name of the planter who bought him on his arrival, but at the time I knew him, he was a slave in a family called Mauel, who resided near Leonardtown. My father was a slave in a family named Hantz, living near the same place. My mother was the slave of a tobacco planter, an old man, who died, according to the best of my recollection, when I was about four years old, leaving his property in such a situation that it became necessary, as I suppose, to sell a part of it to

33. John W. Blassingame, "Using the Testimony of Ex-Slaves: Approaches and Problems," in Charles T. Davis and Henry Louis Gates, eds., *The Slave's Narrative* (Oxford: Oxford University Press, 1990), pp. 81–82.

pay his debts. Soon after his death, several of his slaves, and with others my-self, were sold at public vendue. My mother had several children, my brothers and sisters, and we were all sold on the same day to different pur-chasers. Our new master took us away, and I never saw my mother, nor any of my brothers and sisters afterwards. This was, I presume, about the year 1785. I learned subsequently, from my father, that my mother was sold to a Georgia trader, who soon after that carried her away from Maryland. Her other children were sold to slave-dealers from Carolina, and were also taken away, so that I was left alone in Calvert county, with my father, whose owner lived only a few miles from my new master's residence. At the time I was sold I was quite naked, having never had any clothes in my life; but my new master had brought with him a child's frock or wrapper, belonging to one of his own children; and after he had purchased me, he dressed me in this garment, took me before him on his horse, and started home; but my poor mother when she saw me leaving her for the last time, ran after me, took me down from the horse, clasped me in her arms, and wept loudly and bitterly over me. My master seemed to pity her, and endeavoured to soothe her distress by telling her that he would be a good master to me, and that I should not want anything. She then, still holding me in her arms, walked along the road beside the horse as he moved slowly, and earnestly and im-ploringly besought my master to buy her and the rest of her children, and not permit them to be carried away by the negro buyers; but while thus en-treating him to save her and her family, the slave-driver, who had first bought her, came running in pursuit of her with a raw hide in his hand. When he overtook us he told her he was her master now, and ordered her to give that little negro to its owner, and come back with him.

My mother then turned to him and cried, "Oh, master, do not take me from my child!" Without making any reply, he gave her two or three heavy blows on the shoulders with his raw hide, snatched me from her arms, handed me to my master, and seizing her by one arm, dragged her back to-wards the place of sale. My master then quickened the pace of his horse; and as we advanced, the cries of my poor parent became more and more in-distinct—at length they died away in the distance, and I never again heard the voice of my poor mother. Young as I was, the horrors of that day sank deeply into my heart, and even at this time, though half a century has elapsed, the terrors of the scene return with painful vividness upon my memory. Frightened at the sight of the cruelties inflicted upon my poor mother, I forgot my own sorrows at parting from her and clung to my new master, as an angel and a saviour, when compared with the hardened fiend into whose power she had fallen. . . .

My father never recovered from the effects of the shock, which this sudden and overwhelming ruin of his family gave him. He had formerly been of a gay social temper, and when he came to see us on a Saturday night, he always brought us some little present, such as the means of a poor slave would allow—apples, melons, sweet potatoes, or, if he could procure nothing else, a little parched corn, which tasted better in our cabin, because he had brought it.

He spent the greater part of the time, which his master permitted him to pass with us, in relating such stories as he had learned from his companions, or in singing the rude songs common amongst the slaves of Maryland and Virginia. After this time I never heard him laugh heartily, or sing a song. He became gloomy and morose in his temper, to all but me; and spent nearly all of his leisure time with my grandfather, who claimed kindred with some royal family in Africa, and had been a great warrior in his native country. The master of my father was a hard penurious man, and so exceedingly avaricious, that he scarcely allowed himself the common conveniences of life. A stranger to sensibility, he was incapable of tracing the change in the temper and deportment of my father, to its true cause; but attributed it to a sullen discontent with his condition as a slave, and a desire to abandon his service, and seek his liberty by escaping to some of the free states. To prevent the perpetration of this suspected crime of *running away from slavery,* the old man resolved to sell my father to a southern slave-dealer, and accordingly applied to one of those men, who was at that time in Calvert, to become the purchaser. The price was agreed on, but, as my father was a very strong, active, and resolute man, it was deemed unsafe for the Georgian to attempt to seize him, even with the aid of others, in the day-time, when he was at work, as it was known he carried upon his person a large knife. It was therefore determined to secure him by stratagem, and for this purpose, a farmer in the neighborhood, who was made privy to the plan, alleged that he had lost a pig, which must have been stolen by some one, and that he suspected my father to be the thief. A constable was employed to arrest him, but as he was afraid to undertake the business alone, he called on his way at the house of the master of my grandfather, to procure assistance from the overseer of the plantation. When he arrived at the house, the overseer was at the barn, and thither he repaired to make his application. At the end of the barn was the coach-house, and as the day was cool, to avoid the wind which was high, the two walked to the side of the coach-house to talk over the matter, and settle their plan of operations. It so happened that my grandfather, whose business it was to keep the coach in good condition, was at work at this time, rubbing the plated handles of the doors, and brightening the other metallic parts of the vehicle. Hearing the voice of the overseer without, he suspended his work, and listening attentively, became a party to their councils. They agreed that they would delay the execution of their project until the next day, as it was then late. They supposed they would have no difficulty in apprehending their intended victim, as, knowing himself innocent of the theft, he would readily consent to go with the constable to a justice of the peace, to have the charge examined. That night, however, about midnight, my grandfather silently repaired to the cabin of my father, a distance of about three miles, aroused him from his sleep, made him acquainted with the extent of his danger, gave him a bottle of cider and a small bag of parched corn, and then praying to the God of his native country to protect his son, enjoined him to fly from the destruction which awaited him. In the morning, the Georgian could not find his newly purchased slave, who was never seen or heard of in Maryland from that day. He probably had prudence enough to conceal himself in the day, and travel only at night; by this means making his way slowly up the country, between the Patapsco and Patuxent, until he was able to strike across to the north, and reach Pennsylvania.

After the flight of my father, my grandfather was the only person left in Maryland, with whom I could claim kindred. He was at that time an old man, as he himself said, nearly eighty years of age, and he manifested towards me all the fondness which a person so far advanced in life could be expected to feel for a child. . . .

The name of the man who purchased me at the vendue, and became my master, was John Cox; but he was generally called Jack Cox. He was a man of kindly feelings towards his family, and treated his slaves, of whom he had several besides me, with humanity. He permitted my grandfather to visit me as often as he pleased, and allowed him sometimes to carry me to his own cabin, which stood in a lonely place at the head of a deep hollow, almost surrounded by a thicket of cedar trees, which had grown up in a worn out and abandoned tobacco field. My master gave me better clothes than the little slaves of my age generally received in Calvert, and often told me that he intended to make me his waiter, and that if I behaved well I should become his overseer in time. . . .

Fortune had decreed otherwise. When I was about twelve years old, my master, Jack Cox, died of a disease which had long confined him to the house. I was sorry for the death of my master, who had always been kind to me; and I soon discovered that I had good cause to regret his departure from this world. He had several children at the time of his death, who were all young; the oldest being about my own age. The father of my late master, who was still living, became administrator of his estate, and took possession of his property, and amongst the rest, of myself. This old gentleman treated me with the greatest severity, and compelled me to work very hard on his plantation for several years, until I suppose I must have been near or quite twenty years of age.

One Saturday evening when I came home from the corn field, my master told me that he had hired me out for a year at the city of Washington, and that I would have to live at the navy-yard. On the new-year's-day following . . . my master set forward for Washington, on horseback, and ordered me to accompany him on foot. It was night when we arrived at the navy-yard, and everything appeared very strange to me. I was told by a gentleman who had epaulets on his shoulders that I must go on board a large ship, which lay in the river. . . . This ship proved to be the *Congress* frigate, and I was told that I had been brought there to cook for the people belonging to her. In the course of a few days the duties of my station became quite familiar to me; and in the enjoyment of a profusion of excellent provisions, I felt very happy. I strove by all means to please the officers and gentlemen who came on board, and in this I soon found my account. One gave me a half-worn coat, another an old shirt, and a third a cast off waistcoat and pantaloons. Some presented me with small sums of money, and in this way I soon found myself well clothed, and with more than a dollar in my pocket. My duties, though constant, were not burthensome, and I was permitted to spend Sunday afternoon in my own way. I generally went up into the city to see the new and splendid buildings; often walked as far as Georgetown, and made many new acquaintances among the slaves, and frequently saw large numbers of people of my colour chained together in long trains, and driven off towards the south. At that time the Slave-trade was not regarded with so much indignation and disgust, as it is now. It was a rare thing to hear of a person of colour running away, and escaping altogether from his master: my father being the only one within my knowledge who had before this time obtained his liberty in this manner in Calvert county; and, as before stated, I never heard what became of him after his flight.

I remained on board the *Congress,* and about the navy-yard, two years, and was quite satisfied with my lot, until about three months before the expiration of this period, when it so happened that a schooner, loaded with iron and other materials for the use of the yard, arrived from Philadelphia. She came and lay close by the *Congress,* to discharge her cargo, and amongst her crew I observed a black man, with whom, in the course of a day or two, I became acquainted. He told me he was free, and lived in Philadelphia, where he kept a house of entertainment for sailors, which he said was attended to in his absence by his wife.

His description of Philadelphia, and of the liberty enjoyed there by the black people, so charmed my imagination that I determined to devise some plan of escaping from the *Congress,* and making my way to the north. I communicated my designs to my new friend, who promised to give me his aid. We agreed that the night before the schooner should sail, I was to be concealed in the hold, amongst a parcel of loose tobacco, which he said the captain had undertaken to carry to Philadelphia. The sailing of the schooner was delayed longer than we expected; and, finally, her captain purchased a cargo of flour in Georgetown, and sailed for the West Indies. Whilst I was anxiously awaiting some other opportunity of making my way to Philadelphia, . . . new-year's-day came, and with it came my old master from Calvert, accompanied by a gentleman named Gibson, to whom he said he had sold me, and to whom he delivered me over in the navy-yard. We all three set out that same evening for Calvert, and reached the residence of my new master the next day. Here I was informed that I had become the subject of a law-suit. My new master claimed me under his purchase from old Mr. Cox; and another gentleman of the neighborhood, named Levin Ballard, had bought me of the children of my former master, Jack Cox. The suit continued in the courts of Calvert county more than two years; but was finally decided in favour of him who had bought me of the children

I went home with my master, Mr. Gibson, who was a farmer, and with whom I lived three years. Soon after I came to live with Mr. Gibson, I married a girl of colour named Judah, the slave of a gentleman by the name of Symmes, who resided in the same neighborhood. . . . Mr. Symmes also married a wife about the time I did. The lady whom he married lived near Philadelphia, and when she first came to Maryland, she refused to be served by a black chambermaid, but employed a white girl, the daughter of a poor man, who lived near. . . . After some time Mrs. Symmes dismissed her white chambermaid, and placed my wife in that situation, which I regarded as a fortunate circumstance, as it insured her good food, and at least one suit of clothes. . . .

Some short time after my wife became chamber-maid to her mistress, it was my misfortune to change masters once more. Levin Ballard, who, as before stated, had purchased me of the children of my former master, Jack Cox, was successful in his law suit with Mr. Gibson, the object of which was to determine the right of property in me; and one day, whilst I was at work in the corn-field, Mr. Ballard came and told me I was his property;

asking me at the same time if I was willing to go with him. I told him I was not willing to go; but that if I belonged to him I knew I must. . . .

My change of masters realized all the evil apprehensions which I had entertained. I found Mr. Ballard sullen and crabbed in his temper, and always prone to find fault with my conduct—no matter how hard I had laboured, or how careful I was to fulfill all his orders, and obey his most unreasonable commands. Yet, it so happened, that he never beat me, for which I was altogether indebted to the good character, for industry, sobriety, and humility, which I had established in the neighborhood. I think he was ashamed to abuse me, lest he should suffer in the good opinion of the public; for he often fell into the most violent fits of anger against me, and overwhelmed me with coarse and abusive language. . . . I had determined at last to speak to him to sell me to some person in the neighborhood, so that I might still be near my wife and children—but a different fate awaited me.

My master kept a store at a small village on the bank of the Patuxent river, called ———, although he resided at some distance on a farm. One morning he rose early, and ordered me to take a yoke of oxen and go to the village to bring home a cart which was there, saying he would follow me. He arrived at the village soon after I did, and took his breakfast with the store-keeper. . . . Whilst I was eating in the kitchen, I observed him talking earnestly, but lowly, to a stranger near the kitchen door. I soon after went out, and hitched my oxen to the cart, and was about to drive off, when several men came round about me, and amongst them the stranger whom I had seen speaking with my master. This man came up to me, and, seizing me by the collar, shook me violently, saying I was his property, and must go with him to Georgia. At the sound of these words, the thoughts of my wife and children rushed across my mind, and my heart died away within me. I saw and knew that my case was hopeless, and that resistance was vain, as there were near twenty persons present, all of whom were ready to assist the man by whom I was kidnapped. I felt incapable of weeping or speaking, and in my despair I laughed loudly. My purchaser ordered me to cross my hands behind, which were quickly bound with a strong cord; and he then told me that we must set out that very day for the south. I asked if I could not be allowed to go to see my wife and children, or if this could not be permitted, if they might not have leave to come to see me; but was told that I would be able to get another wife in Georgia.

My new master, whose name I did not hear, took me that same day across the Patuxent, where I joined fifty-one other slaves, whom he had bought in Maryland. Thirty-two of these were men, and nineteen were women. The women were merely tied together with a rope, about the size of a bed cord, which was tied like a halter round the neck of each; but the men, of whom I was the stoutest and strongest, were very differently caparisoned. A strong iron collar was closely fitted by means of a padlock round each of our necks. A chain of iron, about a hundred feet in length, was passed through the hasp of each padlock, except at the two ends, where the hasps of the padlocks passed through a link of the chain. In addition to this, we were handcuffed in pairs, with iron staples and bolts, with a short chain about a foot long uniting the handcuffs and their wearers in pairs. In this manner we were chained alternately by the right and left hand; and the poor man, to whom I was thus ironed, wept like an infant when the blacksmith, with his heavy hammer, fastened the ends of the bolts that kept the staples from slipping from our arms. For my own part, I felt indifferent to my fate. It appeared to me that the worst had come that could come, and that no change of fortune could harm me.

After we were all chained and handcuffed together, we sat down upon the ground; and here reflecting upon the sad reverse of fortune that had so suddenly overtaken me, I became weary of life, and bitterly execrated the day that I was born. It seemed that I was destined by fate to drink the cup of sorrow to the very dregs, and that I should find no respite from misery but in the grave. I longed to die and escape from the hands of my tormentors; but even the wretched privilege of destroying myself was denied me; for I could not shake off my chains, nor move a yard without the consent of my master. Reflecting in silence upon my forlorn condition, I at length concluded that as things could not become worse—and as the life of man is but a continued round of changes, they must, of necessity, take a turn in my favour at some future day. I found relief in this vague and indefinite hope, and when we received orders to go on board the scow, which was to transport us over the Patuxent, I marched down to the water with a firmness of purpose of which I did not believe myself capable, a few minutes before.

We were soon on the south side of the river, and taking up our line of march, we traveled about five miles that evening, and stopped for the night at one of those miserable public houses, so frequent in the lower parts of Maryland and Virginia, called *"ordinaries."*

Our master ordered a pot of mush to be made for our supper; after despatching which, we all lay down on the naked floor to sleep in the handcuffs and chains. The women, my fellow-slaves, lay on one side of the room; and the men who were chained with me, occupied the other. I slept but little this night, which I passed in thinking of my wife and little children, whom I could not hope ever to see again. I also thought of my grand-father, and of the long nights I had passed with him, listening to his narra-tives of the scenes through which he had passed in Africa. I at length fell asleep, but was distressed by painful dreams. My wife and children ap-peared to be weeping and lamenting my calamity; and beseeching and im-ploring my master on their knees, not to carry me away from them. My little boy came and begged me not to go and leave him, and endeavoured, as I thought, with his little hands to break the fetters that bound me.

2.3. A Georgia Bureaucrat Requests the Purchase of Two Hundred Slaves in Maryland or Virginia for Labor on Public Facilities (About 1828)

For people of the deep South the existence of comparatively inexpensive slaves in slave-exporting states had the potential of encouraging expedient acts or decisions, which, though potentially advantageous, might result in contempt for their fellow humans and even serious disregard for the law. An example of this was a suggestion, made by the state engineer of Georgia, that the state legislature purchase some two hundred male slaves in Mary-land or Virginia for temporary labor on unspecified public improvements, with the understanding that, once the work was done, the slaves would be re-sold *on the local market,* allowing the state to recoup its costs and even make a profit. Though it was probably known to the legislators, the state engineer evidently did not inform them that the transfer of two hundred slaves into Georgia from Maryland or Virginia had the potential of pro-ducing a benefit for the state of Georgia.

Enoch Lewis, brother of Quaker abolitionist Evan Lewis and editor of the *African Observer,* called his readers' attention to this proposal, offering a caustic analysis of possible damaging consequences, not only for the slaves, but for members of the state government, who would not only be transformed into veritable slave traders, but also risk criminal penalties, since at that time the importation of slaves into Georgia was illegal. Pun-ishment was unlikely, however, since the law banning entry of slaves into Georgia for sale was rarely enforced (see Michael Tadman, *Speculators and Slaves,* pp. 90–91).

SOURCE: *The African Observer, A Monthly Journal, Containing Essays and Doc-uments Illustrative of The General Character, and Moral and Political Effects, of Negro Slavery,* Philadelphia, Fifth Month, 1828, pp. 307–9.

The Georgia State Engineer advises the Legislature to purchase as many slaves as the nature and extent of certain proposed public improvements in the state may require. He says:

"The number of negroes should be proportionate to the extent of the improvements; and if I am permitted to express an opinion on this subject, I think the number should not be under two hundred. Such a gang of young, healthy, and vigorous hands, I presume, could be purchased in Maryland or Virginia, at a sum not exceeding $80,000, delivered in Georgia; the annual expense of food, clothing, and superintendence, would probably amount to $25,000. The original cost of the negroes may be considered as so much money loaned out of the treasury without interest, for when the state has accomplished such improvements as may be thought necessary, the negroes may be disposed of, and the money returned into the treasury."—*Nat. Gaz.* [National Gazette?]

Whether this proposal has been acted upon by the legislature of Georgia, I am not informed; but what a picture of public feeling does the recommendation itself present to our view! The legislature is gravely advised to engage in, and become a party to a traffic, which is substantially the same as that which the general government has denounced as piracy, and directed its naval commanders to suppress. An act of Congress, passed in 1819, appropriated 100,000 dollars to the suppression of the slave trade, to which subsequent appropriations have been added. No less than 185,140 dollars of the people's money have been actually expended in the efforts which have been made towards the attainment of this momentous object. Yet here we have a proposal to appropriate 80,000 dollars to a trade which differs but little in its character and incidents from that against which the thunders of the American navy are pointed. A journey by land and on foot across the Carolinas is, doubtless, less destructive to negro life than a voyage across the Atlantic, in the hold of a slave ship; but the separation of families, in the case before us, would probably be more complete than in the African trade. "Young, healthy, and vigorous" slaves, to the number of two hundred, would hardly be selected from the slave families in Maryland and Virginia, without inflicting a wound, at which the feeling mind must shudder, on many an anxious relative, as well as on the immediate victims of the trade. This scheme, we may observe, contemplates the revival, to a certain extent, of a prohibited traffic. The importation of slaves from abroad into the state, was constitutionally proscribed in 1798; and their introduction, except under certain limitations, from other states of the Union, was forbidden by law in 1817. Judging of the plan from the terms in which it is couched, I should conclude that an agent or agents are to be appointed by the legislature, to undertake a pilgrimage to the slave manufactories on the Potomac, and collect, as they can, among the slave breeders there, the requisite number of young, healthy, and vigorous slaves, to be transported to Georgia, and employed at the public works. These slaves must of course be *picked,* unless families for sale should be found, in which all the members are young, healthy, and vigorous. These slaves, after being employed, as long as their services are required, on the public works, and thus in some degree domesticated in Georgia, are again to be exposed to sale, probably at auction, to the highest bidder, and endure the pangs of a second separation from their friends, and the scenes with which they had become familiar.

Should this proposal be adopted, the legislature or its agents will be placed in a curious predicament. A traffic will be prosecuted on behalf of the state, for which an individual, not duly authorized, would incur not merely a pecuniary fine, but a three years' imprisonment in the penitentiary.

2.4. Pigs for People

Persons acquiring slaves normally paid for them in cash, but at times traders resorted to arrangements appropriate to their immediate circumstances, including the exchange of various kinds of *property* for slaves, including domesticated animals. Enoch Lewis of the *African Observer,* discovered one case of such bartering—the exchange of pigs for people—a practice he seemed to attribute to the long-standing association of black people with assets in general, even animals thought of as "the less amiable kind." Concerning the pig trade, late in his life H. C. Bruce, a former slave, recalled the heavy movement of swine along a Virginia highway that passed his home. Richmond, he wrote, "being a great pork market, and this old public highway being the most direct route from the west to Richmond, these hog raisers, in order to reach a market for their hogs, were compelled to drive them on foot over the road at a distance of over two hundred miles. I have seen as many as three hundred hogs in one drove pass our old home in one day going towards Richmond" (see H. C. Bruce, *The New Man. Twenty-Nine Years a Slave. Twenty-Nine Years a Free Man* [York, Pa.: P. Anstadt & Sons, 1895; reprint, New York: Negro Universities Press, 1969], pp. 46–47).

SOURCE: *The African Observer. A Monthly Journal Containing Essays and Documents Illustrative of the General Character, and Moral and Political Effects, of Negro Slavery,* Philadelphia, First Month, 1827, pp. 54–55.

A gentleman, who lately visited this city [Philadelphia], informed the editor in the course of conversation, that on a journey from one of the western states to Virginia, during the coldest part of the winter 1826–27, he followed the route on which traders in swine return to Kentucky from the southeastern parts of Virginia, and the adjacent state. These traders, it appears, collect toward the close of summer, from the western parts of Kentucky, immense droves of hogs, which they drive to the southeast in search of a market. At the time in question, these traveling merchants were returning with the produce of their respective adventures. Many of them had collected in exchange for their swine, great numbers of negroes, mostly children and youths of both sexes, with a few women, whom they were conducting to Kentucky. Sometimes he passed a dearborn [a light carriage] loaded with its human merchandise, huddled together in a parcel of straw like the quadrupeds with which they had been purchased, and covered with a few dirty blankets. Sometimes his eyes were disgusted with the sight of a woman perched on a horse with a child in her arms and another cowering at her back, all scantily clothed and exposed to the rigours of the pitiless blast.

At the taverns where he lodged he generally found a number of these suffering children of humanity, who seldom failed to apply to their own accomodation during the night the blankets which the travelers carried under their saddles. These blankets, when found, after necessary search, in the morning were always more injured, both in texture and appearance, by their application to human use during the night than by their station between the saddle and the horse during the day. The dirt with which they were copiously marked bore ample testimony to the situation in which their occupants had been lodged, and the traces of fire to the scantiness of their nocturnal supply.

He endeavored to learn from the traders themselves in what manner these children had been procured, and by what means they were intended to be introduced and sold in Kentucky. With respect to the former, it appeared they were obtained exactly like any other article of trade; one, two or more in a place, without regard to family connection, or any other circumstance, except the convenience or caprice of the parties to the contract; and as to the latter, no important difficulty was present by the prohibitory law; for the law itself had provided the means of its own evasion. An *oath only* was required that the slaves were brought into the state for the proper use of those who brought them; and the sale was easily effected, by *borrowing money* and giving the slaves in pledge, with the condition annexed, that in case the money was not repaid within a limited time, the pledge should be forfeited.

Where the nerves and the conscience have become inured to the purchase and sale of human beings as goods and chattels, perhaps this traffic can be readily reconciled. It may be said, and perhaps with truth, that the removal of these children from the exhausted lands of Virginia to the more fertile soil of Kentucky is an improvement rather than a deterioration of their condition. Still, the traffic is strongly repulsive, on more accounts than one. These children, when fattened and matured for a few years in Kentucky, may very probably become the objects of a second transfer to the great slave markets of Mississippi and the Floridas, a destination which is contemplated, by its victims, with peculiar horror. But exclusive of this consideration, grating as it must be to a feeling mind, the separation of children from parents and the total dissolution of family ties in which this traffic is commenced, and the perjury by which it is consummated, a broad philosophic principle stands opposed to this procedure. The human mind unavoidably forms an association between the *characters* as well as the *values* of things which we are accustomed to exchange for each other. Hence among civilized nations, the almost universal love of *money.* Our attachment to the necessaries and conveniences of life is transferred by association to their representative, or in other words the money by which they may be purchased. The North American Indians, frequently adopt a prisoner into their families, in place of a relative whom they have lost; and, according to the estimation in which the prototype was held, is that of the substitute. No assiduity can raise him above the character and standing of his original. When negro children are habitually and familiarly exchanged for domestic animals, particularly those of the less amiable kind, the comparison thus made of the values of the objects of exchange can scarcely fail to equalize, or at least closely approximate, in the eyes of the traders, the associated races. One predominant idea involves them all; they are viewed as property. Value is supposed to be given for value. The worth of the one species is estimated in terms of the other, and hence the characters are unavoidably, in estimation if not in fact, closely assimilated. Is not this to brutalize the human race, and, as far as possible, to erase the Creator's image from the creatures he has made? Well might these poor degraded children address to their *drivers* the pathetic language of Cowper,

Prove that you have human feelings,
Ere ye proudly question ours.

2.5. A Congressman from Pennsylvania Denounces Slavery and the
Slave Trade in the District of Columbia (1829)

For decades, slavery and the slave trade in the District of Columbia were targets of abolitionists in countless articles, speeches, and petitions. Nevertheless, although *slave trading* in the District was banned in the Compromise of 1850, slavery itself remained legal in the capital until April 1862, when the Civil War at last provided the necessary impetus to reform.

Decades earlier, as interest in the slavery problem intensified, public meetings were held in Pennsylvania and other locations to call attention to the harsh conditions suffered by slaves and free blacks in the South and in the District of Columbia, with the hope that greater knowledge might arouse public concern and hasten an end to slavery. As a result of these meetings, in December 1831, a special committee met in Lancaster County, Pennsylvania, to collect information on slavery and the slave trade, particularly in the nation's capital. The members of this committee lacked the necessary time and knowledge to prepare a statement on the subject and so agreed to print and distribute a speech on the slave trade that Congressman Charles Miner of Pennsylvania had delivered in the House of Representatives some two years before. The members of the committee were impressed by Miner's knowledge and concern for the slaves, but differed with him on what Congress should do. In a motion offered to the House of Representatives Miner had called for a *gradual* end to slavery in the District, but in the judgment of the Lancaster Committee abolition would best be immediate, since in their words "the *just* right of no individual can be injured by doing justice to his fellow man."

SOURCE: *An Extract from a Speech Delivered by Charles Miner, In the House of Representatives of the United States in 1829. On the Subject of Slavery and the Slave Trade in the District of Columbia. With Notes,* in *Legal and Moral Aspects of Slavery: Selected Essays* (New York: Negro Universities Press, 1969).

Mr. Miner observed, that as doubts had been expressed, of the correctness of the allegations set forth in the preamble it became his duty to the House to shew that they were well founded. . . . In Article 1, section 8, of the Constitution, it is declared that Congress shall have power "to exercise exclusive legislation, in all cases whatsoever, over such District (not exceeding ten miles square) as may, by cession of particular States, and the acceptance of Congress, become the seat of Government of the United States." The words are full, clear, and explicit. The power extends to "legislation in all cases whatsoever." We, therefore, are the local as well as general legislature here. Maryland has no longer any authority: Virginia has no longer any legislative power within the District. If evils exist, we alone can remedy them. If injustice and oppression prevail, we are alone responsible. And here, Mr. Speaker, I would earnestly impress upon the House, that those who suffer evils which they alone have the power to prevent, are accountable for those evils. The legislature that permits bad laws to remain in force is not less responsible, before God and the world, for the injustice that results from them, than the legislature that enacts unjust laws, or the Government that perpetrates injustice. I am aware, sir, that the subject of slavery is one of great delicacy, exciting strong feelings whenever it is mentioned; but it exists here, and exercises a large influence in the District; yet since the Federal Government was established in this place, it has been almost wholly neglected. Maryland, in the liberal spirit of the age, has softened the harsher features of her laws in respect to this class of persons. But the ameliorating influence in her statutes extend not within the limits she has ceded to us. The code of Virginia, I believe, has undergone salutary modifications. Our legislation has left the subject where we found it nearly thirty years ago. Gentlemen from the South did not feel it their duty to move in the matter: gentlemen from the North, seeing it created so much excitement whenever mentioned, have passed it by. In consequence of this neglect, as I shall shew you, have grown numerous corruptions, leading to cruelty and injustice, that ought no longer to be tolerated. . . .

Among the allegations in the preamble are these:—That slave-dealers, gaining confidence from impunity, have made the seat of government their headquarters for carrying on the domestic slave trade: that the public prisons have been extensively used for carrying on the domestic slave trade; and that officers of the Federal Government have been employed, and derived emoluments from carrying on this traffic. By papers furnished me by the keeper, it appears that there were sent to prison, for safe keeping, that is, as is well understood, for sale, and imprisoned as runaways:

	Safe keeping	Taken up as runaways
In 1824,	81	52
1825,	124	58
1826 and 1827	156	101
1828,	91	79
	452	290

Debtors, and persons charged with criminal offences, of course, are not included in this statement. So that it would appear, in the last five years, more than four hundred and fifty persons had been confined in the public prison of the city—a prison under the control of Congress, and regulated by its laws—for sale—in the process of the slave trade. . . . Visiting the prison in 1826, and passing through the avenues that led to the cells, I was struck with the appearance of a woman having three or four children with her, one at the breast. She presented such an aspect of woe, that I could not help inquiring her story. It was simply this: she was a slave, but had married a man who was free. By him she had eight or nine children. Moved by natural affection, the father laboured to support the children, but as they attained an age to be valuable in the market, perhaps ten or twelve, the master sold them. One after another was taken away and sold to the slave dealers. She had now come to an age to be no longer profitable as a breeder, and her master had separated her from her husband and all the associations of life, and sent her and her children to your prison for sale. She was waiting for a purchaser, and seemed to me to be more heart-broken than any creature I had ever seen. I am free to say, sir, and I would appeal to every gentleman who hears me, to say, if it is proper that the public prisons under our jurisdiction should be used to carry on a traffic which exhibits scenes like this. Of the four hundred and fifty others I know nothing. I see no reason to suppose that there were not many cases of equal cruelty. Of the two hundred and ninety committed as runaways many were delivered to their masters; some were sold for want of proof that they were free; and some proved their freedom, and were discharged. It seems to me a hardship, that persons born free in New York, Pennsylvania, or elsewhere, who perhaps never thought of a certificate of freedom, should without any charge of crime, if they come within the District, be thrown into prison!

Some proof at least ought to be made, raising a presumption that they are runaway slaves, before they should be deprived of personal liberty. A free man, poor, friendless, and ignorant, so arrested and confined in a cell of little more than ten feet square, would have but slight chance of asserting his rights.

Five that were committed in 1826–7, without any proof of their being slaves, were sold for their jail fees and other expenses. I could wish, sir, we knew what they sold for, and what became of the money. It will be seen on a moment's reflection, how strong the motive would be, on the part of the slave traders, and those who find it their interest to aid them to seize persons who come into the District, to confine them closely in prison, to intercept their letters, to permit them to be sold, and to buy them in. The system naturally leads to fraud and injustice.[34] In August, 1821, a black man

34. This was not unique to the United States. According to Brazilian laws, stray animals, cattle, and slaves were known as "property of the wind" *(bens do evento) and could be seized by police or other authorities and, if owners were not found, sold at public auction.* See Robert Edgar Conrad, *Children of God's Fire: A Documentary History of Black Slavery in Brazil* (Princeton: Princeton University Press, 1983), pp. 322–30. For other Brazilian examples, see Docs. 2.12 and 3.11.

was taken up and imprisoned as a runaway. He was kept confined until October, 1822—405 days. In this time, vermin disease, and misery had deprived him of the use of his limbs. He was rendered a cripple for life, and finally discharged, as no one would buy him. Turned out upon the world, a miserable pauper; disabled by our means from gaining subsistence, he is sometimes supported from the poor house; sometimes craves alms in your streets. I cannot think that these things ought to be so. They appear to me as incompatible with our duty, and the interests of the District, as they are contrary to the principles of justice and the rights of humanity. For their services, it cannot be supposed that the Marshall and his deputies, the keepers of the prison, go unrewarded. They are, I take it, federal officers, deriving their powers from the Federal Government. What is the amount of their fees and their perquisites, I have no means of knowing. Suppose fees and commissions, on each person, of 20 dollars—that would, on 452, multiplied by 20, equal 9040, be upwards of nine thousand dollars in five years. Half that sum would be something considerable. Double this amount, if the prison of Alexandria should yield as much more, would be a large sum. The same amount on the persons imprisoned as runaways would make a large addition to the receipts. If a free man is sold for jail fees; if those fees amount to fifty dollars; and he sells for three hundred, does the marshall retain the balance of three hundred, or does it go into the public treasury? I see no such item in the account of receipts. I mean not, by any remarks I make, to impeach or cast a reflection upon the Marshal or any officers under him. The marshal I have not the pleasure to know, and have no intention to censure. The system is, I presume, as he found it. The system is ours: we are responsible; and if there is blame, it rests mainly at our doors. Of the keeper of the prison, I am bound to say that his deportment has been uniformly correct, so far as it has come to my knowledge. While he is faithful, he is yet humane. Since my remarks on a former occasion, the prison and its discipline appear to be much improved, and the miseries of wretched inmates alleviated as far as circumstances would admit.

Mr. Speaker, I have another case of hardship to bring to your notice. A man was taken up as a runaway, and advertised for sale. He protested that he was a free man. No proof to the contrary appeared. As the time of sale approached, a good deal of interest was excited for him, and two respectable citizens interposed in his behalf. They asked the delay of a short time, that the rights of the man might be ascertained. They went so far as to offer security for the payment of the fees, if the sale could be delayed. But I will read the evidence of what I state. Here Mr. M. read the following:

District of Columbia, *Washington County,*

Appear before me, a Justice of the Peace in and for this county, Ezekiel Young and Hosiah Bosworth, two respectable witnesses, and make oath in due form of law, that, in the last Summer, they were at the jail of the county of Washington, in the said District, in behalf of a black man called James Green, who stated that he was free, and could prove his freedom, and had written on for the purpose: That they did importune with the Deputy Marshal of this District to postpone the sale, and offered security for the fees, yet the said Deputy Marshal said he could not postpone the sale. He was then sold to a man who acknowledged himself a slave dealer, but said he would continue the slave here a few days; but did not. He was sold without a limitation of time of service, and no security was required of the slave dealer to retain him in the District. Given under my hand and seal, this 28th January, 1828.

JNO. CHALMERS, J. P. [L. S.]

So the man was sold, and sent off by the slave dealers into hopeless bondage, though probably having as much right to freedom as we have. Would anyone doubt but our laws need revision? Can anyone who hears me question that this whole matter needs to be looked into with a searching eye? If this event had happened in a distant country, how strongly would it have affected us? There is, in the public prints, an advertisment of a woman as a runaway, and that she will be sold for her jail fees. She is a yellow woman of about nineteen. She seems intelligent, and to have been well brought up. Her story is that she is entitled to her freedom at twenty-five: but that her present master, who is a slave dealer, is trying to make her a slave for life. In this case, I do not think the confinement is intended to aid him. But it will be seen in a moment that when the subject passes by unheeded, a dealer, owning a servant who has two or three years to serve, may cause him to be arrested as a runaway, let him be sold for jail fees, have a trusty friend to buy him in, and thus convert a servant for a term of years into a slave for life. A more expeditious mode of proceeding, by which persons having a limited time to serve are deprived entirely of their rights is thus: They are purchased up at cheap rates by the slave traders. They remove them to a great distance. It will be easily seen how small the chance that such persons would have to preserve the proofs of their freedom, and how little would their protestations be heeded, without proof. They are carried where redress is hopeless. Thus the slave trade, as it exists, and is carried on here, is marked by instances of injustice and cruelty, scarcely exceeded on the coast of Africa. It is a mistake to suppose it is a mere purchase and sale of acknowledged slaves. The District is full of complaints upon the subject, and the evil is increasing.

So long ago as 1802, the extent and cruelty of this traffic produced from a grand Jury at Alexandria a presentment, so clear, strong, and feelingly drawn, that I shall make no apology for reading the whole of it. Here Mr. M. read the following presentment of the Grand Jury:

January Term, 1802.

We the Grand Jury of the county of Alexandria, in the District of Columbia, present as a grievance, the practice of persons coming from distant parts of the United States into this District, for the purpose of purchasing slaves, where they exhibit to our view a scene of wretchedness and human degradation, disgraceful to our characters as citizens of a free government.

True it is, that those dealers in the persons of our fellow men collect within this District, from various parts, numbers of those victims of Slavery, and lodge them in some place of confinement until they have completed their numbers. They are then turned out in our streets and exposed to view, loaded with chains as though they had committed some heinous offence against our laws. We consider it a *grievance,* that citizens from distant parts of the United States should be permitted to come within this District, and pursue a traffic fraught with so much *misery* to a class of beings entitled to our protection by the laws of justice and humanity; and that the interposition of civil authority cannot be had to prevent parents being wrested from their offspring, and children from their parents, without respect to the ties of nature. We consider those grievances demanding legislative redress; especially the practice of making sale of black people, who are, by the will of their masters, designed to be free at the expiration of a term of years, who are sold, and frequently taken to distant parts, where they have not the power to avail themselves of that portion of liberty "which was designed for their enjoyment."

The National Legislature was too much engaged, or from other causes did not interpose, and the slave trade continued to increase in extent and enormity. . . . There are several . . . private prisons within the District; how many, I know not; but from the information given me, I think the feelings of the House would be touched, could they see the cells, the fetters, and chains they contain without even the victims that wear them. I hold some account of one of those prisons in my hand, furnished me by a friend. I cannot read it without mentioning the names of several persons, and as I wish to give neither pain not offence to any one, in any thing I say, I will only advert to the matter generally. In a series of essays published in a re-

SLAVERY

AND THE

SLAVE TRADE

AT THE

NATION'S CAPITAL.

NEW YORK:

PUBLISHED BY WILLIAM HARNED,

FOR THE

AMERICAN AND FOREIGN ANTI-SLAVERY SOCIETY,

5 Spruce Street,

$1 PER 100, $8 PER 1000.

7. Liberty Tract No. 1, *Slavery and the Slave Trade at the Nation's Capital.* Published in New York by William Harned for the American and Foreign Anti-Slavery Society. Courtesy of the Oberlin College Library.

spectable print in the District, in 1827, this subject was treated of.. I know of no motive for exaggeration. Published on the spot where the facts are known, it is fair to presume the picture of the slave trade, as it prevails in the District, is true to the original. Here Mr. M. read from the Alexandria Gazette of June 22, 1827, the following paragraphs:

"Some years ago," says our informant, "a coloured woman who had always been treated with kindness by her master, was sold by him to a person in this neighborhood, in order that she might be near her husband, who was also a slave. In the course of a few years she changed owners several times, and at length fell into the hands of the slave traders, who were making up a company for the Southern market. When these tidings were communicated to her, and she found that she must leave forever all the objects of her affections, to endure a life of misery in a distant land, she could not support the anguish it occasioned, and fell lifeless to the ground."

Scarcely a week passes without some of these wretched creatures being driven through our streets. After having been confined and sometimes manacled in a loathsome prison, they are turned out in public view, to take their departure for the South. The children, and some of the women, are generally crowded into a cart or wagon, while the others follow on foot, not unfrequently handcuffed and chained together. To those who have never seen a spectacle of this kind, no description can give an adequate idea of its horrors. Here you may behold fathers and brothers leaving behind them the dearest objects of affection, and moving slowly along in the mute agony of despair—there the young mother sobbing over her infant, whose innocent smiles seem but to increase her misery. From some you will hear the burst of bitter lamentation, while from others the loud hysteric laugh breaks forth, denoting still deeper agony.

The District of Columbia is now made the depot for this disgraceful traffic.

This traffic, and the views it exhibits, I beg the House to be assured, are as offensive to the people of the District, as they are unjust in themselves, and impolitic in us to countenance. Can it be supposed otherwise without a reproach to the good sense and moral sensibility of its citizens? But the slave dealers feel themselves secure. They do not dread any expression of your displeasure. These scenes have been exhibited here by the slave dealers for nearly thirty years, under your eye, and Congress has not moved to arrest their course. Your silence gives sanction to the trade. If an evil, only you can correct it. If you take no steps to correct it, does not your silence imply acquiescence, if not approbation? Is it then strange that the slave dealers should gain confidence from impunity, and make this their headquarters for carrying on the domestic slave trade? Sir, this is made the great market for the sale and purchase of human flesh. . . .

To give the House a just view of the actual state of things here, Mr. M. said he would read several advertisements from the public prints of the city. They would shew, not only the openness with which the slave dealers proceeded; but they would also shew that the sale of persons, men and women, at public auction was a common practice, warranted by our laws, and permitted by the Federal Legislature. Here Mr. M. read the following advertisement[s], published in this city:

WE WILL GIVE CASH

For one hundred likely Young Negroes of both sexes, between the ages of 8 and 25 years. Persons who wish to sell would do well to give us a call, as the Negroes are wanted immediately. We will give more than any other purchasers that are in market, or may hereafter come into market.

Any letters addressed to the subscribers, through the post office at Alexandria, will be promptly attended to. For information, inquire at the subscribers', West End of Duke street, Alexandria, D.C.

Dec. 15-w3m FRANKLIN & ARMFIELD. . . .

CASH! CASH! CASH!—AND NEGROES WANTED.

The subscriber will give the highest price, in cash, for likely sound young negro men, from 16 to 25 years, provided they can be had in time to be put on board the steamboat Potomac on next Wednesday evening. The subscriber can be seen at McCandless's tavern, High Street, Georgetown, D.C.

Sept. 30-d7t   SAM'L DAWSON.

CONSTABLE'S SALE

By virtue of two writs of fieri facias, issued by Israel Little, a Justice of the Peace for the county of Washington, and to me directed, I shall expose to sale, for cash, on Saturday, 30 of December, 1825, at the Navy Yard Market House, at 8 o'clock, A.M., one Negro Man. Seized and taken as the property of Mrs. Dorothy Wales, to Satisfy debts due to Edward Simmes and William R. Maddox.

Dec. 24—   ENOCH BRYAN, Constable.

So that a Constable has power, the least responsible officer known to our laws, under our Federal Authority, to set up and sell a man or a woman at the public market house. I cannot think that this is right. I do not think that these are proper scenes to be exposed at the seat of the General Government. Such exhibitions, some years ago, were presented in New York; and I recollect that the mechanics and merchants of that city formed an association, resolving that they would do no business with an auctioneer who should sell human beings at auction; and an end was put to the practice. Aside from the injustice and cruelty to individuals practised under the laws as they now exist, permit me, Mr. Speaker, to consider the subject in a more enlarged and national point of view. We are acknowledgedly the principal republic on the globe. Justice and equal rights are professedly at the foundation of our government. The Congress of the United States, and their proceedings, are viewed with solicitude by intelligent men throughout the world. Despotism must look with keen desire for our failure; the friends of civil liberty look with not less anxious hope for our prosperity and success. If we fail, the great cause of freedom will be lost forever. As we succeed, the principles of the rights of man gain strength and will extend their influence. . . . In relation to the moral power of this Government; in regard to the effect, at home and abroad, of our example, it would seem to me that we are called upon by the most weighty considerations to render the laws here as perfect as it is in human powers and human wisdom to make them. Suppose a distinguished foreigner, of correct and expanding views, who has listened with interest to the accounts of our republic, and whose mind is imbued with the liberal principles of the age, is resolved to visit us. He leaves the despotic shores of the European continent with delight. He prays for impelling gales to waft him to this land of justice and freedom. . . . And what objects are here presented to his view? At one market he meets a crowd; and as he passes near, behold it is a constable exhibiting a woman for sale subject to the scoffs and jeers of the unfeeling! He is selling her for a petty debt, under the authority of the sanction of Congress! Well may he exclaim "the age of chivalry is indeed gone forever!" To remove the painful impression, he takes up a newspaper of the District, and reads "cash in market, and the highest prices" for men and women. He walks abroad, and sees a gang of slaves handcuffed together, a long chain running between them and connecting the whole: miserable objects of horror and despair, marching off under the command of the slave-traders! What must be his feelings? . . .

Many thousand citizens have petitioned, from time to time, that Congress would take this matter into consideration, and provide by law for the gradual abolition of slavery at the Seat of General Government. The sentiment is becoming stronger and stronger every day, throughout the Nation, that the power of Congress should be exercised to clear out the mass of iniquity and oppression which has fixed itself here, and like a stagnant pool generates all manner of corruptions, producing a moral pestilence which the interest and honor of the country, equally call upon us to exert our authority to remove. Of the interior of the secret prisons, our knowledge is, of course, extremely imperfect; but a letter which I hold in my hand, written by a gentleman of Alexandria, every way to be relied upon, states,—[Here Mr. Miner read from the letter:]

"Almost every week, droves are brought into town, of ten or twelve, all chained together. Some time since, a person observed twenty-two or three come out of the cellar of a small house, where they had been stowed for some time. He thought it must surely be contrary to the *law,* that so many should be placed in so small an apartment, and inquired of one of the civil officers, how many slaves it was lawful to place in a small damp cellar. The officer replied: 'As many as it will hold.' The same things exist with regard to *shipping* them: they may place as many in a vessel as it will hold."

There is one case more to which I invite attention. . . . The circumstance to which I allude occurred last Winter, during the sitting of Congress. A coloured man, who was free, had married a woman who was a slave. By her he had several children. He was industrious, respectable, had acquired some property, and was the commander of a boat that plied from the place where he lived to Baltimore. The master of his wife died, and the man attended the sale of his effects, and purchased in his wife and children. For all this I have authority which the gentleman will not question. She was then his by marriage, and by purchase, by the double right of the laws of God and man. He left home on a trip to Baltimore, doubtless cheered to increased exertions by the prospect of happiness that opened upon him. On his return, his wife and children were gone: he sought for them in the neighbourhood; they could not be found. I cannot pretend to say, with certainty, what were the feelings of the poor negro on the occasion. I know no reason why he should not feel like ourselves. And what would be the painful surprise, gradually heightened to the agony of despair, if any member of this House who is a husband and a father, should return and find his house desolate, his wife and children gone, he knew not where? The man hastened to his former master for advice and aid. The gentleman to whom he applied, whatever may be his speculative notions on these subjects, is humane: has a tender heart for human suffering, and a quick sense of indignation at injustice. He gave the man a letter to an influential citizen of Alexandria, to make inquiry at a private prison in that city, whether the lost wife and children were there. The inquiry was made. The wife and children had been there, but the slave dealers had removed them beyond reach: they had been marched off with a gang that had been collected from a distant market, and they were lost to him forever. By whose fraud, by what treachery, this dark deed of iniquity was perpetrated, I cannot tell. The crime, though not wholly committed, was consummated in this District. By permitting, and thereby sanctioning the slave trade here, we encourage these scenes of injustice. Sir, if such an event as this had happened in Greece, if the Turks had committed such an outrage on human rights, this whole nation would have been in commotion. Money would have been raised, and sent by thousands, for the relief or redemption of the captives. Aye, sir, and we should send out missionaries to enlighten and convert the misguided heathen who should perpetrate such acts of flagrant cruelty.

The remark has often been made, and the events of our day show its correctness, that examples of time past move men beyond comparison, more than those of their own times. We accustom ourselves to what we see. The inquisition is to us a subject of horror; and yet the man, who, half a century ago, or even at a later time, should in Spain have proposed its abolition, I dare say, by honest but mistaken zeal, would have been deemed impious. Distance and time magnify objects. We feel deeply for the sufferings of Ireland; we weep for the miseries of the Greeks; but we suffer, in a race of a different colour, under our own eye, and our own jurisdiction, scenes of greater cruelty and injustice than are acted on the other side of the Atlantic. We move on the surface of the stream, where the sun-beams play, and where the glittering waves sparkle with hope, and joy, and pleasure; and we pass on, unconscious of the dark counter-current that flows beneath, embittered by the tears, and impelled by the sighs of the wretched. . . .

2.6. Congressman Horace Mann Calls for an End to the Slave Trade in the District of Columbia (1849)

As seen in Document 2.5, in 1829 Congressman Miner of Pennsylvania introduced resolutions in the House of Representatives asking the Committee on the District of Columbia to investigate the laws on slavery in the District and propose amendments to those laws, including gradual abolition of slavery. The debate on these proposals was prolonged, but the committee at last decided it was best to leave things as they were, "with the laws, and the humanity of those who are interested in protecting and taking care of this species of property" (see Mary Tremain, *Slavery in the District of Columbia*, pp. 65–69). Thereafter the "debate" on slavery in the District took the form of internecine conflict with little or nothing achieved, until the dispute was at last transformed by the Compromise of 1850, which, among other changes, admitted California into the Union as a free state, organized

Utah and New Mexico into territories, created a harsher fugitive slave law, and ended the slave trade in the District of Columbia. Nearly two years earlier, Congressman Abraham Lincoln had proposed an end to slavery in the District, which was poorly received, and so, in frustration, the educator and congressman from Massachusetts, Horace Mann, delivered a speech in support of a bill to abolish the *slave trade* only. The following are excerpts from this speech, which was strongly opposed by both northern and southern senators.

SOURCE: Horace Mann, *Slavery: Letters and Speeches* (Boston: B. B. Mussey, 1851), pp. 121–28, 144–47, 150–52.

Speech Delivered in The House of Representatives on Slavery and the Slave Trade in the District of Columbia, on February 23, 1849

Mr. Chairman:

There is a bill upon the speaker's table which provides for abolishing the slave trade in the District of Columbia. For three successive days we have tried in vain to reach it, in the order of business. Its opponents have baffled our efforts. . . . I am not without apprehension that the last sands of this Congress will run out without any action upon the subject. Even should the bill be taken up, it is probable that all debate upon it will be suppressed by that sovereign silencer,—the previous question. Hence I avail myself of the present opportunity, as it is probably the only one I shall have, during the present session, to submit my views upon it.

I frankly avow in the outset, that the bill provides for one part only of an evil, whose remedy, as it seems to me, is not only the object of a reasonable desire, but of a righteous and legal demand. The bill proposes the abolition, not of slavery, but only of the slave trade, in the District of Columbia. My argument will go to show, that, within the limits of this District, slavery ought not to exist in fact, and does not exist in law.

Sir, in the first place, let us inquire what is the state of things in this District on this subject. The gentleman from Indiana, [Mr. R. W. Thompson,] who addressed us a few days since, used the following language:—

"What is the slave trade in the District of Columbia? I have heard a great deal said about 'slave pens,'—about slaves sold at auction,—and about stripping the mother from the child, and the husband from the wife. These things may exist here, but I do not know of them. Since I have been in the habit of visiting the District,—which is from my boyhood,—I have never seen a negro sold here,—I have never seen a band of negroes taken off by the slave trader. I do not remember that I have ever seen the slave trader himself. I know nothing of the 'slave pen' that is so much talked about. It may be here, however, and these things may happen every day before the eyes of gentlemen who choose to hunt them up; but for myself, I have no taste for such things."

Now, sir, if the gentleman means to say that he has no personal knowledge of "slave pens" and of the slave traffic in this District, that is one thing; but if he means to deny or call in question the existence of the traffic itself, or of the dens where its concentrated iniquities make up the daily employment of men, that is quite another thing. Sir, from the western front of this Capitol, from the piazza that opens out from your congressional library, as you cast your eye along the horizon and over the conspicuous objects of the landscape,—the President's Mansion, the Smithsonian Institution, and the site of the Washington Monument, you cannot fail to see the horrid and black receptacles where human beings are penned like cattle, and kept like cattle,—as strictly and literally so as oxen and swine are kept and sold at the Smithfield shambles in London, or at the cattle fair in Brighton. In a communication made during the last session, by the mayor of this city, to an honorable member of this House, *he* acknowledges the existence of slave pens here. Up and down the beautiful river that sweeps along the western margin of the District, slavers come and go, bearing their freight of human souls to be vended in this marketplace; and after they have changed hands, according to the forms of commerce, they are retransported,—the father of the family to go, perhaps to the rice fields of South Carolina, the mother to the cotton fields of Alabama, and the children to be scattered over the sugar plantations of Louisiana or Texas.

Sir, it is notorious that the slave traders of this District advertise for slaves in the newspapers of the neighboring counties of Maryland, to be delivered in any numbers at their slave pens in this city; and that they have agents, in the city and out of it, who are engaged in supplying victims for their shambles. Since the gentleman from Indiana was elected to this Congress, and, I believe, since he took his seat in this Congress, one coffle of about sixty slaves came, chained and driven, into this city; and at about the same time another coffle of a hundred. Here they were lodged for a short period, were then sold, and went on their returnless way to the ingulfing south.

Sir, all this is done under our own eyes, and within hearing of our own ears. All this is done now, and it has been done for fifty years,—ever since the seat of national government was established in this place, and ever since Congress, in accordance with the constitution, has exercised *"exclusive* legislation" over it. But the gentleman from Indiana, though accustomed to

visiting this District from his boyhood, has "never seen a negro sold
here";—he has "never seen a band of negroes taken off by the slave trader";
he does not remember "to have seen the slave trader himself"; he knows
"nothing of the 'slave pen' that is so much talked about." Sir, the eye sees
. . . what the mind is disposed to recognize. The image upon the retina is
nothing, if there be not an inward sense to discern it. The artist sees beauty;
the philosopher sees relations of cause and effect; the benevolent man
catches the slightest tone of sorrow; but the insensate heart can wade
through tears and see no weeping, and can live amidst groans of anguish,
and the air will be a non-conductor of the sound. I know a true anecdote of
an American gentleman who walked through the streets of London with a
British nobleman; and being beset at every step of the way by squalid men-
dicants, the American, at the end of the excursion, adverted to their having
run a gantlet between beggars. "What beggars?" said his lordship, "I have
seen none."

But the gentleman from Indiana says, "But for myself, I have no taste
for such things." His taste explains his vision. Suppose Wilberforce and
Clarkson [British abolitionists] to have had no "taste" for quelling the horrors of the African slave trade. . . .

As far back as 1808, Congress did what it could to abolish the slave
trade on the coast of Africa. In 1820 it declared the foreign slave trade to be
piracy; but on the 31st of January, 1849, a bill was introduced into this
House to abolish the domestic slave trade in this District,—here in the centre and heart of the nation,—and seventy-two representatives voted against
it,—voted to lay it on the table, where, as we all know, it would sleep a
dreamless sleep. This was in the House of Representatives. It is well known
that the Senate is still more resistant of progress than the House; and it is
the opinion of many that, even if a bill should pass both House and Senate,
it would receive the executive veto. By the authority of Congress, the city of
Washington is the Congo of America. . . . The Potomac and the Chesapeake are the American Niger and Bight of Benin; while this District is the
great government barracoon, whence coffles are driven across the country
to Alabama or Texas, as slave ships once bore their dreadful cargoes of
agony and woe across the Atlantic. . . .

But to resume. When the visitor to this city from the north leaves his
lodgings and goes into the public streets, half the people whom he meets
there are of the same degraded class. Their tattered dress and unseemly
manners denote congenital debasement. Their language proclaims their ignorance. If you have occasion to send them on an errand, they cannot read
the direction of a note, or a sign on a shopboard. Their ideas are limited

In the Hands of Strangers

within the narrowest range. They speak the natural language of servility, and they wear the livery of an inferior condition. The conviction of their deplorable state is perpetually forced upon the mind. You do not need their color to remind you of their degradation. Color, sir! They are often almost as white as ourselves. Sir, there is not a member of Congress who has not frequently seen some of his fellow-members, in the spring of the year, with a jaundiced skin more sallow and more yellow than that of many a slave who is bought and sold and owned in this city. I have seen members of this House to whom I have been disposed to give a friendly caution to keep their "free papers" about their persons, lest suddenly, on the presumption from color, they should be seized and sold for runaway slaves. A yellow complexion here is so common a badge of slavery, that one whose skin is colored by disease is by no means out of danger. To enjoy security, a man must do more than take care of his life; he must take care of his health. It is not enough to take heed to the meditations of his heart; he must see also to the secretions of his liver.

But, sir, the stranger from the north visits the courts of justice in this city; he goes into halls set apart and consecrated . . . to the investigation of truth and the administration of justice; but if he sees any specimens of the colored race there, he sees them only as menials. They cannot go there as witnesses. However atrocious the wrongs they may suffer in their own person and character, or in the person or character of wife or children, they cannot appeal to the courts to avenge or redress them. If introduced there at all, it is as a bale of goods is introduced, or as an ox or a horse is brought within their purlieus for the purpose of trying some disputed question of identity or ownership. They go not as suitors, but as sacrifices. In the courts of law; in the temples with which all our ideas of justice, of right between man and man, are associated; where truth goes to be vindicated, where innocence flies to be avenged,—in these courts, an entire portion of the human race are known, not as men, but as chattels, as cattle. Where for them is the Magna Charta that the old barons wrested from King John? Is a whole race to be forever doomed to this outlawry? Are they forever to wear a "wolf's head," which every white man may cut off when he pleases? Sir, it cannot be that this state of things will last forever. If all the rights of the black race are thus withheld from them, it is just as certain as the progress of time that they, too, will have their Runnymede, their Declaration of Independence, their Bunker Hill, and their Yorktown.

Such, sir, are the sights that molest us when we come here from the north,—that molest us in the hotels, that molest us in the streets, that molest us in the courts, that molest us every where. But the week passes away and the Sabbath comes,—the day of rest from worldly toils, the day set apart for social worship, when men come together, and by their mutual presence and assistance, lift up the hearts of each other in gratitude to God. But where now are the colored population, that seemed to be so numerous every where else? Have they no God? Have they no interest in the Savior's example and precepts? Have they no need of consolation, of faith in the Unseen, to help them bear up under the burdens and anxieties of life? Is their futurity so uncertain or so worthless that they need no guide to a better country, or that they can be turned off with a guide as ignorant and blind as themselves?

We go from the courts and the churches to the schools. But no child in whose skin there is a shadow or a shade of African complexion is to be found there. The channels are so cut that all the sacred and healing waters of knowledge flow, not to him, but by him. Sir, of all the remorseless and wanton cruelties ever committed in this world of wickedness and woe, I hold that to be the most remorseless and wanton which shuts out from all means of instruction a being whom God has endued [endowed] with the capacities of knowledge, and inspired with the divine desire *to know.* . . . To one who is permitted to know nothing of the historical past, all the past generations of men are a nonentity. To one whose mind is not made capacious of the future, and opened to receive it, all the great interests of futurity have less of reality than a dream. I say, therefore, in strict, literal, philosophical truth, that whoever denies knowledge to children works devilish miracles. Just so far as he disables and incapacitates them from knowing, he annihilates the objects of knowledge; he obliterates history; he destroys the countless materials in the natural world that might through the medium of the useful arts, be converted into human comforts and blessings; he suspends the sublime order and progression of Nature, and blots out those wonderful relations of cause and effect that belong to her unchangeable laws. . . .

Such, sir, is the spectacle which is presented to all northern men, whenever for duty, for business, or for pleasure, they visit this metropolis. Wherever we go, wherever we are, the odious, abhorred concomitants of this institution are forced upon our observation, and become a perpetual bitterness in the cup of life. The whole system, with all its adjuncts, is irreconcilably repugnant to our ideas of justice. We believe it to be a denial of the rights of man; we believe it to be contrary to the law of God. Whether these feelings wear away by the lapse of time, and the indurating power of custom, I know not; but, for one, I hope never to become hardened and callous to the sight; for it is a case where I could experience no mitigation of my pains, without a corresponding debasement of my nature.

In the Hands of Strangers

Now, in all sincerity, and in all kindness, I ask our southern brethren what there is to them so valuable and desirable in retaining slavery here, as to be a compensation for all the pain and evil which its existence inflicts upon the north? Surely its abandonment here would be a small thing to them, while its continuance is a great thing to us. It is a great thing to us, because we are held responsible for it by the whole civilized world. This District is the common possession of the nation. Congress has power of exclusive legislation over it. Congress, therefore, is responsible for its institutions, as a man is responsible for the condition of his house, and the customs of his family. The general government is not responsible for the local institutions of Massachusetts or of Mississippi. Each of them has supreme control over its own domestic concerns. . . . But it is wholly otherwise with regard to the institutions that prevail in this District; their honor, or their infamy, attaches to us. We are judged by them the world round. We of the Northern States feel it at home; we are made to feel it still more deeply abroad. Throughout every nation in Europe, it is the common language and the common sentiment, that an institution which exists in one half of the states of this Union is in flagrant contrast and contradiction to the theory of our government. When we are reminded of this,—whether in a kindly and expostulatory manner by our friends, or in an offensive and taunting one by our enemies,—we of the north can say, at least, that we are not responsible for it. . . . But they will retort upon us, and say, There is one spot for which you are responsible,—the District of Columbia. You could abolish slavery there if you would; you do not; and therefore the sin of its continuance is yours, as much as if it existed in New York or Massachusetts. Now I ask southern gentlemen how it is consistent with magnanimity and honor, with a fraternal feeling towards the north, for them to force the odium of this inconsistency upon us? Surely they gain no credit, no character by it; we lose both credit and character. The existence of slavery here is no benefit to them; it is of unspeakable injury to us. They would lose nothing by surrendering it; we suffer everything by its continuance. A change would work them no injury; it would be invaluable to us. I ask them, on principles of common fairness and good neighborhood, that they should courteously and voluntarily yield us this point, which would allay so much bitterness and heart-burning at the north, and which, according to their view of the matter, would fill the south with the sweet savor of a generous deed.

I know, sir, that some southern gentlemen profess to see a principle in such a course that debars them from adopting it. They say that if slavery in this District should be surrendered, it would only be giving the adversary a vantage ground, on which he could plant himself to attack slavery in the states. I dissent from this view entirely. Has not the gentleman from Ohio, [Mr. Joshuah Giddings], who is supposed to represent the extreme anti-slavery views which exist in this House,—has he not declared here a hundred times over, that he disclaims all right, that he renounces all legal authority and pretext, under the constitution, to lay the hands of this government, for the purpose of freeing him, on a single slave in the slave states? But clearly the principle is different in regard to slaves in this District, where we possess the power of "exclusive legislation." But if gentlemen at the south see a principle which debars them from surrendering slavery in this District, we at the north see a principle which prompts us, and will prompt us, until the work is accomplished, to renewed exertions. On the same ground on which slavery in this District has been defended for the last fifty years, it can be defended for the next fifty, or the next five hundred years; it can be defended forever. . . .

One more point, sir, and I have done. Why, says my opponent, did not the right to hold slaves continue after the change of jurisdiction, as well as the right to hold horses? For the plainest of all reasons, I answer: for the reason that a horse is *property* by the universal consent of mankind, by the recognition of every civilized court in Christendom, without any positive law declaring it to be the subject of ownership. But a *man* is not property, without positive law; without a law declaring him to be the subject of ownership. There was such a positive law in Maryland; but Congress, for want of constitutional authority, could not enact, revive, or continue it. And such I verily believe would have been the decision of the Supreme Court of the United States, had the question been carried before them immediately subsequent to the act of 1801. But now, as slavery has existed practically in this District for half a century, it is proper to pass a law abolishing it. It is better, under the present circumstances, that slavery should be abolished here by a law of Congress, than by the decision of a court; because Congress can provide an indemnity for the owners, and let the slaves go free. But should it be abolished by a legal adjudication, every slave would be hurried away to the south, and sold, he and his descendants, into perpetual bondage.

In justice, then, to the north, which ought not to bear the opprobrium of slavery in this capital of the nation; in justice to the slaves who are held here in bondage against legal, as well as natural right; and, in more than justice to the masters, whose alleged claims I am willing, under all the circumstances, to satisfy, let a law be forthwith passed for ascertaining and paying the market value of the slaves, and for repealing all laws which uphold slavery in this District.

2.7. "Things as They Are in America." A Scottish Traveler Describes a Downtown Slave Market in Richmond, Virginia (1853)

William Chambers, a Scottish writer and publisher, was co-editor, along with his brother, Robert, of *Chambers's Edinburgh Journal* (after 1853 known as *Chambers's Journal of Popular Literature*). In that year (1853) William Chambers undertook a tour of the United States and Canada, during which he prepared a series of articles for publication in the family journal. Among the results of his travels were two books, *Things as They Are in America,* which appeared in 1854, and *American Slavery and Colour,* published in Edinburgh in 1857.

Among the best of Chambers's impressions of life in the South are his descriptions of Richmond slave markets located on two narrow streets just off the main downtown thoroughfare. A sensitive man, Chambers pondered the behavior and status of two classes of human beings he found there, one white, the other black, one selling, the other being sold, one respectably dressed, the other in coarse clothing, downcast and submissive. Tragic but noteworthy was Chambers's first experience in a slave shop where he watched three black children engaged in a make-believe auction—a small black boy playing the role of auctioneer who is attempting to "sell" a girl to a third child, the ostensible "buyer," who "was rolling about on the floor."

SOURCE: *Chambers's Journal of Popular Literature* (Edinburgh), no. 31, August 5, 1854, pp. 89–92.

Richmond is known as the principal market for the supply of slaves for the south—a circumstance understood to originate in the fact that Virginia, as a matter of husbandry, breeds negro labourers for the express purpose of sale. Having heard that such was the case, I was interested in knowing by what means and at what prices slaves are offered to purchasers. Without introductions of any kind, I was thrown on my own resources in acquiring this information. Fortunately, however, there was no impediment to encounter in the research. The exposure of ordinary goods in a store is not more open to the public than are the sales of slaves in Richmond. By consulting the local newspapers, I learned that the sales take place by auction every morning in the offices of certain brokers, who as I understood by the terms of their advertisements, purchased or received slaves for sale on commission.

Where the street was in which the brokers conducted their business, I did not know; but the discovery was easily made. Rambling down the main street in the city, I found that the subject of my search was a narrow and short thoroughfare, turning off to the left, and terminating in a similar cross thoroughfare. Both streets, lined with brick houses, were dull and silent. There was not a person to whom I could put a question. Looking about, I observed the office of a commission-agent, and into it I stepped. Conceive the idea of a large shop with two windows and a door between; no shelving or counters inside; the interior a spacious, dismal apartment, not well swept; the only furniture a desk at one of the windows, and a bench at one side of the shop, three feet high, with two steps to it to the floor. I say, conceive the idea of this dismal-looking place, with nobody in it but three negro children, who, as I entered, were playing at auctioning each other. An intensely black little negro, of four or five years of age, was standing on the bench, or block, as it is called, with an equally black girl, about a year younger, by his side, whom he was pretending to sell by bids to another black child, who was rolling about the floor.

My appearance did not interrupt the merriment. The little auctioneer continued his mimic play, and appeared to enjoy the joke of selling the girl, who stood demurely by his side.

"Fifty dolla for de gal—fifty dolla—fifty dolla—I sell dis here fine gal for fifty dolla," was uttered with extraordinary volubility by the wooly-headed urchin, accompanied with appropriate gestures, in imitation, doubtless, of the scenes he had seen enacted daily in the spot. I spoke a few words to the little creatures, but was scarcely understood; and the fun went on as if I had not been present: so I left them, happy in rehearsing what was likely soon to be their own fate.

At another office of a similar character, on the opposite side of the street, I was more successful. Here, on inquiry, I was respectfully informed by a person in attendance, that the sale would take place the following morning at half-past nine o'clock.

Next day I set out accordingly, after breakfast, for the scene of operations, in which there was now a little more life. Two or three persons were lounging about, smoking cigars; and, looking along the street, I observed that three red flags were projected from the doors of those offices in which sales were to occur. On each flag was pinned a piece of paper, notifying the articles to be sold. The number of lots was not great. On the first, was the following announcement:—"Will be sold this morning at half-past nine o'clock, a Man and a Boy."

It was already the appointed hour; but as no company had assembled,

I entered and took a seat by the fire. The office, provided with a few deal-forms and chairs, a desk at one of the windows, and a block accessible by a few steps, was tenantless, save by a gentleman who was arranging papers at the desk, and to whom I had addressed myself on the previous evening. Minute after minute passed, and still nobody entered. There was clearly no hurry in going to business. I felt almost like an intruder, and had formed the resolution of departing, in order to look into the other offices, when the person referred to left his desk, and came and seated himself opposite to me at the fire.

"You are an Englishman," said he, looking me steadily in the face; "do you want to purchase?"

"Yes," I replied, "I am an Englishman; but I do not intend to purchase. I am traveling about for information, and I shall feel obliged by your letting me know the prices at which negro servants are sold."

"I will do so with much pleasure," was the answer; "do you mean field-hands or house-servants?"

"All kinds," I replied; "I wish to get all the information I can."

With much politeness, the gentleman stepped to his desk, and began to draw up a note of prices. This, however, seemed to require careful consideration; and while the note was preparing, a lanky person in a wide-awake hat [a low-crowned felt hat], and chewing tobacco, entered and took the chair just vacated. He had scarcely seated himself when, on looking towards the door, I observed the subjects of sale—the man and boy indicated by the paper on the red flag—enter together, and quietly walk to a form at the back of the shop, whence, as the day was chilly, they edged themselves towards the fire, in the corner where I was seated. I was now between the two parties—the white man on the right, and the old and young negro on the left—and I waited to see what would take place.

The sight of the negroes at once attracted the attention of Wide-awake [the man with the felt hat]. Chewing with vigour, he kept keenly eyeing the pair, as if to see what they were good for. Under this searching gaze, the man and boy were a little abashed, but said nothing. Their appearance had little of the repulsiveness we are apt to associate with the idea of slaves. They were dressed in a gray woolen coat, pants, and waistcoat, coloured cotton neckcloths, clean shirts, coarse woolen stockings, and stout shoes. The man wore a black hat; the boy was bareheaded. Moved by a sudden impulse, Wide-awake left his seat, and rounding the back of my chair began to grasp at the man's arms, as if to feel their muscular capacity. He then examined his hands and fingers; and, last of all, told him to open his mouth and shew his teeth, which he did in a submissive manner. Having finished these examinations, Wide-awake resumed his seat, and chewed on in silence as before.

I thought it was but fair that I should now have my turn of investigation, and accordingly asked the elder negro what was his age. He said he did not know. I next inquired how old the boy was. He said he was seven years of age. On asking the man if the boy was his son, he said he was not—he was his cousin. I was going into other particulars, when the office-keeper approached, and handed me the note he had been preparing; at the same time making the observation that the market was dull at present, and that there never could be a more favourable opportunity of buying. I thanked him for the trouble which he had taken; and now submit a copy of his price-current:

"Best Men, 18 to 25 years old,—.	1200 to 1300 dollars.
Fair do.—-do. do.	950 to 1050 . . .
Boys, 5 feet.	850 to 950 . . .
Do., 4 feet, 8 inches	700 to 800 . . .
Do., 4 feet, 5 inches	500 to 600 . . .
Do., 4 feet, ...	375 to 450 . . .
Young Women	800 to 1000. . .
Girls, 5 feet,—	750 to 850 . . .
Do., 4 feet 9 inches, ...	700 to 750 . . .
Do., 4 feet, ...	350 to 452 . . .

(signed) _____,

Richmond, Virginia."

Leaving this document for future consideration, I pass on to a history of the day's proceedings. It was now ten minutes to ten o'clock, and Wide-awake and I being alike tired of waiting, we went off in quest of sales further up the street. Passing the second office, in which also nobody was to be seen, we were more fortunate at the third. Here, according to the announcement on the paper stuck to the flag, there were to be sold "A woman and three children; a young woman, three men, a middle-aged woman, and a little boy." Already a crowd had met, composed, I should think, of persons mostly from the cotton-plantations of the south. A few were seated near a fire on the right-hand side, and others stood round an iron stove in the middle of the apartment. The whole place had a dilapidated appearance. From a back-window, there was a view into a ruinous courtyard; beyond which, in a hollow, accessible by a side-lane, stood a shabby brick house, on which the word *Jail* was inscribed in large black letters on a white background. I imagined it to be a depôt for the reception of negroes.

On my arrival, and while making these preliminary observations, the

In the Hands of Strangers

lots for sale had not made their appearance. In about five minutes afterwards they were ushered in, one after the other, under the charge of a mulatto, who seemed to act as principal assistant. I saw no whips, chains, or any other engine of force. Nor did such appear to be required. All the lots took their seats on two long forms near the stove; none shewed any sign of resistance; nor did any one utter a word. Their manner was that of perfect humility and resignation.

As soon as all were seated, there was a general examination of their respective merits, by feeling their arms, looking into their mouths, and investigating the quality of their hands and fingers—this last being evidently an important particular. Yet there was no abrupt rudeness in making these examinations—no coarse or domineering language was employed. The three negro men were dressed in the usual manner—in gray woolen clothing. The woman, with three children, excited my peculiar attention. She was neatly attired, with a coloured handkerchief bound round her head, and wore a white apron over her gown. Her children were all girls, one of them a baby at the breast, three months old, and the others two and three years old respectively, rigged out with clean white pinafores. There was not a tear or an emotion visible in the whole party. Everything seemed to be considered as a matter of course; and the change of owners was possibly looked forward to with as much indifference as ordinary hired servants anticipate a removal from one employer to another.

While intending purchasers were proceeding with personal examinations of the several lots, I took the liberty of putting a few questions to the mother of the children. The following was our conversation:

"Are you a married woman?"

"Yes, sir."

"How many children have you had?"

"Seven."

"Where is your husband?"

"In Madison County."

"When did you part from him?"

"On Wednesday—two days ago."

"Were you sorry to part from him?"

"Yes, sir," she replied with a deep sigh; "my heart was a'most broke."

"Why is your master selling you?"

"I don't know—he wants money to buy some land—suppose he sells me for that."

There might not be a word of truth in these answers, for I had no means of testing their correctness; but the woman seemed to speak unre servedly, and I am inclined to think that she said nothing but what, if necessary, could be substantiated. I spoke, also, to the young woman who was seated near her. She, like the others, was perfectly black, and appeared stout and healthy, of which some of the persons present assured themselves by feeling her arms and ankles, looking into her mouth, and causing her to stand up. She told me she had several brothers and sisters, but did not know where they were. She said she was a house-servant, and would be glad to be bought by a good master—looking at me, as if I should not be unacceptable.

I have said that there was an entire absence of emotion in the party of men, women, and children, thus seated preparatory to being sold. This does not correspond with the ordinary accounts of slave-sales, which are represented as tearful and harrowing. My belief is, that none of the parties felt deeply on the subject, or at least that any distress they experienced was but momentary—soon passed away and was forgotten. One of my reasons for this opinion rests on a trifling incident which occurred. While waiting for the commencement of the sale, one of the gentlemen present amused himself with a pointer-dog, which at command, stood on its hind-legs, and took pieces of bread from his pocket. These tricks greatly entertained the row of negroes, old and young; and the poor woman, whose heart three minutes before was almost broken, now laughed as heartily as any one.

"Sale is going to commence—this way, gentlemen," cried a man at the door to a number of loungers outside; and all having assembled, the mulatto assistant led the woman and her children to the block, which he helped her to mount. There she stood with her infant at the breast, and one of her girls at each side. The auctioneer, a handsome, gentlemanly personage, took his place, with one foot on an old deal-chair with a broken back, and the other raised on the somewhat more elevated block. It was a striking scene.

"Well, gentlemen," began the salesman, "here is a capital woman and her three children, all in good health—what do you say for them? Give me an offer. (Nobody speaks.) I put up the whole lot at 850 dollars—850 dollars—850 dollars (speaking very fast)—850 dollars. Will no one advance upon that? A very extraordinary bargain, gentlemen. A fine healthy baby. Hold it up. (Mulatto goes up the first step of the block; takes the baby from the woman's breast, and holds it aloft with one hand, so as to shew that it was a veritable sucking baby.) That will do. A woman, still young, and three children, all for 850 dollars. An advance, if you please, gentlemen. (A voice bids 860.) Thank you, sir—860; any one bids more? (A second voice says, 870; and so on the bidding goes as far as 890 dollars, when it stops.) That won't do, gentlemen. I cannot take such a low price. (After a pause, addressing the mulatto): She may go down." Down from the block the woman and her children were therefore conducted by the assistant, and, as if nothing had occurred, they calmly resumed their seats by the stove.

The next lot brought forward was one of the men. The mulatto beckoning to him with his hand, requested him to come behind a canvas screen, of two leaves, which was standing near the back-window. The man placidly rose, and having been placed behind the screen, was ordered to take off his clothes, which he did without a word or look of remonstrance. About a dozen gentlemen crowded to the spot while the poor fellow was stripping himself, and as soon as he stood on the floor, bare from top to toe, a most rigorous scrutiny of his person was instituted. The clear black skin, back and front, was viewed all over for sores from disease; and there was no part of his body left unexamined. The man was told to open and shut his hands, asked if he could pick cotton, and every tooth in his head was scrupulously looked at. The investigation being at an end, he was ordered to dress himself; and having done so, was requested to walk to the block.

The ceremony of offering him for competition was gone through as before, but no one would bid. The other two men, after undergoing similar examinations behind the screen, were also put up, but with the same result. Nobody would bid for them, and they were all sent back to their seats. It seemed as if the company had conspired not to buy anything that day. Probably some imperfections had been detected in the personal qualities of the negroes. Be this as it may, the auctioneer, perhaps a little out of temper from his want of success, walked off to his desk, and the affair was so far at an end.

"This way, gentlemen—this way!" was heard from a voice outside, and the company immediately hived [*sic*] off to the second establishment. At this office there was a young woman, and also a man for sale. The woman was put up first at 500 dollars; and possessing some recommendable qualities, the bidding for her was run as high as 710 dollars, at which she was knocked down to a purchaser. The man, after the customary examination behind a screen, was put up at 700 dollars; but a small imperfection having been observed in his person, no one would bid for him; and he was ordered down.

"This way, gentlemen—this way down the street, if you please!" was now shouted by a person in the employment of the first firm, to whose office all very willingly adjourned—one migratory company, it will be perceived, serving all the slave-auctions in the place. Mingling in the crowd, I went to see what should be the fate of the man and boy, with whom I had already had some communication.

There the pair, the two cousins, sat by the fire, just where I had left them an hour ago. The boy was put up first.

"Come along, my man—jump up; there's a good boy!" said one of the partners, a bulky and respectable-looking person, with a gold chain and bunch of seals; at the same time getting on the block. With alacrity the little fellow came forward, and, mounting the steps, stood by his side. The forms in front were filled by the company; and as I seated myself, I found that my old companion, Wide-awake, was close at hand, still chewing and spitting at a great rate.

"Now, gentlemen," said the auctioneer, putting his hand on the shoulder of the boy, "here is a very fine boy, seven years of age, warranted sound—what do you say for him? I put him up at 500 dollars—500 dollars (speaking quick, his right hand raised up, and coming down on the open palm of his left) 500 dollars. Any one say more than 500 dollars? (560 is bid.) 560 dollars. Nonsense! Just look at him. See how high he is. (He draws the lot in front of him, and shews that the little fellow's head comes up to his breast.) You see he is a fine, tall, healthy boy. Look at his hands."

Several step forward, and cause the boy to open and shut his hands—the flexibility of the small fingers, black on the one side, and whitish on the other, being well looked to. The hands, and also the mouth, having given satisfaction, an advance is made to 570, then to 580 dollars.

"Gentlemen, that is a very poor price for a boy of this size. (Addressing the lot): Go down, my boy, and shew them how you can run."

The boy, seemingly happy to do as he was bid, went down from the block, and ran smartly across the floor several times; the eyes of every one in the room following him.

"Now, that will do. Get up again. (Boy mounts the block, the steps being rather deep for his short legs; but the auctioneer kindly lends him a hand.) Come, gentlemen, you see this is a first-rate lot. 590-600-610-620-630 dollars are bid.) I will sell him for 630 dollars. (Right hand coming down on left.) Last call. 630 dollars once—630 dollars twice. (A pause; hand sinks.) Gone!"

The boy having descended, the man was desired to come forward; and after the usual scrutiny behind a screen, he took his place on the block.

"Well, now, gentlemen," said the auctioneer, "here is a right prime lot. Look at this man; strong, healthy, able-bodied; could not be a better hand for field-work. He can drive a wagon, or anything. What do you say for him? I offer the man at the low price of 800 dollars—he is well worth 1200 dollars. Come, make an advance, if you please. 800 dollars said for the man (a bid), thank you; 810 dollars—810 dollars—810 dollars (several bids)—820-830-850-860-going at 860-going. Gentlemen, this is far below his value. A strong-boned man, fit for any kind of heavy work. Just take a look at him.

(Addressing the lot): Walk down. (Lot dismounts, and walks from one side of the shop to the other. When about to reascend the block, a gentleman who is smoking a cigar, examines his mouth and his fingers. Lot resumes his place.) Pray, gentlemen, be quick (continues the auctioneer); I must sell him, and 860 dollars are only bid for the man—860 dollars. (A fresh run of bids to 945 dollars.) 945 dollars once, 945 dollars twice (looking slowly round, to see if all were done), 945 dollars, going—going (hand drops)—gone!"

During this remarkable scene, I sat at the middle of the front form with my note-book in hand, in order to obtain a full view of the transaction. So strange was the spectacle, that I could hardly dispel the notion that it was all a kind of dream; and now I look back upon the affair as by far the most curious I ever witnessed. The more intelligent Virginians will sympathize in my feelings on the occasion. I had never until now seen human beings sold; the thing was quite new. Two men are standing on an elevated bench, one white and the other black. The white man is auctioning the black man. What a contrast in look and relative position! The white is a most re-spectable-looking person; so far as dress is concerned, he might pass for a clergyman or church-warden. There he stands—can I believe my eyes?—in the might of an Anglo-Saxon, sawing the air with his hand, as if addressing a missionary or any other philanthropic meeting from a platform. Surely that gentlemanly personage cannot imagine that he is engaged in any mortal sin! Beside him is a man with a black skin, and clothed in rough garments. His looks are downcast and submissive. He is being sold, just like a horse at Tattersall's, or a picture at Christie and Manson's—I must be under some illusion. That dark object whom I have been always taught to consider a man, is not a man. True, he may be called a man in advertisements, and by the mouth of auctioneers. But it is only a figure of speech—a term of convenience. He is a man in one sense, and not in another. He is a kind of man—stands upright on two legs, has hands to work, wears clothes, can cook his food (a point not reached by monkeys), has the command of speech, and, in a way, can think and act like a rational creature—can even be taught to read. But nature has thought fit to give him a black skin, and that tells very badly against him. Perhaps, also, there is something wrong with his craniological development. Being, at all events, so much of a man—genus *homo*—is it quite fair to master him, and sell him, exactly as suits your convenience—you being, from a variety of fortunate circumstances, his superior? All this passed through my mind as I sat on the front form in the saleroom of Messrs ———, while one of the members of that well-known firm was engaged in pursuing, by the laws of Virginia, his legitimate calling.

Such were a forenoon's experiences in the slave-market of Richmond. Everything is described precisely as it occurred, without passion or prejudice. It would not have been difficult to be sentimental on a subject which appeals so strongly to the feelings; but I have preferred telling the simple truth. . . .

W.C.

2.8. "When a Hawk Flies over a Barnyard." A Methodist Minister's Impressions of the Slave Trade in Maryland

A lifelong opponent of slavery, the author of the following essays, John Dixon Long, was a pastor of the Methodist Episcopal Church who during his long ministry in his native Maryland made a practice, at some danger to himself, of expounding against slavery to members of the slaveholding class while administering publicly among the slaves. At last, in 1856, in poor health and aware that his four sons were "beginning to imbibe the common prejudices of slave society," he relocated his family in Philadelphia, where to his disappointment, he also encountered much pro-slavery sentiment. Though Long had never written for publication, his frustration with the views he found in the North led him to the decision to "bear testimony" against slavery by means of the written word, though he doubted his ability and feared a loss of friends and even persecution. Not finding a publisher in Philadelphia who would print his book, he paid the costs of publication himself "with no misgivings that the principles I have advocated will be found unsound in the Great Day." Five of Long's brief sketches have been selected for their relevance to aspects of internal slave trading in the United States and for what they reveal about this southern clergyman's atypical opposition to the dogmas of his society.[35]

SOURCE: Rev. John Dixon Long, *Pictures of Slavery in Church and State; Including Personal Reminiscences, Biographical Sketches, Anecdotes, Etc., Etc.* (Published by the author in 1857), pp. 66–70, 93–94, 110–11, 144–47, 210–11.

SLAVE DROVES

In all our country towns are located negro-traders or their agents. If any one doubts this fact, let him read their advertisements in the county papers. Thursdays and Saturdays are the public days in the towns. A great deal of

---

35. For the views of more prominent southerners on the issue of slavery, see Docs. 3.1, 3.2, 3.6, 3.10, and 3.15 through 3.17.

property is sold from various parts of the county at Court House doors, at sheriff's sales. At these auctions, numbers of slaves are sold. The trader or his agent is always present. He also attends the public vendues of deceased persons, where hogs, mules, horses, and negroes are sold. He is also very attentive to private calls from men at their houses. When he has collected a drove of negroes, he starts for the South. Such are the facilities for travel now, that he does not collect so great a number at a time as formerly.

If the reader will take a good map of Maryland, he will find that the Pocomoke River divides Worcester from Somerset County, for more than twenty miles above its mouth. A traveler wishing to go to Norfolk, Va., from Princess Anne, the county town of Somerset, would have to cross this river at the Ferry about a mile above New Town, through which he must pass to Eastville, Va., and thence to Norfolk. To the Ferry my father removed in 1824, where he had bought property. It was here that I spent several years of my life. It was here that I witnessed some of the scenes which I will now attempt to describe, and which are so deeply pictured on my memory as to cast a gloom over the associations of my youthful home.

Picture the following scene, which I have often witnessed: One or two negro-buyers, *mounted on horses,* with *pistols peeping from their pockets,* with large loaded whips in their hands, and cursing the slaves with deep oaths. A large two or four-horse wagon, laden with women and children. Negro men walking, handcuffed and chained around the ankle, two and two; and when the two men were not of the same height, the chains were very painful; or, if the negro was very large, the foot-cuff too small for his ankle, he suffered great agony. I have seen them, at the Ferry, under the necessity of violating the decencies of nature before the women, not being permitted to retire. The first drove I saw, after the love of Christ was shed abroad in my heart, caused me to wring my hands in deep agony. It cast a gloom over me for several days. Slaves from Somerset County could follow their friends as far as the Ferry; here they had to part. Here I have seen mothers part with their children, and brothers with their sisters. Here I have heard them bid adieu thus: "Farewell, mother"; "farewell, child"; "farewell, John"; "farewell, Bill"; and then rend the air with their cries and lamentations. Dear reader, is it unreasonable that I should feel deeply on this subject? This infamous traffic is still carried on in every part of Maryland, but not in so vulgar a manner. The slaves are conveyed in *close carriages* to the steamboats, *via* Baltimore. It is a shameful fact that, in the South, church-members are constantly selling church-members, professed saints selling real ones, and infidels selling the members of Christ's body. Barter and traffic in temples of the Holy Ghost are carried on. Native Americans sell Native

Americans; white *Whigs and Democrats* sell black Whigs and Democrats (for slaves generally profess the politics of their masters); and all this is done in the *"land of the free, and the home of the brave."* What is the fountain that feeds all these streams of negro-droves, outrages, indecencies, handcuffs and blighting separations of the dearest relations of life? The relation of *owner and slave.* Who furnishes the material for these slave factories? The *man who breeds them, lets them be sold for his debts,* wills them to his children, or gives them away during his lifetime, that they may be sold. . . .

SELLING NEGROES BY THE POUND

This idea was suggested to me by a gentleman who stated that he was present when a slave was sold to the traders. A pair of scales being in the house, some of the party weighed the body of the slave, and made a calculation of the price of the slave per pound. A young colored man will bring from seven to eight dollars per pound at this time, and bright mulatto girls a little more. Beef cattle from seven to eight cents per pound. . . .

NEGRO BUYERS

Negro-Buyers—Negro-Traders—Georgia-Traders—Negro-Purchasers. By these four names the dealers in human flesh are designated in the South. "Georgia-trader" is a favorite title among the slaves. I dare not trust myself to describe the extent of my detestation of the moral character and horrible occupation of this class of men. No language is sufficiently strong to paint them in their true colors. Paul uses language, in reference to the old Romans, that comes nearest to that which my subject requires, when he says that they were "filled with all unrighteousness, fornication, wickedness, covetousness, maliciousness, full of envy, murder, malignity, haters of God, despiteful, proud, without natural affection, implacable, unmerciful." What the captain of a slave ship is on the ocean these men are on the land. To this day, when I see one of them, a strange sensation thrills me, and my love of human nature is weakened. To the slave population they are regarded as the impersonation of Satan. When slave mothers wish to keep their children quiet, they threaten them with the negro-buyer; and when one of these men is seen riding up to the master's house by the slaves, terror settles on the faces of all the poor creatures. They feel as much alarmed as a hen and her chickens when a hawk flies over a barn-yard. And well they may! Negro-buyers respect ministers of the Gospel who hate slavery; and it is my opinion that they have the utmost contempt for those preachers who contend that chattel slavery is right. No man knows better than the negro-buyer the awful sin of slavery. And could you see the terrible death-bed scenes of these men, you would think so too. If I believed that to sustain the relation of owner and slave was not a sin, I should regard these men as gentlemen. I should welcome them to the pews of our churches. If it is no sin in an Ohio farmer to raise hogs and horses for the eastern market, it is no sin in any man to buy these hogs and horses, and collect them in droves and sell them in our cities. If it is no sin to hold men as horses, it is no sin to sell them; and the man who collects them in droves commits no sin. It is therefore wrong in pro-slavery church members to treat them with disrespect, and to speak contemptuously of their calling. These men are benefactors; they take away the surplus stock of negro chattels; they provide masters with ready money, which enables them to build churches, to contribute to Bible, Tract, and Missionary Societies—to visit Saratoga, Cape May, the Virginia Springs and Newport—to support pro-slavery preachers, Bible agents, and political and religious newspapers! . . .

SLAVERY ONCE UNPROFITABLE

From 1820 to 1830, slaves were very cheap. A young negro man would only bring from two to three hundred dollars. A colored woman could be hired for eighteen dollars per annum; a colored man for thirty or forty dollars per year. Now [1857] a person of the same class will sell for from 1000 to 1500 dollars, and is hired at from 30 to 100 dollars per year.

It passed into a proverb that the hogs ate the corn, the negroes ate the hogs, and the master ate the negroes.

The negro was the sure crop, though he sold cheap. If the master wanted to build a new house, he sold one or two negroes. If he bought a fine carriage, poor Sambo had to look out. If he got pushed for money, his hope lay in the [slave] quarter. But when the virgin soils of Missouri, Arkansas, Alabama, Florida, and Texas opened, and cotton took a rise, then negroes went up.

If slaves were as cheap now as they were 30 years ago, the South would scarcely thank you for a fugitive slave law. Hundreds of slaveowners would give you all you wanted to get them out of the way. It is not true that the abolitionist has retarded emancipation in the South. The change of sentiment is due to the augmented demand for cotton, sugar, and tobacco. . . .

Whatever may be said against kidnapping the natives on the west coast of Africa, and selling them to the North American States, may be charged against the internal slave-trade of the American Union. Indeed, the latter is far more odious, inhuman and antichristian. This will appear from several considerations. Who are the subjects of the African slave-trade? Heathens, idolators, barbarians, and strangers. Who supplies the subjects of this trade? Outlaws and pirates, by the laws of nations, and by the laws of this great Republic; men whose home is on the "ocean wave;" who speak amid the marshes and jungles of a tropical clime, where the anaconda, the tiger, and the lion crouch. Who are the subjects of the American or internal slave-trade? Women who wiped the cold sweat from the languid and pale faces of our mothers when they suffered the pangs of our nativity; mothers whose juicy breasts have nourished the very men who sell them to the slave-trader; Christian husbands and wives, married by the ministers of the ever-lasting Gospel in the name of the Father, the Son, and the Holy Spirit; brothers sold by brothers in church relationship; children sold by their fa-thers, and sisters by their brothers. This abomination of abominations is perpetrated in sight of our school-houses and churches; in sight of our grave-yards and our cemeteries; at the doors of our courts of justice and our halls of legislation. Yes, more than this: in sight of the Capitol of this *Second Roman Empire,* enlarged and improved, whose proud eagles hold in their claws 4,000,000 of human chattels. Who furnishes the subjects of this inhuman traffic? Those who suffer their slaves to be sold for their debts, or, dying, leave them to be sold by their children. He who condemns the African slave-trade must condemn the internal slave-trade; and he who condemns the internal traffic must condemn the fountain that feeds it. . . .

SLAVERY AND MARRIAGE

Slavery dissolves the marriage relation between slaves, or between a slave man and a free woman, or a free man and a slave woman, at the will of the master. It ignores the authority of God in the conjugal relation, and trammels the conscience of true ministers of Jesus Christ.

Two colored persons called upon the writer in Maryland, to marry them, and before proceeding with the ceremony, I inquired of the man if he was single. He stated that he had been married by a Methodist preacher, but his wife had been sold to Georgia about two years [before]. I was em-barrassed and perplexed. What was to be done under the circumstances? I married them. Did I do wrong? I fear I did. If I had refused, the man would have lived with the woman, and I should have laid a burden of temptation on him that the church would not have touched with her little finger. On the other hand, it seemed like acknowledging the power of the masters as above the command of God. This man's lawful wife was separated from him for a cause other than adultery; she was, perhaps, then living; and, it may be, was already the forced wife or mistress of a slave or master in the far-off South.

The serpent slavery meets the Christian minister at every turn, hissing at the authority and love of Christ. Slavery and the married relation are utterly incompatible. To-day the preacher may, by permission of the master, unite two slaves in holy wedlock, and by Divine Authority, say, "Whom God hath joined together, let no man put asunder," and the next day, the husband or wife can, at the will of the owner, be sent to some distant State. What minister of Christ can justify a system which thus strikes at morality, and openly, unblushingly violates the commands of the Great Jehovah.

2.9. The Buying and Selling of John Brown

The following selection is from a narrative of slave life as told to L. A. Chamerovzow, secretary of the British and Foreign Anti-Slavery Society, by a former slave, one John Brown. In his preface to the volume Chamerovzow described the book as "a plain, unvarnished tale of real Slave-life, conveyed as nearly as possible in the language of the subject of it, and written under his dictation." According to the editor, its publication had two purposes: "to advance the anti-slavery cause by the diffusion of information; and to promote the success of the project John Brown has formed to advance himself by his own exertions, and to set an example to others of his 'race.' "

SOURCE: *Slave Life in Georgia: A Narrative of the Life, Sufferings, and Escape of John Brown, a Fugitive Slave, Now in England,* ed. L. A. Chamerovzow, secretary of the British and Foreign Anti-Slavery Society, 2d ed. (London: W. M. Watts, 1855), pp. 1–21.

My Childhood and First Troubles.

My name is John Brown. How I came to take it, I will explain in due time. When in Slavery, I was called Fed. Why I was so named, I cannot tell. I never knew myself by any other name, nor always by that; for it is common for slaves to answer to any name, as it may suit the humour of the master. I do not know how old I am, but I think I may be at any age between thirty-five and forty. I fancy I must be about thirty-seven or eight; as nearly as I can guess. I was raised on Betty Moore's estate, in Southampton County, Virginia, about three miles from Jerusalem Court house and the little Nottoway river. My mother belonged to Betty Moore. Her name was Nancy; but she was called Nanny. My father's name was Joe. He was owned by a planter named Benford, who lived at Southampton, in the same State. I believe my father and his family were bred on Benford's plantation. His father had been stolen from Africa. He was of the Eboe tribe. I remember seeing him once, when he came to visit my mother. He was very black. I never saw him but that one time, and though I was quite small, I have a distinct recollection of him. He and my mother were separated, in consequence of his master's going further off, and then my mother was forced to take another husband. She had three children by my father; myself, and a brother and sister, twins. My brother's name was Silas, and my sister's Lucy. My mother's second husband's name was Lamb. He was the property of a neighboring planter and miller named Collier. By him she had three children; two boys, Curtis and Cain, and a girl between them called Irene. We all lived together with our mother, in a log cabin, containing two rooms, one of which we occupied; the other being inhabited by my mother's niece, Annikie, and her children. It had a mud floor; the sides were of wattle and daub, and the roof was thatched over. Our sleeping place was made by driving a forked stake into the floor which served to support a cross piece of wood, one end of it resting in the croch, the other against the shingle that formed the wall. A plank or two across, over the top, completed the bedroom arrangements, with the exception of another plank on which we laid straw or cotton-pickings, and over that a blanket.

Our mistress Betty Moore was an old, big woman, about seventy, who wore spectacles and took snuff. I remember her very well, for she used to call us children up to the big house every morning, and give us a dose of garlic and rue to keep us "wholesome," as she said, and make us "grow likely for the market." After swallowing our dose, she would make us run round a great sycamore tree in the yard, and if we did not run fast enough to please her, she used to make us nimbler by laying about us with a cowhide. She always carried this instrument dangling at her side, like ladies in this country [England] wear their scissors. It was painted blue, and we used to call it the "blue lizard." She used to like to see her people constantly employed, and would make us all set to work at night, after our day's labour was over, picking the seed out of cotton. We had a hard time of it with the old lady.

At this period, my principal occupation was to nurse my little brother whilst my mother worked in the field. Almost all slave children have to do the nursing; the big taking care of the small, who often come poorly off in consequence. I know this was my little brother's case. I used to lay him in the shade, under a tree, sometimes, and go to play, or curl myself up under a hedge, and take a sleep. He would wake me by his screaming, when I would find him covered with ants, or musquitos, or blistered from the heat of the sun, which having moved round whilst I was asleep, would throw the shadow of the branches in another direction, leaving the poor child quite exposed.

Betty Moore had three daughters. The eldest was married to one Burrell Williams, who acted as Betty's overseer. The second was the wife of one James Davis; and the third was unmarried, when I first began to notice the persons about us. At last the third got married to one Billy Bell, and then I experience my first serious tribulation.

According to the will left by old Moore, the slave property was to be equally divided amongst the mother and the three daughters, when the youngest married. About a month after this event, it began to be talked about that the distribution was soon going to take place. I remember well the grief this caused us to feel, and how the women and the men used to whisper to one another when they thought nobody was by, and meet at night, or get together in the field when they had an opportunity to talk about what was coming. They would speculate too on the prospects they had of being separated; to whose lot they and their children were likely to fall, and whether the husbands would go with their wives. The women who had young children cried very much. My mother did, and took to kissing us a good deal oftener. This uneasiness increased as the time wore on, for though we did not know when the great trouble would fall upon us, we all knew it would come, and were looking forward to it with very sorrowful hearts. At last, one afternoon, James Davis, the husband of Betty's second daughter, rode into the yard. This man had a dreadful name for cruelty. He was the terror of his own negroes, as well as of his neighbor's. When we young ones saw him, we ran away and hid ourselves. In the evening orders came to the negroes, at their quarters, to be up at the big house by nine the next morning. Then we knew our great trouble was come.

It was a bright, sun-shiny morning, in the autumn season, at about the commencement of tobacco-cutting time. At the appointed hour, nearly the whole of us had congregated in the great yard, under the big sycamore tree. A Fourth part of the negroes on the estate had been kept back by Betty Moore, as her share, her husband's will giving her the right of making a selection. Besides these, she had taken my brother Silas and my sister Lucy, whom she reserved on behalf of her eldest daughter, the wife of Burrell Williams. They were fine, strong children, and it was arranged they should remain with Betty till she died, and then revert to Burrell Williams. All who were there stood together, facing the Executors, or Committee as they were called, who sat on chairs under the same sycamore tree I have spoken of. Burrell Williams, James Davis, and Billy Bell held themselves aloof, and did not in any manner interfere with the proceedings of the Committee, who told us off into three lots, each lot consisting of about twenty-five or thirty, as near as I can recollect. As there was a good deal of difference in the value of the slaves, individually, some being stronger than others, or more likely, the allotments were regulated so as to equalize the value of each division. For instance, my brother Silas and my sister Lucy, who belonged rightly to the gang of which I and my mother and other members of the family formed a part, were replaced by two of my cousin Annikie's children, a boy and a girl; the first called Henry, the other Mason, who were weak and sickly. When the lots had been told off, the names of the men, women, and children composing them were written on three slips of paper, and these were put into a hat. Burrell Williams then came forward and drew. James Davis followed, and Billy Bell came last. The lot in which I and my mother were was drawn by James Davis. Each slip was then signed by the Committee, and the lot turned over to the new owner.

By about two o'clock the business was concluded, and we were permitted to have the rest of the day to ourselves. It was a heart-rending scene when we all got together again, there was so much crying and wailing. I really thought my mother would have died of grief at being obliged to leave her two children, her mother, and her relations behind. But it was of no use lamenting, and as we were to start early next morning, the few things we had were put together that night, and we completed our preparations for parting for life by kissing one another over and over again, and saying good bye till some of us little ones fell asleep.

My New Master: And How He Came To Sell Me.

We were aroused by times in the morning, and were soon ready to set off on our journey. Our destination was Northampton, about forty-five miles from our old home. We expected to be two days on the road, and as there were a good many little children, who could not walk so far, the smallest of these were put into a waggon, which our new master, James Davis, helped to drive. He rode by it on horseback, his wife keeping along with the older coloured people, in her carriage. The weather was very fine, and we went slowly on, many of us looking back sadly at the place we were leaving, and with which we were so familiar. At noon we drew up by the roadside to breakfast off hoe-cake and water, after which we started again, and walked on until dark. We camped out in the wood by the highway that night, James Davis and his wife putting up at a planter's in the neighborhood, who sent relay parties to watch us. We collected a lot of dried sticks and made a fire, in which the women baked some Johnny-cake which they made from our allowance of corn. When we had supped, we raked together the leaves into heaps under the trees, and laid down upon them, covering ourselves with whatever blanketing we could muster. The children slept in the waggon.

At day-break we started afresh, and continued our journey until noon, when we stopped to eat. We had baked sufficient Johnny-cake over night, for the mid-day meal next day, so we were not long refreshing. To encourage us to make good speed, we were promised a feast of boiled black-eyed peas and bacon-rinds, as soon as we got to Northampton, and some of us got a cut with the whip. Any how, we reached James Davis' that afternoon, at about four o'clock. We had our peas and bacon-rinds, and some hard cider was served out to us into the bargain. I remember it very well, for it gave me a very violent cholic. After supper we were driven to our quarters.

And here I may as well tell what kind of a man our new master was. He was of small stature, and thin, but very strong. He had sandy hair, fierce gray eyes, a very red face, and chewed tobacco. His countenance had a very cruel expression, and his disposition was a match for it. He was, indeed, a very bad man, and used to flog us dreadfully. He would make his slaves work on one meal a day, until quite night, and after supper set them to burn brush or to spin cotton. We worked from four in the morning till twelve before we broke our fast, and from that time till eleven or twelve at night. I should say that on the average, and taking all the year round, we laboured eighteen hours a day well told. He was a captain of the patrol, which went out every Wednesday and Saturday night, hunting "stray niggers," and to see that none of the neighbors' people were [away] from quarters.

I remained at James Davis's for nearly eighteen months. Once during that period, I remember he took me into the town to a tavern kept by one Captain Jemmy Duprey. There was a negro speculator there, on the look-out for bargains, but he would not have me. I did not know where I was going when my master took me with him, but when I got back I told my mother, who cried over me, and said she was very glad I had not been sold away from her.

But the time arrived when we were to be finally separated. Owing to a considerable rise in the price of cotton, there came a great demand for slaves in Georgia. One day a negro speculator named Starling Finney arrived at James Davis's place. He left his drove on the highway, in charge of one of his companions, and made his way up to our plantation, prospecting for negroes. It happened that James Davis had none that suited Finney, but being in want of money, as he was building a new house, and Finney being anxious for a deal, my master called me up and offered to sell me. I was then about or nearly ten years of age, and after some chaffering about terms, Finney agreed to purchase me by the pound.[36]

How I watched them whilst they were driving this bargain! and how I speculated upon the kind of man he was who sought to buy me! His venomous countenance inspired me with mortal terror, and I almost felt the heavy thong of the great riding-whip he held in his hand, twisting round my shoulders. He was a large, tall fellow, and might have killed me easily with one blow from his huge fist. He had left his horse at the gate, and when the bargain for me was struck, he went out and led him to the door, where he took the saddle off. I wondered what this was for, though suspicious that it had something to do with me; nor had I long to wait before I knew. A ladder was set upright against the end of the building outside, to one rung of which they made a stilyard fast.[37] The first thing Finney did was to weigh his saddle, the weight of which he knew, to see whether the stilyard was accurately adjusted. Having satisfied himself of this, a rope was brought, both ends of which were tied together, so that it formed a large noose or loop. This was hitched over the hook of the stilyard, and I was seated in the loop. After I had been weighed, there was a deduction made for the rope. I do not recollect what I weighed, but the price I was sold for amounted to three hundred and ten dollars. Within five minutes after, Finney paid the money, and I was marched off. I looked round and saw my poor mother stretching out her hands after me. She ran up and overtook us, but Finney, who was behind me, and between me and my mother, would not let her approach, though she begged and prayed to be allowed to kiss me for the last time, and bid me good bye. I was so stupefied with grief and fright, that I could not shed a tear, though my heart was bursting. At last we got to the gate, and I turned round to see whether I could not get a chance of kissing my mother. She saw me, and made a dart forward to meet me, but Finney gave me a hard push, which sent me spinning through the gate. He then slammed it to and shut it in my mother's face. That was the last time I ever saw her, nor do I know whether she is alive or dead at this hour.

We were in a lane now, about a hundred and fifty yards in length, and which led from the gate to the highway. I walked on before Finney, utterly unconscious of anything. I seemed to have become quite bewildered. I was aroused from this state of stupor by seeing that we had reached the main road, and had come up with a gang of negroes, some of whom were handcuffed two and two, and fastened to a long chain running between the two ranks. There were also a good many women and children, but none of these

36. For an illustration of a slave woman being sold by the pound, see the frontispiece in Michael Tadman's *Speculators and Slaves.* Editor.

37. Stilyard: a water tub suspended from a strong frame. Editor.

were chained. The children seemed to be all above ten years of age, and I soon learnt that they had been purchased in different places, and were for the most part strangers to one another and to the negroes in the coffle. They were waiting for Finney to come up. I fell into the rank, and we set off on our journey to Georgia.

I Am Sold Again. How I Fared.

Our journey lasted six weeks, as we made a good many stoppages by the way, to enable the speculator, Finney, to buy up, and change away, and dispose of his slaves. I do not recollect the names of all the places we passed through. We crossed the Roanoke river by ferry, and went on to Halifax, and from there to Raleigh in North Carolina. Several incidents occurred on the road, of which I will relate only two.

When I joined the coffle, there was in it a negro woman named Critty, who had belonged to one Hugh Benford. She was married, in the way that slaves are, but as she had no children, she was compelled to take a second husband. Still she did not have any offspring. This displeased her master, who sold her to Finney. Her anguish was intense, and within about four days from the time I saw her first, she died of grief. It happened in the night, whilst we were encamped in the woods. We set off in the morning, leaving her body there. We noticed, however, that two of Finney's associates remained behind, as we conjectured to dispose of the corpse. They fetched up with us again about two hours after.

The other incident was the stealing of a young negro girl. An old lady whose name I do not remember, and who was going into Georgia, travelled with the drove for the sake of society. She was accompanied by her waiting-maid, a young woman about twenty years of age, and of smart appearance. When we stopped at night, the old lady would be driven to some planter's house to lodge, and her horses be sent back to feed with ours. The girl remained with us. This was cheaper for the old lady than having to pay for the keep of her horses and her maid. In the morning her horses would be sent to the place where she had lodged, and she would drive on until she overtook us on the road, and then take up her maid. Finney determined to steal this girl. One morning, we being then on our way through South Carolina, the old lady's horses were sent as usual to the house where she had staid [*sic*] the night, and we went on. Instead, however, of keeping the direct road, Finney turned off and went through the woods, so that we gave the poor girl's mistress the slip. She was then forced to get up in the wagon with Finney, who brutally ill-used her, and permitted his companions to treat her in the same manner. This continued for several days, until we got to Augusta, in the state of Georgia, where Finney sold her. Our women talked about this very much, and many of them cried and said it was a great shame.

At last we stopped at one Ben Tarver's place in Jones County, Georgia. This man was a Methodist Minister, and had a cotton plantation and a good many slaves. . . . He was reputed to be a very bad master, but a very good preacher. During the time I staid there, which was two weeks, Finney used to take out his slaves every day to try and sell them, bringing those back whom he failed to dispose of. Those who did not go out with Finney for the market were made to work in Tarver's cotton fields, but they did not get anything extra to eat, though he profited by their labour. In these two weeks Finney disposed of a good many of his drove, and he became anxious to sell the rest, for he wanted to take another journey into Virginia, on a fresh speculation. One day I was dressed in a new pair of pantaloons and a new shirt, made from part of the tilt of a waggon in which we children sometimes slept. I soon found out why I was made so smart, for I was taken to Millidgeville with some other lads and there put up at auction.

This happened to me some time in the month of March. The sale took place in a kind of shed. The auctioneer did not like my appearance. He told Finney in private, who was holding me by the hand, that I was old and hard-looking, and not well grown, and that I should not fetch a price. In truth I was not much to look at. I was worn down by fatigue and poor living till my bones stuck up almost through my skin, and my hair was burnt to a brown red from exposure to the sun. I was not, however, very well pleased to hear myself run down. I remember Finney answered the auctioneer that I should be sure to grow a big-made man, and bade him, if he doubted his judgement, examine my feet, which were large, and proved that I would be strong and stout some day. My looks and my condition, nevertheless, did not recommend me, and I was knocked down to a man named Thomas Stevens for three hundred and fifty dollars: so Finney made forty dollars by me. Thomas Stevens could not pay cash for me, so I went back to Ben Tarver's that night, but next morning Finney and one of his associates, Hartwell Tarver, Ben's brother, took me round to Steven's place, and the money having been paid, I was again handed over to a new master.

2.10. A British Traveler Describes a Coffle of Slaves Fording a Mountain River in Virginia

The author of this piece, George William Featherstonhaugh, was a British geographer who, among other notable achievements, helped to determine the boundary between the United States and Canada under the 1842 Webster-Ashburton Treaty. A traveler in the American and Canadian west early in life, in the 1840s he undertook an extended journey through the United States from Washington, D.C., to the Mexican border, during which he reached a point in Virginia near the sources of streams flowing into both the Gulf of Mexico and the Atlantic Ocean. Here in the Allegheny Mountains early on a cool morning he observed a coffle of slaves fording the New River, a tributary of the Kanawha River, which flows westward into the Ohio. In addition to his description of the slaves crossing the stream, the author offers brief but accurate explanations of the internal traffic and its operation, reasoning that for slaves the trade was "a greater curse than slavery itself," since by its very nature it resulted in the permanent division of families. Like many educated nineteenth-century writers, however, Featherstonhaugh seems to have acquired from his culture some typically false assumptions regarding the nature of black people.

SOURCE: G. W. Featherstonhaugh, F.R.S., F.G.S., *Excursion through the Slave States, from Washington on the Potomac to the Frontier of Mexico; with Sketches of Popular Manners and Geological Notices* (New York: Harper & Brothers, 1844), pp. 36–38.

"A Melancholy Spectacle."

Just as we reached New River in the early grey of the morning, we came up with a singular spectacle, the most striking one of the kind I have ever witnessed. It was a camp of negro slave-drivers, just packing up to start; they had about three hundred slaves with them, who had bivouacked the preceding night in *chains* in the woods; these they were conducting to Natchez, upon the Mississippi River, to work upon the sugar plantations in Louisiana. It resembled one of those coffles of slaves spoken of by Mungo Park [in *Travels in the Interior Districts of Africa,* London, 1799], except that they had a caravan of nine waggons and single-horse carriages, for the purpose of conducting the white people, and any of the blacks that should fall lame, to which they were now putting the horses to pursue their march. The female slaves were, some of them, sitting on logs of wood, whilst others were standing, and a great many little black children were warming themselves at the fires of the bivouac. In front of them all, and prepared for the march, stood, in double files, about two hundred male slaves, *manacled and chained to each other*. I had never seen so revolting a sight before! Black men in fetters, torn from the lands where they were born, from the ties they had formed, and from the comparatively easy condition which agricultural

8. A Coffle of Slaves Passing from Virginia to Tennessee. Courtesy of the Colonial Williamsburg Foundation, Williamsburg, Virginia.

labour affords, and driven by white men, with liberty and equality in their mouths, to a distant and unhealthy country, to perish in the sugar-mills of Louisiana, where the duration of life for a sugar-mill slave does not exceed seven years! To make this spectacle still more disgusting and hideous, some of the principal white slave-drivers, who were tolerably well dressed, and had broad-brimmed hats on, *with black crape round them,* were standing near, laughing and smoking cigars. . . .

[W]e drove on, and having forded the river in a flat-bottomed boat, drew up on the road, where I persuaded the driver to wait until we had witnessed the crossing of the river by the "gang," as it was called.

It was an interesting but melancholy spectacle to see them effect the passage of the river: first, a man on horseback selected a shallow place in the ford for the male slaves; then followed a waggon and four horses, attended by another man on horseback. The other waggons contained the children and some that were lame, whilst the scows, or flat-boats, crossed the women and some of the people belonging to the caravan. There was much method and vigilance observed, for this was one of the situations where the gangs—always watchful to obtain their liberty—often show a disposition to mutiny, knowing that if one or two of them could wrench their manacles off, they could soon free the rest, and either disperse themselves or over-power and slay their sordid keepers, and fly to the Free States. The slave-drivers, aware of this disposition in the unfortunate negroes, endeavour to mitigate their discontent by feeding them well on the march, and by en-couraging them to sing "Old Virginia never tire," to the banjo.

The poor negro slave is naturally a cheerful, laughing animal, and even when driven through the wilderness in chains, if he is well fed and kindly treated, is seldom melancholy; for his thoughts have not been taught to stray to the future, and his condition is so degraded, that if the food and warmth his desires are limited to are secured to him, he is singularly docile. It is only when he is ill-treated and roused to desperation, that his vindictive and sav-age nature breaks out. But these gangs are accompanied by other negroes trained by the slave-dealers to drive the rest, whom they amuse by lively sto-ries, boasting of the fine warm climate they are going to, and the oranges and sugar which are there to be had for nothing: in proportion as they recede from the Free States, the danger of revolt diminishes, for in the Southern Slave-States all men have an interest in protecting this infernal trade of slave-driving, which, to the negro, is a greater curse than slavery itself, since it too often dissevers forever those affecting natural ties which even a slave can form, by tearing, without an instant's notice, the husband from the wife, and the children from their parents; sending the one to the sugar plantations of Louisiana, another to the cotton-lands of Arkansas, and the rest to Texas. . . .

This land traffic . . . has grown out of the wide-spreading population of the United States, the annexation of Louisiana, and the increased culti-vation of cotton and sugar. . . . Hence negroes have risen greatly in price, from 500 to 1000 dollars, according to their capacity. Slaves being thus in demand, a detestable branch of business—where sometimes a great deal of money is made—has very naturally arisen in a country filled with specula-tors. The soil of Virginia has gradually become exhausted with repeated crops of tobacco and Indian corn; and when to this is added the constant subdivision of property which has overtaken every family since the aboli-tion of entails [during and after the Revolutionary War], it follows of course that many of the small proprietors, in their efforts to keep up ap-pearances, have become embarrassed in their circumstances, and, when they are pinched, are compelled to sell a negro or two. The wealthier proprietors also have frequently fractious and bad slaves, which, when they cannot be reclaimed, are either put into jail, or into those depots which exist in all the large towns for the reception of slaves who are sold, until they can be removed. All this is very well known to the slave-driver, one of whose associates goes annually to the Southwestern States, to make his contacts with those planters there who are in want of slaves for the next season. These fellows then scour the country to make purchases. Those who are bought out of jail are always put in fetters, as well as any of those whom they may suspect of an intention to escape. The women and grown-up girls are usually sold into the cotton-growing States, the men and the boys to the rice and sugar plantations. Persons with large capital are actively concerned in this trade, some of whom have amassed considerable fortunes. But occasionally these dealers in men are made to pay fearfully the penalty of their nefarious occupation. I was told that only two or three months before I passed this way a "gang" had surprised their conductors when off their guard, and had killed some of them with axes.

2.11. "How Can We Sing the Lord's Song in a Strange Land?" The Abolitionist and Former Slave, Frederick Douglass, Denounces the Evils of the Domestic Slave Trade (1852)

The remarkable Frederick Douglass—son of a slave woman and a white master, self-educated, a successful fugitive from bondage, a ship's artisan under slavery and later in New Bedford, Connecticut, a lecturer for the Massachusetts Anti-Slavery Society, author of autobiographies, and publisher of the periodicals *North Star* and *Douglass' Monthly* (see Docs. 3.22 and 3.26)—was also in his childhood a witness to the internal slave trade, particularly as it was carried on in Baltimore. This firsthand experience with the traffic may account for the extraordinary emotion and anguish with which Douglass analyzes and denounces it in the following public address, delivered in Corinthian Hall in Rochester, New York, on July 5, 1852.

SOURCE: Philip S. Foner, ed., *The Life and Writings of Frederick Douglass* (New York: International Publishers, 1950), vol. 2, pp. 188–95.

The Meaning of the Fourth of July for the Negro, Speech at Rochester, New York, July 5, 1852.

Fellow-citizens, pardon me, allow me to ask, why I am called upon to speak here to-day? What have I, or those I represent, to do with your national independence? Are the great principles of political freedom and of natural justice, embodied in that Declaration of Independence, extended to us? and am I, therefore, called upon to bring our humble offering to the national altar, and to confess the benefits and express devout gratitude for the blessings resulting from your independence to us?

Would to God, both for your sakes and ours, that an affirmative answer could be truthfully returned to these questions! Then would my task be light, and my burden easy and delightful. For *who* is there so cold, that a nation's sympathy could not warm him? Who so obdurate and dead to the claims of gratitude, that would not thankfully acknowledge such priceless benefits? Who so stolid and selfish, that would not give his voice to swell the hallelujahs of a nation's jubilees, when the chains of servitude had been torn from his limbs? I am not that man. In a case like that, the dumb might eloquently speak, and the "lame man leap as an hart."

But such is not the state of the case. I say it with a sad sense of the disparity between us. I am not included within the pale of this glorious anniversary! Your high independence only reveals the immeasurable distance between us. The blessings in which you, this day, rejoice, are not enjoyed in common.—The rich inheritance of justice, liberty, prosperity and independence, bequeathed by your fathers, is shared by you, not by me. The sunlight that brought light and healing to you, has brought stripes and death to me. This fourth of July is *yours,* not *mine. You* may rejoice, *I* must mourn. To drag a man in fetters into the grand illuminated temple of liberty, and call upon him to join you in joyous anthems, were inhuman mockery and sacrilegious irony. Do you mean, citizens, to mock me, by asking me to speak to-day? If so, there is a parallel to your conduct. And let me warn you that it is dangerous to copy the example of a nation whose crimes, towering up to heaven, were thrown down by the breath of the Almighty, burying that nation in irrevocable ruin! I can to-day take up the plaintive lament of a peeled and woe-smitten people!

"By the rivers of Babylon, there we sat down. Yea! we wept when we remembered Zion. We hanged our harps upon the willows in the midst thereof. For there, they that carried us away captive, required of us a song; and they who wasted us required of us mirth, saying, Sing us one of the songs of Zion. How can we sing the Lord's song in a strange land? If I forget thee, O Jerusalem, let my right hand forget her cunning. If I do not remember thee, let my tongue cleave to the roof of my mouth." [Psalm 137: 1–6.]

Fellow-citizens, above your national, tumultuous joy, I hear the mournful wail of millions! whose chains, heavy and grievous yesterday, are, to-day, rendered more intolerable by the jubilee shouts that reach them. If I do forget, if I do not faithfully remember those bleeding children of sorrow this day, "may my right hand forget her cunning, and may my tongue cleave to the roof of my mouth!" To forget them, to pass lightly over their wrongs, and to chime in with the popular theme, would be treason most scandalous and shocking, and would make me a reproach before God and the world. My subject, then, fellow-citizens, is American slavery. I shall see this day and its popular characteristics from the slave's point of view. Standing there identified with the American bondman, making his wrongs mine, I do not hesitate to declare, with all my soul, that the character and conduct of this nation never looked blacker to me than on this 4th of July! Whether we turn to the declarations of the past, or to the professions of the present, the conduct of the nation seems equally hideous and revolting. America is false to the past, false to the present, and solemnly binds herself to be false to the future. Standing with God and the crushed and bleeding slave on this occasion, I will, in the name of humanity which is outraged, in the name of liberty which is fettered, in the name of the constitution and the Bible which are disregarded and trampled upon, dare to call in question and to denounce, with all the emphasis I can command, everything that serves to perpetuate slavery—the great sin and shame of America! "I will not equivocate; I will not excuse" [words of the abolitionist, William Lloyd Garrison]; I will use the severest language I can command; and yet not one word shall escape me that any man, whose judgment is not blinded by prejudice, or who is not at heart a slaveholder, shall not confess to be right and just.

But I fancy I hear some one of my audience say, "It is just in this circumstance that you and your brother abolitionists fail to make a favorable impression on the public mind. Would you argue more, and denounce less; would you persuade more, and rebuke less; your cause would be much more likely to succeed." But, I submit, where all is plain there is nothing to be argued. What point in the anti-slavery creed would you have me argue? On what branch of the subject do the people of this country need light? Must I undertake to prove that the slave is a man? The point is conceded already. Nobody doubts it. The slaveholders themselves acknowledge it in the enactment of laws for their government. They acknowledge it when they punish disobedience on the part of the slave. There are seventy-two crimes in the State of Virginia which, if committed by a black man (no matter how ignorant he be), subject him to the punishment of death; while only two of the same crimes will subject a white man to the like punishment. What is this but the acknowledgment that the slave is a moral, intellectual, and responsible being? The manhood of the slave is conceded. It is admitted in the fact that Southern statute books are covered with enactments forbidding, under severe fines and penalties, the teaching of the slave to read and write. When you can point to any such laws in reference to the beasts of the field, then I may consent to argue the manhood of the slave. When the dogs in your streets, when the fowls of the air, when the cattle on your hills, when the fish of the sea, and the reptiles that crawl, shall be unable to distinguish the slave from the brute, *then* will I argue with you that the slave is a man!

For the present, it is enough to affirm the equal manhood of the Negro race. Is it not astonishing that, while we are ploughing, planting, and reaping, using all kinds of mechanical tools, erecting houses, constructing bridges, building ships, working in metals of brass, iron, copper, silver and gold; that, while we are reading, writing and ciphering, acting as clerks, merchants and secretaries, having among us lawyers, doctors, ministers, poets, authors, editors, orators and teachers; that, while we are engaged in all manner of enterprises common to other men, digging gold in California, capturing the whale in the Pacific, feeding sheep and cattle on the hillside, living, moving, acting, thinking, planning, living in families as husbands, wives and children, and, above all, confessing and worshipping the Christian's God, and looking hopefully for life and immortality beyond the grave, we are called upon to prove that we are men!

Would you have me argue that man is entitled to liberty? that he is the rightful owner of his own body? You have already declared it. Must I argue the wrongfulness of slavery? Is that a question for Republicans? Is it to be settled by the rules of logic and argumentation, as a matter beset with great difficulty, involving a doubtful application of the principle of justice, hard to be understood? How should I look to-day in the presence of Americans, dividing, and subdividing a discourse, to show that men have a natural right to freedom? speaking of it relatively and positively, negatively and affirmatively. To do so, would be to make myself ridiculous, and to offer an insult to your understanding.—There is not a man beneath the canopy of heaven that does not know that slavery is wrong for *him*.

What, am I to argue that it is wrong to make men brutes, to rob them of their liberty, to work them without wages, to keep them ignorant of their relations to their fellow men, to beat them with sticks, to flay their flesh with the lash, to load their limbs with irons, to hunt them with dogs, to sell them at auction, to sunder their families, to knock out their teeth, to burn their flesh, to starve them into obedience and submission to their masters? Must I argue that a system thus marked with blood, and stained with pollution, is *wrong?* No! I will not. I have better employment for my time and strength than such arguments would imply.

What, then, remains to be argued. Is it that slavery is not divine; that God did not establish it; that our doctors of divinity are mistaken? There is blasphemy in the thought. That which is inhuman cannot be divine. *Who* can reason on such a proposition? They that can, may; I cannot. The time for such argument is passed.

At a time like this, scorching irony, not convincing argument, is needed. O! had I the ability, and could reach the nation's ear, I would, to-day, pour out a fiery stream of biting ridicule, blasting reproach, withering sarcasm, and stern rebuke. For it is not light that is needed, but fire; it is not the gentle shower, but thunder. We need the storm, the whirlwind, and the earthquake. The feeling of the nation must be quickened; the conscience of the nation must be roused; the propriety of the nation must be startled; the hypocrisy of the nation must be exposed; and its crimes against God, and man, must be proclaimed and denounced.

What, to the American slave, is the 4th of July? I answer; a day that reveals to him, more than all other days in the year, the gross injustice and cruelty to which he is the constant victim. To him, your celebration is a sham; your boasted liberty, an unholy alliance; your national greatness, swelling vanity; your sounds of rejoicing are empty and heartless; your denunciation of tyrants, brass fronted impudence; your shouts of liberty and equality, hollow mockery; your prayers and hymns, your sermons and thanksgivings, with all your religious parade and solemnity, are, to Him, mere bombast, fraud, deception, impiety, and hypocrisy—a thin veil to cover up crimes which would disgrace a nation of savages. There is not a nation on the earth guilty of practices more shocking and bloody than are the people of the United States, at this very hour.

Go where you may, search where you will, roam through all the monarchies and despotisms of the Old World, travel through South America, search out every abuse, and when you have found the last, lay your facts by the side of the everyday practices of this nation, and you will say with me, that, for revolting barbarity and shameless hypocrisy, America reigns without a rival.

Take the American slave-trade, which we are told by the papers, is especially prosperous just now. Ex-senator [Thomas Hart] Benton [of Missouri] tells us that the price of men was never higher than now. He mentions the fact to show that slavery is in no danger. This trade is one of the peculiarities of American institutions. It is carried on in all the large towns and cities in one-half of this confederacy; and millions are pocketed every year by dealers in this horrid traffic. In several states this trade is a chief source of wealth. It is called (in contradistinction to the foreign slave trade) *"the internal slave-trade."* It is, probably, called so, too, in order to divert from it the horror with which the foreign slave-trade is contemplated. That trade has long since been denounced by this government as piracy. It has been denounced with burning words, from the high places of the nation, as an execrable traffic. To arrest it, to put an end to it, this nation keeps a squadron, at immense cost, on the coast of Africa. Everywhere, in this country, it is safe to speak of this foreign slave-trade as a most inhuman traffic, opposed alike to the laws of God and man. The duty to extirpate and destroy it, is admitted even by our doctors of divinity. In order to put an end to it, some of these last have consented that their colored brethren (nominally free) should leave this country, and establish themselves on the western coast of Africa! It is, however, a notable fact, that, while so much execration is poured out by Americans upon those engaged in the foreign slave-trade, the men engaged in the slave-trade between the states pass without condemnation, and their business is deemed honorable.

Behold the practical operation of this internal slave trade, the American slave-trade, sustained by American politics and American religion. Here you will see men and women reared like swine for the market. You know what is a swine-drover? I will show you a man-drover. They inhabit all our southern states. They perambulate the country, and crowd the highways of the nation, with droves of human stock. You will see one of these human flesh jobbers, armed with pistol, whip, and bowie-knife, driving a company of a hundred men, women, and children, from the Potomac to the slave market at New Orleans. These wretched people are to be sold singly, or in lots, to suit purchasers. They are food for the cotton-field and the deadly sugar-mill. Mark the sad procession, as it moves wearily along, and the inhuman wretch who drives them. Hear his savage yells and his blood-curdling oaths, as he hurries on his affrighted captives! There, see the old man with locks thinned and gray. Cast one glance, if you please, upon that young mother, whose shoulders are bare to the scorching sun, her briny tears falling on the brow of the babe in her arms. She, too, that girl of thirteen, weeping, *yes!* weeping, as she thinks of the mother from whom she has been torn! The drove moves tardily. Heat and sorrow have nearly consumed their strength; suddenly you hear a quick snap, like the discharge of a rifle; the fetters clank, and the chain rattles simultaneously; your ears are saluted with a scream, that seems to have torn its way to the centre of your soul! The crack you heard was the sound of the slave-whip; the scream you heard was from the woman you saw with the babe. Her speed had faltered under the weight of her child and her chains! that gash on her shoulder tells her to move on. Follow this drove to New Orleans. Attend the auction; see

men examined like horses; see the forms of women rudely and brutally exposed to the shocking gaze of American slave-buyers. See this drove sold
and separated forever; and never forget the deep, sad sobs that arose from
that scattered multitude. Tell me, citizens, where, under the sun, can you
witness a spectacle more fiendish and shocking? Yet this is but a glance at
the American slave-trade, as it exists, at this moment, in the ruling part of
the United States.

I was born amid such sights and scenes. To me the American slave-
trade is a terrible reality. When a child, my soul was often pierced with a
sense of its horrors. I lived on Philpot Street, Fell's Point, Baltimore, and
have watched from the wharves the slave ships in the Basin, anchored from
the shore, with their cargoes of human flesh, waiting for favorable winds to
waft them down the Chesapeake. There was, at that time, a grand slave
mart kept at the head of Pratt Street, by Austin Woldfolk [*sic*]. His agents
were sent into every town and county in Maryland, announcing their arrival, through the papers, and on flaming hand-bills, headed "cash for Negroes." These men were generally well dressed men, and very captivating in
their manners; ever ready to drink, to treat, and to gamble. The fate of
many a slave has depended upon the turn of a single card; and many a child
has been snatched from the arms of its mother by bargains arranged in a
state of brutal drunkenness.

The flesh-mongers gather up their victims by dozens, and drive them,
chained, to the general depot at Baltimore. When a sufficient number have
been collected here, a ship is chartered for the purpose of conveying the forlorn crew to Mobile, or to New Orleans. From the slave prison to the ship,
they are usually driven in the darkness of night; for since the anti-slavery
agitation, a certain caution is observed.

In the deep, still darkness of midnight, I have been often aroused by
the dead, heavy footsteps, and the piteous cries of the chained gangs that
passed our door. The anguish of my boyish heart was intense; and I was
often consoled, when speaking to my mistress in the morning, to hear her
say that the custom was very wicked; that she hated to hear the rattle of the
chains, and the heart-rending cries. I was glad to find one who sympathized
with me in my horror.

Fellow-citizens, this murderous traffic is, to-day, in active operation in
this boasted republic. In the solitude of my spirit I see clouds of dust raised
on the highways of the south; I see the bleeding footsteps; I hear the doleful wail of fettered humanity on the way to the slave-markets, where the
victims are to be sold like *horses, sheep,* and *swine,* knocked off to the highest bidder. There I see the tenderest ties ruthlessly broken, to gratify the

lust, caprice, and rapacity of the buyers and sellers of men. My soul sickens at the sight.

> "Is this the land your fathers loved?
> The freedom which they toil to win?
> Is this the earth wheron they moved?
> Are these the graves they slumber in? . . .

2.12. "No Mere Invention of the Novelist." A Scotsman Reports on the Enslavement of a Free Citizen of Pennsylvania

William Chambers, author of Document 2.7, an account of slave auctions in Richmond, Virginia, declared some years after undergoing that experience: "The sight of a few Slave Sales has a wonderful effect in awakening the feelings on the subject of Slavery. The thing is seen to be an undeniable reality—no mere invention of the novelist.[38] From time to time, the spectacle of an auction-stand on which one man is selling another flashes back upon the mind. For three years I have been haunted by recollections of that saddening scene, and taken a gradually deepening interest in American slavery—its present condition, its mysterious future." One result of Chambers's preoccupation with slavery was the book *American Slavery and Colour* (1857), which analyzes historical aspects of U.S. slavery as well as such problems as the conflict over slavery in Kansas and the emerging national crisis. The excerpt below, drawn from the appendix of Chambers's book, offers another example of an unjust legal anomaly that was long in force not only in the United States but also—unknown to the vast majority of Americans—in faraway Brazil, where its victims were known as *bens do evento,* or "property of the wind" (see Doc. 2.5, note 34).

SOURCE: William Chambers, *American Slavery and Colour* (Edinburgh, Scotland: W. & R. Chambers, 1857), pp. 186–88.

Dangerous Condition of Coloured Persons.

It has been stated that free persons of colour from the northern states are in danger of lapsing into slavery, by merely intruding within the verge of a slave state. In Maryland, there was a law passed in 1839, to prohibit the ingress of free persons of colour, under the penalty of a heavy fine. The en-

38. Probably a reference to Harriet Beecher Stowe. Editor.

The Internal Slave Trade of the United States

actment is as follows: "No free negro or mulatto, belonging to, or residing in any other state, is permitted to come into Maryland, whether such free negro or mulatto intends settling in this state or not, under the penalty of 20 dollars for the first offense." For a second offence, the penalty is 500 dollars; and, failing the payment of such fines, the offender "shall be committed to the jail of the county, and shall be sold by the sheriff at public sale to the highest bidder."

Under this law, a free coloured person wandering inadvertently into Maryland in quest of employment, may be seized, and if poor and unable to pay the fine, sold after a few days' public notice, just as if he were a stray heifer. A case of this kind occurred not long ago.

In 1851, there resided in Philadelphia a negro named Edward Davis, who, finding employment fail, went to the country in quest of the means of subsistence. He could not have possessed very bright intelligence, for he ought to have known that it was dangerous for him to enter the borders of a slave state. His original intention was to go no further than Hollidaysburgh, a flourishing town in Blair county, Pennsylvania; but for some reason he abandoned this design, and crossing the Susquehanna, reached the populous village of Havre de Grace, in Maryland. Here he sought for, and obtained employment; and was thoughtlessly pursuing his occupation when he was arrested and taken before a magistrate, to answer the charge of having violated the law, which prohibits the settlement of free negroes in the state. The offence was clear, and the fine of twenty dollars incurred. Destitute of money, and without friends, he was confined in prison, where he lay about two months. At the end of this period, he was brought out, and after due advertisement, sold by auction to pay his fine and expenses—altogether amounting to fifty dollars. The following is a copy of the sheriff's certificate of sale, which we give as a curiosity:

"State of Maryland, Harford county—I, Robert M'Gan, sheriff of Harford county, do hereby certify, that whereas negro Ned Davis was found guilty by the Orphan Court of Harford county of a violation of the Act of Assembly of the state of Maryland, passed 1839, chapter 38; and the said negro having refused to pay the fine and costs, as in the said law directed, I did, having first given the notice prescribed by law, expose the said negro at public sale, at the court-house doors in Bell Air, and Dr. John G. Archer, of Louisiana, being the highest bidder, became the purchaser of the said negro. Given under my hand and seal, this tenth day of November 1851. Robert M'Gan, sheriff."

Davis, now a slave, was subsequently transferred from master to master; and we find that, in June 1852, he was sold to a Mr. Dean of Macon,

Georgia, for 300 dollars. As this is only about a third of the market-value of an able-bodied negro, we infer that he was past the prime of life, or otherwise defective. In one of the accounts of the transaction, he is spoken of as being thirty-four years of age. Be that as it may, Ned Davis was, to all intents and purposes, a slave; and as such, was first employed to cook for a large number of slaves in Baltimore; and subsequently, on being purchased by Mr. Dean, was sent southward, through Washington and Charleston, to Georgia. On arriving in Macon, he was put to work on a railway; but the labour of an excavator being beyond his strength, his health failed, and, as a relief, he was placed on a cotton-plantation. He was afterwards sent back to the railway. This second time, however, he utterly broke down, and was removed to an hospital. This occurred in July 1853. In the hospital, he related his history to the attending physicians, who, taking pity on him, offered to buy him for 400 dollars; but the price was refused. Although shattered in health and partially lame, the unfortunate Ned was again put to some kind of work, and he continued in servitude till the 12th of March 1854. On this day, after long brooding over his wrongs, he ran away from Macon, and went to Savannah, a seaport from which steam-vessels traded to northern free states. Davis's object was to get on board one of these vessels; and he secreted himself in a stable till the 14th, on which day he went on board the steamer *Keystone State,* which was to sail next morning for Philadelphia. The remainder of the narrative may be given in the words of a New York newspaper:

"At nine o'clock the next morning, the steamer sailed with Davis on board. The following day, the men, while heaving the lead, heard a voice from under the guards of the boat, calling for them to throw him a rope. Upon examination, it was found that the voice proceeded from a coloured man, concealed on a beam under the guards of the wheel-house. He was rescued from his perilous situation, in a state of great exhaustion: his clothes were saturated with sea-water, as the sea had become rough, and he was dipped in the water at every rock of the vessel. The hands furnished him with a dry suit, and made him comfortable; but the commander of the boat was differently disposed. Fearing the effects of the Georgian law, in case he should bring a slave to a free state, he ordered his vessel to put into Newcastle, Delaware, where he had the unfortunate man imprisoned, with the intention, it is stated, of taking him back to Savannah on his return-trip. But the facts of the case having leaked out, public sympathy was enlisted, and a determination shewn that Davis should not go back to Georgia, unless it could be established that he was not entitled to his freedom. On the 20th of March, the case was brought before Justice Bradford, of Newcastle. A number of witnesses were examined, and his freedom clearly proved. On hearing this testimony in his favour, the magistrate discharged him from custody, there being no reason why a free citizen of Pennsylvania should be kept in a Delaware prison, with no crime charged against him. After his discharge, and before he had left the magistrate's office, the commander of the *Keystone State* appeared; made affidavit that he believed Davis to be a fugitive slave, and also a fugitive from justice; whereupon he was detained, and again shut up in prison. On the return of the captain of the steamer to Savannah, measures were adopted to reclaim possession of Davis by legal proceedings. The case came on for trial at Newcastle, April 16; and it was clearly proved by evidence, that the negro had been legally seized and sold in Maryland, and transferred by his owners to his present claimant, Mr. Dean. A decision was given accordingly: the runaway being adjudged to be a slave, and put at the disposal of his proprietor. Whether he was actually taken back to Georgia is not stated. If alive, there can be no doubt of his being still in a condition of slavery. The laws of Pennsylvania possess no power to reclaim a citizen, whose liberty is legally forfeited in another state; and if the friends of Ned Davis fail to buy him, there are, so far as we are aware, no other lawful means by which they can restore him to freedom.

2.13. A Free Man Seized, Jailed, and Advertised for Sale in the Nation's Capital Petitions Congress for His Release

On December 28, 1843, abolitionist congressman Joshua Giddings of Ohio presented the following petition to Congress on behalf of a man named William Jones, who claiming the status of a free-born citizen of Virginia, had nevertheless been seized in the city of Washington as a presumed slave, and after weeks of imprisonment, was advertised for sale by a U.S. marshall. After a bitter debate on the floor of the House of Representatives, Jones's petition was transferred to a congressional committee, which gave him "no satisfaction," but instead initiated legislation to apply the Fugitive Slave Act of 1793 to the District of Columbia. Nothing further is known about the fate of William Jones.

SOURCE: *Congressional Globe,* December 28, 1843, 25th Congress, 1st Session, vol. 13, p. 78; reprinted by Herbert Aptheker in *A Documentary History of the Negro People in the United States* (New York: The Citadel Press, 1971), vol. 1, p. 236.

To the Congress of the United States:

The humble petition of William Jones, now a prisoner in the United States jail in Washington city, respectfully represents:

That your memorialist is a free citizen of the United States, born free in the State of Virginia, and has always been an industrious and honest citizen, chargeable with no crime; that, while enjoying his liberty in this city, he was seized, and, without any charge of crime, was thrown into jail, where he has been confined for several weeks, and is now advertised to be sold as a slave by the marshall of the United States to pay the expenses of his imprisonment, unless his owner shall appear; that your petitioner has no owner but his God, and owes no service but to his country; that it is hard for him to be imprisoned without fault, and then sold to pay the expense. He therefore prays that Congress will exert their powers for the protection of the weak, and procure for him that liberty and justice which are his right, and which he has a special claim for in the District, which is under the exclusive legislation of your honorable body.

2.14. A Creole Woman Describes Her Kidnapping as a Child in Louisiana and Her Life as a French Tutor in the Household of a Kentucky Slave Trader

This report by an elderly Creole woman, Mrs. M. S. Fayman, of her abduction as a child and forced transportation to Kentucky greatly differs from most accounts of the victims of the slave trade, not only in respect to her background and her exceptional occupation and privileged status during her time as a slave, but also concerning her kidnapper's intentions. The latter, a wealthy slave trader and tobacco farmer, seems to have been motivated by high aspirations for his children—so much so that he saw fit to seize an innocent ten-year-old child from her Catholic guardians to supply his offspring with a companion and tutor of French—which, of course, he might well have done without resorting to kidnapping or the use of force. In her account of her experiences the narrator offers glimpses of the lifestyle of a wealthy planter and his family, along with impressions of the harsh conditions he and his overseers inflicted upon 350 plantation workers, and the slaves he bought and sold.

SOURCE: George P. Rawick, ed., *The American Slave: A Composite Autobiography,* series 2, vol. 16, *Maryland Narratives,* pp. 10–13.

I was born in St. Nazaire Parish in Louisiana, about 60 miles south of Baton Rouge, in 1850. My father and mother were Creoles, both of them were people of wealth and prestige in their day and considered very influential. My father's name was Henri de Sales and mother's maiden name, Marguerite Sanchez de Haryne. I had two brothers Henri and Jackson named after General Jackson, both of whom died quite young, leaving me the only living child. Both mother and father were born and reared in Louisiana. We lived in a large and spacious house surrounded by flowers and situated on a farm containing about 750 acres, on which we raised pelicans for sale in the market at New Orleans.

When I was about 5 years old I was sent to a private school in Baton Rouge, conducted by French sisters, where I stayed until I was kidnapped in 1860. At that time I did not know how to speak English; French was the language spoken in my household and by the people in the parish.

Baton Rouge, situated on the Mississippi, was a river port and stopping place for all large river boats, especially between New Orleans and large towns and cities north. We children were taken out by the sisters after school and on Saturdays and holidays to walk. One of the places we went was the wharf. One day in June and on a Saturday a large boat was at the wharf going north on the Mississippi River. We children were there. Somehow, I was separated from the other children. I was taken up bodily by a white man, carried on the boat, put in a cabin and kept there until we got to Louisville, Kentucky, where I was taken off.

After I arrived in Louisville I was taken to a farm near Frankfort [Kentucky] and installed there virtually a slave until 1864, when I escaped through the kindness of a delightful Episcopalian woman from Cincinnati, Ohio. As I could not speak English, my chores were to act as a tutor and companion for the children of Pierce Buckran Haynes, a well known slave trader and plantation owner in Kentucky. Haynes wanted his children to speak French and it was my duty to teach them. I was the private companion of 3 girls and one small boy, each day I had to talk French and write French for them. They became very proficient in French and I in the rudiments of the English language.

I slept in the children's quarters with the Haynes' children, ate and played with them. I had all the privileges of the household accorded me with the exception of one, I never was taken off nor permitted to leave the plantation. While on the plantation I wore good clothes, similar to those of the white children. Haynes was a merciless brutal tyrant with his slaves, punishing them severely and cruelly both by the lash and in the jail on the plantation.

The name of the plantation where I was held as a slave was called Beatrice Manor, after the wife of Haynes. It contained 8000 acres, of which more than 6000 acres were under cultivation, and having about 350 colored slaves and 5 or 6 overseers all of whom were white. The overseers were the overlords of the manor; as Haynes dealt extensively in tobacco and trading in slaves, he was away from the plantation nearly all the time. There was located on the top of the large tobacco waterhouse a large bell, which was rung at sun up, twelve o'clock and at sundown, the year round. On the farm the slaves were assigned a task to do each day and in the event it was not finished they were severely whipped. While I never saw a slave whipped, I did see them afterwards, they were very badly marked and striped by the overseers who did the whipping.

I have been back to the farm on several occasions, the first time in 1872 when I took my father there to show him the farm. At that time it was owned by Colonel Hawkins, a Confederate Army officer.

Let me describe the huts, these buildings were built of stone, each one about 20 feet wide, 50 feet long, 9 feet high in the rear, about 12 feet high in front, with a slanting roof of chestnut boards and with a sliding door, two windows between each door back and front about 2 x 4 feet, at each end a door and window similar to those on the side. There were ten such buildings, to each building there was another building 12 x 15 feet, this was where the cooking was done. At each end of each building there was a fire place built and used for heating purposes. In front of each building there were barrels filled with water supplied by pipes from a large spring, situated about 300 yards on the side of a hill which was very rocky, where the stones were quarried to build the buildings on the farm. On the outside near each window and door there were iron rings firmly attached to the walls, through which an iron rod was inserted and locked each and every night, making it impossible for those inside to escape.

There was one building used as a jail, built of stone about 20 x 40 feet with a hip roof about 25 feet high, 2-story. On the ground in each end was a fire place; in one end a small room, which was used as an office; adjoining, there was another room where the whipping was done. To reach the second story there was built on the outside steps leading to a door, through which the female prisoners were taken to the room. All the buildings had dirt floors.

I do not know much about the Negroes on the plantation who were there at that time. Slaves were brought and taken away always chained together, men walking and women in ox carts. I had heard of several escapes and many were captured. One of the overseers had a pack of 6 or 8 trained blood hounds which were used to trace escaping slaves.

Before I close let me give you a sketch of my family tree. My grand-mother was a Haitian Negress, grandfather a Frenchman. My father was a Creole.

After returning home in 1864, I completed my high school education in New Orleans in 1870, graduated from Fisk University 1874, taught French there until 1883, married Prof. Fayman, teacher of history and English. Since then I have lived in Washington, New York, and Louisiana. For further information, write me c/o Y.W.C.A. (col.), Baltimore, to be forwarded.

2.15. Highborn "Soul Drivers"

The following selection is from a powerful book, *American Slavery As It Is,* collected and edited by the antislavery activist, Theodore D. Weld, with the assistance of his wife, Angelina Grimké Weld, and her sister, Sarah Grimké. The latter were members of a prominent slaveholding family of Charleston, South Carolina, who as young women moved to the North where they became abolitionists and campaigners for women's rights. Weld, a New Englander, was an itinerant lecturer against slavery in the 1830s, editor of publications of the American Anti-Slavery Society, and author of such works as *The Power of Congress over the District of Columbia* (1837), *The Bible against Slavery* (1837), and *Slavery and the Internal Slave Trade in the United States of America* (1841).

The present piece is Weld's caustic response to frequent claims by upper-class southerners that slave traders were "universally despised" and avoided by their own class. Weld argued that it was not the activity of slave trading that wealthy slaveholders despised and avoided, but rather the working-class status and vulgarity of most slave traders, observing at the same time that an individual of "good family" or a "gentleman of property and standing" who engaged in such activities did "not lose caste." He charged that some of the most respected members of the southern elite had been—or still were—actively engaged in the business of buying and selling slaves.

SOURCE: Theodore D. Weld, *American Slavery As It Is: Testimony of a Thousand Witnesses* (New York: American Anti-Slavery Society, 1839), pp. 173–74.

Notwithstanding the mass of testimony which has been presented establishing the fact that in the "public opinion" of the South the slaves find no protection, some may still claim that the "public opinion" exhibited . . . is not that of the *highest class of society at the South,* and in proof of this assertion, refer to the fact that Negro Brokers, Negro Speculators, Negro Auctioneers, and Negro Breeders, &c., are by that class universally despised and avoided, as are all who treat their slaves with cruelty. . . . As to the estimation in which "speculators," "soul drivers," &c. are held, we remark, that they are not despised because they *trade in slaves* but because they are *working* men, all such are despised by slaveholders. White drovers who go with droves of swine and cattle from the free states to the slave states, and Yankee pedlars who traverse the south, and white day-laborers are, in the main, equally despised, or, if negro-traders excite more contempt than drovers, pedlars, and day-laborers, it is because they are, as a class, more ignorant and vulgar, men from low families and boors in their manners. Ridiculous! to suppose that a people who have, *by law,* made men articles of trade equally with swine, should despise men-drovers and traders more than hog-drovers and traders. That they are not despised because it is their business to trade in *human beings* and bring them to market is plain from the fact that when some "gentleman of property and standing" and of a "good family" embarks in a negro speculation, and employs a dozen "soul drivers" to traverse the upper country, and drive to the south coffles of slaves, expending hundreds of thousands in his wholesale purchases, he does not lose caste. It is known in Alabama that Mr. Erwin, son-in-law of HON. HENRY CLAY, and brother of J. P. Erwin, formerly postmaster, and late mayor of the city of Nashville, laid the foundation of a princely fortune in the slave-trade, carried on from the Northern Slave States to the Planting South; that the Hon. H. Hitchcock, brother-in-law of Mr. E., and since one of the judges of the Supreme Court of Alabama, was interested with him in the traffic; and that a late member of the Kentucky Senate (Col. Wall) not only carried on the same business, a few years ago, but accompanied his droves in person down the Mississippi. Not as the *driver,* for that would be vulgar drudgery, beneath a gentleman, but as a nabob in state, ordering his understrappers.

It is also well known that President Jackson was a "soul driver," and that even so late as the year before the commencement of the last war [the War of 1812], he bought up a coffle of slaves and drove them down to Louisiana for sale.

THOMAS N. GADSDEN, Esq., the principal slave auctioneer in Charleston, S.C., is of one of the first families in the state, and moves in the very highest class of society there. He is a descendant of the distinguished General [Christopher] Gadsden of revolutionary memory, the most

9. Outdoor Slave Auction North of the Old Exchange, Charleston, March 10, 1853. From a sketch by Eyre Crowe, in *The Illustrated London News,* November 29, 1856, pp. 555–56.

prominent southern member in the Continental Congress of 1775 and afterwards elected lieutenant governor and then governor of the state. The Rev. Dr. Gadsden, rector of St. Philip's Church, Charleston, and the Rev. Phillip Gadsden, both prominent Episcopal clergymen in South Carolina, and Colonel James Gadsden of the United States army, after whom a county in Florida was recently named,[39] are all brothers of this Thomas N. Gadsden, Esq., the largest slave auctioneer in the state, under whose hammer men, women and children go off by thousands; its stroke probably sunders *daily* husbands and wives, parents and children, brothers and sisters, perhaps to see each other's faces no more. Now who supplies the auction table of this Thomas N. Gadsden, Esq., with its loads of human merchandise? These same detested "soul drivers" forsooth! They prowl through the country, buy, catch, and fetter them, and drive their chained coffles up to his stand, where Thomas N. Gadsden, Esq., knocks them off

39. James Gadsden is best known for the Gadsden Purchase of 1853, which he negotiated against Mexican popular opinion as U. S. ambassador to Mexico. An aide-de-camp of General Jackson, he was also involved in the removal of the Seminole Indians to South Florida.

to the highest bidder, to Ex-Governor Butler perhaps, or to Ex-Governor Hayne, or to Hon. Robert Barnwell Rhett, or to his own reverend brother, Dr. Gadsden. Now this high born, wholesale *soul-seller* doubtless despises the retail "soul-drivers" who give him their custom, and so does the wholesale grocer, the drizzling tapster who sneaks up to his counter for a keg of whiskey to dole out under a shanty in two cent glasses; and both for the same reason.[40]

2.16. The Author and Landscape Artist, Frederick Law Olmsted, Investigates the Domestic Slave Trade

In this selection, Frederick Law Olmsted, noted landscape artist and author of three influential accounts of southern life in the 1850s, offers informed opinions regarding such topics as the rearing of slaves, their improved physical treatment resulting from high prices, the impact of slave trading and slave breeding upon southern society, and the attitudes and practices of the slaveholding class. Of notable interest are several paradoxical effects of high slave prices: a growing reluctance to emancipate slaves, the use of rigorous but less physically damaging instruments of punishment to avoid telltale signs of abuse or insubordination which could reduce market values, and perhaps most reprehensible, stricter laws and restraints on the education of slaves as a way to keep them ignorant and docile and so less likely to run away and deprive their masters of a great deal of wealth. The following excerpts begin with an account of events which the author witnessed on a slow train from Richmond to Petersburg, Virginia.

SOURCE: Frederick Law Olmsted, *Journey in the Seaboard Slave States, with Remarks on Their Economy* (New York: Mason Brothers, 1861), pp. 55–58, 279–81, 283–88.

There were, in the train, two first-class passenger cars, and two freight cars. The latter were occupied by about forty negroes, most of them belonging to traders, who were sending them to the cotton States to be sold. Such kind of evidence of activity in the slave trade of Virginia is to be seen every day; but particulars and statistics of it are not to be obtained by a stranger here. Most gentlemen of character seem to have a special disinclination to

40. According to Frederic Bancroft, Thomas N. Gadsden was a noted figure among the Charleston elite and had probably sold more Negroes than any other South Carolina trader. *Slave Trading*, pp. 168–69.

converse on the subject; and it is denied, with feeling, that slaves are often reared, as is supposed by the Abolitionists, with the intention of selling them to the traders. It appears to me evident, however, from the manner in which I hear the traffic spoken of incidentally, that the cash value of a slave for sale, above the cost of raising it from infancy to the age at which it commands the highest price, is generally considered among the surest elements of a planter's wealth. Such a nigger is worth such a price, and such another is too old to learn to pick cotton, and such another will bring so much, when it has grown a little more, I have frequently heard people say, in the street, or the public houses. That a slave woman is commonly esteemed least for her laboring qualities, most for those qualities which give value to a brood-mare is, also, constantly made apparent.[41]

By comparing the average decennial ratio of slave increase in all the States, with the difference in the number of the actual slave-population of the slave-breeding States, as ascertained by the census, it is apparent that the number of slaves exported to the cotton States is considerably more than twenty thousand a year.

While calling on a gentleman occupying an honorable official position at Richmond, I noticed upon his table a copy of Professor Johnson's Agricultural Tour in the United States. Referring to a paragraph in it, where some statistics of the value of the slaves raised and annually exported from Virginia were given, I asked if he knew how these had been obtained, and whether they were reliable. "No," he replied; "I don't know anything about it; but if they are anything unfavorable to the institution of slavery, you may be sure they are false." This is but an illustration, in extreme, of the manner in which I find a desire to obtain more correct but *definite* information, on the subject of slavery, is usually met by gentlemen otherwise of enlarged mind and generous qualities.

A gentleman, who was a member of the "Union Safety Committee" of New York, during the excitement which attended the discussion of the Fugitive Slave Act of 1850, told me that, as he was passing through Virginia this winter, a man entered the car in which he was seated, leading in a negro girl, whose manner and expression of face indicated dread and grief. Thinking she was a criminal, he asked the man what she had done:

---

41. A slaveholder writing to me with regard to my cautious statements on this subject, made in the *Daily Times*, says: "In the States of Maryland, Virginia, North Carolina, Kentucky, Tennessee and Missouri, as much attention is paid to the breeding and growth of negroes as to that of horses and mules. Further South, we raise them both for use and for market. Planters command their girls and women (married or unmarried) to have children. A breeding woman is worth from one-sixth to one-fourth more than one that does not breed."

"Done? Nothing."

"What are you going to do with her?"

"I'm taking her down to Richmond, to be sold."

"Does she belong to you?"

"No; she belongs to ————; he raised her."

"Why does he sell her—has she done anything wrong?"

"Done anything? No: she's no fault, I reckon."

"Then, what does he want to sell for?"

"Sell her for! Why shouldn't he sell her? He sells one or two every year; wants the money for 'em, I reckon."

The irritated tone and severe stare with which this was said, my friend took as a caution not to pursue his investigation.

A gentleman, with whom I was conversing on the subject of the cost of slave labor, in answer to an inquiry—what proportion of all the stock of slaves on an old plantation might be reckoned upon to do full work?—answered, that he owned ninety-six negroes; of these, only thirty-five were field-hands, the rest being either too young or too old for hard work. He reckoned his whole force as only equal to twenty-one strong men, or *"prime* field-hands." But this proportion was somewhat smaller than usual, he added, "because his women were uncommonly good breeders; he did not suppose there was a lot of women anywhere that bred faster than his; he never heard of babies coming so fast as they did on his plantation; it was perfectly surprising; and every one of them, in his estimation, was worth two hundred dollars, as negroes were selling now, the moment it drew breath."

I asked what he thought might be the usual proportion of workers to slaves, supported on plantations, throughout the South. On the large cotton and sugar plantations of the more Southern States, it was very high, he replied; because their hands were nearly all bought and *picked for work;* he supposed, on these, it would be about one-half; but, on any old plantation, where the stock of slaves had been an inheritance, and none had been bought or sold, he thought the working force would rarely be more than one-third, at most, of the whole number.

This gentleman was out of health, and told me, with frankness, that such was the trouble and annoyance his negroes occasioned him—although he had an overseer—and so wearisome did he find the lonely life he led on his plantation, that he could not remain upon it; and, as he knew everything would go to the dogs if he did not, he was seriously contemplating to sell out, retaining only his foster-mother and a body-servant. He thought of taking them to Louisiana and Texas, for sale; but, if he should learn that there was much probability that Lower California would be made a slave State, he supposed it would pay him to wait, as probably, if that should occur, he could take them there and sell them for twice as much as they would now bring in New Orleans. He knew very well, he said, that, as they were raising corn and tobacco, they were paying nothing at all like a fair interest on their value. . . .[42]

[T]he value of slaves *for sale* has steadily advanced in Virginia, with the extension of cotton fields over the lands conquered or purchased for that purpose of the Indians in Alabama and Florida; of France, in the valley of the Mississippi; and of Mexico, in Texas. The effect of this demand for slaves . . . [has] concentrated the interest of the planter in his slaves, as in old times it had been concentrated in tobacco; the improvement, or even the sustentation of the value of his lands became a matter of minor importance; the taste for improving husbandry, except among the men of leisure, capital, and highly-cultivated minds, was fatally checked. Mr. [Edmund] Ruffin, a gentleman of ultra, and, it seems to a stranger, fanatical devotion to the perpetuation of slavery, yet otherwise a most sensible and reliable observer and thinker, unintentionally gives his evidence against the Slave Trade, by describing the effect of the increased value it gave to negroes:

"A gang of slaves on a farm will increase to four times their original number in thirty or forty years. If a farmer is only able to feed and maintain his slaves, their increase in value may double the whole of his capital originally invested in farming before he closes the term of an ordinary life. But few farms are able to support this increasing expense, and also furnish the necessary supplies to the family of the owner; whence very many owners of large estates, in lands and negroes, are, throughout their lives, too poor to enjoy the comforts of life, or to incur the expenses necessary to improve their unprofitable farming. A man so situated may be said to be a slave to his own slaves. If the owner is industrious and frugal, he may be able to support the increasing numbers of his slaves, and to bequeath them undiminished to his children. But the income of few persons increases as fast as their slaves, and, if not, the consequence must be that some of them will be sold, that the others may be supported, and the sale of more is perhaps afterwards compelled to pay debts incurred in striving to put off that dreaded alternative. The slave at first almost starves his master, and at last is eaten by him—at least, he is exchanged for his value in food."

What a remarkable state of things is here pictured—the labor of a

---

42. Mr. [Henry A.] Wise is reported to have stated, in his electioneering tour, when candidate for governor [of Virginia], in 1855, that if slavery were permitted in California, Negroes would sell for $5,000 apiece.

country almost exclusively applied to agriculture, and yet able to supply *itself,* but in few cases, with the coarsest food!

The interest of the slaves' owners being withdrawn, by their increasing value as transferable property, from their land, a gradual but rapid amelioration of their condition followed, as respects physical comfort. Since 1820, there has been a constant improvement in this respect. They are now worked no harder, in general, than is supposed to be desirable to bring them into high muscular and vital condition; they are better fed, clothed, and sheltered, and the pliant strap and scientific paddle have been substituted, as instruments of discipline, for the scoring lash and bruising cudgel.[43]

No similar progress, it is to be observed, has been made in the mental and moral economy of slavery in Virginia; the laws and customs being a good deal less favorable, than formerly, to the education of the race, which is sufficiently explainable. The opinion being prevalent—and, I suppose, being well-founded—that negro property, as it increases in intelligence, decreases in security; as it becomes of greater value, and its security more important, more regard is naturally paid to the means of suppressing its ambition and dwarfing its intellect.

Of course, this increased care of the slaves' physical well-being adds to the current expenditure of their master, and makes all operations, involving labor, cost more than formerly; and, as its effect is to force more rapid breeding, and the number of slaves does not diminish, no corresponding encouragement is obtained from it for free-labor. Consequently, the internal slave-trade makes the cost of labor greater, and its quality worse, precisely in proportion to its activity. This . . . is the grand reason of the excessively low market value of all real estate, and has occasioned the slow and stingy application of capital to mining and other industrial enterprises, in all other elements for the success of which Virginia is so exceedingly rich.

It was for a long time generally expected that the demand of the cotton-planters would gradually draw off all the slaves from Virginia, and that the State would thus be redeemed to freedom. The objection which had been chiefly urged against Jefferson's scheme of emancipation certainly would have had less weight during thirty years past against a requirement

43. Hon. Humphrey Marshall, of Kentucky . . . thus describes the strap: "The strap, gentlemen, you are probably aware, is an instrument of refined modern torture, ordinarily used in whipping slaves. By the old system, the cow-hide—a severe punishment—cut and lacerated them so badly as to almost spoil their sale when brought to the lower markets. But this strap, I am told, is a vast improvement in the art of whipping negroes; and, it is said, that one of them may be punished by it within one inch of his life, and yet he will come out with no visible injury, and his skin will be as smooth and polished as a peeled onion!"

that all slaves below mature age remaining after a certain future time in the State should be educated, freed, and transported; for the owners, who could not afford to lose the value of their property could at any time have sold away their slaves at very much more than their cost price before the requirement went into effect.

It, therefore, became advisable to stigmatize such a proposition as tyrannical—to claim for a class the power of thus continuing to ruin the State, so long as they found in it their private profit, as a legal and vested right. On January 18, 1832, a member of the legislature, Mr. Gholson, proclaimed this in the following cunning language. Be it observed that all existing nuisances, and those that are a part of them, are always called old-fashioned; which, oddly enough under such circumstances, is considered equivalent to respectable.

"It has always (perhaps erroneously) been considered, by steady and old-fashioned people, that the owner of land had a reasonable right to its annual profit, the owner of orchards to their annual fruits, * * and the owner of female slaves to their increase. * * It is on the justice and inviolability of this maxim that the master forgoes the service of the female slave, has her nursed and attended during the period of gestation, and raises the helpful infant offspring. The value of the property justifies the expense; and I do not hesitate to say that in its increase consists much of our wealth.". . .[44]

The value of slaves has, since then, pretty steadily advanced; the exportation has as steadily augmented; while the stock kept on hand is some three thousand more than it was then. The amiable letter writer, whom the State of Jefferson now delights to honor, tells our simple New York Democrats that if they had not been so foolish as to favor the admission of California as a Free State—if they had been able, as he desired, to force it to become a Slave State—it would have opened such a market for slaves as would have soon drained them all out of Virginia.

I do not believe, if prime field-hands should ever sell for ten thousand

---

44. During a debate on the Brazilian Free Birth Law of 1871 a Brazilian deputy expressed similar opinions. "Once the fact is accepted that slavery is legal, . . . equally legal is the right of ownership over the present slaves, as well as ownership of the slave womb and the children who may emerge from that womb. Our national law . . . always honored and acknowledged the Roman principle *partus sequitur ventrem*. . . . Therefore the fruit of the slave womb belongs to the owner of that womb as legally as the offspring of any animal in his possession." If, however, the fruit of the womb did not yet exist, there was "an acquired right to that fruit which is as valid as that of a tree's owner to the fruit that tree may produce." A noted mulatto senator, Salles Torres-Homem, responded: "I should not have to demonstrate before this august assembly that intelligent creatures, endowed like us with noble qualities, . . . should not be compared, from the point of view of property, to the colt, the calf, the fruit of the trees, and to the living objects of nature that are subject to human domination. An absurd, detestable doctrine!" See Conrad, *Children of God's Fire*, pp. 443, 449. Editor.

dollars a head, there would be one negro less kept in Virginia than there is now, when they are worth but one thousand.

How would this increasing demand be met, then?

Very easily: by the re-importation of breeding-slaves from the consuming States. Connecticut exports bullocks and barren cows by the thousand annually; and the drovers who take the working and fatted stock out, often drive back heifers from the districts in which the breeding of cattle is made less a matter of business, and is, therefore, less profitable than it is in that region of bleak pastures.

2.17. "Let Us Not Require Too Much of Slavery." A Boston Minister
and Onetime Abolitionist Justifies Southern Behavior (1854)

In 1853 a prominent Congregationalist minister, Reverend Nehemiah Adams, pastor of the Essex Street Church in Boston from 1834 to 1878, spent three months in the South to make a study of slavery. The result was *A South-Side View of Slavery,* a slender volume that shocked abolitionists, many of whom were convinced that Adam's account was written to palliate the South and justify its misdeeds. At a meeting, for example, of the Massachusetts Anti-Slavery Society, William Wells Brown, a black man who had endured slavery for eighteen years and professed to know as much about that condition as Reverend Adams, complained that to bolster its declining respectability the Slave Power's policy was "to *buy* up whatever stood in its way," and he cited Adams as an instance of the South's corrupting influence upon politicians and clergymen (*Proceedings of the Massachusetts Anti-Slavery Society,* 1854, 1855, and 1856, p. 36). Having earlier opposed slavery, Adams was aware of its inequities. However, perhaps to achieve believability, he singled out slave auctions and the domestic slave trade as among the "revolting features of slavery," both of which he nevertheless defended. Auctions, he claimed, were often "merely legal appointments to determine claims and settle estates," with no intention of breaking up families. At auctions slaves were allowed "to find masters and mistresses who will buy them" and, "knowing that the sale was a mere form, and that they were already disposed of, did not in such cases suffer to the degree which strangers supposed." Concerning the slave trade, Adams offered a realistic description of a slave coffle but otherwise limited himself to reporting that slave traders were detested in the South. The accusation of "vilely multiplying slaves in Virginia" was exaggerated, he argued, and came down to the fact that Virginia was fully stocked with slaves and that "the surplus black population naturally flows to where their numbers are less." Finally, Adams was gratified by the hypothesis of "an eminent and venerable physician" of the South that for slave women the pain of family separations was "singularly short-lived," since the maternal instincts of slave mothers were much like those of the hen or the partridge, which, though "roused when her young are in danger," will in a few weeks treat them as strangers.

Adams's views regarding auctions and the slave trade may be compared with interviews of elderly ex-slaves in the 1930s (Docs. 2.20, 2.22), or with a giant slave auction in Georgia in 1859 (Doc. 2.24).

SOURCE: Nehemiah Adams, *South-Side View of Slavery; or Three Months at the South* (Boston: T. R. Marvin & B. B. Mussey, 1854), pp. 64–83.

SECTION I.—*Slave Auctions.*

Passing up the steps of a court-house in a southern town with some gentlemen, I saw a man sitting on the steps with a colored infant, wrapped in a coverlet, its face visible, and the child asleep.

It is difficult for some who have young children not to bestow a passing look or salutation upon a child; but besides this, the sight before me seemed out of place and strange.

"Is the child sick?" I said to the man, as I was going up the steps.

"No, master; she is going to be sold."

"Sold! Where is her mother?"

"At home, master."

"How old is the child?"

"She is about a year, master."

"You are not selling the child, of course. How comes she here?"

"I don't know, master; only the sheriff told me to sit down here and wait till twelve o'clock, sir."

It is hardly necessary to say that my heart died within me. Now I had found slavery in its most awful feature—the separation of a child from its mother. . . .

Undetermined whether I would witness the sale, whether I could trust myself in such a scene, I walked into a friend's law office, and looked at his books. I heard the sheriff's voice, the "public outcry," as the vendue is called, but did not go out, partly because I would not betray the feelings which I knew would be awakened.

One of my friends met me in a few minutes after, who had witnessed the transaction.

"You did not see the sale," he said.

In the Hands of Strangers

"No. Was the child sold?"

"Yes, for one hundred and forty dollars."

I could take this case, so far as I have described it, go into any pulpit or upon any platform at the north, and awaken the deepest emotions known to the human heart, harrow up the feelings of every father and mother, and make them pass a resolution surcharged with all the righteous indignation which language can express. All that any speaker who might have preceded me . . . might have said respecting the contentment, good looks, happy relations of the slaves, I could have rendered of no avail to his argument by this little incident. No matter what kindness may be exercised in ten thousand instances; a system in which the separation of an infant from its mother is an essential element can not escape reprobation.

On relating what I had seen to some southern ladies, they became pale with emotion; they were silent; they were filled with evident distress. But before remarking upon this case, I will give another. My attention was arrested by the following advertisement:

"Guardian's Sale.

"Will be sold before the court-house door in ———, on the first Tuesday in May next, agreeably to an order of the ordinary of ——— county, the interest of the minors of ———, in a certain negro girl named ———, said interest being three fourths of said negro."

Three fourths of a negro to be sold at auction! There was something here which excited more than ordinary curiosity: the application of vulgar fractions to personal identity was entirely new. I determined to witness this sale.

An hour before the appointed time, I saw the girl sitting alone on the steps of the court-house. She wore a faded but tidy orange-colored dress, a simple handkerchief on her head, and she was barefoot. Her head was resting upon her hand, with her elbow on her knee. I stood unperceived and looked at her. Poor, lonely thing, waiting to be sold on the steps of that court-house! The place of justice is a bleak promontory, from which you look off as upon a waste of waters—a dreary, shoreless waste. What avails every mitigation of slavery? Had I become a convert to the system, here is enough to counterbalance all my good impressions.

The sheriff arrived at noon, and the people assembled. The purchaser was to have the services of the girl three fourths of the time, a division of property having given some one a claim to one fourth of her appraised value.

The girl was told to stand up. She had a tall, slender form, and was, in all respects, an uncommonly good-looking child.

The bidding commenced at two hundred dollars, and went on in an animated and exciting manner.

The girl began to cry, and wiped her tears with the back of her hand; no one replied to her; the bidding went on; she turned her back to the people. I saw her shoulders heave with her suppressed crying; she said something in a confused voice to a man who sat behind the auctioneer. . . .

She was fourteen years old. A few days before I had sent to a child of mine, entering her fourteenth year, a birthday gift. By this coincidence I was led to think of this slave girl with some peculiar feelings. I made the case my own. She was a child to parents, living or dead, whose hearts, unless perverted by some unnatural process, would yearn over her and be distracted by this sight.

Four hundred and forty-five dollars was the last bid, and the man sitting behind the sheriff said to her kindly, "Well, run and jump into the wagon."

A large number of citizens had assembled to witness the sale of this girl; some of them men of education and refinement, humane and kind. . . . How then, I said to myself as I watched their faces, can you look upon a scene like this as upon an ordinary business transaction, when my feelings are so tumultuous, and all my sensibilities are excruciated? You are not hard-hearted men; you are gentle and generous. . . . Some of you are graduates of Yale College; some of Brown University: you know all that I know about the human heart: I hesitate to believe that I am right and you wrong. If to sell a human being at auction were all which I feel it to be, you must know it as well as I. Yet I cannot yield my convictions. Why do we differ so in our feelings? Instances of private humanity and tenderness have satisfied me that you would not lay one needless burden upon a human being, nor see him suffer without redress. Is it because you are used to the sight that you endure it with composure? or because it is an essential part of a system which you groan under but cannot remove?

To begin with the sale of the infant. During my stay in the place, three or four estimable gentlemen said to me, each in private, "I understand that you saw that infant sold the other day. We are very sorry that you happened to see it. Nothing of the kind ever took place before to our knowledge, and we all feared that it would make an unhappy impression upon you."

The manner in which this was said affected me almost as much as the thing which had given occasion to it. Southern hearts and consciences, I felt reassured, were no more insensible than mine. The system had not steeled the feelings of these gentlemen; . . . every kind and generous emotion was alive in their hearts; they felt that such a transaction needed to be explained and justified. How could they explain it? How could they justify

In the Hands of Strangers

it? With many, if not all of my readers, it is a foregone conclusion, as it had been with me, that the case admits of no explanation or justification.

I received, as I said, three or four statements with regard to the case, and this is the substance of them:—The mother of this infant belonged to a man who had become embarrassed in his circumstances, in consequence of which the mother was sold to another family in the same place, before the birth of the child, and there was some legal doubt with regard to his claim. He was disposed to maintain this claim, and it became a question how the child should be taken from him. A legal gentleman, whose name is familiar to the country, told me that he was consulted, and he advised that through an old execution the child should be levied upon, be sold at auction, and thus be removed from him. The plan succeeded. The child was attached, advertised, and offered for sale. The mother's master bought it, at more than double the ratable price, and the child went to its mother.

Nor was this all. In the company of bidders there was a man employed by a generous lady to attend the sale, and see that the infant was restored to its mother. The lady had heard that the sale was to take place, but did not fully know the circumstances, and her purpose was to prevent the child from passing from the parent. Accordingly her agent and the agent of the mother's master were bidding against each other for some time, each with the same benevolent determination to restore the child to its mother.

Rachel was comforted. Rather she had had no need of being comforted, for the sheriff was in this case to be her avenger and protector. Here was slavery restoring a child to its mother; here was a system which can deal in unborn children, redressing its own wrong. Moreover, the law which forbids the sale of a child under five years was violated, in order to keep the child with its mother. The man who had the claim on the unborn child was from Connecticut.

Had I known the sequel of the story, what a thrilling, effective appeal could I have made at the north by the help of this incident. Then what injustice I should have inflicted upon the people of that place; what stimulus might I have given to the rescue of a fugitive slave; what resuscitation to the collapsing vocabulary of epithets. How might I have helped on the dissolution of the Union; how have led half our tribes to swear that they would have war with the rest forever, when in truth the men and women who had done this thing had performed one of the most tender and humane actions, and did prevent, and, if, necessary, with their earthly all, (for I knew them well,) would have prevented that from ever taking place to which, in my ignorance and passion, I should have sworn that I could bear witness—an infant taken from it's mother's breast and sold.

The Internal Slave Trade of the United States

The "three fourths" of the girl were bought by the owner of the other fourth, who already had possession of her. The sale took place that he might be her sole owner. The word which followed the sale, "Well, run and jump into the wagon," was music to the child. I understood afterward why she turned her back to the crowd, and looked at the man who sat behind the sheriff. He was her master, and he owned her mother; the girl heard the bidding from the company, and heard her master bidding; the conflict she understood; she was at stake, as she felt, for life; it took some time for the bidding to reach four hundred dollars; hope deferred made her heart sick; she turned and kept her eye on her master, to see whether he would suffer himself to be defeated. He sat quietly using his knife upon a stick, like one whose mind was made up; the result of the sale in his favor excited no new feeling in him; but the ready direction, "Well, run and jump into the wagon," was as much as to say, I have done what I meant to do when I came here.

I did not see "Jacob," forty-five years of age, well recommended, who was advertised to be sold at the same time and place. The sheriff announced that the sale of Jacob was merely to perfect a title. There was only one bid, therefore—six hundred dollars; the owner thus going through a form to settle some legal question.

We are all ready to inquire as to the views and feelings of good men at the south with regard to the sale of slaves at auction. I felt great curiosity to know how some of the best of men regarded it.

1. They say that very many of the slaves advertised with full descriptions, looking like invitations to buy, are merely legal appointments to determine claims, settle estates, without any purpose to let the persons offered for sale pass from the families to which they belong.

It was some relief to know as much as this. At home and at the south advertisements in southern papers of negroes for sale at auction, describing them minutely, have often harrowed our feelings. The minute description, they say, is, or may be, a legal defence in the way of proof and identification.

2. However trying a public sale may be to the feelings of the slave, they say that it is for his interest that the sale should be public.

The sale of slaves at auction in places where they are known—and this is the case every where except in the largest cities—excites deep interest in some of the citizens of that place. They are drawn to the sale with feelings of personal regard for the slaves, and are vigilant to prevent unprincipled persons from purchasing and carrying them away, and even from possessing them in their own neighborhood. I know of citizens combining to prevent such men from buying, and of their contributing to assist good men and women in purchasing the servants at prices greatly increased by such competition. In all such places the law requiring and regulating public sales and advertisements of sales prevents those private transfers which would defeat the good intentions of benevolent men. It is an extremely rare case for a servant or servants who have been known in town to be removed into hands which the people of the place generally would not approve.

The sale of a negro at public auction is not a reckless, unfeeling thing in the towns of the south, where the subjects of the sale are from among themselves. In selling estates, good men exercise as much care with regard to the disposition of the slaves as though they were providing homes for white orphan children; and that too when they have published advertisements of slaves in such connections with horses and cattle, that, when they are read by a northerner, his feelings are excruciated. In hearing some of the best of men, such as are found in all communities, largely intrusted with the settlement of estates, men of extreme fairness and incorruptible integrity, speak of the word "chattel" as applied to slaves, it is obvious that this unfeeling law term has no counterpart in their minds, nor in the feelings of the community in general.

Slaves are allowed to find masters and mistresses who will buy them. Having found them, the sheriffs' and administrators' sales must by law be made public, the persons must be advertised, and everything looks like an unrestricted offer, while it is the understanding of the company that the sale has really been made in private.

Sitting in the reading-room of a hotel one morning, I saw a colored woman enter and courtesy *(sic)* to a gentleman opposite.

"Good morning, sir. Please, sir, how is Ben?"

"Ben—he is very well. But I don't know you."

"Ben is my husband. I heard you were in town, and I want you to buy me. My mistress is dead these three weeks, and the family is to be broken up."

"Well, I will buy you. Where shall I inquire?"

All this was said and done in as short a time as it takes to read it; but this woman was probably obliged by law, in the settlement of the estate, to be advertised and described.

All these things go far to mitigate our feelings with regard to the sale of slaves at auction in many cases. But even with regard to these cases, no one who is not used to the sight will ever see it but with repugnance and distress.

I walked with a gentleman, esteemed and honored by his fellow-citizens, and much intrusted with the settlement of estates. I knew that he would appreciate my feelings, and I disclosed them. I asked him if there were no other way of changing the relations of slaves in process of law, except by exposing them, male and female, at auction, on the court-house steps. I told him how I felt on seeing the girl sold, and that the knowledge subsequently of the satisfactory manner in which the case was disposed of did not make me cease to feel unhappy. I could not bear to see a fellow-being made a subject of sale, even in form; and I wondered that any one could look upon it with composure, or suffer it to be repeated without efforts to abolish it.

His reply was, for substance, that so far as he and the people of his town were concerned, no case of hardship in the disposal of a slave had ever occurred there, to his knowledge; that he had settled a large number of estates, and in every case had disposed of the servants in ways satisfactory to themselves; that he had prevented certain men from bidding upon them; that he had prevailed on others not to buy, because he and the servants were unwilling to have these men for their masters; and, therefore, that the question was practically reduced to the expediency of the form of transfer, viz., by public vendue.

He repeated what I have said of the desirableness that the sale or transfer should be public; whether in a room, or on steps, was unimportant, only that every public outcry was ordained to be made at the court-house. He said that the slaves, knowing that the sale was a mere form, and that they were already disposed of, did not in such cases suffer to the degree which strangers supposed.

It was evident from all that he said, that he transfused his own kind, benevolent feelings, and those of his fellow-citizens over every sale within the limits of his town, and could not, therefore, see it with a northerner's eyes and heart. . . .

No human being, innocent of crime, ought to be subjected to the rack of being offered for sale, nor ought fellow-creatures ever to behold that sight. It will be done away. Reproachful words, however, will not hasten the removal of it.

I once stated the subject to a friend in this form: We cannot expect that servants can abide in a house forever. Death breaks up their relations, and they must have other masters. Allowing all you say of their being necessarily a serving class, why not always give them a choice in changing these relations? This is done uniformly in some of your towns. I could name one in which no slave has been disposed of otherwise for ten years at least, except in cases of refractory or troublesome persons.

Then let opportunity be given for private inquiry and examination; let the transfer be made without obliging the slave to be present, and this will approximate as far as possible to the method of obtaining servants at employment offices.

At the Christmas holidays, some of the southern cities and towns are alive with the negroes, in their best attire, seeking employment for the year to come, changing places, and having full liberty to suit themselves as to their employers. The characters and habits of all the masters and mistresses are known and freely discussed by them.

So, instead of selling a family at auction upon the death of a master, it is often the case that letters are written for them to people in different States, where they may happen to have acquaintances, perhaps to relatives of the master's family, known and beloved, asking them to buy; and thus the family is disposed of to the satisfaction of all concerned. Wherever kindness prevails, the evils of slavery can be made to disappear as much as from any condition, especially where the servants are worthy.

But then there are cases in which the feelings of the slaves are wantonly disregarded, and the owners make no distinction, and are incapable of making any, between a negro and a mule.

Then there are slaves who are vicious and disagreeable, whom their owners are glad to sell out of their sight, as other men are glad to be rid of certain apprentices or refractory children, and feel happier the greater the distance to which they remove.

Again, men in pecuniary straits, in the hands of a broker or sheriff, do things which excruciate themselves as much as their slaves. Thus, in part, the domestic slave trade is maintained.

SECTION II.—*Domestic Slave Trade.*

A southern physician described to me a scene in the domestic slave trade. He touched at a landing-place in a steamer, and immediately a slave coffle was marched on board. Men, women, and children, about forty in all, two by two, an ox chain passing through the double file, and a fastening reaching from the right and left hands of those on either side of the chain, composed what is called a *slave coffle.* Some colored people were on the wharf, who seemed to be relatives and friends of the gang. Such shrieks, such unearthly noises, as resounded above the escape of steam, my informant said can not be described. There were partings for life, and between what degrees of kindred the nature of the cries were probably a sign.

When the boat was on her way, my informant fell into conversation with a distinguished planter, with regard to the scene which they had just witnessed. They deplored it as one of the features of a system which they both mourned over, and wished to abolish, or at least correct, till no wrong, no pain, should be the fruit of it which is not incidental to every human lot.

While they were discussing the subject, the slavedealer heard their talk, came up, and made advances to shake hands with the planter. The gentleman drew back and said, "Sir, I consider you a disgrace to human nature." He poured scorn and indignation upon him. He spoke the feelings of the south generally. Negro traders are the abhorrence of all flesh. Even their descendants, when they are known, and the property acquired in the traffic, have a blot on them. I never knew a deeper aversion to any class of men; it is safe to say, that generally it is not surpassed by our feelings toward foreign slave traders.

They go into the States where the trade is not prohibited by law, find men who are in want of money, or a master who has a slave that is troublesome, and for the peace of the plantation that slave is sold, sometimes at great sacrifice; and there are many of whom, under pecuniary pressure, it is not always difficult to purchase.

There are some men whose diabolical natures are gratified by this traffic—passionate, cruel, tyrannical men, seeking dominion in some form to gratify these instincts. The personal examinations which they make, and the written descriptions which they give, of slaves whom they buy, are sometimes disgusting in the extreme. It is beyond explanation that good men at the south do not clamor against this thing, till the transfer of every human being, if he must be a slave, is made with all the care attending the probate of a will.

The charge of vilely multiplying negroes in Virginia is one of those exaggerations of which this subject is full, and is reduced to this—that Virginia, being an old State, fully stocked, the surplus black population naturally flows off where their numbers are less.

I heard this conversation at the breakfast house of a southern railroad. As several of us were warming ourselves at the fire, one of the passengers said to the keeper of the house,—

"Where is Alonzo now?"

"He is in Alabama."

"I thought he had come back."

"Well, he was to come back some time ago; but they keep sending him so many negroes to sell, he can't leave."

Alonzo is probably a negro trader of the better sort; a mere agent or factor. If slaves are to be sold, there must be men to negotiate with regard to them; these are not all of the vilest sort; yet their occupation is abhorred.

The separation of families seems to be an inevitable feature of slavery, as it exists at present. If a man is rich and benevolent, he will provide for his servants, and tax himself to support them, let their number be never so great, buying one plantation after another, chiefly to employ his people. But the time will come when he must die, and his people are deprived of his protection. No one child, perhaps, can afford to keep them together; perhaps he has no children; then they must take their chance of separations to the widest borders of the slave States. But here individual kindness mitigates sorrow and distress. The owner of several plantations at the south, with no children, has made his slaves his heirs, on condition that they remove to Liberia.

It seems to be taken for granted that to be sold is inevitably to pass from a good to an inferior condition. This is as much a mistake as it would be to assert the same of changes on the part of domestic servants in the free States. There are as good masters as those whose death makes it necessary to scatter the slaves of an estate. The change itself is not necessarily an evil.

We must remember that slaves are not the only inhabitants, nor slave families the only families, in the land, that are scattered by the death of others. Sometimes the demand seems to be that slaves should be kept together at all events, and separations never permitted. This is absurd, upon the least reflection. No one ought to demand or expect for them an experience better or worse than the common lot of men. Let the slaves share with us in the common blessings and calamities of divine providence. What would become of our families of five or ten children should their parents die? Can we keep our children about us always? Do none but black children go to the ends of the Union and become settled there? How many white people there are that do this, who—deplorable truth!—cannot read and write, and seldom if ever hear of their relatives from whom they are separated. Let us not require too much of slavery. Let us not insist that the slaves shall never be separated, nor their families broken up; but let it be done as in the course of nature every where, with no more pain, nor pain of any other kind, than must accrue to those who depend upon their own efforts for a living.

Facts connected with this part of the subject have given me deep respect and sympathy for those slaveholders who, from the number of instances which have come to my knowledge, it is evident are by no means few, that suffer hardship and loss in their efforts to keep the members of their slave families together. Our knowledge of distressing cases, and the indisputable truth that slavery gives the power of disposal to the owner at his will, no doubt leads us to exaggerate the number of cases in which suffering is unjustly inflicted. While we are sure to hear of distressing cruelties, ten thousand acts of kindness are not mentioned. These cannot compensate, however, for the liability to abuse which there is in authority almost absolute; but still let us discriminate when we bring charges against a whole community, and let us consider how far the evils complained of are inseparable, not only from a system which is felt to be a burden, but also from human nature in every condition.

As was remarked with regard to sales by auction, it is in vain to expect that painful separations of families in a wanton manner, or by stress of circumstances, can wholly cease, in the present system. . . . [However], it was remarked to me by an eminent and venerable physician at the south, that maternal attachments in slave mothers are singularly shortlived. Their pain and grief at the sale of their children, their jealousy, their self-sacrificing efforts for them, are peculiar; but they are easily supplanted. The hen, and even the timid partridge, is roused when her young are in danger, and her demonstrations of affection then are unsurpassed. Yet in a few weeks she will treat her offspring as strangers. Maternal instincts in slave mothers (my friend observed) were more like this than the ordinary parental feelings of white people.

2.18. "The Profits of Slave-Breeding Are Almost Fabulous." An Abolitionist Ponders the Role of Virginia in the Production of Slaves for Southern Markets (1857)

Contrary to the opinions of Nehemiah Adams on the issue of slave breeding, George M. Weston, a northern journalist and abolitionist, pulled no punches when it came to assessing the importance of that particular commercial enterprise. "It is common to think of Virginia as *slave-breeding* Virginia," he wrote in his book, *The Progress of Slavery in the United States,* from which the following excerpts are taken. "The two ideas are as indissolubly associated as cotton-spinning is with Manchester, or as cutlery is with Sheffield." Weston argued, in fact, that the "production" of slaves in Virginia and other Southern states was a major component of the domestic slave trade without which that trade and the large increase of the slave population would not have been possible.

Obviously many slaveowners were not proud of what seems to have taken place on their estates. As Frederick Law Olmsted observed, "Gentlemen of character seem to have a special disinclination to converse on the subject." Nevertheless, for many in border states such as Virginia and Maryland, the alternative to deliberately increasing their ownership of slaves for future sale was perhaps impoverishment and even a loss of patrician status. Other slaveholders, on the other hand, openly and even eagerly engaged in the business, as revealed in Document 2.20, "Unnatural Selection: Slave Breeding in the South as Told by Former Slaves."

This issue is not entirely settled, in part perhaps because in *Time on the Cross*, Robert Fogel and Stanley Engerman concluded that evidence of slave breeding was "meager indeed," a view that a host of historians responded to avidly.[45] Among the many is Richard Sutch, who has written brilliantly on the topic and recently pointed out that "the subject of slave breeding has an almost unique capacity to arouse strong emotions, feelings that have sometimes interfered with the objectivity of the investigation" (see "Breeding, Slaves," in Randall M. Miller and John David Smith, eds., *Dictionary of Afro-American Slavery* [Westport, Conn.: Praeger, 1997], pp. 83).

SOURCE: George M. Weston, *The Progress of Slavery in the United States* (1857; reprint, New York: Negro Universities Press, 1969), pp. 112–18, 147–49.

Let us see how it has been with Virginia, that *"Guinea"* of the New World, which has *"blackened half America"* by her *"exportation of slaves,"* and will *"blacken"* the whole of it, if she can have her own way. The 293,427 slaves found there in 1790 amounted with their descendants (they quintupled in sixty years) to 1,467,135 in 1850, of whom 472,526 were then living in Virginia, and the balance, 994,609, were living elsewhere, and the census of 1860 will find nearly fourteen hundred thousands of negro slaves of Virginia stock outside of her limits. Can we console ourselves, in the presence of an infliction so enormous and so deplorable, with the belief that Virginia has been relieved of a burden cast upon others, that this vast number of slaves must, at all events, have existed, and that it was a mere question of the place where? We may believe this, if we choose to do so, and may persist in the belief by resolutely closing our ears to facts and common sense, but not otherwise. 1,467,135 negro slaves could not be subsisted in Virginia. The remunerative employment for them is not found there. The numbers actually in Virginia are maintained, not by the profits of their labor, but by selling their annual increase; and it is this increase, with the high value it

45. Among the many scholars involved in the debate see Robert William Fogel and Stanley L. Engerman, *Time on the Cross: the Economics of American Negro Slavery* (New York: Little, Brown, 1974), pp. 78–86; Bancroft, *Slave Trading*, pp. 67–87; Kenneth M. Stampp, *The Peculiar Institution: Slavery in the Ante-Bellum South* (New York: Vintage Books, 1956), pp. 245–51; Sutch, "The Breeding of Slaves for Sale"; Herbert G. Gutman, *The Black Family in Slavery and Freedom, 1750–1925* (New York: Pantheon Books, 1976); and Tadman, *Speculators and Slaves*, pp. 121–29. Tadman was reluctant to accept the existence of slave breeding but conceded that "an almost universal enthusiasm for natural increase from 'slave property'" prevailed in both the Upper and Lower South.

possesses in the market, which causes them to be kept. The breeding of them is deliberately carried on, and carefully looked after, for the purpose of selling them, and not for the purpose of working them. It is, in short, the extended demand for this kind of people, which makes Virginia *"more populous"* in slaves.

In a speech before the Colonization Society, in 1829, [Secretary of State] Henry Clay said:

"It is believed that nowhere in the farming portion of the United States would slave labor be generally employed, if the proprietors were not *tempted to raise slaves by the high price of Southern markets, which keeps it up in their own."*

In his Review of Debates in 1831–32, Professor [Thomas R.] Dew, of Virginia, says:

"Six thousand slaves are yearly exported from Virginia to other states. A full equivalent being left in the place of the slave, this emigration becomes an advantage to the State, and does not check the black population as much as, at first view, we might imagine; because it furnishes every inducement to the master *"to attend to the negroes, to encourage breeding, and to cause the greatest number possible to be raised.* Virginia is, in fact, a negro-raising State for other States.". . .

In the Convention to revise the Constitution of Virginia, (See Debates in Virginia Convention of 1829–30,) Judge Upshur observed that a then recent law of Louisiana had reduced the value of slaves in Virginia, *"in two hours after it was known,"* twenty-five per cent; referring, undoubtedly, to the stringent Louisiana statute of January 31, 1829, which interposed numerous and formidable obstacles to the introduction of slaves into that State. Nothing could more strikingly illustrate the fact, that the price of Virginia slaves depends, not upon real value at home, but upon markets abroad, and that they are raised, not to be worked, but to be sold.

The idea that anything has been gained by providing outlets for the slaves of the northern slave States, is a delusion and a snare; a cheat in those who propagate it, and a pitfall for the unwary. The only one of those States which has made any substantial progress in getting rid of slavery since the Revolution is Delaware; and Delaware prohibits the sale or removal of slaves, and in that prohibition is the sole explanation of her progress. If her citizens could have sold slaves, they would have raised them. Only being permitted to work them, and not finding that profitable, they have not raised them.

In the letter of Hon. Robert J. Walker, advocating the annexation of Texas, in 1844, it was promised that by that measure slavery in Kentucky and

Virginia would be *"greatly diminished in twenty years."* That has not happened, but the reverse. In Virginia, the number of slaves, which had diminished during the previous decade, increased during the decade which was signalized by the annexation of Texas. In Kentucky, slaves increased in both decades, but most rapidly in the last; a little more than ten per cent between 1830 and 1840, but nearly sixteen per cent between 1840 and 1850. It is thus shown by experience, as well as by sound reasoning, that the multiplication of slaves which results from outlets overbalances the number drained off.

There is no reason to believe that there has been any progress for the better in the northern slave States, the slave-breeding States, since 1850; down to which time the census shows that slavery was only confirmed in them, because made profitable, by the faculty of selling the increase to the extreme South.

The Richmond (Va.) *Examiner,* of May 29, 1857, says:

"The mistaken idea seems to prevail, that the slave population of Virginia is annually diminished by the sales of our slaves into more southern States. *This is a very great mistake.* The slave population, so far from diminishing in numbers, is steadily increasing. According to the statistical information which we published in our issue of last Friday, the slaves in Virginia have increased some fifteen thousand since 1850. In our opinion, the Abolition dream of a prospective emancipation of our slaves is utterly and hopelessly visionary and vain. For ourselves, we rejoice to believe that African slavery is as permanently and immovably fixed and fastened to our soil, as the bedded ores of the Alleghanies."

Slaves being taxable property, their numbers are ascertained at frequent intervals.

In Kentucky, from 1850 to 1855, the taxable slaves increased from 196,841 to 202,790.

To no point can we look for any compensation for the vast regions of the Southwest overrun by slavery, unless it be to Missouri. That State, undoubtedly, has been saved from a large slave population, and may yet be reclaimed to freedom, because the States on the Gulf of Mexico have presented greater inducements for the employment of slave labor. But this proves, not that any region has been relieved of slaves by making markets for them, but that a wider space has been opened for slavery than it had the physical capacity to occupy; that for lack of numbers it could not appropriate in fact what it commanded by legislation; and that, in short, by an inexplicable generosity, we have offered to the slave-breeders more than they could possibly take.

Under the actual condition of things in the slave States, the profits of slave-breeding are almost fabulous. Three notices of sales within the present month (May, 1857) have happened to arrest the eye of the writer, and the attention of the reader is requested to the enormous prices paid for children.

Case I. From a Southern paper, copied into the New York *Tribune.*

"Judy, aged twenty-four years, and child, $1,255; Jack, aged four years, $376; Elvina, aged five years, $400; Bettie, aged eight years, $785; Henry, aged twenty-nine years, diseased, $605; Jeff, aged twenty-six years, $1,100; George, aged nineteen years, $1,205."

Case II. From the Baltimore *Sun.* Sale in Prince George's county, adjoining Washington City.

The following slaves, owned by L. H. Chew, have been sold, viz.: one woman and two small girls sold for $1,450. Boy about fifteen years of age sold for $915. Small boy sold for $700. Girl about fourteen years of age sold for $900. Two small girls sold, one for $880 and the other for $350."

Case III. From an account of sales in Morgan county (Missouri), May 2, published in St. Louis *Republican.*

"A negro man, twenty-five years old, brought $1,250; a man, twenty-eight years old, brought $905; a girl, nine years old, brought $805; two boys, the eldest five years old, brought $487; the other, two and a half years old, brought $325."

Is it wonderful [surprising] that the "brood mares," with such prices for their young, should be well fed and well groomed? Is it wonderful that the desire should be most ardent to extend institutions, under which *"Jack, aged four years,"* will sell on the auction block for three hundred and seventy-six good, hard dollars; while three hundred and twenty-five dollars is thought cheap enough for a boy *"two and a half years old?"* And, finally, taking human nature as it is, who is most blameworthy: he who raises *"small girls"* for sale under the temptation of these prices, or he who creates, or connives at creating, the markets upon which such prices depend?

It is too plain for argument, and indeed is admitted, that no such number of negroes could or would be maintained in Virginia, as slaves, as the number of slaves of Virginia stock now scattered over the country; it is hardly affirmed that the actual number kept there as slaves would be kept as such if the faculty of selling abroad was taken away; and it is not denied that the rate of increase of slaves in Virginia is stimulated by prices which result, not from the profits of their labor, but from sales. The argument urged by those who uphold the furnishing of markets for the slaves (at present the chief product) of Virginia, is that although their rate of increase might be diminished by cutting off those markets, it would still be large, and that the number who could not be profitably employed as slaves would still exist in the form of freed negroes; and it never fails to be added that in that form they would flow over into the free States, to their great advantage and annoyance. . . .

The citizens of Virginia indignantly deny that they breed and rear slaves for the purpose of selling them. Not only do those who interpose this denial do so, in the majority of cases, with a consciousness of truth; but, perhaps, in no single instance can it be truly affirmed that any individual slave is raised for the purpose of being sold. The determination to rear slaves is formed and executed this year, while the act of selling may not take place until twenty years hence. The two things are probably never resolved upon and consummated, as parts of one plan. The fallacy of the denial interposed by the people of Virginia consists in this, that although no one slave may be raised with a special view to his sale, yet the entire business of raising slaves is carried on with reference to the price of slaves, and solely in consequence of the price of slaves; and this price depends, as they well know, solely upon the domestic slave trade. Of the men why deny for themselves individually the fact of raising slaves for the purpose of selling them, too many make no scruple in insisting upon markets to keep up the price of slaves. The well-known lamentation of a successful candidate for the Governorship of Virginia [Henry Wise], uttered without rebuke before a Virginia audience, that the closing of the mines in California to slave labor, had prevented the price of an able-bodied negro man from rising to five thousand dollars, is only a single example of the freedom and publicity with which the domestic slave trade is advocated in that State.

The King of Dahomey, on a certain occasion, admitted that he took captives in war, and that he sold into slavery the captives so taken; he admitted that the sale of slaves afforded him his principal revenue; but he denied that he ever went to war for the purpose of procuring captives to be sold as slaves, and for the truth of his denial, he vouched his own honor and the honor of all his ancestors. The King of Dahomey, however, has found it impossible to allay the suspicions of mankind; and it will be equally impossible for Virginia, so long as the selling of slaves is her principal business, to avoid the imputation that she breeds them for sale, and especially when so many of her citizens do not scruple to avow it.

2.19. "It's a Money-Making Business." The Enthusiastic Opinions of a Young Southerner

Evidence supporting Weston's arguments on slave breeding can be found in many sources, particularly in the testimony of numerous ex-slaves who late in life spoke of their encounters—or those of their parents—with this exceptional practice (see Doc. 2.20, "Unnatural Selection"). As we have seen, Southerners often denied the existence of slave breeding, and the obvious truth is that many of them owned slaves who, without much encouragement, enriched them spontaneously. Whether slave owners were deliberate slave breeders or inclined to let things happen as they would, they were at times willing to discuss the matter openly and honestly, especially if by so doing they could impress others with their business acumen and resulting rich returns. An example of the latter appeared in a letter to Horace Greeley's antislavery *New York Daily Tribune* written by an unnamed writer who, having traveled to the South in 1858, was asked to acquaint the northern public with his impressions of slavery and the "moral tone of the community in those States."

Having boarded a train and found a seat, the writer was joined by "a respectable-looking young gentleman" who, as it turned out, was eager to talk about himself. From him the northern traveler learned a great deal, not only about his background and family, but also about his substantial income and assets, including no less than seven children born to his two young female slaves, and another on the way. The young man's entry into the breeding profession seems to have been unplanned, but, if he was accurately quoted, in the short period of five years he had become in his own mind, a zealous, self-declared and prosperous propagator of human beings.

SOURCE: *The New York Daily Tribune*, January 12, 1859.

Southern Experiences.

To the Editor of the N. Y. Tribune. . . .

My friend [on the train] revealed to me that he belonged to the legal profession; had been practising over a year; described the kind of business he did, how it paid, and so forth. From that he went to his domestic relations; how he had recently been married to a young, beautiful and accomplished wife, and rich withal, being the daughter of Judge So-and-so; how much he loved her, and hated to part from her even for a short journey upon business; and this business was also explained; he was going to Georgia to make his annual arrangements for hiring some certain men and women, property of his. He then told how these people loved him, and how much confidence he could place in them to send them anywhere; and how talented they were; what each one of them could do, and [the amount] each one hired for. One was a black-smith, a good mechanic; one was foreman in a factory, a smart boy; one was hired to a planter, and his two women were at service in families. Here the pecuniary phase of the subject was brought up and triumphantly produced by my friend as a final and conclusive argument in favor of Slavery.

"The whole North," he said, "would go at the business of raising niggers at once, if they could only see how profitable it is. There are my five, that I have had over five years; they are worth $900 a year to me, and do not cost me a cent. All I have to do is to hire them for a year, and I never see them again till the next Christmas. My two women hire for $6 a month, except when they are pregnant, when they lose a month or two; but then the child more than pays for the lost time. One of them, Fanny, was just sixteen when I got her, and she had a boy that Spring. That boy is now nearly five years old, and in fifteen years will be worth from $1,500 to $2,000. I am thus paid for the trouble of raising him about $100 a year; and I have no trouble either, for the mother takes care of him until he is old enough to hire, and then he will begin to bring me wages. She has had a child every Spring since, and now she sends me word not to hire her for May, for she expects to have another! That will be five in a little over five years, and in twenty-five years from this time, if they all live, which they are very likely to do, the youngest will be twenty years old, and, if a man, worth at least $1,500. There are now two boys and two girls, and they will be worth at least $5,000 in the aggregate at that time, to say nothing of the one that is coming. And the mother will not stop there; she will have a good many more. If she keeps on as she has done, and has as many boys as girls, she will bring me $20,000 worth of niggers before she stops. My other girl, Bet, has three children. So, you see, the girls are more profitable to us in the long run than the boys, though they do not bring such high prices. Fanny's two girls will be worth $2,000 when they are eighteen years old, but they will both be having children before that time. Bet's three boys are worth an average of $500 apiece to me now. So, you see, it's a money-making business. Why, our richest men have made their fortunes by it. There's old Squire Brown, who didn't use to be worth a red cent, and always was as poor as he could be, now lives in one of the biggest houses in Wilmington, keeps his carriage, and toddles off to the Springs every Summer; and when people wonder how he got rich so fast, he tells them they forget that his niggers increase as fast as other people's!"

Thus ran on my friend for some time, quoting instances of fortunes made in human flesh by persons whom he knew, and giving me all the details of the business; the speculations and calculations of profit and loss, showing how safe it was to invest money in and what large returns were made from the business of raising niggers, as he called them. The reader may wonder how I sat so patiently while this gentleman crammed these loathsome particulars down my throat, morsel by morsel; but I had long before learned, by a more painful experience than this, to keep my tongue dumb while my flesh and blood would cry out, and only to groan in spirit at enormities which could not be altered by my feeble voice.

2.20. "Unnatural Selection." Slave Breeding in the South as Told by Former Slaves

The following personal narratives dictated by ex-slaves in the 1930s to interviewers of the WPA's Federal Writer's Project offer strong evidence that slaveholders in both the Deep South and in slave-exporting states were actively engaged in the practice of rearing slaves for eventual sale. These documents, drawn from many volumes of testimony, prove that slaveholders used duress and sexual manipulation as well as incentives and preferential treatment in order to encourage obedience and the production of abundant children, and even to endow those children with physical characteristics likely to increase their value in the market place. The twenty-two persons whose narratives are included here consist of eight women, twelve men, and two ex-slaves of unknown sex who at the time of their testimony were living in the states of Texas, Florida, North and South Carolina, Missouri, Tennessee, Mississippi, and Virginia. The volumes were published under the editorship of George P. Rawick under the title *The American Slave: A Composite Autobiography.* Sources of documents follow individual statements.

   Despite considerable evidence of slave rearing, the question remains controversial, as pointed out in the introduction to Document 2.18. Especially important therefore is testimony of prominent Southerners on the issue, including the following quotations from Frederic Bancroft's *Slave Trading in the Old South* (pp. 69–71, 75–77). For example, in an 1829 speech Henry Clay of Kentucky stated that "nowhere in the farming portion of the United States would slave labor be generally employed, if the proprietor were not tempted to raise slaves by the high price of the Southern market, which keeps it [the price] up in its own." Claiming that in the last twenty years an annual average of 8,500 slaves had been sent to other southern states, Thomas Jefferson Randolph, a grandson of Thomas Jefferson, wrote: "It is a practice, and an increasing practice in parts of Virginia, to rear slaves for market. How can an honorable mind . . . bear to see this ancient dominion converted into one grand menageries where men are to be reared for market like oxen for the shambles?" Thomas R. Dew, a professor at William and Mary College, told the Virginia legislators in 1832 "that upwards of 6,000 [slaves] are yearly exported to other States. Virginia is, in fact, a *Negro* raising State for other States; she produces enough for her own supply, and six thousand for sale" (see Doc. 3.6). In 1858 Howell Cobb, treasury secretary and president of the Georgia Cotton Planters' convention, asserted: "With us the proprietor's largest source of prosperity is in the Negroes he raises." John C. Reed, a Georgia lawyer and Princeton graduate, wrote: "Although the profits of slave-planting were considerable, the greatest profit of all was what the master thought and talked of all the day long, the natural increase of his slaves, as he called it. Really the leading industry of the South was slave rearing. The profit was in keeping the slaves healthy and rapidly multiplying." Finally, Reverend Moncure D. Conway, a Virginia minister and opponent of slavery, wrote: "As a general thing, the chief pecuniary resource in the border States is the breeding of slaves; and I grieve to say that there is too much ground for the charges that general licentiousness among the slaves, for the purpose of a large increase, is compelled by some masters and encouraged by many. The period of maternity is hastened, the average youth of negro mothers being nearly three years earlier than that of any free race, and an old maid is utterly unknown among the women." All these men were southerners and perhaps only Conway was an outspoken opponent of slavery, who twice was driven from the South.

Lucy Galloway, resident of North Gulfport, Mississippi.

When the writer asked Lucy to tell her something more about the "black girl that came from Africa," her face brightened and she said: "We was all crazy about 'Little Luce.' Dat wuz what we called her, cause she wuz little, but my! she wuz strong and could whup anybody dat fooled wid her. She remembered her mother who wuz also a slave in Africy. Their master over dere wuz a black man and he wuz mean to dem; would beat 'em when dey didn't do to suit him. Luce had one tooth missing in front, which she said she lost while fighting the black boss over dere. She said dat wuz de reason dey sold because she was so bad about fightin' and bitin'—she wuz strong and could fight jes' like a cat.

"When dey wuz fixin' to sell her to de white folks, dey made her grease her long black hair and plait it in braids to hang down her neck, and to wash and grease her legs to make dem shine when she wuz dancing fer dem. De speculators sho' like to see her dance! She said all she wore wuz a full skirt dat come to her knees and a sash tied roun' her waist. She said dat she always brought big money when dey put her on de block to sell. She wuz a good-lookin' gal—jest as black and slick as a—'gutta-pucha button.'

"She was sold over here to a man name Hutson, and she always go by de name of 'Lucy Hutson.'. . . . She married Alf Hutson, one of de black men on de place. She said dat dey dressed her up and told her dat her and Alf had to 'Jump over de Broom.' After dey jumped over de broom. Old Masta said: 'Now salute yer bride!' After dat dey had cake and feasting. Luce wuz a fa-vorite wid all of dem. She said she always took de prize at all de dances. . . ."

Asked about her grandmother—"Frances," she said:

"My grandmother was a 'good breeder,' and dat is de reason she did not have to work as hard as some of de other slaves. She had 22 chillun. It was her job to look after all the slave chillun. She saw dat dey all got fed good. She had two big wooden trays and about four o'clock ever evin' she would fill dem trays wid somethin' to eat and call all de pick-a-ninnies, and dey would all come a-runnin. Den dey didn't git no more till mawnin'—but dey wuz round and fat as butter balls."

Supplement, Series 1, vol. 8, *Mississippi Narratives,* part 3, pp. 807–9.

Thomas Johns of Cleburne, Texas, 90, born in Chambers County, Alabama.

My mother was born and raised in slavery in Virginia, and she married and she and her husban' had a little girl, and my mother and de little girl wuz sol' away from her husban' and brought to Alabama. . . . My father's name was George and my mother's name was Nellie. My father was born in Africa. Him and two of his brothers and one sister was stole and brought to Savannah, Georgy, and sol'. Dey was de children of a chief of de Kiochi tribe (the name of the tribe is spelled phonetically by the writer from Tom's pronunciation). De way dey was stole, dey was asked to a dance on a ship which some white men had, and my aunt said it was early in de mornin' w'en dey foun' dey was away from de lan', and all dey could see was de stars and de water all 'roun'. She said she was a member of de file-tooth tribe of niggers. My father's teeth was so dat only de front ones met together when he closed his mouth. De back ones didn' set together. . . .

Ol' mahster never beat his slaves, and he didn't sell 'em; didn' raise none to sell neither, but some of de owners did. If a owner had a big woman slave and she had a little man for her husban' and de owner had a big man slave, or another owner had a big man slave, den dey would make the woman's little husban' leave, and dey would make de woman let de big man be with her so's dere would be big children, which dey could sell well. If de man and de woman refuse to be together dey would get whipped hard and maybe whipped to death. Course hard whippin' made a slave hard to sell, maybe couldn' be sold 'cause w'en a man went to buy a slave, he would make him strip naked and look him over for whip marks and other blemishes, jus' like dey would a horse. Course even if it did damage de sale of a slave to whip him, dey done it, 'cause dey figured kill a nigger, breed another—kill a mule, buy another.

Supplement, Series 2, vol. 6, *Texas Narratives,* part 5, pp. 1957, 1959–60, 1963–64.

Lewis Jones, 86, resident of Fort Worth, Texas, born in Fayette County, Texas.

My birth am in de yeah 1851. I's bo'n on de plantation ob Marster Fred Tate. Dat am on de Colorado River in Fayette County, Yas Sar! In de State ob Texas. . . .

My mammy am owned by Marster Tate, so am my pappy an' all my brudders an' sistahs. How many brudders an' sistahs I's have? Lawd a mighty! Now, I's will tell yous 'cause yous ask an' dis nigger gives de facts as 'tis. Dat am w'at yous wants, 'taint it?

Now, let's see. Lawd, I's can't 'collect de numbah [of brudders an' sistahs.] My mammy tol' me often but it am hahd fo' to keep in de mind. Now, dere am my mammy. My pappy have 12 chilluns by her an' 12 by Mary. Yous keep de count. Den dere am Eliza, Him have 10 by her, dere am Mandy, him have 8 by her an' dere am Betty, him have five or six by her. Now, let me 'collect some mo'. W-e-l-l, I's can't bring de name to mind but dere am two or three wid jus' one or two chilluns. Now, how many dat make? Dat am right. Close to 50 chilluns. You's don't undahstand dat? 'Tis dis away, my pappy am de breedin' nigger. . . . Yous see, w'en I's meet a culled person on dat plantation, I's sho mos'ly, dat it am my brudder or sistah.

Supplement, Series 2, vol. 6, *Texas Narratives,* part 5, pp. 2108–9.

Mary Gaffney, resident of, Galveston, Texas, born in Mississippi.

Yes, I've seen slaves sold and auctioned off. The first thing they did was to make us clean up good and put clean clothes on, then they would give us some tallow from a beef and grease our face, hands and feet, then they would trot us out before the bidder so he could look us over real good; then he would offer Maser a price. Maser never would take the first bid, he would always get the highest bid he could before he sold; then the fun would take place, all the hollering and bawling you never heard. Well you have sold calves from cows haven't you? and heard them bawl for 3 or 4 days for their calves, that was just the way it was with the slaves. Mostly like burying a slave, because when they sold a slave the new buyers would nearly everytime carry them clear out of the state, and the slaves that were left at home would not even know where the new Maser was carrying them or even his name. They done that so we would not be wanting to go see our son, daughters, mother or father. . . .

When we got sick we had the best of care. If we was bad sick Maser got the white doctor, if we was just ailing Maser got us the old negro Mammy and she would gather all the medicine out of the woods. . . . Maser he seen that we had good care, because if he didn't and let a slave die, he had lost some money, it was not like it is now. If you kill a negro you hire another, that is because the negro is not worth money to them like they was then. I know that we had better care then than we do now, because we do not have the money to pay doctor bills with and therefore we have to do without and suffer it out the best way we can. . . .

When I married it was just home wedding, fact is, I just hated the man I married but it was what Maser said do. When he came to Texas he took up big lots of land and he was going to get rich. He put another negro with my mother, then he put one with me. I would not let that negro touch me and he told Maser and Maser gave me a real good whipping, so that night I let that negro have his way. Maser was going to raise him a lot more slaves, but still I cheated Maser, I never did have any slaves to grow and Maser he wondered what was the matter. I tell you son, I kept cotton roots and chewed them all the time but I was careful not to let Maser know or catch me, so I never did have any children while I was a slave. Then when slavery was over I just kept on living with that negro, his name was Paul Gaffney.

Yes after freedom we had five children, four of them is still living. My grandchildren I don't think I can count them but I thinks they are twenty. I'se had one great-granchild. Yes, they are all here close farming but none of them are doing any good, they are just starving through some way.

Supplement, Series 2, vol. 5, *Texas Narratives*, part 4, pp. 1445, 1451, 1453.

Jepthat Choice, about 102, resident of Houston, Texas, born near Henderson, Texas.

The old Massa was mighty careful about the raisin' of healthy nigger families, and used us strong healthy young bucks to 'stand' the healthy young gals. You see when I was young, they took care not to strain me, an' I was a pretty good nigger, as handsome as a speckled pup, and I was much in demand for breedin'. You see in those days people seemed to know more about such things than they do know. If a young, scrawny nigger was found foolin 'round the women, he was whupped, and maybe sold.

Later on we good strong niggers was 'lowed to marry, and the Massa and old Missus would fix the nigger and gal up in new clo'se and have the doin's in the 'Big House'. White folks would all gather round in a circle with the nigger and gal in the center. Then old Massa would lay a broom down on the floor in front of 'em an' tell 'em to join hands and jump over the broom. That married 'em for good.

When babies were bo'n, old nigger grannies handles 'most all them cases, but until they was about three years old, the children wan't 'lowed 'round our regular living quarters, but were wet nursed by nigger women who did not work in the field and kept in separate quarters. In the evenin', the mammies were let to see them. . . .

Old Massa used to feed us good too, and they was lots of beef and hogs on the plantations and lots of game, too. 'Possum and sweet yams is mighty good. . . . 'Course sometime they was grief, too, when some of the niggers was sold. Iffen old Massa sold a nigger man that was married, he always tried to sell the wife to the same folks so they would not be separated. Children under twelve were thrown in. But sometimes a nigger would be sold to some one, and the woman to some one else; and then they'd be carryings-on. But they was so 'fraid of getting whupped, or maybe killed, that they went peaceful-like—but mighty sorrowful. The children went with the mother. . . . I've been married eight times, but haven't got any legitimate children that I know of. I've got some children from 'outside' women I've had to 'stand' for, but I don't know how many. You see, them old days was different from what it is now!

Supplement, Series 2, vol. 3, *Texas Narratives,* part 2, pp. 709–11.

Sam Meredith Mason, 79, resident of Travis County, Texas.

Why some of them slaves was bred lak hosses. A good, well-built man was hired out among a bunch of wimmen, so as to produce good, healthy chillun.

Supplement, Series 2, vol. 7, *Texas Narratives,* part 6, p. 2599.

William Matthews, 90, resident of Galveston, Texas, born in Franklin Parish, Louisiana.

De quarters was back of de big white house dat de white folks live in de middle of some pine trees. De cabins didn' have no floors in 'em. Dey set plumb on de ground. Dey was build like you build a hog pen. . . . Dey only had 'bout fifty slaves on de place. It was big, big 'nough for a hundred more, but what they do? Dey take the good slaves an' sell 'em, dat's what dey do. Den dey makes de ones dat was lef' do de work. Dey never bought nobody dat I can rec'lect. Sell, sell all de time an' never buy nobody. Dat was dem.

Like I done said, de marster sol' de good slaves in Monroe. I ain' never been sol', an' I ain' seen none of 'em sol', but I know how dey done it, Dey stand 'em on blocks an' bid 'em off. Some other man git 'em. Mothers was taken 'way from dere chillun, husbands was taken 'way from dere wives, wives was taken 'way from dere husbands. You know what happen? After de War when dey was all free, dey marry who dey want to 'an sometimes a long time after dat dey find out dat brothers had married dere sisters, an' mothers had married dere sons, an' things like dat. How I know? I hear 'em talk 'bout it. 'Course I don' know anybody who done it, but on places like ours where dere wasn' no marriages, how you going to know who is your brother an' who ain'?

Nobody marry in dem days. A girl go out an' take a notion for somebody an' dey make a 'greement an' take a house together if it's 'greeable to de white folks an' if she 'low me to come in, I's her husband. Course if a unhealthy nigger take up wit' a healthy stout woman, de white folks sep'rate 'em. Dey matched 'em up like dey wan' em. If a man was a big stout man, good breed, dey give him four, five women. Dat's de God's truth.
Supplement, Series 2, vol. 7, *Texas Narratives,* part 6, pp. 2612–13, 2615–16.

Carl F. Hall, resident of Boyd County, Texas.

The slave trade of importing slaves into the United States, being forbidden about 1820, cut off the supply to such an extent that strong, healthy negroes became very high in price. Many Kentucky slave owners raised slaves for this market just as we today raise live stock on farms.

Only the strong healthy slave women were allowed to have children, and often were not allowed to mate with their own husbands, but were bred like live stock to some male negro who was kept for that purpose because of his strong phisique, which the master wished to reproduce, in order to get a good price for his progeny, just like horses, cattle, dogs and other animals are managed today in order to improve the stock. Often the father of a comely black woman's child would be the master himself, who would heartlessly sell his own offspring to some other master, without regard for his welfare. . . .

There were auction blocks near the court houses where the slaves were sold to the highest bidders. A slave would be placed on a platform and his merits as a specimen of human power and ability to work was enumerated. . . . Young slave girls brought high prices because the more slave children that were born on one's plantation the richer he would be in the future.

Some slaves were kept just for this purpose, the same as prize thorough-
bred stock is kept.

Series 2, vol. 16, Kentucky Narratives, pp. 72, 74.

Sam and Louisa Everett, 86 and 90 years of age, residents of Mulberry, Florida, born near Norfolk, Virginia.

Sam and Louisa Everett, 86 and 90 years of age respectively, have
weathered together some of the worst experiences of slavery, and as they
look back over the years, can relate these experiences as clearly as if they had
happened only yesterday.

Both were born near Norfolk, Virginia, and sold several times on
nearby plantations. It was on the plantation of "Big Jim" McLain that they
met as slave-children and departed after emancipation to live the lives of
free people. . . . Louisa remembers little about her parents and thinks that
she was sold at an early age to a separate master. Her name as nearly as she
could remember was Norfolk Virginia. Everyone called her "Nor." It was
not until after she was freed and had sent her children to school that she
changed her name to Louisa. . . .

On [Big Jim's] plantation were more than 100 slaves who were mated
indiscriminately and without any regard for family units. If their master
thought that a certain man and woman might have strong, healthy offspring, he forced them to have sexual relations, even though they were married to other slaves. If there seemed to be any slight reluctance on the part
of either of the unfortunate ones, Big Jim would make them consummate
this relationship in his presence. He used the same procedure if he thought
a certain couple was not producing children fast enough. He enjoyed these
orgies very much and often entertained his friends in the same manner;
quite often he and his friends would engage in these debaucheries, choosing for themselves the prettiest of the young women. Sometimes they
forced the unhappy husbands and lovers of their victims to look on.

Louisa and Sam were married in a very revolting manner. To quote the
woman:

"Marse Jim called me and Sam ter him and ordered Sam to pull off his
shirt—that was all the McClain niggers wore—and he said to me: Nor, do
you think you can stand this big nigger? He had that old bull whip flung
acrost his shoulder, and Lawd, that man could hit so hard! So I jes said 'yas-
sur, I guess so,' and tried to hide my face so I couldn't see Sam's nakedness,
but he made me look at him anyway.

"Well, he told us what we must git busy and do in his presence, and we
had to do it. After that we were considered man and wife. Me and Sam was

a healthy pair and had fine, big babies, so I never had another man forced on me, thank God. Sam was kind to me and I learnt to love him.

Series 2, vol. 17, *Florida Narratives,* pp. 126–28.

Willie McCullough, resident of Raleigh, North Carolina, born in 1869 in Darlington County, South Carolina.

My mother was named Rilla McCullough and my father was named Marion McCullough. I remember them very well and many things they told me that happened during the Civil War. They belonged to a slave owner named Billy Cannon who owned a large plantation near Marion, South Carolina. The number of slaves on the plantation from what they told me was about fifty. Slaves were quartered in small houses built of logs. They had plenty of rough food and clothing. They were looked after very well in regard to their health, because the success of the master depended on the health of his slaves. A man can't work a sick horse or mule. A slave occupied the same place on the plantation as a mule or horse did, this is a male slave. Some of the slave women were looked upon by the slave owners as a stock raiser looks upon his brood sows, that is from the standpoint of production. If a slave woman had children fast she was considered very valuable because slaves were valuable property.

There was classes of slavery. Some of the half-white and beautiful young women who were used by the marster and his men friends or who was the sweetheart of the marster only, were given special privileges. Some of 'em worked very little. They had private quarters well fixed up and had a great influence over the marster. Some of these slave girls broke up families by getting the marster so enmeshed in their net that his wife, perhaps an older woman, was greatly neglected. Mother and grandmother told me that they were not allowed to pick their husbands.

Mother tole me that when she became a woman at the age of sixteen her marster went to a slave owner nearby and got a six-foot nigger man, almost an entire stranger to her, and told her she must marry him. Her marster read a paper to them, told them they were man and wife and told this negro he could take her to a certain cabin and go to bed. This was done without getting her consent or even asking her about it. Grandmother said that several different men were put to her just about the same as if she had been a cow or sow. The slave owners treated them as if they had been common animals in this respect.

Mother said she loved my father before the surrender and just as soon as they were free they married.

Series 2, vol. 15, *North Carolina Narratives,* part 2, pp. 77–78.

Jacob Manson, 86, resident of Raleigh, North Carolina.

I belonged to Col. Bun Eden. His plantation was in Warren County an' he owned 'bout fifty slaves or more. Dere wus so many of 'em der he did not know all his own slaves. We got mighty bad treatment an' I jest wants to tell you a nigger didn't stan' as much show dere as a dog did. . . .

Marster had no chilluns by white women. He had his sweethearts 'mong his slave women. I ain't no man for tellin false stories. I tells de truth and dat is de truth. At dat time it wus a hard job to find a marster dat didn't have women 'mong his slaves. Dat wus a gineral thing 'mong de slave owners.

One of de slave girls on a plantation near us went to the missus an tole her 'bout her marster forcing her to let him have sumthin to do wid her an her missus tole her, "Well go on you belong to him." Another marster named Jimmie Shaw owned a purty slave gal nearly white an he kept her. His wife caught 'im in a cabin in bed wid her. His wife said sumthin to him 'bout it an' he cussed his wife. She tol him she had caught 'im in de act. She went back to de great house an got a gun. Wen de marster come in de great house she tole 'im he must let de slave girls alone, dat he belonged to her. He cussed her agin an sed she would have to tend to her own dam business an' he would tend to his. Dey had a big fuss an den Marster Shaw started towards her. She grabbed de gun an let him have it. She shot him dead in de hall. . . .

A lot of slave owners had certain strong healthy slave men to serve de slave women. Ginerally dey give one man four women an' dat man better not have nutin to do wid de udder women an' de women better not have nuthin to do wid udder men. De chilluns was looked atter by de ole women who were unable to work in de fields while de mothers of de babies worked. De women plowed and done udder work as de men did. No books or larnin' of any kind was allowed.

Series 2, vol. 15, *North Carolina Narratives,* part 2, pp. 96–98.

Hilliard Yellerday, resident of Raleigh, North Carolina.

My mother and father told me many interesting stories of slavery and of its joys and sorrows. From what they told me there was two sides of the picture. One was extremely bad and the other was good. . . .

My mother was named Maggie Yellerday, and my father was named Sam Yellerday. They belonged to Dr. Jonathan Yellerday, who owned a large plantation and over a hundred slaves. His plantation looked like a small town. He had blacksmith shops, shoe shops, looms for weaving cloth, a corn mill and a liquor distillery. There was a tanyard covering more than a quarter acre where he tanned the hides of animals to use in making shoes. There was a large bell they used to wake the slaves in the morning, and to call them to their meals during the day. He had carriages and horses, stable men and carriage men. . . . His house had eighteen rooms, a large hall, and four large porches. The house set in a large grove about one mile square and the slave quarters were arranged in rows at the back of the master's great house. The nearest cabins were about one hundred yards from it.

Dr. Jonathan Yellerday looked after slaves' health and the food was fair, but the slaves were worked by overseers who made it hard for them, as he allowed them to whip a slave at will. He had so many slaves he did not know all their names. His fortune was his slaves. He did not sell slaves and he did not buy many, the last ten years preceding the war. He resorted to raising his own slaves.

When a girl became a woman she was required to go to a man and become a mother. There was generally a form of marriage. The master read a paper to them telling them they were man and wife. Some were married by the master laying down a broom and the two slaves, man and woman, would jump over it. The master would then tell them they were man and wife and they could go to bed together. Master would sometimes go and get a large hale hearty Negro man from some other plantation to go to his Negro women. He would ask the other master to let this man come over to his place to go to his slave girls. A slave girl was expected to have children as soon as she became a woman. Some of them had children at the age of twelve and thirteen years old. Negro men six feet tall went to some of these children.

Mother said there were cases where these young girls loved someone else and would have to receive the attentions of men of the master's choice. This was a general custom. This state of affairs tended to loosen the morals of the Negro race and they have never fully recovered from its effect. Some slave women would have dozens of men during their life. Negro women who had had a half dozen mock husbands in slavery time were plentiful. The holy bonds of matrimony did not mean much to a slave. The masters called themselves Christians, went to church worship regularly and yet allowed this condition to exist.

Series 2, vol. 15, *North Carolina Narratives*, part 2, pp. 432–35.

Sylvia Watkins, 91, resident of Nashville, Tennessee, born in Bedford County, Tennessee.

Mah mammy was named Mariah. She had six chillun by my daddy en three by her fust husband. . . . [She] wuz sold in Virginia w'en she wuz a gurl. She sez 'bou 60 ob em wuz put in de road en druv down 'yer [here] by a slave trader, lak a bunch ob cattle. Mah mammy en two ob mah sistahs wuz put on a block, sold en carried to Alabama. We neber 'yeard fum dem nomo', en dunno whar dez es. . . .

Durin' slavery if one marster had a big boy an 'nuther had a big gal de marsters made dem libe tergedder. Ef'n de 'oman didn't have any chilluns, she wuz put on de block en sold en 'nuther 'oman bought. You see dey raised de chilluns ter mek money on jes lak we raise pigs ter sell.

Series 2, vol. 16, Tennessee Narratives, pp. 75, 77.

Hannah Jones, about 87, St. Louis, Missouri, born in Cape Girardeau, Missouri.

Hannah Jones was born in Cape Girardeau, Missouri, August 3, about 1850, the daughter of Oil and Noah Thompson. Her story follows:

The niggers had three or four wifes before de war, as many as dey could bear chillun by. But after de war dey had to take one woman and marry her. My mother had three chillun by him and de odder wifes had three and four chillun too. Old man Ben Oil raised my mother. He was an old bachelor but his brothers were all married.

Ben Oil had 100 niggers. He just raised niggers on his plantation. His brother-in-law, John Cross, raised niggers too. We had 125 niggers. He had a nigger farm. His other brother-in-law we call old man English, had 100 niggers. Dey all jes' had nothin' else but niggers. Before de war broke out, Tom Oil and John Oil come up dah and taken all us niggers but eight and eight acres of land he left for Ben Oil's housekeeper. Ole Marse Ben died and after dat Tom carried us all back down der to New Orleans wid him and opened a nigger pen. Dat's a place like a stock yard where dey auction us off. De old ones was de ones dey was anxious to get shet of. We only know our ages by known' we is born in corn plantin' and cotton pickin' time. We never even knowed de days of de week.

I had three aunts to die in all dat huddle of niggers. De doctors make us go walking every day cause dat was de only exercise we git. One of dem aunts dropped dead on de street while walking. De other two died in de slave pen. My grandmother was a fine seamstress. She sewed all de sewing for de white folks. Three days after her first baby was born dey made her git up and make twelve stiff-front, tucked white shirts for her old misstress' boy who be goin' off to college and she was so sick and weak, some of de stitches was crooked. Old Miss ordered de overseer to take her out and beat her 'bout it. Before he did de doctor looked at her and said tain't no use beatin' her she won't do you no more good. She's stone blind, but she can have chillun right on. So dey kept her for dat and she bore twelve more head of chillun after dat.

My mother was black as a crow and her hair was so long she could sit on it. Dey brought a huddle of niggers over amongst de Indians from all over de south and Maryland and intermarried 'em wid dere own sisters, brothers, cousins, nieces and de like. De niggers didn't know for years dey was any kin. When dey want to raise certain kind a breed of chillun or certain color, dey just mixed us up to suit dat taste, and tell de nigger dis is your wife or dis is your husband and dey take each other and not know no better and raise big families to de white folks liking.

Series 2, vol. 11, *Missouri Narratives,* part 7, pp. 214–16.

Mon Ryer Emmanuel, 78, resident of Marion, South Carolina, born in South Carolina.

Oh, my Lord, child, I ain' know nothin bout slavery time no more den we was just little kids dere on de white people plantation. . . . I's been born en bred right over yonder to dat big patch of oak trees bout dat house what you see after you pass de white people church cross de creek dere. De old man Anthony Ross, he been have a good mind to his colored people all de time. Yes, mam, my white folks was proud of de niggers. Um, yes'um, when dey used to have company to de big house, Miss Ross would bring dem to de door to show dem us chillun. En my blessed, de yard would be black wid us chillun all string up dere next de door step lookin up in dey eyes. Old missus would say, "Ain' I got a pretty crop of little niggers comin' on?" De lady, she look so please like. Den Miss Ross say, "Do my little niggers want some bread to gnaw on?" En us chillun say, "Yes'um, yes'um, we do." Den she would go in de pantry en see could she find some cook bread to hand us. She had a heap of fine little niggers, too, cause de yard would be black wid all different sizes. Won' none of dem big enough to do nothin'. No, mam, dey had to be over 16 year old fore old Massa would allow dem to work cause he never want to see his niggers noways stunt up while dey was havin de growing pains.

Series 1, vol. 2, *South Carolina Narratives,* part 2, pp. 11–12.

Willie Blackwell, 103, resident of Fort Worth, Texas, born on the Blackwell plantation in Granville County, North Carolina.

I's been a slave? Sho! I's more'n twenty-five years old when de war broke out 'mongst the north and south, and I 'longed to Marse Willie Blackwell, what am a powerful rich man and bought de first tobaccy factory in Durham, over in North Carolina. . . .

Marse's house am inside two big yards, one takin' in sev'ral acres and de little one close to de house. Even de overseer's house wasn't nigh to de big house, dat plantation am so big. When de poor white folks wants to talk to marse, dey come to de gate in de little yard and hollers. Den marse sends me to see what dey want, and iffen dey won't tell me, marse say, "He can go plumb to Hell." And he meant it too!

I's 'most [almost] born on de Glover plantation. You see, pappy am de Blackwell stud and he am de big powerful nigger what dey wants to breed dey slave stock up with, so he am use on de Glover place. It jus' happen marse buys mammy from de Glovers jus' for I's born.

Dat stud business make de young bucks lots of troublement. I finds dat out when I wants to do some steppin'. Better not step with de stud's wenches or you'll git de whip. Course, dere was lots of steppin' de stud, but dat done 'twixt dark and mornin' and you better not git cotch. . . .

Marse have so many niggers he didn't know he own from somebody else's when he meet dem. We didn't even pay no 'tention to who's kin to who. Dere so much buyin' and sellin' we gits all mix up, too, and jus' don't care. If marse have a big, comely wench he puts her with de stud and no other man to mess with her. But sposin' a nigger buck loves her and she loves him. Marse see dat and git rid of dat buck. Only one thing wrong, iffen he don't sell dat buck a thousand miles away, dat buck come back to see dat wench. Yas, suh, I knows, 'cause I's dere, Johnny on de spot!

Supplement, series 2, vol. 2, *Texas Narratives,* part 1, pp. 303–5.

Charlotte Martin, resident of Live Oak, Florida, born in Sixteen, Florida.

[Judge Wilkerson, owner of a large plantation in Sixteen, Florida,] found it very profitable to raise and sell slaves. He selected the strongest and best male and female slaves and mated them exclusively for breeding. The huskiest babies were given the best of attention in order that they might grow into sturdy youths, for it was those who brought the highest prices at the slave markets. Sometimes the master himself had sexual relations with his female slaves, for the products of miscegenation were very remunerative. These offspring were in demand as house servants.

Series 2, vol. 17, *Florida Narratives,* pp. 166–67.

Douglas Parish, about 87, resident of Monticello, Florida.

Douglas Parish was born in Monticello, Florida, May 7, 1850, to Charles and Fannie Parish, slaves of Jim Parish. Fannie had been bought from a family by the name of Palmer to be a "breeder," that is, a bearer of strong children who could bring high prices at the slave markets. A "breeder" always fared better than the majority of female slaves, and Fannie Parish was no exception. All she had to do was raise children. Charles Parish labored in the cotton fields, the chief product of the Parish plantation.

Series 2, vol. 17, Florida Narratives, p. 257.

Jack Jones, over 90, resident of Oktibbeha County, Mississippi.

Old Uncle Jack Jones of this city, now over 90 years of age, was born on a slave plantation 18 years before the War between the States. . . . Uncle Jack was one of 17 children by the one wife of his father, but had no idea how many others were born of other women sired by this same man. His father was an exceptionally strong, vigorous, and hardy man. As a result, he was a very popular breeder. . . . Uncle Jack's father belonged to one Mr. Jones, who lived below Macon, but for some reason he failed and his slaves were sold out at auction. His father was bid off by Squire Connell; his father's wife was bid off to some other planter. There was no such thing as marriage among the slaves of Squire Connell. He would tell a certain woman to live with a certain man and she followed directions, though if each were strong, there would be no objections on the part of either.

Supplement, Series 1, vol. 8, Mississippi Narratives, part 3, pp. 1212–13.

Mary Jane Jones, about 88 years old, resident of Harrison County, Mississippi.

"I was born in Jefferson County on Little Deer Creek Plantation, the last litter of my mother's children. She was the mother of sixteen head of children and raised eleven of them. You see, my mother was a wedding gift to my marster at the time of his marriage; was given to him as a kind of nest egg to breed slaves for him, and just as soon as he carried her home, he bought a slave husband fur her and children came to both families thick and fast. My mother would have a baby every time my mistress would have one, so that my mother was always the wet nurse for my mistress."

Supplement, Series 1, vol. 8, Mississippi Narratives, part 3, p. 1243.

Harriett Sanders, 70, resident of Oktibbeha County, Mississippi, born in Oktibbeha County.

"I heard my grand pa say . . . dem what breed good or bring forth lots of chillern, was kept from all hard work. He say my mammy was a good breeder and she never worked in de field, jes around de house and tuk care of de chillern."

Supplement, Series 1, vol. 10, Mississippi Narratives, part 5, p. 1912.

2.21. "The Worst Abuse of the System of Slavery Is Its Outrage upon the Family." The Author of *Uncle Tom's Cabin* Refutes the Persistent Southern Claim That Slave Families Were Rarely Divided by Sale

Soon after publication of *Uncle Tom's Cabin,* Harriet Beecher Stowe was forced to respond to a multitude of critics, northern and southern, claiming to be deeply disturbed by the content and argument of her book. An admirer of Mrs. Stowe, A. M. Gangewer, briefly summed up her readers' complaints as follows. They denied that the book was a truthful portrait of slavery. Mrs. Stowe's representations were allegedly exaggerated and the scenes and incidents she described were unfounded. Her critics further denied that families were separated, that children were sold from their parents, wives from their husbands, and so on. Thus the entire work was seen by detractors as a caricature. Mrs. Stowe responded to such criticisms with a thoroughly researched study, *The Key to Uncle Tom's Cabin,* a book that richly documents her story of Uncle Tom, Eliza, Topsy, Simon Legree, and many others in the process offering plentiful evidence that family members were regularly separated by the slave trade and that this was well known throughout the South.

SOURCE: Harriet Beecher Stowe, *The Key to Uncle Tom's Cabin; Presenting the Original Facts and Documents upon Which the Story is Founded, together with Corroborative Statements Verifying the Truth of the Work* (Boston: John P. Jewett, 1853), pp. 133–44.

The worst abuse of the system of slavery is its outrage upon the family; and, as the writer views the subject, it is one which is more notorious and undeniable than any other.

Yet it is upon this point that the most stringent and earnest denial has been made to the representations of "Uncle Tom's Cabin," either indirectly . . . or more directly in the assertions of newspapers, both at the North and at the South. When made at the North, they indicate, to say the least, very great ignorance of the subject; when made at the South, they certainly do very great injustice to the general character of the Southerner for truth and honesty. All sections of [the] country have faults peculiar to themselves. The fault of the South, as a general thing, has not been cowardly evasion and deception. It was with utter surprise that the author read the following sentences in an article in "Fraser's Magazine," professing to come from a South Carolinian.

"Mrs. Stowe's favorite illustration of the master's power to the injury of the slave is the separation of families. We are told of infants of ten months old being sold from the arms of their mothers, and of men whose habit it is to raise children to sell away from their mother as soon as they are old enough to be separated. Were our views of this feature of slavery derived from Mrs. Stowe's book, we should regard the families of slaves as utterly unsettled and vagrant."

And again: "We feel confident that, if statistics could be had to throw light upon this subject, we should find that there is less separation of families among the negroes than occurs with almost any other class of persons."

As the author of this article, however, is evidently a man of honor, and expresses many most noble and praiseworthy sentiments, it cannot be supposed that these statements were put forth with any view to misrepresent, or to deceive. They are only to be regarded as evidences of the facility with which a sanguine mind often overlooks the most glaring facts that make against a favorite idea or theory, or which are unfavorable in their bearings on one's own country or family. Thus parents often think their children perfectly immaculate in just those particulars in which others see them to be most faulty. . . .

But let us open two South Carolina papers, published in the very State where this gentleman is residing, and read the advertisements **FOR ONE WEEK.** The author has slightly abridged them. . . .

ESTATE SALE. FIFTY PRIME NEGROES. BY J. & L. T. LEVÍN.

On the first Monday in January next I will sell, before the Court House in Columbia, 50 of as likely Negroes as have ever been exposed to public sale, belonging to the estate of A. P. Vinson, deceased. The Negroes have been well cared for, and well managed in every respect. Persons wishing to purchase will not, it is confidently believed, have a better opportunity to supply themselves.   Nov. 18.   H. ADAM, Executor.

ADMINISTRATOR'S SALE

Will be sold on the 15th December next, at the late residence of Samuel Moore, in York District, all the personal property of said deceased, consisting of

35 LIKELY NEGROES;

a quantity of Cotton and Corn, Horses and Mules, Farming Tools, Household and Kitchen Furniture, with many other articles.   **SAMUEL E. MOORE. Administrator. . . .**

SHERIFF'S SALES FOR JANUARY 2, 1853.

By virtue of sundry writs of *fieri facias,* to be directed, will be sold before the Court House in Columbia, within the legal hours, on the first Monday and Tuesday in January next—Seventy-four acres of Land, more or less, in Richmond District, bounded on the north and east by Lorick's and on the south and west by Thomas Trapp.

Also, Ten Head of Cattle, Twenty-five Head of Hogs, and Two Hundred Bushels of Corn, levied on the property of M. A. Wilson, at the suit of Samuel Gardner v. M. A. Wilson. SEVEN NEGROES, named Grace, Frances, Edmund, Charlotte, Emuline, Thomas, and Charles levied on the property of Bartholomew Turnipseed. 450 acres of Land more or less, in Richmond District, bounded on the north &c. &c.

LARGE SALE OF REAL AND PERSONAL PROPERTY.— ESTATE SALE.

On Monday, the (7th) seventh day of February next, I will sell at auction, without reserve, at the Plantation, near Linden, all the Horses, Mules, Waggons, Farming Utensils, Corn, Fodder, &c.

And on the following Monday (14th), the fourteenth day of February next, at the Court House, at Linden, in Marengo County, Alabama, I will sell at public auction, without reserve, to the highest bidder,

110 PRIME AND LIKELY NEGROES,

belonging to the Estate of the late John Robinson, of South Carolina. Among the negroes are four valuable Carpenters, and a very superior Blacksmith.

NEGROES FOR SALE.

By permission of Peter Wyies, Esq., Ordinary for Chester District, I will sell, at public auction, before the Court House, in Chesterville, on the first Monday in February next,

FORTY LIKELY NEGROES,

belonging to the Estate of F. W. Davie.—-   **W. D. DE SAUSSURE.,**

Executor. . . .

GREAT SALE OF NEGROES AND THE SALUDA FACTORY, BY J. & L. LEVIN.

On Thursday, December 30, at 11 o'clock, will be sold at the Court House in Columbia

ONE HUNDRED VALUABLE NEGROES.

It is seldom such an opportunity occurs as now offers. Among them are only four beyond 45 years old, and none above 50. There are twenty-five prime young men, between 16 and 30; forty of the most likely young women, and *as fine a set of children as can be shown!!* Terms, &c.   Dec/ 18, '52.

NEGROES AT AUCTION.—BY J. & L. T. LEVIN.

Will be sold, on Monday, the 3rd January next, at the Court House at 10 o'clock, 22 LIKELY NEGROES, the larger number of which are young and desirable. Among them are Field Hands, Hostlers, and Carriage Drivers, House Servants, &c., and of the following ages: Robinson, 40, Elsey 34, Yanky 13, Sylla 11, Anikee 8, Robinson 6, Candy 3, Infant 9, Thomas 35, Die 38, Amey 18. Eldridge 13, Charles 6, Sarah 60, Baket 50, Mary 18, Betty 16, Guy 12, Tilla 9, Lydia 24, Rachel 4, Scipio 2.

The above negroes are sold for the purpose of making some other investment of the proceeds; the sale will, therefore, be positive. . . .

LIKELY AND VALUABLE GIRL AT PRIVATE SALE

A LIKELY GIRL, about seventeen years old (raised in the up-country), a good Nurse and House Servant, can wash and iron, and do plain cooking, and is warranted sound and healthy. She may be seen at our office, where she will remain until sold.

ALLEN & PHILLIPS *Dec. 15, '49.* Auctioneers and Com. Agents.

PLANTATION AND NEGROES FOR SALE

The subscriber, having located in Columbia, offers for sale his Plantation in St. Matthew's Parish, six miles from the Railroad, containing 1,500 acres, now in a high state of cultivation, with Dwelling House and all necessary Out-buildings.

ALSO
50 LIKELY NEGROES, with provisions, &c.

Dec. 6, '41.   **T. J. GOODWIN.**

FOR SALE

A Likeley Negro Boy, about twenty-one years old, a good waggoner and field hand. Apply at this office.   Dec. 20, 1852. . . .

These papers of South Carolina are not exceptional ones; they may be matched by hundreds of papers from any other State.

Let the reader now stop one minute, and look over again these two weeks' advertisements. This is not novel-writing—*this* is fact. See these human beings tumbled promiscuously out before the public with horses, mules, second-hand buggies, cotton-seed, bedsteads, &c., &c.; and Christian ladies, in the same newspaper, saying that they prayerfully study God's word, and believe their institutions have his sanction! Does he suppose that here, in these two weeks, there have been no scenes of suffering?—Imagine the distress of these families—the nights of anxiety of these mothers and children, wives and husbands, when these sales are about to take place! Imagine the scenes of the sales! A young lady, a friend of the writer, who spent a winter in Carolina, described to her the sale of a woman and her children. When the little girl, seven years of age, was put on the block, she fell into spasms with fear and excitement. She was taken off—recovered and put back—the spasms came back—three times the experiment was tried, and at last the sale of the *child* was deferred!

See also the following, from Dr. Elwood Harvey, editor of a western paper, to the *Pennsylvania Freeman*, Dec. 25, 1846:—

We attended a sale of land and other property, near Petersburg, Virginia, and unexpectedly saw slaves sold at public auction. The slaves were told they would not be sold, and were collected in front of the quarters, gazing on the assembled multitude. The land being sold, the auctioneer's loud voice was heard, "Bring up the niggers!" A shade of astonishment and affright passed over their faces, as they stared first at each other, and then at the crowd of purchasers, whose attention was now directed to them. When the horrible truth was directed to their minds that they were to be sold, and nearest relations and friends were to be parted forever, the effect was indescribably agonizing. Women snatched up their babes, and ran screaming into the huts. Children hid behind the huts and trees, and the men stood in mute despair. The auctioneer stood on the portico of the house, and the "men and boys" were ranging in the yard for inspection. It was announced that no warranty of *soundness* was given, and purchasers must examine for themselves. A few old men were sold at prices from thirteen to twenty-five dollars, and it was painful to see old men, bowed with years of toil and suffering, stand up to the jests of brutal tyrants, and to hear them tell their disease and worthlessness, fearing that they would be bought by traders for the Southern market.

A white boy, about fifteen years old, was placed on the stand. His hair was brown and straight, his skin exactly the same hue as other white persons, and no discernible trace of negro features in his countenance.

Some vulgar jests were passed on his colour, and two hundred dollars were bid for him; but the audience said "that it was not enough to begin on for such a likely nigger." Several remarked that they "would not have him as a gift." Some said a white nigger was more trouble than he was worth. One man said it was wrong to sell *white* people. I asked him if it was more wrong than to sell black people. He made no reply. . . .

But let us further reason upon the testimony of advertisements. What is to be understood by the following, of the *Memphis Eagle and Inquirer,* Saturday, Nov. 13, 1852?

75 NEGROES.

I have just received from the East 75 assorted A No. 1 negroes. Call soon, if you want to get the first choice.   **BENJ. LITTLE.** No. II.

CASH FOR NEGROES.

I will pay as high cash prices for a few likely young negroes as any trader in this city. Also, will receive and sell on commission at Byrd Hill's old stand, on Adams-street, Memphis.

BENJ. LITTLE.

500 NEGROES WANTED.

We will pay the highest cash price for all good negroes offered. We invite all those having negroes for sale to call on us at our mart, opposite the lower steamboat landing. We will also have a large lot of Virginia negroes for sale in the fall. We have as safe a jail as any in the country, where we can keep negroes safe for those that wish them kept.

BOLTON, DICKINS, & CO.

Under the head of Advertisement No. 1, let us humbly inquire what *"assorted A No. 1 Negroes"* means. Is it likely that it means negroes sold in families? What is meant by the invitation, *"Call soon if you want to get the first choice?"*

Let us now propound a few questions to the initiated on No. 2. What does Mr. Benjamin Little mean by saying that he *"will pay as high a cash price for a few likely young negroes as any trader in the city?"* Do *families* commonly consist of *likely young negroes?"*

On the third advertisement we are also desirous of some information. Messrs. BOLTON, DICKINS, & CO. state that they expect to receive a large lot of *Virginia* negroes in the fall. Unfortunate Messrs. Bolton, Dickins, & Co.! Do you suppose that Virginia families will sell their negroes? Have you read Mr. J. Thornton Randolph's last novel, and have you not learned that old Virginia families *never* sell to traders? and, more than that,

that they *always* club together and buy up the negroes that are for sale in their neighborhood, and the traders when they appear on the ground are hustled off with very little ceremony? One would really think that you had got your impressions on the subject from "Uncle Tom's Cabin." For we are told that all who derive their views of slavery from this book "regard the families of slaves as utterly unsettled and vagrant."

But before we recover from our astonishment on reading this, we take up the *Natchez* (Mississippi) *Courier* of Nov. 20th, 1852, and there read:

NEGROES

The undersigned would respectfully state to the public that he has leased the stand in the Forks of the Road, near Natchez, for a term of years, and that he intends to keep a large lot of NEGROES on hand during the years. He will sell as low or lower than any other trader at this place or in New Orleans. He has just arrived from Virginia with a very likely lot of Field Men and Women; also House Servants, three Cooks, and a Carpenter. Call and see. A fine Buggy Horse, a Saddle Horse, and a Carryall, on hand, and for sale.

Natchez, Sept. 28, 1852.   **THOMAS G. JAMES.**

Where in the world did this lucky Mr. THOS. G. JAMES get this likely Virginia **"assortment?"** And had no families been separated to form that assortment? We hear of a lot of field men and women. Where are their children? We hear of a lot of house-servants—of "three cooks," and "one carpenter," as well as a "fine buggy horse." Had these unfortunate cooks and carpenters no relations? Did no sad natural tears stream down their dark cheeks when they were being "assorted" for the Natchez market?

Still further we see in the same paper the following:

SLAVES! SLAVES! SLAVES!

FRESH ARRIVALS WEEKLY.—Having established ourselves at the Forks of the Road, near Natchez, for a term of years, we have now on hand, and intend to keep throughout the entire year, a large and well-selected stock of Negroes, consisting of field-hands, house-servants, mechanics, cooks, seamstresses, washer, ironers, &c., which we can and will sell as low or lower than any other house here or in New Orleans.

Persons wishing to purchase would do well to call on us before making purchases elsewhere, as our regular arrivals will keep us supplied with a good and general assortment. Our terms are liberal. Give us a call.—

GRIFFIN & PULLAM

Natchez, Oct. 15, 1852. "Free Trader and Concordia Intelligencer" copy as above.

Indeed! Messrs. Griffin and Pullam, it seems, are equally fortunate.

10.

"Negroes Wanted." Slave Advertisements, Lexington, Kentucky. From J. Winston Coleman, Jr., *Slavery Times in Kentucky.* Courtesy of the University of North Carolina Press.

They are having fresh supplies weekly, and are going to keep a large, well-selected stock constantly on hand, to wit, "field-hands, house-servants, me-chanics, cooks, seamstresses, washers, ironers, etc."

Let us respectfully inquire what is the process by which a trader ac-quires a well-selected stock. He goes to Virginia to *select.* He has had orders, say, for one dozen cooks, for half a dozen carpenters, for so many house-ser-vants, &c. &c. Each one of these individuals have their own ties; besides being cooks, carpenters, and house-servants, they are also fathers, mothers, husbands, wives; but what of that? They must be *selected*—it is an assort-ment that is wanted. The gentleman who has ordered a cook does not, of course, want her five children; and the planter who has ordered a carpenter does not want the cook, his wife. A carpenter is an expensive article, at any rate, as they cost from a thousand to fifteen hundred dollars; and a man who has to pay out this sum for him cannot always afford himself the luxury of indulging his humanity; and as to the children, they must be left in the slave-raising State. For when the ready-raised article is imported *weekly* into Natchez or New Orleans, is it likely that the inhabitants will encumber themselves with the labour of raising children? No; there must be division of labour in all well-ordered business. The Northern slave States raise the article, and the Southern ones consume it. The extracts have been taken from the papers of the more Southern states. If, now, the reader has any curiosity to explore the *selecting* process in the Northern States, the daily prints will further enlighten him. In the *Daily Virginian* of November 19th, 1852, Mr. J. B. McLendon thus announces to the Old Dominion that he has settled himself down to attend to the selecting process:

NEGROES WANTED.

The subscriber, having located in Lynchburg, is giving the highest cash prices for negroes between the ages of 10 and 30 years. Those having negroes for sale may find it to their interest to call on him at the Washington Hotel, Lynchburg, or address him by letter.

All communications will receive prompt attention.

J. B. MCLENDON.

Mr. McLendon distinctly announces that he is not going to take any children under ten years of age, nor any grown people over thirty. Likely *young* negroes are what he is after:—families, of course, never separated!

Again in the same paper, Mr. Seth Woodroof is desirous of keeping up the recollection in the community that he also is in the market, as it would appear he has been some time past. He, likewise, wants negroes between ten and thirty years of age; but his views turn rather on mechanics, blacksmiths, and carpenters—witness his hand:

NEGROES WANTED

The subscriber continues in market for Negroes, of both sexes, between the ages of 10 and 30 years, including Mechanics, such as Blacksmiths, Carpenters, and will pay the highest market prices in cash. His office is a newly-erected brick building on 1st or Lynch-street, immediately in rear of the Farmers' Bank, where he is prepared (having erected buildings with that view) to board negroes sent to Lynchburg for sale, or otherwise, on as moderate terms, and keep them as secure, as if they were placed in the jail of the Corporation.—   *Aug.* 26.

SETH WOODROOF.

There is no manner of doubt that this Mr. Seth Woodroof is a gentleman of humanity, and wishes to avoid the separation of families *as much as possible*. Doubtless he ardently wishes that all his blacksmiths and carpenters would be considerate, and never have any children under ten years of age; but, if the thoughtless dogs have got them, what's a humane man to do? He has to fill out Mr. This, That, and the Other's order—that's a clear case; and therefore John and Sam must take their last look at their babies, as Uncle Tom did of his when he stood by the rough trundle bed and dropped into it great, useless tears. . . .

But the good trade is not confined to the Old Dominion. See the following extract from a Tennessee paper, the *Nashville Gazette*, November 23rd, 1852, where Mr. A. A. McLean, general agent in this kind of business, makes known his wants and intentions:

WANTED

to purchase immediately twenty-five likely **NEGROES**—male and female—between the ages of 15 and 25 years; for which I will pay the highest prices in cash.

A. A. MCLEAN, General Agent, Cherry Street.

Mr. McLean, it seems, only wants those between the ages of fifteen and twenty-five. This advertisement is twice repeated in the same paper, from which fact we may conjecture that the gentleman is very much in earnest in his wants, and entertains rather confident expectations that somebody will be willing to sell. Further, the same gentleman states another want.

WANTED.

I want to purchase, immediately, a Negro man, Carpenter, and will give a good price. *Sept. 29* **A. A. MCLEAN,—** **Gen'l Agent.**

Mr. McLean does not advertise for his wife and children, or where this same carpenter is to be sent—whether to the New Orleans market, or up the Red River, or off to some far bayou of the Mississippi, never to look upon wife or child again. But, again, Mr. McLean in the same paper tells us of another want:

WANTED IMMEDIATELY.

A Wet Nurse. Any price will be given for one of good character, constitution, &c..

Apply to **A. A. MCLEAN,—** **Gen'l Agent.**

And what is to be done with the baby of this wet nurse? Perhaps, at the moment that Mr. McLean is advertising for her, she is hushing the little thing in her bosom, and thinking, as many another mother has done, that it is about the brightest, prettiest little baby that ever was born; for, singularly enough, even black mothers do fall into this delusion sometimes. No matter for all this—she is wanted for a wet nurse! Aunt Prue can take

In the Hands of Strangers

her baby, and *raise* it on corn-cake, and what not. Off with her to Mr. McLean!

See, also, the following advertisement of the good State of Alabama, which shows how the trade is thriving there.

Mr. S. N. Brown, in the *Advertiser* and *Gazette,* Montgomery, Alabama, holds forth as follows:

NEGROES FOR SALE

S. N. Brown takes this method of informing his old patrons, and others waiting to purchase Slaves, that he has now on hand, of his own selection and purchasing, a lot of likely young *Negroes,* consisting of Men, Boys, and Women, Field Hands, and superior House Servants, which he offers and will sell as low as the times will warrant. Office on Market-street, above the Montgomery Hall, at Lindsay's Old Stand, where he intends to keep slaves for sale on his own account, and not on commission; therefore thinks he can give satisfaction to those who patronized him. *Montgomery, Ala., Sept.* 13, 1852.

Where were these boys and girls of Mr. Brown *selected?* let us ask. How did their fathers and mothers feel when they were *"selected?"* Emmeline was taken out of one family, and George out of another. The judicious trader has travelled through wide regions of the country, leaving in his track wailing and anguish. A little incident, which has recently been the rounds of the papers, may perhaps illustrate some of the scenes he has occasioned:

INCIDENT OF SLAVERY

A negro woman belonging to Geo. M. Garrison, of Polk Co., killed four of her children, by cutting their throats while they were asleep, on Thursday night, the 2nd instant, and then put an end to her own existence by cutting her throat. Her master knows of no cause for the horrid act, unless it be that she heard him speak of selling her and two of her children, and keeping the others.

The uncertainty of the master in this case is edifying. He knows that negroes cannot be expected to have the feelings of cultivated people; and yet, here is a case where the creature really acts unaccountably, and he can't think of any cause except that he was going to sell her from her children.

But, compose yourself, dear reader; there was no great harm done. These were all *poor* people's children, and some of them, though not all, were black; and that makes all the difference in the world, you know!

But Mr. Brown is not alone in Montgomery. Mr. J. W. Lindsey wishes to remind the people of his depot.

100 NEGROES FOR SALE.

At my depot, on Commerce-street, immediately between the Exchange Hotel and F. M. Hilmer, Jr.'s Warehouse, where I will be receiving, from time to time, large lots of Negroes during the season, and will sell on as accomodating terms as any house in the city. I would respectfully request my old customers and friends to call and examine my stock.

Montgomery, Nov. 2, 1852.   **JNO. W. LINSEY.**

Mr. Lindsey is going to be receiving, from time to time, all the season, and will sell as cheap as anybody; so there's no fear of the supply falling off. And, lo! in the same paper, Messrs. Sanders & Foster press their claims also on the public notice.

NEGROES FOR SALE.

The undersigned have bought out the well-known establishment of Eckles and Brown, where they have now on hand a large lot of likely young Negroes, to wit: Men, Women, Boys and Girls, good field-hands. Also several good House Servants and Mechanics of all kinds. The subscribers intend to keep constantly on hand a large assortment of Negroes, comprising every description. Persons wishing to purchase will find it much to their interest to call and examine previous to buying elsewhere.

April 13.   **SANDERS & FOSTER.**

Messrs Sanders and Foster are going to have an *assortment* also. All their negroes are to be young and likely; the trashy old fathers and mothers are all thrown aside like a heap of pigweed, after one has been weeding a garden. . . .

But let us search the Southern papers, and see if we cannot find some evidence of that humanity which avoids the separation of families, *as far as possible.* In the *Argus,* published at Weston, Missouri, Nov. 5, 1852, see the following:

A NEGRO FOR SALE.

I wish to sell a black girl, about 24 years old, a good cook and washer, handy with a needle, can spin and weave. I wish to sell her in the neighborhood of Camden Point; if not sold there in a short time, I will hunt the best market; or I will trade her for two small ones, a boy and girl.

M. DOYAL.

Considerate Mr. Doyal! He is opposed to the separation of families, and, therefore, wishes to sell this woman in the neighborhood of Camden Point, where her family ties are—perhaps her husband and children, her brothers or sisters. He will not separate her from her family if it is possible to avoid it; that is to say, if he can get as much for her without; but, if he can't, he will *"hunt the best market."* What more would you have of Mr. Doyal?

How speeds the blessed trade in the state of Maryland?—Let us take the *Baltimore Sun* of Nov. 23, 1852.

Mr. J. S. Donovan thus advertises the Christian public of the accomodation's jail:

CASH FOR NEGROES.

The undersigned continues, at his old stand, No. 13, **CAMDEN ST.,** to pay the highest price for NEGROES. Persons bringing Negroes by railroad or steamboat will find it very convenient to secure their Negroes, as my Jail is adjoining the Railroad Depot and near the Steamboat Landings. Negroes received for safe keeping. **J. S. DONOVAN.**

In another column, however, Mr. John Denning has his season advertisement, in terms which border on the sublime.

5000 NEGROES WANTED.

I will pay the highest prices, in cash, for 5000 NEGROES, with good titles, slaves for life or for a term of years, in large or small families or single negroes. I will also purchase negroes restricted to remain in the State, that sustain good characters. Families never separated. Persons having Slaves for sale will please call and see me, as I am always in the market with cash. Communications promptly attended to, and liberal commissions paid, by **JOHN N. DENNING,** No. 18, S. Frederick-street, between Baltimore and Second streets, Baltimore, Maryland. Trees in front of the house.

Mr. John Denning, also, is a man of humanity. He never separates families. Don't you see it in his advertisement? If a man offers him a wife without her husband, Mr. John Denning won't buy her. Oh, no! His five thousand are all unbroken families; he never takes any other; and he transports them whole and entire. This is a comfort to reflect upon, certainly. . . .

We are occasionally reminded, by the advertisements for runaways, to how small an extent it is found *possible to avoid* the separation of families; as in the *Richmond Whig* of Nov. 5, 1852.

10 DOLLARS REWARD.

We are requested by Henry P. Davis to offer a reward of 10 dollars for the apprehension of a negro man named HENRY, who ran away from the said Davis' farm near Petersburg, on Thursday, the 27th October. Said slave came from near Lynchburg, Va., purchased of————Cock, and has a wife in Halifax county, Va. He has recently been employed on the South Side Railroad. He may be in the neighborhood of his wife.

PULLIAM & DAVIS, Aucts., Richmond.

It seems to strike the advertiser as *possible* that Henry may be in the neighborhood of his wife. We should not at all wonder if he were. . . .

In order to give some little further idea of the extent to which this kind of property is continually changing hands, see the following calculation, which has been made from sixty-four Southern newspapers, taken very much at random. The papers were all published in the last two weeks of the month of November, 1852.

The negroes are advertised sometimes by name, sometimes in definite numbers, and sometimes in "lots," "assortments," and other indefinite terms. We present the result of this estimate, far as it must fall from a fair representation of the facts, in a tabular form.

Here is recorded, in *only eleven papers,* the sale of eight hundred and forty-nine slaves in *two weeks* in Virginia; the State where [the Virginia novelist] Mr. J. Thornton Randolph describes such an event as a separation of families being a thing that "we read of in *novels* sometimes."

States where Published	Number of Papers Consulted	Number of Negroes Advertised	Number of Lots	Number of Runaways
Virginia	11	849	15	7
Kentucky	5	238	7	1
Tennessee	8	385	17	4
S. Carolina	12	852	7	2
Georgia	6	98	0	2
Alabama	10	549	5	5
Mississippi	8	669	6	5
Louisiana	4	460	35	4
Totals	64	4,100	92	30

The total, in *sixty-four papers,* in different states, for only two weeks, is four thousand one hundred, besides ninety-two *lots,* as they are called.

From the poor negro, exposed to bitterest separation, the law jealously takes away the power of writing. For him the gulf of separation yawns black and hopeless, with no redeeming signal. Ignorant of geography, he knows not whither he is going, or where he is, or how to direct a letter. To all intents and purposes it is a separation hopeless as that of death, and as final.

2.22. "Trustin' Was the Only Hope of de Pore Critters in Them Days." Slave Selling, Public Auctions, Family Separations, and Overland Transportation, as Recalled by Former Slaves

As in Document 2.20, the following narratives are drawn from the many volumes of slave testimony collected during the 1930s by the WPA's Federal Writers' Project, and published under the general editorship of George P. Rawick under the title, *The American Slave: A Composite Autobiography.* These selections deal mainly with the general themes of this part of the book, that is, with the buying and selling of slaves, public auctions, division of families and associated matters. Inevitably, however, many other grievances and sorrows spring forth from those who testified, and no attempt has been made to keep them out. As in Document 2.20, the name, age, place of residence at the time of interview, and the birthplace of each person interviewed are at the head of each statement, whenever available. The sources of the documents follow the individual statements.

Jordon Smith, 86, resident of Marshall, Texas, born in Georgia.

I was bo'n in Georgia, next to the line of North Carolina on the Widder (Widow) Hick's place. I don't 'member her husband 'cause he died 'fore I was bo'n. My father died 'fore I was bo'n too, but my mother was named Aggie, and belonged to Widder Hicks. Her name was changed after my ole Mistress died, and we fell to her nephew, Ab Smith. I had seven brothers and sisters live to be grown. They was Tom, Willie, Wash, Jane, Hannah, Kate and Lizza. I 'members my mother's father and mother. They come from up North somewhere, and was full blood Africans. I couldn't understand their talk.

When my ole Mistress died, they divide her property up between Ab and Will Smith, her two nephews what lived with her since I can 'member. I don't know how much munney and land they got, but each one of them drew twelve slaves a piece. Me, my mother, and some uncles and aunts was in the draw and went to Ab Smith. The rest of the slaves was put on the block and sold and carried to Knoxville. I'se hear men begging to buy their wife or some of their fo'ks so they could be together. Lots of times the buyer say "I don't want her, or him," speaking of some of his fo'ks. That caused a big separation. Some of the old Mistress' slaves never seed their fo'ks after they was sold at the "dividement" of the property.

Master Ab then come down south in Georgia and put us to work on a big farm he bought. [He] had hundreds of acres of wheat and made the wimmen stack hay in the fiel'. Sometimes one of them got sick and wanted to go to the house, but he made them lay down on a straw-pile in the fiel'. Lots of chil'ren was bo'n on a straw-pile in the fiel'. After the chile was bo'n he sent them to the house. That's not what I heard, but what I seed with these eyes.

They [Ab and Will Smith] had two trader yards. One was in Virginia, and one in New Orleans. Sometimes a thousand slaves would be there waiting to be sold. When the traders knowed that some big men from Texas and Tennessee was comin' to buy slaves, they made them all clean up. They greased their mouths with meat skins to make the buyers think they was feeding them plenty of meat. When the buyers come, they lined the slaves up in two rows, women on one side and men on the other. A buyer would

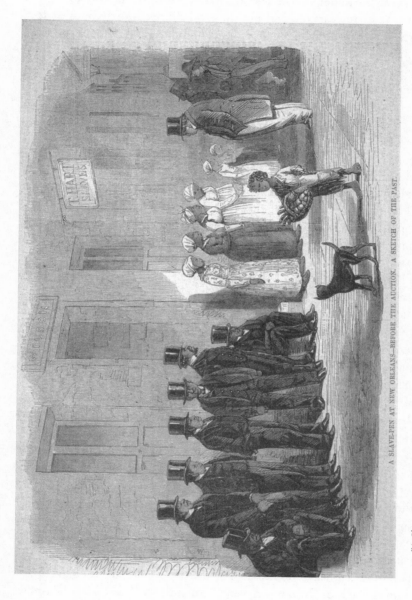

A SLAVE-PEN AT NEW ORLEANS—BEFORE THE AUCTION. A SKETCH OF THE PAST.

11. "A Slave Pen at New Orleans—Before the Auction." *Harpers Weekly,* January 24, 1863. Courtesy of the Special Collections Department, University of Pittsburgh Library System.

In the Hands of Strangers

walk up between the two rows and grab a woman and try to throw her down, and feel of her to see how she was put up. If she was pretty strong, he would say to the trader, "Is she a good breeder? How much is she worth?" If a girl was 18 or 19 years old and put up good she was worth 'bout $1,500. Then the buyer would pick out a strong, young nigger boy 'bout the same age and buy him. When he got them home he say to them, "I want you to stay together. I want young niggers." He wouldn't take no 'mount of munney for that kind.

Supplement, Series 2, vol. 9, *Texas Narratives,* part 8, pp. 3637–41.

Willie Williams, 86, resident of Forth Worth, Texas, born in Tennessee.

I don't know when I was born, 'cause I was taken from my folks when I was a baby, but massa told me I was born in de spring of de year, in 1851. I know I been in dis world a long time, but I has have good white folks. I was born on Massa Benford's place in Tennessee and my mama's name was Martha Birdon. She say my pappy's name Milton Wade, but I never seed him. And I didn't know my mama a long time, 'cause she's sold away from Massa Benford's place, and I was sold with her, den he took me back, and I never seed my mama no mo'.

After I was sold back to Massa Benford, he puts me in de nigger yard. Dat whar de massa kep' slaves what he traded. It was jus' a bunch of shacks throwed together and dirty was no name for it, it was worse than a pig pen. De man what watch over us in dat nigger yard was de meanest man what ever lived. He'd take a club and beat de daylight out of us, 'cause de club wouldn't leave scars like de bullwhip, and didn't bring de price down when we is sold.

One day Massa Benford takes us to town and puts us on dat auction block and a man named Bill Dunn bought me. I was 'bout seven years old. Talkin' 'bout somethin' awful, you should have been dere. De slave owners was shoutin' and sellin' chillen to one man and de mama and pappy to 'nother. De slaves cries and takes on somethin' awful. If a woman had lots of chillen she was sold for mo' [more], 'cause it a sign she a good breeder.

Right after I was sold to Massa Dunn, dere was a big up-risin' in Tennessee and it was 'bout de Union, but I don't know what it was all about, but dey wanted Massa Dunn to take some kind of a oath, and he wouldn't do it and he had to leave Tennessee. He said dey would take the slaves 'way from him, so he brought me and Sallie Armstrong to Texas. Dere he trades us to Tommy Ellis for some land and dat Massa Ellis, he de best white man what ever lived. He was so good to us we was better off dan when we's free.

Series 1, vol. 5, *Texas Narratives,* part 4, pp. 170–71.

The Internal Slave Trade of the United States

Rose Williams, over 90, resident of Fort Worth, Texas, born in Bell County, Texas.

What I say am de facts. If I's one day old, I's over 90, and I's born in Bell County, right here in Texas, and am owned by Massa William Black. He owns mammy and pappy, too. Massa Black has a big plantation but he has more niggers dan he need for work on dat place, 'cause he am a nigger trader. He trade and buy and sell all de time.

Massa Black am awful cruel and he whip de cullud folks and works 'em hard and feed dem poorly. We'uns have for rations de cornmeal and milk and 'lasses and some beans and peas and meat once a week. We'uns have to work in de field every day from daylight till dark and on Sunday we'uns do us washin' Church? Shucks, we'uns don't know what dat mean.

I has de correct mem'randum of when de war start. Massa Black sold we'uns right den. Mammy and Pappy powerful glad to git sold, and dey and I is put on de block with 'bout ten other niggers. When we'uns gits to de tradin' block, dere lots of white folks dere what come to look us over. One man shows de intres' in pappy. His name Hawkins. He talk to pappy and pappy talk to him and say, "Dem my woman and chiles. Please buy all of us and have mercy on we'uns." Massa Hawkins say, "Dat gal am a likely lookin' nigger, she am portly and strong, but there am more dan I wants, I guesses."

De sale start and 'fore long pappy am put on de block. Massa Hawkins wins de bid for pappy and when mammy am put on de block, he wins a bid for her. Den dare am three or four other niggers sold befo' my time comes. Den Massa Black calls me to de block and de auction man say, "What am I offer fer dis portly, strong young wench. She never been 'bused [abused] and will make a good breeder."

I wants to hear Massa Hawkins bid, but him say nothin'. Two other men am biddin' 'gainst each other and I sho' has de worryment. Dere am tears comin' down my cheeks 'cause I's been sold to some man dat would make sep'ration from my mammy. One man bids $500 and de auction man ask, "Do I hear more? She am gwine at $500.00." Den someone say, $525.00, and de auction man say, "She am sold for $525.00 to Massa Hawkins. Am I glad and 'cited! Why, I's quiverin' all over.

Massa Hawkins takes we'uns to his place and it am a nice plantation. Lots better am dat place dan Massa Black's. Dere is 'bout 50 niggers what is growed and lots of chillen. De first thing massa do when we'uns gits home am give we'uns rations and a cabin. You mus' believe dis nigger when I says dem rations a feast for us. Dere plenty meat and tea and coffee and white flour. I's never tasted white flour and coffee and mammy fix some biscuits and coffee. Well, de biscuits was yum, yum, yum to me, but de coffee I doesn't like.

De quarters am purty good. Dere am twelve cabins all made from logs and a table and some benches and bunks for sleepin' and a fireplace for cookin' and de heat. Dere am no floor, jus' de ground.

Massa Hawkins am good to de niggers and not force 'em work too hard. Dere am as much diff'ence 'tween him and old Massa Black in de way of treatment as 'twixt de Lawd and de devil. Massa Hawkins 'lows he niggers have reason'ble parties and go fishin', but we'uns am never tooken to church and has no books for larnin'. Dere am no edumcation for de niggers.

Dere am one thing Massa Hawkins does to me what I can't shunt from my mind. I knows he don't do it for meanness, but I allus holds it 'gainst him. What he done am force me to live with dat nigger, Rufus, 'gainst my wants.

After I been at he place 'bout a year, de massa come to me and say, "You gwine live with Rufus in dat cabin over yonder. Go fix it for livin'." I's 'bout sixteen year old and has no larnin', and I's jus' igno'mus chile. I's thought dat him mean for me to tend de cabin for Rufus and some other niggers. Well, dat am start de pestigation for me.

I's took charge of de cabin after work am done and fixes supper. Now, I don't like dat Rufus, 'cause he a bully. He am big and 'cause he so, he think everybody do what him say. We'uns has supper, den I goes here and dere talkin', till I's ready for sleep and den I gits in de bunk. After I's in, dat nigger come and crawl in de bunk with me 'fore I knows it. I says, "What you mean, you fool nigger?" He say for me to hush de mouth. "Dis am my bunk, too," he say.

"You's teched in de head. Git out," I's told him, and I puts de feet 'gainst him and give him a shove and out he go on de floor 'fore he knew what I'm doin'. Dat nigger jump up and he mad. He look like de wild bear. He starts for de bunk and I jumps quick for de poker. It am 'bout three foot long and when he comes at me I lets him have it over de head. Did dat nigger stop in he tracks? I's say he did. He looks at me steady for a minute and you's could tell he thinkin' hard. Den he go and set on de bench and say, "Jus wait. You thinks it am smart, but you's am foolish in de head. Dey's gwine larn you somethin'."

"Hush yous big mouth and stay 'way from dis nigger, dat all I wants," I say, and jus' sets and hold dat poker in de hand. He jus' sets, lookin' like de bull. Dere we'uns sets and sets for 'bout an hour and den he go out and I bars de door.

De nex' day I goes to de missy and tells her what Rufus wants and missy say dat am de massa's wishes. She say, "Yous am de portly gal and Rufus am de portly man. De massa wants you-uns for to bring forth portly chillen.

I's thinkin' 'bout what de missy say, but say to myse'f. "I's not gwine live with dat Rufus." Dat night when him come in de cabin, I grabs de poker and sits on de bench and says, "Git 'way from me, nigger, 'for I busts yous brains out and stomp on dem." He say nothin' and git out.

De nex' day de massa call me and tell me, "Woman, I's pay big money for you and I's done dat for de cause I wants yous to raise me chillens. I's put you to live with Rufus for dat purpose. Now, if you doesn't want whippin' at de stake, yous do what I wants."

I thinks 'bout massa buyin' me offen de block and savin' me from bein' sep'rated from my folks and 'bout bein' whipped at de stake. Dere it am. What am I's to do? So I 'cides to do as de massa wish and so I yields.

When we'uns am given freedom, Massa Hawkins tells us we can stay and work for wages or share crop de land. Some stays and some goes. My folks and me stays. We works on de land on shares for three years, den moved to other land near by. I stays with my folks till they dies.

If my mem'randum am correct, it am 'bout thirty years since I come to Fort Worth. Here I cooks for white folks till I goes blind 'bout ten years ago.

I never marries, 'cause one 'sperience am 'nough for dis nigger. After what I does for de massa, I's never wants no truck with any man. [Rose Williams forced Rufus to leave her after she had given birth to two of his children.] De Lawd forgive dis cullud woman, but he have to 'scuse me and look for some others to 'plenish de earth.

Series 1, vol. 5, *Texas Narratives,* part 4, pp. 174–78.

Ben Simpson, 90, resident of Madisonville, Texas, born in Norcross, Georgia.

Boss, I's born in Georgia, in Norcross, and I's ninety years old. My father's name was Roger Stielszen and my mother's name was Betty. Massa Earl Stielszen captures them in Africa and brung them to Georgia. He got kilt and my sister and me went to his son. His son was a killer. He got in trouble there in Georgia and got him two good-stepping hosses and the covered wagon. Then he chains all he slaves round the necks and fastens the chains to the hosses and makes them walk all the way to Texas. My mother and my sister had to walk. Emma was my sister. Somewhere on the road it went to snowin' and massa wouldn't let us wrap anything round our feet. We had to sleep on the ground, too, in all that snow.

Massa have a great, long whip platted out of rawhide and when one [of] the niggers fall behind or give out, he hit him with that whip. It take the hide every time he hit a nigger. Mother, she give out on the way, 'bout the line of Texas. Her feet got raw and bleedin' and her legs swoll plumb out of shape. Then massa, he jus' take out he gun and shot her, and whilst she lay dyin' he kicks her two, three times and say, "Damn a nigger what can't stand nothin'." Boss, you know that man, he wouldn't bury mother, jus' leave her layin' where he shot her at. You know, then there wasn't no law 'gainst killin' nigger slaves. He come plumb to Austin through that snow. He takin' up farmin' and changes he name to Alex Simpson, and changes our names, too. He cut logs and builded he home on the side of them mountains. We never had no quarters. When night-time come he locks the chain round our necks and then locks it round a tree. Boss, our bed were the ground. All he feed us was raw meat and green corn. Boss, I et many a green weed. I was hongry. He never let us eat at noon, he worked us all day without stoppin'. We went naked, that the way he worked us. We never had any clothes.

He brands us. He brand my mother befo' us left Georgia. Boss, that nearly kilt her. He brand her in the breast, then between the shoulders. He brand all us.

My sister, Emma, was the only woman he have till he marries. Emma was wife of all seven Negro slaves. He sold her when she's 'bout fifteen, jus' before her baby was born. I never seen her since.

Boss, massa was a outlaw. He come to Texas and deal in stolen hosses. Jus' befo' he's hung for stealin' hosses, he marries a young Spanish gal. He sho' mean to her. Whips her 'cause she want him to leave he slaves alone and live right. Bless her heart, she's the best gal in the world. She was the best thing God ever put life in the world. She cry and cry every time massa go off. She let us a-loose and she feed us good one time while he's gone. Missy Selena, she turns us a-loose and we wash in the creek clost by. She jus' fasten the chain on us and give us great big pot cooked meat and corn. And up he rides. Never say a word but come to see what us eatin'. He pick up he whip and whip her till she falls. If I could have got a-loose I'd kilt him. I swore if I ever got a-loose I'd kill him. But befo' long after that he fails to come home, and some people finds him hangin' to a tree. Boss, that long after war he got hung. He didn't let us free. We wore chains all the time. When we work, we drug them chains with us. At night he lock us to a tree to keep us from runnin' off. He didn't have to do that. We were 'fraid to run. We knew he'd kill us. Besides, he brands us and they no way to git it off. If a slave die, massa made the rest of us tie a rope round his feet and drug him off. Never buried one, it was too much trouble.

Massa allus say he be rich after the war. He stealin' all the time. He have a whole mountain side where he keep he stock. Missy Selena tell us one day we sposed to be free, but he didn't turn us a-loose. It was 'bout three years after the war they hung him. Missy turned us a-loose. I had a hard time then. All I had to eat was what I could find and steal. I was 'fraid of everybody. I jus' went wild and to the woods, but, thank God, a bunch of men taken they dogs and run me down. They carry me to they place. Gen. Houston had some niggers and he made them feed me. He made them keep me till I git well and able to work. Then he give me a job. I marry one the gals befo' I leaves them. I'm plumb out of place there at my weddin'. Yes, suh, boss, it wasn't one year befo' that I'm the wild nigger. We had thirteen chillen. . . .

Series 1, vol. 5, *Texas Narratives*, part 4, pp. 27–29.

Fannie Moore, 88, resident in Asheville, N.C., Place of birth unknown.

Nowadays when I heah folks a'growlin an' a'grumblin bout not habbin this an' that I jes think what would they done effen they be brought up on de Moore plantation. De Moore plantation b'long to Marse Jim Moore, in Moore, South Carolina. De Moores had own de same plantation and de same niggers and dey children for yeahs back. When Marse Jim's pappy die he leave de whole thing to Marse Jim, effen he take care of his mammy. She shore was a rip-jack. She say niggers didn't need nothin' to eat. Dey jes like animals, not like other folks. She whip me, many time wif a cow hide, til I was black and blue. . . .

Marse Jim own de bigges' plantation in de whole country. Jes thousands acres ob lan'. An de ole Tiger Ribber [River] a runnin' right through de middle ob de plantation. On one side ob de ribber stood de big house, whar de white folks lib and on the other side stood the quarters. De big house was a purty thing all painted white, a standin' in a patch of oak trees. . . .

It was a tubble [terrible] sight to see de speculators come to de plantation. Dey would go through de fields and buy de slaves dey wanted. Marse Jim nebber sell pappy or mammy or any ob de chillun. He allus like pappy. When de speculator come all de slaves start a shakin'. No one know who is a goin'. Den sometime dey take 'em an' sell 'em on de block. De "breed woman" always bring mo' money den de res', ebben de men. When dey put her on de block dey put all her chillun aroun her to show folks how fas [fast] she can hab chillun. When she sold her family nebber see her agin. She nebber know how many chillun she hab. Some time she hab colored children an' sometime white. Taint no use to say anything case effen she do

In the Hands of Strangers

she jes git whipped. . . . Many boys and girls marry dey own brothers and sisters an' nebber know de difference lest they get to talkin' bout dey parents and where dey uster lib.

Series 2, vol. 15, *North Carolina Narratives,* part 2, pp. 128, 131–32.

Delia Garlic, 100, resident of Montgomery, Alabama, born in Powhatan, Virginia.

Delia Garlic lives at 43 Stone Street, Montgomery, and insists she is 100 years old. Unlike many of the old Negroes of the South, she has no good words for slavery days or the old masters, declaring: "Dem days was hell."

She sat on her front porch and assailed the taking of young children from mothers and selling them in different parts of the country.

"I was growed up when de war come," she said, "an' I was a mother befo' it closed. Babies was snatched from dere mother's breas' an' sold to speculators. Chilluns was separated from sisters an' brothers an' never saw each other ag'in.

"Course dey cry; you think dey not cry when dey was sold lak cattle? I could tell you 'bout it all day, but even den you couldn't guess de awfulness of it.

"It's bad to belong to folks dat own you soul an' body; dat can tie you up to a tree, wid yo' face to de tree an' yo' arms fastened tight aroun' it; who take a long curlin' whip an' cut de blood ever' [every] lick.

"Folks a mile away could hear dem awful whippings. Dey was a turrible part of livin'.

Delia said she was born at Powhatan, Virginia, and was the youngest of thirteen children.

"I never seed none of my brothers an' sisters 'cept brother William," she said. "Him an' my mother an' me was brought in a speculator's drove to Richmon' an' put in a warehouse wid a drove of other niggers. Den we was all put on a block an' sol' to de highes' bidder.

"I never seen brother William ag'in. Mammy an' me was sold to a man by de name of Carter, who was de sheriff of de county.

"No'm, dey warn't no good times at his house. He was a widower an' his daughter kept house for him. I nursed for her, an' one day I was playin' wid de baby. It hurt its little han' an' commenced to cry, an' she whirl on me, pick up a hot iron an' run it all down my arm an' han'. It took off the flesh when she done it. . . .

I kept on stayin' dere, an' one night de marster come in drunk an' set at de table wid his head lollin' aroun'. I was waitin' on de table, an' he look up an' see me. I was skeered, an' dat made him awful mad. He called an overseer an' tol' him: 'Take her out an' beat some sense in her.'

"I begin to cry an' run an' run in de night; but finally I run back by de quarters an' heard mammy callin' me. I went in, an' raght [right] away dey come for me. A horse was standin' in front of de house, an' I was took dat very night to Richmon' an' sold to a speculator ag'in. I never seed my mammy anymore.

"I has thought many times through all dese years how mammy looked dat night. She pressed my han' in bofe of hers an' said: 'Be good an' trus' in de Lawd.'

"Trustin' was de only hope of de pore critters in dem days. Us jest prayed for strength to endure it to de end. We didn't 'spect nothin' but to stay in bondage 'till we died.

"I was sol' by de speculator to a man in McDonough, Ga. I don't ricollec' his name, but he was openin' a big hotel at McDonough an' bought me to wait on tables. But when de time come aroun' to pay for me, his hotel done fail. Den de Atlanta man dat bought de hotel bought me, too. 'Fo long, dough, [before long, though] I was sol' to a man by de name of Garlic, down in Louisiana, an' I stayed wid him 'till I was freed. I was a regular fiel' han', plowin' an' hoein' an' choppin' cotton.

Series 1, vol. 6, *Alabama and Indiana Narratives,* part 1, pp. 129–31.

Mintie Maria Miller, 85, resident of Galveston, Texas, born in Tuscaloosa, Alabama in 1852.

I was born in Tuscaloosa, Alabama, in 1852. I don' 'member who we belong to for I was too little. My mother told me, but I forgot now. My mother's name was Hannah. I don' know my father's name.

When I was still pretty little my brother, uncle, aunt, an' mother was sold an' I went with 'em. My father wasn' sold so he couldn' go. De marster told us we was going to Texas, dat we belong to Dr. Massie now.

Dey brought us to Texas on an ox cart. My sister got on de wagon to go, too, an' de marster said, "Adeline, you can' [can't] come. You got stay here with Mistress." Dat's de last I ever seen my sister. She was four years old den.

It took us three months to come to Texas on de ox cart. I don' know how far we come in one day, but it sure was tiresome. Dere was two crowds of us. My mother, uncle, aunt an' me an' my brother was in one wagon. Another man with some more slaves was in de other wagon. He was going to a dif'runt place from us. De marster didn' come, he left Capt'in White to take care of us. At night we slept in de wagon.

After we come to Texas we live on a big place. It was somewhere 'round Lynchburg. Dr. Massie own it. He had two girls an' I use' to sleep on de foot of dere bed. . . .

I didn' do no work when I was little. My mother was de cook for de white folks. Dey treated us fine but some of de white folks treated dere slaves awful bad. Dere was a girl in Lynchburg, I can't 'member her name jus' now, she was little, 'bout eight or nine I guess, an' she run 'way from her marster. She had to swim de Trinity River an' it was winter an' her feet got frozen. Someone got her an' sold her to a poor white man cheap. He had ten chillun of his own an' he jus' work out for other white folks. He put dis girl's feet in de fire to kind of thaw 'em out, an' burn 'em.

Well, dere was a law in Lynchburg dat iffen you treat a slave like dat dey can take 'em away from you an' sell 'em again. So Dr. Frost took 'er away from dis man an' give 'er to Miss Nancy to take care of 'til she got well. Miss Nancy was de mistress dere at Dr. Massie's place. Dis girl was light, like a Mexican. Miss Nancy wouldn't have any light people. She said dey had white blood in 'em an' she wouldn' have dem. But she said she'd take care of dis girl 'til she got well, so she stay with us. But some of dem sure treated dere people bad. Some of dem whipped dere people awful bad iffen dey did anything wrong or didn' work, 'specially de field hands. I always belong to nice people. Once in a while de marster whipped some of de field hands dat didn' work, but dat was all. . . .

Den dey said dey was going to sell me. Miss Nancy's father-in-law died an' dey got rid of some of us. Young Miss Nancy didn' want to give me up an' she tol' me to be sassy an' no one would buy me. De next dey took me to Houston. De marster didn' bring me dere. A man from de market come an' got us dat was to be sold in a wagon an' brought us dere an' brought us home again in de evenin' iffen we wasn' sold dat day. I was too small to 'member where de market was located. I know it was in Houston, but I don' know where 'bouts. I know a man name George Fraser sold de slaves. De market was an open house, more like a shed. Dey had high blocks of wood in dere where de men an' women stood so de white men could see 'em good. We all stood together to one side 'til our turn come. Sometimes de white men come an' look at us so dey could know which one was de best an' bid on him. We jus' stand still an' wait. Dere wasn' nothin' you could do.

Dey stood me on a block of wood an' a man bid me in. I felt mad. You see I was young den, too young to know better. I don' know how much dey sold me for. I know dat de man dat bought me made me open my mouth while he look at my teeth. Dey did all de slaves dat way. Sold dem jus' like you sell a horse.

Den my old marster tol' me goodbye an' tried to give me a dog. But I 'membered what Miss Nancy had tol' me an' I sassed him an' slapped de dog out of his hand. Den de new man who had bought me said, "When one o'clock come you got to sell 'er again for she's sassy. If she did me dat way I'd kill 'er." So dey sold me twice in de same day.

Dey usually sold in de morning I think. Dey had two sessions de day I was sold, but I don' know if that was usual. When de white folks in Louisiana an' Mississippi knew dey wasn' going to win de war dey sold as many of dere slaves as dey could. Dey brought some of de slaves from New Orleans an' sold dem in Houston. I heard dem say one time dat dey sold a hundred in one day.

Supplement, series 2, *Texas Narratives,* part 6, pp. 2687–91.

Polly Shine, about 90, resident of Madisonville, Texas, born in Shreveport, Louisiana, in 1848.

Yes, I have seen slaves sold and auctioned off. They made us wash and clean up real good first, then grease our hands and feet also our legs up to our knees and greased our neck, face and ears good so we would look real fat and slick. Then they would trot us out to and fro before our buyers and let them look us over real good. They felt of our legs, arms and so on before they would offer a price for us. We would be awful sad because we did not know what kind of Maser we were going to have, didn't know but what he would be real mean to us or would take us plum out of the state where we never would see or hear of our people any more. But I am going to tell you child, that they did not let us know very much about our people, or that is they took us away from our parents when we was real young so that when they got ready to trade us we would not put on too much demonstration or holler and take on too much.

Of course, when they traded us we took on more or less anyway because we never knew what was going to become of us after our Maser traded us to another Maser and he carried us to another country, then we had to get use to the way of our new Maser and the other slaves, as they all had different ways and rules to go by.

Sometimes when they traded us they would put the women to bed with this negro man and then the other to find out which one would be suited together the best, of course that never suited us much but we had to do just like our Masers made us, as we could not do any other way. If we refused they would whip or be so mean to us and we had to do just what our Masers wanted us to do, no back-firing on our part.

Well the way we traveled as slaves was just about like you have seen people drive cattle to market. Our Maser would put us in the road ahead of them and they would be on horses behind us as we traveled and they would follow and we had to travel pert, no laggin on behind if we did, he always had whip that he would tap us with, boy! when he hit us across the legs we could step real lively and I don't mean maybe either. In these days we did not have trucks to travel in or for our Masers to haul us in and if there was a very large bunch of us negroes to be moved from one place to another, we had to hit it on foot.

Yes, I have seen a few slaves in chains because they would be so unruly that their Maser would have to put them in chains. We had one slave there on our plantation that Maser could not do anything with in the way of keeping him at home. When night come he had him a girl that lived over on another plantation joining ours and that negro would go over there when Maser told him to go to bed in his quarters, and just as soon as Maser got to bed he would get up and slip off over to see his girl, and he would not come back to his quarters until just before daylight, then he would not be any account at all that day. So Maser he tried ever [every] way to get along with that negro without putting him in chains, he whipped him and the patterrollers [patrollers] they got hold of him several times but that did not do any good so he finally got him some chains and put around that negroes legs and then he would get him a pole and hop around on, he would get over there some way to see his girl. They got to where they could get them chains off that negro, and Maser he would not be out done so he fixed that negro a shed and bed close to a tree there on the plantation and chained his hands and feet to that tree so he could not slip off to see his girl. Of course that fixed the negro slave so he could not travel at night to see his girl, but still that did not do any good but Maser finally did put a stop to the negro man running around at night, then his girl started. She would come over there to his shed and bed and they would lay around there, talk and go on all night, so that negro he would lose so much sleep that he still was not any account. Still they could not out do Maser. He put that negro up for sale and not one that lived there close by would . . . offer to buy him as they knew how he was, but there was a man that came in there from another state offered to buy him from Maser and he sold him, and when that negro found out that his Maser had sold him he began to beg him not to. He promised Maser if he would not sell him and take him away from his girl and would let him go to see his girl . . . once a week, he would stay at home and be a real good negro, as him and this girl had one child by now. But Maser would not listen to that negro as he had done too much trouble with him already and let the man have him. The man told him he could not go to see any girl there where he was carrying him as there was not any girls there for him to slip off to see. They like to have killed that negro but it did not do any good.

2.23. "Gone, Gone—Sold and Gone." The Slave Trade in Verse, Prose, and Song

Each concerned observer of the American scene in slavery times naturally used his or her own medium of expression. Six authors, some obscure and some well known, but all with something important to say about American slavery, are considered here one by one, beginning with brief statements about their lives and concluding with one or two of their works.

SOURCES: Benjamin Brawley, *Early Negro American Writers* (New York: Dover Publication, 1970), pp. 39–40, 228–33, 292–93; John Greenleaf Whittier, *Anti-Slavery Poems: Songs of Labor and Reform* (New York: Arno Press, 1969); Harriet Beecher Stowe, *Uncle Tom's Cabin or Life Among the Lowly* (New York: D. Appleton, 1898), pp. 131–36; and a collection of sheet music at Stephen Foster Memorial Building, University of Pittsburgh.

Phillis Wheatley, born in Africa about 1754, was captured and shipped as a slave to Massachusetts and there sold on the block at the age of seven. Entering the home of a prosperous and enlightened family, Wheatley "in sixteen Months Time from her Arrival," in the words of her master, "attained the English Language, to which she was an utter Stranger before, to such a Degree, as to read . . . the most difficult Parts of the Sacred Writings, to the great Astonishment of all who heard her." In 1773, still a slave, she published her first book of verse and for this and her later poetry won wide acclaim. Wheatley's life was brief and often hard, but she became "the first black, the first slave, and the third woman in the United States to publish a book of poems."[46] The short excerpt below from one of her poems reveals her deep regard for the oppressed of Africa and lingering concern for her parents whom she was forced to leave behind.

From Phillis Wheatley,
Poems on Various Subjects, Religious and Moral.
No more, America, in mournful strain,
Of wrongs, and grievances unredress'd complain;
No longer shall thou dread the iron chain
Which wanton Tyranny, with lawless hand
Had made, and with it meant t'enslave the land.

---

46. See Sidney Kaplan and Emma Nogrady Kaplan, *The Black Presence in the Era of the American Revolution,* rev. ed. (Amherst: University of Massachusetts Press), pp. 170–71.

In the Hands of Strangers

Should you, my lord, while you peruse my song,
Wonder from whence my love of Freedom sprung,
Whence flow these wishes for the common good,
By feeling hearts alone best understood,
I, young in life, by seeming cruel fate
Was snatchd from Afric's fancied happy seat:
What pangs excruciating must molest,
What sorrows labour in my parent's breast!
Steeled was that soul, and by no misery moved,
That from a father seized his babe beloved:
Such, such my case. And can I then but pray
Others may never feel tyrannic sway?

John Greenleaf Whittier wrote many poems on the topic of slavery. One of
the best was "The Farewell of a Virginia Slave-Mother to Her Daughters,
Sold into Southern Bondage," which appears below.

John Greenleaf Whittier
"The Farewell of a Virginia Slave-Mother to Her Daughters,
Sold into Southern Bondage."

Gone, gone—sold and gone,
To the rice-swamp dank and lone.
Where the slave-whip ceaseless swings,
Where the noisome insect stings,
Where the fever demon strews
Poison with the falling dews,
Where the sickly sunbeams glare
Through the hot and misty air—
Gone, gone—sold and gone,
To the rice-swamp dank and lone,
From Virginia's hills and waters—
Woe is me, my stolen daughters!

Gone, gone—sold and gone,
To the rice-swamp dank and lone.
There no mother's eye is near them,
There no mother's ear can hear them;
Never, when the torturing lash
Seams their back with many a gash,
Shall a mother's kindness bless them,

The Internal Slave Trade of the United States

Or a mother's arms caress them,
Gone, gone—sold and gone,
To the rice-swamp dank and lone,
From Virginia's hills and waters—
Woe is me, my stolen daughters!

Gone, gone—sold and gone,
To the rice-swamp dank and lone,
Oh, when weary, sad, and slow,
From the fields at night they go,
Faint with toil and racked with pain,
To their cheerless homes again—
There no brother's voice shall greet them,
There no father's welcome meet them.
Gone, gone—sold and gone,
To the rice-swamp dank and lone,
From Virginia's hills and waters—
Woe is me, my stolen daughters!

Gone, gone—sold and gone,
To the rice-swamp dank and lone,
From the tree whose shadow lay
On their childhood's place of play
From the cool spring where they drank;
Rock, and hill, and rivulet bank;
From the silent house of prayer,
And the holy counsels there—
Gone, gone—sold and gone,
To the rice-swamp dank and lone,
From Virginia's hills and waters—
Woe is me, my stolen daughters!

Gone, gone—sold and gone,
To the rice-swamp dank and lone;
Toiling through the weary day,
And at night the spoiler's prey
Oh, that they had earlier died,
Sleeping calmly side by side,
Where the tyrant's power is o'er
And the fetter galls no more!
Gone, gone—sold and gone,

To the rice-swamp dank and lone,
From Virginia's hills and waters—
Woe is me, my stolen daughters!

James M. Whitfield was born free in Boston and worked as a barber in Buffalo. By 1852 he was writing verses for newspapers and in 1853 he published a book of poetry entitled *America and Other Poems.* Excerpts from his poem "America" contrast the accomplishments of blacks in the Revolutionary War with their conditions under slavery.

James M. Whitfield,
America

America, it is to thee,
Thou boasted land of liberty,—
It is to thee I raise my song,
Thou land of blood, and crime, and wrong.
It is to thee, my native land,
From which has issued many a band,
To tear the black man from his soil,
And force him here to delve and toil;
Chained on your blood-bemoistened sod,
Cringing beneath a tyrant's rod,
Stripped of those rights which Nature's God
Bequeathed to all the human race,
Bound to a petty tyrant's nod,
Because he wears a paler face.
Was it for this that freedom's fires
Were kindled by your patriot sires?
Was it for this they shed their blood,
On hill and plain, on field and flood? . . .
The thought ne'er entered in their brains
That they endured those toils and pains,
To force fresh fetters, heavier chains
For their own children, in whose veins
Should flow that patriotic blood,
So freely shed on field and flood.
Oh, no; they fought, as they believed,
For the inherent rights of man;
But mark, how they have been deceived
By slavery's accursed plan. . . .

Could they have looked, with prophet's ken,
Down to the present evil time,
Seen free-born men, uncharged with crime,
Consigned unto a slaver's pen,—
Or thrust into a prison cell,
With thieves and murderers to dwell—
While that same flag whose stripes and stars
Had been their guide through freedom's wars
As proudly waved above the pen
Of dealers in the souls of men!
Almighty God! 'Tis this they call
The land of liberty and law;
Part of its sons in baser thrall
Than Babylon or Egypt saw—
Worse scenes of rapine, lust and shame,
Than Babylonian ever knew,
Are perpetrated in the name
Of God, the holy, just and true; . . .
We do not before thy throne,
With carnal weapons drenched in gore,
Although our blood has freely flown,
In adding to the tyrant's store. . . .
For while thou'rt holy, just and good,
The battle is not to the strong;
But in the sacred name of peace,
Of justice, virtue, love and truth,
We pray, and never mean to cease,
Till weak old age and fiery youth
In freedom's cause their voices raise,
And burst the bonds of every slave;
Till north and south, and east and west,
The wrongs we bear shall be redressed.

Harriet Beecher Stowe chose to write a serialized novel, *Uncle Tom's Cabin*, to express her aversion to slavery. The extract from that work below features four characters: Mr. Haley, a slavetrader; Uncle Tom (Haley's recently purchased property), a slave woman broken with age called Aunt Hagar, and her fourteen-year-old son Albert, who are sold at a public auction in the town of Washington, Kentucky. The piece, though fictional, greatly resembles a giant slave auction held in Savannah, Georgia, in 1859 (see Doc. 2.25).

From Harriett Beecher Stowe's *Uncle Tom's Cabin*.
Chapter XII

Mr. Haley and Tom jogged onward in their wagon, each, for a time absorbed in his own reflections. Now, the reflections of two men sitting side by side are a curious thing,—seated on the same seat, having the same eyes, ears, hands, and organs of all sorts, and having pass before their eyes the same objects,—it is wonderful what a variety we shall find in these same reflections!

As, for example, Mr. Haley: he thought first of Tom's length, and breadth, and height, and what he would sell for, if he was kept fat and in good case till he got him into market. He thought of how he should make out his gang; he thought of the respective market value of certain supposititious men and women and children who were to compose it, and other kindred topics of the business; then he thought of himself, and how humane he was, that whereas other men chained their "niggers" hand and foot both, he only put fetters on the feet, and left Tom the use of his hands, as long as he behaved well; and he sighed to think how ungrateful human nature was, so that there was even room to doubt whether Tom appreciated his mercies. He had been taken in so by "niggers" whom he had favored; but still he was astonished to consider how good-natured he yet remained! . . .

Mr. Haley pulled out of his pocket sundry newspapers, and began looking over their advertisements, with absorbed interest. He was not a remarkably fluent reader, and was in the habit of reading in a sort of recitative half-aloud, by way of calling in his ears to verify the deductions of his eyes. In this tone he slowly recited the following paragraph:—

"'EXECUTOR'S SALE,—NEGROES!—Agreeably to order of court, will be sold, on Tuesday, February 20, before the Court-house door, in the town of Washington, Kentucky, the following negroes: Hagar, aged 60; John, aged 30; Ben, aged 21; Saul, aged 25; Albert, aged 14. Sold for the benefit of the creditors and heirs of the estate of Jesse Blutchford, Esq.

SAMUEL MORRIS, THOMAS FLINT, *Executors.*'

"This yer I must look at," said he to Tom, for want of somebody else to talk to.

"Ye see, I'm going to get up a prime gang to take down with ye, Tom; it'll make it sociable and pleasant like,—good company will, ye know. We must drive right to Washington first and foremost, and then I'll clap you into jail, while I does the business."

Tom received this agreeable intelligence quite meekly, simply wondering, in his own heart, how many of these doomed men had wives and children, and whether they would feel as he did about leaving them. It is to be confessed, too, that the naive, offhand information that he was to be thrown into jail by no means produced an agreeable impression on a poor fellow who had always prided himself on a strictly honest and upright course of life. Yes, Tom, we must confess it, was rather proud of his honesty, poor fellow,—not having very much else to be proud of;—if he had belonged to some of the higher walks of society, he, perhaps, would never have been reduced to such straits. However, the day wore on, and the evening saw Haley and Tom comfortably accomodated in Washington,—the one in a tavern, and the other in a jail.

About eleven o'clock the next day, a mixed throng was gathered around the court-house steps,—smoking, chewing, spitting, swearing, and conversing, according to their respective tastes and turns,—waiting for the auction to commence. The men and women to be sold sat in a group apart, talking in a low tone to each other. The woman who had been advertised by the name of Hagar was a regular African in feature and figure. She might have been sixty, but was older than that by hard work and disease, was partially blind, and somewhat crippled with rheumatism. By her side stood her only remaining son, Albert, a bright-looking little fellow of fourteen years. The boy was the only survivor of a large family, who had been successively sold away from her to a southern market. The mother held on to him with both her shaking hands, and eyed with intense trepidation every one who walked up to examine him.

"Don't be feard, Aunt Hagar," said the oldest of the men, "I spoke to Mas'r Thomas 'bout it, and he thought he might manage to sell you in a lot both together."

"Dey needn't call me worn out yet," said she, lifting her shaking hands. "I can cook yet, and scrub, and scour,—I'm wuth a buying, if I do come cheap;—tell 'em dat ar,—you *tell 'em,*" she added earnestly.

Haley here forced his way into the group, walked up to the old man, pulled his mouth open and looked in, felt of his teeth, made him stand and straighten himself, bend his back, and perform various evolutions to show his muscles, and then passed on to the next, and put him through the same trial. Walking up last to the boy, he felt of his arms, straightened his hands, and looked at his fingers, and made him jump, to show his agility.

"He ain't gwine to be sold widout me!" said the old woman, with passionate eagerness; "he and I goes in a lot together; I's rail strong yet, Mas'r, and can do heaps o' work,—heaps on it, Mas'r."

"On plantation?" said Haley, with a contemptuous glance. "Likely story!" and, as if satisfied with his examination, he walked out and looked, and stood with his hands in his pockets, his cigar in his mouth, and his hat cocked on one side, ready for action.

"What think of 'em?" said a man who had been following Haley's examination, as if to make up his own mind from it.

"Wal," said Haley, spitting, "I shall put in, I think, for the youngerly ones and the boy."

"They want to sell the boy and the old woman together," said the man.

"Find it a tight pull;—why, she's an old rack o'bones,—not worth her salt."

"You wouldn't, then?" said the man.

"Anybody'd be a fool 'twould. She's half blind, crooked with rheumatis, and foolish to boot."

"Some buys up these yer old critturs, and ses there's a sight more wear in 'em than a body'd think," said the man reflectively.

"No go, 'tall," said Haley; "wouldn't take her for a present,—fact,—I've *seen* now."

"Wal, 'tis kinder pity, not to buy her with her son,—her heart seems so sot on him,—s'pose they fling her in cheap."

"Them that's got money to spend that ar way, it's all well enough. I shall bid off on that ar boy for a plantation-hand;—wouldn't be bothered with her, no way,—not if they'd give her to me," said Haley.

"She'll take on despit," said the man.

"Nat'lly, she will," said the trader, coolly.

The conversation was here interrupted by a busy hum in the audience; and the auctioneer, a short, bustling, important fellow, elbowed his way into the crowd. The old woman drew in her breath, and caught instinctively at her son.

"Keep close to yer mammy, Albert,—close,—dey'll put us up togedder," she said.

"Oh, mammy, I'm feared they won't," said the boy.

"Dey must, child; I can't live, noways, if they don't," said the old creature, vehemently.

The stentorian tones of the auctioneer, calling out to clear the way, now announced that the sale was about to commence. A place was cleared, and the bidding began. The different men on the list were soon knocked off at prices which showed a pretty brisk demand in the market; two of them fell to Haley.

"Come, now, young'un," said the auctioneer, giving the boy a touch with his hammer, "be up and show your springs, now."

"Put us two up togedder, togedder,—do, please, Mas'r," said the old woman, holding fast to her boy.

"Be off ," said the man, gruffly, pushing her hands away; "you come last. Now, darkey, spring"; and, with the word, he pushed the boy toward the block, while a deep heavy groan rose behind him. The boy paused, and looked back; but there was no time to stay, and, dashing the tears from his large, bright eyes, he was up in a moment.

His fine figure, alert limbs, and bright face, raised an instant competition, and half a dozen bids simultaneously met the ear of the auctioneer. Anxious, half frightened, he looked from side to side, as he heard the clatter of contending bids,—now here, now there,—till the hammer fell. Haley had got him. He was pushed from the block toward his new master, but stopped one moment, and looked back, when his poor old mother, trembling in every limb, held out her shaking hands toward him.

"Buy me too, Mas'r, for de dear Lord's sake!—buy me,—I shall die if you don't!"

"You'll die if I do, that's the kink of it," said Haley,—"no!" And he turned on his heel.

The bidding for the poor creature was summary. The man who had addressed Haley, and who seemed not destitute of compassion, bought her for a trifle, and the spectators began to disperse.

The poor victims of the sale, who had been brought up in one place together for years, gathered round the despairing old mother, whose agony was pitiful to see.

"Couldn't dey leave me one? Mas'r allers said I should have one,—he did," she repeated over and over, in heart-broken tones.

"Trust in the Lord, Aunt Hagar," said the oldest of the men, sorrowfully.

"What good will it do?" she said, sobbing passionately.

"Mother, mother,—don't! don't!" said the boy. "They say yous got a good master."

"I don't care,—I don't care. Oh, Albert! Oh, my boy! You's my last baby. Lord, how ken I?"

"Come, take her off, can't some of ye?" said Haley, dryly; "don't do no good for her to go on that ar way."

The old men of the company, partly by persuasion and partly by force, loosed the poor creature's last despairing hold, and, as they led her off to her new master's wagon, strove to comfort her.

"Now!" said Haley, pushing his three purchases together, and producing a bundle of handcuffs, which he proceeded to put on their wrists; and fastening each handcuff to a long chain, he drove them before him to the jail.

In the Hands of Strangers

The Pittsburgh composer, Stephen Foster, also touched on slavery and the slave trade in song and verse. In 1845, at the age of nineteen, he belonged to a singing society which met at the Foster home, and, since "Negro melodies" were popular, he began to compose in that genre with such titles as "Louisiana Belle," "Uncle Ned," "Way Down South, Where de Cane Grows," and at the age of 23, "Nelly Was a Lady," a song about "a dark Virginny bride" who dies while traveling down the Mississippi River, probably on an involuntary journey to the deep South. In the opinion of Harold Milligan, author of *Stephen Collins Foster* (New York: G. Schirmer, 1920), this was "not the negro of 'Jump Jim Crow' and 'Zip Coon,' but of 'Uncle Tom's Cabin.' " The Foster verses included here, though at times lighthearted, convey a tragic message, a "feeling of sadness and sorrow," in the words of J. Winston Coleman, "that permeates Stephen Collins Foster's immortal song, *My Old Kentucky* Home." [47] Much the same is true of Foster's "Farewell My Lily Dear."

Stephen Foster
"Farewell My Lilly Dear"
Lilly dear, it grieves me
The tale I have to tell;
Old massa sends me roaming,
So Lilly, fare-you-well!
Oh! fare-you-well my true love.
Farewell old Tennessee,
Then let me weep for you love,
But do not weep for me.
Farewell forever to old Tennessee;
Farewell my Lilly dear, Don't weep for me.

I's guine to roam the wide world
In lands I've never hoed,
With nothing but my banjo
To cheer me on the road;
For when I'm sad and weary
I'll make the banjo play,
To mind me of my true love
When I am far away.
Farewell forever to old Tennessee;
Farewell my Lilly dear, Don't weep for me.

47. See *Slavery Times in Kentucky,* pp. 194–95.

I wake up in the morning.
And walk out on the farm;
Oh! Lilly am a darling—
She take me by the arm.
We wander through the clover
Down by the river side,
I tell her that I love her
And she must be my bride.
Farewell forever to old Tennessee;
Farewell my Lilly dear, Don't weep for me.

Oh! Lilly dear 'tis mournful
To leave you here alone,
You'll smile before I leave you
And weep when I am gone,
The sun can never shine, love
So bright for you and me,
As when I worked beside you
In good old Tennessee.
Farewell forever to old Tennessee;
Farewell my Lilly dear, Don't weep for me.

The author of the final poem, Frances E. W. Harper, was born free in Baltimore in 1825. She became a teacher, a supporter of the Underground Railroad, and an eloquent antislavery lecturer in Maine and in the South after the Civil War. She was the author of a novel and several collections of poetry.

Frances E. W. Harper
Bury Me in a Free Land

Make me a grave where'er you will,
In a lowly plain, or a lofty hill;
Make it among earth's humblest graves,
But not in a land where men are slaves.
I could not rest if around my grave
I heard the steps of a trembling slave;
His shadow above my silent tomb
Would make it a place of fearful gloom.
I could not rest if I heard the tread
Of a coffle gang to the shambles led,
And the mother's shriek of wild despair

Rise like a curse on the trembling air.
I could not sleep if I saw the lash
Drinking her blood at each fearful gash,
And I saw her babes torn from her breast,
Like trembling doves from their parent nest.
I'd shudder and start if I heard the bay
Of bloodhounds seizing their human prey,
And I heard the captive plead in vain
As they bound afresh his galling chain.
If I saw young girls from their mothers' arms
Bartered and sold for their youthful charms,
My eye would flash with a mournful flame,
My death-paled cheek grow red with shame.
I would sleep, dear friends, where bloated might
Can rob no man of his dearest right;
My rest shall be calm in any grave
Where none can call his brother a slave.
I ask no monument, proud and high,
To arrest the gaze of the passers-by;
All that my yearning spirit craves,
Is Bury me not in a land of slaves.

2.24. A Great Auction Sale of Slaves at Savannah, Georgia, March 2
and 3, 1859

In 1859, Mortimer Thomson, a correspondent for Horace Greeley's *New York Tribune,* traveled to Savannah, Georgia, to report on an auction of some 450 "long cotton and rice negroes," an unusually large number to be sold at a single auction. As we have seen, the *Tribune* was an established critic of the Southern labor system, and therefore Thomson attended the auction posing as a wealthy slave-buying planter, even making occasional bids of his own, though not enough to result in a purchase. The slaves involved in the sale were the property of Pierce Butler, one of two male heirs to the properties of their grandfather, a planter and politician perhaps best known for his participation in the Constitutional Convention of 1787 and his writing of the Constitution's fugitive-slave clause (see Paul Finkelman, *An Imperfect Union: Slavery, Federalism, and Comity* [Chapel Hill: University of North Carolina Press, 1981], pp. 26–28, 239–42). No less fascinating, the younger Pierce Butler whose slaves were to be sold in Savannah was the divorced husband of the noted English actress, Fannie Kemble, who resided for a time at the Butler estate on the Altamaha River in Georgia and there wrote distinctly negative accounts of the condition and treatment of the Butler slaves (see Frances Anne Kemble, *Journal of a Residence on a Georgia Plantation in 1838–1839* [Athens: University of Georgia Press, 1984]). For more on the younger Pierce Butler and the financial dealings that forced him to sell his slaves, and on Joseph Bryan, the leading slave dealer of Georgia who was in charge of the sale, see Frederic Bancroft's *Slave Trading in the Old South*, pp. 75, 222–36, 378.

SOURCE: "Great Auction Sale of Slaves, at Savannah, Georgia, March 2d and 3d, 1859. Reported for The Tribune" (New York: American Anti-Slavery Society, 1859).

SALE OF SLAVES.

The largest sale of human chattels that has been made in Star-Spangled America for several years took place on Wednesday and Thursday of last week, at the Race Course near the City of Savannah, Georgia. The lot consisted of four hundred and thirty-six men, women, children and infants, being that half of the negro stock remaining of the old Major Butler plantations which fell to one of the two heirs to that estate. Major Butler, dying, left a property valued at more than a million of dollars, the major part of which was invested in rice and cotton plantations, and the slaves thereon, all of which immense fortune descended to two heirs, his [grand]sons, Mr. John A. Butler, sometime deceased, and Mr. Pierce M. Butler, still living, and resident in the City of Philadelphia, in the free State of Pennsylvania. Losses in the great crash of 1857–8, and other exigencies of business, had compelled the latter gentleman to realize on his Southern investments, that he may satisfy his pressing creditors. This necessity led to a partition of the negro stock on the Georgia plantations, between himself and the representative of the other heir, the widow of the late John A. Butler, and the negroes that were brought to the hammer last week were the property of Mr. Pierce M. Butler of Philadelphia, and were in fact sold to pay Mr. Pierce M. Butler's debts. The creditors were represented by Gen. Cadwallader, while Mr. Butler was present in person, attended by his business agent, to attend to his own interests.

The sale had been advertised largely for many weeks, though the name of Mr. Butler was not mentioned; and as the negroes were known to be a choice lot and very desirable property, the attendance of buyers was large. The breaking up of an old family estate is so uncommon an occurrence that the affair was regarded with unusual interest throughout the South. For several days before the sale every hotel in Savannah was crowded with negro speculators from North and South Carolina, Virginia, Georgia, Alabama and Louisiana, who had been attracted hither by the prospects of making good bargains. Nothing was heard for days, in the bar-rooms and public rooms, but talk of the great sale, criticisms of the business affairs of Mr. Butler, and speculations as to the probable prices the stock would bring. The office of Joseph Bryan, the negro broker who had the management of the sale, was thronged every day by eager inquiries in search of information, and by some who were anxious to buy, but were uncertain as to whether their securities would prove acceptable. Little parties were made up from the various hotels every day to visit the Race Course, distant some three miles from the city, to look over the chattels, discuss their points, and make memoranda for guidance on the day of sale. The buyers were generally of a rough breed, slangy, profane and bearish, being for the most part from the back river and swamp plantations, where the elegancies of polite life are not, perhaps, developed to their fullest extent. In fact, the humanities are sadly neglected by the petty tyrants of the rice fields that border the great Dismal Swamp, their knowledge of the luxuries of our best society comprehending only revolvers and kindred delicacies.[48]

Your correspondent was present at an early date; but as he easily anticipated the touching welcome that would, at such a time, be officiously extended to a representative of *The Tribune,* and being a modest man withal, and not desiring to be the recipient of a public demonstration from the enthusiastic Southern population, who at times overdo their hospitality and their guests, he did not placard his mission and claim his honors. Although he kept his business in the background, he made himself a prominent figure in the picture, and, wherever there was anything going on, there was he in the midst. At the sale might have been seen a busy individual, armed with pencil and catalogue, doing his little utmost to keep up all the appearance of a knowing buyer pricing "likely nigger fellers," talking confidentially to the smartest ebon maid, chucking the round-eyed youngsters under the chin, making an occasional bid for a large family, (a low bid—so low that somebody always instantly raised him twenty-five dollars, when the busy man would ignominiously retreat), and otherwise conducting himself like a rich planter, with forty thousand dollars where he could put his finger on it. This gentleman was much condoled with by some sympa-

48. The author perhaps meant the Okefenokee Swamp, mentioned later, about forty miles southwest of the Butler properties. The Dismal Swamp straddles the border between North Carolina and Virginia. Editor.

thizing persons, when the particularly fine lot on which he had fixed his eye was sold and lost to him forever, because he happened to be down stairs at lunch just at the interesting moment.

WHERE THE NEGROES CAME FROM.

The negroes came from two plantations, the one a rice plantation near Darien in the State of Georgia, not far from the Okefenokee Swamp, and the other a cotton plantation on the extreme northern point of St. Simon's Island, a little bit of an island in the Atlantic, cut off from [the] Georgia main land by a slender arm of the sea. Though the most of the stock had been accustomed only to rice and cotton planting, there were among them a number of very passable mechanics, who had been taught to do all the rougher sorts of mechanical work on the plantations. There were coopers, carpenters, shoemakers and blacksmiths, each one equal in his various craft to the ordinary requirements of a plantation. . . . Though probably no one of all these would be called a superior, or even an average, workman, among the masters of the craft, their knowledge of these various trades sold in some cases for nearly as much as the man—that is, a man without a trade, who would be valued at $900, would readily bring $1,600 or $1,700 if he was a passable blacksmith or cooper.

There were no light mulattoes in the whole lot of the Butler stock, and but very few that were even a shade removed from the original Congo blackness. They have been little defiled by the admixture of degenerate Anglo-Saxon blood, and, for the most part, could boast that they were of as pure a breed as the best blood of Spain—a point in their favor in the eyes of the buyer as well as physiologically, for too liberal an infusion of the blood of the dominant race brings a larger intelligence, a more vigorous brain, which, anon, grows restless under the yoke, and is prone to inquire into the definition of the word liberty, and the meaning of the starry flag which waves, as you may have heard, o'er the land of the free. . . .

None of the Butler slaves have ever been sold before, but have been on these two plantations since they were born. Here have they lived their humble lives, and loved their simple loves; here were they born, and here have many of them had children born unto them; here had their parents lived before them, and are now resting in quiet graves on the old plantations that these unhappy ones are to see no more forever; here they left not only the well-known scenes dear to them from very babyhood by a thousand fond memories, and homes as much loved by them, perhaps as brighter homes by men of brighter face; but all the clinging ties that bound them to living hearts were torn asunder, for but one half of each of these two happy little communities were sent to the shambles *to be scattered to the*

In the Hands of Strangers

four winds, and the other half was left behind. And who can tell how closely intertwined are the affections of a little band of four hundred persons living isolated from all the world beside, from birth to middle age? Do they not naturally become one great family, each man a brother unto each?

It is true they were sold "in families"; but let us see: a man and his wife were called a "family," their parents and kindred were not taken into account; the man and wife might be sold to the pine woods of North Carolina, their brothers and sisters be scattered through the cotton fields of Alabama and the rice swamps of Louisiana, while the parents might be left on the old plantation to wear out their weary lives in heavy grief, and lay their heads in far-off graves over which their children might never weep. And no account could be taken of loves that were as yet unconsummated by marriage; and how many aching hearts have been divorced by this summary proceeding, no man can ever know. And the separation is as utter, and is infinitely more hopeless than that made by the Angel of Death, for then the loved ones are committed to the care of a merciful Deity; but in the other instance, to the tender mercies of a slave-driver. These dark-skinned unfortunates are perfectly unlettered, and could not communicate by writing even if they should know where to send their missives. And so to each other, and to the old familiar places of their youth, clung all their sympathies and affections, not less strong, perhaps, because they are so few. The blades of grass on all the Butler estates are outnumbered by the tears that are poured out in agony at the wreck that has been wrought in happy homes, and the crushing grief that has been laid on loving hearts.

But, then, what business have "niggers" with tears? Besides, didn't Pierce Butler give them a silver dollar apiece? . . . And, sad as it is, it was all necessary, because a gentleman was not able to live on the beggarly pittance of half a million, and so must needs enter into speculations which turned out adversely.

HOW THEY WERE TREATED IN SAVANNAH.

The negroes were brought to Savannah in small lots, as many at a time as could be conveniently taken care of, the last of them reaching the city the Friday before the sale. They were consigned to the care of Mr. J. Bryan, Auctioneer and Negro Broker, who was to feed and keep them in condition until disposed of. Immediately on their arrival they were taken to the Race Course, and there quartered in the sheds erected for the accomodation of the horses and carriages of gentlemen attending the races. Into these sheds they were huddled pell-mell, without any more attention to their comfort than was necessary to prevent their becoming ill and unsalable. Each "family" had one or more boxes or bundles, in which were stowed such scanty articles of their clothing as were not brought into immediate requisition, and their tin dishes and gourds for their food and drink. . . .

In these sheds were the chattels huddled together on the floor, there being no sign of bench or table. They eat and sleep on the bare boards, their food being rice and beans, with occasionally a bit of bacon and corn bread. Their huge bundles were scattered over the floor, and thereon the slaves sat or reclined, when not restlessly moving about, or gathered into sorrowful groups, discussing the chances of their future fate. On the faces of all was an expression of heavy grief; some appeared to be resigned to the hard stroke of Fortune that had torn them from their homes, and were sadly trying to make the best of it; some sat brooding moodily over their sorrows, their chins resting on their hands, their eyes staring vacantly, and their bodies rocking to and fro, with a restless motion that was never stilled; few wept, the place was too public and the drivers too near, though some occasionally turned aside to give way to a few quiet tears. They were dressed in every possible variety of uncouth and fantastic garb, in every style and of every imaginable color; the texture of the garments was in all cases coarse, most of the men being clothed in the rough cloth that is made expressly for the slaves. The dresses assumed by the negro minstrels, when they give imitations of plantation character, are by no means exaggerated; they are, instead, weak and unable to come up to the original. There was every variety of hat, with every imaginable slouch; and there was every cut and style of coat and pantaloons, made with every conceivable ingenuity of misfit, and tossed on with a general appearance of perfect looseness that is perfectly indescribable except to say that a Southern negro always looks as if he could shake his clothes off without taking his hands out of his pockets. The women, true to the feminine instinct, had made, in almost every case, some attempt at finery. All wore gorgeous turbans, generally manufactured in an instant out of a gay-colored handkerchief by a sudden and graceful twist of the fingers; though there was occasionally a more elaborate turban, a turban complex and mysterious, got up with care and ornamented with a few beads or bright bits of ribbon. Their dresses were mostly coarse stuff, though there were some of gaudy calicoes; a few had earrings, and one possessed the treasure of a string of yellow and blue beads. The little children were always better and more carefully dressed than the older ones, the parental pride coming out in the shape of a yellow cap pointed like a mitre, or a jacket with a strip of red broadcloth round the bottom. The children were of all sizes, the youngest being fifteen days old. The babies were generally good-natured; though when one would set up a yell, the complaint soon attacked the others, and a full chorus would be the result.

The slaves remained at the race-course, some of them for more than a week and all of them for four days before the sale. They were brought in thus early that buyers who desired to inspect them might enjoy that privilege, although none of them were sold at a private sale. For these preliminary days their shed was constantly visited by speculators. The negroes were examined with as little consideration as if they had been brutes indeed; the buyers pulling their mouths open to see their teeth, pinching their limbs to find how muscular they were, walking them up and down to detect any signs of lameness, making them stoop and bend in different ways that they might be certain there was no concealed rupture or wound; and in addition to all this treatment, asking them scores of questions relative to their qualifications and accomplishments. All these humiliations were submitted to without a murmur, and in some instances with good-natured cheerfulness—where the slave liked the appearance of the proposed buyer, and fancied that he might prove a kind "mas'r."

The following curiously sad scene is the type of a score of others that were there enacted:

"Elisha," chattel No. 5 in the catalogue, had taken a fancy to a benevolent-looking middle-aged gentleman who was inspecting the stock, and thus used his powers of persuasion to induce the benevolent man to purchase him, with his wife, boy and girl, Molly, Israel and Sevanda, chattels Nos. 6, 7 and 8. The earnestness with which the poor fellow pressed his suit, knowing as he did that perhaps the happiness of his whole life depended on his success, was touching, and the arguments he used most pathetic. He made no appeal to the feelings of the buyer; he rested no hope on his charity and kindness, but only strove to show how well worth his dollars were the bone and blood he was entreating him to buy.

"Look at me, Mas'r: am prime rice planter; sho' you won't find a better man den me; no better on de whole plantation; not a bit old yet; do mo' work den ever; do carpenter work, too, little; better buy me, Mas'r; I'se be good sarvant, Mas'r. Molly, too, my wife, Sa, fus' rate rice hand; mos as good as me. Stan' out yer, Molly, and let the gen'lm'n see."

Molly advances, with her hands crossed on her bosom, and makes a quick short curtsy, and stands mute, looking appealingly in the benevolent man's face. But Elisha talks all the faster.

"Show mas'r yer arm, Molly—good arm dat, Mas'r—she do a heap of work mo' with dat arm yet. Let good Mas'r see yer teeth, Molly—see dat, Mas'r, teeth all reg'lar, all good—she'm young gal yet. Come out yer, Israel, walk aroun' an let the gen'lm'n see how spry you be."

Then pointing to the three-year-old girl who stood with her chubby hand to her mouth, holding on to her mother's dress, and uncertain what to make of the strange scene.

"Little Vardy's only a chile yet; make prime gal by-and-by. Better buy us, Mas'r, we'm fus' rate bargain."—and so on. But the benevolent gentleman found where he could drive a closer bargain, and so bought somebody else.

Similar scenes were transacting all the while on every side—parents praising the strength and cleverness of their children, and showing off every muscle and sinew to the very best advantage, not with the excusable pride of other parents, but to make them the more desirable in the eyes of the man-buyer; and, on the other hand, children excusing and mitigating the age and inability of parents, that they might be more marketable and fall, if possible, into kind hands. Not unfrequently these representations, if borne out by the facts, secured a purchaser. The women never spoke to the white men unless spoken to, and then made the conference as short as possible. And not one of them all, during the whole time they were thus exposed to the rude questions of vulgar men, spoke the first unwomanly or indelicate word, or conducted herself in any regard otherwise than as a modest woman should do; their conversation and demeanor were quite as unexceptionable as they would have been had they been the highest ladies in the land, and through all the insults to which they were subjected they conducted themselves with the most perfect decorum and self-respect.

The sentiment of the subjoined characteristic dialogue was heard more than once repeated:

"Well, Colonel, I seen you looking sharp at shoemaker Bill's Sally. Going to buy her?"

"Well, Major, I think not. Sally's a good, big, strapping gal, and can do a heap o' work; but it's five years since she had any children. *She's done breeding, I reckon.*"

In the intervals of more active labor, the discussion of the reopening of the slave trade was commenced, and the opinion seemed to generally prevail that its reëstablishment is a consummation devoutly to be wished, and one red-faced Major or General or Corporal clenched his remarks with the emphatic assertion that "We'll have all the niggers in Africa over here in three years—we won't leave enough for seed."

THE SALE.

The Race Course at Savannah is situated about three miles from the city, in a pleasant spot, nearly surrounded by woods. As it rained violently during the two days of the sale, the place was only accessible by carriages, and the result was that few attended but actual buyers, who had come from long distances, and could not afford to lose the opportunity. . . .

The negroes looked more uncomfortable than ever; the close confinement indoors for a number of days, and the drizzly, unpleasant weather, began to tell on their condition. They moved about more listlessly, and were fast losing the activity and springiness they had at first shown. This morning they were all gathered into the long room of the building erected as the "Grand Stand" of the Race Course, that they might be immediately under the eye of the buyers. The room was about a hundred feet long by twenty wide, and herein were crowded the poor creatures, with much of their baggage, awaiting their respective calls to step upon the block and be sold to the highest bidder. This morning Mr. Pierce Butler appeared among his people, speaking to each one, and being recognized with seeming pleasure by all. The men obsequiously pulled off their hats and made that indescribable sliding hitch with the foot which passes with a negro for a bow; and the women each dropped the quick curtsy which they seldom vouchsafe to any other than their legitimate master and mistress. Occasionally, to a very old or favorite servant, Mr. Butler would extend his gloved hand, which mark of condescension was instantly hailed with grins of delight from all the sable witnesses.

The room in which the sale actually took place immediately adjoined the room of the negroes, and communicated with it by two large doors. The sale room was open to the air on one side, commanding a view of the entire Course. A small platform was raised about two feet and a half high, on which were placed the desks of the entry clerks, leaving room in front of them for the auctioneer and the goods.

At about 11 o'clock the business men took their places and announced that the sale would begin. Mr. Bryan, the negro-broker, is a dapper little man, wearing spectacles and a yachting hat, sharp and sudden in his movements, and perhaps the least bit in the world obtrusively officious—as earnest in his language as he could be without actually swearing, though acting much as if he would like to swear a little at the critical moment; Mr. Bryan did not sell the goods, he merely superintended the operation, and saw that the entry clerks did their duty properly. . . .

Mr. Walsh [the auctioneer] mounted the stand and announced the terms of the sale, "one-third cash, the remainder payable in two equal annual instalments, bearing interest from the day of sale, to be secured by approved mortgage and personal security, or approved acceptances in Savannah, Ga., or Charleston, S. C. Purchasers to pay for papers." The buyers, who were present to the number of about two hundred, clustered around the platform; while the negroes, who were not likely to be immediately wanted, gathered into sad groups in the background to watch the progress of the selling in which they were so sorrowfully interested. The wind howled outside, and through the open side of the building the driving rain came pouring in; the bar down stairs ceased for a short time its brisk trade; the buyers lit fresh cigars, got ready their catalogues and pencils, and the first lot of human chattels was led upon the stand, not by a white man, but by a sleek mulatto, himself a slave, and who seems to regard the selling of his brethren, in which he so glibly assists, as a capital joke. It had been announced that the negroes would be sold in "families," that is to say, a man would not be parted from his wife, or a mother from a very young child. There is perhaps as much policy as humanity in this arrangement, for thereby many aged and unserviceable people are disposed of, who otherwise would not find a ready sale.

The first family brought out were announced on the catalogue as

NAME	AGE	Remarks
1. George 27	. . . .	.Prime Cotton Planter.
2. Sue 26	. . . .	.Prime Rice Planter.
3. George 6	. . . .	.Boy Child.
4. Harry 2	. . . .	.Boy Child.

The manner of buying was announced to be, bidding a certain price apiece for the whole lot. Thus George and his family were started at $300, and were finally sold at $600 each, being $2,400 for the four. To get an idea of the relative value of each one, we must suppose George worth $1,200, Sue worth $900, Little George worth $200, and Harry worth $100. Owing, however, to some misapprehension on the part of the buyer as to the manner of bidding, he did not take the family at this figure, and they were put up and sold again, on the second day, when they brought $620 each, or $2,480 for the whole—an advance of $80 over the first sale. . . .

It seems as if every shade of character capable of being implicated in the sale of human flesh and blood was represented among the buyers. . . . These gentry, with quiet step and subdued voice, moved carefully about among the live stock, ignoring, as a general rule, the men, but tormenting the women with questions which, when accidentally overheard by the disinterested spectator, bred in that spectator's mind an almost irresistible desire to knock somebody down. And then, all imaginable varieties of rough backwood rowdies, who began the day in a spirited manner, but who, as its hours progressed, and their practice at the bar became more prolific in results, waxed louder and talkier and more violent, were present and added a characteristic feature to the assemblage. Those of your readers who have read "Uncle Tom's Cabin"—and who has not?—will remember with peculiar feelings, Legree, the slave-driver and woman-whipper. That that character is not overdrawn or too highly colored, there is abundant testimony. Witness the subjoined dialogue: A party of men were conversing on the fruitful subject of managing refractory "niggers"; some were for severe whipping, some recommending branding, one or two recommended other modes of torture, but one huge brute of a man, who had not taken an active part in the discussion, save to assent with approving nod to any unusually barbarous proposition, at last broke his silence by saying, in an oracular way, "You may say what you like about managing niggers; I'm a driver myself, and I've had some experience, and I ought to know. You can manage ordinary niggers by lickin' 'em and givin' 'em a taste of hot iron once in a while when they're extra ugly; but if a nigger really sets himself up against me, I can't never have any patience with him. I just get my pistol and shoot him right down; and that's the best way."

And this brute was talking to gentlemen, and his remarks were listened to with attention, and his assertions assented to by more than one in the knot of listeners. But all this time the sale was going on, and the merry Mr. Walsh, with many a quip and jest, was beguiling the time when the bidding was slow. The expression on the faces of all who stepped on the block was always the same, and told of more anguish than it is in the power of words to express. Blighted homes, crushed hopes and broken hearts was the sad story to be read in all the anxious faces. Some of them regarded the sale with perfect indifference, never making a motion save to turn from one side to the other at the word of the dapper Mr. Bryan, that all the crowd might have a fair view of their proportions, and then, when the sale was accomplished, stepped down from the block without caring to cast even a look at the buyer, who now held all their happiness in his hands. Others, again, strained their eyes with eager glances from one buyer to another as the bidding went on, trying with earnest attention to follow the rapid voice of the auctioneer. Sometimes two persons only would be bidding for the same chattel, all the others having resigned the contest, and then the poor creature on the block, conceiving an instantaneous preference for one of the buyers over the other, would regard the rivalry with intense interest, the expression of his face changing with every bid, settling into a half smile of joy if the favorite buyer persevered unto the end and secured the property, and settling down into a look of hopeless despair if the other won the victory.

DAPHNEY'S BABY.

The family of Primus, plantation carpenter, consisting of Daphney his wife, with her young babe, and Dido, a girl of three years old, were reached in due course of time. Daphney had a large shawl, which she kept carefully wrapped round her infant and herself. This unusual proceeding attracted much attention, and provoked many remarks, such as these:

"What do you keep your nigger covered up for? Pull off her blanket."

"What's the matter with the gal? Has she got the headache?"

"What's the fault of the gal? Ain't she sound? Pull off her rags and let us see her."

"Who's going to bid on that nigger, if you keep her covered up? Let's see her face."

And a loud chorus of similar remarks, emphasized with profanity, and mingled with sayings too indecent and obscene to be even hinted at here, went up from the crowd of chivalrous Southern gentlemen.

At last the auctioneer obtained a hearing long enough to explain that there was no attempt to practise any deception in the case—the parties were not to be wronged in any way; he had no desire to palm off on them an inferior article; but the truth of the matter was that Daphney had been confined only fifteen days ago, and he thought that on that account she was entitled to the slight indulgence of a blanket, to keep from herself and child the chill air and the driving rain.

Will your lady readers look at the circumstances of this case. The day was the 2d day of March. Daphney's baby was born into the world on St. Valentine's happy day, the 14th of February. Since her confinement, Daphney had travelled from the plantation to Savannah, where she had been kept in a shed for six days. On the sixth or seventh day after her sickness, she had left her bed, taken a railroad journey across the country to the shambles, was there exposed for six days to the questionings and insults of the negro speculators, and then on the fifteenth day after her confinement was put up on the block, with her husband and her other child, and with her new-born baby in her arms, sold to the highest bidder.

It was very considerate of Daphney to be sick before the sale, for her wailing babe was worth to Mr. Butler all of a hundred dollars. The family sold for $625 apiece, or $2,500 for the four. . . . While on the subject of babies, it may be mentioned that Amity, chattel No. 316, wife of Prince, chattel No. 315, had testified her earnest desire to contribute all in her power to the worldly wealth of her master by bringing into the world at one time chattels Nos. 317 and 318, being a fine pair of twin boys, just a year old. It is not in evidence that Amity received from her master any testimonial of his appreciating her good behavior on this occasion, but it is certain that she brought a great price, the four, Prince, Amity, and the twins selling for $670 apiece, being a total of $2,680.

Many other babies, of all ages of babyhood, were sold, but there was nothing particularly interesting about them. There were some thirty babies in the lot; they are esteemed worth to their master a hundred dollars the day they are born, and to increase in value at the rate of a hundred dollars a year till they are sixteen or seventeen years old, at which age they bring the best price.

THE LOVE STORY OF JEFFREY AND DORCAS.

Jeffrey, chattel No. 319, marked as a "prime cotton hand," aged 23 years, was put up. Jeffrey being a likely lad, the competition was high. The first bid was $1,100, and he was finally sold for $1,310. Jeffrey was sold alone; he had no incumbrance in the shape of an aged father or mother, who must necessarily be sold with him; nor had he any children, for Jeffrey was not married. But Jeffrey, chattel No. 319, being human in his affections, had dared to cherish a love for Dorcas, chattel No. 278; and Dorcas, not having the fear of her master before her eyes, had given her heart to Jeffrey. Whether what followed was a just retribution on Jeffrey and Dorcas, for daring to take such liberties with their master's property as to exchange hearts, or whether it only goes to prove that with black as with white the saying holds that "the course of true love never did run smooth," cannot now be told. Certain it is that these two lovers were not to realize the consummation of their hopes in happy wedlock. Jeffrey and Dorcas had told their loves, had exchanged their simple vows, and were betrothed, each to the other as dear, and each by the other as fondly loved, as though their skins had been of fairer color. And who shall say that, in the sight of Heaven and all holy angels, these two humble hearts were not as closely wedded as any two of the prouder race that call them slaves?

Be that as it may, Jeffrey was sold. He finds out his new master; and, hat in hand, the big tears standing in his eyes, and his voice trembling with emotion, he stands before that master and tell his simple story, praying that his betrothed may be bought with him. Though his voice trembles, there is not embarrassment in his manner; his fears have killed all the bashfulness that would naturally attend such a recital to a stranger, and before unsympathizing witnesses; he feels that he is pleading for the happiness of her he loves, as well as for his own, and his tale is told in a frank and manly way.

"I loves Dorcas, young Mas'r; I loves her well and true; she says she loves me, and I know she does; de good Lord knows I loves her better than I loves any one in de wide world—never can love another woman half so well. Please buy Dorcas, Mas'r. We're be good sarvants to you long as we live. We're be married right soon, young mas'r, and de chillun will be healthy and strong, Mas'r, and dey'll be good sarvants, too. Please buy Dorcas, young Mas'r. We loves each other a heap—do, really, true, Mas'r."

THE PARTING "Buy us too".

12. *The Parting* "Buy Us Too." Courtesy of the Virginia Historical Society, Richmond, Virginia.

In the Hands of Strangers

Jeffrey then remembers that no loves and hopes of his are to enter into the bargain at all, but in the earnestness of his love he has forgotten to base his plea on other ground till now, when he bethinks him and continues, with his voice not trembling now, save with eagerness to prove how worthy of many dollars is the maiden of his heart.

"Young Mas'r, Dorcas prime woman—A1 woman, sa. Tall gal, sir; long arms, strong, healthy, and can do a heap of work in a day. She is one of de best rice hands on de whole plantation; worth $1,200 easy, mas'r an' fus'-rate bargain at that."

The man seems touched by Jeffrey's last remarks, and bids him fetch out his "gal, and let's see what she looks like."

Jeffrey goes into the long room and presently returns with Dorcas, looking very sad and self-possessed, without a particle of embarrassment at the trying position in which she is placed. She makes the accustomed curtsy, and stands meekly with her hands clasped across her bosom, waiting the result. The buyer regards her with a critical eye, and growls in a low voice that the "gal has good p'ints." Then he goes on to a more minute and careful examination of her working abilities. He turns her round, makes her stoop, and walk; and then he takes off her turban to look at her head that no wound or disease be concealed by the gay handkerchief; he looks at her teeth, and feels of her arms, and at last announces himself pleased with the result of his observations, whereat Jeffrey, who has stood near, trembling with eager hope, is overjoyed, and he smiles for the first time. The buyer then crowns Jeffrey's happiness by making a promise that he will buy her, if the price isn't run too high. And the two lovers step aside and congratulate each other on their good fortune. But Dorcas is not to be sold till the next day, and there are twenty-four long hours of feverish expectation.

Early next morning is Jeffrey alert, and, hat in hand, encouraged to unusual freedom by the greatness of the stake for which he plays, he addresses every buyer, and of all who listen he begs the boon of a word to be spoken to his new master to encourage him to buy Dorcas. And all the long morning he speaks in his homely way with all who know him that they will intercede to save his sweetheart from being sold away from him forever. No one has the heart to deny a word of promise and encouragement to the poor fellow, and, joyous with so much kindness, his hopes and spirits gradually rise until he feels almost certain that the wish of his heart will be accomplished. And Dorcas, too, is smiling, for is not Jeffrey's happiness her own?

At last comes the trying moment, and Dorcas steps up on the stand.

But now a most unexpected feature in the drama is for the first time unmasked: *Dorcas is not to be sold alone,* but with a family of four others.[49] Full of dismay, Jeffrey looks to his master, who shakes his head, for, although he might be induced to buy Dorcas alone, he has no use for the rest of the family. Jeffrey reads his doom in his master's look, and turns away, the tears streaming down his honest face.

So Dorcas is sold, and her toiling life is to be spent in the cotton fields of South Carolina, while Jeffrey goes to the rice plantation of the Great Swamp.

And to-morrow, Jeffrey and Dorcas are to say their tearful farewell, and go their separate ways in life, to meet no more as mortal beings.

But didn't Mr. Pierce Butler give them a silver dollar apiece? Who shall say there is no magnanimity in slaveowners?

In another hour I see Dorcas in the long room, sitting motionless as a statue, with her head covered with a shawl. And I see Jeffrey, who goes to his new master, pulls off his hat and says, "I'se very much obliged, Mas'r, to you for tryin' to help me. I knows you would have done it if you could—thank you, Mas'r—thank you—but—its—berry—hard"—and here the poor fellow breaks down entirely and walks away, covering his face with his battered hat, and sobbing like a very child.

He is soon surrounded by a group of his colored friends who, with an instinctive delicacy most unlooked for, stand quiet, and with uncovered heads, about him.

Anson and Violet, chattles Nos. 111 and 112, were sold for $250 each, both being old, and Anson being down in the catalogue as "ruptured and as having one eye." Violet was sold as being sick. Her disease was probably consumption, which supposition gave rise to the following feeling conversation between two buyers:

"Cheap gal that, Major."

"Don't think so. They may talk about being sick; it's no easy sickness she's got. She's got consumption, and the man that buys her'll have to be doctorin' her all the time, and she'll die in less than three months. I won't have anything to do with her—don't want any half dead niggers about me."

THE MARKET VALUE OF AN EYE.

Guy, chattel No. 419, "a prime young man," sold for $1,280, being without blemish; his age was twenty years, and he was altogether a fine article. His next-door neighbor, Andrew, chattel No. 420, was his very counterpart in all marketable points, in size, age, skill, and everything save that

49. The Bryan catalogue listed Dorcas and an accompanying child as follows: "345-Dorcas, 17 [years old]; cotton, prime woman. 346-Joe, 3 months. Sold for $1,260 each." Bancroft, *Slave Trading,* p. 227, thus assumed that, contrary to what Jeffrey had been told, Joe was "Dorcas's babe and the only member of her 'family' present." Editor.

he had lost his right eye. Andrew sold for only $1,040, from which we argue that the market value of the right eye in the Southern country is $240. . . .

And so the Great Sale went on for two long days, during which time there were sold 429 men, women and children. There were 436 announced to be sold, but a few were detained on the plantations by sickness.

At the close of the sale, on the last day, several baskets of champagne were produced, and all were invited to partake, the wine being at the expense of the broker, Mr. Bryan.

The total amount of the sale foots up to $303,850-the proceeds of the first day being $161,480, and of the second day $142,370.

The highest sum paid for any one family was given for Sally Walker, and her five children, who were mostly grown up. The price was $6,180.

The highest sum paid for a single man was $1,750, which was given for William, a "fair carpenter and caulker."

The highest price paid for a woman was $1,250, which was given for Jane, "cotton hand and house servant."

The lowest price paid was for Anson and Violet, a gray-haired couple, each having numbered more than fifty years; they brought but $250 apiece.

MR. PIERCE BUTLER GIVES HIS PEOPLE A DOLLAR APIECE.

Leaving the Race buildings, where the scenes we have described took place, a crowd of negroes were seen gathered eagerly about a white man. That man was Pierce M. Butler of the free city of Philadelphia, who was solacing the wounded hearts of the people he had sold from their firesides and their homes, by doling out to them small change at the rate of a dollar a head. To every negro he had sold, who presented his claim for the paltry pittance, he gave the munificent stipend of one whole dollar, in specie; he being provided with two canvas bags of 25 cent pieces, fresh from the mint, to give an additional glitter to his generosity.

And now come the scenes of the last partings—of the final separations of those who were akin, or who had been such dear friends from youth that no ties of kindred could bind them closer—of those who were all in all to each other, and for whose bleeding hearts there shall be no earthly comfort—the parting of parents and children, of brother from brother, and the rending of sister from a sister's bosom; and O, hardest, cruelest of all, the tearing assunder of loving hearts, wedded in all save the one ceremony of the Church—these scenes pass all description; it is not meet for pen to meddle with tears so holy.

As the last family stepped down from the block, the rain ceased, for the first time in four days the clouds broke away, and the soft sunlight fell on the scene. The unhappy slaves had many of them been already removed, and others were now departing with their new masters.

That night, not a steamer left that Southern port, not a train of cars sped away from that cruel city, that did not bear each its own sad burden of those unhappy ones, whose only crime is that they are not strong and wise. Some of them maimed and wounded, some scarred and gashed, by accident or by the hand of ruthless drivers—all sad and sorrowful as human hearts can be.

But the stars shone out as brightly as if such things had never been, the blushing fruit trees poured their fragrance on the evening air, and the scene was as calmly sweet and quiet as if Man had never marred the glorious beauty of Earth by deeds of cruelty and wrong.

2.25. "It Was Evil, Wretchedly Evil." A North Carolina Minister Remembers the Local Slave Trade

In a book of over four hundred pages on the old South and the aftermath of the Civil War, the Reverend Jethro Rumple of Rowan County, North Carolina, devoted only three pages to "African slavery" and slightly more than a single page to the domestic slave trade. Nevertheless Rumple's single paragraph on the local buying and selling of slaves deserves full citation, if for no other reason because it was written by a respected local resident who, despite an essentially conservative disposition, tended to verify the testimony of ex-slaves, travelers, and abolitionist writers—the practice, for example, of slaves being urged or required to sing or to play musical instruments or even to carry patriotic symbols while on their overland journeys.

As elsewhere in the United States, the age-old practices of the African slave trade hovered over North Carolina, where even the vocabulary of that traffic had found its way into regular usage, in this case in the form of the word "barracoon," derived from Spanish *barracón*, or Portuguese *barracão*, a large hut or cabin. In the parlance of the African coast a barracoon was a rude, often roofless enclosure where slaves were confined while awaiting shipment to the Americas. In Rowan County, North Carolina, it was a structure where the "rebellious" and the "unwilling" were incarcerated prior to setting off on their long treks to the lower South.

SOURCE: *A History of Rowan County North Carolina Containing Sketches of Prominent Families and Distinguished Men with an Appendix by Rev. Jethro Rumple* (Salisbury, N.C.: J. J. Bruner, 1881), pp. 254–55.

Occasionally there were cruel hardships suffered by [the slaves]. When the thriftless master got in debt, or when the owner died and his estate was sold at vendue, or if the heartless master chose, the negro husband and wife might be separated, or parent and child might be sold from each other, one party falling into the hands of a negro trader, and carried off to Alabama or Mississippi. Such cases occurred at intervals, and under the laws there was no help for it. But in all such cases the feelings of humane and Christian elements of the community were shocked. Generally, however, arrangements were made to purchase, and keep in the neighborhood all deserving negroes. As sales would come on it was the habit of the negroes to go to some man able to buy them and secure their transfer to a desirable home. Sometimes, however, all this failed, and the "negro trader" having the longest purse would buy and carry off to the West husbands or wives or children against their will. Older citizens remember the gangs of slaves that once marched through our streets with a hand of each fastened to a long chain, in double file, sometimes with sorrowful look, and sometimes with a mockery of gayety. The house of the trader was, perhaps, a comfortable mansion, in some shady square of town. Near the center of the square, and embowered in trees and vines, was his "barracoon," or prison for the unwilling. There a dozen or two were carefully locked up and guarded. Other cabins on the lot contained those who were submissive and willing to go. On the day of departure for the West, the trader would have a grand jollification. A band, or at least a drum and fife, would be called into requisition, and perhaps a little rum be judiciously distributed to heighten the spirits of his sable property, and the neighbors would gather in to see the departure. First of all one or two closely covered wagons would file out from the "barracoon," containing the rebellious and unwilling, in handcuffs and chains. After them the rest, dressed in comfortable attire, perhaps dancing and laughing, as if they were going on some holiday excursion. At the edge of the town, the fife and drum ceased, the pageant faded away, and the curious crowd who had come to witness the scene returned to their homes. After months had rolled away the "trader's" wagons came back from Montgomery, Memphis, Mobile, or New Orleans, loaded with luxuries for his family. In boxes and bundles, in kegs and caskets, there were silks and laces, watches and jewelry, ribbons and feathers, candies and tropical fruits, wines and cordials, for family use and luxurious indulgence, all the profits of an accursed traffic in human flesh and blood, human tears and helpless anguish and oppression. This was the horrible and abominable side of this form of social institution. It was evil, wretchedly evil.

Conflict and Crisis of the Union on the Road to Civil War

The documents in this section are concerned with the struggle between the North and the South over slavery. Within that broad theme they pertain to such issues as the African slave trade to the United States, efforts to colonize free American blacks in Africa and other tropical lands, and the dispute with Mexico over slavery in Texas leading to the annexation of Texas and the Mexican-American War. Other issues dealt with are the southern drive to expand slavery into the tropics, black racism in the northern states, the scriptural issue of whether God and the New and Old Testaments sanctioned or opposed slavery, efforts to renew the African slave trade in the 1850s, the bitter struggle between slavery and freedom in Kansas, the Dred Scott Decision of 1857, which, among other wrongs, denied citizenship to black Americans, the Underground Railroad and the conflict over the fugitive slave law of 1850, the endemic problem of slavery in the District of Columbia, the Civil War and the valiant responses of southern slaves to that extraordinary transition, and finally, Frederick Douglass's eloquent inquiry: "What Shall Be Done with the Negro?"

From the very beginning of the American republic serious conflicts broke out between North and South. Already in 1776 the two sections were at odds over state tax apportionments, northerners suggesting that these be based on state populations including slaves, a plan so offensive to slaveholders that South Carolina threatened disunion even before the nation had become a firm reality. This dispute was solved by basing tax assessments on land values and improvements, a concession to the South, but a new threat to national unity developed in 1786–87, when John Jay, secretary for foreign affairs, suggested to Congress that, in return for commercial concessions, the United States surrender the right of free navigation on the lower Mississippi River (then controlled by Spain), a proposal that aroused threats of secession from both southern and western states.[1]

Obviously the slavery issue also brought discord and threats of secession in the early years of the Republic. For example, when in 1790 Congressman William Smith of South Carolina addressed his colleagues concerning the hypothetical authority of Congress to free the slaves, he inquired: "Would the Southern States acquiesce in such a measure without a struggle? Would the citizens of that country tamely suffer their property to be torn from them? . . . If you injure the Southern States, the injury would reach our Northern and Eastern brethren; for the States are links of one chain; if we break one, the whole must fall to pieces." In the same debate Congressman Thomas Tucker of South Carolina asked his fellow representatives: "Do these men [Quakers] expect a general emancipation of slaves by law? This would never be submitted to by the Southern States without a Civil War." Representative James Jackson of Georgia offered similar opinions: "Let me ask if it is good policy to bring forward a business at this moment likely to light up the flame of civil discord: for the people of the Southern States will resist one tyranny as soon as another. The other parts of the Continent may bear them down by force of arms, but they will never suffer themselves to be divested of their property without a struggle."[2]

As seen above, even issues less important than slavery brought calls for secession. Protective tariffs, for example, which raised consumer prices in the South and allegedly benefited only the North, aroused great concern among South Carolinians in the 1820s, causing Thomas Cooper, a secessionist and president of South Carolina College, to urge citizens of his state "to 'calculate the value' of a Union which was bringing ruin upon them."[3] In 1836, a young congressman from South Carolina, James H. Hammond, asserted that antislavery petitions (then a major source of conflict) were intended "to subvert the institutions of the South," and that a congressional step toward emancipation would result in his return to South Carolina to preach secession, even if this resulted in war.[4] Similarly, when in 1838, Congressman William Slade, holding in his hand a petition signed by nearly five hundred citizens of Ver-

1. Glover Moore, *The Missouri Compromise, 1819–1821* (Lexington: University of Kentucky Press, 1953), pp. 3–5.

2. *Annals of Congress,* 1st Congress, 2 Session, pp. 1198, 1200, 1455, 1460. See Docs. 3.1 and 3.2.

3. Laura A. White, *Robert Barnwell Rhett: Father of Secession* (Gloucester, Mass.: Peter Smith, 1965), pp. 12–17.

4. Clement Eaton, *The Mind of the Old South* (Baton Rouge: Louisiana State University Press, 1967), pp. 48–49.

mont, called for a bill to abolish slavery and the slave trade in the District of Columbia, he was met with "a paroxysm of rage" among southern congressmen.[5] Following an abrupt adjournment, "fire-brand" legislator Robert Barnwell Rhett, also of South Carolina, informed his colleagues of a statement he had written, said to express the will of the South. A published version of this document, intended to force continuation of the so-called gag-rule blocking antislavery petitions, proposed: "And the constitution of the United States having proved inadequate to protect the southern States in the peaceable enjoyment of their rights and *property*, it is expedient that the said constitution should be amended or the Union of the States be dissolved. Resolved—that a Committee of two members from each State in the Union be appointed, to report upon the expediency and practicability of amending the Constitution, or the best means of peaceably dissolving the Union."[6]

During the debate on the Compromise of 1850 there were many warnings of secession on the part of southerners.[7] The Georgia legislature, for example, threatened to leave the Union if California was admitted as a free state, if slavery was abolished in the District of Columbia, if Congress passed the Wilmot Proviso (intended to ban slavery in territories seized in the war with Mexico), or if northern states obstructed the return of fugitive slaves to the South.[8] Six years later, an ardent supporter of southern nationalism, Edmund Ruffin of Virginia, published an article in the New Orleans journal, *De Bow's Review*, in which he predicted a victory for the new Republican Party in 1860, and so urged southerners to "use this time of truce to thoroughly examine, understand, and strengthen our position, and so be prepared to meet and repel every future attack on our constitutional rights and our rightful interests." As Ruffin admitted, what he was proposing was certain to bring disaster, but he rejected submission to "unjust oppression" and called for preservation of southern property and political rights through "a struggle for freedom, with all the certain disasters and incalculable dangers of a war with a nation of ten-fold their power."[9] To cite one

5. For Slade's enduring involvement in the antislavery movement in Congress and otherwise, see Wilbur H. Siebert, *Vermont's Anti-Slavery and Underground Railroad Record* (1937; reprint, New York: Negro Universities Press, 1969), pp. 22, 37–39, 50.

6. William Lee Miller, *Arguing about Slavery: The Great Battle in the United States Congress* (New York: Alfred A. Knopf, 1996), pp. 279–81; White, *Robert Barnwell Rhett*, pp. 37–39. Italics added.

7. Henry Wilson, *History of the Rise and Fall of the Slave Power in America* (Boston: Houghton, Mifflin, 1872), vol. 2, pp. 211–20.

8. Stanley W. Campbell, *The Slave Catchers: Enforcement of the Fugitive Slave Law, 1850–1860* (New York: W. W. Norton, 1972), p. 17.

9. See Paul F. Paskoff and Daniel J. Wilson, eds., *The Cause of the South: Selections from De Bow's Review, 1846–1867* (Baton Rouge: Louisiana State University Press, 1982), pp. 201–8.

more remarkable example of southern support of secession, Leonidas W. Spratt, an outspoken advocate of renewal of the African slave trade in the 1850s, wrote in 1858 that the South was not under "any special obligations of sentiment or interest to preserve the Union," was, in fact, "committed to leave it" if the North did not desist in its abuses (see Doc. 3.16). Yet, when this same zealot learned soon after secession that the Confederate constitution had retained the ban on the African slave trade, he confessed his movement's defeat, yet called for a new revolution. "It may be painful," he admitted, "but we must make it." [10]

Even northerners favored secession, especially as the conflict deepened in the 1830s. One northerner who decidedly supported disunion was William Lloyd Garrison, editor of the antislavery journal, *The Liberator.* Already in 1836, in an appearance before a committee of the Massachusetts legislature, Garrison had declared: "Sir, we loudly boast of our free country, and of the union of these states, yet I have no country! As a New Englander and as an Abolitionist I am excluded by a bloody proscription from one-half of the national territory, and so is every man who is known to regard slavery with abhorrence. Where is our Union? . . . The right of free and safe locomotion from one part of the land to the other is denied to us, except on peril of our lives. . . . Therefore . . . the Union is now virtually dissolved." What had become apparent to Garrison in 1836 had solidified by 1842. By then he had recognized, in the words of his biographer, Archibald H. Grimke, "that the Union was the strong tower of the slave-power, which would never be destroyed until the fortress which protected it was first utterly destroyed." Soon after reaching this conclusion Garrison wrote to his brother-in-law: "We must dissolve all connection with those murderers of fathers and murderers of mothers, and murderers of liberty, and traffickers of human flesh, and blasphemers against the Almighty at the South. What have we in common with them? Are not their principles, their pursuits, their policies, their interests, their designs, their feelings, utterly diverse from ours? Why, then, be subject to their dominion?" Soon after in *The Liberator* Garrison called for "repeal of the Union between the North and the South" and "for throwing all the means, energies, actions, purposes, and appliances of the genuine friends of liberty and republicanism into this one channel. . . . Divorced from Northern protection, [slavery] dies; with

10. Emory M. Thomas, *The Confederate Nation: 1861–1865* (New York: Harper & Row, 1979), p. 44. For the highly controversial plan to renew the African slave trade, see Docs. 3.15 and 3.16, and Ronald T. Takaki's important book, *A Pro-Slavery Crusade: The Agitation to Reopen the African Slave Trade* (New York: The Free Press, 1971). For the article containing Spratt's remarks, see John F. Cairnes, *The Slave Power: Its Character, Career and Probable Designs* (London: Macmillan, 1863), pp. 390–410.

that protection it enlarges its boundaries, multiplies its victims, and extends its ravages."[11]

Many of Garrison's followers opposed his call for disunion, but most leading abolitionists strongly favored his proposal. Already in January 1842, before Garrison's announcement in *The Liberator*, John Quincy Adams had presented a petition to the House of Representatives from citizens of Massachusetts asking Congress to take steps to dissolve the Union and offering three reasons for doing so. First, the Union did not offer reciprocal benefits to the North; second, "a vast proportion" of northern revenues was being drained off each year to support the objectives of the South; and third, because, if conditions remained as they were, the South would overwhelm and destroy the nation. The petition from Massachusetts was "laid upon the table," as were countless others, but, according to a report of the event, southern congressmen "stood aghast, when they found that the card which they had always counted upon as sure to win the game, in the last resort might be played by their adversaries as well as by themselves. It seemed like a new interference, on the part of the North, with another of their 'peculiar institutions,' a violation of their ancient monopoly of dissolving the Union."[12] Much more, however, was taking place. In March 1842, for example, Representative Joshua Giddings presented a petition from his Ohio constituents asking Congress "to take measures to procure an amicable division of the United States, by a line running between the Slave and Free States." This petition was also tabled, but breaking up the Union had become an acceptable topic of discussion in the North as in the South.[13]

The issue of slavery was obviously paramount in this enduring struggle, but both before and long after the Civil War southerners denied that it was the main cause of conflict. In 1868, for example, Alexander H. Stephens, former vice president of the Confederacy, admitted that slavery was "the main exciting proximate cause" of the war, but the "real cause" was northern violation of southern constitutional rights. Decades later former

---

11. Archibald H. Grimke, *William Lloyd Garrison: The Abolitionist* (New York: Funk & Wagnalls, 1891), pp. 246, 307–11. For an 1855 statement by Garrison on disunion, see William E. Crain, ed., *William Lloyd Garrison and the Fight against Slavery: Selections from The Liberator* (Boston: Bedford Books of St. Martin's Press, 1995), pp. 141–44.

12. One historian has stated that during the Missouri crisis southerners began to learn "how effectively the threat of disunion could be used as a weapon of southern defense." See Don E. Fehrenbacher, *The South and Three Sectional Crises* (Baton Rouge: Louisiana State University Press, 1980), p. 21. For more examples of prominent northern disunionists in the 1840s and 1850s, see Eric Foner, *Free Soil, Free Labor, Free Men* (London: Oxford University Press, 1970), pp. 138–41.

13. *Eleventh Annual Report Presented to the Massachusetts Anti-Slavery Society by Its Board of Managers, January 25, 1843* (Boston: Massachusetts Anti-Slavery Society, 1843), pp. 4–10.

In the Hands of Strangers

Confederate president Jefferson Davis was even more unyielding. Slavery, he wrote, was "in no wise the cause of the conflict, but only an incident." It was "Northern violation of constitutional guarantees" that had forced the South to secede.[14] The arguments of Stephens, Davis, and other southern writers were popular well into the twentieth century. The Constitution guaranteed slavery, the North refused to abide by that guarantee, and so the South was "compelled to leave the Union for its own protection."[15] The real offender was—not slavery—but "the fanaticism of the abolition attack" upon southern rights.

Such opinions may not have seemed entirely unreasonable from the southern point of view. Bit by bit, in response to southern realities, anti-slavery sentiment had grown into a dynamic force in the 1820s and 1830s, as a growing corps of activists spread their message across the North and even into slaveholding states, at times meeting fierce opposition but gradually enlightening the citizenry and, in the process, further radicalizing the South. In response to abolitionist agitation, and to such events as Nat Turner's rebellion in Virginia and the alarming discovery of the radical pamphlet, *Walker's Appeal,* in the possession of southern blacks (see Doc. 3.4), southern lawmakers attempted to restrain the black population through such measures as banning meetings of free blacks, mulattoes, and slaves for purposes of basic education, confining black seamen to their ships while in port, and prohibiting black peddlers from selling goods outside their home counties, or from reentering states where they had previously lived.[16] To cite one example of such legislation, soon after Nat Turner's 1831 revolt a Virginia law was passed providing that "all meetings of free Negroes or mulattoes at any school house, church, meeting house or other place for teaching them reading or writing, either in the day or the night shall be considered an unlawful assembly. Warrants shall direct any sworn officer to enter and disperse such Negroes and inflict corporal punishment on the offenders at the discretion of the justice, not exceeding twenty lashes. Any white person assembling to instruct free Negroes to read or write shall be fined not over $50.00, also be imprisoned not exceeding two months." Such laws perhaps achieved the desired effect among the less defiant, but they antagonized the North, gave impetus to the abolitionist

14. Howard K. Beale, "What Historians Have Said about the Causes of the Civil War," reprint of "Theory and Practice in Historical Study," *Social Science Research Council Bulletin,* no. 54 (1946): 62.

15. Elbert B. Smith, *The Death of Slavery: The United States, 1837–65* (Chicago: University of Chicago Press, 1967), p. 6.

16. Charles S. Sydnor, *The Development of Southern Sectionalism, 1819–1848* (Baton Rouge: Louisiana State University Press, 1968), pp. 223–29.

cause, and of course, denied blacks "the great advantages which civilized and polished nations enjoy."[17]

Prominent among the incidents, crises, and controversies that intensified the struggle between North and South was a conflict brought on by Missouri's application for admission to the Union as a slave state in 1817, a request opposed by the North not only because of its opposition to the spread of slavery, but also because Missouri's status as a slave state would increase pro-slavery representation in Congress. In February 1819, during a series of debates, Congressman James Tallmadge of New York unexpectedly offered an amendment to the Missouri bill prohibiting "further introduction of slavery or involuntary servitude" and freeing all children of slaves born in Missouri after its admission into the Union, though such children could be "held to service" until the age of twenty-five. After an acrimonious debate that might have ended in war, secession, or both, a compromise was reached and signed by President Monroe in March 1820, allowing Missouri and Maine to enter the union as slave and free states respectively, in exchange for a southern pledge to forbid slavery in the vast Louisiana Territory west of the new state of Missouri and north of latitude 36° 30'. This agreement settled for a time the question of slavery in the territories, but it brought comfort to southerners and disapproval in the North, since Missouri was to be a slave state. A New Hampshire newspaper admitted, for example, that "something has been gained in the exclusion of Slavery from the territories. . . . But still we have suffered a disgraceful defeat." At about that time Secretary of State John Quincy Adams wrote in his journal: "I take it for granted that the present [Missouri] question is mere preamble—a title page to a great, tragic volume."[18]

It might reasonably be suggested, in fact, that the "author" of this "tragic volume," was hard at work even before passage of the Missouri Compromise, and continued to pursue his (or her) task until Lee's surrender at Appomattox forty-five years later. To carry the analogy further, the

17. June Purcell Guild, *Black Laws of Virginia* (1936; reprint, New York: Negro Universities Press, 1969), pp. 175–76. In contrast to the 1831 law, an act of 1796 stated that "the great advantages which civilized and polished nations enjoy are principally derived from the invention and use of letters, and upon a review of the history of mankind it seems that, however favorable government founded on liberty, justice and order may be to human happiness, no permanency can be hoped for if the minds of the citizens are not rendered liberal and humane; so it is enacted that certain aldermen shall consider the expediency of establishing schools and at every one of these schools there shall be taught reading, writing and common arithmetic, and all the *free* children, male and female, shall be entitled to receive tuition gratis for the term of three years." Ibid., p. 174. Italics added.

18. Glover Moore, *The Missouri Compromise, 1819–1821* (University of Kentucky Press, 1953), pp. 33–64, 199; William J. Cooper, Jr., *Liberty and Slavery: Southern Politics to 1860* (New York: Alfred A. Knopf, 1983), pp. 134–42; Miller, *Arguing about Slavery,* p. 180.

first chapter of this hypothetical volume might well have been called "Expansionism," or "Imperialism," since acquisition of new lands for slavery had begun before the Missouri debate, gained momentum in successive years, and remained a major cause of discord until the Civil War, the South's objectives being acquisition of vast new territories for agriculture, new markets for slaves, and of course, an increase of pro-slavery representation in Congress.

An important example of such expansion was the acquisition of Texas. After the ban on the slave trade to the United States in 1808, illegal slave traders began landing Africans on the Texas coast where dealers could acquire them cheaply, transport them to nearby Louisiana where a local law allowed "informers" to acquire the smuggled slaves, and then sell them in local markets for a large profit.[19] About this same time Americans began to enter Texas with their slaves, establishing themselves in fertile lands beyond the Louisiana border. Then in 1820, about the time the Missouri debate was coming to a close, Moses Austin of that same state received a grant from the Spanish government to establish a Catholic colony in Texas, an arrangement inherited the following year by his son, Stephen F. Austin, whose contract gave his colonists eighty acres of land for each slave in their possession. In 1821, when Mexico won independence from Spain, the legality of slavery in Texas became less certain, since Mexico's liberal leaders were unfriendly to the practice. Mexico, in fact, soon passed laws to free native-born slave children at the age of fourteen and to ban the purchase and sale of slaves entering Mexico (meaning, of course, Texas). Then in 1827, when Mexico banned slave importations "under any pretext," Texans responded by adopting a facsimile of that country's age-old system of debt peonage. This allowed them to make contracts with "indentured servants" by which de facto slaves were obliged theoretically to make annual payments to reimburse their purchase prices, the costs of migration to Texas, and other debts or obligations, a scheme clearly intended to legitimize a condition of lifelong servitude.

In 1829 Mexico finally abolished slavery, but persuaded by concerned Texans, exempted Texas from the decree on grounds that many slaves were "so extremely ignorant as to unfit them for freedom." In 1830 Mexico banned immigration of American citizens into Texas and ordered enforcement of rules prohibiting slave importations, and this was followed in 1832 by an order that servants and daylaborers entering Texas could not be made

19. Randolph B. Campbell, *An Empire for Slavery: The Peculiar Institution in Texas* (Baton Rouge: Louisiana State University Press, 1989), pp. 11–12.

to serve more than ten years. As historian Randolph B. Campbell summed up the situation, "Slavery appeared thoroughly hemmed in by restrictions,"[20] and so it is not surprising that, given the commitment of Texans to slavery, they waged a war in 1835–36 to break their ties with Mexico.[21] In March 1837, the U.S. government recognized Texas's independence, and according to William Jay, "the whole slave region, with scarcely an exception, demanded a union with the new State."[22] Strong antislavery sentiment delayed Texas's annexation for nearly ten years, but in 1845, the United States took that controversial step, then soon launched an incursion into territory beyond the Nueces River to which the United States had no rightful claim, crossing the Rio Grande and marching on into the heart of Mexico largely supported and led by southern interests.[23] Of course such episodes sharpened appetites for new adventures and the wealth and fame they might produce. In any case, there were strong links between the Texas war of 1835–36, the Mexican-American war of 1846–48, filibustering expeditions in the 1850s into neighboring tropical countries, and even the extraordinary campaign of the late 1850s to renew the African slave trade.

One individual associated with such proceedings was John A. Quitman, a New Yorker who in his youth migrated to Natchez, Mississippi, and there became a successful lawyer, slaveholder, politician, soldier, governor, and member of Congress. In 1836 Quitman journeyed to Texas to participate in the independence war, arriving too late, however, to take part in the battle of San Jacinto, which brought defeat to Mexico and de facto independence to Texas. Quitman regretted having missed the fight, but ten years later his appetite for conquest was richly gratified by his involvement in the Mexican-American War. When Congress voted for war in May, the ever belligerent Quitman offered his services to President Polk and was commissioned a brigadier general with orders to report to General Zachary Taylor deep inside Mexican territory on the Rio Grande.[24] In Mexico he took part in two major battles: the first at Monterrey and the second in Mexico City where a brief but deadly encounter took place at Chapultepec Castle, Quitman's soldiers overwhelming the defenders, among them the

20. Ibid., pp. 16–19, 23–29.

21. For an important account of these events from an abolitionist's point of view, see Benjamin Lundy, *The War in Texas; A Review of Facts and Circumstances* . . . (Philadelphia: Mettihew and Gunn, 1836).

22. William Jay, *A View of the Action of the Federal Government on Behalf of Slavery* (Miami: Mnemosyne, 1969), pp. 152–56.

23. Fehrenbacher, *The South and Three Sectional Crises,* pp. 33–34.

24. Robert E. May, *John A. Quitman: Old South Crusader* (Baton Rouge: Louisiana State University Press, 1985), pp. 76–89, 147–61.

celebrated cadets of the Military Academy, the Niños Héroes, who ostensibly leaped to their deaths rather than submit. Acting as governor of the city after its fall, Quitman remained a stalwart expansionist, suggesting in a letter that "this beautiful & rich country [be made] a portion of the United States." In the Treaty of Guadalupe Hidalgo, which ended the war, Mexico lost fifty-five percent of its territory, including present-day California, Arizona, New Mexico, and Texas, as well as parts of Utah, Nevada, and Colorado, for which the United States paid fifteen million dollars (see Docs. 3.7 through 3.9).[25] Some years later, having been involved in attempts to seize Cuba for the United States, Quitman publicly demanded Cuban independence from Spain and called upon the "Caucasian white race to carry humanity, civilization and progress to the rich and fertile countries . . . south of us, which now, in the occupation of inferior and mixed races, lie undeveloped and useless."[26]

About this time another American of the white race was attempting to "carry humanity, civilization and progress" to Latin America. This was William Walker, a native of Nashville, educated in medicine, law, and journalism, but known to history as a freebooter. In 1853 Walker and forty-seven followers sailed from San Francisco for the Mexican territory of Baja California where they captured and plundered the territorial capital and declared Lower California an independent republic with Walker as president. Repulsed from Baja California, Walker returned to San Francisco where he was acquitted of violating the neutrality laws and so set out with a small army for Nicaragua, enticed by offers of land and military pay and later "a contract of colonization" for himself and his followers.[27] In Nicaragua Walker soon rose to power, capturing the important city of Granada, involving himself in a cross-country transit route, fending off rivals, winning the Nicaraguan presidency in a sham election, and attempting to restore slavery in Nicaragua, an idea certain to advance his standing in the South. This was followed by other schemes attractive to southerners: plans to annex Nicaragua to the United States, to "free" Cuba from Spanish rule, and to give land grants to Americans to transform Nicaragua into a "home for Southern men." These designs were never carried out, however,

---

25. Ibid., pp. 187–99; Barbara A. Tenenbaum, "Mexico, 1810–1910," in Barbara A. Tenenbaum, ed., *Encyclopedia of Latin American History and Culture* (New York: Charles Scribner's Sons, 1996), vol. 4, pp. 9–10. For a notable account of the Mexican war, see William Jay, *A Review of the Causes and Consequences of the Mexican War* (Boston: Benjamin B. Mussey, 1849).

26. May, *John A. Quitman*, pp. 236–52, 270–95; Arthur F. Corwin, *Spain and the Abolition of Slavery in Cuba, 1817–1886* (Austin: University of Texas Press, 1967), pp. 99–103; Franklin W. Knight, *Slave Society in Cuba during the Nineteenth Century* (Madison: University of Wisconsin Press, 1970), pp. 137–46.

27. Gen'l William Walker, *The War in Nicaragua* (Tucson: University of Arizona Press, 1985).

since Walker, overwhelmed by Central American forces, sought refuge in the United States. Later he landed in northern Honduras, but, threatened by local troops, surrendered to a British naval officer who turned him over to Honduran authorities. The latter executed Walker by firing squad less than three months before South Carolina seceded from the Union.[28]

Perhaps even more disturbing than Walker's efforts to conquer Nicaragua were the many U.S. attempts to annex Cuba from Spain in the years before the Civil War. The most famous of these incidents occurred in 1854 when President Franklin Pierce instructed his secretary of state to order U.S. ambassadors to Britain, France, and Spain to meet in Europe to discuss American acquisition of Cuba. The result was the infamous Ostend Manifesto, which proposed that the United States offer Spain a price for Cuba allegedly much higher than its true value, but that if a purchase was not quickly arranged, "then, by every law, human and divine, we shall be justified in wresting it from Spain, if we possess the power."[29] The Ostend Manifesto, the essence of which soon became known to the world, forced President Pierce to deny its authenticity, but the urge to annex persisted. "Cuba must and shall be ours," said slavery enthusiast Senator Albert Gallatin Brown of Mississippi in 1859, in what amounted to a personal Ostend Manifesto. If Spain was willing to sell, he would willingly pay, he said, but otherwise he would seize Cuba as "indemnity for the past." His reasons for desiring Cuba remained the same as always: to gain new territory, to increase American commerce and to expand slavery.[30]

The decade of the 1850s was among the most turbulent of the antebellum period. Among the more ominous events was the Compromise of 1850, which admitted California into the Union as a free state, but balanced that concession to the North by allowing the "organization" of the territories of New Mexico and Utah for eventual admission into the Union without restrictions as to slavery. A concession to the North was a ban on slave trading in the District of Columbia, though slavery would remain legal there and residents could sell their slaves to other residents or to persons removing them from the District, presumably for transportation to the Deep South. In exchange for this arrangement, southerners received a harsh new Fugitive Slave Law, seen by abolitionists as an insult to the Republic, and

28. Robert E. May, *The Southern Dream of a Caribbean Empire, 1854–1861* (Athens: University of Georgia Press, 1989), pp. 77–135 and passim.

29. James A. Rawley, *Race and Politics: "Bleeding Kansas" and the Coming of the Civil War* (Lincoln: University of Nebraska Press, 1969), pp. 135–36.

30. May, *Southern Dream*, pp. 138, 147–55; Wilson, *Rise and Fall*, vol. 2, pp. 610–13; C. Stanley Urban, "The Africanization of Cuba Scare, 1853–1855," *Hispanic American Historical Review* 37, no. 1 (1957): 29–45.

above all to the many fugitive slaves who risked their lives to win freedom in Canada and northern states (see Docs. 3.20 and 3.21).[31]

A particularly serious cause of conflict between North and South was the Kansas-Nebraska Bill of 1854. This legislation repealed the Missouri Compromise of 1820, which had banned slavery in the Louisiana territory north of latitude 36° 30' and provided that "all questions pertaining to slavery" in the new states and territories would be "left to the people residing therein."[32] This principle, known as "Popular Sovereignty," set off a firestorm of conflict as northern free-soil settlers eager to establish themselves in a new territory journeyed to Kansas from New England and other northern states assisted by emigrant aid societies. There they encountered armed pro-slavery residents of Missouri (so-called "border ruffians") who crossed into Kansas determined to cast ballots for slavery and, failing that, to add a new slave state to the Union by any necessary means (see Doc. 3.13). Among the results was open warfare on the western plains popularly known as "Bleeding Kansas" which brought John Brown to prominence prior to his unsuccessful attack on the U.S. military arsenal at Harper's Ferry.

Other sources of conflict included the Dred Scott Decision of 1857 in which Chief Justice of the Supreme Court Roger B. Taney asserted, among other extraordinary utterances, that blacks were "so far inferior that they had no rights which the white man was bound to respect" (see Doc. 3.14). They included attempts in the late 1850s on the part of a small body of southerners, motivated by an appetite for cheap labor, to renew the African slave trade (see Docs. 3.15 through 3.19). The atmosphere of bad feeling was aggravated by members of the clergy, North and South, who insisted that slavery was ordained by God, and even supported by the Bible (see especially Doc. 3.10). These and other conflicts and controversies, and perhaps above all, Lincoln's election to the presidency in 1860, led to southern secession, the Confederate attack on Fort Sumter, and the outbreak of war. The latter set off a runaway movement affecting tens of thousands of slaves, hastened an end to slavery in the District of Columbia, and in the North, revived interest in the misguided and impractical goal of colonizing part or all of the free black population outside the borders of the United States (see Docs. 3.23 and 3.24).[33]

It has often been argued that the antagonism between North and

---

31. Cooper, *Liberty and Slavery,* pp. 228–35; Fehrenbacher, *The South and Three Sectional Crises,* pp. 40–41; Wilson, *Rise and Fall,* vol. 2, pp. 296.

32. Fehrenbacher, *The South and Three Sectional Crises,* pp. 17–18; Campbell, *The Slave Catchers,* pp. 81–83.

33. Wilson, *Rise and Fall,* vol. 2, pp. 462–565 and passim.

South—and between slavery and freedom
years, produced an "irrepressible conflict,"
the extreme nature of the differences betwee
so. Historian David Donald brilliantly sun
the two sections no longer spoke the same la
code, or obeyed the same law, when their re
conflict in the halls of Congress, thinking r
wonder how the Union could longer endur
fessor Donald quoted these words of Ralph
how a barbarous community and a civilized community can constitute one
state. I think we must get rid of slavery, or we must get rid of freedom." [34]

3.1. Early Signs of Crisis: A Georgia Congressman Demands Continuation of the African Slave Trade and Benjamin Franklin Pokes Fun at His Assertions (1790)

During the first session of Congress in 1789–90 the Philadelphia Society of Friends (Quakers), fearing that with the end of the War for Independence the African slave trade might be renewed, petitioned Congress to do whatever it could to prevent a resurgence of the traffic. These petitions, one of which was signed by Benjamin Franklin, president of the Pennsylvania Society for Promoting the Abolition of Slavery, were reviewed by a special committee which decided that, concerning slavery, Congress lacked power to intervene in the internal affairs of the states, but would nevertheless use their authority to favor the petitioners' request. A committee of the whole House, however, opposed the petitioners, pointing out that, according to the Constitution, importing slaves into states wishing to receive them could not be prohibited until 1808, and that the states alone had the power to free slaves or to regulate their treatment. In support of these opinions, a Georgia rice planter and congressman, James Jackson, defended the slave trade and the rights of slaveholders in the House, outlining the dire effects, as he saw them, of ending the trade.

Having read Jackson's speech, Franklin wrote a parody of it, inventing for his purposes a fictional pro-slavery spokesman, Sidi Mehemet Ibrahim of Tripoli. The views of this supposed representative of the infamous Barbary states closely paralleled those of Jackson, though for most Americans

34. David Donald, *Charles Sumner and the Coming of the Civil War* (New York: Alfred A. Knopf, 1965), p. 311.

epting that particular supporter of the pro-slavery position
seemed awkward at best. Several facts add to the interest of
cuments. First, like many persons of his age, Franklin as a young
had owned, rented, and even traded in slaves (see Carl Van Doren,
enjamin Franklin [New York: Viking Press, 1938], pp. 128–29, 197). Second, some years earlier, rumors that Franklin had been captured by "Barbary Pirates" on a return voyage from France had aroused deep concern for the fate of *white* Americans enslaved by North African seamen, and Franklin himself might well have been inspired by that incident to write his parody.

SOURCE: "Debates on the Slave Trade," *The African Observer. A Monthly Journal, Containing Essays and Documents Illustrative of the General Character, and Moral and Political Effects of Negro Slavery* (Philadelphia, 1828), pp. 235–38.

A Summary of Congressman Jackson's Speech.

"Slavery is an evil habit—but in some situations, such as S. Carolina and Georgia were in, it was a necessary habit. Large tracts of fertile lands were uncultivated for want of population. The climate was unfavourable to northern constitutions. What is to be done with this land? Is the rice trade to be banished from our shores? Will congress give up the revenue arising from it? And for what? To gratify the supposed feelings, the theoretical speculations or humanity of the Quakers? The Africans were ruled by despots in their own country. All the people are bound to appear in the field when required by their sovereigns. The slaves there are not protected by law; but here, in addition to the ties of humanity, the law interposes in favour of the aged and decrepit. With respect to emancipation, what is to be done with the slaves when freed? They must be incorporated with the white citizens or colonized." Here Jefferson's notes are cited to show the difficulty and danger of incorporation. "Though the Quakers may choose to intermarry with them, there are others among us, who will choose to preserve their race unsullied. Where will you colonize them? To send them to their own country would be to exchange one slavery for another. If we colonize them at home, will not the danger of their natural dispositions exist? Would they be able to support a government to advantage? The Indians would either destroy or enslave them. What people ever engaged in the slave trade have abolished it? England dares not touch it. Shall we undertake it, to gratify a volunteering society of Quakers? for the gratification of a man, who, trembling under the lash of an evil conscience, to atone for his numerous hoard of former sins, emancipated his negroes?[35] I call it not an act of humanity. It was a death-bed repentance; the fear of torments in another world, and the terrors of eternal damnation. Christianity is not repugnant to slavery. This may be seen by several passages. The case of Onesimus is one. The apostle did not require Philemon to set him free. Romans 13, 1. Ephes. 6, 5. Colos. 4, 1. 1. Tim. 5–1, 2. Titus 2, 9–10. &c. Neither was slavery prohibited by Moses. Justice forbids interference. I hold one thousand acres of rice land on the Altemaha. Importations [of slaves] being expected, this land is worth three guineas an acre; take away this expectation and you destroy the value; restrict importations, and you diminish that value one half. Numbers in S. Carolina and Georgia are in the predicament. How are they to be compensated? Have the Quakers a purse sufficient? and are they willing to carry justice and humanity so far as to give it? Have congress a treasury sufficient for this purpose?"

Franklin's Parody.

"Reading in the newspapers the speech of Mr. Jackson in congress, against meddling with the affair of slavery, or attempting to mend the condition of slaves, it put me in mind of a similar speech, made about an hundred years since, by Sidi Mehemet Ibraham, a member of the Divan of Algiers, which may be seen in Martin's account of his consulship, 1687. It was against granting the petition of the sect, called Erika or Purists, who prayed for the abolition of piracy and slavery, as being unjust. Mr. Jackson does not quote it; perhaps he has not seen it. If, therefore, some of its reasonings are to be found in his eloquent speech, it may only show that men's interests operate and are operated on, with surprising similarity, in all countries and climates, whenever they are under similar circumstances. The African's speech, as translated, is as follows:

"Allah Bismallah, &c. God is great, and Mahomet is his Prophet. Have the *Erika* considered the consequences of granting their petition? If we cease our cruises against the Christians, how shall we be furnished with the commodities their countries produce, and which are so necessary for us? If we forbear to make slaves of their people, who, in this hot climate, are to cultivate our lands? Who are to perform the common labours of our families? Must we not then be our own slaves? And is there not more compassion and favour to be shown to us Musselmen, than to these Christian dogs? We have now about fifty thousand slaves, in and near Algiers. This

---

35. Here the orator had the politeness to name, as the object of these coarse invectives, a Friend then present, who early in life had emancipated his slaves, and whose general philanthropy had induced Brissott de Warville [a French revolutionary and founder of the Societé des Amis des Noirs] to bestow on its possessor the appelation of an angel of peace.

number, if not kept up by fresh supplies, will soon diminish, and be gradually annihilated. If, then, we cease taking and plundering the infidel ships, and making slaves of the seamen and passengers, our lands will become of no value, for want of cultivation; the rents of houses in the city will sink one half; and the revenues of government, arising from the share of prizes, must be totally destroyed And for what? to gratify the whim of a whimsical sect, who would have us not only forbear making more slaves, but even manumit those we have. But who is to indemnify their masters for the loss? will the state do it? is our treasury sufficient? will the Erika do it? can they do it? or would they, to do what they think justice to the slaves, do a greater injustice to their owners? And if we set our slaves free, what is to be done with them? Few of them will return to their native countries; they know too well the greater hardships they must there be subject to. They will not embrace our holy religion—they will not adopt our manners: our people will not pollute themselves by intermarrying with them. Must we then maintain them as beggars in our streets? or suffer our property to be the prey of their pillage? For men accustomed to slavery, will not work for a livelihood unless compelled. And what is there so pitiable in their present condition? Were they not slaves in their own countries? Are not Spain, Portugal, France, and the Italian states governed by despots, who hold all their subjects in slavery without exception? Even England treats her sailors as slaves; for they are, whenever the government pleases, seized, and confined in ships of war, condemned not only to work, but to fight for small wages, or a mere subsistence, not better than our slaves are allowed by us. Is their condition then made worse by their falling into our hands? No; they have only exchanged one slavery for another; and I may say a better: for they are brought into a land where the sun of Islamism gives forth its light, and shines in full splendor, and they have an opportunity of making themselves acquainted with the true doctrine, and thereby saving their immortal souls.—Those who remain at home have not that happiness. Sending the slaves home, then, would be sending them out of light into darkness.

"I repeat the question, what is to be done with them? I have heard it suggested, that they may be planted in the wilderness, where there is plenty of land for them to subsist on, and where they may flourish as a free state. But they are, I doubt, too little disposed to labour without compulsion, as well as too ignorant to establish a good government: and the wild Arabs would soon molest and destroy, or again enslave them. While serving us, we take care to provide them with every thing; and they are treated with humanity. The labourers in their own countries are, as I am informed, worse fed, lodged, and clothed. The condition of most of them is therefore already mended, and requires no further improvement. Here their lives are in safety. They are not liable to be impressed for soldiers and forced to cut one another's Christian throats, as in the wars of their own countries. If some of the religious mad bigots, who now teaze us with their silly petitions, have in a fit of blind zeal freed their slaves, it was not generosity, it was not humanity, that moved them to the action; it was from the conscious burthen of a load of sins, and a hope, from the supposed merits of so good a work, to be excused from damnation. How grossly are they mistaken in imagining slavery to be disavowed by the Alcoran! Are not the two precepts, to quote no more, "Masters, treat your slaves with kindness," "Slaves, serve your masters with cheerfulness and fidelity," clear proofs to the contrary? Nor can the plundering of infidels be in that sacred book forbidden; since it is well known from it, that God has given the world, and all that it contains, to his faithful Mussulmen, as fast as they can conquer it. Let us then hear no more of this detestable proposition; the manumission of Christian slaves, the adoption of which would be depreciating our lands and houses, and thereby depriving so many good citizens of their property, create universal discontent, and provoke insurrections, to the endangering of government, and producing general confusion. I have, therefore, no doubt, that this wise council will prefer the comfort and happiness of a whole nation of true believers, to the whim of a few Erika and dismiss this petition.

"The result was, as Martin tells us, that the Divan came to this resolution: 'That the doctrine, that plundering and enslaving the Christians is unjust, is at best problematical; but that it is the interest of this state to continue the practice is clear; therefore, let the petition be rejected.' And it was rejected accordingly."

3.2. "If This Is an Evil, It Is One for Which There Is No Remedy."
A South Carolina Congressman Defends Slavery and the African Slave Trade (1790)

The speech of the Georgia planter and congressman, James Jackson, opposing the Quaker petitions (see Doc. 3.1) was not published in the *Annals of Congress,* the latter (p. 1451) merely stating that "Mr. Jackson spoke largely on the subject, and in opposition to the [Committee's] report." Thus, the speech below of Congressman Smith of South Carolina, delivered the day after Jackson spoke, will offer more developed impressions of the opinions of congressmen representing pro-slavery states such as Geor-

In the Hands of Strangers

gia and South Carolina. It appears, in fact, that Smith repeated some of Jackson's arguments, including his opposition to colonizing the blacks "in some foreign region," a plan allegedly advocated by opponents of slavery.

SOURCE: *Annals of Congress,* 1st Congress, 2nd Session, pp. 1453–64.

Mr. Smith of South Carolina, March 17, 1790.

Mr. Smith of South Carolina said he lamented much that this subject had been brought before the House, that he had deprecated it from the beginning, because he foresaw that it would produce a very unpleasant discussion; that it was a subject of a nature to excite the alarms of the Southern members, who could not view, without anxiety, any interference in it on the part of Congress. . . .

The memorial from the Quakers contained, in his opinion, a very indecent attack on the character of those States which possess slaves. It reprobated slavery as bringing down reproach on the Southern States, and expatiates on the detestation due to the licentious wickedness of the African trade, and the inhuman tyranny and blood guiltiness inseparable from it. He could not but consider it as calculated to fix a stigma of the blackest nature on the State he had the honor to represent and to hold its citizens up to public view as men divested of every principle of honor and humanity. . . .

The memorial from the Pennsylvania Society applied, in express terms, for an emancipation of slaves, and the report of the committee appeared to hold out the idea that Congress might exercise the power of emancipating after the year 1808: for it is said that Congress could not emancipate slaves prior to that period. He remarked that either the power of manumission still remained with the several States, or it was exclusively vested in Congress; for no one would contend that such a power would be concurrent in the several States and the United States. He then showed that the State Governments clearly retained all the rights of sovereignty which they had before the establishment of the Constitution, unless they were exclusively delegated to the United States; and this could only exist where the Constitution granted in express terms an exclusive authority to the Union, or where it granted in one instance an authority to the Union, and in another prohibited the States from exercising the like authority, or where it granted an authority to the Union, to which a similar authority in the States would be repugnant.

He applied these principles to the case in question; and asked, whether the Constitution had in express terms, vested the Congress with the power of manumission? Or whether it restrained the States from exercising that power? Or whether there was any authority given to the Union, with which the exercise of this right by any State would be inconsistent? If these questions were answered in the negative, it followed that Congress had not an exclusive right to the power of manumission. Had it a concurrent right with the States? No gentleman would assert it, because the absurdity was obvious. For a State regulation on the subject might differ from a Federal regulation, in which case one or the other must give way. As the laws of the United States were paramount to those of the individual States, the Federal regulations would abrogate those of the States. Consequently the States would thus be divested of a power which it was evident they now had and might exercise whenever they thought proper. But admitting that Congress had the authority to manumit the slaves in America, and were disposed to exercise it, would the Southern States acquiesce in such a measure without a struggle? Would the citizens of that country tamely suffer their property to be torn from them? Would even the citizens of the other States, which did not possess this property, desire to have all the slaves let loose upon them? Would not such a step be injurious even to the slaves themselves? It was well known that they were an indolent people, improvident, averse to labor: when emancipated they would either starve or plunder. Nothing was a stronger proof of the absurdity of emancipation than the fanciful schemes which the friends of the measure had suggested; one was, to ship them out of the country, and colonize them in some foreign region. This plan admitted that it would be dangerous to retain them within the United States after they were manumitted: but surely it would be inconsistent with humanity to banish these people to a remote country, and to expel them from their native soil, and from places to which they had a local attachment. It would be no less repugnant to the principles of freedom, not to allow them to remain here, if they desired it. How could they be called freemen, if they were, against their consent, to be expelled from the country? Thus did the advocates for emancipation acknowledge that the blacks, when liberated, ought not to remain here to stain the blood of the whites by a mixture of the races.

Another plan was to liberate all those who should be born after a certain limited period. Such a scheme would produce this very extraordinary phenomenon that the mother would be a slave, and her child would be free. These young emancipated negroes, by associating with their enslaved parents, would participate in all the debasement which slavery is said to occasion. But allowing that a practicable scheme of general emancipation could be devised, there can be no doubt that the two races would still remain distinct. It is known from experience, that the whites had such an idea of their superiority over the blacks, that they never even associated with them; even the warmest friends to the blacks kept them at a distance, and rejected all intercourse with them. Could any instance be quoted of their intermarrying; the Quakers asserted that nature had made all men equal, and that the difference of color should not place negroes on a worse footing in society than the whites; but had any of them ever married a negro, or would any of them suffer their children to mix their blood with that of a black? They would view with abhorrence such an alliance.

Mr. S. then read some extracts from Mr. Jefferson's Notes on Virginia, proving that negroes were by nature an inferior race of beings; and that the whites would always feel a repugnance at mixing their blood with that of the blacks. Thus, he proceeded, that respectable author, who was desirous of countenancing emancipation, was, on a consideration of the subject, induced candidly to avow that the difficulties appeared insurmountable. . . .

Various objections, said he, had at different times been alleged against the abominable practice, as it has been called, of one man exercising dominion over another; but slavery was no new thing in the world. The Romans, Greeks, and other nations of antiquity, held slaves at the time Christianity first dawned on society, and the professors of its mild doctrines never preached against it. . . .

Another objection was that the public opinion was against slavery. How did that appear? Were there any petitions on the subject excepting that from the Pennsylvania Society and a few Quakers? And were they to judge for the whole Continent? Were the citizens of the Northern and Eastern States to dictate to Congress on a measure in which the Southern States were so deeply interested? There were no petitions against slavery from the Southern States, and they were the only proper judges of what was for their interest. The toleration of slavery in the several States was a matter of internal regulation and policy, in which each State had a right to do as she pleased, and no other State had a right to intermeddle with her policy or laws. If the citizens of the Northern States were displeased with the toleration of slavery in the Southern States, the latter were equally disgusted with some things tolerated in the former. . . . The Northern States knew that the Southern States had slaves before they confederated with them. If they had such an abhorrence for slavery, why, said Mr. S., did they not cast us off and reject our alliance? The truth was that the best informed part of the citizens of the Northern States knew that slavery was so ingrafted into the policy of the Southern States, that it could not be eradicated without tearing up by the roots their happiness, tranquility, and prosperity; that if it were an evil, it was one for which there was no remedy, and therefore, like wise men, they acquiesced in it. We, on the other hand, knew that the Quaker doctrines had taken such deep root in some of the States, that all resistance to them must be useless; we therefore made a compromise on both sides—we took each other with our mutual bad habits and respective evils, for better, for worse; the Northern States adopted us with our Slaves, and we adopted them with their Quakers. There was then an implied compact between the Northern and Southern people that no step should be taken to injure the property of the latter, or to disturb their tranquility. . . .

But some persons have been of opinion, that if the further importation of slaves could be prohibited, there would be a gradual extinction of the species. Having shown the absurdity of liberating the *postnati* without extending it to all the slaves old and young, and the great absurdity and even impracticability of extending it to all, I shall say a few words with regard to the extinction. That would be impossible, because they increase; to occasion an extinction, Congress must prohibit all intercourse between the sexes; this would be an act of humanity they would not thank us for, nor would they be persuaded that it was for their own good, or Congress must, like Herod, order all the children to be put to death as soon as born. If, then, nothing but evil would result from emancipation, under the existing circumstances of the country, why should Congress stir at all in the business, or give any countenance to such dangerous applications? . . . If some citizens, from misinformation and ignorance, have imbibed prejudices against the Southern States, if ill-intentioned authors have related false facts and gross misrepresentations tending to traduce the character of a whole State, and to mislead the citizens of other States, is that a sufficient reason why a large territory is to be depopulated, merely to gratify the wish of some misinformed individuals? But what have the citizens of the other States to do with our slaves? Have they any right to interfere with our internal policy?

This is not an object of general concern, for I have already proved that it does not weaken the Union; but admit that it did, will the abolition of slavery strengthen South Carolina? It can only be cultivated by slaves; the climate, the nature of the soil, ancient habits, forbid the whites from performing the labor. Experience convinces us of the truth of this. Great Britain made every attempt to settle Georgia by whites alone, and failed, and was compelled at length to introduce slaves; after which that State increased very rapidly in opulence and importance. If the slaves are emancipated, they will not remain in that country—remove the cultivators of the soil, and the whole of the low country, all the fertile rice and indigo swamps will be deserted and become a wilderness. What, then, becomes of its strength? Will such a scheme increase it? Instead of increasing the population of the whites, there will be no whites at all. If the low country is deserted, where will be the commerce, the valuable exports of that country, the large revenue raised from its imports and from the consumption of the rich planters? In a short time the Northern and Eastern States will supply us with their manufactures; if you depopulate the rich low country of South Carolina and Georgia, you will give us a blow which will immediately recoil on yourselves. Without the rice swamps of Carolina, Charleston would decay; so would the commerce of that city: this would injure the back country. If you injure the Southern States, the injury would reach our Northern and Eastern brethren; for the States are links of one chain; if we break one, the whole must fall to pieces. Thus it is manifest, that in proportion to the increase of our agriculture will our wealth be increased; the increase of which will augment that of our sister States, which will either supply us with their commodities, or raise a large revenue upon us, or be the carriers of our produce to foreign markets.

It has been said, that the toleration of slavery brings down reproach on America. It only brings reproach on those who tolerate it, and we are ready to bear our share. We know that none but prejudiced and uncandid persons who have hastily considered the subject, and are ignorant of the real situation of the Southern States, throw out these insinuations. We found slavery ingrafted in the very policy of the country when we were born, and we are persuaded of the impolicy of removing it; if it be a moral evil, it is like many others which exist in all civilized countries, and which the world quietly submit to. . . . The French, so far from curbing and cramping the African trade with needless regulations, give large premiums upon every negro landed on their islands; in some instances as much as two hundred livres per head. Is that nation more debased than others? Are they not a polished people, sensible of the rights of mankind, and actuated by proper sentiments of humanity? The Spaniards encourage slavery; they are people of the nicest honor, proverbially so. The Romans and Greeks had slaves, and are not their glorious achievements held up as excitements to great and magnanimous actions? Sparta teemed with slaves at the time of her greatest fame as a valiant Republic. . . . Much had been said of the cruel treatment of slaves in the West Indies and the Southern States; with respect to the latter, he denied the fact from experience and accurate information, and believed in his conscience that the slaves in South Carolina were a happier people than the lower order of whites in many countries he had visited. With regard to the West Indies, *Lord Rodney* and *Admiral Barrington* had both declared that they had spent some time in the West Indies, and that they had never heard of a negro being cruelly treated; that they had often spoken of their happiness in high terms, declaring that they should rejoice exceedingly if the English day laborer was half as happy. Some have said that slavery is unnecessary; so far from it, that several essential manufactures depended on it. Indigo, cochineal, and various other dying materials, which are the produce of the West Indies, could only be raised by slaves; the great staple commodities of the South would be annihilated without the labor of slaves. It is well known that when the African slaves were brought to the [African] coast for sale, it was customary to put to death all those who were not sold; the abolition of the slave trade would therefore cause the massacre of the people.

The cruel mode of transportation was another motive to this abolition; but was it to be presumed that the merchants would so far attend to their own interests as to preserve the lives and the health of the slaves on the passage. All voyages must be attended with inconveniences, and those from Africa to America not more than others. As to their confinement on board, it was no more than necessary; as to the smallness of space allotted them, it was more than was allotted to soldiers in a camp; . . . it was full as much as was allotted in ships of war to seamen, who by the laws of England were frequently, on their return to their families, after a long and dangerous voyage, seized by violence, hurried away by a press-gang, and forced on another voyage more tedious and perilous than the first, to a hot and sickly climate where several hundreds of them were stowed away in the hold of a vessel. . . .

Having thus removed the force of the observations which have been advanced against the toleration of slavery, by a misguided and misinformed humanity, I shall only add that I disapprove of the whole of the report; because it either states some power sufficiently expressed in the Constitution, which is unnecessary, or it sets forth some power which I am clear Congress do not possess. . . . In short, Mr. Chairman, the whole of this business has been wrong from beginning to end, and as one false step generally leads to others, so has the hasty commitment of these memorials involved us in all this confusion and embarrassment. . . .

3.3. A North-South Exchange of Accusations on the African Slave Trade (1806)

Regarding the following selection, Elizabeth Donnan wrote: "This is one of a number of editorials which appeared during 1806, which expressed the growing resentment of Carolina against outside criticism of the traffic in slaves, whether it emanated from northern states or from Maryland, Virginia, or North Carolina." In fact, the writer of this editorial, printed in the *Charleston Courier* on July 10, 1806, perhaps had reasons to be righteous. What Carolinians were doing was entirely "legal," it could be argued, since slaves were being brought *into* the state and not being taken to foreign countries. Introducing slaves into South Carolina had been legalized in 1803, allegedly owing to a large contraband traffic in Africans, the certainty that the African trade would be outlawed in 1808, and an increasing likelihood of a huge demand for slaves in the newly acquired Louisiana Territory that was certain to enrich South Carolina's merchants and planters. In contrast, the slave trade carried on by citizens of Massachusetts, Rhode Island, and Pennsylvania had not been legal for nearly twenty years—if, that is, Africans were being brought into those northern states; and since 1794, if merchants were transporting slaves from Africa to foreign destinations such as Cuba or South America. It is conceivable that some were doing both.[36]

SOURCE: Elizabeth Donnan, ed., *Documents Illustrative of the History of the Slave Trade to America* (Washington, D.C.: Carnegie Institution of Washington, 1935), vol. 4, pp. 517–19.

"What Epithet Shall We Apply to Those Reptiles?"

Editorial: We have, for a considerable time past, seen with the utmost indignation, the many scandalous and scurrilous paragraphs which have appeared in several of the Northern papers, against the citizens of this State, for doing that which the laws of their country permit them to do, and for embarking in a trade which the necessities of the State require. A more extensive cultivation of land from the increase of our population, renders it necessary that more labourers should be employed to till the soil; the advantages of which not only result in private interest, but the public coffers of the nation ultimately feel its beneficial influence. These considerations led to the decision of the Legislature.

It is not for us now to call in question the morality of the trade, for our readers will recollect that we have uniformly opposed the introduction of so many new negroes, as repugnant to the principles of sound policy, as well as of morality; or, in the emphatic language of our Governor, because

36. For the banning of the African trade into the three northern states in 1787 and 1788, the outlawing of the trade to foreign countries in 1794, and the legalization of the traffic to South Carolina in 1803, see DuBois, *The Suppression of the African Slave Trade*, pp. 36, 85–86, 229, 231–33, 237, 240.

"it increased our weakness, and not our strength." The delegates of the people when sitting in solemn general assembly, deemed it essentially necessary for the interest of the state to permit the importation of slaves from Africa, and those merchants who embark in this trade, do no more than carry the intentions and wishes of the government of their country into operation.

Readers! mark the following paragraph, copied from a Philadelphia paper of June 13. After quoting the paragraph from our paper of the 31st of May last, relative to the pardon of Valentine, under the gallows, for negro stealing, the editor proceeds—"From the same paper we have selected the following advertisements, offering for sale, publicly, and in the face of day, one thousand seven hundred and eleven human beings, stolen from Africa, and no effort is made to bring to justice the detestable Thieves who dragged them, by violence, from their native homes!" Then follow the advertisements at full length, of Gibson and Broadstreet, Henry and John Ker, John Watson and Co., Wm. Boyd, John S. Adams, T. W. Rawlinson, etc.

The only truth contained in the Editor's observation is, the number of slaves offered for sale. The rest is a flourish to catch the feelings of the ignorant, at the expense of truth; and as to the epithet of thieves, which he applies to those who bring Slaves from Africa, we shall presently see whether we cannot apply it to the pure, the immaculate, and demure Philadelphian, and some other of the Northern cities, where they are bellowing out, humanity! humanity! humanity! Oh, the rights of dear insulted human nature!

On the 14th of February last there were at Montevideo, in the River Plate, the following vessels, with slaves from Mozambique and the Gold Coast.

————Ship *Juliana,* Nicols of Boston
————*Pigou,* Collet of Philadelphia
————*Swift,* Mayberry of Newport
————*Espasia,* Moore of Philadelphia
————*Ann,* Donaldson of Newport
————*John,* Watson of Charleston

Out of the six slave ships on the coast:
Two belonged to Philadelphia.
One to Boston.
Two to Newport.
One to Charleston

Of these, the one from Charleston was the only one which was authorized to slave by the laws of his country. Neither Philadelphia, Boston, or Newport, are authorized by the laws of their respective states, to equip vessels for slave voyages—and yet it is a fact known to every citizen of Charleston, that where there is one ship belonging to this port, employed in the slave trade, there are three vessels from the northern states. If villainy is to be attached to the characters of those who engage in this trade, under the sanction of the laws of their country, what epithet shall we apply to those reptiles, who, in defiance of the laws of their state, and in defiance of the opinions of their fellow-citizens, engage in, to them, an unlawful and prohibited commerce? Such fellows would set their country in a blaze for money, and then run away by the light of it. [Elizabeth Donnan added this footnote: "The remainder of the editorial attacks an advertisement for the sale of a 'German boy' which appeared in the Philadelphia paper under consideration."]

3.4. "We Have Enriched America with Our Blood and Tears." *Walker's Appeal* and the Colonization Movement

In 1816 a group of prominent men, chiefly southerners, met in Washington and took steps leading to creation of the American Colonization Society, an organization which, according to its constitution, proposed to remove the free people of color to Africa or to some other "expedient" location. Those attending included Bushrod Washington, nephew of George Washington, Henry Clay of Kentucky, John Randolph of Virginia, Francis Scott Key of Maryland and Elias B. Caldwell, who resided in Washington and had close ties to both the North and the South.[37]

Many blacks, led by such men as James Forten of Philadelphia and Bishop Richard Allen, founder of the African Methodist Episcopal Church, publicly opposed colonization, whereas some critics of slavery such as William Lloyd Garrison endorsed it for a time until recognizing that the Society's leaders were primarily motivated by a desire to reduce or eliminate the free black population in order to strengthen and preserve slavery. Some free blacks, driven perhaps by desperation, were disposed or "persuaded" to accept colonization (see Doc. 3.5), but few looked forward to leaving the land of their birth to be sent to a faraway destination. Despite their rejection of the plan, however, as we will see (Docs. 3.23 and 3.24), the idea of colonizing American blacks in distant parts of the world retained its vitality until the Civil War— was, in fact, invigorated by the circumstances produced by that conflict.

37. For the first meeting of the Colonization Society and some reactions to it, see P. J. Staudenraus, *The African Colonization Movement, 1816–1865* (New York: Columbia University Press), pp. 23–35.

David Walker, the author of this selection, was an ardent opponent of colonization. Born in 1785 in Wilmington, North Carolina, the son of a free black woman, in his youth he developed an intense hatred of slavery, and so left the South in search of a better life. Settling in Boston, he sold used clothing for a living, taught himself to read and write, and worked for the antislavery cause, contributing articles to *Freedom's Journal,* the first black newspaper of the United States.[38] In 1829 he published "Walker's Appeal," a radical tract that forthrightly accepted violence as a way to end slavery. Southerners, of course, responded with alarm and soon offered rewards for Walker, dead or alive, and in fact he soon died.[39] In his "Appeal," Walker attributed the misery of black people to slavery, ignorance, "religion" (as inflicted on slaves by the master class), and the devious agenda of the American Colonization Society.

SOURCE: Herbert Aptheker, *"One Continual Cry": David Walker's Appeal to the Colored People of the World (1829–1830)* (New York: Humanities Press, 1965), pp. 109–13, 115–17, 120–27, 134–38.

"Our Wretchedness in Consequence of the Colonizing Plan"

My dearly beloved brethren:—This is a scheme on which so many able writers, together with that very judicious colored Baltimorean, have commented, that I feel my delicacy about touching it. . . . Previous, however, to giving my sentiments, either for or against it, I shall give that of Mr. Henry Clay, together with that of Mr. Elias B. Caldwell, Esq. of the District of Columbia, as extracted from the National Intelligencer, by Dr. [Jesse] Torrey, author of a series of "Essays on Morals, and the Diffusion of Useful Knowledge."

At a meeting which was convened in the District of Columbia, for the express purpose of agitating the subject of colonizing us in some part of the world, Mr. Clay was called to the chair, and . . . he rose and spake, in substance, as follows: says he—

38. On October 30, 1828, the following notice appeared in *Freedom's Journal:* "Clothing kept constantly on hand for sale by David Walker, No. 42 Brattle Street, Boston. A great variety of second-hand clothing. He also cleans all kinds of woolen clothing in the neatest manner and on the most reasonable terms." Philip S. Foner and Ronald L. Lewis, *The Black Worker: A Documentary History from Colonial Times to the Present* (Philadelphia: Temple University Press, 1978), p. 129.

39. In *To Awaken My Afflicted Brethren: David Walker and the Problem of Antebellum Slave Resistance* (University Park: Pennsylvania State University Press, 1997), p. 269, Peter P. Hinks has uncovered evidence from the Boston Index of Deaths, Boston City Hall, that Walker died of consumption at the age of thirty-three.

That class of the mixt population of our country [coloured people] was peculiarly situated; they neither enjoyed the immunities of freemen, nor were they subjected to the incapacities of slaves, but partook, in some degree, of the qualities of both. From their condition, and the unconquerable prejudices resulting from their colour, they never could amalgamate with the free whites of this country. It was desirable, therefore, as it respected them, and the residue of the population of the country, to drain them off. Various schemes of colonization had been thought of, and a part of our continent, it was supposed by some, might furnish a suitable establishment for them. But, for his part, Mr. C[lay]. said, he had a decided preference for some part of the Coast of Africa. There ample provision might be made for the colony itself, and it might be rendered instrumental in the introduction into that extensive quarter of the globe, of the arts, civilization, and Christianity.

(Here I ask Mr. Clay, what kind of Christianity? Did he mean such as they have among the Americans—distinction, whip, blood, and oppression? I pray the Lord Jesus Christ to forbid it.)

"There, said he, was a peculiar, a moral fitness, in restoring them to the land of their fathers, and if instead of the evils and sufferings which we had been the innocent cause of inflicting upon the inhabitants of Africa, we can transmit to her the blessings of our arts, our civilization, and our religion. May we not hope that America will extinguish a great portion of that moral debt which she has contracted to that unfortunate continent?" . . .

Before I proceed any further, I solicit your notice, brethren, to the foregoing part of Mr. Clay's speech, in which he says, (look above) "and if, instead of the evils and sufferings, which we had been the innocent cause of inflicting," &c.—What this very learned statesman could have been thinking about, when he said in his speech, "we had been the innocent cause of inflicting," etc., I have never been able to conceive. Are Mr. Clay and the rest of the Americans, innocent of the blood and groans of our fathers and us, their children? Every individual may plead innocence, if he pleases, but God will, before long, separate the innocent from the guilty, unless something is speedily done—which I suppose will hardly be, so that their destruction may be sure. Oh Americans! let me tell you, in the name of the Lord, it will be good for you, if you listen to the voice of the Holy Ghost, but if you do not, you are ruined!!! Some of you are good men; but the will of my God must be done. Those avaricious and ungodly tyrants among you, I am awfully afraid will drag down the vengeance of God upon you.—When God Almighty commences his battle on the continent of America, for the oppression of his people, tyrants will wish they never were born.

But to return to Mr. Clay, whence I digressed. He says,

> It was proper and necessary distinctly to state, that he under-
> stood it constituted no part of the object of this meeting, to touch
> or agitate in the slightest degree, a delicate question, connected
> with another portion of the coloured population of our country. It
> was not proposed to deliberate upon or consider at all, any ques-
> tion of emancipation, or that which was connected with the aboli-
> tion of slavery. It was upon that condition alone, he was sure, that
> many gentlemen from the South and the West, whom he saw pres-
> ent, had attended, or could be expected to co-operate. It was upon
> that condition only, that he himself had attended.

That is to say, to fix a plan to get those of the coloured people, who are said to be free, away from among those of our brethren whom they unjustly held in bondage, so that they may be enabled to keep them the more secure in ignorance and wretchedness, to support them and their children, and consequently they would have the more obedient slave. For if the free are al-lowed to stay among the slave, they will have intercourse together, and, of course, the free will learn the slaves *bad habits,* by teaching them that they are **MEN,** as well as other people, and certainly *ought* and *must* be **FREE. . . .**

This gentleman (Mr. Henry Clay) not only took an active part in this colonizing plan, but was absolutely chairman of a meeting held at Wash-ington, the 21st day of December, 1816, to agitate the subject of colonizing us in Africa. . . . Do you believe that Mr. Henry Clay, late Secretary of State, and now in Kentucky, is a friend to the blacks, further, than his per-sonal interest extends? Is it not his greatest object and glory upon earth, to sink us into miseries and wretchedness by making slaves of us, to work his plantation to enrich him and his family? Does he care a pinch of snuff about Africa—whether it remains a land of Pagans and of blood, or of Christians, so long as he gets enough of her sons and daughters to dig up gold and silver for him? If he had no slave, and could obtain them in no other way, if it were not repugnant to the laws of his country, which pro-hibit the importation of slaves (which act was, indeed, more through ap-prehension than humanity) would he not try to import a few from Africa to work his farm? Would he work in the hot sun to earn his bread, if he could make an African work for nothing, particularly if he could keep him in ignorance and make him believe that God made him for nothing else but to work for him? Is not Mr. Clay a white man, and too delicate to work in the hot sun? Was he not made by his Creator to sit in the shade, and make the blacks work without remuneration for their services, to support him and his family? I have been for some time taking notice of this man's speeches and public writings, but never to my knowledge have I seen any thing in his writings which insisted on the emancipation of slavery. . . .

I shall now pass in review the speech of Mr. Elias B. Caldwell, Esq. of the District of Columbia, extracted from the same page on which Mr. Clay's will be found. Mr. Caldwell, giving his opinion respecting us, at that ever memorable meeting, he says: "The more you improve the condition of these people, the more you cultivate their minds, the more miserable you make them in their present state. You give them a higher relish for those privileges which they can never attain, and turn what we intend for a blessing into a curse." Let me ask this benevolent man, what he means by a blessing intended for us. Did he mean sinking us and our children into ignorance and wretchedness, to support him and his family? . . . "No," said he, "if they must remain in their present situation, keep them in the *lowest state of degradation and ignorance. The nearer you bring them to the condition of brutes, the better chance do you give them of possessing their apathy.*"

Extract from the speech of Mr. John Randolph of Roanoke:
Said he:

> "It had been properly observed by the Chairman, as well as by the gentlemen from this District [meaning Messrs. Clay and Caldwell] that there was nothing in the proposition submitted to consideration which in the smallest degree touches another very important and delicate question, which ought to be left as much out of view as possible [Negro Slavery].
>
> There is no fear, [Mr. R. said,] that this proposition would alarm the slave-holders; they had been accustomed to think seriously of the subject.—There was a popular work on agriculture, by John Taylor of Caroline, which was widely circulated and much confided in, in Virginia. In that book, much read because coming from a practical man, this description of people [referring to us half free ones] were pointed out as a great evil. They had indeed

been held up as the greater bug-bear to every man who feels an inclination to emancipate his slaves, not to create in the bosom of his country so great a nuisance. If a place could be provided for their reception, and a mode of sending them hence, there were hundreds, nay thousands of citizens who would, by manumitting their slaves, relieve themselves from the cares attendant on their possession. The great slave-holder, [Mr. R. said,] was frequently a mere sentry at his own door—bound to stay on his plantation to see that his slaves were properly treated. &c. [Mr. R. concluded by saying,] that he had thought it necessary to make these remarks being a slave-holder himself, to shew that, so far from being connected with abolition of slavery, the measure proposed would prove one of greatest securities to enable the master to keep in possession his own property."

Here is a demonstrative proof of a plan got up by a gang of slave-holders to select the free people of colour from among the slaves, that our more miserable brethren may be the better secured in ignorance and wretchedness, to work their farms and dig their mines, and thus go on enriching the Christians with their blood and groans. What our brethren could have been thinking about, who have left their native land and home and gone away to Africa, I am unable to say. This country is as much ours as it is the whites, whether they will admit it now or not, they will see and believe it by and by. They tell us about prejudice—what have we to do with it? Their prejudices will be obliged to fall like lightning to the ground, in succeeding generations; not, however, with the will and consent of all the whites, for some will be obliged to hold on to the old adage, viz.: the blacks are not men, but were made to be an inheritance to us and our children forever!!!!!![40] . . .

The Americans say that we are ungrateful—but I ask them for heaven's sake, what we should be grateful to them for—for murdering our fathers and mothers? Or do they wish us to return thanks to them for chaining and handcuffing us, branding us, cramming fire down our throats, or for keeping us in slavery, and beating us nearly or quite to death to make us work in ignorance and miseries, to support them and their families. They certainly think that we are a gang of fools. . . .

Before I proceed further with this scheme, I shall give an extract from the letter of the truly Reverend Divine (Bishop Allen) of Philadelphia, re-

40. From Leviticus.

specting this trick. At the instance of the Editor of the Freedom's Journal,[41] he says,

> Dear Sir, I have been for several years trying to reconcile my mind to the Colonizing of Africans in Liberia, but there have always been, and there still remain great and insurmountable objections against the scheme. We are an unlettered people, brought up in ignorance, not one in a hundred can read and write, not one in a thousand has a liberal education; is there any fitness for such to be sent into a far country, among heathens, to convert or civilize them, when they themselves are neither civilized or Christianized? See the great bulk of the poor, ignorant Africans in this country, exposed to every temptation before them: all for the want of their morals being refined by education and proper attendance paid unto them by their owners, or those who had the charge of them. It is said by the Southern slave-holders, that the more ignorant they can bring up the Africans, the better slaves they make, "go and come." Is there any fitness for such people to be colonized in a far country to be their own rulers? Can we not discern the project of sending the free people of colour away from their country? Is it not for the interest of the slave-holders to select the free people of colour out of the different states, and send them to Liberia? Will it not make their slaves uneasy to see free men of colour enjoying liberty? It is against the law in some of the Southern states, that a person of colour should receive an education, under a severe penalty. Colonizationists speak of America being first colonized; but is there any comparison between the two? America was colonized by as *wise, judicious* and *educated* men as the world afforded. **WILLIAM PENN** did not want for *learning, wisdom, or intelligence.* If all the people were as ignorant, and in the same situation as our brethren, what would become of the world? Where would be the principle or piety that would govern the people? We were *stolen* from our mother country, and brought *here.* We have *tilled* the ground and made fortunes for thousands, and still they are not weary of our services. *But they who stay to till the ground must be slaves.* Is there not land enough in America, or corn enough in

41. *Freedom's Journal* was owned and edited by Samuel Cornish (later editor of the "Colored American") and John Russwurm, who in 1829 emigrated to Liberia where he held high offices in the Colonization Society. For Russwurm's conversion from an opponent of the Society to a fervent supporter and editor of the Liberia *Herald,* see Staudenraus, *African Colonization Movement,* p. 191. Editor.

Egypt? Why should they send us into a far country to die? See the thousands of foreigners emigrating to America every year: and if there be ground sufficient for them to cultivate, and bread for them to eat; why would they wish to send the *first tillers* of the land away? Africans have made fortunes for thousands, who are yet unwilling to part with their services; but the free must be sent away, and those who remain must be *slaves*. I have no doubt that there are many good men who do not see as I do, and who are sending us to Liberia; but they have not duly considered the subject—they are not men of colour.—This land which we have watered with our *tears* and *our blood*, is now our *mother country*, and we are well satisfied to stay where wisdom abounds and the gospel is free."

"**RICHARD ALLEN,**
"*Bishop of the African Methodist Episcopal*
"*Church in the United States.*"

I have given you, my brethren, an extract verbatim from the letter of that godly man as you may find it on the aforementioned page of Freedom's Journal. I know that thousands, and perhaps millions of my brethren in these States, have never heard of such a man as Bishop Allen—a man whom God many years ago raised up among his ignorant and degraded brethren, to preach Jesus Christ and him crucified to them—who notwithstanding, had to wrestle against principalities and the powers of darkness to diffuse that gospel with which he was endowed, among his brethren—but who having overcome the combined powers of devils and wicked men, has under God planted a Church among us which will be as durable as the foundation of the earth on which it stands. Richard Allen! . . . See him and his ministers in the states of New York, New Jersey, Pennsylvania, Delaware and Maryland, carrying the gladsome tidings of free and full salvation to the colored people.

Tyrants and false christians, however, would not allow him to penetrate far into the South for fear that he would awaken some of his ignorant brethren, whom they held in wretchedness and miseries—for fear, I say, that he would awaken and bring them to a knowledge of their Maker. O my Master! my Master! I cannot but think upon Christian Americans!! What kind of people can they be? . . . Yet those men tell us that we are the seed of Cain, and that God put a dark stain upon us, that we might be known as their slaves!!! . . .

However, let us be the seed of *Cain, Harry, Dick, or Tom!!!* God will show the whites what we are, yet. I say from the beginning, I do not think that we were natural enemies to each other. But the whites having made us so wretched, by subjecting us to slavery, and having murdered so many millions of us, in order to make us work for them, and out of devilishness—and they taking our wives, whom we love as we do ourselves—our mothers who bore the pains of death to give us birth—our fathers and dear little children, and ourselves, and strip and beat us one before the other—chain, handcuff and drag us about like rattle-snakes—shoot us down like wild bears, before each other's faces, to make us submissive to, and work to support them and their families. They (the whites) know well if we are *men*. . . .

Thus we see, my brethren, the two very opposite positions of those great men, who have written respecting this "Colonizing Plan." (Mr. Clay and his slave holding party,) men who are resolved to keep us in eternal wretchedness, are also bent upon sending us to Liberia. While the Reverend Bishop Allen, and his party, men who have the fear of God, and the welfare of their brethren at heart. The Bishop in particular, whose labours for the salvation of his brethren, are well known to a large part of those, who dwell in the United States, are completely opposed to the plan—and advise us to stay where we are. Now we have to determine whose advice we will take respecting this all important matter, whether we will adhere to Mr. Clay and his slave-holding party, who have always been our oppressors and murderers, and who are for colonizing us, more through apprehension than through humanity, or to this godly man who has done so much for our benefit, together with the advice of all the good and wise among us and the whites. Will any of us leave our homes and go to Africa? I hope not. Let them commence their attack upon us as they did on our brethren in Ohio, driving and beating us from our country, and my soul for theirs, they will have enough of it.[42] Let no man of us budge one step, and let slave-holders come to beat us from our country. America is more our country than it is the whites—we have enriched it with our *blood and tears*. The greatest riches in all America have arisen from our blood and tears:—and will they drive us from our property and homes, which we have earned with our *blood?* They must look sharp or this very thing will bring swift destruction upon them. . . .

But to return to the colonizing trick. It will be well for me to notice here at once that I do not mean indiscriminately to condemn all the members and advocates of this scheme, for I believe that there are some friends

---

42. Walker refers to anti-black rioting in Cincinnati by a local branch of the Colonization Society. Mob attacks forced more than half the blacks of the city to flee to Canada and other parts of the United States. See August Meier and Elliott Rudwick, *From Plantation to Ghetto,* 3d ed. (New York: Hill & Wang, 1976), p. 124. Editor.

to the sons of Africa, who are laboring for our salvation, not in words only but in truth and in deed, who have been drawn into this plan. Some, more by persuasion than anything else; while others, with humane feelings and lively zeal for our good, seeing how much we suffer from the afflictions poured upon us by unmerciful tyrants, are willing to enroll their names in any thing which they think has for its ultimate end our redemption from wretchedness and miseries; such men, with a heart truly overflowing with gratitude for their past services and zeal in our cause, I humbly beg to ex-amine this plot minutely, and see if the end which they have in view will be completely consummated by such a course of procedure. . . .

Do the colonizationists think to send us off without first being recon-ciled to us? Do they think to bundle us up like brutes and send us off, as they did our brethren of the State of Ohio? Methinks colonizationists think they have a set of brutes to deal with, sure enough. Do they think to drive us from our country and homes, after having enriched it with our blood and tears, and keep back millions of our dear brethren, sunk in the most barbarous wretchedness, to dig up gold and silver for them and their chil-dren? . . . See the African Repository and Colonial Journal [the principal Colonization periodical], from its commencement to the present day—see how we are, through the medium of that periodical, abused and held up by the Americans, as the greatest nuisance to society, and throat-cutters in the world. But the Lord sees their actions. . . .

Now let us reason—I mean you of the United States, whom I believe God designs to save from destruction, if you will hear. . . . I say, let us rea-son; had you not better take our body, while you have it in your power, and while we are yet ignorant and wretched, not knowing but a little, give us education, and teach us the pure religion of our Lord and Master, which is calculated to make the lion lay down in peace with the lamb, and which millions of you have beaten us nearly to death for trying to obtain since we have been among you, and thus, at once, gain our affection, while we are ignorant? Remember, Americans, that we must and shall be free and en-lightened as you are, will you wait until we shall, under God, obtain our liberty by the crushing arm of power? Will it not be dreadful for you? I speak Americans for your good. We must and shall be free I say, in spite of you. You may do your best to keep us in wretchedness and misery, to enrich you and your children, but God will deliver us from under you. And wo, wo, will be to you if we have to obtain our freedom by fighting. . . .

The Americans may say and do as they please, but they have to raise us from the condition of brutes to that of respectable men, and to make a na-tional acknowledgement to us for the wrongs they have inflicted on us. As unexpected, strange, and wild as these propositions may to some appear, it is no less a fact, that unless they are complied with, the Americans of the United States, though they may for a little while escape, God will yet weigh them in a balance, and if they are not superior to other men, as they have represented themselves to be, he will give them wretchedness to their very heart's content.

3.5. "A Most Detestable Plan of Persecution." How Free Blacks Were Coerced to Emigrate to Liberia

The abolitionist, William Lloyd Garrison, rejected the more radical aspects of "Walker's Appeal," but was almost certainly influenced by Walker when he published his own severe denunciation of the Colonization Society in 1832. This heavily documented study, *Thoughts on Colonization,* made the following general accusations: The Society was apologetic to both slavery and slaveholders. It was pledged not to oppose slavery. It recognized slaves as property, which elevated slave prices. It opposed abolition, was nurtured by selfishness and fear, worked to accomplish a total removal of the black population from the land of their birth, deprecated free blacks, denied that they could ever improve their conditions while in the United States, sought to deny them education, and finally, worked to deceive and mislead the country.

Six years after Garrison's book appeared, William Jay published his own highly critical and well-documented study of the Colonization Society, from which the following excerpt is taken. Here Jay brilliantly reveals the role of the Colonization Society and its supporters, Northerners and Southerners alike, in compelling free blacks to migrate to Liberia *against their will.* The Society's constitution stated clearly that its "exclusive" goal was to colonize free blacks, *with their consent,* in Africa, or such other place as Congress might deem expedient. Jay, however, assembled a long list of examples of how the consent of blacks to emigrate was, to use his words, "extorted by the most abominable persecution."

SOURCE: William Jay, *Inquiry into the Character and Tendency of the American Colonization, and American Anti-Slavery Societies* (1838; reprint, New York Universities Press, 1969), pp. 47–54.

Compulsory Emigration.

It has never been denied that good men belong to the Colonization Society; and it ought not to be denied that even good men are fallible, and subject to erroneous opinions and unwarrantable prejudices. To us it appears unquestionable that the facts developed in the preceding pages prove a tendency in the Society to excite in the community a persecuting spirit towards the free blacks. That the pious and respectable members of the Society detest the horrible outrages recently committed upon these people in New York, Philadelphia, and elsewhere, it would be both foolish and wicked to doubt; and yet no one who candidly and patiently investigates the whole subject can fail to be convinced that these outrages never would have happened, had the Society never existed. The assertion is not hazardous, that of the multitudes composing the [anti-] negro mobs, there was not an individual less disposed than the Canterbury town meeting to laud the "benevolent Colonization system." [43] Every wretch who participated in beating, and plundering free negroes would rejoice in their expulsion from their country, and in the Society he beholds an instrument for the accomplishment of his wishes.

But how is it possible that the best and the worst of men can unite in supporting the same institution? In the first place, these good men, as is abundantly evident from their own confessions, are actuated by motives of supposed public policy, as well as benevolence in promoting the colonization of people whom they regard as nuisances; and in the second place, there are in the constitution three talismanic words which through the influence of existing prejudices have blinded the eyes of these good men to the *practical* operation of the Society on the colored people. The words are **"WITH THEIR CONSENT."** It is speciously argued, if the free blacks *consent* to go to Africa, why not send them? if they do not wish to go, they are at liberty to remain. This argument seems for the most part to have benumbed the consciences and understandings of Colonizationists, as to the cruel persecution which their Society necessarily encourages. They would be horrified at the idea of their agents scouring the country, and seizing men, women, and children, placing them on the rack till, as joint after joint was dislocated, the suffering wretched *consented* to go to Africa; and yet the Society feels no compunction in countenancing legal oppression having the same ultimate object in view, and in transporting negroes whose *consent* they well know, has been extorted by the most abominable persecution. Many feel disposed to deny the truth of these assertions; but not, we trust, after seeing the proof of them, which we will now proceed to offer.

We have already adverted to the cruel laws by which these people are

---

43. Jay refers to the persecution suffered by a young white woman, Prudence Crandall, and her black students, whose school for colored girls in Canterbury, Connecticut, was attacked and demolished. Editor.

oppressed, and kept, purposely kept, in ignorance and degradation. Now let it be recollected that, with but few exceptions, these laws have been either enacted, or are kept in force by legislatures, which have formally and in their legislative capacity, passed resolutions in favor of the Society. Fourteen States have thus avowed their attachment to Colonization. Now had these States, including *Connecticut,* Ohio, and several of the slave States, repealed their laws against the free blacks, and forborne to enact new ones; their sincerity in approving a plan for the removal of these people *with their consent* would have been less questionable, than it is now, when they persist in a course of policy well calculated to *coerce* that consent. The Society appears to be a particular favorite with the slave States, with the exception of South Carolina, where its true character seems to have been misunderstood.

Now hear the acknowledgment of a Southern writer. We have before us the fourth edition, 1834, of "A Treatise on the Patriarchal System of Society" by a Florida slave holder. It is a treatise, in sober earnestness, on the means of perpetuating slavery, and increasing its profits. The author says, p. 12—"Colonization in Africa has been proposed to the free colored people: *to forward which,* a general system of persecution against them, upheld from the pulpit, has been *legalized* throughout the Southern States." The writer does not explain his allusion to the Southern pulpit; but we may judge of its influence on the condition of the free blacks, from the avowal already quoted from the Southern *Religious Telegraph,* of its repugnance to these people being taught to *read,* because such an acquirement would be an inducement with them to remain in this country; or, in other words, that the better they were treated here, the less likely would they be to consent to go to Africa.[44]

The Legislatures of Maryland and Virginia, it is well known, have made large appropriations for Colonization, and yet these Legislatures are among the most malignant persecutors of free blacks. The original bill, making the Virginia appropriation, contained a clause for the *compulsory* transportation of free blacks. Let it be recollected that: the Colonization Society has ever been the peculiar favorite of Virginia, and that her most distinguished citizens have been enrolled among its officers; and let us now see *how* Colonization has been promoted in that State. On a motion to strike out the compulsory clause, Mr. Brodnax thus expressed himself *against* the motion:

44. The quotation is as follows: "If the free people of color were generally taught to read, it might be an inducement to them to remain in this country; we would offer them no such inducements." *Southern Religious Telegraph,* February 19, 1831. Editor.

"IT IS IDLE TO TALK ABOUT NOT RESORTING TO FORCE.

Every body must look to the introduction of force of some kind or other. If the free negroes are willing to go, they will go; if not willing, **THEY MUST BE COMPELLED TO GO.** Some gentlemen think it politic *now* to insert this feature in the bill, though they *proclaim their readiness to resort to it when it becomes necessary;* they think that for a year or two a sufficient number will consent to go, and **THEN THE REST CAN BE COMPELLED.** For my part, I deem it better to approach the question and settle it at once, and avow it openly. The intelligent portion of the free negroes know very well what is going on. Will they not see your debates? Will they not see that **COERCION IS ULTIMATELY TO BE RESORTED TO.** I have already expressed it as my opinion, that few, *very few,* will *voluntarily* consent to emigrate, if no *compulsory measures be adopted.* Without it, you will still, no doubt, have applicants for removal equal to your means. Yes, sir, people who will not only consent, but beg you to deport them. But what *sort of consent*—a consent extorted by a species of oppression, calculated to render their situation among us insupportable! Many of those who have been already sent off went with their avowed consent, but under the influence of a more decided compulsion than any which this bill holds out. I will not express in its fullest extent the idea I entertain of *what has been done, or what enormities will be perpetrated to induce this class of persons to leave the State.* Who does not know that when a free negro, by crime or otherwise, has rendered himself obnoxious to a neighborhood, how easy it is for a party to visit him one night, take him from his bed and family, and apply to him the gentle admonition of a severe flagellation, to induce him to go away. In a few nights the dose can be repeated, perhaps increased, until, in the language of the physicians, *quantum suff.* has been administered, to produce the desired operation, and the fellow becomes perfectly willing to move away. I have certainly heard, (if incorrectly, the gentleman from Southampton[45] will put me right) that *all the large cargo of emigrants, lately transported from that country to Liberia, all of whom professed to be willing to go, were rendered so by some such ministration as I have described.* Indeed, sir, *all of us* look to **FORCE** of some kind or other, direct or indirect, moral or physical, legal or illegal."

Another member, Mr. Fisher, in opposing the motion, said, "If we wait till the free negroes *consent* to leave the State, we shall wait until time is no more. They never will give their consent. He believed if the compulsory

---

45. An allusion to the rebellion led by Nat Turner, a slave, in Southampton County, Virginia, in August 1831. Editor.

principle were stricken out, this class would *be forced to leave by the harsh treatment of the whites."*

The compulsory clause was stricken out, but we have the assurance of Mr. Brodnax, that they who objected to it at *present,* were ready to resort to force, whenever it should become necessary; and he tells us that *all* look to *force* of some kind or other; and he might have added, "all of us look to the Colonization Society as the instrument by which the forcible expulsion of the free negroes is to be effected." Nor do they look in vain. At the very time that the negroes of Southampton were suffering the barbarities he describes, the managers of the Society addressed their auxiliaries, urging them to increased efforts in raising funds, and alluding to the excitement occasioned by the insurrection at Southampton, remarked, "the free people of color have awakened from their slumber, to a *keen* sense of their situation, and *are ready* in large numbers to emigrate to the Colony of Liberia." *Address,* 17th *Nov.* 1831.

A large number of these miserable people did indeed consent to go to Africa, and the managers well knew *how* their consent was obtained. "I *warned* the managers against this Virginia business," said Mr. Breckenridge in his speech before the Society, "and *yet* they sent out two shiploads of vagabonds, not fit to go to such a place, and that were *coerced* away as truly as if it had been done with a cartwhip."

Hear the confession of Mr. Gurley, the Secretary of the Society, on this subject—"Our friends at Norfolk appealed to us, and said the people were persecuted, and that it was a matter of humanity to take them. Our agent said they were *driven* from the county, and had appealed to him, and begged to go to Liberia." *Speech before the Society.*

Hear the testimony of Thomas C. Brown from Liberia, given in May, 1834. "I am acquainted with several from Southampton County, Virginia, who informed me that they received several hundred lashes from the patroles [*sic*] to make them willing to go. In one instance, a man was several times compelled to witness the lashes inflicted on his wife, and then to be severely flogged himself. In another instance, a family received information from their white neighbors that unless they went to Liberia, they should be whipped. Having no means of redress, they were obliged to go."

Hear the New York Colonization Society, when addressing the *public*— "We say to them (the free blacks) we think you may improve your condition by going thither, but if you prefer remaining here, you will be *protected* and *treated with kindness."* Proceedings of New York Col. Soc., 1831.

Hear the same Society, when addressing the *Legislature*—"We do not ask that the provisions of our constitution and statute book should be modified as to *relieve* and exalt the condition of the colored people while they remain with us. Let these provisions stand **IN ALL THEIR RIGOR,** to work out the ultimate and unbounded *good* of this people." In plain English, to coerce their consent to go to Africa. *Memorial to New York Legislature,* 1832.

We have seen what are the Connecticut and Virginia plans for promoting Colonization—now for the Pennsylvania plan. At a public meeting held in the borough of Columbia (Penn.) at the Town Hall, 23rd August, 1834, the following, among other resolutions, were unanimously passed.

"Resolved, that we will not purchase any articles that can be procured elsewhere, or give our **VOTE** for any office whatever, to any one who employs negroes to do that species of labor white men have been accustomed to perform.

"Resolved, that the Colonization Society ought to be supported by all the citizens favorable to the removal of the blacks from this country."

Here we find the support of the Society avowedly coupled with a most detestable plan of persecution. And now for the practical operation of this meeting of the friends of the "benevolent Colonization system." It appears from a Columbia paper that one or two nights after the meeting, a mob collected, and partly tore down the dwelling of a black man; they then proceeded to the office of another black man, who had the presumption to *deal in lumber,* "a species of labor *white* men had been accustomed to perform," broke out the windows and door, rifled the desk, scattered the papers in the street, and attempted to overturn the building. Surely the Society may reasonably anticipate the consent of the blacks to emigrate, when in Connecticut, Pennsylvania, and Virginia, such cogent arguments are used to obtain it. Were the Society governed, as it ought to be, by Christian principles, it would shrink from encouraging persecution by accomplishing its object, the exportation of its victims. It would say explicitly to the authors of these atrocities, "you shall gain nothing by your cruelty, through our instrumentality. . . . But alas, it has virtually given official notice that it will transport all whose consent can be obtained, no matter by what barbarity. Hear the declaration of Mr. Gurley, the Secretary of the Society.

"Should they (free blacks) **BE URGED BY ANY STRESS OF CIRCUMSTANCES** to seek an asylum beyond the limits of the United States, humanity and religion will alike dictate that they should be assisted to remove and establish themselves in freedom and prosperity in the land of their **CHOICE.**" *Letter to gentlemen in New York.*

True it is, the free blacks have been rendered by prejudice and persecution an ignorant and degraded class; but they are still competent to appreciate the practical character of Colonization philanthropy.

The following resolutions, passed by a meeting of free blacks in New Bedford, in 1832, express the unanimous opinion of all their brethren who have intelligence to form, or courage to express an opinion on the subject.

"Resolved, that in whatever light we view the Colonization Society, we discover nothing in it but terror, prejudice, and oppression. The warm and beneficent hand of philanthropy is not apparent in the system, but the influence of the Society on public opinion is more prejudicial to the interests and welfare of the people of color in the United States, than slavery itself.

"Resolved, that the Society, to effect its purpose, the removal of free people of color (not the slaves) through its agents, teaches the public to believe that it is patriotic and benevolent to withhold from us knowledge, and the means of acquiring subsistence; and to look upon us as unnatural and illegal residents in this country, and thus by the force of prejudice, if not by law, endeavor to compel us to embark for Africa, and that too apparently by our own free will and consent."

And now let us ask what purpose is to be answered by persecuting this people, and keeping them ignorant and degraded? Does any one believe that they will ever be removed from this country? They now amount to 362,000. In 16 years, 2,162 have been sent away, some at first voluntarily, but many of them through coercion. But can cruelty, be it ever so extreme, furnish the Society with funds and ships sufficient to transport such a multitude? They must, in spite of Connecticut and Virginia persecution, remain with us. And if they are to remain with us, what conduct towards them do policy and religion prescribe? Conduct precisely opposite to that pursued by the Society. We must instruct and elevate them, if we would not be encumbered by an ignorant and depraved population; we must treat them with justice and kindness if we would avoid the displeasure to **HIM** who has declared, "Ye shall not oppress one another."

3.6. "When Our Ancestors First Settled on this Continent, the Savages Were Around and Among Them. . . . Now Where Are They?" Professor Thomas R. Dew of William and Mary College Reflects the Tenor of His Times

A succession of shocking practices and events—including forced migration of blacks to Liberia—took place in the United States in the first half of the nineteenth century, all calling to mind the current term "ethnic cleansing."

For example, under the leadership of General Andrew Jackson, Florida Indians and their African American allies were attacked and subdued in the First Seminole War. Pacified at last, the Seminoles coexisted for a time with Florida whites, but hostilities were renewed in 1832 and continued for a decade until the Seminoles agreed at last to migrate to lands west of the Mississippi River. White citizens of Georgia (and other states) also yearned to be rid of native peoples, and so when gold was discovered in Georgia and miners arrived to reap the wealth, President Jackson granted that state the right to survey Indian lands and to impose state laws upon the Cherokees. After years of discord the latter were forced to move en masse to the west on what was known as the "Trail of Tears," a cruel fate suffered by Creeks, Choctaws, Chickasaws, and Seminoles as well.[46]

The following excerpts from a major discourse delivered in 1831 by Professor Thomas R. Dew reveal a brilliant mind, but little compassion for either blacks or native Americans. As he reminded his fellow legislators, a slave revolt in Virginia led by the slave rebel Nat Turner had spread fear and consternation throughout the South, in the case of Virginia frightening members of the legislature to the point that some were prepared to abandon slavery altogether, while others supported removal of Virginia's blacks to Liberia. Clearly, Dew's purpose was to bring "reason" to the assembly in order to convince slaveowners and politicians to return to more conventional thinking as a way to preserve their threatened labor system.

SOURCE: *The Pro-Slavery Argument; as Maintained by the Most Distinguished Writers of the Southern States, Containing the Several Essays, on the Subject, of Chancellor Harper, Governor Hammond, Dr. Simms, and Professor Dew* (New York: Negro Universities Press, 1968), pp. 287, 289–90, 355–64, 372–74, 451–54, 457.

PROFESSOR DEW ON SLAVERY.

In looking to the texture of the population of our country, there is nothing so well calculated to arrest the attention of the observer, as the existence of negro slavery throughout a large portion of the confederacy. A race of people, differing from us in color and in habits, and vastly inferior in the scale of civilization, have been increasing and spreading, "growing with our growth, and strengthening with our strength," until they have become intertwined and intertwisted with every fibre of society. Go through

46. See Lewis Filler and Allen Guttman, eds., *The Removal of the Cherokee Nation: Manifest Destiny or National Dishonor?* (Malabar, Fla.: Robert E. Krieger, 1988), and Theda Perdue and Michael D. Green, eds., *The Cherokee Removal: A Brief History with Documents* (Boston: Bedford Books of St. Martin's Press, 1995).

our Southern country, and every where you see the negro slave by the side of the white man; you find him alike in the mansion of the rich, the cabin of the poor, the workshop of the mechanic, and the field of the planter. Upon the contemplation of a population framed like this, a curious and interesting question readily suggests itself to the inquiring mind:—Can these two distinct races of people, now living together as master and servant, be ever separated? Can the black be sent back to his African home, or will the day ever arrive when he can be liberated from his thraldom, and mount upwards in the scale of civilization and rights, to an equality with the whites? . . .

In our Southern slaveholding country, the question of emancipation has never been seriously discussed in any of our legislatures, until the whole subject, under the most exciting circumstances, was, during the last winter, brought up for discussion in the Virginia Legislature, and plans of partial or total abolition were earnestly pressed upon the attention of that body. It is well known that, during the last summer, in the county of Southampton, in Virginia, a few slaves, led on by Nat Turner, rose in the night, and murdered, in the most inhuman and shocking manner, between sixty and seventy of the unsuspecting whites of that county. The news, of course, was rapidly diffused, and, with it, consternation and dismay were spread throughout the State, destroying, for a time, all feeling of security and confidence; and, even when subsequent development had proved that the conspiracy had been originated by a fanatical negro preacher, (whose confessions prove, beyond a doubt, mental aberration,) [47] and that this conspiracy embraced but few slaves, all of whom had paid the penalty of their crimes, still the excitement remained, still the repose of the commonwealth was disturbed, for the ghastly horrors of the Southampton tragedy could not immediately be banished from the mind—and *rumor,* too, with her thousand tongues, was busily engaged in spreading tales of disaffection, plots, insurrections, and even massacres, which frightened the timid, and harassed and mortified the whole of the slaveholding population. During this period of excitement, when reason was banished from the mind, and the imagination was suffered to conjure up the most appalling phantoms, . . . we are not to wonder that, even in the lower part of Virginia, many should have seriously inquired if this supposed monstrous evil could not be removed from our bosom? Some looked to the removal of the free people of

47. For Nat Turner's published "Confession," see Kenneth S. Greenberg, ed., *The Confessions of Nat Turner and Related Documents* (Boston: Bedford Books of St. Martin's Press, 1996), pp. 44–58. For a detailed account of Nat Turner's revolt, see Herbert Aptheker, *American Negro Slave Revolts* (New York: Columbia University Press, 1943), pp. 293–324. Editor.

color, by the efforts of the Colonization Society, as an antidote to all our ills. Some were disposed to strike at the root of the evil: to call on the General Government for aid, and, by the labors of *Hercules,* to extirpate the curse of slavery from the land. Others again, who could not bear that Virginia should stand towards the General Government . . . in the attitude of a suppliant, looked forward to the legislative action of the State, as capable of achieving the desired result. In this state of excitement and unalloyed apprehension, the Legislature met, and plans for abolition were proposed, and earnestly advocated in debate. . . .

In the late Virginia Legislature, where the subject of slavery underwent the most thorough discussion, all seemed to be perfectly agreed in the necessity of removal in case of emancipation. Several members from the lower counties, which are deeply interested in this question, seemed to be sanguine in their anticipations of the final success of some project of emancipation and deportation to Africa, the original home of the negro. "Let us translate them," said one of the most respected and able members of the Legislature, (Gen. Brodnax,) "to those realms from which, in evil times, under auspicious influences, their fathers were unfortunately abducted.— Mr. Speaker, the idea of restoring these people to the region in which nature had planted them, and to whose climate she had fitted their constitutions—the idea of benefiting not only our condition and their condition, by the removal, but making them the means of carrying back to a great continent, lost in the profoundest depths of savage barbarity, unconscious of the existence even of the God who created them, not only the arts and comforts and multiplied advantages of civilized life, but what is of more value than all, a knowledge of true religion—intelligence of a Redeemer—is one of the grandest and noblest, one of the most expansive and glorious ideas which ever entered into the imagination of man. The conception, whether to the philosopher, the statesman, the philanthropist, or the christian *(sic)*, of rearing up a colony which is to be the nucleus around which future emigration will concentre *(sic)*, and open all Africa to civilization, and commerce, and science, and arts, and religion—when Ethiopia shall stretch out her hands, indeed, is one which warms the heart with delight." (*Speech of Gen. Brodnax of Dinwiddie,* pp. 36 and 37.) We fear that this splendid vision, the creation of a brilliant imagination, influenced by the pure feelings of a philanthropic and generous heart, is destined to vanish at the severe touch of analysis. . . .

We take it for granted, that the right of the owner to his slave is to be respected, and, consequently, that he is not required to emancipate him, unless his full value is paid by the State. Let us, then, keeping this in view, proceed to the very simple calculation of the expense of emancipation and deportation in Virginia. The slaves, by the last census (1830,) amounted within a small fraction to 470,000; the average value of each one of these is $200; consequently the whole aggregate value of the slave population of Virginia in 1830, was $94,000,000; and allowing for the increase since, we cannot err far in putting the present value at $100,000,000. The assessed value of all the houses and lands in the State amount to $206,000,000, and these constitute the material items in the wealth of the State, the whole personal property besides bearing but a very small proportion to the value of slaves, lands, and houses. Now, do not these very simple statistics speak volumes upon this subject? It is gravely recommended to the state of Virginia to give up a species of property which constitutes nearly one-third of the wealth of the whole State, and almost one-half of that of Lower Virginia, and with the remaining two-thirds to encounter the additional enormous expense of transportation and colonization on the coast of Africa. But the loss of $100,000,000 of property is scarcely the half of what Virginia would lose, if the immutable laws of nature could suffer (as fortunately they cannot) this tremendous scheme of colonization to be carried into full effect. Is it not population which makes our lands and houses valuable? . . . It is, in truth, the slave labor in Virginia which gives value to her soil and her habitations; take away this, and you pull down the Atlas that upholds the whole system; eject from the State the whole slave population, and we risk nothing in the prediction, that on the day in which it shall be accomplished, the worn soils of Virginia will not bear the paltry price of the government lands in the West, and the Old Dominion will be a "waste howling wilderness,"—"the grass shall be seen growing in the streets, and the foxes peeping from their holes."

But the favorers of this scheme say they do not contend for the sudden emancipation and deportation of the whole black population; they would send off only the increase, and thereby keep down the population to its present amount, while the whites, increasing at their usual rate, would finally become relatively so numerous as to render the presence of the blacks among us for ever afterwards entirely harmless. This scheme, which at first, to the unreflecting, seems plausible, and much less wild than the project of sending off the whole, is nevertheless impracticable and visionary, as we think a few remarks will prove. It is computed that the annual increase of the slaves and free colored population of Virginia is about six thousand. Let us first, then, make a calculation of the expense of purchase and transportation. At $200 each, the six thousand will amount in value to $1,200,000. At $30 each, for transportation, which we shall soon see is too little, we have the whole expense of purchase and transportation $1,380,000, an expense to be annually incurred by Virginia to keep down her black population to its present amount. And let us ask, is there any one who can seriously argue that Virginia can incur such an annual expense as this for the next twenty-five or fifty years, until the whites have multiplied so greatly upon the blacks, as in the *opinion* of the *alarmists,* for ever to quiet the fears of the community? Vain and delusive hope, if any were ever wild enough to entertain it! Poor old Virginia, the leader of the *poverty stricken team,* which have been for years so heavily dragging along under the intolerable burthen of the Federal Government, must inevitably be crushed, whenever this new weight is imposed on her, in comparison with which federal exactions are light and mild. We should as soon expect the *Chamois,* the hardy rover over Alpine regions, by his unassisted strength to hurl down the snowy mantle which for ages has clothed the lofty summit of Mount Blanc, as that Virginia will be ever able, by her own resources, to purchase and colonize on the coast of Africa six thousand slaves for any number of years in succession.

But this does not develop to its full extent, the monstrous absurdity of this scheme. There is a view of it yet to be taken, which seems not to have struck very forcibly any of the speakers in the Virginia Legislature, but which appears to us, of itself perfectly conclusive against this whole project. We have made some efforts to obtain something like an accurate account of the number of negroes every year carried out of Virginia to the South and Southwest. We have not been enabled to succeed completely; but from all the information we can obtain, we have no hesitation in saying, that up-wards of six thousand are yearly exported to other states. Virginia is in fact a *negro* raising State for other States; she produces enough for her own sup-ply, and six thousand for sale. Now, suppose the government of Virginia enters the slave market resolved to purchase six thousand for emancipation and deportation, is it not evident that it must overbid the Southern seeker, and thus take the very slaves who would have gone to the South? The very first operation, then, of this scheme, provided slaves be treated as property, is to arrest the current which has been hitherto flowing to the South, and to accumulate the evil in the State. As sure as the moon in her transit over the meridian arrests the current which is gliding to the ocean, so sure will the action of the Virginia government, in an attempt to emancipate and send off 6,000 slaves, stop those who are annually going out of the State; and when 6,000 are sent off in any one year, (which we never expect to see,) it will be found, on investigation, that they are those who would have been sent out of the State by the operation of our slave trade, and to the utter astonishment and confusion of our abolitionists, the black population will be found advancing with its usual rapidity—the only operation of the scheme being to substitute our government, *alias, ourselves,* as purchasers, instead of the planters of the South. This is a view which every legislator in the State should take. He should beware, lest in his zeal for action, this efflux, which is now so salutary to the State, and such an abundant source of wealth, be suddenly dried up, and all the evils of slavery be increased instead of diminished. If government really could enter with capital and zeal enough into the boundless project, we might even in a few years see the laws of nature reversed, and the tide of slavery flowing from the south in Virginia, to satisfy the philanthropic demand for colonization. The only means which the government could use to prevent the above described effect, would be either arbitrarily to fix the price of slaves below their market value, which would be a clear violation of the right of property, (which we shall presently notice,) or to excite a feeling of insecurity and apprehension as to this kind of property, and thus dispose the owner to part with it at less than its true value: but surely no statesman would openly avow such an object, although it must be confessed that some of the speakers, even, who contended that slaves should ever be treated as property, avowed sentiments which were calculated to produce such a result.

It is said, however, that the southern market will at all events be closed against us, and consequently that the preceding argument falls to the ground. To this we answer, that as long as the demand to the south exists, the supply will be furnished in some way or other, if our government do not unwisely tamper with the subject. Bryan Edwards[48] has said, that "an attempt to prevent the introduction of slaves into the West Indies would be like chaining the winds, or giving laws to the ocean." We may with truth affirm, that an attempt to prevent a circulation of this kind of property through the slave-holding States of our confederacy would be equally if not more impracticable. But there is a most striking illustration of this now exhibiting before our eyes—the Southampton massacre produced great excitement and apprehension throughout the slave-holding States, and two of them, hitherto the largest purchasers of Virginia slaves, have interdicted their introduction under severe penalties. Many in our State looked forward to an immediate fall in the price of slaves from this cause; and what has been the result? Why, wonderful to relate, Virginia slaves are now higher than they have been for many years past; and this rise in price has no doubt been occasioned by the number of southern purchasers who have visited our

48. A British West Indian merchant and author of *History of the British Colonies in the West Indies.* Editor.

State, under the belief that Virginians had been frightened into a determination to get clear of their slaves at all events; "and from an artificial demand in the slave purchasing States, caused by an apprehension on the part of the farmers of those States, that the regular supply of slaves would speedily be discontinued by the operation of their non-importation regulations; [49] and we are, consequently, at this moment exporting slaves more rapidly, through the operation of the internal slave trade, than for many years past.

Let us now examine a moment into the object proposed to be accomplished by this scheme. It is contended, that free labor is infinitely superior to slave labor in every point of view, and therefore it is highly desirable to exchange the latter for the former, and that this will be gradually accomplished by emancipation and deportation; because the vacuum occasioned by the exportation of the slaves will be filled up by the influx of freemen from the north and other portions of the Union—and thus, for every slave we lose, it is contended that we shall receive in exchange a free laborer, much more productive and more moral. If we are not greatly mistaken, this, on analysis, will be found to be a complete specimen of that arithmetical *school boy* reasoning, which has ever proved so deceptive in politics, and so ruinous in its practical consequences; and first, let us see whether anything will be gained in point of productiveness, by this exchange of slave labor for free, even upon the avowed principles of the abolitionists themselves. The great objections to slave labor, seem to be—First, that it is unproductive, or at least, not as productive as free labor; and secondly, that it is calculated to repel free labor from the sphere in which it is exercised. . . . In the first place, then, we say upon their own principles, even, they cannot expect free labor to take the place of slave, for every one acknowledges it utterly impossible to send away, at once, all our slaves—there is scarcely we presume, a single abolitionist in Virginia, who has ever supposed, that we can send away more than the annual increase. Now, then, we ask, how can any one reasonably expect that the taking away of two or three negroes from a body of one hundred, (and this is a much greater proportion than the abolitionists hope to colonize,) can destroy that prejudice against laboring with the blacks, which is represented, as preventing the whites from laboring, and as sending them in multitudes to the West. If we are too proud to work in a field with fifty negro men this year, we shall

---

49. From Louisiana, many of the farmers themselves have come into our State, for the purpose of purchasing their own slaves, and thereby evading the laws. There are, in fact, so many plans which will effectually defeat all these preventive regulations, that we may consider their rigid enforcement utterly impracticable; and moreover, as the excitement produced by the late insurrection in Virginia, dies away, so will these laws be forgotten, and remain as dead letters on the statute books.

surely be no more disposed to do it next year, because one negro, the increase of fifty, has been sent to Liberia; and consequently the above reasoning, if it prove any thing, proves that we must prevent our laboring classes (the blacks) from increasing, because whites will not work with them—although the whites will be just as averse to working with them after you have checked their increase as before! . . .

Now, under these circumstances, an imposition of an additional burthen of 1,380,000 dollars for the purpose of purchase and deportation of slaves, would add so much to the taxes of the citizens—would subtract so much from the capital of the state, and increase so greatly the embarrassments of the whole population, that fewer persons would be enabled to support families, and consequently to get married.—This great tax, added to those we are already suffering under, would weigh like an incubus upon the whole state—it would operate like the blighting hand of Providence that should render our soil barren and our labor unproductive. It would diminish the value of the *fee simple* of Virginia, and not only check the natural increase of population within the commonwealth, but would make every man desirous of quitting the scenes of his home and his infancy, and fleeing from the heavy burthen which would for ever keep him and his children buried in the depths of poverty. His sale of negroes would partly enable him to emigrate; and we have little doubt, that whenever this wild scheme shall be seriously commenced, it will be found that more whites than negroes will be banished by its operation from the state. And there will be this lamentable difference between those who are left behind; a powerful stimulus will be given to the procreative energies of the blacks, while those of the whites will be paralyzed and destroyed. Every emigrant from among the whites will create a *vacuum* not to be supplied—every removal of a black will stimulate to the generation of another. The *poverty* stricken master would rejoice in the prolificness of his female slave, but pray Heaven in its kindness to strike with barrenness his own spouse, lest in the plenitude of his misfortunes, brought on by the wild and Quixotic philanthropy of his government, he might see around him a numerous offspring unprovided for and destined to galling indigence.

It is almost useless to inquire whether this deportation of slaves to Africa would, as some seem most strangely to anticipate, invite the whites of other states into the commonwealth. Who would be disposed to enter a state with worn out soil and a black population mortgaged to the payment of millions *per annum,* for the purpose of emancipation and deportation, when in the West the most luxuriant soils, unencumbered with heavy exactions, could be purchased for the paltry sum of $1.25 per acre? . . .

It is said slavery is wrong, in the *abstract* at least, and contrary to the spirit of Christianity. To this we answer as before, that any question must be determined by its circumstances, and if, as really is the case, we cannot get rid of slavery without producing a greater injury to both the masters and slaves, there is no rule of conscience or revealed law of God which *can* condemn us. The physician will not order the spreading cancer to be extirpated although it will eventually cause the death of his patient, because he would thereby hasten the fatal issue. So if slavery had commenced even contrary to the laws of God and man, and the sin of its introduction rested upon our hands, and it was even carrying forward the nation by slow degrees to final ruin—yet if it were *certain* that an attempt to remove it would only hasten and heighten the final catastrophe—that it was in fact a "vulnus immedicabile" on the body politic, which no legislation could safely remove, then, we would not only not be found to attempt the extirpation, but we would stand guilty of a high offense in the sight of both God and man, if we should rashly make the effort. But the original sin of introduction rests not on our heads, and we shall soon see that all those dreadful calamities which the false prophets of our day are pointing to, will never in all probability occur. With regard to the assertion, that slavery is against the spirit of Christianity, we are ready to admit the general assertion, but deny most positively that there is any thing in the Old or New Testament, which would go to show that slavery, when once introduced, ought at all events to be abrogated, or that the master commits any offense in holding slaves. The children of Israel themselves were slave holders, and were not condemned for it. All the patriarchs themselves were slave holders—Abraham had more than three hundred—Isaac had a "great store" of them,—and even the patient and meek Job himself had *"a very great household."* When the children of Israel conquered the land of Canaan, they made one whole tribe "hewers of wood and drawers of water," and they were at that very time under the special guidance of Jehovah; they were permitted expressly to purchase slaves of the heathens, and keep them as an inheritance for their posterity—and even the Children of Israel might be enslaved for six years. When we turn to the New Testament, we find not one single passage at all calculated to disturb the conscience of an honest slave holder. No one can read it without seeing and admiring that the meek and humble Saviour of the world in no instance meddled with the established institutions of mankind—he came to save a fallen world, and not to excite the black passions of men and array them in deadly hostility against each other. From no one did he turn away; his plan was offered alike to all—to the monarch and the subject—the rich and the poor—the master and the slave. . . . "Let every man (says Paul,) abide in the same calling wherein he is called. Art thou called *being* a servant? care not for it; but if thou mayest be made free use *it* rather." (1 *Corinthians,* vii. 20, 21.) . . . These, and many other passages in the New Testament, most convincingly prove, that slavery in the Roman world was nowhere charged as a fault or crime upon the holder, and everywhere is the most implicit obedience enjoined.[50]

We beg leave, before quitting this topic, to address a few remarks to those who have conscientious scruples about the holding of slaves, and therefore consider themselves under an obligation to break all the ties of friendship and kindred—dissolve all the associations of happier days, to flee to a land where this evil does not exist. We cannot condemn the conscientious actions of mankind, but we must be permitted to say, that if the assumption even of these pious gentlemen be correct, we do consider their conduct as very unphilosophical, and we will go further still: we look upon it as even immoral upon their own principles. Let us admit that slavery is an evil, and what then? Why, it has been entailed upon us by no fault of ours, and must we shrink from the charge which devolves upon us, and throw the slave in consequence into the hands of those who have no scruples of conscience—those who will not perhaps treat him so kindly? . . .

Let us now look a moment to the slave, and contemplate his position. Mr. Jefferson has described him as hating, rather than loving his master, and as losing, too, all that *amor patriæ* which characterizes the true patriot. We assert again, that Mr. Jefferson is not borne out by the fact. We are well convinced that there is nothing but the mere relations of husband and wife, parent and child, brother and sister, which produce a closer tie, than the relation of master and servant.[51] We have no hesitation in affirming, that throughout the whole slaveholding country, the slaves of a good master, are his warmest, most constant, and most devoted friends; they have been accustomed to look up to him as their supporter, director and defender. Every one acquainted with southern slaves, knows that the slave rejoices in the elevation and prosperity of his master; and the heart of no one is more gladdened at the successful debut of young master or miss on the great theatre of the world, than that of either the young slave who has grown up with them, and shared in all their sports, and even partaken of all their delicacies—or the aged one who has looked on and watched them from birth to manhood, with the kindest and most affectionate solicitude, and has ever met from them all the kind treatment and generous sympathies of feeling, tender hearts. . . .

50. See Ephesians, vi, 5, 9, Titus, ii. 9, 10. Philemon. Colossians, iii, 22, and iv. 1.

51. There are hundreds of slaves in the southern country who will desert parents, wives or husbands, brothers and sisters, to follow a kind master—so strong is the tie of master and slave.

3.7. "The Sun of American Freedom Will Set in an Ocean of Blood."
A Massachusetts Abolitionist Warns of the Perils Inherent in the
Annexation of Texas (1837)

The following is an account of events involving Texas and Mexico, as reported in the *Fifth Annual Report of the Massachusetts Anti-Slavery Society*,
dated January 25, 1837. The unnamed author recounts the events of the preceding decade, highlighting the turbulent creation of a self-governing
Texas and that entity's legalization of a cruel and unchangeable slavery,
then predicts a series of catastrophic events that in his opinion will become
reality unless slavery's opponents join together to block the annexation of
the new state of Texas. Divisible as the new "Republic" was into as many as
nine states, its annexation, he warned, would make the slave states invincible in Congress, open an enormous region to the internal slave trade, supply a precedent for additional conquests of Mexican territories, and
"inevitably" lead to violent destruction of the Union.

SOURCE: *Fifth Annual Report of the Board of Managers of the Massachusetts Anti-
Slavery Society, with Some Account of the Annual Meeting, January 25, 1837,* pp. 42–51.

Texas.

For the last ten years, the slaveholders of the South have been looking
to the acquisition of Texas to the Union, with a burning thirst of avarice
which nothing but human blood can allay, and a cannibal appetite for
human flesh which nothing but hecatombs of sable victims can satisfy.
Whether it should be obtained by purchase, revolution, or conquest, has
been a matter of indifference to them—to GET IT is all that they have
wanted. The value of such a prize to the South, (aside from political considerations,) may be inferred from the following brief statement. The slave
population of the country now amounts to 2,500,000, which Mr. [John
C.] CALHOUN, in his Report to the Senate, estimates to be worth "equal
at least to $950,000,000"—averaging $380 per head. This is undoubtedly a
low estimate, as their market value is at present exorbitantly high, able-
bodied men selling for $1,000 each. It is estimated that the acquisition of
Texas would raise their price fifty per cent. at least—thus it would at once
be a gain to the South of $375,000,000! The act of the government of Mex-
ico in 1829 proclaiming liberty throughout all the land, and the refusal of
that country to part with Texas, as a matter of sale, frustrated the hopes of
the slave-speculators, of a peaceful acquisition. Many of them, therefore,
boldly emigrated to Texas, carrying their slaves with them, and evading the

law of Mexico by indenting them as apprentices for the term of ninety-nine years! Their latent design was to revolutionize that country as soon as a favorable opportunity should present itself. That opportunity—favorable beyond their most sanguine expectations—was found in the unnatural conduct of the North toward the abolitionists. It was indeed a masterstroke of policy on the part of the South, to inflame the mind of the North to madness against the principles and measures of a large portion of the philanthropic citizens, and to frighten her into subjection by threats of disunion, and thus to commit her on the side of southern interests, step by step, beyond the possibility of retreat; so that she should be unable, or at least unwilling to interpose a barrier to the annexation of Texas to the American Union. Let it not be forgotten that the invasion of Texas was made by the South at a time when the fires of persecution, kindled to consume all who should dare to doubt or deny the divine right of slavery, were blazing all over the nominally free States! This invasion excited the liveliest sympathy throughout the country, and was generally applauded by the newspaper press. It was impudently compared to the revolutionary struggle of 1776, and eulogized in the U.S. Senate, by Mr. PRESTON, as "a struggle for rights and free institutions"! Volunteers from almost every section of the Union, but chiefly from the slaveholding States, poured into Texas, in order to reinstate slavery upon its soil. Of the character of the leaders in this black crusade, the Boston Atlas of April 16th, (a paper opposed to the abolitionists,) speaks in the following emphatic terms:

"Who are the LEADERS in this 'heroic struggle'? General Houston, once Governor of Tennessee, but since that, a chief of the Cherokees, a miserable vagabond and brawler, lately enacting Lynch's law at Washington, now the apostle of Texian freedom. Robert Potter, once a member of Congress, but infamous throughout the Union for his bloody brutality and universal scoundrelism—lately the tenant of the state prison; expelled with scorn and contempt from the legislature of North Carolina; now a 'great character' in Texas. Add to these all the murderers, swindlers, and horse-thieves, who have fled from the Southern States for the last ten years, and the list of Texian heroes will be complete. These people may be, in the opinion of North Americans, fit to instruct the poor benighted Mexicans in the science of liberty and good government; but the only discoveries they have yet offered to introduce among them are SLAVERY and LYNCH'S LAW—two grand republican panaceas, of which, if Mexicans cannot yet apprehend the *sublime* merits, the extreme darkness of their ignorance must be their excuse."

The following paragraph from the Mobile Advertiser contains a frank avowal of the object of the South in attempting the conquest of Texas territory:

"The South wish to have Texas admitted into the Union for two reasons: First, to equalize the South with the North, and secondly, as a convenient and safe place calculated from its peculiarly good soil and salubrious climate for a slave population.—Interest and political safety both alike prompt the action and enforce the argument. . . . *They have an awful foe in all those who demand the emancipation of their slaves, and who call upon them to give up their property now and forever.*"

The New-York Sunday News gives the following additional evidence:

"Their determination so generally expressed in favor of the incorporation of Texas into the Union is based upon the fact that the measure is necessary, *in order to strengthen the South against the machinations of the Northern abolitionists. If the Union continues, the South must be aided by the addition of four or five new States carved out of Texas,* and one new State formed by the territory of Florida. There are now twelve slaveholding States out of twenty-six in the Union; and the addition of five more will give them a majority of *six* members in the Senate of the United States, and enable them to hold in check the radicalism of Northern representation in the House of Representatives."

The manner in which the faith of our treaties with Mexico has been kept may be seen in the following paragraph from the Vicksburg (Miss.) Register:

"THREE THOUSAND MEN FOR TEXAS.—Gen. Dunlap, of Tennessee, is about to proceed to Mexico with the above number of men. The whole corps are now at Memphis. They will not, it is said, pass this way. Every man is completely armed, the corps having been originally raised for the Florida war [the second Seminole War]. This force, we have no doubt, will be able to carry everything before it."

And the following from the Louisville (Ky.) Journal:

"A field battery of six guns—four six pounders and two twenty-four pound howitzers—with all the implements for service, and one thousand balls, shells, and canisters, presented to the Republic of Texas by Maj. Gen. T. J. Chambers, arrived in this city under the charge of Major McLeod, on the 27th inst. They are splendid pieces of artillery. They will be in Texas in three or four weeks, and the way their wide mouths will talk to the Mexicans will be a caution for all the foes of liberty." (!!)

The Pensacola Gazette states that "General Gaines[52] sent an officer of the United States army into Texas to reclaim some deserters. He found

---

52. Edmund Pendleton Gaines, a professional soldier who in that same year (1837) participated in the Second Seminole War in Florida, where he was severely wounded. Editor.

them already enlisted in the Texian service, to the number of two hundred. *They still wore the uniform of our army,* but refused to return." Gen. Gaines himself crossed the boundary line with his army, and marched seventy miles into Mexican territory, to the military post of Nacogdoches—ostensibly, it is true, to prevent or punish Indian depredations, but evidently in order to countenance the Texian rebels.

This is our *neutrality,* as a nation, in the face of the following solemn contract with the Mexican republic:

"There shall be a firm, inviolable, and universal peace, and a true and sincere friendship between the United States of America, and the United Mexican States, in all the extent of their possessions and territories, between their people and citizens respectively, without distinctions of persons or places."

The forbearance of the Mexican government, in view of this atrocious violation of the faith of treaties, is remarkable. Let us reverse the case. Let us suppose that some Mexican adventurers had settled in some part of Louisiana; that to them had been granted by our government unusual privileges and exemptions;[53] that on some false and frivolous pretences, they had raised the standard of rebellion, and called upon their Mexican brethren to come over to their aid; that they had sent some of their number to Mexico to enlist troops and obtain supplies; that the presses of that country had generally justified their rebellion; that Mexican soldiers, even without changing their uniform, had flocked to their standard from all quarters of the country; that Mexican Senators and Representatives, in Congress assembled, had precipitately urged upon that body a recognition of the independence of the State of Louisiana; that the Mexican government had winked at all these movements, or, after a long delay, had at last issued an equivocal message, recommending the observance of strict neutrality between the contending parties; and, finally, that the independence of the rebels and invaders had been acknowledged by the Mexican Congress;—would not this country have been roused to madness, and have declared war with Mexico, as a nation basely recreant to her faith?—ay, even before one-half of these events had transpired? And yet the Mexican insurrectionists might have pleaded that their object was to secure universal

---

53. The reception of the Texas settlers by the Mexican government has been hospitable and liberal beyond example. Land had been given to them, they have been exempted from taxes and duties during ten years, on the one hand, and protected by a high tariff against foreign competition in the markets for their produce, on the other hand; they have the unprecedented indulgence of legal proceedings in their *own language,* a matter into which national punctilio might be expected to enter; and they have enjoyed as perfect civil and religious liberty, as it seems possible for human beings to secure." *Quarterly Anti-Slavery Magazine.*

emancipation in Louisiana, without regard to complexional caste; but the Texians avow that they are stimulated by a determination to re-establish slavery and the slave-trade upon the soil which has been purged from these abominations. They abhor the idea of emancipation, and are eager to administer Lynch law to every abolitionist.[54] By the Constitution which they have adopted, none but 'free WHITE PERSONS' can become citizens of this Republic. The 9th Section is in the following words:

"SEC. 9. All persons of color, who were slaves for life previous to their emigration to Texas, and all who *are now held in bondage,* shall remain in the like state of servitude, provided the said slaves shall be the bona fide property of the person so holding said slave as aforesaid. *Congress shall pass no laws to prohibit emigrants from the United States of America from bringing their slaves into the Republic with them,* and holding them by the same tenure by which slaves were held in the United States; *nor shall Congress have the power to emancipate slaves; nor shall any slaveholder be allowed to emancipate his or her slave or slaves, without the consent of Congress,* unless he or she shall send his or her slave or slaves without the limits of the Republic. No *free* person of African descent, either in whole or in part, shall be *permitted to reside permanently in the Republic,* without the consent of Congress; and the importation or admission of Africans or negroes into this Republic, EXCEPTING FROM THE UNITED STATES OF AMERICA, is forever prohibited, and declared to be piracy.

It seems, then, that in this *free, republican* territory, slavery is not only made constitutional, but Congress has no power to prohibit the foreign slave-trade between Texas and the United States[55]—nor to emancipate slaves on the soil; nor are slaveholders themselves allowed to abandon their oppression, except by expelling their victims beyond the limits of the Republic! It is in vain that we search the annals of slavery, to find a parallel to a section like this! The clause which prohibits the importation of slaves from Africa, and other places, can be easily evaded, as the following article from the Boston Atlas of April 19th [1936] demonstrates:

"Slaves are constantly arriving at the Havana; and we state upon the best authority, that "a gentleman of Texas," the brother of one high in office under the Federal government, is, or not long ago was, in the United States,

54. Benjamin Lundy, a veteran advocate of emancipation, states that he was near being robbed *twice* in his late tour in Texas that the "tar and feathers" were prepared, and would have been applied, had not a *Mexican* officer been near, and informed him of the proceeding.

55. "The land of the free and the asylum of the oppressed," allowed, by way of a special favor, to be the GUINEA of Texian marauders and rapacious man-stealers! This is done to secure the cooperation of the South.

for the purpose of procuring *American* vessels to proceed to Havana, and there to take in cargoes of slaves for the Texian market. When it was suggested to this gentleman that this would be engaging in the slave-trade, and that by our laws the slave-trade was piracy, the Texian stopped the objector's mouth by referring to a late decision by a learned judge of the Supreme Court of the United States, that to take slaves as *passengers* from one point of the African coast to another is *not* engaging in the slave-trade; and he argued—and the argument seems difficult to refute—that to take slaves as *passengers,* (and this was all he wanted of the ship-owners,) from Havana to Texas, would fall under the same rule. The same gentleman assured our informant that the two or three thousand AFRICAN SLAVES now in Texas seemed to be very happy and contented—they only complained a little at being separated from their wives and children!" . . .

One other step remains to be taken by this country, to reach the climax of her iniquity: it is to annex the REPUBLIC (?) of Texas to the American Union! To what scenes of misery and horror may not this recognition and annexation give rise! In the opinion of JOHN QUINCY ADAMS, it is more than probable that we shall be involved in "a Mexican war; a war with Great Britain, if not with France; a general Indian war; a servile war; and, as an inevitable consequence of them all, a civil war."

But, be the consequences to this country what they may, the admission of Texas into the Union, at the next session of Congress, is regarded by the southern States as a certain event! They have not invaded that country, and made havoc of human life, and poured out their blood and treasure, merely to have the satisfaction of witnessing its independence. They claim it as their own, and they mean to possess it. They have many powerful motives in seeking its acquisition:—it can be divided into NINE STATES, each as large as Kentucky:—It will give the South omnipotent political power over the North, in Congress:—It will open a new world for the prosecution of the domestic slave trade:—It will furnish a precedent for *making new conquests of Mexican territory.* For if Texas may be forcibly separated from Mexico, and annexed to the American Union, why not Coahuila, Tamaulipas, and Santa Fe? And most assuredly they will be, unless the people of the Northern States lift up their voices UNITEDLY and INSTANTLY, in inflexible opposition to the admission of Texas! If they yield in this instance, THEY ARE LOST—the Union will inevitably be dashed in pieces—and the sun of American freedom will set in an ocean of blood. It is impossible that LIBERTY and SLAVERY can reign together—one or the other must perish; they are mortal enemies, who are now engaged in a death-struggle for victory. Wo[e] to the non-slaveholding States, if they consent to remain under the dominion of SLAVERY! if they conspire to take the life of LIBERTY! Let the prospect of the annexation of Texas agitate, alarm, inflame, UNITE, their entire population; let the measure be resisted with invincible energy; let their Senators and Representatives in Congress witness such an expression of public sentiment, that not one of them shall dare "to go with the South"; let the pulpit and the press be faithful to their high trust; let public meetings be held in every city, town and village; and let all political and sectarian feuds be banished, that there may be a perfect union of feeling and action on this momentous question. Why should there not be this union? The question is not whether abolitionists are right or wrong; nor whether slavery should be immediately or gradually abolished; nor whether Congress has, or has not, the power to emancipate the slaves in the District of Columbia; but it is, whether such a weight of political power shall be thrown into the scale of southern slavery, as to make northern liberty kick the beam: whether a foreign territory shall be added to our republic, for the express purpose of extending the empire of slavery, and invigorating both the foreign and domestic slave-trade; whether a FREE LABOR or SLAVE-DRIVING policy shall govern the nation; whether, in fine, we shall run the hazard of the bloody wars enumerated by Mr. ADAMS, or, for self-preservation, unyielding refuse our assent to the admission of Texas into the Union. All other questions, at the present crisis, sink into insignificance in comparison. No labor, no expense, can be too great in bringing Congress to a decision.

3.8. "This Doleful Removal." In an Open Letter to Martin Van Buren, the Essayist and Poet Ralph Waldo Emerson Urges the President-Elect to Reject Forced Dislodgment of the Cherokee Indians from Their Native Georgia into Lands Beyond the Mississippi

As observed in the introduction to Document 3.6, native peoples of the United States—Creeks, Choctaws, Cherokees, Chickasaws, Seminoles, and others—endured much suffering at the hands of whites. Not only were thousands enslaved. Equally shocking, as whites migrated southward early in the nineteenth century, the Cherokees, many of whom had adopted European customs, were increasingly threatened with compulsory removal to remote western lands, a course of action upheld by leaders such as Andrew Jackson. In 1838, as Jackson was about to cede his presidency to Martin Van Buren, elements of the press revealed to the public that a bogus treaty had been signed in 1835 with the Cherokee nation to trade their Georgia lands for faraway locations in the west. Encouraged by his wife, Lidian, and other residents of Concord, Massachusetts, Emerson wrote to Van Buren to avert the impending tragedy, arguing that the alleged treaty was a fraud, and that "out of eighteen thousand souls composing the Cherokee nation, fifteen thousand six hundred and sixty-eight" had strongly rejected it. Van Buren, however, seems to have ignored Emerson's letter, and later that same year, with General Winfield Scott in command, the Cherokees were forced to assemble and to trek hundreds of miles westward to lands beyond the Mississippi.

SOURCE: James Elliot Cabot, *A Memoir of Ralph Waldo Emerson* (Cambridge: The Riverside Press, 1887), vol. 2, pp. 697–702.

Concord, Mass., *April* 23, 1838

Sir,—The seat you fill places you in a relation of credit and nearness to every citizen. By right and natural position, every citizen is your friend. Before any acts contrary to his own judgment or interest have repelled the affections of any man, each may look with trust and loving anticipation to your government. Each has the highest right to call your attention to such subjects as are of a public nature and properly belong to the chief magistrate; and the good magistrate will feel a joy in meeting such confidence. In this belief and at the instance of a few of my friends and neighbors, I crave of your patience a short hearing for their sentiments and my own: and the circumstances that my name will be utterly unknown to you will only give the fairer chance to your equitable construction of what I have to say.

Sir, my communication respects the sinister rumors that fill this part of the country concerning the Cherokee people. The interest always felt in the aboriginal population—an interest naturally growing as that decays—has been heightened in regard to this tribe. Even in our distant State some good rumor of their worth and civility has arrived. We have learned with joy their improvement in the social arts. We have read their newspapers. We have seen some of them in our schools and colleges. In common with the great body of the American people, we have witnessed with sympathy the painful labors of these red men to redeem their own race from the doom of eternal inferiority, and to borrow and domesticate in the tribe the arts and customs of the Caucasian race. And notwithstanding the unaccountable apathy with which of late years the Indians have been sometimes abandoned to their enemies, it is not to be doubted that it is the good pleasure and the understanding of all humane persons in the republic, of the men and the matrons sitting in the thriving independent families all over the land, that they shall be duly cared for, that they shall taste justice and love from all to whom we have delegated the office of dealing with them.

The newspapers now inform us that in December, 1835, a treaty, contracting for the exchange of all the Cherokee territory was pretended to be made by an agent on the part of the United States with some persons appearing on the part of the Cherokees; that the fact afterwards transpired that these deputies did by no means represent the will of the nation; and that, out of eighteen thousand souls composing the nation, fifteen thousand six hundred and sixty-eight have protested against the so-called treaty. It now appears that the government of the United States choose to hold the Cherokees to this sham treaty, and are proceeding to execute the same. Almost the entire Cherokee nation stand up and say, "This is not our act. Behold us. Here are we. Do not mistake that handful of deserters for us"; and the American President [Andrew Jackson] and the Cabinet, the Senate and the House of Representatives, neither hear these men nor see them, and are contracting to put this active nation into carts and boats, and to drag them over mountains and rivers to a wilderness at a vast distance beyond the Mississippi. And a paper purporting to be an army-order fixes a month from this day as the hour for this doleful removal.

In the name of God, sir, we ask you if this be so. Do the newspapers rightly inform us? Men and women with pale and perplexed faces meet one another in the streets and churches here, and ask if this be so? We have inquired if this be a gross misrepresentation from the party opposed to the government and anxious to blacken it with the people. We have looked in the newspapers of different parties, and find a horrid confirmation of the tale. We are slow to believe it. We hoped the Indians were misinformed, and that their remonstrance was premature, and would turn out to be a needless act of terror.

The piety, the principle that is left in these United States,—if only in its coarsest form, a regard to the speech of men,—forbid us to entertain it as a fact. Such a dereliction of all faith and virtue, such a denial of justice, and such deafness to screams for mercy were never heard of in times of peace and in the dealing of a nation with its own allies and wards, since the earth was made. Sir, does this government think that the people of the United States are become savage and mad? From their minds are the sentiments of love and a good nature wiped clean out? The soul of man, the justice, the mercy that is the heart's heart in all men, from Maine to Georgia, does abhor this business.

In speaking thus the sentiments of my neighbors and my own, perhaps I overstep the bounds of decorum. But would it not be a higher indecorum coldly to argue a matter like this? We only state the fact that a crime is projected that confounds our understandings by its magnitude,—a crime that really deprives us as well as the Cherokees of a country; for how could we call the conspiracy that should crush these poor Indians our government, or the land that was cursed by their parting and dying imprecations our country, any more? You, sir, will bring down that renowned chair in which you sit into infamy if your seal is set to this instrument of perfidy; and the name of this nation, hitherto the sweet omen of religion and liberty, will stink to the world.

You will not do us the injustice of connecting this remonstrance with any sectional and party feeling. It is in our hearts the simplest commandment of brotherly love. We will not have this great and solemn claim upon national and human justice huddled aside under the flimsy plea of its being a party-act. Sir, to us the questions upon which the government and the people have been agitated during the past year, touching the prostration of the currency and of trade, seem but motes in comparison. The hard times, it is true, have brought the discussion home to every farm-house and poor man's house in this town; but it is the chirping of grasshoppers beside the immortal question whether justice shall be done by the race of civilized to the race of savage man;—whether all the attributes of reason, of civility, of justice, and even of mercy, shall be put off by the American people, and so vast an outrage upon the Cherokee nation and upon human nature shall be consummated.

One circumstance lessens the reluctance with which I intrude at this time on your attention: my conviction that the Government ought to be admonished of a new historical fact, which the discussion of this question has disclosed, namely, that there exists in a great part of the Northern people a gloomy diffidence in the *moral* character of the government.

On the broaching of this question, a general expression of despondency, of disbelief that any good will accrue from a remonstrance on an act of fraud and robbery, appeared in those men to whom we naturally turn for aid and counsel. Will the American government steal? Will it lie? Will it kill?—we ask triumphantly. Our counselors and old statesmen here say that ten years ago they would have staked their life on the affirmation that the proposed Indians measures could not be executed; that the unanimous country would put them down. And now the steps of this crime follow each other so fast, at such fatally quick time, that the millions of virtuous citizens, whose agents the government are, have no place to interpose, and must shut their eyes until the last howl and wailing of these tormented villages and tribes shall afflict the ear of the world.

I will not hide from you, as an indication of the alarming distrust, that a letter addressed as mine is, and suggesting to the mind of the executive the plain obligations of man, has a burlesque character in the apprehensions of some of my friends. I, sir, will not beforehand treat you with the contumely of this distrust. I will at least state to you this fact, and show you how plain and humane people, whose love would be honor, regard the policy of the government, and what injurious inferences they draw as to the minds of the governors. A man with your experience in affairs must have seen cause to appreciate the futility of opposition to the moral sentiment. However feeble the sufferer and however great the oppressor, it is in the nature of things that the blow should recoil upon the aggressor. For God is in the sentiment, and it cannot be withstood. The potentate and the people perish before it; but with it, and as its executor, they are omnipotent.

I write thus, sir, to inform you of the state of mind these Indian tidings have awakened here, and to pray with one voice more that you, whose hands are strong with the delegated power of fifteen millions of men, will avert with that might the terrific injury which threatens the Cherokee tribe.

With great respect, sir, I am, your fellow citizen.

RALDO WALDO EMERSON.

3.9. "God Only Knows What Doctrines We Shall Next Be Called to Listen To." A Congressman Calls for an End to the War Against Mexico

The following abridged address was delivered in Congress by Josuah R. Giddings, a representative of Ashtabula County, Ohio, at the height of the war with Mexico. The issue under debate was the Wilmot Proviso, an amendment which David Wilmot of Pennsylvania had attached to a House bill in 1846 to forbid establishment of slavery in territories acquired as a result of the war with Mexico. The Senate rejected the Proviso, but in February 1847 it was added to a bill to grant President James K. Polk three million dollars to bring an end to the war. Giddings strongly favored the Proviso, but in his speech preferred to emphasize such issues as the heavy casualties among combatants on both sides, and the far greater losses suffered by Mexican civilians, all of which were the result, in his opinion, of the South's iniquitous intention of spreading slavery into a country where it had long been illegal. As much as any other document in this book, this selection reveals the high degree of animosity in North-South relations, greatly magnified in those years by the expansion of slavery into Texas and the invasion of Mexico, undertakings which many southerners hoped would carry slavery to the shores of the Pacific Ocean.

In the Hands of Strangers

During his long career in Congress Giddings often spoke out against the internal slave trade and slavery in the District of Columbia. He opposed the Seminole War in Florida (1837–43), and the Fugitive Slave Act of 1850, and with John Quincy Adams, tenaciously upheld the right of citizens to petition Congress for redress of grievances, a privilege denied by the so-called gag-rule of 1836, which brought automatic tabling of antislavery petitions sent to Congress. In 1844 the gag-rule was at last repealed as unconstitutional.

SOURCE: Josuah R. Giddings, *Speeches in Congress* (Boston: John P. Jewett, 1853), pp. 202–14.

THE WILMOT PROVISO

MR. SPEAKER,—The proposition now before us is one of that plain and distinct character, which enables every member to comprehend it at the first view. We are engaged in a war with Mexico. It is most obviously a war of conquest, intended by the Executive to obtain further territory, over which to extend the curse of slavery; and the proposition before us is to make such territory *free*, by attaching to it what is called the "Wilmot Proviso."

Every person who has heard, or read the debates of this body, during its present session, must be convinced that questions of no ordinary magnitude are pending before us. The fierce conflict of opinion, the criminations and recriminations, the stern defiance, the solemn appeals, the impassioned eloquence, show conclusively that we are approaching a crisis of deep and pervading interest. Indeed, we must soon decide, so far as this present House of Representatives can determine, whether or not the blood and treasure of this nation shall be poured out on Mexican soil, for the purpose of establishing slavery upon territory hitherto consecrated to freedom. The advocates of oppression from the North, and from the South, will arrange themselves in the affirmative, and the friends of freedom will be found in the negative. A few yet remain apparently undecided. The seductions of Executive favor are held to entice them to enlist under the black flag of slavery; while the still, small voice of reason and of conscience is beckoning them to the ranks of freedom.

Gentlemen from the South, with deep emotions, have solemnly warned us, that if we persist in our determination, the *"Union will be dissolved."* I do not doubt their sincerity. But I would rather see this Union rent into a thousand fragments than have my country disgraced, and its moral purity sacrificed, by the prosecution of a war for the extension of human bondage. Nor would I avoid this issue, were it in my power. For many years I have seen the rights of the North, and the vital principles of our Constitution, surrendered to the haughty vaporings of southern members. For many years have I exerted my humble influence to stimulate northern members to the maintenance of our honor and of the Constitution. And now I devoutly thank that God, who has permitted me to witness the union of a portion of northern members of both political parties, upon a question so vital to our interests and honor, as well as to humanity.

I also rejoice that this is a question which admits of no compromise. Slavery and freedom are antagonisms. They must necessarily be at war with each other. There can be no compromise between right and wrong, or between virtue and crime. The conflicting interests of slave and free labor have agitated this government from its foundation, and will continue to agitate it, until truth and justice shall triumph over error and oppression. Should the proposition now before us [the Wilmot Proviso] fail, it will surely succeed at the next session of Congress; for it is very evident that public sentiment in the free States is daily becoming more and more in favor of it.[56] The legislatures in six of those States have instructed their Senators and requested their Representatives to vote for this measure. Few gentlemen on this floor will disregard those resolutions when we come to the vote. Whigs and democrats will then be found acting together. Our party attachments will be disregarded, and the interests of the nation will receive our attention. . . .

The objects and ulterior designs of this war have lately been so fully avowed; and are now so generally understood, that it would be a work of supererogation to repeat them. All, I believe, are aware, and admit, that the extension of slavery over territory now free, and under the jurisdiction of Mexican laws, constitutes the object for which such a vast expenditure of blood and treasure is to be made; and I repeat that each member who is in favor of that object will, of course, vote against the amendment which will prohibit slavery within such territory as we may acquire, if any; and those in favor of the "self-evident truths" put forth by our fathers in 1776, will vote for the amendment offered. The war in which we are engaged has precipitated this issue upon us; and I rejoice that it is thus presented for our decision. . . . The acquisition of slave territory, is substantially the same question which was propounded to us when we were called to annex Texas to these States. The subject is more generally understood, and better appreciated at this time than it was then.

You, Mr. Chairman, well recollect that the evening on which the reso-

56. The Proviso never became law. Editor.

lutions for annexing Texas passed this body, "the loud-mouthed cannon," from the terrace in front of the Capitol announced to the friends of that measure its final success. I was pensively wending my way to my lodgings, when my ears were saluted by the roar of those guns, which I then regarded as "minute guns," announcing the final overthrow of the Union which had been formed by our patriot fathers. I clearly saw, or thought I saw, my country involved in a system of territorial aggrandizement; involved in aggressive war; expending the blood and treasure of the nation, for the extension of an institution odious to man, and forbidden by the laws of God. As I then looked forward to the circumstances which now surround us, I was generally depressed with their contemplation.

Sir, long before this war commenced, I declared, in this hall, that "I would rather see a war with Great Britain, with all its horrors, and its devastation of public morals, than to see the people of the free States quietly submit to the annexation of Texas." I then deeply felt what I said. I felt that our Constitution had ceased to limit the powers of either Congress or the Executive; I saw the union of 1787 broken up and abandoned, for the purpose of bringing into our political association a foreign slave-holding government; I saw that foreigners, as destitute of constitutional qualifications as any other foreigners, were to be placed in this hall, to strike down the interests and to control the rights of my constituents, and of the free States; I saw this war in prospect, with its crimes and guilt; I saw the national debt that has been, and is to be, incurred, the disgrace that is to rest upon our nation, the strife and contention in which we are now engaged among ourselves; and I clearly saw that this career of conquest, if persisted in, must prove the grave of our republic. And I repeat, that unless the friends of the Constitution and of humanity can not stop this policy of acquiring territory, the end of this government draws near.

During our present session, I have received petitions from various States of this Union, numerously signed, praying that our political association with Texas may be dissolved. The petitioners base their requests upon the fact, that the people of the free States have never authorized Congress to place their rights or interests at the disposal of foreigners. They feel that they have been transferred, like southern slaves, to an association with Texians; not by the votes of their own Representatives, but by the votes of members from the slave States, who felt that it would be for the benefit of slavery that the freemen of the North should be controlled by southern votes. Believe you that this feeling is to die away while this war, designed still further to degrade the North, shall be continued? Will our people become satisfied while northern freemen are called upon to go to Mexico, and sacrifice their lives that the slave power may be increased, and the North still further disgraced? I assure you, Sir, that our people are becoming aroused to the dangers which threaten them; and although men of high character and of commanding talents may deem it bad policy to speak forth unwelcome truths, yet, Sir, there are instrumentalities at work which will inform the public mind of the true political condition of the free States; and when the people of those States shall understand fully the manner in which their interests have been silently surrendered, and their constitutional rights subverted, they will take care to place more faithful sentinels upon the watchtowers of liberty.

But, Sir, we have been told here, that "the whig party are in favor of prosecuting this war." Sir, I know not on what authority gentlemen make this assertion. I deny that Representatives from Pennsylvania are authorized to express on this floor the wishes of the whig party of Ohio; or that gentlemen from Philadelphia have authority to declare the views of my constituents. The congressional district which I have the honor to represent, gives the largest whig majority of any in the United States. And I have longer represented my constituents consecutively than any other whig member of this body, except my venerable friend from Massachusetts [John Quincy Adams]. I shall, therefore, speak for them as I was commissioned to do. Nor shall I silently allow any other gentleman to represent them as so ignorant of their moral and political duties, or so lost to a just sense of their obligations to mankind, and to God, as to be willing to lend any assistance in that work of human butchery now going on in Mexico.

Why, Sir, when the brigade in which the commercial city of Cleveland is situated, was called on for volunteers to aid this war, only about thirty human beings could be found sunk so low in the depths of moral depravity as to be willing to join in cutting the throats of their fellow men in Mexico. Another brigade in my district, after searching all the haunts of vice and dissipation, was able to furnish only *three* volunteers for this war. It should be borne in mind that not one of the whole number was a whig. When the other brigade was called on, they replied with one voice—"We will fight for liberty, but not for slavery;" and to their honor be it said, not a man of either political party would lend his influence to the prosecution of this nefarious war. Sir, let gentlemen speak for themselves, or for their own districts; but let no man presume to slander my people by representing them as favorable to the prosecution of our conquests in Mexico. . . .

But, while the North possess the power to exclude farther slave territory, our danger consists in our own party divisions, and in the far-reaching policy of southern statesmen. But two days since, a distinguished senator in the other end of the capitol (Mr. Calhoun) brought forward a proposition the most dangerous to northern rights that could be devised under existing circumstances. Forseeing, as all reflecting men do, that the army must be withdrawn, if the opponents of the war remain firm to their purpose, he proposes to compromise the matter, by bringing back the troops to the Rio Grande; to occupy that river from the mouth to the "Passo del Norte," [El Paso] and from thence, to erect a line of fortifications due west to the Gulf of California; holding possession of the whole Mexican territory on this side of the line thus indicated, until peace shall be restored.

It should be borne in mind, that the Mexican government and the officers of their army are pledged against all attempts at negotiating a peace with us, while our army occupies any portion of their territory. If, therefore, this plan be adopted, we shall be at the expense of holding military occupation of the country for an indefinite period. The Mexicans will not submit to a despotism wielded by our military officers, and, therefore, will leave the country; and slave-holders, with their human chattels, will occupy their places. Our army will act as a guard to keep the slaves in subjection, while their professed object will be to defend the country against Mexicans. In this way, a sparse slave-holding population will be scattered over it, and, perhaps at some future time, Mexico, exhausted and disheartened, may consent to cede it to us. If so, there being so many slaves already there, will be urged upon us as a conclusive reason why slavery shall continue throughout that vast extent of country. If, on the other hand, a peace shall be concluded, without obtaining a title to the country, then a revolution, after the example of Texas, will take place, and annexation to this Union, with a vast increase of the slave power in the councils of the nation, will be the result; for it should be borne in mind, that the territory thus proposed to be occupied by us, is of sufficient extent to be divided into fourteen such states as Ohio.

Some northern men appear to regard this proposal with a degree of favor which alarms me. In truth, Mr. Chairman, we have been so long accustomed to surrender our rights to the demands of the South, that some of our friends appear to think it improper for us to take a firm position in support of the honor and the interests of our free States. They seem willing to surrender a portion of our rights to appease slave-holding rapacity. Sir, this policy has already brought us to the verge of political ruin; continue it a little longer, and the people of the free States will themselves be slaves. Let the proposition alluded to be adopted, and the power of the free States will dwindle to insignificance in the other branch of the Legislature. We shall then be regarded as useful to the Union, only as instruments to support slavery. Northern rights and northern honor will be looked upon as among the things that *were;* they will be unknown to the future. I would not solemnly caution every man against consenting to this proposed policy. Its effect will be to extend the boundaries of Texas to the Rio Grande.[57] That was stated by the distinguished Senator to whom I have alluded, to be one of the great objects of the war. That plan, once adopted, must prove fatal to the free States. I repeat, let us stand immovably upon the maxim of having "no more slave territory," *"no more slave States."* Let this be our watchword here and in our State Legislatures, and among the entire people of the free States, including all political parties, and, I assure you, we shall have peace at no distant day.

Again, some northern men who are opposed to extending slavery, appear willing to obtain further territory, under the impression that it will remain free. I greatly fear, Sir, if we add to the extent of our south-western border, it will prove an extension of slavery. I am, therefore, opposed to obtaining any more territory in that direction. I would confine Texas to the precise limits occupied by her at the time of the annexation. Beyond that, I would not extend the power of the slave-holder to recapture his slave. I would leave the whole country beyond the valley of the Nueces *free.* Let it be a place of refuge, unpolluted by the footsteps of the slave-catcher, where the panting fugitive may rest in safety; where no Texian master shall have power to seize or re-enslave him, as he may now do in our free States.

I desire to call attention to the immense sacrifice of human life now making to carry on this war. The official documents before us show that *twenty-three thousand nine hundred and ninety-eight officers and men* entered the service during the first eight months of this war; that fifteen thousand four hundred and eighty-six remained in service at the close of that time; that three hundred and thirty-one had deserted; and that two thousand two hundred and two had been discharged; leaving five thousand nine hundred and nineteen unaccounted for. Thus, in little more than eight months, this war has cost the lives of nearly six thousand American troops, or about one third of the whole number sent to Mexico. A distinguished senator (Mr. Calhoun) estimates our loss at one third of those who go to

---

57. The border between Texas and the Mexican province of Tamaulipas had long been the Nueces River, not the Rio Grande. Regarding President Polk's involvement in the seizure of this territory between the Nueces and the Rio Grande, Senator Henry Wilson wrote: "Not content with occupying ground on and westward of the Nueces, [Polk] issued, on the 13th of January, 1846, the fatal order to General [Zachary] Taylor to advance and 'occupy positions on or near the left bank of the Rio del Norte.' That movement of the army from Corpus Christi to the Rio Grande, a distance of more than one hundred miles, was an invasion of Mexican territory,—an act of war for which the President was and must ever be held responsible by the general judgement of mankind." Wilson, *Rise and Fall,* vol. 2, p. 9. Editor.

In the Hands of Strangers

that country. I presume the Mexican loss to be about one third as great as ours,[58] and the whole number of human beings sacrificed in this attempt to extend slavery, is now about one thousand per month. Sir, what should be the reflections of those gentlemen who have contributed their votes and their influence to send their neighbors and friends in such numbers to Mexican graves? I regard every regiment that marches for that country as a funeral procession, one third of whom are going to their resting-place in that vast charnel-house beyond the Rio Grande, and another third to return with shattered constitutions, doomed to early graves. How long will the free States continue to furnish victims for this sacrifice?

But I return to the question more particularly under consideration. It has been seriously argued that we have no power to prohibit slavery from such territory as we may acquire. . . . On the contrary, I should be obliged to any man who will point me to the power which Congress possesses under the Constitution, to repeal the law of nature and of nature's God,— to take from man his right of self-defence, and make him the property of his fellow man.

If we possess the power to degrade one half or two thirds of the people, and convert them into *property,* and vest the title to them in the other portion of [our] community, we may surely vest in one man, or in a larger number of men, the title to all the others. Sir, is such doctrine to be listened to in an American Congress? We hold "that all men are created free and equal, and are endowed by their Creator with certain inalienable rights, among which are life, liberty, and the pursuit of happiness; that to secure these rights, governments are instituted among men." But it is now said that we have no constitutional power to form a government for such purposes in any territory which we possess, or which we may hereafter acquire. I think such doctrine will be heard with astonishment by the people of this government, as well as by those of other nations. Our revolution was based on those "self-evident truths" to which I have alluded, and our government was founded on them. But we are now told that we have no right to legislate for freedom; that our legislative functions can only be exerted in extending and increasing the curse of human bondage. God only knows what doctrines we shall next be called to listen to.

Gentlemen from the South have constantly referred to what they term "the guaranties of slavery in the Federal Constitution." I am myself unable to comprehend their meaning, by the use of that language. I have made the

---

58. This view was nearly correct as to the *army;* but the loss of Mexican lives, including peasants, women, and children murdered, and who died of pestilence, was far greater than that of the Americans. Editor.

inquiry on this floor for the article or section in which such guaranty may be found; but, to this day, I have found no lawyer, statesman, or jurist, who could point me to it. . . . During the debate, we have heard it asserted repeatedly, that the slave is the *property* of his master. On what right does the master claim title to his slave as property? It is the same title by which the pirate claims title to the goods of his victim. It is the same by which the highwayman claims title to your purse. It is founded in violence, and maintained by crime. Whenever the slave becomes possessed of physical force sufficient, he may relieve himself from bondage by any means in his power, provided he does not injure innocent persons. He may, without incurring any moral guilt, use such violence as he may deem necessary to effect his release from bondage, even to the taking of his master's life. He is called *property* by southern gentlemen. But suppose the slaves of the South were to rise and overpower their masters, and compel them to labor by aid of chains and scourges; they would then have precisely the same title to their present owners as *property* which their masters now have to them. This, Sir, is the only property which man can hold in man.

3.10. "God Sent Ham to Africa, Shem to Asia, Japheth to Europe." Slavery Ordained by God

In the turbulent decades before the Civil War the Bible was often used both to defend and to oppose slavery. This conflict, which was spirited and uncompromising, appears to have reached a high point in the 1840s and 1850s, when publication after publication appeared on the subject. These include, for example, James Henry Hammond's *Two Letters on Slavery in the United States, Addressed to Thomas Clarkson, Esq.* (1845), in which Hammond, a governor of South Carolina, maintains that God had "authorized his chosen people to purchase 'bondsmen forever' from the heathen," as recorded in the Book of Leviticus; Reverend George D. Armstrong's *The Christian Doctrine of Slavery* (1857), which affirmed that Christ and his Apostles had taught that slave-holding was not a sin or an offense to the Church; and in contrast, Reverend William Hosner's *Slavery and the Church* (1853), in which the author declared that slavery was "a sin under all circumstances" and was sanctioned by neither the Old or the New Testament. The Methodist Church, the Presbyterians, and other denominations separated, in fact, along sectional lines, with northerners often rejecting the belief that slavery was ordained by God, whereas southerners tended to hold the opposite opinion.

The following selection, a speech by the Reverend Frederick Ross of Alabama delivered to a New York audience in 1856, uses the story of Noah to prove that God was partial to slavery and not at all opposed to the buying and selling of human beings—a concept bitterly opposed by the abolitionist cleric, Reverend George B. Cheever, in his book, *God Against Slavery* (1857). The latter firmly declared: "The claim set up by Americans, eighteen hundred and fifty-seven years after Christ, to hold the African race as their chattel property, by reason of the curse pronounced on Canaan two thousand three hundred and forty-seven years *before* Christ, exceeds in the extravagance of its impudence and madness any Christian or pagan hallucination ever assumed by any nation under heaven. You will say it is too ridiculous to receive a sober notice; but I have had to meet it as a grave and serious claim, put forward by a professedly religious person, who deliberately urged it as a proof that slavery could not be sinful in the sight of God!"

This "professedly religious person" was either Reverend Frederick Ross, author of the following arguments, or a person much like him, since Ross, like other writers friendly to slavery, used the story of Noah and his sons (along with racist doctrine) to uphold the legitimacy of slavery.

SOURCE: Rev. Fred [*sic*] A. Ross, D.D., *Slavery Ordained by God*. (New York: J. B. Lippincott, 1859), pp. 32, 34–36, 50–58, 60–64, 66–68.

"Find Fault with God, Ye Anti-Slavery Men, If You Dare"
Speech Delivered in the General Assembly, New York, 1856.

I am not a slave-holder. Nay, I have shown some self-denial in that matter. I emancipated slaves whose money-value would now be $40,000. In the providence of God, my riches have entirely passed from me. I do not mean that, like the widow, I gave all the living I had. My estate was then greater than that slave-property. I merely wish to show I have no selfish motive in giving, as I shall, the true Southern defence of slavery. (Applause.) I speak from Huntsville, Alabama, my present home. That gem of the South, that beautiful city where the mountain softens into the vale,—where the water gushes, a great fountain, from the rock,—where around that living stream there are streets of roses, and houses of intelligence and gracefulness and gentlest hospitality,—and, withal, where so high honor is ever given to the ministers of God.

Speaking then from that region where *"Cotton is king,"* I affirm, contrary as my opinion is to that most common in the South, that the slavery agitation has accomplished and will do great good. I said so, to ministerial and political friends, twenty-five years ago. I have always favored the agitation,—just as I have always countenanced discussion upon all subjects. I felt that the slavery question needed examination. I believed it was not understood in its relations to the Bible and human liberty. Sir, the light is spreading North and South. 'Tis said, I know, this agitation has increased the severity of slavery. True, but for a moment only, in the days of the years of the life of this noble problem. . . . The political controversy, however fierce and threatening, is only for power. But the moral agitation is for the harmony of the Northern and Southern mind, in the right interpretations of Scripture on this great subject, and, of course, for the ultimate union of the hearts of all sensible people, to fulfill God's intention,—to bless the white man and the black man in America. I am sure of this. I take a wide view of the progress of the destiny of this vast empire. I see God in America. I see him in the North and in the South. I see him more honored in the South to-day than he was twenty-five years ago; and that that higher regard is due, mainly, to the agitation of the slavery question. Do you ask how? Why, sir, this is how. Twenty-five years ago the religious mind of the South was leavened by wrong Northern training, on the great point of the right and wrong of slavery. Meanwhile, powerful intellects in the South, following the mere light of a healthy good sense, guided by the common grace of God, reached the very truth of this great matter,—namely, that the relation of the master and slave is not sin; and that, notwithstanding its admitted evils, it is a connection between the highest and the lowest races of man, revealing influences which may be, and will be, most benevolent for the ultimate good of the master and the slave. . . .

When Ham [the second son of Noah] in his antediluvian recklessness, laughed at his father [Noah], God took occasion to give to the world the rule of the superior over the inferior. *He cursed him. He cursed him because he left him unblessed.* The withholding of the father's blessing, in the Bible, was curse. . . . Ham was cursed to render service, forever, to Shem and Japheth. The *special* curse on Canaan [son of Ham] made the general curse on Ham conspicuous, historic, and explanatory, simply because his descendants were to be brought under the control of God's peculiar people. Shem was blessed to rule over Ham. Japheth was blessed to rule over both. God sent Ham to Africa, Shem to Asia, Japheth to Europe.[59]

---

59. A modern black scholar, Leslie B. Rout, Jr., has pointed out that in the mid-fifteenth century when Portugal was initiating the direct African slave trade, Gomes Eannes de Azurara wrote in his *Chronicle* (see Doc. 1.1) that "in accordance with ancient custom, which I believe to have been because of the curse, which after the Deluge Noah laid on his son Cain [Canaan] cursing him in this way: that his race would be subject to all other races of the world." See Rout's *African Experience in Spanish America,* p. 12. Editor.

Mr. Moderator, you have read Guyot's *"Earth and Man."* That admirable book is a commentary upon this part of Genesis. It is the philosophy of geography. And it is the philosophy of the rule of the higher races over the inferior, written on the very face of the earth. He tells you why the continents are shaped as they are shaped; why the mountains stand where they stand; why the rivers run where they run; why the currents of the sea and the air flow as they flow. And he tells you that the earth south of the Equator makes the inferior man. That the oceanic climate makes the inferior man in the Pacific Islands. That South America makes the inferior man. That the solid, unindented Southern Africa makes the inferior man. That the huge, heavy, massive, magnificent Asia makes the huge, heavy, massive, magnificent man. That Europe, indented by the sea on every side, with its varied scenery, and climate, and Northern influences, makes the varied intellect, the versatile power and life and action, of the master man of the world. And it is so. Africa, with here and there an exception, has never produced men to compare with the men of Asia. For six thousand years, save the unintelligible stones of Egypt, she has had no history. Asia has had her great men and her name. But Europe has ever shown, and now, her nobler men and higher destiny. Japheth has now come to North America, to give us his greatness and his transcendent glory. (Applause.) And, sir, I thank God our mountains stand where they stand; and that our rivers run where they run. Thank God they run not across longitudes, but across latitudes, from north to south. If they crossed longitudes, we might fear for the Union. But I hail the Union,—made by God, strong as the strength of our hills, and ever to live and expand,—like the flow and swell of the current of our streams. (Applause.) . . .

I now come to particular illustrations of the world-wide law that service shall be rendered by the inferior to the superior. The relations in which such service obtains are very many. Some of them are these:—husband and wife; parent and child; teacher and scholar; commander and soldier,—sailor; master and apprentice; master and hireling; master and slave. Now, sir, all these relations are ordained of God. They are all directly commanded, or they are the irresistible law of his providence, in conditions which must come up in the progress of depraved nature. The relations themselves are all good in certain conditions. And there may be no more of evil in the lowest than in the highest. . . .

Why, sir, the wife everywhere, except where Christianity has given her elevation, *is the slave*. And, sir, I say, without fear of saying too strongly, that for every sigh, every groan, every tear, every agony of stripe or death, which has gone up to God from the relation of master and slave, there have been more sighs, more groans, more tears, and more agony in the rule of the husband over the wife. Sir, I have admitted, and do again admit, without qual-ification, that every fact in Uncle Tom's Cabin has occurred in the South. But, in reply, I say deliberately, what one of your first men told me, that he who will make the horrid examination will discover in New York City, in any number of years past, more cruelty from husband to wife, parent to child, *than in all the South from master to slave* in the same time. I dare the investigation. And you may extend it further, if you choose,—to all the re-sults of honor and purity. I fear nothing on this subject. I stand on rock,— the Bible,—and therefore, just before I bring the Bible, to which all I have said is introductory, I will run a parallel between the relation of master and slave and that of husband and wife. . . .

Do you say, The slave is held to *involuntary service?* So is the wife. Her re-lation to her husband, in the immense majority of cases, is made for her, and not by her. And when she makes it for herself, how often, and how soon, does it become involuntary! How often, and how soon, would she throw off the yoke if she could! Oh ye wives, I know how superior you are to your hus-bands in many respects,—not only in personal attraction, (although in that particular, comparison is out of place,) in grace, in refined thought, in pas-sive fortitude, in enduring love, and in a heart to be filled with the spirit of heaven. Oh, I know all this. Nay, I know you may surpass him in his own sphere of boasted prudence and worldly wisdom about dollars and cents. Nevertheless, he has authority, from God, to rule over you. You are under service to him. You are bound to obey him *in all things.* Your service is very, very, very often involuntary from the first, and, if voluntary at first, becomes hopeless necessity afterwards. I know God has laid upon the husband to love you as Christ loved the church, and in that sublime obligation has placed you in the light and under the shadow of a love infinitely higher, and purer, and holier than all talked about in the romances of chivalry. But the husband may not so love you. He may rule you with the rod of iron. What can you do? Be divorced? God forbids it, save for crime. Will you say that you are free,— that you will go where you please, do as you please? Why, ye dear wives, your husbands may forbid. And listen, you cannot leave New York, nor your palaces, any more than your shanties. No; you cannot leave your parlor, nor your bedchamber, nor your couch, if your husband commands you to stay there! What can you do? Will you run away, with your stick and your bun-dle? He can advertise you!! What can you do? You can, and I fear some of you do, wish him, from the bottom of your hearts, at the bottom of the Hudson. Or, in your self-will, you will do just as you please. (Great laughter.) . . .

But to proceed:—

Do you say the slave is *sold and bought ?* So is the wife the world over.

Everywhere, always, and now as the general fact, however done away or modified by Christianity. The savage buys her. The barbarian buys her. The Turk buys her. The Jew buys her. The Christian buys her,—Greek, Armenian, Nestorian, Roman Catholic, Protestant. The Portuguese, the Spaniard, the Italian, the German, the Russian, the Frenchman, the Englishman, the New England man, the New Yorker,—especially the upper ten,—*buy the wife*—in many, very many cases. She is seldom bought in the South, and never among the slaves themselves; for they always marry for love. (Continued laughter.) Sir, I say the wife is bought in the highest circles, too often, as really as the slave is bought. Oh, she is not sold and purchased in the public market. But come, sir, with me, and let us take the privilege of spirits out of the body to glide in that gilded saloon, or into that richly comfortable family room, of cabinets, and pictures, and statuary: see the parties, there, to sell and buy that human body and soul, and make her a chattel! See how they sit, and bend towards each other, in earnest colloquy, on sofa of rosewood and satin,—*Turkey* carpet (how befitting!) under feet, sunlight over head, softened through stained windows: or it is night, and the gas is turned nearly off, and the burners gleam like stars through the shadow from which the whisper is heard, in which that old ugly brute, with gray goatee—how fragrant!—bids one, two, five, ten hundred thousand dollars, and *she* is knocked off to him,—that beautiful young girl asleep up there, amid flowers, and innocent that she is sold and bought. Sir, that young girl would as soon permit a baboon to embrace her, as that old, ignorant, gross, disgusting wretch to approach her. Ah, has she not been sold and bought for money? But—But what? But, you say, she freely, and without parental authority, accepted him. Then she sold herself for money, and was guilty of *that* which is nothing better than legal prostitution. I know what I say; you know what I say. Up there in the gallery you know: you nod to one another. Ah! you know the parties. Yes, you say: All true, true, true. (Laughter.)

Now, Mr. Moderator, I will clinch all I have said by nails sure, and fastened from the word of God. . . . Sir, God sanctioned slavery then, and sanctions it now. He made it right, they know, then and now. Having thus taken the last puff of wind out of the sails of the anti-slavery phantom ship, turn to the twenty-first chapter of Exodus, vs. 2–5. God, in these verses, gave the Israelites his command how they should buy and hold the Hebrew servant,—how under certain conditions, he went free,—how, under other circumstances, he might be held to service forever, with his wife and her children. There it is. Don't run into the Hebrew. (Laughter.)

But what have we here?—vs. 7–11:—"And if a man sell his daughter to be a maid-servant, she shall not go out as the men-servants do. If she please not her master, who hath betrothed her to himself, then shall he let her be redeemed: to sell her unto a strange nation he shall have no power, seeing he hath dealt deceitfully with her. And if he hath betrothed her unto his son, he shall deal with her after the manner of daughters. If he take him another wife, her food, her raiment, and her duty of marriage shall he not diminish. And if he do not these three unto her, than shall she go out free without money." Now, sir, the wit of man can't dodge that passage, unless he runs away into the Hebrew. (Great laughter.) For what does God say? Why, this:—that an Israelite might sell his own daughter, not only into servitude, but into polygamy,—that the buyer might, if he pleased, give her to his son for a wife, or take her to himself. If he took her to himself, and she did not please him, he should not sell her unto a strange nation, but should allow her to be redeemed by her family. But, if he took him another wife before he allowed the first one to be redeemed, he should continue to give the first one her *food,* her *raiment,* and her *duty of marriage;* that is to say, *her right to his bed.* If he did not do *these three things,* she should go out free; *i.e.* cease to be his slave, without his receiving any money for her. There, sir, God sanctioned the Israelite father in selling his daughter, and the Israelite man to buy her, into slavery and into polygamy. And it was right, because God made it right. In verses 20 and 21, you have these words:—"And if a man smite his servant or his maid with a rod, and he die under his hand, he shall be severely punished; notwithstanding, if he continue a day or two, he shall not be punished: for he is his money." What does this passage mean? Surely this: if the master gave his slave a hasty blow with a rod, and he died under his hand, he should be punished. But, if the slave lived a day or two, it would so extenuate the act of the master he should not be punished, inasmuch as he would be in that case sufficiently punished in losing his money in his slave. Now, sir, I affirm that God was more lenient to the degraded Hebrew master than Southern laws are to the higher Southern master in like cases. But there you have what was the divine will. Find fault with God, ye anti-slavery men, if you dare. In Leviticus, xxv. 44–46, "Both thy bondmen and thy bondmaids, which thou shalt have, shall be of the heathen that are round about you; of them shall ye buy bondmen and bondmaids. Moreover, of the children of the strangers that do sojourn among you, of them shall ye buy, and of their families that are with you, which they beget in your land: and they shall be your possession. And ye shall take them as an inheritance for your children after you, to inherit them for a possession; they shall be your bondsmen forever."

Sir, I do not see how God could tell us more plainly that he did command his people to buy slaves from the heathen round about them, and from the stranger, and of their families sojourning among them. The passage has no other meaning. Did God merely permit sin?—did he merely tolerate a dreadful evil? God does not say so anywhere. He gives his people law to buy and hold slaves of the heathen forever, on certain conditions, and to buy and hold Hebrew slaves in variously-modified particulars. Well, how did the heathen, then, get slaves to sell? Did they capture them in war?—did they sell their own children? Wherever they got them, they sold them; and God's law gave his people the right to buy them. . . . Why, sir, if a man can hold three slaves, with a right heart and the approbation of God, he may hold thirty, three hundred, three thousand, or thirty thousand. It is a mere question of heart, and capacity to govern. The Emperor of Russia holds sixty millions of slaves: and is there a man in this house so much of a fool as to say that God regards the Emperor of Russia a sinner because he is the master of sixty millions of slaves? Sir, that Emperor has certainly a high and awful responsibility upon him. But, if he is good as he is great, he is a god of benevolence on earth. And so is every Southern master. His obligation is high, and great, and glorious. It is the same obligation, in kind, he is under to his wife and children, and in some respects immensely higher, by reason of the number and the tremendous interests involved for time and eternity in connection with this great country, Africa, and the world. Yes, sir, I *know,* whether Southern masters fully know it or not, that *they hold from God,* individually and collectively, *the highest and the noblest responsibility ever given by Him to individual private men on all the face of the earth.* For God has intrusted to them to train millions of the most degraded in form and intellect, but, at the same time, the most gentle, the most amiable, the most affectionate, the most imitative, the most susceptible of social and religious love, of all the races of mankind,—to train them, and to give them civilization, and the light and the life of the gospel of Jesus Christ. And I thank God he has given this great work to that type of the noble family of Japheth best qualified to do it,—to the Cavalier stock,—the gentleman and the lady of England and France, born to command, and softened and refined under our Southern sky. May they know and feel and fulfill their destiny! Oh, may they "know that they also have a Master in heaven."

3.11. "The Geography of Prejudice." A New Yorker Analyzes the Many Varieties of Racist Oppression in Northern Free States

In this selection the abolitionist, William Jay (see Docs. 1.12 and 3.5), examined anti-black racism in the northern free states, revealing widespread rejection of civil liberties for so-called people of color. Such abuses included denial of the right to vote and to participate in state and local government, to travel freely from state to state, to establish permanent residences without undue obstacles and bogus obligations, and to petition government for redress of grievances. Blacks in the North could not serve in the military, hold legal offices, act as witnesses in courts of law, obtain access to education and unobstructed participation in religious worship, or practice professions of their own choosing. They were the frequent victims of personal insult and abuse, were denied unobstructed access to public transportation, and perhaps most deplorable of all, were never entirely free from the threat of seizure and illegal enslavement. Though long opposed to *southern* slavery, Jay declared that it was "a fact of acknowledged notoriety that however severe may be the laws against the colored people at the South, the prejudice against their *persons* is far weaker than among ourselves."

SOURCE: William Jay, *Miscellaneous Writings on Slavery* (Boston: John P. Jewett, 1853), pp. 371–95.

ON THE CONDITION OF THE FREE PEOPLE OF COLOR
IN THE UNITED STATES.

Colonizationists have taken great pains to inculcate the opinion that prejudice against color is implanted in our nature by the Author of our being; and whence they infer the futility of every effort to elevate the colored man in this country, and consequently the duty and benevolence of sending him to Africa, beyond the reach of our cruelty. The theory is as false in fact as it is derogatory to the character of that God whom we are told is LOVE. With what astonishment and disgust should we behold an earthly parent exciting feuds and animosities among his own children; yet we are assured, and that too by professing Christians, that our heavenly Father has implanted a principle of hatred, repulsion and alienation between certain portions of his family on earth, and then commanded them, as if in mockery, to "love one another.". . .

Were we to inquire into the geography of this prejudice, we should find that the localities in which it attains its rankest luxuriance, are not the rice-swamps of Georgia, nor the sugar-fields of Louisiana, but the hills and valleys of New England, and the prairies of Ohio! It is a fact of acknowledged notoriety, that however severe may be the laws against the colored people of the South, the prejudice against their *persons* is far weaker than among ourselves.

It is not necessary for our present purpose to enter into a particular investigation of the condition of free negroes in the slave States. We all know that they suffer every form of oppression which the laws can inflict upon persons not actually slaves. That unjust and cruel enactments should proceed from a people who keep two millions of their fellow-men in abject bondage, and who believe such enactments essential to the maintenance of their despotism, certainly affords no cause for surprise. We turn [rather] to the free States, where slavery has not directly steeled our hearts against human suffering, and where no supposed danger of insurrection affords a pretext for keeping the free blacks in ignorance and degradation; and we ask, What is the character of the prejudice against color *here?* Let the Rev. Mr. Bacon, of Connecticut, answer the question. This gentleman, in a vindication of the Colonization Society, assures us, "The *Soodra* [Sudra, a Hindu of the lowest caste] is not farther separated from the *Brahmin* in regard to all his privileges, civil, intellectual, and moral, than the negro from the white man by the prejudices which result from the difference made between them by the GOD OF NATURE." (Report of the American Colonization Society, p. 87.) . . .

With these preliminary remarks we will now proceed to take a view of the condition of the free people of color in the non-slave-holding States; and will consider in order, the various disabilities and oppressions to which they are subjected, either by law or the customs of the society.

1. GENERAL EXCLUSION FROM THE ELECTIVE FRANCHISE.

Were this exclusion founded on the want of property, or any other qualification deemed essential to the judicious exercise of the franchise, it would afford no just cause of complaint; but it is founded solely on the color of the skin, and is therefore irrational and unjust. That taxation and representation should be inseparable, was one of the axioms of the fathers of the Revolution, and one of the reasons they assigned for their revolt from the crown of Britain. But *now,* it is deemed a mark of fanaticism to complain of the disfranchisement of a whole race, while they remain subject to the burden of taxation. It is worthy of remark, that of the thirteen original States, only *two* were so recreant to the principles of the Revolution, as to make a *white skin* a qualification for suffrage. But the prejudice has grown with our growth, and strengthened with our strength; and it is believed that in *every* State constitution subsequently formed or revised, (excepting Vermont and Maine, and the revised constitution of Massachusetts,) the crime of a dark complexion has been punished by debarring its possessor from all approach to the ballot box.

2. DENIAL OF THE RIGHT OF LOCOMOTION.

It is in vain that the Constitution of the United States expressly guarantees to "the citizens of each State, all the privileges and immunities of citizens in the several States":—It is in vain that the Supreme Court of the United States has solemnly decided that this clause confers on every citizen of one State the right to "pass through, or reside in any other State for the purposes of trade, agriculture, professional pursuits, or *otherwise.*" It is in vain that "the members of the several State Legislatures" are required to "be bound by oath or affirmation to support" the Constitution conferring this very guaranty. Constitutions and judicial decisions and religious obligations are alike outraged by our State enactments against people of color. There is scarcely a slave State in which a citizen of New York, with a dark skin, may visit a dying child without subjecting himself to legal penalties. But in the slave States we look for cruelty; we expect the rights of humanity and the laws of the land to be sacrificed on the altar of slavery. In the free States, we had reason to hope for a greater deference to decency and morality. Yet even in those States we behold the effects of a miasma wafted from the South. The Connecticut Black Act, prohibiting under heavy penalties the instruction of any colored person from any State, is well known. . . . But among all the free States, OHIO stands preëminent for the wickedness of her statutes against this class of our population. These statutes are not merely infamous outrages on every principle of justice and humanity, but are gross and palpable violations of the State constitution, and manifest an absence of moral sentiment in the Ohio Legislature, as deplorable as it is alarming. . . . By the Constitution of New York, the colored inhabitants are expressly recognized as "citizens." Let us suppose, then, a New York freeholder and voter of this class, confiding in the guaranty given by the Federal constitution, removes into Ohio. No matter how much property he takes with him; no matter what attestations he produces to the purity of his character, he is required by the Acts of 1807, to find, within twenty days, two freehold sureties in the sum of five hundred dollars for his *good behavior;* and likewise for his *maintenance,* should he at any future period, from any cause whatever, be unable to maintain himself, and in default of procuring such sureties, he is to be removed by the overseers of the poor. The Legislature well knew that it would generally be utterly impossible for a stranger, and especially a *black* stranger, to find such sureties. It was the *design* of the Act, by imposing impracticable conditions, to prevent colored emigrants from remaining within the State; and in order more certainly to effect this object, it imposes a pecuniary penalty on every inhabitant who shall venture to "harbor," that is, receive under his roof, or who shall even "employ" an emigrant who has not given the required sureties; and it moreover renders such inhabitant so harboring, or employing him legally liable for his future maintenance! That the law has not been universally enforced proves only that the people of Ohio are less profligate than their legislators; that it has remained on the statute book for thirty-two years proves the depraved state of public opinion and the horrible persecution to which the colored people are legally exposed. But let it not be supposed that this vile law is in fact obsolete, and its very existence forgotten.

In 1829, a very general effort was made to enforce this law, and about *one thousand free blacks* were in consequence of it driven out of the State, and sought a refuge in the more free and Christian country of Canada. Previous to their departure, they sent out a deputation to the Governor of the Upper Province to know if they would be admitted, and received from Sir James Colebrook this reply:—"Tell the *republicans* on your side of the line that we royalists do not know men by their *color*. Should you come to us, you will be entitled to all the privileges of the rest of his majesty's subjects." This was the origin of the Wilberforce colony in Upper Canada.

Now what says the Constitution of Ohio? "ALL are born free and independent, and have certain natural, inherent, inalienable rights; among which are the enjoying, and defending life and liberty, *acquiring, possessing and protecting property,* and pursuing and attaining happiness and safety." Yet men . . . impose a pecuniary penalty and grievous liabilities on every man who shall give to an innocent fellow-countryman a night's lodging, or even a meal of victuals in exchange for his honest labor![60]

3. DENIAL OF THE RIGHT OF PETITION.

We explicitly disclaim all intention that the several disabilities and cruelties we are specifying are of universal application. The laws of some States in relation to the people of color are more wicked than others; and the spirit of persecution is not in every place equally active and malignant. In none of the free States have these people so many grievances to complain of as in Ohio, and for the honor of our country we rejoice to add that in no other State in the Union has their right to petition for redress of their grievances been denied.

On the 14th of January, 1839, a petition for relief from certain legal disabilities, from colored inhabitants of Ohio, was presented to the *popular* branch of the Legislature, and its rejection was moved by George H. Flood. . . . Mr. Flood's motion was lost by a majority of only *four* votes; but this triumph of humanity and republicanism was as transient as it was meagre. The *next* day the House, by a large majority, resolved

"That the blacks and mulattoes who may be residents within this State

60. For the Black Laws of Ohio and related matters, see Foner and Lewis, *Black Worker,* pp. 152–57. Editor.

have no constitutional right to present their petitions to the General Assembly for any purpose whatsoever, and that any reception of such petitions on the part of the General Assembly is a mere act of privilege or policy, and not imposed by any expressed or implied power of the Constitution."

The phraseology of this resolution is as clumsy as its assertions are base and sophistical. The meaning intended to be expressed is simply that the constitution of Ohio, neither in terms nor by implication, confers on such residents as are negroes or mulattoes any right to offer a petition to the Legislature for any object whatever; nor imposes on that body any obligation to notice such a petition; and whatever attention it may please to bestow upon it ought to be regarded as an act not of duty, but merely of favor or expediency. Hence it is obvious that the *principle* on which the resolution is founded is that the reciprocal right and duty of offering and hearing petitions *rests solely on constitutional enactment,* and not on moral obligation. The *reception* of negro petitions is declared to be a mere act of *privilege or policy.* Now it is difficult to imagine a principle more utterly subversive of all the duties of rulers, the rights of citizens, and the charities of private life. The victim of oppression or fraud has no *right* to appeal to the constituted authorities for redress, nor are those authorities under any obligation to consider the appeal; the needy and unfortunate have no right to implore the assistance of their more fortunate neighbors; and all are at liberty to turn a deaf ear to the cry of distress. The eternal and immutable principles of justice and humanity, proclaimed by Jehovah, and impressed by him on the conscience of man, have no binding force on the Legislature of Ohio, unless expressly adopted and enforced by the State constitution! . . .

4. EXCLUSION FROM THE ARMY AND MILITIA.

The Federal Government is probably the only one in the world that forbids a portion of its subjects to participate in the national defence, not from any doubts of their courage, loyalty, or physical strength, but merely on account of the tincture of their skin! To such an absurd extent is this prejudice against color carried, that some of our militia companies have occasionally refused to march to the sound of a drum when beaten by a black man. To declare a certain class of the community unworthy to bear arms in defence of their native country is necessarily to consign that class to general contempt.

5. EXCLUSION FROM ALL PARTICIPATION IN THE ADMINISTRATION OF JUSTICE.

No colored man can be a judge, juror, or constable. Were the talents and acquirements of a Mansfield or a Marshall veiled in a sable skin, they would be excluded from the bench of the humblest court in the American republic. In the slave States generally, no black man can enter a court of justice as a witness against a white one. Of course a white man may, with perfect impunity, defraud or abuse a negro to any extent, provided he is careful to avoid the presence of any of his own caste at the execution of his contract, or the indulgence of his malice. We are not aware that an outrage so flagrant is sanctioned by the laws of any *free* State, with one exception. That exception the reader will readily believe can be none other than OHIO. A statute of this State enacts, "that no black or mulatto *person* or *persons* shall hereafter be permitted to be sworn, or give evidence in any court of record or elsewhere in this State, in any cause depending, or matter of controversy, when either party to the same is a WHITE person; or in any prosecution of the State against any WHITE person.". . .

6. IMPEDIMENTS TO EDUCATION.

No people have ever professed so deep a conviction of the importance of popular education as ourselves, and no people have ever resorted to such cruel expedients to perpetuate abject ignorance. More than one third of the whole population of the slave States are prohibited from learning even to read, and in some of them free men, if with dark complexions, are subject to stripes for teaching their own children. If we turn to the free States, we find that in all of them, without exception, the prejudices and customs of society oppose almost insuperable obstacles to the acquisition of a liberal education by colored youth. . . . Colored children are very generally excluded from our common schools, in consequence of the prejudices of teachers and parents. In some of our cities there are schools *exclusively* for their use, but in the country the colored population is too sparse to justify such schools; and white and black children are rarely seen studying under the same roof; although such cases do sometimes occur, and then they are confined to elementary schools. . . .

It may not be useless to cite an instance of the malignity with which the education of the blacks is opposed. The efforts made in Connecticut to prevent the establishment of schools of a higher order than usual for colored pupils are too well known to need a recital here; and her BLACK ACT, prohibiting the instruction of colored children from other States, although now expunged from her statute books through the influence of abolitionists, will long be remembered to the opprobrium of her citizens. We ask attention to the following illustration of public opinion in another New England State.

In 1834 an academy was built by subscription in CANAAN, New Hampshire, and a charter granted by the Legislature; and at a meeting of the proprietors it was determined to receive all applicants having "suitable moral and intellectual recommendations, without other distinctions;" in other words, without reference to *complexion*. When this determination was made known, a town meeting was forthwith convened, and the following resolutions adopted, viz.:

"Resolved, that we view with *abhorrence* the attempt of the abolitionists to establish in this town a school for the instruction of the sable sons and daughters of Africa, in common with our sons and daughters.

"Resolved, that we will not associate with, nor in any way countenance, any man or woman who shall hereafter persist in attempting to establish a school in this town for the *exclusive* education of blacks, *or* for their education in conjunction with the whites. . . ."

The proprietors of the academy supposing, in the simplicity of their hearts, that in a free country they might use their property in any manner not forbidden by law, proceeded to open their school, and in the ensuing spring had twenty-eight white and fourteen colored scholars. The crisis had now arrived when the cause of prejudice demanded the sacrifice of constitutional liberty and of private property. Another town meeting was convoked, at which, without a shadow of authority, and in utter contempt of law and decency, it was ordered that the academy should be forcibly removed, and a committee was appointed to execute the abominable mandate. Due preparations were made for the occasion, and on the 10th of August three hundred men with about two hundred oxen assembled at the place, and taking the edifice from off its foundation, dragged it to a distance, and left it a ruin. No one of the actors in this high-handed outrage was ever brought before a court of justice to answer for this criminal and riotous destruction of the property of others.[61]

7. IMPEDIMENTS TO RELIGIOUS INSTRUCTION

The impediments to education already mentioned necessarily render the acquisition of religious knowledge difficult, and in many instances impracticable. In the northern cities the blacks have frequently churches of their own, but in the country they are too few and too poor to build churches and maintain ministers. Of course they must remain destitute of public worship and religious instruction, unless they can enjoy these blessings in company with the whites. Now there is hardly a church in the United States, not exclusively appropriated to the blacks, in which one of their number owns a pew, or has a voice in the choice of a minister. There

61. For other notable cases of women who established schools for black children before the Civil War, see Philip S. Foner and Josephine F. Pacheco, *Three Who Dared: Prudence Crandall, Margaret Douglass, Myrtilla Miner: Champions of Antebellum Black Education* (Westport, Conn.: Greenwood Press, 1985). Editor.

are usually, indeed, a few seats in a remote part of the church, set apart for their use, and in which no white man is ever seen. It is surely not surprising, under all the circumstances of the case, that these seats are rarely crowded. Colored ministers are occasionally ordained in the different denominations, but they are kept at a distance by their white brethren in the ministry, and are rarely permitted to enter their pulpits; and still more rarely, to sit at their tables, although acknowledged to be ambassadors of Christ. The distinction of *caste* is not forgotten, even in the celebration of the Lord's Supper, and seldom are colored disciples permitted to eat and drink of the memorials of the Redeemer's passion till after every white communicant has been served.

8. IMPEDIMENTS TO HONEST INDUSTRY.

In this country ignorance and poverty are almost inseparable companions; and it is surely not strange that those should be poor whom we compel to be ignorant. The liberal professions are virtually sealed against the blacks, if we except the church, and even in that, admission is rendered difficult by the obstacles placed in their way in acquiring the requisite literary qualifications; and when once admitted, their administrations are confined to their own color. Many of our most wealthy and influential citizens have commenced life as ignorant and as penniless as any negro who loiters in our streets. Had their complexion been dark, notwithstanding their talents, industry, enterprise, and probity, they would have continued ignorant, and penniless, because the paths to learning and to wealth would then have been closed against them. There is a conspiracy embracing all the departments of society to keep the black man ignorant and poor. As a general rule, admitting few if any exceptions, the schools of literature and of science reject him—the counting house refuses to receive him as a book-keeper, much worse as a partner—no store admits him as a clerk—no shop as an apprentice. Here and there a black man may be found keeping a few trifles on the shelf for sale; and a few acquire, as if by stealth, the knowledge of some handicraft; but almost universally these people, both in town and country, are prevented by the customs of society from maintaining themselves and their families by any other than menial occupations. . . .

9. LIABILITY TO BE SEIZED, AND TREATED AS SLAVES.

An able-bodied colored man sells in the southern market for from eight hundred to a thousand dollars; of course he is worth stealing. Colonizationists and slave-holders, and many northern divines, solemnly affirm that the situation of a slave is far preferable to that of a free negro; hence it would seem an act of humanity to convert the latter into the former. Kidnapping being both a lucrative and a benevolent business, it is not strange that it should be extensively practised. In many of the States this business is regulated by law, and there are various ways in which the transmutation is legally effected. Thus, in South Carolina, if a free negro "entertains" a runaway slave, it may be his own wife or child, he himself is turned into a slave. In 1827, *a free woman and her three children* underwent this benevolent process for *entertaining* two fugitive children of six and nine years old. In Virginia all emancipated slaves remaining twelve months in the State are kindly restored to their former condition. In Maryland a free negro who marries a white woman thereby acquires all the privileges of a slave—and generally throughout the slave region, including the District of Columbia, every negro not known to be free is mercifully considered a slave, and if his master cannot be ascertained, he is thrown into a dungeon and there kept till by a public sale a master can be provided for him. But often the law grants colored men, *known to be free,* all the advantages of slavery. Thus, in Georgia, every *free* colored man coming into the State, and unable to pay a fine of one hundred dollars, becomes a slave for life; in Florida, insolvent debtors, *if black,* are SOLD for the benefit of their creditors; and in the District of Columbia a free colored man, thrown into jail on suspicion of being a slave and, proving his freedom, is required by law to be sold as a slave, if too poor to pay his jail fees. Let it not be supposed that these laws are all obsolete and inoperative. They catch many a northern negro who, in pursuit of his own business, or on being decoyed by others, ventures to enter the slave region; and who, of course, helps to augment the wealth of our southern brethren.[62] . . .

But it is not at the South alone that freemen may be converted into slaves "according to law." The Act of Congress respecting the recovery of fugitive slaves affords most extraordinary facilities for this process, through official corruption and individual perjury. By this Act, the claimant is permitted to *select* a justice of the peace, before whom he may bring or send his alleged slave, and even to prove his property by *affidavit.* Indeed, in almost every State in the Union, a slave-holder may recover at law a human being as his beast of burden, with far less ceremony than he could his pig from the possession of his neighbor. In only three States is a man, claimed as a slave, entitled to trial by jury. . . .

Another mode of legal kidnapping still remains to be described. By the Federal Constitution, fugitives from *justice* are to be delivered up, and under this constitutional provision, a free negro may be converted into a slave without troubling even a justice of the peace to hear the evidence of

---

62. For a tragic example of this type of enslavement, see Doc. 2.12. Editor.

the captor's claim. A fugitive slave is of course a felon; he not only steals himself, but also the rags on his back, which belong to his master. It is understood he has taken refuge in New York, and his master naturally wishes to recover him with as little noise, trouble, and delay as possible. The way is simple and easy. Let the Grand Jury indict A. B. for stealing wearing apparel, and let the indictment with an affidavit of the criminal's flight be forwarded by the Governor of the State to his Excellency of New York, with a requisition for the delivery of A. B. to the agent appointed to receive him. A warrant is, of course, issued to "any constable of the State of New York," to arrest A. B. For what purpose?—to bring him before a magistrate where his identity may be established?—no, to deliver him up to the foreign agent. Hence, the constable may pick up the first likely negro he finds in the street, and ship him to the South; and should it be found on his arrival on the plantation that the wrong man has come, it will also probably be found that the mistake is of no consequence to the planter.

10. SUBJECTION TO INSULT AND OUTRAGE.

The feeling of the community towards these people, and the contempt with which they are treated, are indicated by the following notice, lately published by the proprietors of a menagerie in New York. "The proprietors wish it to be understood that people of color are not permitted to enter, *except when in attendance upon children and families.*" For two shillings any white scavenger would be freely admitted, and so would negroes, provided they came in a capacity that marked their dependence; their presence is offensive, *only* when they come as independent spectators, gratifying a laudable curiosity.

Even death, the great leveller, is not permitted to obliterate, among Christians, the distinction of caste, or to rescue the lifeless form of the colored man from the insults of his white brethren. In the porch of a Presbyterian Church, in Philadelphia, in 1837, was suspended a card containing the form of a deed to be given to purchasers of lots in a certain burial ground, and to enhance the value of the property, and to entice buyers, the following clause was inserted: "No person of *color,* nor any one who has been the subject of *execution,* shall be interred in said lot." Our colored fellow-citizens, like others, are occasionally called to pass from one place to another; and in doing so are compelled to submit to innumerable hardships and indignities. They are frequently denied seats in our stage coaches; and although admitted upon the *decks* of our steamboats, are almost universally excluded from the cabins. Even women have been forced, in cold weather, to pass the night upon deck, and in one instance the wife of a colored clergyman lost her life in consequence of such an exposure. . . .

The facts we have now exhibited abundantly prove the extreme cruelty and sinfulness of that prejudice against color which we are impiously told is an ORDINATION OF PROVIDENCE. Colonizationists, assuming the prejudice to be natural and invincible, propose to remove its victims beyond its influence. Abolitionists, on the contrary, remembering with the Psalmist, that "It is He that hath made us, and not we ourselves," believe that the benevolent Father of us all requires us to treat with justice and kindness every portion of the human family, notwithstanding any particular organization he has been pleased to impress upon them.

3.12. Negro Mania

John Campbell, a resident of Philadelphia, publisher and author of books on such topics as the French Revolution, and the English corn laws, was also a man of extremist views on the question of race. The following quotations from one of his books, *Negro-Mania,* clearly reveals the nature of his thinking. Campbell's opinions are largely based on skin color, but even more on hair texture, as the following introductory diatribe implies: "What wooly-headed Homers, Virgils, Dantes, Molieres, or Shakespeares," he asked his readers, "ever inscribed their names upon the pillar of fame, by the numbers of immortal song? What wooly-headed Xenophons, Tacituses, Gibbons, Voltaires, Humes, and Bancrofts ever depicted the actions of wooly-headed heroes, patriots and soldiers? What wooly-headed Epaminondases, Caesars, Alexanders, Washingtons, Napoleons and Wellingtons ever led their marshalled battalions upon the principles of military science to either liberty, victory, or death? What wooly-headed Solons or Numas, or Alfreds, or Jeffersons, ever framed a code of laws to direct and guide the destinies of a great nation? . . . What wooly-headed Columbuses, or Hudsons, or Drakes ever ventured across the wide wilderness of waters in search of distant, unknown and undiscovered continents? In fine, have the wooly-headed races of men ever produced . . . even . . . one man famous as either a lawgiver, statesman, poet, priest, painter, historian, orator, architect, musician, soldier, sailor, engineer, navigator, astronomer, linguist, mathematician, anatomist, chemist, physician, naturalist [or] philosopher?"

To respond to Campbell's question, if he had tried he could easily have found many accomplished blacks in Philadelphia: persons such as Richard Allen, abolitionist and founder of the African Methodist Episcopal Church; Robert Purvis, affluent businessman and co-founder of the Philadelphia

Underground Railroad and the American Anti-Slavery Society; Charles Reason, an educator at the Institute for Colored Youth in Philadelphia and later professor of French and *belles lettres* at Central College, New York; the musician Frank Johnson, whose military band entertained Victoria and Albert in England; and William Still, a freed slave who rose to leadership of the Philadelphia branch of the Underground Railroad and chronicled the battle for freedom of fugitive slaves (see Doc. 3.20). Most prominent blacks in Campbell's time were clergymen, antislavery leaders, or both, but under more normal conditions they could have become, as Campbell would have it, lawgivers, statesmen, architects, navigators, astronomers, or even leaders of "marshalled battalions." Despite the times, in fact, some of the persons mentioned above, and others like them, *were,* in fact, orators, linguists, writers, musicians and philosophers, and, more important, unlike Campbell, countless blacks, educated or not, made giant contributions to the struggle for freedom and the progress of humanity.

SOURCE: John Campbell, *Negro-Mania: Being an Examination of the Falsely Assumed Equality of the Various Races of Men* (Philadelphia: Campbell & Power, 1851), pp. 6, 8–10, 543–49.

From Campbell's Closing Pages.

A couple of years ago men were afraid in Philadelphia to speak out their opinions of the Negro; that day is past—his equality and humanity can be talked of now in any and every company. Were one to have said that no amount of education, or circumstances, or food, or climate, or all united, could ever make aught of a negro than a negro, there were not wanting a certain number of sham humanitarians, fierce as wolves, ready to pounce upon the unfortunate utterer of the truth, and willing to hunt him to the death. This evil had to be arrested—public opinion had to be changed—and the only way to accomplish this was by open and free discussion. I dared the abolitionists to the contest; nearly every speaker was upon their side at the commencement, but one after another changed their opinions, the nature of the evidence, and the character of the authority I cited were so irresistible that the *honest and disinterested, having no selfish motives to blind their eyes to the evidence adduced* [italics in original], readily adopted the ideas of the great names who had made the science of man and the history of races their especial study.

Open, full, and free discussion will settle this question. In every contest of this kind the Negroites have been ignominiously driven from their strongholds. This must ever be the case where truth and falsehood come in contact. The truth must and shall prevail; and I am of opinion that a new turn will be given to public opinion in the free States, and the fact be believed, that whenever the white man and the Negro inhabit a warm climate together, there is no other state of society than mastery for the whites and slavery for the black race; but this has been so clearly demonstrated by Hammond, Blackwood, and others, that I need not do more than allude to it.

In this place it may not be inappropriate to say something about the free colored people. I speak now of Pennsylvania. Here we have a negroid population numbering over fifty-three thousand. I hold that he would be a pure patriot, and a philanthropist, in every sense of the term, who could rid us of this intolerable curse; who could point out a plan by which this vicious, idle, lazy, mongrel race would be safely deposited in Liberia.

The Shams denounce any attempt at colonization as cruel and tyrannical, thereby displaying their usual ignorance of negro nature. They claim for this species of man the same rights the whites possess; whereas, if they understood the matter, they would know that Negro nature is not Celtic or Saxon nature; they would know that the destiny, constitution, intellect, and even diseases of the negro are all essentially different from the white. These things the abolitionists know, or ought to know. The plain fact of the matter is, that we must take efficient steps ere long to get rid of our negroes, either by *colonization or otherwise* [italics in original]; but get rid of them we must, and must is the word. We must appropriate a certain sum annually, to enable those who are willing to emigrate so to do. We must prohibit the introduction of free negroes into our State. We must alter our State constitution for the purpose of enabling us to get rid of this population. And after we have made ample provision to send them in comfort to Africa, should there be any left who would prefer being slaves to the whites instead of free blacks in Liberia, they should have the power to choose, but they must either go there as free, or remain here as slaves. Aside of us they cannot be on terms of equality.

Will the white race ever agree that blacks shall stand beside us on election day, upon the rostrum, in the ranks of the army, in our places of amusement, in places of public worship, ride in the same coaches, railway cars, or steamships? Never! Never! nor is it natural, or just that this kind of equality should exist. God never intended it; had he so willed it, he would have made all one color. We see clearly that God himself has made the distinction—has made him inferior to the white. Could any body or tribe of negroes maintain the warlike attitude which the Circasian, a typical stock of the Caucasian race, do against the armed forces of the Russian Bear.

This, I presume, none will attempt to answer in the affirmative. Why, then, all this rant about negro equality, seeing that neither nature or nature's God ever established any such equality. . . .

An abolition meeting is held at a town in Ohio, New York, or Pennsylvania; speeches are made, negro wrongs are dwelt upon, Burns is quoted, "A man's a man for a' that," and Terence also, *"Homo sum et nihil a me alienum puto,"* "My black brother," and "all men are created free and equal." The meeting terminates, an impression is made, and frequently even upon strong minds. There are no libraries within reach of them; the different authors' works are too expensive, and the abolition poison runs through the mental system precisely as hydrophobia does through the physical, until the patient becomes a rabid, raving fanatic. Now this book popularizing this subject, and placing the best authorities for examination, bringing the whole question of races before them in a compact form, will destroy the influence of the knaves and demagogues who care nothing for the happiness of either Negro or white, provided they can accomplish their own selfish purposes. But the grand secret of the separation, or rather of the separate existence of race is to be found in the love of the beautiful, that instinctive and innate feeling wisely implanted by the Creator in us, will keep forever and ever the higher race always distinctive from the inferior ones.

Man, even savage man will stop to gaze at a beautiful statue or picture, and the fair haired white Caucasian woman has been always sought as a wife by every race; while on the other hand the white race of men have drawn back in disgust from anything like general intermingling with the females of the inferior races. So long as this feeling exists, all attempts at establishing an equality of races is silly; nay, more, it is wicked. If the Negro is equal to the white why do not the Negro-maniacs produce the names of such negroes as have become eminent for any one great quality in art, science, literature, or in any other way; this cannot be done, and the abolitionists know it.

From the evidence laid down in the preceding pages, it is proven that the constitution of the white man is not adapted to out-door labor in the Southern States. As such is the fact, would it be politic to abandon the rice, cotton, tobacco, and sugar plantations to the negroes, place them upon terms of political equality with the whites, allow an ignorant, brutal, and degraded race to perpetrate crimes and excesses similar to what were enacted in Hayti? This will never be tolerated by white men—by Americans.

The destiny of the negro when among the whites in tropical climes is slavery; and would it not be well that those slaves who, according to Jacob Omnium, are worked under the lash eighteen hours in Cuba, by the Spaniard, that their destiny were changed—that the mild system of slavery in practice in the Southern States were introduced into Cuba, or that Cuba fell into the possession of the United States, would not the physical condition of the African be made better by this change?

If it be true that the Negro is our equal, and that we enslave him, then we are acting unjustly, and the day of retribution will certainly come; but if it will be found upon investigation that he is naturally the white man's inferior, and that he alone is capable of undergoing tropical labor, then his proper place is in subjection to his natural master. The more this question is discussed, the more certain is it to be decided against Negro equality.

Should this volume be favorably received it will give me much satisfaction; should it not, I console myself with the reflection that one hundred years hence it will matter little. I have said what I thought, and spoken what I felt, regardless of consequences; believing as I do, in the language of the Apostle, "Prove all things; hold fast that which is good."

3.13. "The Crime against Kansas." Popular Sovereignty and the Struggle between Freedom and Slavery on the Western Plains

In May 1856, Senator Charles Sumner of Massachusetts delivered a sensational two-day address to the Senate, strongly criticizing southern attempts to impose slavery upon the territory of Kansas. Condemning southern intrusions into Kansas on behalf of slavery, he criticized President Franklin Pierce and members of Congress, notably Senators Andrew P. Butler of South Carolina and Stephen A. Douglas of Illinois, who in Sumner's words, had "raised themselves to eminence on this floor in championship of human wrongs." Butler and Douglas, he charged, could be compared to Miguel de Cervantes' characters, Don Quixote de la Mancha and Sancho Panza, the first of whom had "chosen a mistress who . . . , though ugly to others, is always lovely to him; I mean the harlot, Slavery." These and other blunt remarks provoked angry responses from southern senators and inspired a violent act of vengeance by Congressman Preston Brooks of South Carolina, a nephew of Senator Butler. Brooks stalked Sumner following his speech and at the first opportunity he physically assaulted him in the Senate Chamber. With a "gutta-percha" walking stick, he struck Sumner again and again, knocking him to the floor and inflicting severe damage to his health from which he never entirely recovered.

13. "Southern Chivalry—Argument versus Club's." Courtesy of Crown Publishers, New York.

Sumner's speech and the southern response it produced may be seen as a microcosm of the revulsion and anger that had developed on the issue of slavery throughout the United States, so unyielding and irreversible that far more damaging acts of mayhem seemed inevitable. As historian David Donald observed, "Northern outrage" over the attack on Sumner "can best be judged . . . in letters and diaries of unimportant citizens," and he offered the following remarkable example. " 'We are in great indignation here,' a Connecticut school girl told her parents. 'I don't think it is of very much use to stay any longer in High School, as the boys would better be learning to hold muskets, and the girls to make bullets.' " [63]

SOURCE: *The Crime against Kansas, Speech of Hon. Charles Sumner in the Senate of the United States, 19th and 20th May, 1856* (Cleveland: John P. Jewett, 1856), pp. 4–29.

MR. PRESIDENT:

Take down your map, sir, and you will find that the Territory of Kansas, more than any other region, occupies the middle spot of North

63. For a brilliant account of Sumner's speech, Brooks's assault on Sumner, and northern and southern responses to these events, see Donald, *Charles Sumner*, pp. 279–311.

America, equally distant from the Atlantic on the east, and the Pacific on the west. . . . Against this territory, thus fortunate in position and population, a Crime has been committed, which is without example. . . . Sir, speaking in an age of light and in a land of constitutional liberty, where the safeguards of elections are justly placed among the highest triumphs of civilization, I fearlessly assert that the wrongs of much abused Sicily, thus memorable in [Roman] history, were small by the side of the wrongs of Kansas, where the very shrines of popular institutions, more sacred than any heathen altar, have been desecrated; where the ballot box . . . has been plundered; where the cry "I am an American citizen" has been interposed in vain against outrage of every kind, even upon life itself. Are you against sacrilege?—I present it for your execration. Are you against robbery?—I hold it up for your scorn. Are you for the protection of American citizens?—I show you how their dearest rights have been closed down, while a tyrannical usurpation has sought to install itself on their very necks!

But the wickedness which I now begin to expose is immeasurably aggravated by the motive which prompted it. Not in any common lust for power did this uncommon tragedy have its origin. It is the rape of a virgin Territory, compelling it to the hateful embrace of Slavery; and it may be clearly traced to a depraved longing for a new slave State, the hideous offspring of such a crime, in the hope of adding to the power of Slavery in the National Government. Yes, sir, when the whole world . . . is rising up to condemn this wrong, and to make it a hissing to the nations, here in our Republic, *force*—ay, sir, **FORCE**—has been openly employed in compelling Kansas to this pollution, and all for the sake of political power. . . .

But this enormity, vast beyond comparison, swells to dimensions of wickedness which the imagination toils in vain to grasp, when it is understood that for this purpose are hazarded the horrors of intestine feud, not only in this distant Territory, but everywhere throughout the country. Already the muster has begun. The strife is no longer local, but national. Even now, while I speak, portents hang on all the arches of the horizon, threatening to darken the broad land, which already yawns with the mutterings of civil war. The fury of the propagandists of Slavery, and the calm determination of their opponents, are now diffused from the distant Territory over wide-spread communities, and the whole country, in all its extent—marshalling hostile divisions, and foreshadowing a strife, which, unless happily averted by the triumph of Freedom, will become war—fratricidal, parricidal war—with an accumulated wickedness beyond the wickedness of any war in human annals; justly provoking the avenging judgment of Providence and the avenging pen of history, and constituting a strife . . .

more than *foreign,* more than *social,* more than *civil;* but something compounded of all these strifes, and in itself more than war. . . .

But before entering upon the argument, I must say something of a general character, particularly in response to what has fallen from senators who have raised themselves to eminence on this floor in championship of human wrongs; I mean the senator from South Carolina [Mr. BUTLER], and the senator from Illinois [Mr. DOUGLAS], who, though unlike as Don Quixote and Sancho Panza, yet like this couple, sally forth together in the same adventure. . . . The senator from South Carolina has read many books of chivalry, and believes himself a chivalrous knight, with sentiments of honor and courage. Of course he has chosen a mistress to whom he has made his vows, and who, though ugly to others, is always lovely to him; though polluted in the sight of the world, is chaste in his sight;—I mean the harlot Slavery. For her his tongue is always profuse with words. Let her be impeached in character, or any proposition made to shut her out from the extension of her wantonness, and no extravagance of manner or hardihood of assertion is then too great for this senator. The frenzy of Don Quixote in behalf of his wench Dulcinea del Toboso is all surpassed. The asserted rights of Slavery, which shock equality of all kinds, are cloaked by a fantastic claim of equality. If the slave states cannot enjoy what, in mockery of the great fathers of the Republic, he misnames equality under the constitution,—in other words, the full power in the National Territories to compel fellow-men to unpaid labor, to separate husband and wife, and to sell little children at the auction-block,—then, sir, the chivalric senator will conduct the State of South Carolina out of the Union! Heroic knight! Exalted senator! A second Moses come from a second exodus!

But, not content with this poor menace, which we have been twice told was "measured," the senator, in the unrestrained chivalry of his nature, has undertaken to apply opprobrious words to those who differ from him on the floor. He calls them "sectional and fanatical;" and opposition to the usurpation in Kansas he denounces as "uncalculating fanaticism." To be sure, these charges lack all grace of originality, and all sentiment of truth; but the adventurous senator does not hesitate. He is the uncompromising, unblushing representative on this floor of a flagrant *sectionalism,* which now domineers over the Republic; and yet, with a ludicrous ignorance of his own position,—unable to see himself as others see him,—or with an effrontery which even his white head ought not to protect from rebuke, he applies to those here who resist his *sectionalism* the very epithet which designates himself. . . .

But I have done with the senator. There is another matter, regarded by him of such consequence, that he interpolated it into the speech of the senator from New Hampshire [Mr. HALE], and also announced that he had prepared himself with it, to take in his pocket all the way to Boston, when he expected to address the people of that community. . . . The North, according to the senator, was engaged in the slave-trade, and helped to introduce slaves into the Southern States; and this undeniable fact he proposed to establish by statistics, in stating which, his errors surpassed his sentences in number. But I let this pass for the present, that I may deal with his argument. Pray, sir, is the acknowledged turpitude of a departed generation to become an example for us? And yet the suggestion of the senator, if entitled to any consideration in this discussion, must have this extent. I join my friend from New Hampshire in thanking the senator from South Carolina for adducing this instance; for it gives me an opportunity to say that the northern merchants, with homes in Boston, Bristol, Newport, New York, and Philadelphia, who catered for Slavery during the years of the slave-trade, are the lineal progenitors of the northern men, with homes in these places, who lend themselves to Slavery in our day; and especially that all, whether north or south, who take part, directly or indirectly, in the conspiracy against Kansas, do but continue the work of the slave-traders, which you condemn. It is true—too true, alas!—that our fathers were engaged in this traffic; but that is no apology for it. . . .

As the senator from South Carolina is the Don Quixote, the senator from Illinois [Mr. DOUGLAS] is the squire of Slavery, its very Sancho Panza, ready to do all its humiliating offices. . . . Standing on this floor, the senator issued his rescript,[64] requiring submission to the usurped power of Kansas; and this was accompanied by a manner—all his own—such as befits the tyrannical threat. Very well. Let the senator try. I tell him now that he cannot enforce any such submission. The senator, with the slave power at his back, is strong, but he is not strong enough for this purpose. . . . Against him are stronger battalions than any marshalled by mortal arm— the inborn, ineradicable, invincible, sentiments of the human heart; against him is nature in all her subtle forces; against him is God. Let him try to subdue these. . . .

It belongs to me now, in the first place, to expose the CRIME AGAINST KANSAS, in its origin and extent. . . . I say Crime, and deliberately adopt this strongest term, as better than any other denoting the consummate transgression. . . . I do not go too far, when I call it the *Crime against Nature,* from which the soul recoils and which language refuses to describe. To lay bare this enormity I now proceed. . . .

64. The written answer of a Roman emperor or pope. Editor.

It has been well remarked by a distinguished historian of our country, that [in the Missouri debate] the slave interest, hitherto hardly recognized as a distinct element in our system, started up portentous and dilated, with threats and assumptions, which are the origin of our existing national politics. This was in 1820. The discussion ended with the admission of Missouri as a slaveholding State, and the prohibition of Slavery in all the remaining territory west of the Mississippi, and north of 36° 30', leaving the condition of other territory, south of this line, or subsequently acquired, untouched by the arrangement. Here was a solemn act of legislation, called at the time a compromise, a covenant, a compact, first brought forward in this body by a slaveholder, vindicated by slaveholders in debate, finally sanctioned by slaveholder votes, also upheld at the time by the essential approbation of a slaveholding President, James Monroe, and his Cabinet, of whom a majority were slaveholders, including Mr. Calhoun himself; and this compromise was made the condition of the admission of Missouri, without which that State could not have been received into the Union. This bargain was simple, and was applicable, of course, only to the territory named. Leaving all other territory to await the judgment of another generation, the South said to the North, Conquer your prejudices so far as to admit Missouri as a slave State, and, in consideration of this much-coveted boon, Slavery shall be prohibited forever in all the remaining Louisiana Territory above 36° 30'; and the North yielded.

In total disregard of history, the President [Franklin Pierce], in his annual message, has told us that this compromise "was *reluctantly* acquiesced in by the Southern States." Just the contrary is true. It was the work of slaveholders, and was crowned by their concurring votes upon a reluctant North. At the time it was hailed by slaveholders as a victory. Charles Pinckney of South Carolina, in an oft-quoted letter, written at three o'clock of the night of its passage, says, "It is considered here by the slaveholding States as a great triumph." At the North it was accepted as a defeat, and the friends of Freedom everywhere throughout the country bowed their heads with mortification. But little did they know the completeness of their disaster. Little did they dream that the prohibition of Slavery in the Territory, which was stipulated as the price of their fatal capitulation, would also at the very moment of its maturity be wrested from them.

Time passed, and it became necessary to provide for this Territory an organized government. Suddenly, without notice in the public press, or the prayer of a single petition, or one word of recommendation from the President,—after an acquiescence of thirty-three years, and the irreclaimable possession by the South of its special share under this compromise,—in vi-

olation of every obligation of honor, compact, and good neighborhood,—
and in contemptuous disregard of the sentiments of an aroused North, this
time-honored prohibition, in itself a Landmark of Freedom, was over-
turned, and a vast region now known as Kansas and Nebraska was opened
to Slavery. It was natural that a measure thus repugnant in character should
be pressed by arguments mutually repugnant. It was urged on two principal reasons, so opposite and inconsistent as to slap each other in the face;
one being that, by the repeal of the prohibition, the Territory should be left
open to the entry of slaveholders with their slaves, without hindrance; and
the other being that the people would be left absolutely free to determine
the question for themselves, and to prohibit the entry of slaveholders with
their slaves, if they should think best. With some, it was openly the extension of Slavery; and with others, it was openly the establishment of Freedom, under the guise of Popular Sovereignty. Of course, the measure thus
upheld in defiance of reason, was carried through Congress in defiance of
all the securities of legislation; and I mention these things that you may see
in what foulness the present crime was engendered.

It was carried, *first*, by *whipping in* to its support, through Executive influence and patronage, men who acted against their own declared judgment,
and the known will of their constituents. *Secondly*, by *foisting out of place*,
both in the Senate and House of Representatives, important business, long
pending, and usurping its room. *Thirdly*, by *trampling under foot* the rules of
the House of Representatives, always before the safeguard of the minority.
And, *fourthly*, by *driving it to a close* during the very session in which it originated, so that it might not be arrested by the indignant voice of the people.
Such are some of the means by which this snap judgment was obtained. If
the clear will of the people had not been disregarded, it could not have
passed. If it had been left to its natural place in the order of business, it could
not have passed. If the rules of the House and the rights of the minority had
not been violated, it could not have passed. . . . Sir, the Nebraska Bill was in
every respect a swindle. It was a swindle by the South of the North. It was, on
the part of those who had already completely enjoyed their share of the Missouri Compromise, a swindle of those whose share was yet absolutely untouched; and the plea of unconstitutionality set up—like the plea of usury
after the borrowed money has been enjoyed—did not make it less a swindle.
Urged as a Bill of Peace, it was a swindle of the whole country. Urged as
opening the doors to slave-masters with their slaves, it was a swindle of the
asserted doctrine of Popular Sovereignty. Urged as sanctioning Popular Sovereignty, it was a swindle of the asserted rights of slave-masters. It was a swindle of a broad territory, thus cheated of protection against Slavery. . . .

Its character was still further apparent in the general structure of the bill. Amidst overflowing professions of regard for the sovereignty of the people in the Territory, they were despoiled of every essential privilege of sovereignty. They were not allowed to choose their Governor, Secretary, Chief Justice, Associate Justices, Attorney or Marshal—all of whom are sent from Washington; nor were they allowed to regulate the salaries of any of these functionaries, or the daily allowance of the legislative body.

Mr. President, men are wisely presumed to intend the natural consequences of their conduct, and to seek what their acts seem to promote. Now, the Nebraska Bill, on its very face, openly cleared the way for Slavery, and it is not wrong to presume that its originators intended the natural consequences of such an act, and sought in this way to extend Slavery. Of course, they did. And this is the first stage in the Crime against Kansas.

But this was speedily followed by other developments. The bare-faced scheme was soon whispered, that Kansas must be a slave State. In conformity with this idea was the Government of this unhappy Territory organized in all its departments; and thus did the President, by whose complicity the Prohibition of Slavery had been overthrown, lend himself to a new complicity—giving to the conspirators a lease of connivance, amounting even to copartnership. The Governor, Secretary, Chief Justice, Associate Justices, Attorney and Marshal, with a whole caucus of other stipendiaries, nominated by the President and confirmed by the Senate, were all commended as friendly to slavery. . . . With such auspices the conspiracy proceeded. Even in advance of the Nebraska Bill, secret societies were organized in Missouri, ostensibly to protect her institutions, and afterwards, under the name of "Self-Defensive Associations," and of "Blue Lodges," these were multiplied throughout the western counties of that State, *before any counter-movement from the North.* It was confidently anticipated, that by the activity of these societies, and the interest of slaveholders everywhere, with the advantage derived from the neighborhood of Missouri, and the influence of the Territorial Government, Slavery might be introduced into Kansas, quietly but surely, without arousing a conflict; that the crocodile egg might be stealthily dropped in the sunburnt soil, there to be hatched unobserved until it sent forth its reptile monster.

But the conspiracy was unexpectedly balked. The debate, which convulsed Congress, had stirred the whole country. Attention from all sides was directed upon Kansas, which at once became the favorite goal of emigration. The Bill had loudly declared that its object was "to leave the people perfectly free to form and regulate their domestic institutions in their own way;" and its supporters everywhere challenged the determination of the question between Freedom and Slavery by a competition of emigration. Thus, while opening the Territory to Slavery, the Bill also opened it to emigrants from every quarter, who might by their votes redress the wrong. The populous North, stung by a strong sense of outrage, and inspired by a noble cause, poured into the debatable land, and promised soon to establish a supremacy of numbers there, involving, of course, a just supremacy of Freedom.

Then was conceived the consummation of the Crime against Kansas. What could not be accomplished peaceably, was to be accomplished forcibly. The reptile monster, that could not be quietly and securely hatched there, was to be pushed full-grown into the Territory. All efforts were now given to the dismal work of forcing Slavery on Free Soil. In flagrant derogation of the very Popular Sovereignty whose name helped to impose this Bill upon the country, the atrocious object was now distinctly avowed. And the avowal has been followed by the act. Slavery has been forcibly introduced into Kansas, and placed under the formal safeguards of pretended law. How this was done, belongs to the argument.

In depicting this consummation, the simplest outline, without one word of color, will be best. . . . I begin with an admission of the President himself, in whose sight the people of Kansas had little favor. And yet, after arraigning the innocent emigrants from the North, he was constrained to declare that their conduct was "far from justifying the *illegal* and *reprehensible* counter-movement which ensued." Then by reluctant admission of the Chief Magistrate, there was a counter-movement, at once "*illegal* and *reprehensible.*" I thank thee, President, for teaching me these words; and now I put them in the front of this exposition, as in themselves a confession. Sir, this "illegal and reprehensible counter-movement" is none other than the dreadful Crime—under an apologetic *alias*—by which, through successive invasions, Slavery had been forcibly planted in this Territory.

Next to this Presidential admission must be placed the details of the invasions, which I now present as not only "illegal and reprehensible," but also unquestionable evidence of the resulting Crime. The violence, for some time threatened, broke forth on the 29th November, 1854, at the first election of a Delegate to Congress, when companies from Missouri, amounting to upwards of one thousand, crossed into Kansas, and, with force and arms, proceeded to vote for Mr. Whitfield, the candidate of Slavery. An eye-witness, General Pomeroy, of superior intelligence and perfect integrity, thus describes the scene:

"The first ballot-box that was opened upon our virgin soil was closed to us by overpowering numbers and impending force. So bold and reckless were our invaders, that they cared not to conceal their attack. They came upon us, not in the guise of voters, to steal away our franchise, but boldly and openly, to snatch it with a strong hand. They came directly from their own homes, and in compact and organized bands, with arms in hand, and provisions for the expedition, marched to our polls, and, when their work was done, returned whence they came."

Here was an outrage at which the coolest blood of patriotism boils. Though, for various reasons unnecessary to develop, the busy settlers allowed the election to pass uncontested, still the means employed were none the less "illegal and reprehensible."

This infliction was a significant prelude to the grand invasion of the 30th March, 1855, at the election of the first Territorial Legislature under the organic law, when an armed multitude from Missouri entered the Territory, in larger numbers than General Taylor commanded at Buena Vista, or than General Jackson had within his lines at New Orleans—larger than our fathers rallied on Bunker Hill. Or they came as an "army of banners," organized in companies, with officers, munitions, tents, and provisions, as though marching on a foreign foe, and breathing loud-mouthed threats that they would carry their purpose, if need be, by the bowie-knife and revolver. Among them, according to his own confessions, was David R. Atchison, belted with the vulgar arms of his vulgar comrades.[65] Arrived at their destination on the night before the election, the invaders pitched their tents, placed their sentries, and waited for the coming day. The same trustworthy eye-witness whom I have already quoted says, of one locality:

"Baggage-wagons were there, with arms and ammunition enough for a protracted fight, and among them two brass field-pieces, ready charged. They came with drums beating and flags flying, and their leaders were of the most prominent and conspicuous men of their State."

Of another locality he says:

"The invaders came together in one armed and organized body, with trains of fifty wagons, besides horsemen, and, the night before the election, pitched their camp in the vicinity of the polls; and, having appointed their own judges in place of those who, from intimidation or otherwise, failed to attend, they voted without any proof of residence."

With force they were able on the succeeding day, in some places, to intimidate the judges of elections; in others, to substitute judges of their own appointment; in others, to wrest the ballot boxes from their rightful pos-

---

65. Senator from Missouri, advocate of the Kansas-Nebraska Bill, and leader of raids against Kansas. Editor.

sessors, and everywhere to exercise a complete control of the election, and thus, by a preternatural audacity of usurpation, impose a Legislature upon the free people of Kansas. . . . But it was not enough to secure the Legislature. The election of a member of Congress recurred on the 2d October, 1855, and the same foreigners, who had learned their strength, again manifested it. Another invasion, in controlling numbers, came from Missouri, and once more forcibly exercised the electoral franchise in Kansas.

At last in the latter days of November, 1855, a storm, long brewing, burst upon the heads of the devoted people. The ballot boxes had been violated, and a Legislature installed, which had proceeded to carry out the conspiracy of the invaders; but the good people of the Territory, born to Freedom, and educated as American citizens, showed no signs of submission. Slavery, though recognized by pretended law, was in many places practically an outlaw. To the lawless borderers, this was hard to bear; and, like the Heathen of old, they raged particularly against the town of Lawrence, already known, by the firmness of its principles and the character of its citizens, as the citadel of the good cause. On this account they threatened in their peculiar language, to "wipe it out." Soon the hostile power was gathered for this purpose. The wickedness of this invasion was enhanced by the way in which it began. A citizen of Kansas, by the name of Dow, was murdered by one of the partisans of Slavery, under the name of "law and order." Such an outrage naturally aroused indignation, and provoked threats. The professors of "law and order" allowed the murderer to escape; and still further to illustrate the irony of the name they assumed, seized the friend of the murdered man, whose few neighbors soon rallied for his rescue. This transaction, though totally disregarded in its chief front of wickedness, became the excuse for unprecedented excitement. The weak Governor, with no faculty higher than servility to Slavery,—whom the President, in his official delinquency, had appointed to a trust worthy only of a well-balanced character,—was frightened from his propriety. By proclamation he invoked the Territory. By telegraph he invoked the President. The Territory would not respond to his senseless appeal. The President was dumb; but the proclamation was circulated throughout the border counties of Missouri; and Platte, Clay, Carlisle, Sabine, Howard, and Jefferson [counties], each of them contributed a volunteer company, recruited from the roadsides, and armed with weapons which chance afforded—known as the "shot-gun militia,"—with a Missouri officer as commissary-general, dispensing rations, and another Missouri officer as general-in-chief; with two wagon-loads of rifles, belonging to Missouri, drawn by six mules, from its arsenal at Jefferson City; with seven pieces of cannon, belonging to the United States, from its arsenal at Liberty; and this formidable force, amounting to at least eighteen hundred men, terrible with threats, with oaths, and with whiskey, crossed the borders, and encamped in larger part of Wacherusa, over against the doomed town of Lawrence, which was now threatened with destruction.[66] With these invaders was the Governor, who by this act levied war upon the people he was sent to protect. . . . Thus was this invasion countenanced by those who should have stood in the breach against it. For more than a week it continued, while deadly conflict seemed imminent. I do not dwell on the heroism by which it was encountered, or the mean retreat to which it was compelled; for that is not necessary to exhibit the Crime which you are to judge. But I cannot forbear to add other additional features, furnished in the letter of a clergyman, written at the time, who saw and was a part of what he describes:

"Our citizens have been shot at, *and, in two instances, murdered,* our houses invaded, hay-ricks burnt, corn and other provisions plundered, cattle driven off, all communication cut off between us and the States, wagons on the way to us with provisions stopped and plundered, and the drivers taken prisoners, and we in hourly expectation of an attack. *Nearly every man has been in arms in the village.* Fortifications have been thrown up, by incessant labor, night and day. The sound of the drum, and the tramp of armed men, resounded through our streets; *families fleeing, with their household goods, for safety.* Day before yesterday, the report of cannon was heard at our house from the direction of Lecompton. Last Thursday, one of our neighbors,—one of the most peaceable and excellent men, from Ohio,—on his way home, was set upon by a gang of twelve men on horseback, and shot down. Over eight hundred men are gathered, under arms, at Lawrence. As yet, no act of violence has been perpetrated by those on our side. *No blood of retaliation stains our hands. We stand and are ready to act purely in the defence of our homes and lives."* . . .[67]

Five several times, and more, have these invaders entered Kansas in armed array; and thus five several times, and more, have they trampled upon the organic law of the Territory. But these extraordinary expeditions are simply the extraordinary witnesses to successive uninterrupted violence. They stand out conspicuous, but not alone. The spirit of evil, in which they had their origin, was wakeful and incessant. . . . Sir, what is man, what is

---

66. The day before Brooks assaulted Sumner the town of Lawrence was attacked. The "sack of Lawrence" marked the beginning of the frontier warfare known as "Bleeding Kansas." See Rawley, *Race and Politics,* p. 129. Editor.

67. Lecompton was the site of a referendum that illegally passed a proslavery constitution.

government, without security; in the absence of which, nor man nor government can proceed in development, or enjoy the fruits of existence? Without security, civilization is cramped and dwarfed. Without security, there can be no true Freedom. Nor shall I say too much, when I declare that security, guarded, of course, by its offspring Freedom, is the true end and aim of government. Of this indispensable boon the people of Kansas have thus far been despoiled—absolutely, totally. . . . Scenes from which civilization averts her countenance have been a part of their daily life.

3.14. The Dred Scott Decision (1857)

In the words of Don E. Fehrenbacher, an authority on the notorious Dred Scott case, the complex exposition of that case by Chief Justice Roger Taney before the Supreme Court on the eve of the Civil War "was not only a statement of southern assumptions and arguments but also an expression of the southern mood—fearful, angry, and defiant—in the late stages of national crisis." Fehrenbacher's keen analysis reveals, in fact, not only Judge Taney's biases, but a generalized commitment to inaccuracy and even some juggling of evidence needed to support his case. It is not true, for example, as Taney repeatedly told the Court, that blacks in the United States had never been and could not become citizens "within the meaning of the Constitution."[68]

The principal plaintiff in this case was a slave named Dred Scott whose owner, Dr. John Emerson, had taken him in 1834 from the slave state of Missouri to the Rock Island military post in the free state of Illinois where they resided until 1836, at which time Scott went with Emerson to Fort Snelling, a military base in the Louisiana Purchase territory where slavery had been banned by the Missouri Compromise of 1820. In 1836, while still at Fort Snelling, Emerson bought Harriet, a slave woman, who, with Emerson's consent, married Dred Scott. Then in 1838 the Army transferred Emerson to Jefferson Barracks in Missouri; and Dred Scott, his wife, and their infant daughter Eliza accompanied him to that slave state.

In 1846, the Scotts, by then parents of two girls, sued for their freedom in the Missouri Circuit Court of St. Louis, on grounds that, having resided in the Louisiana territory where slavery was illegal, they and their children were free. Although it was not unusual in Missouri and other border states

---

68. See Don E. Fehrenbacher, *Slavery, Law, and Politics: The Dred Scott Case in Historical Perspective* (New York: Oxford University Press, 1981).

for blacks to seek their freedom by legal means, their case was thwarted by technical weakness and in time transferred to the Missouri Supreme Court. During the following years, however, the case continued to be heard, until finally, with the possible support of abolitionists, it was taken on appeal to the U.S. Supreme Court in Washington. Argued in 1855–56, the Court concluded in 1857 (with two dissenting members), that Dred Scott was not a citizen of Missouri "in the sense in which that word is used in the Constitution." As a result, that court had no jurisdiction in the case, and the suit was dismissed. The Scott family had failed to gain their freedom, but two months later were transferred to another owner and promptly liberated. Dred Scott died of consumption only sixteen months after he became free.

SOURCE: *The Dred Scott Case, Three Volumes in One* (Plainview, N.Y.: The Black Heritage Library Collection, 1973), vol. 2, *The Dred Scott Decision: Opinion of Chief Justice Taney,* pp. 15, 17–22, 24, 29–32, 41–44.

Mr. Chief Justice TANEY delivered the opinion of the court. . . .

The question is simply this: Can a Negro, whose ancestors were imported into this country, and sold as slaves, become a member of the political community formed, and brought into existence by the Constitution of the United States, and as such become entitled to all the rights, and privileges, and immunities, guaranteed by that instrument to the citizen? One of which rights is the privilege of suing in a court of the United States in the cases specified in the Constitution.

It will be observed, that the plea applies to that class of persons only whose ancestors were negroes of the African race, and imported into this country, and sold and held as slaves. The only matter in issue before the court, therefore, is whether the descendants of such slaves, when they shall be emancipated, or who are born of parents who had become free before their birth, are citizens of a State, in the sense in which the word citizen is used in the Constitution of the United States. And this being the only matter in dispute on the pleadings, the court must be understood as speaking in this opinion of that class only, that is, of those persons who are the descendants of Africans who were imported into this country, and sold as slaves.

The situation of this population was altogether unlike that of the Indian race. The latter, it is true, formed no part of the colonial communities, and never amalgamated with them in social conditions or in government. But although they were uncivilized, they were yet a free and independent people, associated together in nations or tribes, and governed by their own laws. Many of these political communities were situated in territories to which the white race claimed the ultimate right of dominion. But that claim was acknowledged to be subject to the right of the Indians to occupy it as long as they thought proper, and neither the English nor colonial Governments claimed or exercised any dominion over the tribe or nation by whom it was occupied, nor claimed the right to the possession of the territory, until the tribe or nation consented to cede it. These Indian Governments were regarded and treated as foreign Governments, as much so as if an ocean had separated the red man from the white; and their freedom has constantly been acknowledged, from the time of the first emigration to the English colonies to the present day, by the different Governments which succeeded each other. Treaties have been negociated with them, and their alliance sought for in war; and the people who compose these Indian political communities have always been treated as foreigners not living under our Government. It is true that the course of events has brought the Indian tribes within the limits of the United States under subjection to the white race; and it has been found necessary, for their sake as well as our own, to regard them as in a state of pupilage, and to legislate to a certain extent over them and the territory they occupy. But they may, without doubt, like the subjects of any other foreign Government, be naturalized by the authority of Congress, and become citizens of a State, and of the United States; and if an individual should leave his nation or tribe, and take up his abode among the white population, he would be entitled to all the rights and privileges which would belong to an emigrant from any other foreign people.

We proceed to examine the case as presented by the pleadings.

The words "people of the United States" and "citizens" are synonymous terms, and mean the same thing. They both describe the political body who, according to our republican institutions, form the sovereignty, and who hold the power and conduct the Government through their representatives. They are what we familiarly call the "sovereign people," and every citizen is one of this people, and a constituent member of this sovereignty. The question before us is, whether the class of persons described in the plea in abatement compose a portion of this people, and are constituent members of this sovereignty? We think they are not, and that they are not included, and were not intended to be included, under the word "citizens" in the Constitution, and can therefore claim none of the rights and privileges which that instrument provides for and secures to citizens of the United States. On the contrary, they were at that time considered as a subordinate and inferior class of beings, who had been subjugated by the dominant race, and, whether emancipated or not, yet remained subject to their authority, and had no rights or privileges but such as those who held the power and the government might choose to grant them.

It is not the province of the court to decide upon the justice or injustice, the policy or impolicy, of these laws. The decision of that question belonged to the political or law-making power; to those who formed the sovereignty and framed the Constitution. The duty of the court is, to interpret the instrument they have framed, with the best lights we can obtain on the subject, and to administer, as we find it, according to its true intent and meaning when it was adopted.

In discussing this question, we must not confound the rights of citizenship which a State may confer within its own limits, and the rights of citizenship as a member of the Union. It does not by any means follow, because he has all the rights and privileges of a citizen of a State, that he must be a citizen of the United States. He may have all the rights and privileges of the citizen of a State, and yet not be entitled to the rights and privileges of a citizen in any other State. For, previous to the adoption of the Constitution of the United States, every State had the undoubted right to confer on whomsoever it pleased the character of a citizen, and to endow him with all its rights. But this character of course was confined to the boundaries of the State, and gave him no rights or privileges in other States beyond those secured to him by the laws of nations and the comity of States. Nor have the several States surrendered the power of conferring these rights and privileges by adopting the Constitution of the United States. Each State may still confer them upon an alien, or any one it thinks proper, or upon any class or description of persons; yet he would not be a citizen in the sense in which that word is used in the Constitution of the United States, nor entitled to sue as such in one of its courts, nor to the privileges and immunities of a citizen in the other States. . . .

The question then arises, whether the provisions of the Constitution, in relation to the personal rights and privileges to which the citizen of a State should be entitled, embraced the negro African race, at that time in this country, or who might afterwards be imported, who had then or should afterwards be made free in any State; and to put it in the power of a single State to make him a citizen of the United States, and endue him with the full rights of citizenship in every other State without their consent? Does the Constitution of the United States act upon him whenever he shall be made free under the laws of a State, and raised there to the rank of a citizen, and immediately clothe him with all the privileges of a citizen in every other State, and in its courts?

The court think the affirmative of these propositions cannot be maintained. And, if it cannot, the plaintiff in error could not be a citizen of the State of Missouri, within the meaning of the Constitution of the United States, and, consequently, was not entitled to sue in its courts. . . .

It becomes necessary, therefore, to determine who were citizens of the several States when the Constitution was adopted. And in order to do this, we must recur to the governments and institutions of the thirteen colonies, when they separated from Great Britain and formed new sovereignties, and took their places in the family of independent nations. We must inquire who, at that time, were recognized as the people or citizens of a State, whose rights and liberties had been outraged by the English Government; and who declared their independence, and assumed the powers of Government to defend their rights by force of arms.

In the opinion of the court, the legislation and histories of the times, and the language used in the Declaration of Independence, show, that neither the class of persons who had been imported as slaves, nor their descendants, whether they had become free or not, were then acknowledged as a part of the people, nor intended to be included in the general words used in that memorable instrument.

It is difficult at this day to realize the state of public opinion in relation to that unfortunate race, which prevailed in the civilized and enlightened portions of the world at the time of the Declaration of Independence, and when the Constitution of the United States was framed and adopted. But the public history of every European nation displays it in a manner too plain to be mistaken.

They had for more than a century before been regarded as beings of an inferior order, and altogether unfit to associate with the white race, either in social or political relations; and so far inferior, that they had no rights which the white man was bound to respect; and that the negro might justly and lawfully be reduced to slavery for his benefit. He was bought and sold, and treated as an ordinary article of merchandise and traffic, whenever a profit could be made by it. This opinion was at that time fixed and universal in the civilized portion of the white race. It was regarded as an axiom in morals as well as in politics, which no one thought of disputing, or supposed to be open to dispute; and men in every grade and position in society daily and habitually acted upon it in their private pursuits, as well as in matters of public concern, without doubting for a moment the correctness of this opinion.

And in no nation was this opinion more firmly fixed or more uniformly acted upon than by the English Government and English people. They not only seized them on the coast of Africa, and sold them or held them in slavery for their own use; but they took them as ordinary articles of merchandise to every country where they could make a profit on them, and were far more extensively engaged in this commerce than any other nation in the world.

The opinion thus entertained and acted upon in England was naturally impressed upon the colonies they founded on this side of the Atlantic. And, accordingly, a negro of the African race was regarded by them as an article of property, and held, and bought and sold as such, in every one of the thirteen colonies which united in the Declaration of Independence, and afterwards formed the Constitution of the United States. The slaves were more or less numerous in the different colonies, as slave labor was found more or less profitable. But no one seems to have doubted the correctness of the prevailing opinion of the time. . . .

Indeed, when we look to the condition of this race in the several States at the time, it is impossible to believe that these rights and privileges were intended to be extended to them.

It is very true that in that portion of the Union where the labor of the negro was found to be unsuited to the climate and unprofitable to the master, but few slaves were held at the time of the Declaration of Independence; and when the Constitution was adopted, it had entirely worn out in one of them, and measures had been taken for its gradual abolition in several others. But this change had not been produced by any change of opinion in relation to this race; but because it was discovered, from experience, that slave labor was unsuited to the climate and productions of these States: for some of the States, where it had ceased or nearly ceased to exist, were actively engaged in the slave trade, procuring cargoes on the coast of Africa, and transporting them for sale to those parts of the Union where their labor was found to be profitable, and suited to the climate and productions. And this traffic was openly carried on, and fortunes accumulated by it, without reproach from the people of the States where they resided. And it can hardly be supposed that, in the States where it was then countenanced in its worst form—that is, in the seizure and transportation—the people could have regarded those who were emancipated as entitled to equal rights with themselves. . . . We need not refer, on this point, particularly to the laws of the present slaveholding States. Their statute books are full of provisions in relation to this class. . . . They have continued to treat them as an inferior class, and to subject them to strict police regulations, drawing a broad line of distinction between the citizen and the slave races, and legislating in relation to them upon the same principle which prevailed at the time of the Declaration of Independence. As relates to these States, it is too plain for argument, that they have never been regarded as a part of the people or citizens of the State, nor supposed to possess any political rights which the dominant race might not withhold or grant at their pleasure. And as long ago as 1822, the Court of Appeals of Kentucky decided that free negroes and mulattoes were not citizens within the meaning of the Constitution of the United States.

The legislation of the States therefore shows, in a manner not to be mistaken, the inferior and subject condition of that race at the time the Constitution was adopted, and long afterwards, throughout the thirteen States by which that instrument was framed; and it is hardly consistent with the respect due to these States, to suppose that they regarded at that time, as fellow-citizens and members of the sovereignty, a class of beings whom they had thus stigmatized. . . . It cannot be supposed that they intended to secure to them rights, and privileges, and rank, in the new political body throughout the Union, which every one of them denied within the limits of its own dominion. More especially, it cannot be believed that the large slaveholding States regarded them as included in the word citizens, or would have consented to a Constitution which might compel them to receive them in that character from another State. For if they were so received, and entitled to the privileges and immunities of citizens, it would exempt them from the operation of the special laws and from the police regulations which they considered to be necessary for their own safety. It would give to persons of the negro race, who were recognised as citizens in any one State of the Union, the right to enter every other State whenever they pleased, singly or in companies, without pass or passport, and without obstruction, to sojourn there as long as they pleased, to go where they pleased at every hour of the day or night without molestation, unless they committed some violation of law for which a white man would be punished; and it would give them the full liberty of speech in public and in private upon all subjects upon which its own citizens might speak; to hold public meetings upon political affairs, and to keep and carry arms wherever they went. And all of this would be done in the face of the subject race of the same color, both free and slaves, and inevitably producing discontent and insubordination among them, and endangering the peace and safety of the State. It is impossible, it would seem, to believe that the great men of the slaveholding States, who took so large a share in framing the Constitution of the United States, and exercised so much influence in procuring its adoption, could have been so forgetful or regardless of their own safety and the safety of those who trusted and confided in them. . . .

No one, we presume, supposes that any change in public opinion or feeling, in relation to this unfortunate race, in the civilized nations of Europe or in this country, should induce the court to give to the words of the Constitution a more liberal construction in their favor than they were intended to bear when the instrument was framed and adopted. Such an argument would be altogether inadmissible in any tribunal called on to interpret it. . . . What the construction was at that time, we think can hardly admit of doubt. We have the language of the Declaration of Independence and of the Articles of Confederation, in addition to the plain words of the Constitution itself; we have the legislation of the different States, before, about the time, and since, the Constitution was adopted; we have the legislation of Congress, from the time of its adoption to a recent period; and we have the constant and uniform action of the Executive Department, all concurring together, and leading to the same result. And if anything in relation to the construction of the Constitution can be regarded as settled, it is that which we now give to the word "citizen" and the word "people."

And upon a full and careful consideration of the subject, the court is of opinion, that, upon the facts stated in the plea in abatement, Dred Scott was not a citizen of Missouri within the meaning of the Constitution of the United States, and not entitled as such to sue in its courts; and, consequently, that the Circuit Court had no jurisdiction of the case, and that the judgment on the plea in abatement is erroneous. We are aware that doubts are entertained by some of the members of the court, whether the plea in abatement is legally before the court upon this writ of error; but if that plea is regarded as waived, or out of the case upon any other ground, yet the question as to the jurisdiction of the Circuit Court is presented on the face of the bill of exception itself, taken by the plaintiff at the trial; for he admits that he and his wife were born slaves, but endeavors to make out his title to freedom and citizenship by showing that they were taken by their owner to certain places hereinafter mentioned, where slavery could not by law exist, and that they thereby became free, and upon their return to Missouri became citizens of that State.

Now, if the removal of which he speaks did not give them their freedom, then by his own admission he is still a slave; and whatever opinions may be entertained in favor of the citizenship of a free person of the African race, no one supposes that a slave is a citizen of the State or of the United States. If, therefore, the acts done by his owner did not make them free persons, he is still a slave, and certainly incapable of suing in the character of a citizen. . . .

In considering this part of the controversy, two questions arise: 1. Was he, together with his family, free in Missouri by reason of the stay in the territory of the United States hereinbefore mentioned? And, 2. If they were not, is Scott himself free by reason of his removal to Rock Island, in the State of Illinois . . . ?

We proceed to examine the first question.[69]

The act of Congress, upon which the plaintiff relies [the Missouri Compromise of 1820], declares that slavery and involuntary servitude, except as a punishment for crime, shall be forever prohibited in all that part of the territory ceded by France, under the name of Louisiana, which lies north of thirty-six degrees thirty minutes north latitude, and not included within the limits of Missouri. And the difficulty which meets us at the threshold of this part of the inquiry is, whether Congress was authorised to pass this law under any of the powers granted to it by the Constitution; for if the authority is not given by that instrument, it is the duty of this court to declare it void and inoperative, and incapable of conferring freedom upon any one who is held as a slave under the laws of any one of the States.

The counsel for the plaintiff has laid much stress upon that article in the Constitution which confers on Congress the power "to dispose of and make all needful rules and regulations respecting the territory or other property belonging to the United States:" but, in the judgement of the court, that provision has no bearing on the present controversy, and the power there given, whatever it may be, is confined, and was intended to be confined, to the territory which at that time belonged to, or was claimed by, the United States, and was within their boundaries as settled by the treaty with Great Britain, and can have no influence upon a territory afterwards acquired from a foreign Government. It was a special provision for a known and particular territory, and to meet a present emergency and nothing more. . . .[70]

At the time when [the Louisiana Purchase] was obtained from France, it contained no population fit to be associated together and admitted as a State; and it therefore was absolutely necessary to hold possession of it, as a Territory belonging to the United States, until it was settled and inhabited by a civilized community capable of self-government, and in a condition to be admitted on equal terms with the other States as a member of the

69. In the final paragraphs included here Taney presented arguments intended to invalidate that part of the Missouri Compromise banning slavery north of 36° 30' north latitude and, for good measure, offered a precedent from Kentucky law intended to prove that by the laws of Missouri Scott and his family were not free persons upon their entry into the state of Missouri. Editor.

70. The reference is to the Northwest Ordinance, which banned slavery in the territory north of the Ohio River, with the exception of French-owned slaves already there. Editor.

Union. But, as we have before said, it was acquired by the General Government, as the representative and trustee of the people of the United States, and it must therefore be held in that character for their common and equal benefit; for it was the people of the several States, acting through their agent and representative, the Federal Government, who in fact acquired the Territory in question, and the Government holds it for their common use until it shall be associated with the other States as a member of the Union.

Upon these considerations, it is the opinion of the court that the act of Congress which prohibited a citizen from holding and owning property of this kind [slaves] in the territory of the United States north of the line therein mentioned, is not warranted by the Constitution, and is therefore void; and that neither Dred Scott himself, nor any of his family, were made free by being carried into this territory; even if they had been carried there by the owner, with the intention of becoming a permanent resident.

We have so far examined the case, as it stands under the Constitution of the United States, and the powers thereby delegated to the Federal Government.

But there is another point in the case which depends on State power and State law. And it is contended, on the part of the plaintiff, that he is made free by being taken to Rock Island, in the State of Illinois, independently of his residence in the territory of the United States; and being so made free, he was not again reduced to a state of slavery by being brought back to Missouri.

Our notice of this part of the case will be very brief; for the principle on which it depends was decided in this court, upon much consideration in the case of Strader et al. *v.* Graham, reported in 10th Howard, 82. In that case, the slaves had been taken from Kentucky to Ohio, with the consent of the owner, and afterwards brought back to Kentucky. And this court held that the *status* or condition, as free or slave, depended upon the laws of Kentucky, when they were brought back into that State, and not of Ohio; and that this court had no jurisdiction to revise the judgment of a State court upon its own laws. . . .

So in this case. As Scott was a slave when taken into the State of Illinois by his owner, and was there held as such, and brought back in that character, his *status,* as free or slave, depended on the laws of Missouri, and not of Illinois.

It has, however, been urged in the argument, that by the laws of Missouri he was free on his return, and that this case, therefore, cannot be governed by the case of Strader et al. *v.* Graham, where it appeared, by the laws of Kentucky, that the plaintiffs continued to be slaves on their return from Ohio. But whatever doubts or opinions may, at one time, have been entertained upon this subject, we are satisfied, upon a careful examination of all the cases decided in the State courts of Missouri referred to, that it is now firmly settled by the decisions of the highest court in the State, that Scott and his family upon their return were not free, but were, by the laws of Missouri, the property of the defendant; and that the Circuit Court of the United States had no jurisdiction, when, by the laws of the State, the plaintiff was a slave and not a citizen. . . .

Upon the whole, therefore, it is the judgement of this court, that it appears by the record before us that the plaintiff in error is not a citizen of Missouri, in the sense in which that word is used in the Constitution; and that the Circuit Court of the United States, for that reason, had no jurisdiction in the case, and could give no judgement in it. Its judgement for the defendant must, consequently, be reversed, and a mandate issued, directing the suit to be dismissed for want of jurisdiction.[71]

3.15. "Slavery Fortifies in a Free People the Love of Liberty." A South Carolinian Calls for the Reopening of the African Slave Trade (1857)

As early as 1839 the abolitionist William Jay predicted that as the field for labor expanded in the South, southerners would begin to call for a renewal of the African slave trade with the alleged purposes of advancing the wealth and enterprise of the Southern states and Christianizing Africa's pagan people (see Bayard Tuckerman, *William Jay and the Constitutional Movement for the Abolition of Slavery* [New York, 1893], p. 151). At that time, in fact, some southerners were already calling for renewal of the traffic, a movement eventually led in the 1850s by Leonidas W. Spratt, editor of the Charleston *Standard* and author of articles and speeches on this controversial question (see Doc. 3.16). Typical of this variety of zealous propaganda is the following address to a local audience by one C. W. Miller of South Carolina.

71. Slavery was abolished in 1865 by the Thirteenth Amendment to the Constitution; and more relevant to Taney's views on citizenship, the Fourteenth Amendment states: "All persons born or naturalized in the United States, and subject to the jurisdiction thereof, are citizens of the United States, and of the State wherein they reside. No State shall make or enforce any law which shall abridge the privileges or immunities of citizens of the United States; nor shall any State deprive any person of life, liberty, or property, without due process of law." Editor.

Miller's arguments may be summed up as follows: Africans were needed to expand cotton and sugar production, to advance industry and commerce, and to elevate the South to new heights of progress and development. Slavery was sanctioned by God, by Jesus, and by his apostles. Reopening the African traffic would be moral and philanthropic, since it would rescue slaves from despotic bondage in Africa and transfer them to a "mild, humane servitude under Christian masters." Reopening the traffic would reduce the high slave prices caused by the banning of the African slave trade in 1808, allowing poor southerners to buy slaves and thus become more identified with slavery. Concerning the internal slave trade, Miller argued reasonably that if the African traffic was "wrong," it was no less wrong to buy and sell slaves internally. In his more exulted moments, he dreamt of new conquests that would elevate the South to splendorous heights. "Latin American lands," he intoned, "rich in soil and minerals . . . are destined for our possession." "The Southern people will have Mexico whenever it is needed," he claimed, and Cuba "beckon[s] us to come and possess her and enjoy her treasures." Finally, Miller's admission—that, in the event of a general slave emancipation, colonization to some other land would be indispensable—suggests that his supposed sympathy for the oppressed people of Africa was not deeply felt.

SOURCE: *Address on Re-opening the Slave Trade, by C. W. Miller, Esq., of South Carolina, to the Citizens of Barnwell at Wylde-Moore, August 29, 1857* (Columbia, S.C.: Steam Power Press of the Carolina Times, 1857).

Fellow Citizens: . . . We have reason to rejoice that we, in common with our fellow-citizens of the Union, are this day enjoying, in peace and prosperity, the blessings of civil and religious liberty, under a republican government; and our rising glory is brilliant and dazzling, even in comparison with the Majestic pomp, power and parade of trans-Atlantic and Oriental nations. Nevertheless, our Confederacy, and especially the slave-holding States, have not yet reached their culminating point of civilization, wealth and splendor. Great as we are, we are still in a state of progress; and the South will be slow in attaining her full and due growth in national greatness without the necessary additional labor which is alone to be supplied by re-opening the African Slave Trade. This subject I propose to discuss; and the time is come, not only for discussion, but for action. Europe clamors for more cotton than the world at present supplies; France has already contracted for 10,000 African slaves, called apprentices, to be employed in the West Indies; while the South, with 1,000,000 of square miles of territory, embracing cotton lands enough to supply the world, cultivates but 5,000,000 of acres in cotton—only one acre in 128 of her soil; and this is the best that can be done till Africa shall pour in upon us more of her population to reclaim our fertile lands. The high price and scarcity of cotton have stopped thousands of looms, and manufacturers are confining their operations to the finer fabrics, The want of labor has made sugar so dear as to be almost a mere article of luxury; and population, all the world over, is pursuing its natural law of out-running production. Nature has ordained that our best lands can only be cultivated, under our burning sun, by African muscle; and we see that with the requisite labor, our vast territory may sustain in comfort a population larger than that of China; that we may make every wilderness and every swamp now under the dominion of water a blooming garden, beautiful as a rice field; improve the whole face of the country with roads, canals, residences, churches, schools, colleges, manufactures, and other monuments of civilization; make ourselves independent, and the producers of grain and raw materials for the world; and on the wings of our own commerce carry them to every corner of the earth; so that the South may proudly lift her head pre-eminent among the nations, crowned with a chaplet more enviable than the diadems of Eastern royalty. But with this prospect before us, and the boon within our grasp, by re-opening the African slave trade, supine procrastination or political intrigue advises us to postpone discussion and action upon the subject. It is a subject of too much importance for delay; and, in discussing it, I will consider—

1. The morality of holding slaves and of reopening the slave trade.
2. The philanthropy of acquiring and holding African slaves.
3. The benefit to the South of re-opening the slave trade.
4. And the practicality of effecting it.

In the first place, I shall show, in few words, that the servitude of the African is in accordance with the will of Almighty God; and he who does the will of God cannot be in the wrong. . . . After the flood, when Noah and his three sons, Shem, Ham, and Japheth, were on earth the curse of servitude was denounced on the African race, through Noah, by inspiration from God.—(Brown's Bible Dc., Noah.)—Ham, after the flood, became the father of Canaan. Noah began to be a husbandman, and planted a vineyard. He, doubtless ignorantly and innocently, drank too freely of the wine which he had made; and as the book of Genesis (chap. 9) relates, becoming intoxicated and uncovered in his tent, Ham saw him and spoke of it to his two brothers.:

"And Ham, the father of Canaan, saw the nakedness of his father and told his brethren without.

"And Shem and Japheth took a garment and laid it upon both their shoulders, and went backward, and covered the nakedness of their father: and their faces were backward, and they saw not their father's nakedness.

"And Noah awoke from his wine and knew what his younger son had done unto him.

"And he said, Cursed be Canaan; a servant of servants shall he be unto his brethren.

"And he said, Blessed be the Lord God of Shem; and Canaan shall be his servant.

"God shall enlarge Japheth, and he shall dwell in the tents of Shem; and Canaan shall be his servant."

Both the curse and the blessings of Noah have been fulfilled in a wonderful manner. The descendants of Japheth conquered those of Shem and dwelt in their tents; and the posterity of Ham have been servants everywhere. . . . The curse of Noah upon Ham's posterity, as proclaimed against his son, Canaan, for the sin of the father, fell with awful severity on all his race, both in Asia and Africa. The Canaanites in Asia felt the scourge of a broken law, when conquered by the Hebrews; and in Africa the condition past and present of Ham's offspring but shows the certainty of God's avenging wrath. . . .

If any one doubts that slavery is sanctioned by Heaven, let him remember that even the Hebrews—God's chosen people—under their theocracy, held slaves. The patriarchs held slaves; and the good Abraham, the father of the faithful, had three hundred or more. In the march of the Israelites through the wilderness, after the Exodus, Heaven-directed by fire at night and by cloud in the day, slavery existed and accompanied them; and in the thunderings, and in the lightnings, in the earthquake, the smoke, and the trumpet-sounds of Sinai, when God delivered the ten commandments to Moses *(our moral law)*, slavery was recognized and impliedly sanctioned. In two of the commandments we find this: in that concerning the Sabbath, saying, "In it thou shalt do no work, thou, nor thy son, nor thy daughter, not thy *man servant, nor thy maid servant;* and also that concerning covetousness, saying, "Thou shalt not covet thy neighbor's house, *nor his man servant, nor his maid servant,"* &c. Would God have tolerated sin? When Jesus Christ came incarnate into the world he found slavery existing in Greece, Rome, Egypt, Judea, and almost everywhere among the nations. He came to inculcate a system of true religion and morality, as well as to atone with His blood for the sins of the world. He was God, and His mission divine. He fearlessly denounced wickedness everywhere. He attacked not only the religion of the Pagans, but what, in many instances, was politically, because morally wrong; and if he had thought slavery a sin, he would have denounced, condemned and forbidden it. But there is not a word in his teachings, nor those of his apostles, against it. On the contrary, we find it noticed and sanctioned in many places in the New Testament. . . . Paul, in his Epistle to the Collosians (chap. 3d), says: "Servants, obey in all things your masters, according to the flesh; not with eye-service, as men-pleasers, but in singleness of heart, fearing God; and whatsoever ye do, do it heartily as to the Lord, and not unto men; knowing that of the Lord, ye shall receive the reward of the inheritance, for ye serve the Lord Christ." What can the human mind discern in this Scripture, but an approval of slavery; that the servant is ordered to serve his master; and in so doing he serves God? All this is consistent with the law of God, which ordained slavery before Christ came, who came not to abrogate, but to fulfill the law. . . .

It will be useful, in this discussion, but curious and mournful, to take a rapid view of the government and some of the customs which prevail in Western Africa; whereby we shall be able to learn how important it is to the native African to be brought hither into contact with American civilization. The whole of Western Africa is divided into small kingdoms, governed by kings who rule over their people with the unrestrained authority of masters, exercising the most cruel and unmitigated despotism. Polygamy is universal with all classes, and the wife is the slave of her dusky lord, who has as many wives as he can buy; his respectability being great in proportion to their number. The parent is allowed to sell his offspring into slavery; and the price of a wife is generally some trifle—a few trinkets, a few yards of cotton cloth, a bottle of whiskey, or a cow. The rich buy all the women, and the poor young men are left to sigh and burn in despair with hopeless passion, or resort to artifices for stolen and unlawful gratification, which generally is connived at by the husband when grown, because his children being slaves, increase his wealth and power; and with a large number of wives, he gladly subsidizes the vigor or winks at the amorous intrigues of love-lorn poverty. Thus the land becomes broadcast with shameless adultery. I speak from knowledge derived from missionaries who have been among them for years, and who have found it utterly impossible to exterminate this system of abomination. There are, however, laws in Africa against conjugal infidelity, which sometimes are enforced. They have a curious institution in Senegambia, called *Mumbo Jumbo,* by which an erring wife, or anyone who has offended her husband, is punished and disgraced. . . . Such are some of the customs which, with indolence, theft, lying and cannibalism, make the native African the most corrupt and degraded human being on earth; and missionary labor has done little to Christianize, civilize or reform him; and never will effect much while he remains on his native soil. . . . But these people must and will be Christianized, because it is the will of God; and He has graciously made the white man instrumental in bringing thousands of them from their bondage and barbarism in Africa, and introducing them here to a mild, humane servitude, under Christian masters. . . .

It is not proposed, in re-opening the African slave trade, to institute anew the system of kidnapping, once practised, but to establish a lawful commerce in purchasing, for fair market value in Africa, such slaves as are held by masters there; and surely no one will say that it is wrong to purchase a slave from a barbarious [*sic*] tyrant in Guinea or Congo, to bring him hither, where he will have a good Christian owner, who will instruct him and provide for all his wants, and especially endeavor to illuminate the midnight darkness of his soul with rays of blissful light. If we are wrong to do this, we are equally or more wrong to buy slaves from each other in America. All that has been said of the horrors of the middle passage would be avoided in a lawful trade, since by the employment of steamers, doubt-less manned by abolitionists [?], negroes may be comfortably brought in a short time across the Atlantic, to our shores.

We see that re-opening the African slave trade is consistent with Chris-tianity and beneficial to the African; and now let us consider the benefits which will result from it to the Caucasian race; and especially to the South-ern section of the United States.

It is indispensibly necessary to have more slave labor to develop the agricultural and other resources of the Southern States, and to elevate our section to the highest condition of which it is capable, in wealth, intelli-gence and power. The slave holding States contain an area of 1,000,000 of square miles, or 640,000,000 of acres. Of this vast territory, only one acre in ten has been improved (see census of 1850), and this improved land em-braces all that has been merely fenced and used for uncleared pasture. Only 500,000 acres are planted in cotton, or one acre in 128. In the South West-ern States, where the best lands lie, only one acre in 20 has been improved, and of these improved lands a large portion is not cleared or planted. The best lands in the South lie under the dominion of water, subject to miasma, and the African race alone can reclaim them. The white man never will do this without the aid of negro slavery. Small as the proportion of land is that is cultivated, in the South, the cotton crop is over 3,000,000 of bales in good seasons, and the whole crops constituting the domestic exports of the South are, in round numbers, worth $172,000,000, while those of the Northern States are worth only $83,000,000 (see last report of U.S. Sec. of the Treasury). This shows what we are, and what we might be in the South, if our land was under extensive cultivation, instead of the small portion now producing crops; and the cultivation of even one half would leave forest land in abundance for all the uses to which it might be applied and for which it would be wanted in civilized life. If we wait for the natural increase of our 4,000,000 of slaves to supply us with labor to bring our country to a high state of improvement, we shall wait in vain. The world will grow hoary with age; generations will pass away; and the forests will perish and spring again out of their dust and ashes, before this desirable consummation will take place. We owe it to ourselves and posterity to make progress in this grand road to national greatness and individual prosperity, while we are on the earth and able to work. Then let us have no delay. If it be said that we have too many slaves, and their labor would thus be unprofitable, I answer that the number to be introduced from Africa may be graduated to the wants of the country by law so as to prevent too great an influx of slaves at one time. When new, untaught negroes come, it will require time to teach them, as well as time to procure them, and by proper laws the trade may be regulated for the public good. We cannot begin this enterprize too soon; we have not time to spare.

The number of slaves would not be too great if it was gradually increased to four times that of the white population of the South. At present, the white population doubles that of the slaves in our section—8,000,000 of white people against 4,000,000 of slaves.

Some ingenious writer has recently said that the area of the Mississippi basin is large enough and rich enough to sustain a population equal to that of the whole number of the human race on the globe. I am sure that comparing the Southern territory with that of Ireland and China, a population of 500,000,000 might be sustained in the slaveholding States, with more comfort than is enjoyed in either of those countries. . . . A member of Congress lately said that in one bend of the Mississippi river there was land enough to employ all the slaves in Virginia. This, too, is land which will produce 2000 pounds of seed cotton per acre, and ten bales may be made per hand.

By supplying the demand for slaves in the Western States from Africa, we will stop the drain from the Eastern and older States and thus keep them identified with the new States in supporting the institution.

The African slave trade must be opened to bring down the price of negroes. The demand for slaves in the Western states is so insatiable that ere long the cotton-growing region of the old Eastern States, South Carolina, North Carolina, Virginia and Maryland, will be exhausted of slave population. At sixteen cents a pound for cotton, the Western planter, in a good crop season, can make $1,000 a year per hand. He can afford to pay $2000 for a good negro man. The owners in the cotton region of the Eastern States cannot resist the temptation to sell their slaves at such prices; and in a few years there will be no slaves in these States, except among the rice-planters. What will be the effect of this? The low country rice planters, few in number, will have all the taxes to pay for the support of the State government; but they will have the preponderance in votes in the Legislature and will rule the upper country. I suppose they will hardly agree to pay all the taxes for the pleasure of ruling, and so they will sell their slaves too, and leave the State a pauper; for the wealth of the State consists chiefly in slaves. . . .

Fear has been expressed of insurrections if native Africans should be introduced. It will be seen that there is no danger from this source, when it is remembered that in many districts the slaves greatly outnumber the white people. In Georgetown, for instance, on some plantations, there are 500 slaves to one white man, and yet there is a perfect state of subordination. Successful insurrection would defeat the fiat of God which dooms the African to servitude. The negroes are utterly destitute of mental capacity to institute military combinations and campaigns.

By increasing the number of slaves here, the African slave trade would give additional strength and stability to the institution of slavery; and, certainly, when the fanatical spirit of the world is arraying a formidable opposition to the South, it is the part of wisdom and duty to fortify ourselves in every way and as speedily as possible. In the South, at least one half of the people are not slave-holders, because the price of slaves is so high that the honest poor man cannot buy them. Let the number be increased so as to bring down the price, and all the industrious, aspiring poor people will become slave-owners, become identified in feeling and interest with the institution; and when this is done, a pillar will be erected under the fabric of slavery which will render it impregnable against all the combined powers of abolitionists. It cannot be disguised that the man who is shut out by poverty and the high price of negroes from holding and enjoying this property, now held only by the rich or fortunate, will not have the same sympathy with slaveholders which interest would inspire. Nevertheless, I believe that the patriotic poor man, though not a slaveowner, who sees his country's power and glory dependent, as they are, on the continued existence of slavery, will arm and fight side by side with the rich in its defence. If, therefore, his condition and that of the country may be benefitted by re-opening the slave-trade, it is due to him, it is right and imperatively demanded by justice and the common good, that all classes in the South should unite to institute so desirable a measure of public policy.

All classes, rich and poor, will be benefitted. If the price of slaves be diminished, the rich can buy more, and all are slave-buyers. No one desires to sell, unless compelled by debt or some other cause to do so; and if slave labor is increased land will rise in price, because there will be greater demand for it; and this will more than compensate for any loss in the value of negroes. If cotton should fall in value, more can be made with additional and cheaper labor, more lands brought under cultivation and reclaimed, plantations better improved, better residences built, and all the comforts and luxuries of life increased. . . . Is it not tantalyzing to our people to know that they have millions of acres of the richest land in the world, and that a cruel legal restriction prevents them from acquiring the labor necessary to till them and to realize those visions of prosperity which are floating before their minds. . . . Labor is needed for clearing and draining new and fertile lands, for making railroads, for manufacturers and the mechanic arts. It is a proposition too well proved, that no nation can attain the highest degree of liberty, independence and power without the trinity of agriculture, manufactures and commerce. . . .

We cannot lift the veil which is spread before the future, but the probability is that when slavery shall reclaim our forests, drain our rich swamps, drive Neptune with his trident into the ocean, bring under cultivation all that is desirable in our present wide-extended country, Caucasian civilization will find then, and perhaps before then, other fields provided for its extension and for the employment of African labor. Toppling and crumbling governments in the South seem to invoke our aid, and lands rich in soil and minerals, now almost desolate, are destined for our possessions. The Southern people will have Mexico whenever it is needed; and Cuba, the beautiful queen of the Gulf, smiling upon us through her tears, "like gleams of sunshine 'mid renewing storms," beckon us to come and possess her and enjoy her treasures. African labor alone can make these fair realms valuable and profitable. With that the South will grow in wealth, beauty and power. Without it, rude nature will overrun all our improvements—assert her ancient empire over a howling wilderness—and our people will be doomed to a slow, terrapin progress, if not to a mournful retrogression.

The attempt of the Northern abolitionists to emancipate is so ridiculous and absurd as scarcely to deserve a notice. The present plan, as suggested by Elihu Burritt, is to raise money by contribution throughout the Union and elsewhere, to buy all the slaves at $250 each.[72] The value of

---

72. A New England Quaker and former blacksmith, known as the "Learned Blacksmith," Elihu Burritt, was a pacifist, abolitionist, and gifted linguist, who as a young man allegedly could read nearly fifty languages. Editor.

4,000,000 slaves at $500 each—about their market worth—would be $2,000,000,000, and at $250 each, just half that sum. Southern men, even if disposed to sell their slaves, would not take half price to please crazy abolitionists; and, if they could be induced to do so, fanaticism has not so overcome the love of money as to furnish the means to pay so large a sum. Besides this, there is no proposal to take the emancipated negroes away, or colonize them in another land. This would be indispensable to us, but would require so much more money as to make the scheme appear what it is, a mere vision of distempered fancy. . . .

Slavery fortifies in a free people the love of liberty and devotion to country. Men who are accustomed to be masters will not submit to aggression on their rights, or pale before the countenance of insolent tyranny. Slavery is one of the elements constituting Southern chivalry; and nowhere among the colonies of the Revolution was the motto of "Liberty or Death" followed and obeyed with more self-sacrificing enthusiasm than by the Southern people. . . .

The re-opening of the slave trade is practicable. The Constitution of the United States does not prohibit it, but simply provides that it should not be prohibited by Congress prior to 1808. After that period, Congress passed a law making it piracy to engage in this trade. Congress can repeal this law by a bare majority, and re-open the slave trade, with such regulations and restrictions as the interest of the South may dictate.

It is the true interest of the North to create this new order of things, because, among other investments, the North has $600,000,000 invested in manufactures, and would be benefitted by increased supplies of cotton and diminished prices of the article. The whole manufacturing world would be benefitted in the same way. . . . I believe that if we are true to ourselves in pressing this measure before Congress that the slave trade will be re-opened. If we put the issue to the North of dissolving the Union if the slave trade is not re-opened by Congress, we will succeed; because the North loves the Union more than it hates slavery. The South can do well without the Union, but the North cannot. . . . If Congress will not re-open the slave trade, it will be evidence that the North is resolved to go on in her struggle for emancipation, and to accomplish her own ruin by the pursuit of an *ignis fatuus*. If they abolish slavery, they abolish cotton, and thereby abolish manufactures; but I cannot think that they have lost their cunning and cupidity in following a vain phantom. The truth is there is a controlling conservative party at the North which will grant any reasonable demands of the South, rather than dissolve the Union. But if I am mistaken in this, and if the North shall refuse to re-open the slave trade, through

Congress, then let the Union perish; and we shall be able to form our own confederacy in the South. Whenever we do this, and re-establish the slave trade, the crippled North will woo us back into the Union with love charms and songs of melody, and wreathed smiles and flattering incense. We shall have the choice of accepting the proffered re-union, or of remaining content with the divorce. But should the North, on the other hand, assume an attitude of defiance, and refuse to allow us to leave the Union, for the purpose of treading freely our course to individual prosperity and national grandeur, we shall not be terrified. The contest will be settled on our own soil; and fighting, if it should come to war, for our own rights, it will only be necessary to show that we are not alarmed—that we are determined not to yield—and our astute enemy will politely retire. Who believes that in this civilized country, one section will invade another in a cause clearly wrong? The abolitionists may urge it, but the great mass of the northern people who, though free soilers, are sensible and conservative, will rebuke and crush the enterprise. . . . We need have no fear that war will come, and no fear if war should come.

Let us keep this ball in motion. Press our friends in Congress to make no delay in asking and even demanding a repeal of the law prohibiting the slave trade, and a new law re-opening it, with proper restrictions. When the abolitionists of the North learn that we are in earnest about this thing, they may be seized with dismay and strange horrors, but we must pursue our interest and our high destiny, by treading with firm and unfaltering steps the course which will lead us to prosperity, power and renown. The civilized world now looks to the South with wonder and respect; but it sees only an infant giant; it beholds only the dawn of our prosperity, the roseate and blushing Aurora, obscurely bright, gilding the sky with morn; but let the slave trade be re-opened, and soon, in a blaze of living light, our mid-day sun will shine.

3.16. "Every White Man of Capacity Will Own His Slave." L. W. Spratt Calls for a New Slave Trade and a New South (1858)

Horace Greeley of the New York *Tribune* dubbed the writer of the following essay, Leonidas. W. Spratt, of Charleston, South Carolina, "the philosopher of the new African slave trade," and according to Ronald Takaki, a historian of the movement to restore that trade, he "deserved the appellation" (see Takaki, *A Pro-Slavery Crusade*, p. 1). Greeley referred to Spratt's relentless involvement in the campaign to flood the South with Africans in order to achieve some bizarre and perhaps unachievable results: expansion of southern political power, reversal of the economic and social decline caused by prohibition of the African traffic half a century before, the arrival of new slaves, thereby increasing the population and offering new opportunities to less prosperous whites. Economic values would rise as Africans entered the country. By their presence they would halt the internal slave trade. Labor costs would decline. Cheap labor would increase land prices, adding to the wealth and progress of Southern society, and every enterprising white man would own his slave and enjoy his place in the system.

Spratt's zealotry seems to have triumphed over his logic. He appears to have given too little thought, for example, to the fact that the market for slaves in the deep South propped up slave prices in slave-exporting states, and therefore those states would not readily support renewal of the African traffic. Predictably, as much of the South was seceding from the Union following Lincoln's election, the state of Virginia, unwilling to jeopardize its southern slave market, refused to join the Confederacy if the foreign traffic in slaves was legalized. Since Virginia was seen as essential to the Confederacy, the writers of the Confederate constitution were obliged to maintain the ban on the African traffic. Spratt called this decision "a great calamity" and a "brand" upon slavery (see Takaki, *A Pro-Slavery Crusade,* pp. 232–43).

SOURCE: L. W. Spratt, *The Foreign Slave Trade. The Source of Political Power— of Material Progress, of Social Integrity, and of the Social Emancipation to the South* (Charleston, S.C.: Steam Power Press of Walker, Evans & Co., 1858).

No. I.
THE SOURCE OF POLITICAL POWER TO THE SOUTH.

The first consideration in favor of the Foreign Slave Trade is in the fact that it will give political power to the South. It were a fatal blindness to ignore the truth that the two great sections of this country are distinct, and a fatal error to suppose that there can ever be an equality of rights without an equality of political power to sustain them. If the North shall have an excess of population, and an excess of States, the North will govern. If the South shall have an excess of population, and an excess of States, the South will govern. . . . At present the North has a majority of two votes in the Federal, and of more than fifty in the Representative branch of the National Legislature; the North has a population of 16,000,000, while the South has a population of but 10,000,000. . . . Under such circumstances it were simplicity to suppose that political power between them can be equal. . . .

The slave trade will give us political power. Every 50,000 slaves that come will give us the right to 30,000 votes in the National Legislature,[73] and thus . . . will contribute directly to the political power of the South. But more than this. The labor basis at the South is too small to sustain even our present superstructure of direction. Slave labor is too efficient and too cheap to permit of hireling labor in competition with it. . . . There is no room, therefore, in the present condition of our labor system for the emigrant from other countries. By his own labor, he cannot live in competition with the slave here, and employing slave labor at cotton prices, he cannot live in competition with mechanical enterprises elsewhere. But by an increase of slaves the bases of our system would be widened. With more abundant operatives, there would be an occasion for more abundant intelligences to direct them. The 4,000,000 slaves we have, give employment and support to 6,000,000 white people; 1,000,000 more would but add to their capacity. In this regard, therefore, each slave might be said to bring his master with him, and thus to add more than twice his political value to the fortunes of the South.

Nor is this all. We have wanted Kansas,[74] and men have periled their lives and have perished to preserve it; but its preservation would have been easy with the Slave Trade. Ten thousand masters have failed to effect the social condition of that Territory. . . . But if, instead of 10,000 masters, we had sent 10,000 slaves, we would have effected every object we could have wished. Ten thousand of the rudest Africans that ever set their foot upon our shores, imported in Boston ships by Boston capital, and under a Boston slave driver, would have swept the free soil party from that land. There is not one amongst them who would not have purchased a slave at $150, (which would give an ample profit on the costs of importation,) and there is not a free-soiler alive, who, purchasing a slave at $150, would not be as strong a propagandist of slavery as ever lived. . . .

So taking Kansas, with her population of 100,000; so also we could take another State in Texas; another, or three or four, in New Mexico; another in Lower California; and as the slave, under the discipline and economies of slavery, has been capable of enduring any climate to which he has been taken, so also might we take Kansas, Utah, Oregon, and perhaps drive hireling labor back to its sterile fastnesses in New England. . . .

Slaves constitute the condition of slavery. Without them, there is no

73. The result of the "three-fifths compromise" in the Constitution by which five slaves were counted as three persons for purposes of taxation and representation in the House of Representatives. Editor.

74. A reference to the violent struggle in the 1850s between Free Soilers and pro-slavery settlers popularly referred to as "Bleeding Kansas." See Doc. 3.13. Editor.

hope of making a slave State; but with them, and representing as they do the cheapest form of labor, we may send them into any market where labor is to be paid for; and with them, therefore, in numbers sufficient to supply the wants of the expanding South, we must come to equality with the North in the popular branch of the national Legislature; we must equal and must soon surpass the North in States, and in this way, therefore, the road is direct and open to the utmost possible security of political power.

No. II.

THE FOREIGN SLAVE TRADE—
VALUE TO VESTED INTERESTS.

Another consideration in favor of the Foreign Slave Trade is in the fact that it will advance the value of vested interests at the South. In respect of such interests the South has been singularly unfortunate. At the North men sleep to opulence. Hemmed in by more restricted limits, and with a vast foreign population poured upon them, whose energies have given progress to every line of business, and value to every article of property; wealth rose around them; one road constructed paid from its profits the capital for another; lands purchased one year were worth twice as much the next; material space, opportunity, and steam and water power, all came to have a market. The constant tendency was upward; every object touched by human want was turned to gold, and thus it was that, without any extraordinary degree of enterprise, without any special, natural or political advantages, the people of that section have spread their sails upon billows of wealth, and have come to be regarded as the most enterprising people upon earth.

Not so, however, at the South. Here our limits were more extended by two hundred and forty-four thousand square miles, the energies and wants of no foreign people have been poured upon our soil, every source of external labor was cut off by the suppression of the Slave Trade. With a smaller population, and a larger surface, there has been no rise in the value of lands, for there have been no limits to rise against; no market for opportunity or powers, for there were enough for all; no want of space except in the vicinity of large cities; no profits, except in rare instances, for the want of a more abundant population, to canals and railroads. . . .

Such is not the future promised to our early history. In passing over the rural parishes of Charleston District, we are met by the remains of a most magnificent civilization. Upon the Ashley and Cooper Rivers there are mansions, some sustained and some in ruins, which attest prosperity and princely wealth. The Oaks, Otranto, Crawfield, Bloomingdale, Oak Hall, Archdale, Accabe and others must have been the scenes of a most expanded hospitality. They are yet surrounded by the lines of costly pleasure grounds, and are approached by avenues of oaks, perhaps the finest in the world. They were expanded to beauty and grandeur by the native Africans. Turned from the marts of Charleston upon the plantations of the District, they gave value to every foot of surface; they were purchased at moderate prices; the profits of one year's service were sufficient to purchase as many more the next; property accumulated in the hands of proprietors; every dollar invested was productive of another; swamps were drained; the landscape brightened; trades were started; arts flourished; commerce took up here her American home; ships sailed to every quarter of the globe; and a land so favored and so promising was never seen as that adjacent to the metropolis of South Carolina.

Such was the state of facts coincident with the importation of crude labor into South Carolina. . . . But when the fertilizing stream of labor was cut off, when the opening West had no fresh supply to meet its requisitions, it made demands upon the accumulations of the seaboard; the limited amount became a prize to be contended for. Land in the interior offered itself at less than one dollar per acre. Land on the seaboard had been raised to fifty dollars per acre, and labor, forced to elect between them, took the cheaper. . . . Lands on the seaboard were forced to seek for purchasers; purchasers came to the seaboard to seek for slaves. Their price was elevated to their value, not upon the seaboard, where lands were capital, but in the interior, where the interest upon the cost of labor was the only charge upon production. Labor, therefore, ceased to be profitable in the one place as it became profitable in the other. Estates which were wealth to their original proprietors became a charge upon the descendants who endeavored to sustain them. Neglect soon came to the relief of unprofitable care; decay followed neglect. Mansions became tenantless and roofless. Trees spring in their deserted halls and waive [*sic*] their branches through dismantled windows. Drains filled up; the swamps returned. Parish churches, in imposing styles of architecture, and once attended by a goodly company in costly equipages, are now abandoned. Lands which had ready sale at fifty dollars per acre now sell for less than five dollars; and over all these structures of wealth, with their offices of art, and over these scenes of festivity and devotion there now hangs the pall of an unalterable gloom.

It was thus that the tide of African labor swept upon the seaboard of the South to brighten every spot it touched; and thus, as it swept on, it left to gloom and desolation the ungrateful coasts so closed against it. It was a grave mistake—as grave in morals as in policy—to shut our ports upon the African. The civilization we possess was less a property than a trust for all the human race, and it was not for us to shut its light from those who, in no other way, could take its brightness. . . .

The experience of the Charleston District has been the experience, to a greater or lesser extent, of every other section of the South. Along the whole Atlantic seaboard, and, in fact, throughout all the Atlantic States, while the Slave Trade was open and labor came in excess of lands redeemed from the Western wilderness, lands rose in value, space was in requisition, improvements paid a profit, and every subject of human want came to value and found a market; but when lands came to be in excess of labor, values rolled off to the West. Extending over such a surface, they could not be sustained to elevation at any particular point, and, like Charleston District, almost the entire South has felt its interests vibrate with the tide of labor.

So vibrating once, it is reasonably certain that, from the same cause, they will so vibrate again. Foreign slave labor might not stop now, as it did before, on the seaboard. It may roll into the interior; but, in either case, the result will be the same. If it shall stop upon the seaboard, values will rise there, and roll, step by step, with labor to the West; or if it shall go first to the West, it will satisfy the wants for labor there. It will arrest the transportation of labor from the older States, and force it back to work upon itself. In either case, population would be increased, labor would become more abundant, and to the extent to which these results shall be effected will there be advancement to vested interests at the South. . . .

That slave labor for all the ruder offices of life, with the slave trade, will be cheaper than free labor, there can be no question. The slave can be landed on our coast for fifty dollars; his training may cost fifty dollars more; he can be fed and clothed under the economies of a plantation for less than twenty-five dollars per annum, and twenty-five dollars therefore and the interest and insurance on $100 will be all the cost of his employment. . . . If this cheaper labor will give increased value to lands, so also will it give increased value to timber, mines, water-power, factories, establishments for industry and art, and to every other thing in fact which can become the subject of its employment; and lands will rise, and swamps will be drained and rendered property—timber, mines, ways, powers and privileges will come to market. Values will swell around us.

It will doubtless be excepted to the sufficiency of this argument that imported slaves will lower the price of those already in the country, and that thus . . . what may be gained in one species of property may be lost in another. But the objection is invalid. The Slave Trade will not cheapen slaves, but will only give a cheaper form of slave labor. Those we have will not be less valuable to us (the products of slave labor being as profitable as they are,) if native Africans were offered in the market at $100 per head. We would not sell, but we would buy, and all we have would be of even greater value in bringing the recruits into subjection. There are men in debt who look to the sale of slaves to pay them out; but even these would find it cheaper to double their force and pay their debts by their production.

The products of slave labor would still be as profitable. It is possible, if the energies of a much larger force were concentrated upon cotton, the price of that single staple might sink at least to the point at which it would stop production in Egypt and the East; but it is to be doubted whether this would be a very great calamity. . . . [S]lave labor is by no means dependent upon cotton: sugar, coffee, rice, tobacco, hemp, the fruits and the grains, the grasses and the arts, are waiting and ready at hand. For the reason that it is the most efficient form of labor this world has ever known, it has taken the monopoly of cotton; and for the reason that cotton is the most common want of the world, it has found in that pursuit alone, a sufficient sphere for its employment. But let it drug the world with cotton, and it will find the harvest of a monopoly in every other field on which it enters. The value of slave labor remaining the same, it can be no cause of complaint that slaves may be purchased cheaper. But if foreign slaves shall be purchased cheaper, it by no means follows that trained slaves will be cheaper also. On the contrary, it is to be questioned whether they will not be elevated to the higher office of instruction, and in that office find even a higher range of value.

No. III.

THE FOREIGN SLAVE TRADE— REINTEGRATION OF SOCIETY AT THE SOUTH.

Another consideration in favor of the Foreign Slave Trade is in the fact that it will tend to restore integrity to the social system of the South. . . . Our society is good, the best perhaps the world has ever seen, and much of its excellence is attributable to the fact that, to an extent at least, it is effected by the condition of domestic slavery. But the system has not been formed to perfect purity. Up to the suppression of the Foreign Slave Trade the two constituents were free to come. The white race took the offices of direction, the black the offices of labor. When direction was in excess it attracted labor, when labor was in excess it attracted direction, and hand in hand they went together to the formation of a balanced system. But when colored labor was cut off there was no possibility of continuing further the process of a natural formation. Without more slaves there was no room in slavery for more white men; such as came must come not to union with the slaves, but to competition with him. . . .

Now this condition is not natural and necessary to the South. Free laborers are not in competition with our slaves from any fancy which they have for that position. Each would own a slave if he could get him, and owning one slave would be as much a slave owner as if he held a hundred. But under present circumstances there is no chance to alter his position. . . . But with slaves in excess of whites, there would be none excluded from a chance of sharing in the system, and with slaves at prices approaching to the costs of importation, there is no laboring man who could not raise the fund, and scarce a man who would not make the purchase.

It is thus that the differences at the South will be harmonized by the Foreign Slave Trade. Every white man of capacity will own his slave. Every man of enterprise will own his labor. All of the ruling race will come to the same social stand point; all will cast their votes from the same position; as well at home as abroad, they will have a common interest, and a common cause; the institution of American slavery will become reintegrated and erect and so compact and firm, will stand not only to sustain itself, but to sustain the South, sublime and composed among all the storms that rage among other nations of the earth. . . .

No. IV.
THE FOREIGN SLAVE TRADE NECESSARY TO THE SOCIAL EMANCIPATION OF THE SOUTH.

Another consideration in favor of the Foreign Slave Trade is the fact that it will give social emancipation to the South. In after years it will be curious to look back upon the present position of the South. I have no doubt but that slavery will stand; and standing with this Union or without it, will come to be the constituent of a most imposing nationality. When this will happen it will be difficult to realize that we have ever stood in our present social and political relations to the North. The slave States were parties to the original contest for American Independence; they shared in the perils and privations of that struggle; they came as equal members to the convention that formed the Constitution; they took their equal stations under the present Government; they brought a social system as vital to themselves as is the democratic system to the North. That system exhibited as many evidences of propriety and power; it has been distinguished by as many indications of Divine approval; it has contributed as much to raise the character of the nation; it gives order to the South; it is the stay of order in the Union; by its peculiar products, it binds the world in peace towards us; it gives elevated names to history—fair and virtuous women to their homes—three million five hundred thousand of a race of savages to the works of civilization, and three-fourths of our exports to the commerce of the country; and yet, through this career of great achievements, it has borne the brand of reprobation. The North takes credit for piety and virtue in condemning us, and we ourselves, . . . the depositors of the great trust, have shrunk from its affirmance. . . .

It is not my present purpose to inquire as to the correctness of this position. Slavery may seem right or wrong to Congress, but it is enough for us that it is our form of society—the institution with which our hopes and fortunes are associated . . . ; and it is time that the social emancipation of the South should come; it is time that Congress should stand before the world in equal relations to the North and South; and time, therefore, that the discrimination to the prejudice of slavery, consisting in restriction on the Foreign Slave Trade, should be removed. . . .

No. V.
THE FOREIGN SLAVE TRADE—OBJECTIONS: FIRST, THAT IT IS WRONG.

Having presented the most obvious considerations in favor of the Foreign Slave Trade, I come next in order to objections. . . .

There are slaves in Africa—writers say that these amount to five-sixths of the entire population. The number may be overestimated, but of the fact of the existence of that condition, there can be no doubt. Now, it is asserted that it is wrong to import these slaves, while it is not wrong to transport domestic slaves from the seaboard to the west. But is there ground for this distinction? . . . With respect to the slave that is offered in the markets of Charleston, I am as far from the ownership by prescription [long-term ownership] as I am of the slave that is offered on the coast of Guinea; and if I may buy him and transport him where I please, for the reason that he is already in a condition of subjection in the one case, so also may I in the other, and he who finds no wrong in purchasing a slave he never owned at home has nothing to say to me for purchasing a slave I never owned abroad. . . . If slavery be right, there can be no wrong in the foreign, whatever there may be in the domestic slave trade. It may be wrong to drag the slave about and tear him from the roots of his affections, but it can never be wrong to bring him to the point at which his union with a higher race is possible, and where he may become the part of a living system of the social world.

No. VI.
OBJECTION SECOND—INHUMANITY OF THE SLAVE TRADE.

It is further objected to the Foreign Slave Trade, that it is attended by too many barbarities to be tolerated by a civilized people; and men who see no wrong in slavery or in the trade in slaves, at home, are yet intensely sensitive of some great enormity in such a traffic the instant it extends beyond the water. . . .

Are there indeed grounds for this distinction? The native African is a poor, uninformed, brutal creature—at best the slave of his appetites and passions; and, if a slave, the slave of appetites and passions as brutal as his own. If a slave, therefore, there can be no question of advantage in his advancement to a life of service in a civilized community. But if a freeman, even, he presents but little claim to commisseration. He comes from barbarism to civilization; from heathenism to Christianity, from a life of war to one of peace; from liability to be taken and eaten at any moment by a lurking adversary, to a condition in which external harm can never happen to him, and though this be a life of servitude, it is one of usefulness, and one in which there is abundant room for the exercise of virtue and every valuable power he may possess. In this there is little to excite the commisseration of enlightened philanthropy, and it is indeed to be doubted whether there have been other savages born in the wastes of Africa, or upon the wastes of any other savage country, so truly blessed as have been the 400,000 Africans who, during the continuance of the slave trade, were transported to the South. . . .

There are those, however, whose chief objection to the Foreign Slave Trade is in the horrors that attended its operation. They are taught to believe that the masters of slave vessels are cruel and blood-thirsty; that the vessels are necessarily small; that the accomodations and comforts are necessarily insufficient; that a large proportion must die, and be thrown overboard; and that the rest can scarcely live. Much of this, as a fact, has been doubtless true. The earlier navigators were rather rude; there was less philanthropy, perhaps less humanity, in those days than there is at present. The lives of slaves were not much regarded, and it is probable, therefore, that in the slave trade, as in most great movements during the 17th and 18th century, there was much to disapprove of; but of these pictures the larger part was doubtless fancy. About the beginning of the present century it became fashionable, and afterwards profitable, to decry the slave trade. . . . With abuse on one side, and without defence on the other, it could not chance but that the truth should be lost sight of. But I would ask whether it ever could have happened but that the slave on board the vessel was not worth his value to the owner . . . and whether, while then, as now, men were considerate of their interests, it could have been that these owners threw away their slaves unnecessarily? or that they did not take every reasonable care of them? . . .

It is urged, however, as another ground of humanity, that the trade in slaves will start the tribes to war upon each other. This, if true, would be important, but is it true that those tribes would be at peace without the slave trade? On the contrary, it is the testimony of all who have ever known that country, that there never was, there is not, and as far as human judgement goes, there never will be a period when they are not at war upon each other. They were at war before the slave trade was started with the Western World; they were at war while the slave trade lasted, and they have been at war since it was supposed to have been arrested. It is, in fact, the condition of savage life—not in Africa alone, but the world over, that they are to war upon each other until each poor tribe is exterminated by the one that, by some accident, becomes the stronger. It is so with the tribes in Africa and the Southern and Pacific Islands. It was so with the savages on this continent, and it must be so while there is a race on earth that cannot find sufficient range for its energies in arts or peace. . . .

I have said that if our sympathies are for the negro race, it were as well to give a share to those amongst us, and in one respect the stoppage of the slave trade has not advanced their fortunes. When the Foreign Slave Trade was in operation, the location of the slave was permanent. When planted upon one spot, he was generally permitted to remain, and further importations, to a great extent, supplied the further requisitions of the West. While that condition lasted he was in the way of advancing from the nature of a mere chattel to a kind of inheritance in the estate. In fact it had become the custom to sell lands and slaves together, and even yet there is the feeling in this State for such relation, and there is unwillingness to sell or buy the one without the other. . . . But when the slave trade was arrested, the wants of the West came rudely in; they tore him from home; his little community was scattered; his customs broken up; he was taken to one place but to be removed to another; all sense of his right to a permanent relation to the soil has been lost, and he is now as mere a chattel as was his progenitor when he was landed one hundred years ago upon our shores. . . .

No. VII.
FOREIGN WAR—VIOLATION OF THE CONSTITUTION—DISSOLUTION OF THE UNION.

In the course of this discussion I have shown, or sought to show, that "The Foreign Slave Trade will restore political power to the South;" "that it will give material progress to the South;" "that it will give value to vested interests of the South;" "that it will give integrity to society at the South;" and "that it will give social emancipation to the South." . . . But if I shall have succeeded in establishing all these propositions, I am conscious, still, that I will not have cleared the question. We are still assured that this movement will occasion foreign war; that it will violate the Constitution; and last and worst of all, that it will certainly cause a dissolution of the Union; and to the consideration of these questions I will devote the closing number of this series.

If the Foreign Slave Trade will lead to war, it is, perhaps, enough to say we cannot shrink from even that emergency. Vested with the trusts of a great truth, if we can only advance to the greatness and glory of its promise through the fiery trials of a foreign war, then to even that ordeal we must commit the arbitrament of the great question.

But there will be no foreign war. It is a mistake that European States are tender on the score of human rights. . . . Nor have they repugnance to slavery. Russia has the serfdom of an equal race, with no crusade against her; Spain has slaves and incurs no war in adding to their number; Turkey has slaves, and States combine to bolster up her nationality; England still retains her fleet in the Black Sea to keep open the trade in Circassians to the markets of Constantinople; both England and France are taking slaves (though under subterfuge, 'tis true,) from Africa to their West India Islands, and the very Africa for whose rights and interests it is supposed they will go to war, has four-fifths of her savages in hopeless bondage to masters as savage as themselves. . . .

With respect to the objection that the Foreign Slave Trade would violate the compromises of the Constitution, but little need be said. If true that the Constitution has been found restrictive of advancement in any section of the Union, that of itself would be sufficient to justify a change of that instrument. But it is not true. The Constitution says the slave trade shall not be arrested before the year 1808, but it no where says that it shall be arrested then or at any other time, and as the "powers not expressly granted to Congress" are "reserved to the States respectively," it may be justly argued that not only was it not obligatory on Congress to restrict the Slave Trade, but that there never was the power to do so, and that the States are still as sovereign with respect to this power and as much at liberty to continue that branch of commerce as they were before the Constitution was adopted. . . .

Nor is there danger of a dissolution of the Union. The North wants cotton. She is scarcely less dependent upon it than England, and the logic is conclusive to the common mind, that more slaves will give more cotton. She also wants profits from her capital and the use of her ships, and no trade in the world will pay so much as the trade in Foreign Slaves. The proposition to reopen the Foreign Slave Trade, therefore addresses the two most powerful interests of the North. . . .

Nor is it true that the North would thus be left in possession of the common glories of the country. It is true they write our history, and industriously assume the first position upon its pages, and, with extreme solicitude to claim advantages, they might possibly, to some extent, secure them; but there are facts of our country's history, of which they can never rob us. They can never rob us of the names of Washington, Jefferson, Henry, Campbell, Shelby, Morgan, Rutledge, Laurens, Pinckney, Marion, Sumter, and a host of others; they can never rob us of the battle fields of Eutaw, King's Mountain, Cowpens, Yorktown, and the recollection of the facts that while the Union fought the battles of the North throughout the Revolutionary war, the South through many dreary years of that contest, sustained herself unaided and alone.

It is not safe, therefore, to assume that the South is under any especial obligations of sentiment or interest to preserve the Union. The Union is dear to us—dear from the history of its achievement, and dear from the advantages which have resulted and which can yet result. Under its cover from external interference we have securely framed the most admirable contrivances for civil liberty, and if secure under its protection, we yet may make still greater progress; but dear as [the Union] is, there are objects dearer—dearer are the rights which we have inherited, and dearer are the hopes and duties of advancement; and, dear as is this Union, if we can only share it with delirium and ribaldry—if our life of existence is to be an eternal war with madmen, whose only checks are the guards we have the strength to throw around them, without a helping hand from that society whose proper charge it is to relieve us from the pressure and the peril, and if the trust of our society is a trespass upon these, and its progress is an outrage for which it is merit and magnanimity to drag us before the tribunals of the world, then are we committed to leave it.

3.17. "Moral Antiques." The Letters of C. A. L. Lamar, Slave Trader, and Promoter of a New African Slave Trade (1857–1859)

Thirty years after the Civil War an unnamed person on a summer vacation allegedly discovered in a New England paper mill a notebook containing copies of letters written by one C. A. L. Lamar of Savannah, Georgia, a cousin, he correctly surmised, of Lucius Quintus Cincinnatus Lamar, President Cleveland's secretary of the interior. The journal, its finder decided, had perhaps been confiscated during Sherman's march to the sea and taken north, where it had possibly fallen into "unappreciative hands" and so was intended for destruction. Aware of the historical importance of the letters, however, their discoverer arranged to publish excerpts from them in *The North American Review.* "Mr. Lamar's views are no longer entertained," he wrote in his preface, "even in Georgia and the Carolinas; but they seem too good, in their historical aspect, not to be given to the public. They are moral antiques which still form a very interesting study."

Unlike most slave traders, who entered that business to enrich themselves, a wealthy man like Lamar might have done so mainly on ideological grounds, or to gain favor with pro-slavery associates. Whatever the case, it was only after the irascible Lamar had lost much of his personal wealth in uncompromising efforts to renew the traffic that he at last made it known to a friend that he was "in it for the dollars."

SOURCE: *The North American Review* 360 (November 1886): 449–60.

Lamar to the Secretary of the Treasury, Howell Cobb, Complaining of the Seizure of one of His Slave Ships, July 27, 1857.

I am loth to trouble you again, but your damned sap-head of a Collector [one John Boston] refused to do anything. . . . He detained my vessel eight days after she was ready for sea, and after she had applied for her clearance-papers. Mr. Boston said she was not "seized," but merely "detained." He said the Department would respond to any demand I might make for damages, &c. The District Attorney, and all the lawyers to whom he applied for advice, told him that there was nothing to cause suspicion to attach to the vessel, and he had best discharge her. . . . I claim $150 per day, damages, for said detention. That I did not expect him to pay, without referring it to the Department. But then I have a claim for storage and wharfage of the cargo, . . . and he declined to pay it. . . . I appeal to you for both claims: viz.—

> 8 days' detention at $150 per day $1,200
> Wharfage, landing, shipping and storage . . . . <u>120</u>
> $1,320

Will you please give the matter your attention? . . . I did not, in my other communication, disclaim any intention of embarking in the Slave-trade, nor did I say anything to warrant you in supposing I was not engaged in it. I simply declared that there was nothing aboard except what was on the manifest, and that I insist there was nothing suspicious on it. I will now say, as the vessel is 1,000 miles from here, that she was as unfit for a voyage to import negroes as any vessel in port. . . . What she may hereafter do, is another matter, which don't concern the present issue. John Boston had her detained because he says he knew she would be engaged in the trade, and had heard that from men who confessed that they were eavesdroppers, who hung around my windows to listen to all conversations that took place. I applied to Ward to write you. He says Boston is unfit for office and ought to be turned out, but the question with him is, who would do to put in. . . . It is a notorious fact that Boston is a natural "Know Nothing." He knows nothing of what is going on in the office:—leaves everything in the hands of John Postell, who is an "acquired K. N., and still hangs on, notwithstanding the abolition tendency of the party North. . . ."

Lamar to his father, Gazaway Bugg Lamar, Who Clearly Doubted the Wisdom of His Son's Activities, October 31, 1857.

I have yours of the 30th. . . . You need give yourself no uneasiness about the Africans and the Slave-Trade. I was astonished at some of the remarks in your letter; they show that you have been imbued with something more than the "panic" by your association North. . . . For example, you say: "An expedition to the moon would have been equally sensible, and no more contrary to the laws of Providence. May God forgive you for all your attempts to violate his will and his laws." Following out the same train of thought, where would it land the whole Southern community? Did not the negroes all come originally from the Coast of Africa? What is the difference between going to Africa and Virginia for negroes? And, if there is a difference, is not the difference in favor of going to Africa? You need not reproach yourself for not interposing with a stronger power than argument and persuasion, to prevent the expedition. There was nothing you or the Government could have done to prevent it. Let all the sin be on me. I am willing to assume it all. . . .

Lamar to N. C. Trowbridge, a Fellow Slave Trader from New Orleans, Reporting on an Early Failure and Future Plans, November 5, 1857.

Dear Trow: . . . I am truly glad to find that Grant [commander of Lamar's ship] is at least honest. He has acted badly, and sacrificed our interest most shamefully. His clearance-papers would have taken him anywhere he wanted to go, unmolested. Why did he not return directly to Savannah? What took him to the West Indies? Why did he sell any of the outfit? He knew the vessel was fitted for nothing else but the trade, and ought to have known we would want to send her back. Put her up for freight for Savannah, and send her here. I will send her on a trip to Cuba, and in the meantime consummate arrangements for another go. Grant ought to receive no pay, refund what he got, and make good all deficiencies. He had $18,000 in

American coin [probably intended for buying slaves in Africa]. Whitney says he sold the cargo, and used $1,800 of the gold, up to the time he left. . . . What excuse does Grant make? Why did he not go to the Coast? He knew, before he undertook the command, that there were armed vessels on the Coast, and a number of them. He ought to have known that he was running no risk—that the captain and crew are always discharged. The captain of the "Albert Devereux" was here the other day. The British cruiser even let him take his gold. If Grant had been equal to the emergency, we would all have been easy in money-matters. . . .

Lamar to Theodore Johnston, Another Business Associate from New Orleans, December 23, 1857.

In reference to Grant, discharge him, pay him nothing, and hope with me that he will speedily land in hell. If you think it best to start her from New Orleans to the Coast, and can make the necessary arrangements for her outfit, and the procurement of a cargo without the money, do so. I am unwilling to trust any more money in the hands of irresponsible hands. If you think you can recover anything from Grant, you can commence the action in my name. I don't care a continental about its being used in connection with an enterprise that the intelligence of the country must recognize sooner or later. The legislature of South Carolina has commenced a movement calculated, in time, say at his next session, to startle the opponents of the measure. The committee to whom was referred so much of Gov. [James] Adam's message as related to the Slave-Trade, made a very able report in favor of it. It was received, printed, and laid over till the next session, to enable the masses to digest it. Something ought to be done *at once* with the "Rawlins." If you can't do anything with her, send her here in ballast.

Lamar to L. Viana of New York City Requesting His Collaboration and Advice on the Slave Trade, December 26, 1857.

Dear Sir: I am this morning in receipt of yours of the 23rd of Dec. I have been expecting you here daily since the 15th, and it was only on the 24th that I wrote Messrs. Johnston and Trowbridge, at New Orleans, to send the bark "E. A. Rawlins" here in case you were not there, or if you were and they failed to make satisfactory arrangements with you. I am anxious to have you interested in the next expedition, and would be pleased to have you say what interest you would like, and give your views generally as to the manner the whole should be conducted. I would like you to say, too, what number you would contract to land at a designated point by your own or others' vessels, the price per head, and the time of probable delivery: I to take all the trouble, expense and *risk,* after they are safely landed. Or, if you would prefer it, make some proposition of the nature of a joint-account speculation. I think I can manage two or three cargoes to much profit. I have been agitating the subject of reopening the Trade, and, in connection with others, think there is a marked difference of opinion in the public mind. Of course great prudence and caution are necessary; for, though the authorities will take no particular pains to look after anything of the kind, yet, if it is brought to their attention, they will be bound to notice and to prosecute. I can show you, when we meet, the place or places I propose to land them,—where you can go in and out by one tide—the bar straight and deep, and no persons about—and the men, both in reference to standing in the community and reliability in case of difficulty—who own the place. One thing is certain. Nothing can be done in the way of conviction. If the worst should happen, we could only lose the cargo.

Lamar to N. C. Trowbridge or Theodore Johnston, New Orleans, February 2, 1858.

Dear Sir: This will be handed you by Captain Wm. Ross Postell, whom I have engaged to go out as supercargo of the bark "E. A. Rawlins," to the coast of Africa. He is a Gent., reliable in every way, and a thorough sailor and navigator, and understands our coast most thoroughly. He is promised two negroes out of every one hundred that the vessel may land, and $80 per month to his family during his absence for four months. I hope now there will be no farther delays, but that the vessel will go immediately to sea, and return with a full cargo in 90 days.

A Confidential Letter from Lamar to Thomas Barrett of Augusta, Georgia, Soliciting His Investment in a Forthcoming Expedition to Africa, May 24, 1858.

I have in contemplation, if I can raise the necessary amount of money, the fitting out of an expedition to go to the coast of Africa, for a cargo of African apprentices, *to be bound for the term of their natural lives,* and would like your co-operation. No subscription will be received for a less amount than $5,000. The amount to be raised is $300,000, cash. I will take $20,000 of the stock, and go myself. I propose to purchase the "Vigo," an iron screw-steamer of 1,750 tons, now in Liverpool for sale at £30,000, cash. She cost £75,000. G. B. Lamar [Lamar's father] can give you a description of her. . . . She is as good as new, save her boilers, and they can be used for several months. If I can buy her, I will put six Paixhan guns on deck, and man her with as good men as are to be found in the South. The fighting men will all be stockholders and gentlemen, some of whom are known to you, if not personally, by reputation. My estimate runs thus:

Steamer $150,000; Repairs, guns, small arms, coal, &c. $50,000 . . . . . .$200,000

Supplies $25,000; Money for purchase of cargo, 75,000 100,000

$$\underline{300,000}$$

I have, as you know, a vessel now afloat, but it is to my mind extremely doubtful whether she gets in safely, as she had to wait on the Coast until her cargo could be collected. If she ever gets clear of the Coast, they can't catch her. She ought to be due in from 10 to 30 days. I have another now ready to sail, which has orders to order a cargo of 1,000 to 1,200 to be in readiness the 1st of September, but to be kept, if necessary, until the 1st of October—which I intend for the steamer—so that no delay may occur. With her I can make the voyage there and back, including all detentions, bad weather if I encounter it, etc., in 90 days certain and sure; and the negroes can be sold as fast as landed at $650 per head. I can contract for them "to arrive" at that figure, *Cash*. The "Vigo" can bring 2,000 with ease and comfort, and I apprehend no difficulty or risk, save shipwreck, and that you can insure against. I can get one of the first-lieutenants in the Navy to go out in command, and we can whip anything, if attacked, that is on that station, either English or American. But I would not propose to fight; for the "Vigo" can steam 11 knots, which would put us out of the way of any of the cruisers. If you know of any who would like to take an interest, mention it to them *confidentially,* and let me know who they are. I want none but reliable men, and men who will have the money the moment it is called for. I can raise 100,000 *here*. What can I raise in and about Augusta? . . . If the "Rawlins" gets in with her cargo, I shall want very little money; for I will take all that is wanting myself.

Lamar to L. W. Spratt of Charleston, a Leading Advocate of the Reopening of the African Traffic, May, 1858.

I have in your port the ship "Richard Cobden," that is represented by Messrs. E. Lafitte & Co. I applied for a clearance for her, and declared, on the manifesto, the intention of the voyage was to go to the coast of Africa for a cargo of apprentices, to return to some port in the U.S. or the Island of Cuba. This application was made two months ago. Mr. Colcock said, as a lawyer he admitted my right, but as a government official he would have to report it to Washington. I have written twice to the Treasury Department, urging a prompt decision, and, if a refusal, the reason for such refusal. But, though I have been promised that I should "have it in a day or two," it is not yet on hand. I know the Secretary [Howell Cobb] will refuse it. If he does, he will have many a battery opened on him. . . . I am determined to have the trade opened.

An Open Letter from Lamar to Howell Cobb of Georgia, Secretary of the Treasury, Who on May 22, 1858, Forbade the Collector of Customs at Charleston to Grant a Clearance to Lamar's Ship, the "Richard Cobden," to Sail to Africa to Acquire African Emigrants for Importation into the United States. [No date.]

Your objection to the form of the application, as "involving the subject in some embarrassment," is groundless. Viewed as a matter of legal rights, the question is simply this: Has any one a legal right to land African emigrants, *bond or free* at any port in the United States? . . . You virtually admitted the right to land such emigrants in some of the non-slave-holding States, but added that you were "not aware of a single State where these newcomers would receive a tolerant, much less cordial, reception." Has Northern public opinion, then, acquired the force of law? . . . Upon the return of the ship to the United States, the *status* of the Africans on board, and all other matters affecting the legality of the voyage, could have been tested in the federal courts. You have . . . closed the courts of the country against me. . . . I proposed to you, in writing, that if you would grant the vessel protection on the coast of Africa, I would land the cargo on the levee in New Orleans, and test the legality of the matter in the courts of the United States. . . . The application which is now before you for a clearance for the same vessel for almost a similar voyage, is not amenable to the objections urged against the other; and I am in hopes you will give an immediate answer to it, and let the South know whether she has any rights in the Union or not.

Lamar to N. C. Trowbridge Complaining of the Government's Seizure of Lamar's Slave Yacht, "Wanderer," December 18, 1858.

I returned this morning from Augusta. I distributed the negroes as best I could; but I tell you things are in a hell of a fix; no certainty about anything. The Government has employed H. R. Jackson to assist the prosecution, and are determined to press matters to the utmost extremity. The yacht has been seized. The examination commenced today, and will continue for thirty days, at the rate they are going on. They have all the pilots and men who took the yacht to Brunswick, here to testify. *She will be lost certain and sure,* if not the negroes. Mr. Hazlehurst testified that he attended the negroes and swore they were Africans, and of recent importation. . . . I don't calculate to get a new dollar for an old one. All these men must be *bribed.* I must be paid for my time, trouble and advances. . . . Six of those left at Mont's who were sick, died yesterday. I think the whole of them now sick will die: they are too enfeebled to administer medicine to. I am paying fifty cents per day to each for all those I took up the country. It was the best I could do. It won't take long at that rate for a large bill to run up. . . . I tell you hell is to pay. I don't think they will discharge the men, but turn them over for trial; if so, there is no telling when we can dispose of the negroes.

Lamar to Theodore Johnson. [No date.]

I am astonished at what Gov. Phiniz has written me, and must believe, until it is confirmed, that he has been misinformed. The idea of a man's taking negroes to keep at fifty cents a head per day, and then refusing to give them up when demanded, simply because the law does not recognize them as property, is worse than stealing. . . . I can get nothing from any one. . . . I shall not only lose the original investment, but the most or at least a part of the advances I have made. The yacht is gone, I think. . . . I shall do all that can be done, but my attorneys say it is a bad showing.

Lamar to Trowbridge. [No date.]

Don't sell any of the negroes for anything but money. I would not give a damn for all the notes that have been sent me. I want the money. Money alone will pay my obligations. Keep the negroes if they can't be sold for cash, and I will send them West.

Lamar to Captain N. D. Brown, January 28, 1859.

Your attorneys will visit you before the trial. If a true bill can be found against you by the grand jury, it will be done upon the evidence of Club and Harris, and of course they will testify to the same thing. In that case I think you all ought *to leave,* and I will make arrangements for you to do so, if you agree with me. I have offered Club and Harris $5,000 not to testify; but the Government is also trying to buy them. I don't think you will have much difficulty in getting out. . . . I am afraid they will convict me, but my case is only seven years and a fine. If I find they are likely to do so, I shall go to Cuba, until I make some compromise with the Government. Matters look badly enough just now. . . .

Lamar Challenges Henry Jarvis Raymond, Founder and Editor of *The New York Times,* to a Duel, April 4, 1859.

Sir: My prolonged and continued absence from home, taken in connection with the fact that I viewed your editorial of the 21st of March [see *Times* editorial in Doc. 3.18] as having been written by an irresponsible party, who did not recognize that responsibility which attaches to gentlemen, is the excuse I have to offer for not having before noticed your remarks, which were personal and offensive to myself. I hope the above will satisfactorily account for any apparent neglect. I have been informed by friends that I have been mistaken in my estimate of your character (and they derived their information from personal friends of yours), and that you would respond to any call made upon you. The object of this is to inquire if you have been properly represented by your friends. It is my purpose to go to Cuba next week, unless circumstances should arise to prevent, and a telegram, which will be paid for here, announcing your decision, will much oblige.

Respectfully yours, &c.
C. A. L. Lamar.

Lamar to Henry Jarvis Raymond, Editor of *The New York Times*, Who Refused to Engage in a Duel, Since Lamar Had "Avowed His Connection with a Traffic Which the Laws of His Country Denounced as Piracy." [No date.]

Sir: I received yours of the 4th this morning. You have taken the usual refuge of a coward, who, afraid to fight, undervalues his adversary. Common as is this course in your meridian, *the boast of your friends* induced me to believe that you would hold yourself responsible to those whom you have offended. But for this, and the previous impression I had formed of your character, I would have had no correspondence with you. When we meet, I have determined upon my course.

Lamar to B. R. Alden, New York [no date].

I shall simply put an indignity upon him in a public manner—such for instance as slapping his face; and then, if he don't resent it, why, I shall take no further notice of him.

Lamar to C. C. Cook, Blakely, Georgia, June 20, 1859.

You are aware that it is a risky business. *I lost two out of three.* To be sure, at first I knew nothing of the business. I have learned something since, and I hope I can put my information to some account. I have been in for "grandeur," and been fighting for a principle. Now I am in for the dollars.

Lamar to Trowbridge, New Orleans, July 21, 1859.

The "Wanderer" is going to China, and may return with coolies. They are worth from $340 to $350 each in Cuba, and cost but $12 and their passage. . . .

3.18. Newspaper Reports on Charles Lamar and the Yacht *Wanderer* (March 14 to April 1, 1859)

Early in 1859 the flagrantly illegal activities of C. A. L. Lamar (see Doc. 3.17) began to attract the attention of northern and even southern newspapers, especially after the extraordinary events involving Lamar's yacht, *Wanderer.* On November 28, 1858, this vessel had landed four hundred African slaves on tiny Jekyll Island, Georgia, some twenty-five miles north of St. Marys Island and nearby Amelia Island, Florida, both of which had been centers of operations for illegal slave trading in the years following its abolition.

Among the most outspoken critics of Lamar's activities were the *New York Times* and the *New York Daily Tribune,* both of which published editorials and letters from readers which excoriated the Georgian slave trader not only for his illegal and brutal introduction of Africans, but also for what the *New York Times* referred to as his "chivalric swindling"—a reference to Lamar's high social position in the city of Savannah in contrast with the less than gentlemanly procedures he used in carrying on his personal and business affairs. Lamar's letters in the preceding section (3.17), the five articles from two New York newspapers below, and a letter written to an Alabama newspaper by a resident of Montgomery, provide a valid impression not only of Charles Lamar but also offer insights into the movement to reopen the African slave trade—a proposition that probably even most Southerners opposed.

SOURCES: *New York Daily Tribune,* March 14, 16, 17 and 21, 1859; *New York Times,* March 21, 1859; and James Benson Sellers, *Slavery in Alabama* (Tuscaloosa: University of Alabama Press, 1950), pp. 152–53.

The *New York Daily Tribune*, March 14, 1859: The *Wanderer.*

The evidence upon which the yacht Wanderer was condemned as a slaver appears to have been perfectly complete. The witnesses were the pilot who brought the vessel over the St. Andrew's bar and a person connected with the light-house at Cumberland Island, on the south shore of St. Andrew's Sound, through whom the pilot was obtained. The latter testified that on the 28th of November last, two men came to the light-house in a boat in the evening, one of whom called himself Captain Cole, and said that he had a ship outside the bar on a pleasure excursion, and wanted a pilot to take her into Jekyl Island, where he wished to take some gentlemen on board. The witness went with Cole to Jekyl Island, where Cole told him that his real name was Corrie, and his ship the Wanderer, just arrived from Congo with four hundred negroes.

The pilot testified that, on going aboard the Wanderer with the person who called himself Captain Cole, he saw negroes on board and was told there were 400. He saw 40 or 50 on deck, huddled together like pigs, mostly naked. The vessel smelt very badly, and was full of cock roaches. Some of the negroes appeared sick, and as they were coming over the bar, one dead one was thrown overboard. After passing the bar, he anchored the vessel near the beach of Jekyll Island and they commenced landing the negroes in boats. He saw one dead one on the Island. After they were all landed the captain requested him to take the vessel up to the mouth of the Little Saltillo [Satilla], which he did. The other witness assisted in this operation, and returning to Jekyl Island, saw the negroes there.

Thus far the whole history of the voyage of the Wanderer, including her leaving New York, where the object and intention were suspected, her figuring away as a pleasure yacht on the coast of Africa, her voyage up the Congo, the unsuccessful pursuit of her by our ships on the coast, her arrival, the landing of the negroes, and everything that happened to the vessel, down to the present time of her condemnation, has been fully brought out. It is much to be hoped that the subsequent dealings with the negroes after they were landed may yet be exposed with equal fullness. On that point there is yet very little information. Two or three of the negroes who fell into the hands of the Marshal were subsequently stolen from him. We have had various vague rumors as to bodies of these negroes transported by railroad, and seen at various points. Recently we have had reports by telegraph of the seizure of fifty of them by the United States authorities, and subsequently of their rescue, with intimations of bloodshed, but nothing definite yet. We trust, however, that the whole story will come out, and that the purchasers of these African slaves, if they cannot be punished, may at least be exposed. The evidence above recited is amply sufficient to convict Captain Corrie and all on board the vessel, at least all American citizens, of the capital crime of piracy; but, if we recollect aright, Captain Corrie, having been first indicted, we know not why, with all this evidence against him, as guilty of fitting out a vessel for the slave-trade, was dismissed on bail, and at present is not in custody. Very likely, however, he may brave it out, relying on the favor of a Southern jury for an acquittal. It is not very creditable to the detective skill employed, or at least it argues a great disinclination among the people of the South, to give information on the subject, that three months should have passed since the landing of the negroes, and so little yet be known of their whereabouts.

The sale of the Wanderer took place last Saturday. Charles Lamar bought her for $4,000. Who is he? A speculator who wishes to fit her out for another voyage? The Spanish slave-traders used to attend the sales at Sierra Leone, and buy in all the quick-sailing vessels, condemned as slavers, with the intent again to employ them in the same trade; nor were the English able to put a stop to this, except by ordering captured slavers, instead of being sold, to be broken up.

The *New York Daily Tribune,* March 16, 1859:
The *Wanderer's* Negroes.

To the Editor of the N. Y. Tribune.

Sir: In the morning edition you inquire what has become of the Wanderer's slaves?

They are sold throughout the South. I have known of their being offered in Augusta, Geo., and in Western Alabama—in the latter region they brought $700 to $900; similar negroes of home raising [native born] bringing $1,200 to $1,500.

One authority—a Southern editor—informed me in private conversation, that they looked well, but evidently were easily cowed. Another gentleman, a strong believer in the peculiar institution, writes me: "They are a miserable-looking set, baboon-looking, little bone or muscle, and scarcely able to move, which is not to be wondered at, as they prefer to eat acorns and raw corn.". . .

The *New York Daily Tribune,* March 17, 1859.
The Sale of the *Wanderer.*

Correspondence of the N. Y. Tribune.

Savannah, Ga., March 12, 1859.

An incident occurred at the sale of the condemned slaver Wanderer to-day, which shows the true sentiment of this slave-stricken city. At the hour appointed, the United States Marshal took his stand on Capt. Corrie's trunk, in front of the Custom House, read the decree of the Court, and offered the vessel at auction, whereupon Mr. Chas. L. Lamar stated that the vessel was his property in the hands of the United States officers, and hoped no one would bid against him. The first bid was $500-$800-$1,000-and from there up to $4,000, the bids were $25 at a time by Mr. Van Horn, the Jailer here, a quite, respectable person, who was doubtless authorized to bid by the Collector. Soon it reached $4,000, and was knocked off quickly to Lamar, who instantly rushed on Van Horn, and struck him a severe blow which laid him senseless. Lamar is well known here as a desperate slave-dealer, although holding an influential position in this community. There was a general shout of approbation at his conduct, with the cry "kill him, Charley, kill him," and for the moment it looked as if pistols and knives would be used.

The whole matter was preconcerted so that no bidding should be allowed against Lamar. The vessel was richly worth a much greater sum, and would have brought it but for the bullying of the slave-dealers present, who openly avow their intention to bring another cargo of the chattels by the same vessel. This Lamar is the person who took the wild Africans from the prison here last week, also the owner of the fifty captured in Telfair County [about 130 miles west of Savannah]. No doubt he will get possession of these in the same manner. The United States laws are all a farce in suppressing the slave trade. It is boasted that the next cargo will pay better than those by the Wanderer, and they will know better how to manage in landing.

The *New York Times*, March 21, 1859.
Chivalric Swindling.

It will be remembered that when certain stolen negroes were landed from the now infamous yacht, *Wanderer*, they were hurried into the interior of Georgia, with all the haste suggested by the fear of detection. They were subsequently sought by the officers of the Government, and some of them were brought back to Savannah. It is needless to add that, according to law, they should have been returned to Africa in the same manner as were the negroes rescued from the *Echo* [assumed name of the brig *Putnam*, captured by the U.S. brig *Dolphin* allegedly bound for Key West with 316 slaves aboard]. The vessel herself was confiscated, and, according to the requirements of an act of Congress, should have been sold at auction for account of the Government. An auction of the yacht was accordingly held, but with very remarkable results, and under very strange auspices.

One Mr. Lamar, the original owner, under false pretences, of the *Wanderer,* appeared at the sale and claimed the negroes from the Yacht as his "property." The officers of the law at Savannah, with a remarkable disregard of their duty, obeyed the mandate of this swindler, and quietly transferred the Africans to Mr. Lamar, who now detains them. As for the yacht, Mr. Lamar said that, it being also "his property," as a matter of course no *gentleman* would bid against him for his vessel. The appeal was so far successful that no one in the crowd took any part in the bidding, except a Mr. Van Horn, who ran up to four thousand dollars this splendid yacht (worth perhaps twenty or thirty thousand at the least), and received immediately afterwards a sound pummelling for his pains at the hands of the valiant

THE AFRICANS OF THE SLAVE BARK "WILDFIRE."—[From our own Correspondent.]

THE SLAVE DECK OF THE BARK "WILDFIRE," BROUGHT INTO KEY WEST ON APRIL 30, 1860.—[From a Daguerreotype.]

14. "The Africans of the Slave Bark 'Wildfire.' " *Harper's Weekly,* June 2, 1860. Courtesy of the Special Collections Department, University of Pittsburgh Library System.

Lamar, and some half-dozen friends, and in the presence of the law officers of the Federal Government.

Now if the yacht and the negroes landed from her were in reality Mr. Lamar's *property,* as he so insolently claimed them to be, then Mr. Lamar is a slave-dealer, a kidnapper of negroes, a felon guilty of an act equivalent in the meaning of the statute to piracy, and he should have been arrested on the spot. Instead of which, he was suffered to stand there, after his public and defiant avowal of a crime punishable by imprisonment and fine, and dictate terms at the auction of the vessel. Still worse—he was suffered to wrest from the hand of legal mercy the victims of his unpunished fraud.

Whether the matter is to rest where it is, or justice and law are to be vindicated, we confess we are somewhat curious to learn. It cannot be altogether needless to ascertain how far such a precedent may be employed, and to what lengths it may be made to go. If considerations of vulgar interest are sufficient to induce a community to side with any impudent thief who, like this fellow Lamar, may choose to snap his fingers in the face of the law, then the sooner respectable States are informed of the fact the better for the quiet transaction of our Federal affairs. If Georgia chooses to assume the responsibility of this sort of cowardly pilfering and spiritless piracy, it is quite time that the United States should be put in a position either to coerce her into decency, or to shake off the disgraceful imputations to which her conduct will give color and shape.

The *New York Daily Tribune,* March 21, 1859.
C. L. A. LAMAR.

We inquired, the other day, in relation to the sale of the slave-yacht the Wanderer, who might be Mr. C. L. A. Lamar to whom she was bid off to the trifling sum of $4,000. We are now able to answer that question somewhat more definitely.

In the first place, Mr. C. L. A. Lamar is a member of the principal mercantile firm in Savannah, and though but a young man, and a fast man at that, is thought to have prodigious business talent—for Savannah; and is believed to carry pretty much the whole of that place in his breeches pocket. Whatever Mr. C. L. A. Lamar lays down as the law, is the law of Savannah; and not only the law, but in the opinion of the mass of the citizens, right, proper, expedient and just.

In the second place, Mr. Lamar is the leading and active spirit in the present attempt to revive the African slave-trade. It was by him that the Wanderer was owned and fitted out, Captain Corrie being, after all, but a very secondary personage. It seems to have been the first intention to have got the slaves across the Atlantic, under pretense that they were being carried as apprentices to some West-India port, and it seems to have been with this object in view, that Mr. Lamar entered into correspondence with the Treasury Department, sometime since published, in which he sought for a clearance for such a voyage. . . .

If, indeed, the Government have the least wish or the least intention to cause the laws against the slave-trade to be respected, instead of confining themselves to prosecutions against the crew of the Wanderer, they will proceed at once against Mr. Lamar himself. If anything was before lacking to the chain of evidence against him, he has himself amply supplied it by his public declarations already quoted. In the meantime, we take it, he will be proceeded against for his high-handed contempt of Court, in attempting, and, for that matter, succeeding in turning the Marshal's sale into a farce, by preventing competition in the first place, and, after the sale was over, violently assaulting the only man who had dared to compete with him. It is hardly possible to imagine a more audacious contempt of Court, and if it is not desired and intended to deprive the District Courts of the United States of all respect and authority, steps surely will be taken to bring this bold nullifier to account. If there be any truth in the oft-repeated assertion that the great bulk of the people of the Southern States are opposed to the revival of the African Slave-trade, there ought to be no difficulty in trying Mr. Lamar, nor, in spite of his fists and his bowie-knives, convicting him as well.

The Writer of a Letter to the *Tuskegee Republican,* Calling Himself L'Écrire, Offers an Uncharitable Description of a Group of African Slaves from the *Wanderer* Who Were Transported Down the Alabama River from Some Point above Montgomery. Reprinted in the *Dallas Gazette,* Cahaba, Alabama, January 7, 1859.

Well, what do you think? Twenty-five or thirty of the Africans, a part of the cargo of the schooner *Wanderer,* passed through this place on last Friday on their way down the river somewhere. They were mostly young negroes, not more than two or three of them having any appearance of a beard. They were not what in plantation parlance would be called likely negroes. But then you must recollect that they were just off a long sea voyage, which must have very much jaded them; and the climate even here is very much colder than what they have been accustomed to. Most of them were dull, sleepy, obtuse looking negroes, having no curiosity about anything. Many of them seem to be laboring under a cutaneous affection, which kept them upon the "scratch" all the time. Nevertheless, the younger ones were more intelligent looking, and I have no doubt will grow up into very good field hands. When contrasted to our own negroes, who have descended from the same stock, they show how much the breed is improved by the Southern mode of treatment—being made to do healthful work, well fed, well clothed, attended to when sick, and well taken care of generally.

They all had on breeches and jackets, and they kept their blankets well wrapped around them. The females had on precisely the same clothing as the males, and I was told there were five or six of them, but without examination it was impossible to distinguish the sexes. I only know that there was one woman among them from the fact that an old negro man, who had gone on board to see them, had the curiosity to investigate matters, and brought to light what I suppose in Africa (where the assortment of female charms must be rather small, anyway) pass for breasts; but they were very much more like the dugs of a feminine dog than anything belonging to humanity.

3.19. "A Battle Is in Progress Between Liberty and Slavery." A Northern Minister Issues a Warning Against Renewal of the African Slave Trade (1860)

The author of this piece, the Reverend Rufus W. Clark, condemned the project to renew the African slave trade, fervently warning that to do so would be to perpetuate slavery, worsen the plight of existing slaves, lower national standards in every field of activity, end all hope of future emancipation, and—prophetically—divide and dissolve the nation. Clark's book was published, in fact, just prior to establishment of the Confederacy and the outbreak of the Civil War.

SOURCE: Rev. Rufus W. Clark, *The African Slave Trade* (Boston: American Tract Society, 1860), pp. 7–9, 85–101.

It is certainly surprising, that in this nineteenth century, and under the light of free and Christian institutions, we should be called upon to discuss anew the subject of the African slave trade. It was supposed that the inexpediency and iniquity of this traffic were universally conceded; that the efforts of philanthropic and Christian men, upon two continents, to lighten public opinion, had been successful; and that the action of our government, and the governments of Europe, in abolishing said traffic, was regarded as final.

But for several years past there has been growing up in the community a power that plants itself in direct antagonism to the teachings of our religion, the professed aim of our political institutions, the influence of our educational systems, and the sentiments inculcated in our national literature. A battle is in progress between liberty and slavery, God's truth and the vile passions of men, that perils the existence of this republic, and touches every vital interest. And, to crown the triumphs of the slave power, we again have vessels fitting out in our ports, north and south, to bring to our shores the suffering children of Africa, and entail anew upon that continent and our own, the evils and horrors of this accursed traffic.

It may be a delicate question to inquire who, in the various States of this Union, are responsible for the growth of this evil; who, by their direct action, their silence, or their apologies for slavery, have made contributions to its strength. To his own conscience, and before God, each man must answer.

When benevolent societies, ecclesiastical bodies, an influential press, churches professing to be Christian, unite with a demoralized public opinion, and an oppressive secular authority, to perpetuate or extend a system of iniquity, there is created a force for evil, against which even millions of free Christian men find it difficult to contend. The virus enters the arteries and muscles of the national life, palsies the sinews of the national strength, and poisons the fountains of national existence. And who will answer for the consequences of fostering such an evil in the heart of a country blessed as ours has been by Heaven? Have we received any special license to sin, with an exemption from the action of those eternal laws that bind the penalty to the transgression? Is it not true now, as of the past, that "the nation and kingdom that will not serve Thee shall perish, yea, those nations shall be utterly wasted?". . .

It would be a libel upon the Southern States of our confederacy to say that, as a body, they were in favor of the revival of the slave trade, or to say that the southern people were unanimous in their approval of slavery.

We know, from personal acquaintance, that there are many noble men and women at the South, who see and acknowledge the evils of the system, and deeply deplore its existence. There are thousands, also, who abhor the slave trade, and deprecate the efforts that are being made for its resuscitation. And our desire is to fortify such in their opinions, and secure their coöperation with the power of the North and West, in resisting these efforts. Unless there is such coöperation, to enlighten the people in reference to the dangers that threaten them, the public opinion may become corrupt upon this topic, as it has in years past upon other questions growing out of slavery.

Some may take the ground that the foreign slave trade is an evil too stupendous to allow us to think for a moment of its extensive revival in this country. But does history prove that this country is averse to fostering stupendous evils? Has the government, or the people, shown any great timidity in trampling under foot the principles of right, the dictates of humanity, the pledges of the past? Have solemn contract preserved soil consecrated to freedom from invasion of the slave power? Has an enlightened conscience secured deference to God's government, when the laws of human government have clashed with it? Do not multitudes regard the sentiment of a "higher law" as a jest? an "overruling Providence" as an obsolete idea?

The traffic is conducted with so much secrecy, and such vigilance is exercised to escape detection, that it is difficult to obtain full evidence of its extent in this country. Still, there is proof enough to show that it is carried on in Cuba and Brazil to an alarming degree, and that American citizens are guilty of participating in it.

The state of the trade at the present time may be learned from Harper's Cyclopædia of Commerce, published in New York in 1858,—a reliable authority. Under the article "Slave Trade (Page 1728), the following statement is made:

"Passing over the interval from the period when the slave trade was declared to be piracy, to the year 1840, we find the number introduced into Brazil from that year to 1851, inclusive, was 348,609, or a little more than 30,000 a year. During the same period, the number imported into Cuba amounted to an average of about 6,000 a year. . . . As perhaps not more than three fourths of the whole number was reported to the mixed commission, the yearly average for this period (for both countries) may be set down at 45,000. . . .

"It is estimated that in the port of New York alone, about twelve vessels are fitted out every year for the slave trade, and that Boston and Baltimore furnish each about the same number, making a fleet of thirty-six vessels, all engaged in a commerce at which the best feelings of our nature revolt. If to these be added the slavers fitted out in Eastern ports besides Boston, we will have a total of about forty, which is rather under than over the actual number. Each slaver registers from 150 to 250 tons, and costs, when ready for sea, with provisions, slave equipments, and everything necessary for a successful trip, about $8,000.

"Here, to start with, we have a capital of $320,000, the greater part of which is contributed by Northern men."

A table of costs is then given, and,—

"From this estimate, it will be seen that the amount of capital required to fit out a fleet of slavers, is about $1,500,000, upon which the profits are so immense as almost to surpass belief. In a single voyage of the fleet, 24,000 human beings are carried off from different points on the slave coasts; and of these, 4,000, or one sixth of the whole number, become victims to the horrors of the middle passage, leaving 20,000 fit for market. For each of these, the trader obtains an average of $500, making a total for the whole 20,000 or $10,000,000.

"Now if we estimate the number of trips made by each vessel in a year at two, we will have this increased to $20,000,000. Each vessel, it is true, can make three, and sometimes four trips; but as some are destroyed after the first voyage, we have placed the number at the lowest estimate. The expenses and profits of the slave trade for a single year compare as follows:

Total expenses of two voyages $3,000,000
Total receipts of two voyages . . . .<u>$20,000,000</u>
       Profits $17,000,000

The case of the slave yacht Wanderer [See Docs. 3.17 and 3.18] is fresh in the memories of the people. Her cargo of human beings has been distributed over various plantations, the slaves having been sold for $800 and $1000 each, and some even as high as $1,500. Against the captain the Grand Jury for the District of Georgia found indictments, but the United States Judge in South Carolina refused to issue a warrant for his arrest. So much for justice, and obedience to the laws of the land!

The Echo was seized in the act of attempting to land slaves on the coast of Cuba. The bark E. A. Rawlins was seized in the Bay of St. Joseph, where she had taken upon herself the new name of Rosa Lee. Last December, she cleared from Savannah, with rice on board. At that time there were suspicions that she was a slaver, but she escaped. Two and a half months later, she was taken in St. Joseph's bay, an unfrequented place, westward of Apalachicola River. There was abundant evidence to believe that she had been to Africa, taken on board her living freight, subjected the victims to all the horrors of the "middle passage," and landed them at Cuba and on the coast of the Gulf of Mexico.

A suspicious looking vessel was seen off the mouth of the Apalachicola, avoiding the pilots who approached her, her papers irregular, and the captain having taken an assumed name. A Spanish captain had been on board, who, the crew confessed, had been murdered.

Another case occurred near Mobile, and the crew were arrested, and brought before the Grand Jury of South Carolina. But these grave representatives of American justice, these protectors of innocence, refused to find indictments against the guilty men, and the United States judge for that district was equally resolute in refusing to enforce the laws against the slave trade.

So bold are some in their movements that recently imported Africans are publicly offered for sale. The following is from the Richmond Reporter (Texas), of the 14th of June, 1859:

FOR SALE.—Four hundred likely negroes, lately landed upon the coast of Texas. Said negroes will be sold upon the most reasonable terms. One third down; the remainder in one or two years, with eight per cent interest. For further information, inquire of C. K. C., Houston, or L. R. G., Galveston.

And the Tribune quotes from the Vicksburg True Southron of the 13th, an account of an African Labor Supply Association, of which the Hon. J. B. D. De Bow is President.[75]

Thus it is evident that this trade is to be encouraged in defiance of the law, and organized efforts are to be made to secure the repeal of the laws enacted by our fathers against this evil.

A Washington correspondent of the New York Herald, said to be an accurate and reliable writer, stated, on the authority of a United States senator, that the number of cargoes of African slaves landed on the coast of the United States, and smuggled into the interior, since May, 1858, a period of fifteen months, amounts to sixty or seventy, and twelve vessels more are expected within ninety days. If grand juries and judges refuse to enforce the laws against the slave trade, it may be indefinitely increased. And from despatches received at the Navy Department, from the frigate Cumberland, dated at Porto Praya, April 15, 1859, it appears that during the last year the traffic has greatly increased. Those despatches state that yachts, schooners, and trading vessels are engaged in the business, and that small armed vessels are required, that can sail up the rivers and capture the slavers.

To encourage the trade, it is stated that eighteen slaveholders in Enterprise, Miss., recently pledged themselves to buy 1000 negroes, at a certain price, if they were brought from Africa.

But I will let the southern papers and politicians speak for themselves. They have spoken, and their dark schemes of infamy and cruelty are before the nation.

The Apalachicola (Fla.) Advertiser says:

"Until the slave trade is opened and made legal, the South will push slavery forward, as a seasoning for every dish. This is the settled and determined policy of a party at the South. We do not pretend to belong to the ultra-southern party, but we believe it is a duty which the general government owes to the South, that the slave trade should be legitimate, that her vast domain may receive cultivation."

If this paper does not belong to the ultra southern party, we should be

---

75. DeBow was editor of the journal *DeBow's Review* of New Orleans, a supporter of Southern interests including the reopening of the African slave trade. Editor.

In the Hands of Strangers

glad to have it define its position. If there is any wickedness, beyond rendering "the slave trade legitimate," we have yet to be informed of it.

In April, 1859, the citizens of Matagorda, Texas, passed the following resolution:

Resolved, That our delegates to the Convention be requested to inquire into the expediency of obtaining negro laborers suited to our climate and products, from some foreign country, and recommend measures by which the importation can be carried on under the supervision and protection of the State."

At a meeting held in Hanesville, Appling County, Georgia, Col. Goulding, of Liberty, (!) offered several resolutions, which were adopted, one of which was, "that all laws of the federal government, interdicting the right of the southern people to import slaves from Africa, are unconstitutional, and violative of the rights of the South; and that said laws are null and void, and a disgrace to the statute book."

The New York Tribune of March 17, 1859, states that Dr. Daniel Lee, Professor of Agriculture and kindred sciences in the Georgia University, has written a letter in favor of reopening the slave trade,—or, rather, in favor of African importations,—the better to develop the agricultural resources of the South.

The necessity of more slaves to develop the resources of the South, and settle new territories, is becoming a favorite argument with the advocates of the revival of the foreign trade. And it will doubtless become more and more prominent in the discussions which the subject of the African trade will awaken in the future.

The Augusta Constitutionalist reports on the speech delivered by the Hon. A. H. Stephens[76] to a large concourse of people assembled in the City Park Hall, in July last, on the occasion of his resignation as representative in Congress, when he used the following language:

"As he said, in 1850, he would repeat now, there is very little prospect of the South settling any territory outside of Texas; in fact, little or no prospect at all, unless we increase our African stock.

"The question his hearers should examine in its length and breadth; he would do nothing more than present it; but it is as plain as any thing, that unless the number of African stock be increased, we have not the population, and might as well abandon the race with our brethren of the North, *in the colonization of the territories.* It was not for him to advise on these questions: he only presented them. The people should think and act upon

---

76. Soon to be vice president of the Confederacy. Editor.

them. If there are but few more slave States, it is not because of abolition-ism, or the Wilmot Proviso, but simply for want of people to settle them. We cannot make States without people; rivers and mountains do not make them; and slave States *can not be made without Africans."*

This language was addressed to the gentlemen and ladies of the city, and is said to have been received with great applause.

At Fort Valley, Ga., there is published a newspaper, called "The Nine-teenth Century," which holds the following language in regard to the slave trade:

"Necessity will demand it at no distant day, and we also believe that the necessity will bring about the object of itself, without much noise or confu-sion on the part of the southern people."

So it seems that the flood gates of this stream of moral and physical death are to be opened quietly, without much disturbance of the public conscience, a few light tremors, perhaps, and without much "noise" from that unfortunate class whose nerves are affected by the horrors of the mid-dle passage. Perhaps the soothing influences of the "Nineteenth Century" will aid in this matter, and the introduction of modern improvements may render the African more submissive to his fate.

There is still another argument for the revival of the slave trade alluded to by the "Southern Confederacy," published at Atlanta, Ga.

That paper declares that "The African slave trade is the hope and bul-wark of southern interests. It is the basis underlying the future greatness and permanency of the slave States. Without its establishment, the institu-tion (slavery) will soon become useless. . . . "

The word "piracy" greatly troubles the friends of the slave trade. In May, 1859, at a meeting held in Parker County, Texas, it was

"Resolved, That we demur to any law of Congress making the foreign slave trade piracy, as a usurpation of power not warranted by the Constitu-tion of the United States, and ought to be repealed."

We come now to a document that deserves our careful attention. In May, the Savannah Republican published an indignant protest of the grand jury which recently indicted parties suspected of being engaged in the slave trade. The jurymen, being under oath to find a bill according to law, state that they did so *against their will.* The protest concludes thus:

"Heretofore, the people of the South, firm in their consciousness of right and strength, have failed to place the stamp of condemnation upon such laws as reflect upon the institution of slavery, but have permitted, un-rebuked, the influence of foreign opinion to prevail in their support.

"Longer to yield to a sickly sentiment of pretended philanthropy, and

In the Hands of Strangers

diseased mental observation of 'higher law' fanatics, the tendency of which is to debase us in the estimation of civilized nations, is weak and unwise. They then unhesitatingly advocate the repeal of all laws which directly or indirectly condemn the institution, and think it the duty of the southern people to require their legislators to unite their efforts for the accomplishment of this object." (Signed)

CHARLES GRANT,	BENEDICT BOURGEIN,
H. S. BYRD, M. D.	JNO. J. JACKSON,
S. PALMER,	GEO W. GARMY.

This is certainly a very remarkable production. That it represents an extensive southern opinion, we will not believe without farther evidence. Its authors are alone responsible for it.

We know that such sentiments are received with disgust by thousands at the South. Many distinguished men have already spoken out against the slave trade. Let such men be multiplied and sustained, and the South may be saved from self-destruction, and the nation from the guilt of that gigantic crime into which many are so madly plunging.

We rejoice that our northern State legislatures are waking up to the magnitude of this evil.

The following resolution against this traffic was passed April 12, 1859, by the New York State Assembly, by a vote of 101 to 6:

"*Resolved* (if the Senate concur), That the citizens of this State look with surprise and detestation upon the virtual opening of the slave trade within the Federal Union: that against this invasion of our laws, of our feelings, and of the dictates of Christianity, we solemnly protest: that we call upon the citizens of the Union to make cause in the name of religion and humanity, and as friends of the principles underlying our system of government, to unite in bringing to immediate arrest and punishment all persons engaged in the unlawful and wicked trade, and hereby instruct our senators and representatives in Congress to exert all lawful power for the immediate suppression of this infamous traffic.

Resolved, That the Executive of this State be required to transmit a copy of this resolution to the legislatures of the several States of this Union, and earnestly request their coöperation in arresting this great wickedness."

Would that every legislature that professes to love liberty, would follow the noble example of the Empire State! . . .

It only remains for us to allude to some of the inevitable effects of re-opening a traffic, so revolting to every feeling of humanity, every dictate of conscience, and every law of God.

There is no need of extended argument to show that the importation of Africans into this country would directly and fearfully augment that evil which already to so great an extent is paralyzing industry, blighting commerce, and destroying the best interests of society. The disastrous influence of American slavery upon agriculture, the mechanical arts, education, public virtue, religion, has been fully set forth by others. Measures have been proposed to mitigate the evils growing out of the system, and good men, North and South, have looked forward to the time when the nation would be relieved of this burden. But the revival of the foreign traffic will perpetuate and extend the system, and blast the hopes that have been entertained of its speedy removal. It will embarrass every measure for the elevation and improvement of those in bondage, tighten the chains of the oppressed, and discourage all effort at even gradual emancipation.

The establishment of the American slave trade would also be a source of irritation between the North and the South. Already the ill feeling produced by the encroachments of slavery is sundering fraternal relations, impeding the progress of trade, and exasperating one portion of the community against another. And let this additional firebrand be thrown in, and the flames of animosity would be kindled over the whole country.

On the one side would be this evil, with its cruelties, its violations of all the principles of justice and humanity; and on the other the intelligence, moral rectitude, and Christian virtue of millions of freemen. And to suppose that these elements can lie quietly side by side, is to suppose an utter impossibility. Our system of education must be corrupted to the very core; our literature must be poisoned by the sentiments of the dark ages; all traces of right and justice must be obliterated from our statute books, and our religion must become a dead form, before such a result can be anticipated. Oil and water will not mingle. Barbarism and Christianity were not made to dwell together in peace. . . .

In conclusion, it is the solemn duty of every American patriot and Christian to rise up and decree that, let the consequences be what they may, another slave shall not pollute our coast, and that, God helping them, they will resist now and for ever, every attempt to revive this accursed traffic. To allow it is to increase and perpetuate the evils that to-day threaten the very existence of the republic. It puts in peril the American Union, and what is more, endangers the liberties of the whole nation. No greater calamity could befall us, no greater curse could smite us, than the reopening of the slave trade. War, pestilence, and famine might not damage us as much as this iniquity. For we might resist the war, and recover from the effects of the pestilence and famine, but this accursed thing strikes at the vitals of the republic. It breaks down the principles of the nation. It corrupts the morals, poisons the religion, and exposes us to the burning wrath of Jehovah. . . .

We appeal to the patriotism of American citizens, and we ask them whether they are willing to see this great republic, freighted with so many human hopes, blessed as it has been of heaven, sacrificed at the altar of this great iniquity? Shall we peril the brilliant prospects of the nation, provoke the wrath of God, become a hissing and a by-word throughout Christendom, by madly clinging to that which is evil, and only evil, and that continually?

3.20. The Underground Railroad: Selected Narratives of Arrivals of Fugitive Slaves in Philadelphia by William Still, Chairman of the Vigilance Committee

In the preface to his book, *The Underground Rail Road,* William Still briefly described the arduous and frightening experiences of runaway slaves who arrived in Philadelphia. "In these Records," he wrote,

> will be found interesting narratives of many men, women and children, from the prison-house of bondage; from cities and plantations; from rice swamps and cotton fields; from kitchens and mechanic shops; from Border States and Gulf States; from cruel masters and mild masters;—some guided by the north star alone, penniless, braving the perils of land and sea, eluding the keen scent of the blood-hound as well as the more dangerous pursuit of the savage slave-hunter; some from secluded dens and caves of the earth, where for months and years they had hidden away waiting for the chance to escape; from mountains and swamps, where indescribable suffering from hunger and other privations had patiently been endured. Occasionally fugitives came in boxes and chests, and not infrequently some were secreted in steamers and vessels, and in some instances journeyed hundreds of miles in skiffs. Men disguised in female attire and women dressed in the garb of men have under very trying circumstances triumphed in thus making their way to freedom. And here and there when all other modes of escape seemed cut off, some, whose fair complexions have rendered them indistinguishable from their Anglo-Saxon brethren, feeling that they could endure the yoke no longer, with assumed airs of importance, such as they had been accus-

Conflict and Crisis of the Union

tomed to see their masters show when traveling, have taken the usual modes of conveyance and have even braved the most scrutinizing inspection of slave-holders, slave-catchers and car conductors, who were ever on the alert to catch those who were considered base and white enough to practice such deception. Passes have been written and used by fugitives, with their masters' and mistresses' names boldly attached thereto. . . . They were determined to have liberty even at the cost of life.

SOURCE: William Still, *The Underground Rail Road. A Record of Facts, Authentic Narratives, Letters, &c., Narrating the Hardships, Hair-breadth Escapes and Death Struggles of the Slaves in their Efforts for Freedom, as Related by Themselves and Others, or Witnessed by the Author; together with Sketches of some of the Largest Stockholders, and Most Liberal Aiders and Advisers on the Road* (Philadelphia: Porter & Coates, 1872), pp. 1–2, 368–71, 394–95, 441–44, 528–31.

"THE MOTHER OF TWELVE CHILDREN."
OLD JANE DAVIS—FLED TO ESCAPE THE AUCTION-BLOCK.

The appended letter, from Thomas Garrett, will serve to introduce one of the most remarkable cases that it was our privilege to report or assist:

WILMINGTON, 6 MO., 9th, 1857.

ESTEEMED FRIEND—WILLIAM STILL:—We have here in this place, at Comegys Munson's an old colored woman, the mother of twelve children, one half of which has been sold South. She has been so ill used, that she was compelled to leave husband and children behind, and is desirous of getting to a brother who lives at Buffalo. She was nearly naked. She called at my house on 7th day night, but being from home, did not see her till last evening. I have procured her two under garments, one new; two skirts, one new; a good frock with cape; one of my wife's bonnets and stockings, and gave her five dollars in gold, which, if properly used, will put her pretty well on the way. I also gave her a letter to thee. Since I gave them to her she has concluded to stay where she is till 7th day night, when Comegys Munson says he can leave his work and will go with her to thy house. I write this so that thee may be prepared for them; they ought to arrive between 11 and 12 o'clock. Perhaps thee may find some fugitive that will be willing to accompany her. With desire for thy welfare and the cause of the oppressed, I remain thy friend,

THOS. GARRET.

Jane did not know how old she was. She was probably sixty or seventy. She fled to keep from being sold. She had been "whipt right smart," poorly fed and poorly clothed, by a certain Roger McZant, of the New Market District, Eastern Shore of Maryland. His wife was a "bad woman too." Just before escaping, Jane got a whisper that her "master" was about to sell her; on asking him if the rumor was true, he was silent. He had been asking "one hundred dollars" for her.

Remembering that four of her children had been snatched away from her and sold South, and she herself was threatened with the same fate, she was willing to suffer hunger, sleep in the woods for nights and days, wandering towards Canada, rather than trust herself any longer under the protection of her "kind" owner. Before reaching a place of repose she was *three weeks in the woods,* almost wholly without nourishment.

JANE, doubtless, represented thousands of old slave mothers, who, after having been worn out under the yoke, were frequently either offered for sale for a trifle, turned off to die, or compelled to eke out their existence on the most stinted allowance.

ARRIVAL FROM DUNWOODY COUNTY, 1858
DARIUS HARRIS

One of the most encouraging signs connected with the travel *via* the Underground Rail Road was, that passengers traveling thereon were, as a general rule, young and of determined minds. Darius, the subject of this sketch, was only about twenty-one when he arrived. It could be seen in his looks that he could not be kept in the prison-house unless constantly behind bars. His large head and its formation indicated a large brain. He stated that "Thomas H. Hamlin, a hard case, living near Dunwoody," had professed to own him. Darius alleged that this same Hamlin, who had thus stripped him of every cent of his earnings was doing the same thing by sixty others, whom he held in his grasp.

With regard to "feeding and clothing" Darius set Hamlin down as "very hoggish;" he also stated that he would sell slaves whenever he could. He (Darius) had been hired out in Petersburg [Virginia] from the age of ten; for the last three years previous to his escape he had been bringing one hundred and fifty dollars a year into the coffers of his owners. Darius had not been ignorant of the cruelties of the slave system up to the time of his escape, for the fetters had been galling his young limbs for several years; especially had the stringent slave laws given him the horrors. Loathing the system of slavery with his whole heart, he determined to peril all in escaping therefrom; seeking diligently, he had found means by which he could carry his designs into execution. In the way of general treatment, however, Darius said that bodily he had escaped "abuses tolerably well." He left in slavery his father and mother, four brothers and one sister. He arrived by one of the Richmond boats.

ARRIVAL FROM DORCHESTER CO., 1860.

HARRIET TUBMAN'S LAST "TRIP" TO MARYLAND.

The following letter from Thomas Garrett throws light upon this arrival:

WILMINGTON, 12th mo., 1st, 1860.

RESPECTED FRIEND:—WILLIAM STILL:—I write to let thee know that Harriet Tubman is again in these parts. She arrived last evening from one of her trips of mercy to God's poor, bringing two men with her as far as New Castle. I agreed to pay a man last evening, to pilot them on their way to Chester county; the wife of one of the men, with two or three children, was left some thirty miles below, and I gave Harriet ten dollars, to hire a man with a carriage, to take them to Chester county. She said a man had offered for that sum, to bring them on. I shall be very uneasy about them, till I hear they are safe. There is now much more risk on the road, till they arrive here, than there has been for several months past, as we find that some poor, worthless wretches are constantly on the look out on two roads, that they cannot well avoid more especially with carriage, yet, as it is Harriet who seems to have had a special angel to guard her on her journey of mercy, I have hope.

Thy Friend,   THOMAS GARRETT.

N. B. We hope all will be in Chester county to-morrow.

These slaves from Maryland, were the last that Harriet Tubman piloted out of the prison-house of bondage, and these "came through great tribulation."

Stephen, the husband, had been a slave of John Kaiger, who would not allow him to live with his wife (if there was such a thing as a slave's owning a wife). She lived eight miles distant, hired her time, maintained herself, and took care of her children (until they became of service to their owner), and paid ten dollars a year for her hire. She was owned by Algier Pearcy. Both mother and father desired to deliver their children from his grasp. They had too much intelligence to bear the heavy burdens thus imposed without feeling the pressure a grievous one.

Harriett Tubman being well acquainted in her neighborhood, and knowing of their situation, and having confidence that they would prove true, as passengers on the Underground Rail Road, engaged to pilot them within reach of Wilmington, at least to Thomas Garrett's. Thus the father and mother, with their children and a young man named John, found aid and comfort on their way, with Harriet for their "Moses." A poor woman escaping from Baltimore in a delicate state, happened to meet Harriet's party at the station, and was forwarded on with them. They were cheered with clothing, food, and material aid, and sped on to Canada. Notes taken at that time were very brief; it was evidently deemed prudent in those days, not to keep as full reports as had been the wont of the secretary, prior to 1859. The capture of John Brown's papers and letters, with names and plans in full, admonished us that such papers and correspondence as had been preserved concerning the Underground Rail Road, might perchance be captured by a pro-slavery mob. For a year or more after the Harper's Ferry battle, as many will remember, the mob spirit of the times was very violent in all the principal northern cities, as well as southern ("to save the Union.") Even in Boston, Abolition meetings were fiercely assailed by the mob. During this period, the writer omitted some of the most important particulars in the escapes and narratives of fugitives. Books and papers were sent away for a long time, and during this time the records were kept simply on loose slips of paper.

CROSSING THE BAY IN A BATTEAU.
SHARP CONTEST WITH PURSUERS ON WATER, FUGITIVES VICTORIOUS.

THOMAS SIPPLE, and his wife, MARY ANN, HENRY BURKETT, and ELIZABETH, his wife, JOHN PURNELL, and HALE BURTON. This party were slaves, living near Kunkletown, in Worcester county, Maryland, and had become restive in their fetters. Although they did not know a letter of the alphabet, they were fully persuaded that they were entitled to their freedom. In considering what way would be safest for them to adopt, they concluded that the water would be less dangerous than any other route. As the matter of freedom had been in their minds for a long time, they had frequently counted the cost, and had been laying by trifling sums of money which had fallen perchance into their hands. Among them all they had about thirty dollars. As they could not go by water without a boat, one of their number purchased an old batteau for the small sum of six dollars. The Delaware Bay lay between them and the Jersey shore, which they desired to reach. They did not calculate, however, that before leaving the Delaware shore they would have to contend with the enemy. That in crossing, they would lose sight of the land they well understood. They managed to find out the direction of the shore, and about the length of time that it might take them to reach it. Undaunted by the perils before them the party repaired to the bay, and at ten o'clock, P. M., embarked direct for the other shore.

Near Kate's Hammock, on the Delaware shore, they were attacked by five white men in a small boat. One of them seized the chain of the fugitive's boat, and peremptorily claimed it. "This is not your boat, we bought this boat and paid for it," spake one of the brave fugitives. "I am an officer, and must have it," said the white man, holding onto the chain. Being armed, the white men threatened to shoot. Manfully did the black men stand up for their rights, and declare that they did not mean to give up their boat alive. The parties speedily came to blows. One of the white men dealt a heavy blow with his oar upon the head of one of the black men, which knocked him down, and broke the oar at the same time. The blow was immediately returned by Thomas Sipple, and one of the white men was laid flat on the bottom of the boat. The white men were instantly seized with a panic, and retreated; after getting some yards off they snapped their guns at the fugitives several times, and one load of small shell was fired into them. John received two shot in the forehead, but was not dangerously hurt. George received some in the arms, Hale Burton got one about his temple, and Thomas got a few in one of his arms; but the shot being light, none of the fugitives were seriously damaged. Some of the shot will remain in them as long as life lasts. The conflict lasted for several minutes, but the victorious bondmen were only made all the more courageous by seeing the foe retreat. They rowed with a greater will than ever, and landed on a small island. Where they were, or what to do they could not tell. One whole night they passed in gloom on this sad spot. Their hearts were greatly cast down; the next morning they set out on foot to see what they could see. The young women were very sick, and the men were tried to the last extremity; however, after walking about one mile, they came across the captain of an oyster boat. They perceived that he spoke in a friendly way, and they at once asked directions with regard to Philadelphia. He gave them the desired information, and even offered to bring them to the city if they would pay him for his services. They had about twenty-five dollars in all. This they willingly gave him, and he brought them according to agreement. When they found the captain they were not far from Cape May light-house.

Taking into account the fact that it was night when they started, that their little boat was weak, combined with their lack of knowledge in relation to the imminent danger surrounding them, any intelligent man would have been justified in predicting for them a watery grave, long before the bay was half crossed. But they crossed safely. They greatly needed food, clothing, rest, and money, which they freely received, and were afterwards forwarded to John W. Jones, Underground Rail Road agent at Elmira [New York]. The sub-joined letter giving an account of their arrival was duly received:

ELMIRA, June 6th, 1860.

FRIEND WM. STILL:—All six came safe to this place. The two men came last night, about twelve o'clock; the man and woman stopped at the depot, and went east on the next train, about eighteen miles, and did not get back till to-night, so that the two men went this morning, and the four went this evening.

O old master don't cry for me,

For I am going to Canada where colored men are free.

P.S. What is the news in the city? Will you tell me how many you have sent over to Canada? I would like to know. They all send their love to you. I have nothing new to tell you. We are all in good health. I see there is a law passed in Maryland not to set any slaves free. They had better get the consent of the Underground Rail Road before they passed such a thing. Good night from your friend.

JOHN W. JONES.

WILLIAM AND ELLEN CRAFT
FEMALE SLAVE IN MALE ATTIRE, FLEEING AS A PLANTER, WITH HER HUSBAND AS HER BODY SERVANT

A quarter of a century ago, William and Ellen Craft were slaves in the State of Georgia. With them, as with thousands of others, the desire to be free was very strong. For this jewel they were willing to make any sacrifice, or to endure any amount of suffering. In this state of mind they commenced planning. After thinking of various ways that might be tried, it occurred to William and Ellen, that one might act the part of master and the other the part of servant.

Ellen being fair enough to pass for white, of necessity would have to be transformed into a young planter for the time being. All that was needed, however, to make this important change was that she should be dressed elegantly in a fashionable suit of male attire, and have her hair cut in the style usually worn by young planters. Her profusion of dark hair offered a fine opportunity for the change. So far this plan looked very tempting. But it occurred to them that Ellen was beardless. After some mature reflection, they came to the conclusion that this difficulty could be very readily obviated by having the face muffled up as though the young planter was suffering badly with the face or toothache; thus they got rid of this trouble. Straightway, upon further reflection, several other very serious difficulties stared them in the face. For instance, in traveling, they knew that they would be under the necessity of stopping repeatedly at hotels, and that the custom of registering would have to be conformed to, unless some very good excuse could be given for not doing so.

Hence they again thought much over matters, and wisely concluded that the young man had better assume the attitude of a gentleman very much indisposed. He must have his right arm placed carefully in a sling; that would be a sufficient excuse for not registering, etc. Then he must be a little lame, with a nice cane in the left hand; he must have large green spectacles over his eyes, and withal he must be very hard of hearing and dependent on his faithful servant (as was no uncommon thing with slave-holders), to look after all his wants.

William was just the man to act this part. To begin with, he was very "likely-looking;" smart, active and exceedingly attentive to his young master—indeed he was almost eyes, ears, hands and feet for him. William knew that this would please the slave-holders. The young planter would have nothing to do but hold himself subject to his ailments and put on a bold air of superiority; he was not to deign to notice anybody. If while traveling, gentlemen, either politely or rudely, should venture to scrape acquaintance with the young planter, in his deafness he was to remain mute; the servant was to explain. In every instance when this occurred, as it actually did, the servant was fully equal to the emergency—none dreaming of the disguises in which the Underground Rail Road passengers were traveling.

They stopped at a first-class hotel in Charleston, where the young planter and his body servant were treated, as the house was wont to treat the chivalry. They stopped also at a similar hotel in Richmond, and with like results.

They knew that they must pass through Baltimore, but they did not know the obstacles that they would have to surmount in the Monumental City. They proceeded to the depot in the usual manner, and the servant asked for tickets for his master and self. Of course the master could have a ticket, but "bonds will have to be entered before you can get a ticket," said the ticket master. "It is the rule of this office to require bonds for all negroes applying for tickets to go North, and none but gentlemen of well-known responsibility will be taken," further explained the ticket master.

The servant replied, that he knew "nothing about that"—that he was "simply traveling with his young master to take care of him—he being in a very delicate state of health, so much so, that fears were entertained that he might not be able to hold out to reach Philadelphia, where he was hastening for medical treatment," and ended his reply by saying, "my master can't be detained." Without further parley, the ticket master very obligingly waived the old "rule," and furnished the requisite ticket. The mountain being thus removed, the young planter and his faithful servant were safely in the cars for the city of Brotherly Love.

In the Hands of Strangers

Scarcely had they arrived on free soil when the rheumatism departed—the right arm was unslung—the toothache was gone—the beardless face was unmuffled—the deaf heard and spoke—the blind saw—and the lame leaped as an hart, and in the presence of a few astonished friends of the slave, the facts of this unparalleled Underground Rail Road feat were fully established by the most unquestionable evidence. The constant strain and pressure on Ellen's nerves, however, had tried her severely, so much so, that for days afterwards, she was physically very much prostrated, although joy and gladness beamed from her eyes, which bespoke inexpressible delight within.

Never can the writer forget the impression made by their arrival. Even now, after a lapse of nearly a quarter of a century, it is easy to picture them in a private room, surrounded by a few friends—Ellen in her fine suit of black, with her cloak and high-heeled boots, looking, in every respect, like a young gentleman; in an hour after having dropped her male attire, and assumed the habiliments of her sex the feminine only was visible in every line and feature of her structure.

Her husband, William, was thoroughly colored, but was a man of marked natural abilities, of good manners, and full of pluck, and possessed of perceptive faculties very large.

It was necessary, however, in those days, that they should seek a permanent residence, where their freedom would be more secure than in Philadelphia; therefore they were advised to go to headquarters, directly to Boston. There they would be safe, it was supposed, as it had been about a generation since a fugitive had been taken back from the Old Bay State, and through the incessant labors of William Lloyd Garrison, the great pioneer, and his faithful coadjutors, it was conceded that another fugitive slave case could never be tolerated on the free soil of Massachusetts. So to Boston they went.

On arriving, the warm hearts of abolitionists welcomed them heartily, and greeted and cheered them without let or hindrance. They did not pretend to keep their coming a secret, or hide it under a bushel; the story of their escape was heralded broadcast over the country—North and South, and indeed over the civilized world. For two years or more, not the slightest fear was entertained that they were not just as safe in Boston as if they had gone to Canada. But the day the Fugitive Bill passed, even the bravest abolitionist began to fear that a fugitive slave was no longer safe anywhere under the stars and stripes, North or South, and that William and Ellen Craft were liable to be captured at any moment by Georgia slave hunters. Many abolitionists counselled resistance to the death at all hazards. Instead of running to Canada, fugitives generally armed themselves and thus said, "Give me liberty or give me death."

William and Ellen Craft believed that it was their duty, as citizens of Massachusetts, to observe a more legal and civilized mode of conforming to the marriage rite than had been permitted them in slavery, and as Theodore Parker had shown himself a very warm friend of theirs, they agreed to have their wedding over again according to the laws of a free State. After performing the ceremony, the renowned and fearless advocate of equal rights (Theodore Parker), presented William with a revolver and a dirk-knife, counseling him to use them manfully in defence of his wife and himself, if ever an attempt should be made by his owners or anybody else to re-enslave them.

But, notwithstanding all the published declarations made by abolitionists and fugitives, to the effect that slave-holders and slave-catchers in visiting Massachusetts in pursuit of their runaway property, would be met by just such weapons as Theodore Parker presented William with, to the surprise of all Boston, the owners of William and Ellen actually had the effrontery to attempt their recapture under the Fugitive Slave Law.

3.21. "Show Me a Bill of Sale from the Almighty." The Abolitionist
Lydia Maria Child Exhorts the Legislature of Massachusetts to
Defy the Fugitive Slave Law (1860)

The following selection, published just before the Civil War, was written to persuade the members of the Massachusetts Legislature that the Fugitive Slave Law of 1850, which obliged the authorities of that state to hunt down and return runaway slaves to their masters, was "utterly wicked and should never be obeyed." The author of this message, Lydia Maria Child, was a gifted novelist, biographer, poet, short-story writer, editor, and uncompromising abolitionist who appealed to the legislators through discussions of many aspects of slavery. These included the causes and effects of slave trading, the ban against teaching blacks to read and write, biblical justifications of servitude, the antics, pastimes and debaucheries of members of the slaveholding class, the mystery of how it was that among slaves "brown and yellow complexions came to be so common," brutal punishments inflicted upon slaves, and Chief Justice Roger Taney's notorious Dred Scott Decision of 1857 (see Doc. 3.14).

Still more convincing, perhaps, were the tragic anecdotes Mrs. Child related to the legislators, based on authentic experiences of slaves who strived to improve their lives and those of their loved ones but in the end saw their hopes and ambitions wrecked. Still more relevant to the question mainly at hand—the enforcement of the Fugitive Slave Law in Massachusetts—were the parts of her appeal that more than hint at the reasons slaves risked their lives to secure safe and permanent havens from tyranny.

SOURCE: L. Maria Child, *The Duty of Disobedience to the Fugitive Slave Act: An Appeal to the Legislators of Massachusetts* (Boston: American Anti-Slavery Society, 1860). In *Anti-Slavery Tracts,* series 2, no. 9, *New Series,* pp. 3–23.

I feel there is no need of apologizing to the Legislature of Massachusetts because a woman addresses them. . . . I therefore offer no excuses on that score. But I do feel as if it required some apology to attempt to convince men of ordinary humanity and common sense that the Fugitive Slave Law is utterly wicked and consequently ought never to be obeyed. Yet Massachusetts consents to that law! Some shadow of justice she grants, inasmuch as her Legislature have passed what is called a Personal Liberty Bill, securing trial by jury to those claimed as slaves. Certainly it is *something* gained, especially for those who may get brown by working in the sunshine, to prevent our Southern masters from taking any of us, at a moment's notice, and dragging us off into perpetual bondage. It is *something* gained to require legal proof that a man is a slave, before he is given up to arbitrary torture and unrecompensed toil. But is *that* the measure of justice becoming the character of a free Commonwealth? *"Prove* that the man is property, according to *your* laws, and I will drive him into your cattle-pen with sword and bayonet," is what Massachusetts practically says to Southern tyrants. "Show me a Bill of Sale from the Almighty!" is what you *ought* to say. No other proof should be considered valid in a Christian country.

One thousand five hundred years ago, Gregory, a Bishop in Asia Minor, preached a sermon in which he rebuked the sin of slaveholding. Indignantly he asked, "Who can be the possessor of human beings save God? Those men that you say belong to you, did not God create them free? Command the brute creation; that is well. Bend the beasts of the field beneath your yoke. But are your fellow-men to be bought and sold, like herds of cattle? Who can pay the value of a being created in the image of God? The whole world itself bears no proportion to the value of a soul, on which the Most High has set the seal of his likeness. This world will perish, but the soul of man is immortal. Show me, then, your titles of possession. Tell me whence you derive this strange claim. Is not your own nature the same with that of those you call your slaves? Have they not the same origin with your-selves? Are they not born to the same immortal destinies?"

Thus spake a good old Bishop, in the early years of Christianity. Since then, thousands and thousands of noble souls have given their bodies to the gibbet and the stake, to help onward the slow progress of truth and free-dom; a great unknown continent has been opened as a new, free starting point for the human race; printing has been invented, and the command, "Whatsoever ye would that men should do unto you, do ye even so unto them," has been sent abroad in all the languages of the earth. And here, in the noon-day light of the nineteenth century, in a nation claiming to be the freest and most enlightened on the face of the globe, a portion of the pop-ulation of fifteen States have thus agreed among themselves: "Other men shall work for us, without wages, while we smoke, and drink, and gamble, and race horses, and fight. We will have their wives and daughters for con-cubines, and sell their children in the market with horses and pigs. If they make any objection to this arrangement, we will break them into subjec-tion with the cow-hide and the bucking-paddle. They shall not be permit-ted to read or write, because that would be likely to 'produce dissatisfaction in their minds.' If they attempt to run away from us, our blood-hounds shall tear the flesh from their bones, and any man who sees them may shoot them down like mad dogs. If they succeed in getting beyond our frontier, into States where it is the custom to pay men for their work, and to protect their wives and children from outrage, we will compel the people of those States to drive them back into the jaws of our blood-hounds."

And what do the people of the other eighteen States of that enlight-ened country answer to this monstrous demand? What says Massachusetts, with the free blood of the Puritans coursing in her veins, and with the sword uplifted in her right hand, to procure "peaceful repose under lib-erty"? Massachusetts answers: "O yes. We will be your blood-hounds, and pay our own expenses. Only prove to our satisfaction that the stranger who has taken refuge among us is one of the men you have agreed upon your-selves to whip into working without wages, and we will hunt him back for you. Only prove to us that this woman, who has run away from your harem, was bought for a concubine, that you might get more drinking-money by the sale of the children she bears you, and our soldiers will hunt her back with alacrity."....

Legislators of Massachusetts, can it be that you really understand what Slavery *is,* and yet consent that a fugitive slave, who seeks protection here, shall be driven back to that dismal house of bondage? For sweet charity's sake, I must suppose that you have been too busy with your farms and your merchandise ever to have imagined yourself in the situation of a slave. Let me suppose a case for you; one of a class of cases occurring by hundreds every year. Suppose your father was Governor of Carolina and your mother was a slave. The Governor's wife hates your mother, and is ingenious in inventing occasions to have you whipped. *You* don't know the reason why, poor child! but your mother knows full well. If they would only allow her to go away and work for wages, she would gladly toil and earn money to buy you. But that your father will not allow. His laws have settled it that she is his property, "for all purposes whatsoever," and he will keep her as long as suits his convenience. The mistress continually insists upon her being sold far away South; and after a while she has her will. Your poor mother clings to you convulsively; but the slave-driver gives you both a cut of his whip, and tells you to stop your squalling. They drive her off with the gang, and you never hear of her again; but, for a long time afterward, it makes you very sad to remember the farewell look of those large loving eyes. Your poor mother had handsome eyes; and this was one reason her mistress hated her.

You are also your father's property; and when he dies, you will be the property of your whiter brother. You black his shoes, tend upon him at table, and sleep on the floor in his room, to give him water if he is thirsty in the night. You see him learning to read, and you hear your father read wonderful things from the newspapers. Very naturally, you want to read, too. You ask your brother to teach you the letters. He gives you a kick, calls you a "damned nig," and informs his father, who orders you to be flogged for insolence. Alone on the floor at night, still smarting from your blows, you ponder over the great mystery of knowledge, and wonder why it would do *you* any more harm than it does your brother. Henceforth, all scraps of newspapers you can find are carefully laid by. Helplessly you pore over them, at stolen moments, as if you expected some miracle would reveal the meaning of those printed signs. Cunning comes to your aid. It is the only weapon of the weak against the strong. When you see white boys playing in the street, you trace a letter in the sand, and say, "My young master calls that B." "That ain't B, you damned nigger. That's A"! they shout. Now you know what shape is A; and diligently you hunt it out, wherever it is to be found on your scraps of newspaper. By slow degrees you toil on, in similar ways, through all the alphabet. No student of Greek or Hebrew ever deserved so much praise for ingenuity and diligence. But the years pass on, and still you cannot read. Your master-brother now and then gives you a copper. You hoard them and buy a primer; screening yourself from suspicion, by telling the bookseller that your master wants it for his sister's little boy. You find the picture of a cat, with three letters by its side; and now you know how cat is spelt. Elated with your wonderful discovery, you are eager to catch a minute to study your primer. Too eager, alas! for your mistress catches you absorbed in it, and your little book is promptly burned. You are sent to be flogged, and your lacerated back is washed with brine to make it heal quickly. But in spite of all their efforts, your intelligent mind is too cunning for them. Before twenty years have passed, you have stumbled along into the Bible; alone in the dark, over a rugged road of vowels and consonants. You keep the precious volume concealed under a board in the floor, and read it at snatches by the light of a pine knot. You read that God has created of one blood all the nations of the earth; and that his commandment is, to do unto others as we would that they should do unto us. You think of your weeping mother, torn from your tender arms by the cruel slavetrader; of the interdicted light of knowledge; of the Bible kept as a sealed book from all whose skins have a tinge of black, or brown, or yellow; of how those brown and yellow complexions came to be so common; of yourself, the son of the Governor, yet obliged to read the Bible by stealth, under the penalty of a bleeding back washed with brine. These and many other things revolve in your active mind, and your unwritten inferences are worth whole folios of theological commentaries.

As youth ripens into manhood, life bears for you, as it does for others, its brightest, sweetest flower. You love young Amy, with rippling black hair, and large dark eyes, with long, silky fringes. You inherit from your father, the Governor, a taste for beauty warmly-tinted, like Cleopatra's. You and Amy are of a rank to make a suitable match; for you are the son of a Southern Governor, and she is the daughter of a United States Senator, from the North, who often shared her master's hospitality, and he being large-minded enough to "conquer prejudices." You have good sympathy in other respects also, for your mothers were both slaves; and, as it is conveniently and profitably arranged for the masters that "the child shall follow the condition of the *mother*," you are consequently both of you slaves. But there are some compensations for your hard lot. Amy's simple admiration flatters your vanity. She considers you a prodigy of learning because you can read the Bible, and she has not the faintest idea how such skill can be acquired. She gives you her whole heart, full of the blind confidence of a first love. The divine spark, which kindles aspirations for freedom in the human soul, has been glowing more and more brightly since you have emerged from boyhood, and now her glances kindle it into a flame. For her dear sake you long to be a free man, with power to protect her from the degrading incidents of a slave-girl's life. Wages acquire new value in your eyes, from a wish to supply her with comforts, and enhance her beauty by becoming dress.

In the Hands of Strangers

For her sake, you are ambitious to acquire skill in the carpenter's trade, to which your master-brother has applied you as the best investment of his human capital. It is true, he takes all your wages; but then, by acquiring uncommon facility, you hope to accomplish your daily tasks in shorter time, and thus obtain some extra hours to do jobs for yourself. These you can eke out by working late into the night, and rising when the day dawns. Thus you calculate to be able in time to buy the use of your own limbs. Poor fellow! Your intelligence and industry prove a misfortune. They charge twice as much for the machine of your body on account of the soul-power which moves it. Your master-brother tells you that you would bring eighteen hundred dollars in the market. It is a large sum. Almost hopeless seems the prospect of earning it, at such odd hours as you can catch when the hard day's task is done. But you look at Amy, and are inspired with faith to remove mountains. Your master-brother graciously consents to receive payments by instalments. These prove a convenient addition to the whole of your wages. They will enable him to buy a new race horse, and increase his stock of choice wines. While he sleeps off drunkenness, you are toiling for him, with the blessed prospect of freedom far ahead, but burning brightly in the distance, like a Drummond Light, guiding the watchful mariner over a midnight sea.

When you have paid five hundred dollars of the required sum, your lonely heart so longs for the comforts of a home, that you can wait no longer. You marry Amy, with the resolution of buying her also, and removing to those Free States, about which you have often talked together, as invalids discourse of heaven. Amy is a member of the church, and it is a great point with her to be married by a minister. Her master and mistress make no objection, knowing that after the ceremony she will remain an article of property, the same as ever. Now come happy months, during which you almost forget that you are a slave, and that it must be a weary long while before you can earn enough to buy yourself and your dear one, in addition to supporting your dissipated master. But you toil bravely on, and soon pay another hundred dollars toward your ransom. The Drummond Light of Freedom burns brighter in the diminished distance.

Alas! in an unlucky hour, your tipsy master-brother sees your gentle Amy, and becomes enamored of her large dark eyes, and the rich golden tint of her complexion. Your earnings and your ransom-money make him flush of cash. In spite of all your efforts to prevent it, she becomes his property. He threatens to cowhide her, if you ever speak to her again. You remind him that she is your wife; that you were married by a minister. "Married, you damned nigger!" he exclaims; "what does a slave's marriage amount to? If you give me any more of your insolence, you'll get a taste of the cowhide."

Anxious days and desolate nights pass. There is such a heavy pain at your heart, it is a mystery to yourself that you do not die. At last, Amy contrives to meet you, pale and wretched as yourself. She has a mournful story to tell of degrading propositions, and terrible threats. She promises to love you always, and be faithful to you till death, come what may. Poor Amy! When she said that, she did not realize how powerless is the slave, in the hands of an unprincipled master. Your interview was watched, and while you were sobbing in each other's arms, you were seized and ordered to receive a hundred lashes. While you are lying in jail, stiff with your wounds, your master-brother comes to tell you he has sold you to a trader from Arkansas. You remind him of the receipt he has given you for six hundred dollars, and ask him to return the money. He laughs in your face, and tells you his receipt is worth no more than so much brown paper; that no contracts with a slave are binding. He coolly adds, "Besides, it has taken all my spare money to buy Amy." Perhaps you would have killed him in that moment of desperation, even with the certainty of being burnt to cinders for the deed, but you are too horribly wounded by the lash to be able to spring upon him. In that helpless condition, you are manacled and carried off by the slave-trader. Never again will Amy's gentle eyes look into yours. What she suffers you will never know. She is suddenly wrenched from your youth, as your mother was from your childhood. The pall of silence falls over all her future. She cannot read or write; and the post-office was not instituted for slaves.

Looking back on that dark period of desolation and despair, you marvel how you lived through it. But the nature of youth is elastic. You have learned that law offers colored men nothing but its *penalties;* that white men engross all its *protection;* still you are tempted to make another bargain for your freedom. Your new master seems easy and good-natured, and you trust he will prove more honorable than your brother has been. Perhaps he would; but unfortunately, he is fond of cards; and when you have paid him two hundred dollars, he stakes them, and you also, at the gaming-table, and loses. The winner is a hard man, noted for severity to his slaves. Now you resolve to take the risk of running away, with all its horrible chances. You hide in a neighboring swamp, where you are bitten by a venomous snake, and your swollen limb becomes almost incapable of motion. In great anguish, you drag it along through the midnight darkness, to the hut of a poor plantation-slave, who binds on a poultice of ashes, but dares not, for fear of his life, shelter you after the day has dawned. He helps you to a deep gully, and there you remain till evening, half-famished for food. A man in the neighborhood keeps blood-hounds, well trained to hunt runaways. They get on your track, and tear flesh from the leg which the snake had spared. To escape them, you leap into the river. The sharp ring of rifles meets your ear. You plunge under water. When you come up to take breath, a rifle ball lodges in your shoulder, and you plunge again. Suddenly, thick clouds throw their friendly veil over the moon. You swim for your life, with balls whizzing round you. Thanks to the darkness and the water, you baffle the hounds, both animal and human. Weary and wounded, you travel through the forests, your eye fixed hopefully on the North Star, which seems ever beckoning you onward to freedom, with its bright glances through the foliage. In the day-time, you lie in the deep holes of swamps, concealed by rank weeds and tangled vines, taking such rest as can be obtained among swarms of mosquitoes and snakes. Through incredible perils and fatigues, foot-sore and emaciated, you arrive at last in the States called Free. You allow yourself little time to rest, so eager are you to press on further North. You have heard the masters swear with peculiar violence about Massachusetts, and you draw the inference that it is a refuge for the oppressed. Within the borders of that old Commonwealth, you breathe more freely than you have ever done. You resolve to rest awhile, at least, before you go to Canada. You find friends, and begin to hope that you may be allowed to remain and work, if you prove yourself industrious and well behaved. Suddenly you find yourself arrested and chained. Soldiers escort you through the streets of Boston, and put you on board a Southern ship, to be sent back to your master. When you arrive, he orders you to be flogged so unmercifully, that the doctor says you will die if they strike another blow. The philanthropic city of Boston hears the bloody tidings, and one of the men in authority says to the public: "Fugitive slaves are a class of foreigners, with whose rights Massachusetts has nothing to do. It is enough for *us*, that they have no right to be *here*." [77] And the merchants of Boston cry, Amen.[78]

Legislators of Massachusetts! if *you* had been thus continually robbed of your rights by the hand of violence, what would *you* think of the com-

77. Said by the U. S. Commissioner, George Ticknor Curtis, at a Union Meeting, in the old Cradle of Liberty.

78. This account was probably based on the experiences of Thomas Sims, a slave who fled Georgia in 1851 and escaped to Massachusetts, where he was seized as a fugitive and sent back to Georgia. In 1860 Lydia Child read a letter from Sims in which he expressed an intense desire for freedom, and so she asked for contributions to pay the $1,800 his master was asking for Sims, a skilled mechanic. Charles Devens, the marshal who ordered Sims's recapture in Boston but later had a change of heart, offered to pay Sims's full price, but Sims remained a slave until 1863 when he escaped to Grant's army in Vicksburg. See *Letters of Lydia Maria Child* (New York: AMS Press, 1971), pp. 144–45, 189. Editor.

pact between North and South to perpetuate your wrongs, and transmit them to your posterity? Would you not regard it as a league between highwaymen, who had "no rights that you were bound to respect"?[79] I put the question plainly and directly to your consciences and your common sense, and they will not allow you to answer, No. Are you, then, doing right to sustain the validity of a law for *others,* which you would vehemently reject for *yourselves,* in the name of outraged justice and humanity? . . .

You have all heard of Margaret Garner, who escaped from Kentucky to Ohio, with her father and mother, her husband and four children. The Cincinnati papers described her as "a dark mulatto, twenty-three years of age, of an interesting appearance, considerable intelligence, and a good address." Her husband was described as "about twenty-two years of age, of a very lithe, active form, and rather a mild, pleasant countenance." These fugitives were sheltered by a colored friend in Ohio. There the hounds in pay of the United States, to which "price of blood" you and I and all of us contribute, ferreted them out, and commanded them to surrender. When they refused to do so, they burst open the door, and assailed the inmates of the house with cudgels and pistols. They defended themselves bravely, but were overpowered by numbers and disarmed. When Margaret perceived that there was no help for her and her little ones, she seized a knife and cut the throat of her most beautiful child. She was about to do the same by the others, when her arm was arrested. The child killed was nearly white, and exceedingly pretty. The others were mulattoes, and pretty also. What history lay behind this difference of complexion the world will probably never know. But I have talked confidentially with too many fugitive women not to know that very sad histories do lie behind such facts. Margaret Garner knew very well what fate awaited her handsome little daughter, and that nerved her arm to strike the death-blow. . . .

These slaves were soon after sent down the Mississippi to be sold in Arkansas. The boat came in collision with another boat and many were drowned. The shock threw Margaret overboard, with a baby in her arms. She was too valuable a piece of property to lose, and they drew her out of the water; but the baby was gone. She evinced no emotion but joy, still saying it was better for their children to die than to be slaves. . . .

79. The author paraphrases the Dred Scott Decision of 1857 (see Doc. 3.14), in which Chief Justice Roger Taney claimed that for more than a century blacks had been regarded as "beings of an inferior order and altogether unfit to associate with the white race, either in social or political relations; *and so far inferior that they had no rights which the white man was bound to respect,* and that the negro might justly and lawfully be reduced to slavery for his benefit." Editor.

15. "The Modern Medea: The Story of Margaret Garner." *Harper's Weekly,* May 18, 1867. Courtesy of the Special Collections Department, University of Pittsburgh Library System.

Again I ask, what would be your judgment of this law, if your *own* daughter and infant grand-daughter had been its victims? You know very well, that had it been your *own* case, such despotism, calling itself law, would be swept away in a whirlwind of indignation, and men who strove to enforce it would be obliged to flee the country.[80]

What satisfactory reasons can be alleged for submitting to this degradation? What good excuse can be offered? Shall we resort to the Old Testament argument, that anodyne for the consciences of "South-Side" divines?[81] Suppose the descendants of Ham were ordained to be slaves to the end of time, for an offence committed thousands of years ago, by a progenitor they never heard of. Still, the greatest amount of theological research leaves it very uncertain who the descendants of Ham are, and where they are. I presume you would not consider the title to

80. According to Carolyn L. Karcher, editor of an edition of Child's book, *An Appeal in Favor of That Class of Americans Called Africans* (Amherst: University of Massachusetts Press, 1996), Toni Morrison's novel *Beloved* was based on Child's account of Margaret Garner. For discussions of Garner, see Campbell, *The Slave Catchers,* pp. 144–47, and Julian Yanuck, "The Garner Fugitive Slave Case," *Mississippi Valley Historical Review* 40 (June 1953): 47–66. Editor.

81. A reference to Reverend Nehemiah Adams's apology for slavery in *A South-Side View of Slavery* (see Doc. 2.17). Editor.

even one acre of land satisfactorily settled by evidence of such extremely dubious character; how much less, then, a man's ownership of himself! Then, again, if we admit that Africans are descendants of Ham, what is to be said of thousands of slaves, advertised in Southern newspapers as "passing themselves for white men, or white women"? Runaways with "blue eyes, light hair, and rosy complexions"? Are these sons and daughters of our Presidents, our Governors, our Senators, our Generals, and our Commodores, descendants of Ham? Are *they* Africans? . . .

In the name of oppressed humanity, of violated religion, of desecrated law, of tarnished honor, of our own freedom endangered, of the moral sense of our people degraded by these evil influences, I respectfully, but most urgently, entreat you to annul this infamous enactment, so far as the jurisdiction of Massachusetts extends. Our old Commonwealth has been first and foremost in many good works; let her lead in this also. And deem it not presumptuous, if I ask it likewise for my own sake. I am a humble member of the community; but I am deeply interested in the welfare and reputation of my native State, and that gives me some claim to be heard. I am growing old; and on this great question of equal rights I have toiled for years, sometimes with a heart sickened by "hope deferred." I beseech you to let me die on Free Soil! . . .

If you cannot be induced to reform this great wickedness, for the sake of outraged justice and humanity, then do it for the honor of the State, for the political welfare of our own people, for the moral character of our posterity. For, as sure as there is a Righteous Ruler in the heavens, if you continue to be accomplices in violence and fraud, God will *not* "save the Commonwealth of Massachusetts."

L. MARIA CHILD.[82]

82. In the month of Lincoln's inauguration, March 1861, Massachusetts added a provision to its personal liberty law denying state officials the right to remove runaway slaves from the custody of federal marshals, thus recognizing the responsibility of the national government to capture fugitives and return them to their owners under due process of law. See Campbell, *The Slave Catchers*, p. 183.

The Fugitive Slave Law, deemed unconstitutional by many members of Congress, contained the following provisions: A U.S. marshal who refused to enforce the law could be fined one thousand dollars, and if a fugitive in his custody escaped, he was "liable for his full value." A slaveholder could pursue and reclaim a fugitive by obtaining a warrant, or by simply arresting him. Judges were required to hear cases "in a summary manner" and to grant certificates allowing claimants to remove fugitives to the state or territory from which they had allegedly escaped. The testimony of a fugitive was not admissible in court. A person aiding a runaway could be fined a thousand dollars and imprisoned for six months. A judge was to receive ten dollars for each runaway he returned to a claimant, but if the fugitive was not returned the judge would receive half that amount. Finally, if a slaveholder feared his slave might be rescued, the officer in charge was required to transport him to the state from which he was thought to have fled, hiring as many men as he thought necessary, expenses to be paid by the U.S. Treasury. Editor.

3.22. "Like Thrusting a Walking Stick into an Ant Hill." The Beginnings of the Civil War and the Outbreak of a Major Runaway Movement

W. E. B. Du Bois wrote regarding the first phase of the Civil War: "So long as the Union army stood still and talked, the Negro kept quiet and worked. The moment the Union army moved into slave territory, the Negro joined it. Despite all argument and calculation and in the face of refusals and commands, wherever the Union armies marched, appeared the fugitive slaves. It made no difference what the obstacles were, or the attitudes of the commanders. It was 'like thrusting a walking stick into an ant hill,' says one writer. And yet the army chiefs at first tried to regard it as an exceptional and temporary matter, a thing which they could control, when as a matter of fact it was the meat and kernel of the war." As Du Bois implied, this was the start of a "general strike" among the slaves of the South which revealed the fugitives' determination to escape their servitude and make a better life for themselves and their families.[83]

When three runaway slaves entered Fortress Monroe, Virginia, in May 1861, soon after the start of the Civil War, the camp commander, General Benjamin F. Butler, set them free, contrary to the wishes of a southern officer, whose encounter with Butler (under a flag of truce) went roughly as follows:

"MAJOR CARY (the Confederate officer): I am informed that three Negroes, belonging to Colonel Mallory, have escaped into your lines. I am Colonel Mallory's agent and have charge of his property. What do you intend to do with regard to these Negroes?

"GENERAL BUTLER: I propose to retain them.

"MAJOR CARY: Do you mean, then, to set aside your constitutional obligations?

"GENERAL BUTLER: I mean to abide by the decision of Virginia, as expressed in her ordinance of secession. I am under no constitutional obligations to a foreign country, which Virginia now claims to be.

"MAJOR CARY: But you say we *can't* secede, and so you cannot consistently detain the Negroes.

"GENERAL BUTLER: But you say you *have* seceded, and so you can-

---

83. See W. E. B. DuBois, *Black Reconstruction in America* (Cleveland: World Publishing, 1962), pp. 55–83. For the runaway movement, see Benjamin Quarles, *The Negro in the Civil War* (Boston: Little, Brown, 1969), pp. 54–77. For the Butler-Cary discussion, see Quarles, pp. 59–60, and for a brilliant account of the blacks in the Union Army, see Thomas Wentworth Higginson, *Army Life in a Black Regiment* (New York: Colliers Books, 1962).

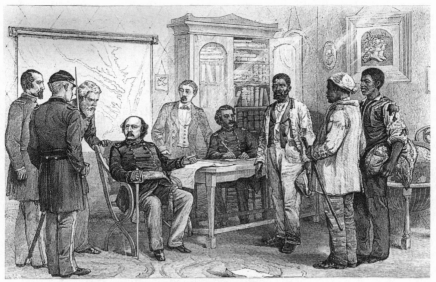

CONTRABAND OF WAR.

16. "Contraband of War." Sketch by special artist in Fortress Monroe. Courtesy of the
Casemate Museum, Fort Monroe, Virginia.

not consistently claim them. I shall detain the Negroes as contraband of
war. You are using them on the batteries. It is merely a question whether
they shall be used for or against the government. Nevertheless, although I
greatly need the labor that has providentially fallen into my hands, if
Colonel Mallory will come into the fort and take the oath of allegiance to
the United States, he shall have his Negroes, and I will endeavor to hire
them from him." Butler's use of the term "contraband of war" in this context allowed him and other Union commanders to reject slaveholder demands for restitution of their slaves, thus encouraging slaves to abandon
their masters and take to the road. Almost at once they were streaming into
Fortress Monroe, eight one day, fifty-nine the next, and so forth, some 900
arriving in the first two months. "Contraband" camps were soon set up to
receive fugitives, and, although the policy of freeing and protecting runaways was controversial during much of the war, "contrabands" often received protection, shelter, opportunities to work for wages, and other
advantages, and tens of thousands of black northerners and former slaves
served honorably in the Union army. The following documents prove that
many runaway slaves were betrayed, some by northern soldiers, but that
others grasped the opportunities offered by the war and so became a vital

factor in the triumph of the Union and the winning of their own freedom. Many others, however, were assembled and sent wholesale to the South by their masters, as a way to preserve their threatened assets.

SOURCES: *Douglass Monthly,* October 1861, p. 543; December 1861, pp. 564–65; Ira Berlin, *The Destruction of Slavery* (New York: Cambridge University Press, 1985), pp. 88–90.

Stealing Slaves to Sell South, from *Douglass Monthly,* October, 1861.

Negroes who have recently sought refuge within the Federal lines at Fortress Monroe agree in representing that there are bands of kidnappers scouring the country for miles around that region. These land-pirates systematically steal all the able-bodied, salable negroes they can, and run them off to the Southern markets and pocket the proceeds. The system of land-piracy has, according to representation, been carried to a considerable extent. So that, between the flight of the negroes and the stealing by the land-pirates, the owners of this species of property in that region are likely to fare badly. This fact illustrates the morals of the rebels, and their proclivity for the slave trade. In this section property in slaves some time since ceased to have any real value. The standard of valuation is completely broken down, and sales of slaves are not heard of. The relation of master and slave does not exist, and it involves no one in the charge of Abolitionism to predict that there is hardly any likelihood of its ever being revived. This state of things must necessarily have a radical effect in landed and every other species of property related to labor. Indeed, every other kind of property has but little more real value than that in negroes. If the lands in that part of the State are ever again cultivated, it must be by free labor. Some of the finest estates in Virginia were in that part of the State. Nearly all of them are now abandoned.

Dealings with Slavery and the Contrabands. Facts, Scenes and Incidents from *Douglass Monthly,* December, 1861.

The recent orders of the government in relation to the contraband negroes have set the newspaper correspondents on the track of investigation, and the testimony that they give is quite curious. Their accounts of the condition and sentiments of the blacks in the rebellious regions into which our armies have penetrated confirm the statements recently made by **Mr. Pierce** in the Atlantic Monthly. The negroes at the South, so far from being degraded animals, are shown to be as keenly alive to the events going on about them as the majority of their masters, and quite ready to take their freedom in any way that is presented to them.

Here are some specimens of the evidence. The first is from a Maryland letter in the Boston Journal:

In a former letter I spoke of the opinions of "my host," that he considered this to be an abolition war. He is not alone in the opinion; for the negroes also look upon it as such. The question arises: how did the negroes form this opinion in regard to it? It is plain they do not read the papers; neither have they been informed of it by abolition emissaries. They have formed their opinions by hearing it discussed by their masters, or by that instinctive feeling which all men have that they are entitled to freedom. Not a few have availed themselves of the commotion of the times, and as riches take to themselves wings, so they have taken to themselves legs, and ran away. Some masters, seeing the storm approaching, sold their slaves last spring. Some who loved secession more than the Union emigrated to Dixie, leaving their negroes behind, who in turn have emigrated to points unknown. It is evident that through all this region the people consider that their hold upon human flesh as property is very much weakened, and the negroes are accordingly treated with great kindness. In reality it is weakened. Every negro has heard of the North, but now, with soldiers all over the country, it is certain that they will obtain a definite knowledge of geography. They are becoming restless, and though the soldiers pass on, the influence of their advent will not be lost. The negroes will remember it, especially the younger ones, who on some future morning, quite likely, will not answer when the master calls. I do not think that the soldiers encourage the slaves to run away, but it is an inevitable consequence from the occupation of the country by the troops that they should learn more of freedom than they knew before, and it would be strange, indeed, if knowing more they did not feel the kindling desire to make the best of their knowledge.

The next is from a letter in the Boston Traveler, written at Hall's Hill, Va.:

When I have been on picket guard I have sometimes had opportunities to visit houses, and have talked with a number of slaves.—They all talk the same way with slight variations. The following conversation with one that came into our camp a few days since will serve as a specimen of the whole.

"How were you treated, Robert?"

"Pretty well, sar."

"Did your master give you enough to eat and clothe you comfortably?"

"Pretty well, till dis year. Massa hab no money to spend dis year. Don't get many clothes dis year."

"If you had a good master, I suppose you were contented?"

"No, sar."

"Why not, if you had enough to eat and clothes to wear?"

"Cause I want to be *free.*"

"You say you have a wife and children owned by another man; that they are treated well, and you had a chance to see them once a fortnight. If you were all free how would you manage to support your wife and children?"

His eyes sparkled as he answered, "I'd hire a little cabin with a little garden, and keep a pig and cow. I'd work out by the day, and I would save money. I've got eight dollars now that I laid up dis summer. But if I didn't save a cent, I should feel better to be **FREE**."

"Can you read and write?"

"No, sar. Massa know we can't read a word; but dis summer he's skeered to hab us see a paper."

"What do the slaves say about the war?"

"Dey tink Lincoln is gwine to free us."

"Where did they hear that?"

"Massa said so, last fall, afore he was President."

"Did you ever hear of John Brown?"

"I did so, sar. Ebery body hear 'bout him. Dar was great time when he come to Harper's Ferry. Folks was all skeered to death. Dey went up from all round here to see him hung."

"Do you think he was a good man?"

"Yes, sar, a mighty fine man."

The Chicago Tribune's correspondent at Paducah, Ky., writes:

A few days ago there was a "scene" at Gen Paine's headquarters worth describing. Some time previous, a black woman, accompanied by a child, came to the General's quarters, desiring protection; and in reply to the question "if she was a slave," stated that she was not, and that her free parents were at Clarksville, Tenn. She was employed to assist in the housework, which she continued to do up to the time we mention, when a lady who lived a few miles from town came to the headquarters and inquired for Gen. Paine, and on being presented to him as Mrs. F——, asked him if he had "her nigger" there. The general, supposing that she meant a negro man for whom unsuccessful search had just been made, replied that he had not. "Why," said she, "haven't you got my nigger woman and child here?" "Negro woman and child," said the general; "perhaps so; come and see." The woman was called and came to the door. "That's the one; she's mine. She left me [at such a time] and stole a horse and a lot of other things, the mean thing," &c., &c., with divers epithets more emphatic than refined. "Stole a horse!" said the General, in a tone of utter amazement, "I don't see how that can be. One piece of property steal another? I've heard of a horse running away with a wagon, and pigs getting into the garden and eating up the potatoes, but I never heard that called stealing." The hit was so palpable that of a room full every one laughed outright, even to the lady's father; but she did not seem to see the joke, and maintained a sour gravity.

A venerable looking gentleman, the lady's father, who was sitting near, spoke up and said: "Daughter, take the oath and be a good loyal woman." But still she hesitated, and thought as she was a woman she ought to have her "nigger" without taking the oath, when the General assured her that she not only couldn't get the negro without taking the oath, but that if she violated the oath after taking it, that he would be sure to know it, and that she would in that case not only lose her negro, but whatever property she had beside. . . .

The Washington correspondent of the N. Y. Post, under date of Nov. 8th, says:

The little steamer Stepping Stones the other night brought up a half-dozen contrabands, picked up by a tug-boat in the lower Potomac. Their escape from the Virginia shore was almost miraculous. The six got into a canoe made of a pine log, and floated out into the stream in the night, where they were lucky enough to find the tug-boat Bailey, which took them on board at once. Two of them left wives behind, whom they did not venture to trust with their secret of escape. They express the opinion that a large number of fugitives have been drowned in the Potomac, as the runaway slaves, when they get to the river, become desperate in the fear of pursuing masters.

From the accounts given by those and other fugitives from Virginia, the slave population there is suffering very much because of a lack of clothing and provisions. The master takes care of himself first, as a matter of course, and the rebel troops must be fed and clothed next, while the slave comes in last for his share, which is very small indeed.—Under this state of things, many negroes run away to the land of plenty, and thousands of others expect soon to do the same thing, if an opportunity occurs. The far-seeing men of the South are looking forward to the [Christmas] holidays with much anxiety, for that is the time on which the great negro insurrections have always occurred. Should this season be passed in peace, they are confident that the negroes can be kept down through the war.

The Washington correspondent of the New York Tribune relates the following:

Widow Triplet, who lives near Alexandria, and whose sympathies are believed to be with the rebels, unaccountably lost eight slaves.—She thought that they were within the lines of General Heintzelman's command and applied to that officer for relief. Foreseeing one possible objection to the return of her chattels, she backed her position with a penal bond, pledging herself not to sell them South. The bond, Gen. Heintzelman told her he was lawyer enough to know to be worthless, because without a consideration. The slaves he declined to search for or surrender, adding that he was no "negro-catcher." It is said that this reply has excited great apprehension in the minds of Widow Triplet's slaveholding neighbors.

Running Negroes South
Harper's Weekly, November 8, 1862.

On pages 712 and 713 we publish an illustration of an event of very frequent occurrence at the present time in Virginia: namely the DRIVING OF NEGROES SOUTH in order to escape the approach of our army. The poor creatures are collected in gangs, handcuffed or chained together, and driven off under the lash or at the point of the bayonet.

One authority says:

"A refugee from the vicinity of Leesburg states that a rebel cavalry force appeared in that place on Monday last and forcibly carried South all the Negroes who had previously been collected together there, and placed in confinement, by order of General Lee.

The Times correspondent says:

While at Aldie, on Thursday last, two citizens named Moore and Ball, came within our lines and were detained as prisoners. The first name is a son of the proprietor of Moore's flour mills at Aldie, on a branch of Goose Creek, and the latter is a large planter in the same town. They have "done nothing," so they said, and were neither bushwhackers nor soldiers, and were surprised at being detained within our lines, when so near their homes, from which they had been absent some time. Upon being questioned closely, they admitted that they had just come from the James River; and finally owned up that they had been running off "niggers," having just taken a large gang, belonging to themselves and neighbors, southward in *chains,* to avoid losing them under the emancipation proclamation. I understand from various sources, that the owners of this species of property, throughout this section of the State, are moving it off toward Richmond as fast as it can be spared from the plantations, and the slaveholders boast that there will not be a Negro left in all this part of the States by the 1st of January next.

17. "Negroes Driven South by the Rebel Officers." *Harper's Weekly*, November 8, 1862. Courtesy of the Special Collections Department, University of Pittsburgh Library System.

Another correspondent says:

The rebels in Secessia are busily engaged just now in running off to Richmond and beyond Negroes and conscripts. A Union man, just from below Culpepper, says he saw droves of Negroes and white men on the road at different points—all strongly guarded. He does not exactly know which excited his pity most, the white or black men.

Testimony of the Superintendent of Contrabands at Fortress Monroe, Virginia, before the American Freedmen's Inquiry Commission[84]

[*Fortress Monroe, Va.,*] May 9, 1863.

Question How many of the people called contrabands, have come under your observation?

Answer Some 10,000 have come under our control, to be fed in part, and clothed in part, but I cannot speak accurately in regard to the number. This is the rendezvous. They come here from all about, from Richmond and 200 miles off in North Carolina. There was one gang that started from Richmond 23 strong and only 3 got through. . . .

Q In your opinion, is there any communication between the negroes and the black men still in slavery?

A Yes Sir, we have had men here who have gone back 200 miles.

Q In your opinion would a change in our policy which would cause them to be treated with fairness, their wages punctually paid and employment furnished them in the army, become known and would it have any effect upon others in slavery?

A Yes—Thousands upon Thousands. I went to Suffolk [about 30 miles south of Fortress Monroe beyond the James River] a short time ago to enquire into the state of things there—for I found I could not get any foot hold to make things work there, through the Commanding General, and I went to the Provost Marshall and all hands—and the colored people actually sent a deputation to me one morning before I was up to know if we put black men in irons and sent them off to Cuba to be sold or set them at work and put balls on their legs and whipped them, just as in slavery; because that was the story up there, and they were frightened and didn't know what to do. When I got at the feelings of these people I found they were not afraid of the slaveholders. They said there was nobody on the plantations but women and they were not afraid of them. One woman came through 200 miles in Men's clothes. The most valuable information we received in regard to the Merrimack and the operations of the rebels came from the

84. From Ira Berlin's *The Destruction of Slavery* (New York: Cambridge University Press), pp. 88–90.

colored people and they got no credit for it. I found hundreds who had left their wives and families behind. I asked them, "Why did you come away and leave them there?" and I found they had heard these stories, and wanted to come and see how it was. "I am going back again after my wife" some of them have said "When I have earned a little money." "What as far as that?" "Yes" and I have had them come to me to borrow money, or to get their pay, if they had earned a months wages, and to get passes. "I am going for my family" they say. "Are you not afraid to risk it?" "No I know the Way" Colored men will help colored men and they will work along the by paths and get through. In that way I have known quite a number who have gone up from time to time in the neighborhood of Richmond and several have brought back their families; some I have never heard from. As I was saying, they do not feel afraid now. The white people have nearly all gone, the blood hounds are not there now to hunt them and they are not afraid, before they were afraid to stay. There are hundreds of negroes at Williamsburgh with their families working for nothing. They would not get pay here and they had rather stay where they are. "We are not afraid of being carried back," a great many have told us and "if we are, we can get away again." Now that they are getting their eyes open they are coming in. Fifty came this morning from Yorktown who followed Stoneman's Cavalry when they returned from their raid. The officers reported to their Quartermaster that they had so many horses and fifty or sixty negroes. "What did you bring them for?" "Why they followed us, and we could not stop them." I asked one of the men about it and he said they would leave their work in the field as soon as they found the Soldiers were Union men and follow them sometimes without hat or coat. They would take the best horses they could get and every where they rode they would take fresh horses, leave the old ones follow on and so they came in. I have questioned a great many of them and they do not feel much afraid; and there are a great many courageous fellows who have come from long distances in rebeldom. Some men who came here from North Carolina, knew all about the [Emancipation] Proclamation and they started on the belief in it; but they had heard these stories and they wanted to know how it was. Well, I gave them the evidence and I have no doubt their friends will hear of it. Within the last two or three months the rebel guards have been doubled on the line and the officers and the privates of the 99th New York between Norfolk and Suffolk have caught hundreds of fugitives and got pay for them.

Q   Do I understand you to say that a great many who have escaped have been sent back?

A   Yes Sir, The masters will come in to Suffolk in the day time and with the help of some of the 99th carry off their fugitives and by and by smuggle them across the lines and the soldier will get his $20. Or $50.

3.23. "The Greatest Possible Blessing That Could Be Bestowed upon the Freed Negro." A Plan to Colonize American Blacks in Brazil (1862)

In his first annual message to Congress in December 1861, President Lincoln, concerned about the many slaves confiscated from rebel masters and the government's obligation to provide for slaves who might yet be freed as a result of the Southern rebellion, recommended that such persons be regarded as free and that steps be taken for "colonizing" them "at some place or places in a climate congenial to them. It might be well to consider, too," he added, "whether the free colored people already in the United States could not, so far as individuals may desire, be included in such colonization." Lincoln understood that to carry out such a plan, territory might have to be purchased, in which case money would have to be appropriated. "If it be said," he added, "that the only legitimate object of acquiring territory is to furnish homes for white men, this measure affects that object, *for the emigration of colored men leaves additional room for white men remaining or coming here.*"[85]

Diplomatic contacts with Britain, France, Holland, Denmark, and Central America were soon initiated on the matter, though without success.[86] Meanwhile, however, Lincoln's ambassador to Brazil, James Watson Webb, was inspired by the president's words to prepare a colonization plan of his own. This scheme, to begin with some 50,000 black migrants, had the potential, in his opinion, of eventually providing Brazil with as many as a million workers, while it would have the "benefit" of "ridding" the United States of an equal number of freed slaves.

Webb's proposal was analyzed by Secretary of State William H. Seward, who commended him for his ideas but politely explained that the president could not accede to his request without additional consideration. Among the problems: It was not known whether the emperor of Brazil

85. James D. Richardson, ed., *A Compilation of the Messages and Papers of the Presidents* (Washington, D.C.: Bureau of National Literature, 1912), vol. 5, pp. 3255. Italics added.

86. See N. Andrew N. Cleven, "Some Plans for Colonizing Liberated Negro Slaves in Hispanic America," *Journal of Negro History* 11 (1926): 36–41. For more colonization schemes during the war, see Staudenraus, *African Colonization Movement*, pp. 240–50.

would prefer an "expelled caste" over other possible sources of labor. The question of whether slavery was "an eradicable evil" remained open and was still "vehemently discussed." Furthermore, it was not yet decided whether, or how, slavery might be ended, whether it would be immediate or gradual, with or without compensation. Colonization itself remained in dispute, as did the question of whether freed persons would be permitted to remain at home, would be sent to a foreign colony or somewhere within U.S. jurisdiction, or even whether their participation would be voluntary or compulsory.

Ironically, no mass migration to Brazil of American ex-slaves took place, but some two thousand white Southerners did settle there after the war, along with at least three former slaves, two of whom came with their former owners and might have been slaves in Brazil. A total of 2,687 colonists were, however, sent to Liberia in the five years following the Civil War, more than seventeen percent of all those sent there from 1817 through 1899.[87]

SOURCE: *Message of the President of the United States to the Two Houses of Congress at the Commencement of the Third Session of the Thirty-Seventh Congress,* vol. 1 (Washington, D.C.: Government Printing Office, 1862), pp. 704–15.

Petrópolis, [Brazil], May 20, 1862.

Sir: I perceive by allusions in the public press, although the message itself, *in extenso,* has not come under my observation, that the President, in suggesting the means of carrying out the gradual manumission of the negro, alludes to the necessity of obtaining a place of colonization for the persons manumitted. The wisdom of such a suggestion is too manifest to require discussion; but the purchase of territory for this wise and philanthropic purpose may be attended with difficulties so embarrassing as, in a measure, to defeat the object in view. It has occurred to me, therefore, that the labor question of Brazil, upon the early solution of which so much depends, and to which I have heretofore referred, may be rendered auxiliary to our own difficulty in disposing of the freed negro.

The rapidly increasing value of the negro in the province of Rio de Janeiro and all the southern provinces of the empire, and the steadily advancing price of coffee, added to the well ascertained fact that the *slave* population is on the *decrease* instead of increase, as with us, where the

---

87. See Frank P. Goldman, *Os pioneiros americanos no Brasil* (São Paulo, 1972), pp. 122–23, and table in Staudenraus, *African Colonization Movement,* p. 251.

African is of a far lower type than those brought to Brazil, is rapidly depopulating the northern provinces of the empire. Every coasting vessel brings its ten to thirty slaves for sale at Rio, for the supply of labor in this vicinity and on the coffee plantations; and the cry is heard from the provinces of Pará, Maranham, Piauhi, Parahiba, Pernambuco, and even Bahia, that they are being depopulated for the benefit of the southern provinces, by the inevitable law of demand and supply. It is now conceded, too, that the negroes on the opposite coast of Africa, whence Brazil was supplied, are a very superior race to the tribes further north, which furnished the slave for the West Indies and the United States. The latter are an ignorant and docile people, and, with few exceptions, they yield themselves naturally to servitude, even in their native Africa. Not so the *Minas* and tribes further south, and from which Brazil was furnished with laborers. They are a fierce, warlike, and intellectual people, to whom slavery is as much a burden as to many of the Caucasian races, and they are not only ready for insurrection and capable of extensive combinations and conspiracies to effect their liberation, as the insurrection in Bahia some years since abundantly proved, but it is now susceptible of demonstration that, throughout the slave population of Brazil, there exists, to a greater or lesser extent, an organized conspiracy to prevent the increase of slavery by the mothers committing infanticide! Of course, *nature* is too powerful in the breasts of women to render such a combination universal, or slavery would cease in a single generation. It is proved, however, that there are sufficient of the fiercer traits among the slaves to render infanticide so frequent as to prevent their increase; and the slave trade being at an end, and colonization from Europe checked by unwise and selfish laws, well may the statesmen of Brazil tremble at the prospect which the future presents. To me it is clearly manifest that, unless the southern provinces of Brazil are supplied with laborers from abroad, which can only be in consequence of a change in the colonization laws of the empire and some special legislation, those provinces lying under the equator will be robbed of their laborers by reason of the higher price which the slave commands in this region, and, in consequence, the north will revert to the possession of the native Indian and the wild beasts, from whom it was conquered by the introduction of African labor.

Is there no remedy for this great evil now pressing with such force upon Brazil? I think there is, and that Providence is pointing out the mode of relief by the events now transpiring in the United States. In one word, the finger of God, in my mind, points to the northern provinces of Brazil as the future home of the manumitted negro of the United States; and thus, by the simplest of all means, the United States, Brazil, and the freed negro are all to be equally benefited by one and the same measure, viz.: a treaty between the United States and Brazil, by which all the freed negroes of the United States shall be transplanted to the region of the Amazon at the expense of the United States, and there be endowed with land gratuitously by Brazil, and at the expiration of a term of years become citizens of Brazil, with all the rights and privileges of the free negro population of the empire; all of whom, by the constitution, are the recognized equals of the white man, and equally eligible with him to the highest offices of the empire, and where already the social distinction between the white and black races, which once existed, have been nearly eradicated. On the bench and in the legislative halls, in the army and the navy, in the learned professions, and among the professors in her colleges, as also in the pulpit and in the social relations of life, the wooly-headed and thick-lipped descendant of Africa has his place side by side with his white "brother" in Brazil, and not unfrequently jostles him for his position.[88]

Under these circumstances it appears to me quite impossible that the government of Brazil could hesitate to enter into any reasonable arrangement which might be suggested and which does not involve the expenditure of money. It is of vital importance to prevent the further depopulation of the northern provinces; and how can that be done so effectually as to introduce free negro labor, and what is more experienced and practical, negro labor? No person familiar with the subject can for a moment doubt but the government of Brazil, with all its apprehension of negro insurrection, would willingly purchase, at $250 per head, 50,000 Africans for the supply of laborers in the northern provinces. This would be a sum of $12,500,000; and it would cost as much more to qualify these Africans for the performance of the duties required of them—say $25,000,000 for the 50,000 Africans.

Now I insist that 50,000 freed negroes from the United States would be worth to Brazil more than 100,000 slaves from Africa; and being free men and citizens, all apprehension of insurrection would cease, while of necessity they would adhere to the soil where originally planted, instead of being shipped off and sold as *chattels* to some other part of the empire where slave labor happened to be in demand. And I propose to *give* Brazil ten or twenty

---

88. Webb misinformed Seward on at least two matters: he claimed that racial prejudice hardly existed in Brazil, and that Brazilian blacks were on their way to achieving something like full equality, which was not at all true. He also exaggerated the importance of infanticide as the cause of the decline of the Brazilian slave population, perhaps because the real reasons—brutal treatment much like that suffered by slaves in the West Indies—would have severely undermined his argument. Editor.

times that number of freed, practical laborers gratuitously, or in return for land now utterly valueless. . . .

Now, my belief is—but of course it is only an opinion, and it will require time to discuss and consider it in all its bearings—that ten thousand, a hundred thousand, or even a million of manumitted slaves may be comfortably transported to Brazil, and here become valuable auxiliaries and useful citizens without one dollar of expense to our government, and solely at the expense of the colonist himself. . . .

I propose, then, simply as suggestions for your consideration and for the consideration of all the philanthropists of the United States or throughout the world, that a joint stock colonization company be created, the liability of every subscriber to which shall be limited to the amount of his subscription, and that the president of such company, and one-fifth of the directors, shall be appointed by the President of the United States: that for every dollar subscribed and paid in, the government shall loan the company, at five per cent, per annum, an equal amount, the sum to be subscribed in the first place to be limited to $3,000,000, to be increased from time to time, according to the demands for colonization. This would give the company an active capital of $6,000,000. The contrabands, or manumitted slaves, should be then transferred to this company to be transported to Brazil, or such other place as may be agreed upon, and the company to have a claim for their services for three years from the time of their arrival. At the expiration of their apprenticeship the freed negroes to receive a certain amount of land, of which at least five acres shall have been cleared, have a hut on it, and shall be rendered suitable for immediate cultivation at the expense of the company; and the emancipated colonist also to have bestowed upon him certain agricultural implements and—dollars in money. Is this feasible? I have not a doubt of it; and if feasible, then beyond all peradventure, it is a project well worthy of the consideration of the philanthropist, the capitalist, and the governments of the United States and Brazil.

1st. Brazil should, and no doubt would, willingly set apart a tract of country in a healthy locality or localities on the shores of the Amazon or in that region, and convey in fee to the company at least one hundred acres of land for every colonist freed, and a proportionate number of acres for all children born to the colonists during their apprenticeship, who, of course, would be liberated with their parents.

2d. Only one fifth or some specific portion of the land thus granted should be required to be conveyed to the liberated apprentice; the remainder to belong to the company as *profits*, to be sold by them to the colonists or whomsoever they please, under certain restrictions, to remunerate it for having cleared a portion of the land for the liberated apprentices, and erected him a hut, and furnished him with implements of industry, &c., &c., in addition to the expenses of his transportation to the colony and caring for him during his apprenticeship.

3d. Beyond all question, the value of the [illegible] of the colonist, during the three years of apprenticeship would quadruple his cost to the company in transporting him to the colony: and thus the company would not really be in a condition to repay its loans from the government of the United States, but to return to the capitalists their entire investment, before the expiration of the manumitted slave's term of apprenticeship! and at the same time be in a condition to add largely to the quantity of land and other gratuities extended to the liberated apprentice.

4th. This project, if applicable and successful in relation to twenty or thirty thousand colonists, would be equally applicable and far more successful when applied to hundreds of thousands.

5th. It would take from our shores our negro population as rapidly as emancipated, *without the cost of one dollar to our government,* and by simply the loan of a sum which it would cost to transport them to any distant colony.

6th. It would insure to the liberated negro the probationary education so necessary to enable him to enjoy freedom and become a useful citizen of a great empire.

7th. It would be immensely remunerative to the philanthropists who would embark in and, under a certain control from the government, direct its operations.

8th. It would be an inappreciable blessing to the United States, by *getting rid of the liberated slave without any future political questions connecting him with the country.* [Italics added.]

9th. It would be the greatest possible blessing that could be bestowed upon the freed negro, and accomplish his redemption, and conversion into a free man in the shortest conceivable time.

10th. It would save to Brazil her northern provinces, and in the course of a few years add a million of *free,* experienced, and orderly laborers to aid in developing her inexhaustible resources.

11th. It would, in process of time, furnish the markets of the world with a never-failing supply of cotton and sugar, the produce of free labor. . . .

And such is the project of negro colonization from the United States in Brazil, his education there at his own expense, and his becoming a free citizen of a great empire. The United States will be blessed by his *absence* and the riddance of a curse, which has well nigh destroyed her; Brazil will receive precisely the species of laborers and citizens calculated to develop her resources and make her one of the great nations of the earth; and the miserable, ignorant, and down-trodden slave, who is now a mere *chattel,* with body and soul alike uncared for, will have his shackles worked off, be liberated, educated for freedom, and have bestowed upon him the great boon of personal liberty. . . .

J. Watson Webb.

Hon. WILLIAM H. SEWARD. *Secretary of State.*

3.24. In a Debate on a Bill to End Slavery in the District of Columbia, Massachusetts Senator Henry Wilson Clashes with a Kentucky Senator Demanding Deportation of Newly Liberated Slaves (1862)

In the midst of war, a bill to free the slaves of the District of Columbia was taken up by Congress and, after complex discussions, was passed into law and signed by President Lincoln. Some 3,100 slaves were thus freed at a cost of nearly a million dollars, compensation to "owners" having been limited to $300.00 per slave. To protect the District's black population, the legislation provided that persons kidnapping or removing free persons from the District for purposes of sale or reenslavement would be subject to a maximum of twenty years in prison (see Mary Tremain, *Slavery in the District of Columbia,* p. 95; *Douglass Monthly,* May, 1862, p. 651).

On March 27, 1862, Senator Henry Wilson of Massachusetts, a self-educated cobbler as a child and later vice president under Grant, gave a powerful speech in favor of the legislation. Wilson, however, also took a strong stand against an amendment proposed by one Senator Davis of Kentucky intended to remove from the District, *and from the United States,* all persons freed under the provisions of the bill, on the grounds that whenever a government liberates a numerous body of slaves living among people of another race, a violent conflict will inevitably break out, leading either to exile or extermination of one race or the other.

The opinions expressed by Senator Davis (as disclosed by Senator Wilson) seem to place the Kentucky senator in the same category as Lincoln's minister to Brazil (see Doc. 3.23), or the members of the American Colonization Society (Docs. 3.4 through 3.6), who since 1816 had labored to remove free black Americans to Liberia or some other faraway destination. As the War between the States had made partial or total emancipation seem more likely than ever, this point of view had reemerged strongly, even the president of the United States revealing his colonization sentiments. The new situation, in fact, created a profound crisis in the minds of many people who in the past had encountered little difficulty in living among black men and women who *belonged to themselves or their white neighbors.* The prospect, however, of living among those same people—without bosses, masters or overseers to order them about—was somehow perilous, unacceptable, inappropriate, demeaning, and intolerable and cried out for a strong solution. The solution, as Senator Davis and others saw it, was to send them somewhere else.

The following excerpt from Senator Wilson's speech challenges the opinions of Senator Davis and others like him who believed that the two races could not and should not live together in freedom and equality, even in the United States of America.

SOURCE: "Speech of Hon. Henry Wilson, of Mass., In the Senate, On the Bill to Abolish Slavery in the District of Columbia, March 27, 1862" (Washington, D. C.: Scammel, 1862), pp. 6–8.

. . . This bill promises to strike the chains from the limbs of three thousand bondmen in the District of Columbia, to erase the word "slave" from their foreheads, to convert them from personal chattels into free men, to lift them from the degradation of personal servitude to the dignity and responsibilities of manhood, to place them in the ranks of free colored men, to perform with them the duties and bear with them the responsibilities of life. This bill, if it shall become law, will simply take three thousand men from humiliating and degrading servitude and add them to the twelve thousand free colored men of the District, to be absorbed in the mass of industrious and law-abiding population. The passage of this bill by the Congress of the United States will not, cannot, disturb for a moment the peace, the order, the security of society. Its passage will excite in the bosoms of the enfranchised not wrath nor hatred nor revenge, but love, joy, and gratitude. These enfranchised bondmen will be welcomed by the free colored population with bounding hearts, throbbing with gratitude to God for inspiring the nation with the justice and courage to strike the chains from the limbs of their neighbors, friends, relatives, brothers, and lifting from their own shoulders the burdens imposed upon them by the necessities, the passions, and the pride of slave-holding society.

This bill, to give liberty to the bondman, deals justly, aye, generously, by the master. The American people, whose moral sense has been outraged by slavery and the black codes enacted in the interests of slavery in the District of Columbia, whose fame has been soiled and dimmed by the deeds of cruelty perpetrated in their national Capital, would stand justified in the forum of nations if they should smite the fetter from the bondman, regardless of the desires or interests of the master. With generous magnanimity this bill tenders compensation to the master out of the earnings of the toiling freemen of America. In the present condition of the country the proposed compensation is full, ample, equitable.

But the Senator from Kentucky [Mr. DAVIS] raises his warning voice against the passage of this measure of justice and beneficence. He assumes to speak like one having authority. He is positive, dogmatic, emphatic, and prophetic. He repeatedly assures the Senate that he gave utterance to what he knew, that his warnings and predictions were infallible prophecies. The senator predicted in excited, if not angry tones, that the passage of this bill, giving freedom to three thousand bondmen, will bring into this District beggary and crime; that the "liberated negroes will become a sore, a burden, and a charge;" that "they will be criminals;" that "they will become paupers;" that they will be engaged in crimes and petty misdemeanors;" that "they will become a charge and a pest upon this society." The senator emphatically declared, "I know what I talk about!" "I speak from what I know." Assured, confident, defiant, the senator asserts that "a negro's idea of freedom is freedom from work;" that after they acquire their freedom they become "lazy," "indolent," "thriftless," "worthless," "inefficient," "vicious," "vagabonds."

The Senator from Kentucky, who speaks with so much assurance, may have the right to speak in these terms of emancipated slaves in Kentucky; but he has no authority so to speak of the twelve thousand free colored men of the District of Columbia. One sixth part of the population of this District are free persons of color. Under the weight of oppressive laws and a public opinion poisoned by slavery, they have by their industry, their obedience to law, their kindly charities to each other, established a character above such reproaches as the Senator from Kentucky applies to emancipated bondmen. As a class, the free colored people of this District are not worthless, vicious, thriftless, indolent vagabonds, criminals, paupers, nor are they a charge and a pest upon this society. The Senator from Kentucky, sir, has no right to apply to them these disparaging epithets. Do they not support themselves by their industry and thrift? Do they not support their own churches? Do they not support their own schools? Do they not also support schools for the education of white children, from which their own are excluded? Do they not care for their sick and their dying? Do they not bury their dead free of public charge? What right, then, has the Senator from Kentucky to come into this Chamber and attempt to deter us from executing this act of emancipation, by casting undeserved reproaches upon the free colored population of the District? Their condition this day demonstrates the utter absurdity of the doctrines and prophecies so oracularly announced by the Senator from Kentucky.

But the Senator from Kentucky, upon this simple proposition to emancipate in the national capital three thousand bondmen, with compensation to loyal masters, chooses to indulge in the vague talk about "aggressive and destructive schemes," "unconstitutional policy," the "horrors of the French Revolution," the "heroic struggle of the peasants of La Vendée," and the "deadly resistance" which the "whole white population of the slaveholding States, men, women, and children, would make to unconstitutional encroachments." Why, sir, does the Senator indulge in such allusions? Have not the American people the constitutional right to relieve themselves from the guilt and shame of upholding slavery in their national Capital? Would not the exercise of that right be sanctioned by justice, humanity, and religion? Does the Senator suppose that we, the representatives of American freemen, will cowardly shrink from the performance of the duties of the hour before these dogmatic avowals of what the men and women of the slaveholding States will do? Sir, I tell the Senator from Kentucky that the day has passed by in the Senate of the United States for intimidation, threat, or menace, from the champions of slavery.

I would remind the Senator from Kentucky that the people, whose representatives we are, now realize in the storms of battle that slavery is, and must ever be, the relentless and unappeasable enemy of free institutions in America, of the unity and perpetuity of the Republic. Slavery—perverting the reason, blinding the conscience, extinguishing the patriotism of vast masses of its supporters—plunged the nation into the fire and blood of the rebellion. The loyal people of America have seen hundreds of thousands of brave men abandon their peaceful avocations, leave their quiet homes and their loved ones, and follow the flag of their country to the field, to do a soldier's duties, and fill, if need be, soldiers' graves, in defence of their periled country; they have seen them fall on fields of bloody strife beneath the folds of the national flag; they have seen them suffering, tortured by wounds or disease, in camps and hospitals; they have seen them returning home maimed by shot or shell, or bowed with disease; they have looked with sorrowful hearts upon their passing coffins, and gazed sadly upon their graves among their kindred or in the land of the stranger; and they know—yes, sir, they know—that slavery has caused all this blood, disease, agony, and death. Realizing all this—aye, sir, knowing all this, they are in no temper to listen to the threats or menaces of apologists, or defenders of the wicked and guilty criminal that now stands with uplifted hand to strike a death blow to the national life. While the brave and loyal men of the Republic are facing its shots and shells on bloody fields, their representatives will hardly quail before the frowns and menaces of its champions in these Chambers.

The Senator from Kentucky proposes by his amendment to remove from the District, from the United States, the persons emancipated under the provisions of this bill. He tells us that "whenever any power, constitutional or unconstitutional, assumes the responsibility of liberating slaves where slaves are numerous, they establish, as inexorably as fate, a conflict between the races that will result in the exile or extermination of the one race or the other." *"I know it!"* exclaims the Senator. How does the Senator know it? In what age and in what country has the emancipation of one race resulted in the extermination of the one race or the other? In what chapter of the history of the world is such exterminating warfare recorded? Nearly a quarter of a century ago England struck the chains from eight hundred thousand of her West India bondmen. There has been no conflict there between the races. Other European nations have emancipated their colonial bondmen. No wars of races have grown out of those deeds of emancipation. One sixth part of the population of the District of Columbia are free colored persons—emancipated slaves or the children of emancipated slaves. The existence of this numerous class of liberated slaves has not here established, "as inexorably as fate," a conflict between the races. More than one sixth of the population of Delaware are free colored persons—emancipated slaves, or the descendants of emancipated slaves. The existence in Delaware of this large class of emancipated slaves has not produced a war of races. The people of Delaware have never sought to hunt them like beasts and exterminate them. One eighth of the population of Maryland are free men of African descent. No exterminating warfare of races rages on the soil of Maryland. No, sir; no! Emancipation does not inevitably lead to an exterminating war of races. In our country the enfranchizement of the bondman has tended to elevate both races, and has been productive of peace, order, and public security. The doctrines so confidently proclaimed by the Senator from Kentucky have no basis whatever to rest upon, either in reason or history. The Senate, I am sure, will not close the chapters of history which record the enfranchizement of bondmen, nor will they ignore the results of their own experience and observation, under the influence of the positive, impassioned, and emphatic assertions of the Senator from Kentucky.

CELEBRATION OF THE ABOLITION OF SLAVERY IN THE DISTRICT OF COLUMBIA BY THE COLORED PEOPLE, IN WASHINGTON, April 19, 1866.—[Sketched by F. Dielman.]

18. "Celebration of the Abolition of Slavery in the District of Columbia by the Colored People." *Harper's Weekly,* May 12, 1866. Courtesy of the Special Collections Department, University of Pittsburgh Library System.

This bill, Mr. President, for the release of persons held to service or labor in the District of Columbia, and the compensation of loyal masters from the Treasury of the United States, was prepared after much reflection and some consultation with others. The committees on the District of Columbia in both houses, to whom it was referred, have agreed to it, with a few amendments calculated to carry out more completely its original purposes and provisions. I trust that the bill, as it now stands, after the adoption of the amendments proposed by the Senator from Maine [Mr. MORRILL] will speedily pass, without any material modifications. If it shall become the law of the land, it will blot out slavery forever from the national Capital, transform three thousand personal chattels into freemen, obliterate oppressive, odious, and hateful laws and ordinances, which press with merciless force upon persons, bond or free, of African descent, and relieve the nation from the responsibilities now pressing upon it. An act of beneficence like this will be hailed and applauded by the nations, sanctified by justice, humanity, and religion, by the approving voice of conscience, and by the blessing of Him who bids us "break every yoke, undo the heavy burden, and let the oppressed go free."

3.25. The Execution of Amy Spain (1865)

Many acts of unjustifiable violence and abuse are revealed in this book. A particularly shocking example is depicted in the present document, which seems to imply a generalized unwillingness on the part of many white Americans, particularly in times of strife, to respect the hopes and aspirations of their black neighbors—or even to tolerate their optimistic responses to events that seemed to foretell for them happier, safer, and more satisfying lives. It implies that white Southerners were not ready to do justice to them, much less to accept them as fellow citizens (as Chief Justice Taney argued in 1857), despite the Thirteenth, Fourteenth, and Fifteenth Amendments, which ended legalized slavery and "guaranteed" their right to vote.

The incident described here by a northern correspondent involved a slave woman named Amy Spain, a resident of a small South Carolina town. Having spent her life in slavery, she impulsively expressed her pleasure and delight upon seeing Yankee soldiers enter the town, only to be hanged in the town square as an example to other blacks upon the return of local whites. This ugly spectacle that allegedly involved most white citizens of the town might well be described as an act of public vengeance.

SOURCE: *Harper's Weekly,* September 30, 1865.

AMY SPAIN.

One of the martyrs of the cause which gave freedom to her race was that of a colored woman named AMY SPAIN, who was a resident of the town of Darlington, situated in a rich cotton-growing district of South Carolina. At the time a portion of the Union army occupied the town of Darlington she expressed her satisfaction by clasping her hands and exclaiming, "Bless the Lord the Yankees have come!" She could not restrain her emotions. The long night of darkness which had bound her in slavery was about to break away. It was impossible to repress the exuberance of her feelings; and although powerless to aid the advancing deliverers of her caste, or to injure her oppressors, the simple expression of satisfaction at the event sealed her doom. AMY SPAIN died in the cause of freedom. A section of SHERMAN'S cavalry occupied the town, and without doing any damage passed through. Not an insult nor an unkind word was said to any of the women of that town. The men had, with guilty consciences, fled; but on their return, with their traditional chivalry, they seized upon poor AMY, and ignominiously hung her to a sycamore-tree standing in front of the court-house, underneath which stood the block from which was monthly

VIEW OF DARLINGTON COURT-HOUSE AND THE SYCAMORE-TREE WHERE AMY SPAIN, THE NEGRO SLAVE, WAS HUNG BY THE CITIZENS OF DARLINGTON, SOUTH CAROLINA.—[SKETCHED BY N. N. EDWARDS.]

19. "View of Darlington Courthouse and the Sycamore Tree Where Amy Spain, the Negro Slave, Was Hung by the Citizens of Darlington, South Carolina." *Harper's Weekly,* September 30, 1865. Courtesy of the Special Collections Department, University of Pittsburgh Library System.

exhibited the slave chattels that were struck down by the auctioneer's hammer to the highest bidder.

AMY SPAIN heroically heard her sentence, and from her prison bars declared she was prepared to die. She defied her persecutors; and as she ascended the scaffold declared she was going to a place where she would receive a crown of glory. She was rudely interrupted by an oath from one of her executioners. To the eternal disgrace of Darlington her execution was acquiesced in and witnessed by most of the citizens of the town. AMY was launched into eternity and the "chivalric Southern gentlemen" of Darlington had fully established their bravery by making war upon a defenseless woman. She sleeps quietly, with others of her race, near the beautiful village. No memorials mark her grave, but after-ages will remember this martyr of liberty. Her persecutors will pass away and be forgotten, but AMY SPAIN's name is now hallowed among the Africans, who, emancipated and free, dare, with the starry folds of the flag of the free floating over them, speak her name with holy reverence.

3.26. "What Shall Be Done with the Negro?" Frederick Douglass
Speaks Out against Old Prejudices and Deceptive Solutions and
Calls Instead for Justice

As we have seen, the prospect of a rapid end to slavery in the United States
inspired proposals for solving the "problem" of the emancipated blacks.
Among those who sought such a solution was Abraham Lincoln who, having invited a committee of prominent "negroes" to the White House, informed the members of that committee, including Frederick Douglass,
that Congress had appropriated money to assist the colonization in some
country, "of the people, or a portion of them, of African descent." He had
long been inclined, Lincoln said, to favor this cause, since the physical differences between the races were a disadvantage to both, and because there
was "an unwillingness on the part of our people, harsh as it may be, for you
free-colored people to remain with us." Lincoln then spoke positively of
Liberia and Central America as potential destinations for the black people
of the United States, the latter being particularly attractive because of its location on "a great line of travel" and its "great material resources and advantages, and especially because of the similarity of climate of your native
land, thus being suited to your physical condition." (Douglass wrote in the
September 1862 edition of *Douglass' Monthly* that he had given only the
substance of Lincoln's remarks on colonization.)

Lincoln's White House meeting with "the committee of colored men"
took place on August 14, 1862. Seven months earlier (in January 1862) Douglass had already written and published the following article offering *his*
thoughts on "What Shall Be Done with the Slaves if Emancipated?" His
opinions are, of course, strikingly different from those of Abraham Lincoln.

SOURCE: Frederick Douglass, *Douglass Monthly,* January 1862, pp. 579–80.

"What Shall Be Done with the Slaves if Emancipated?"

It is curious to observe, at this juncture, when the existence of slavery is
threatened by an aroused nation, when national necessity is combining
with an enlightened sense of justice to put away the huge abomination forever, that the enemies of human liberty are resorting to all the old and ten
thousand times refuted objections to emancipation with which they con-
fronted the abolition movement twenty-five years ago. Like the one stated
above, these pro-slavery objections have their power mainly in the slavery-
engendered prejudice, which everywhere pervades the country. Like all
other great transgressions of the law of eternal rectitude, slavery thus pro-

duces an element in the popular and depraved moral sentiment favorable to its own existence. These objections are often urged with a show of sincere solicitude for the welfare of the slaves themselves. It is said, what will you do with them? they can't take care of themselves; they would all come to the North; they would not work; they would become a burden upon the State, and a blot upon society; they'd cut their masters' throats; they would cheapen labor, and crowd out the poor white laborer from employment; their former masters would not employ them, and they would necessarily become vagrants, paupers and criminals, overrunning all our alms houses, jails and prisons. The laboring classes among the whites would come in bitter conflict with them in all the avenues of labor, and regarding them as occupying places and filling positions which should be occupied and filled by white men; a fierce war of races would be the inevitable consequence, and the black race would, of course (being the weaker) be exterminated. In view of this frightful, though happily somewhat contradictory picture, the question is asked, and pressed with a great deal of earnestness at this momentous crisis of our nation's history. What shall be done with the four million slaves if they are emancipated?

This question has been answered, and can be answered in many ways. Primarily, it is a question less for man than for God—less for human intellect than for the laws of nature to solve. It assumes that nature has erred; that the law of liberty is a mistake; that freedom, though a natural want of the human soul, can only be enjoyed at the expense of human welfare, and that men are better off in slavery than they would or could be in freedom; that slavery is the natural order of human relations, and that liberty is an experiment. What shall be done with them?

Our answer is, do nothing with them; mind your business, and let them mind theirs. Your *doing* with them is their greatest misfortune. They have been undone by your doings, and all they now ask, and really have need of at your hands, is just to let them alone. They suffer by every interference, and succeed best by being let alone. The negro should have been let alone in Africa—let alone when the pirates and robbers offered him for sale in our Christian slave markets—(more cruel and inhuman than the Mohammedan slave markets)—let alone by courts, judges, politicians, legislators and slave-drivers—let alone altogether, and assured that they were thus to be let alone forever, and that they must now make their own way in the world, just the same as any and every other variety of the human family. As colored men, we only ask to be allowed to *do* with ourselves, subject only to the same great laws for the welfare of human society which apply to other men, Jews, Gentiles, Barbarian, Scythian. Let us stand upon our own legs, work with our own hands, and eat bread in the sweat of our own brows. When you, our white fellow-countrymen, have attempted to do anything for us, it has generally been to deprive us of some right, power or privilege which you yourselves would die before you would submit to have taken from you. When the planters of the West Indies used to attempt to puzzle the pure-minded WILBERFORCE with the question, How shall we get rid of slavery? his simple answer was, "quit stealing." In like manner, we answer those who are perpetually puzzling their brains with questions as to what shall be done with the negro, "let him alone and mind your own business." If you see him plowing in the open field, leveling the forest, at work with a spade, a rake, a hoe, a pick-axe, or a bill—let him alone; he has a right to work. If you see him on his way to school, with spelling books, geography, and arithmetic in his hands—let him alone. Don't shut the door in his face, nor bolt your gates against him; he has a right to learn—let him alone. Don't pass laws to degrade him. If he has a ballot in his hand, and is on his way to the ballot-box to deposit his vote for the man who he thinks will most justly and wisely administer the Government which has the power of life and death over him, as well as others—let him ALONE; his right of choice as much deserves respect and protection as your own. If you see him on his way to the church, exercising religious liberty in accordance with this or that re-ligious persuasion—let him alone—Don't meddle with him, nor trouble yourselves with any questions as to what shall be done with him.

The great majority of human duties are of this negative character. If men were born in need of crutches, instead of having legs, the fact would be otherwise. We should then be in need of help, and would require outside aid; but according to the wiser and better arrangement of nature, our duty is done better by not hindering than by helping our fellow-men; or, in other words, the best way to help them is just to let them help themselves.

We would not for one moment check the outgrowth of any benevolent concern for the future welfare of the colored race in America or elsewhere; but in the name of reason and religion, we earnestly plead for justice before all else. Benevolence with justice is harmonious and beautiful; but benevo-lence without justice is a mockery. Let the American people, who have thus far only kept the colored race staggering between partial philanthropy and cruel force, be induced to try what virtue there is in justice. First pure, then peaceable—first just, then generous.—The sum of the black man's misfor-tune and calamities are just here: He is everywhere treated as an exception to all the general rules which should operate in the relations of other men. He is literally scourged beyond the beneficent range of truth and justice.— With all the purifying and liberalizing power of the Christian religion, teaching, as it does, meekness, gentleness, brotherly kindness, those who profess it have not yet even approached the position of treating the black man as an equal man and a brother. The few who have thus far risen to this requirement, both of reason and religion, are stigmatized as fanatics and enthusiasts.

What shall be done with the negro if emancipated? Deal justly with him. He is a human being, capable of judging between good and evil, right and wrong, liberty and slavery, and is as much a subject of law as any other man; therefore, deal justly with him. He is like other men, sensible of the motives of reward and punishment. Give him wages for his work, and let hunger pinch him if he doesn't work. He knows the difference between fullness and famine, plenty and scarcity. "But will he work?" Why should he not? He is used to it, and is not afraid of it. His hands are already hardened by toil, and he has no dreams of ever getting a living by any other means than by hard work. But would you turn them all loose? Certainly! We are no better than our Creator. He has turned them loose, and why should not we?

But would you let them all stay here? Why not? What better is *here* than *there?* Will they occupy more room as freemen than as slaves? Is the presence of a black freeman less agreeable than that of a black slave? Is an object of your injustice and cruelty a more ungrateful sight than of your justice and benevolence? You have borne the one more than two hundred years—can't you bear the other long enough to try the experiment? "But would it be safe?" No good reason can be given why it should not be. There is much more reason for apprehension from slavery than from freedom. Slavery provokes and justifies incendiarism, murder, robbery, assassination, and all manner of violence.—But why not let them go off by themselves? That is a matter we would leave exclusively to themselves. Besides, when you, the American people, shall once do justice to the enslaved colored people, you will not want to get rid of them. Take away the motive which slavery supplies for getting rid of the free black people of the South, and there is not a single State, from Maryland to Texas, which would desire to be rid of its black people. Even with the obvious disadvantage to slavery, which such contact is, there is scarcely a slave State which could be carried for the unqualified expulsion of the free colored people. Efforts at such expulsion have been made in Maryland, Virginia and South Carolina, and all have failed, just because the black man as a freeman is a useful member of society. To drive him away, and thus deprive the South of his labor, would be as absurd and monstrous as for a man to cut off his right arm, the better to enable himself to work.

In the Hands of Strangers

There is one cheering aspect of this revival of the old and thread-bare objections to emancipation—it implies at least the presence of danger to the slave system. When slavery was assailed twenty-five years ago, the whole land took the alarm, and every species of argument and subterfuge was resorted to by the defenders of slavery. The mental activity was amazing; all sorts of excuses, political, economical, social, ethical, theological and ethnological, were coined into barricades against the advancing march of anti-slavery sentiment. The same activity now shows itself, but has added nothing new to the argument for slavery or against emancipation.—When the accursed slave system shall once be abolished, and the negro, long cast out from the human family, and governed like a beast of burden, shall be gathered under the divine government of justice, liberty and humanity, men will be ashamed to remember that they were ever deluded by the flimsy nonsense which they have allowed themselves to urge against the freedom of the long enslaved millions of our land. That day is not far off.

O hasten it in mercy, gracious Heaven!

INDEX

abolitionism, in Pennsylvania, xiv, 19–21

Adams, John Quincy, 307, 309–10, 360, 369

Adams, Reverend Nehemiah (of Boston), 212–23

advertisements for slaves (U.S.), 37, 112–13, 116–19, 130, 153, 247–49, 251–59

African Repository and Colonial Journal, 337

African slave trade, xiii–xiv, 5–19, 22–27; by Africans, 13, 15–16, 27–29, 34, 41–46; attempted legalization of in nineteenth-century America, xv, 91–92, 314; condoned by members of U.S. government, 81–92; diseases and mortality at sea, 12, 18–19, 22, 37, 39, 49–50, 67–68, 71–72, 78–79; food aboard ships, 47–48, 102; harsh conditions at sea, 16–18, 26–27, 29, 46–50, 78–80; rebellions aboard slave ships, xiv, 18, 29, 30–34, 50, 101–4; trading methods, 14–16, 22–26; in the United States, xiii, xiv, 69, 70, 73, 325–28

Allen, Richard, 328, 333–35, 336

American Colonization Society, 328–47, 381, 382

asientos, 2–3

Atchison, David R., 404

auctions of slaves (U.S.), 115, 118, 130, 133, 164–73, 185, 194–95, 203–6, 212–20, 250–51, 256; as told by former slaves, 260, 263, 267, 268, 270–71, 284–301

Austin, Stephen F., 310

Azurara, Gomes Eannes de, 5–11

Ball, Charles, 131–40

Barbados, 13

Bay Islands (Honduras), 72–73

Benton, Thomas Hart, 193

Blassingame, John W., 132

Brazil: alleged slaveholder ownership of the slave womb and resulting children, 211; illegal American involvement in, 98–101; slavery in, xiv, 1–2, 71–72, 92–104, 111, 196

breeding of slaves, xiv, 69, 70, 78, 85, 121, 175, 206–8, 223, 224, 228; as told by former slaves, 231–45, 262, 265, 267, 271, 291

British Royal African Company, 12, 14–15

Brodnax of Dinwiddie, W. H., 347

Brooks, Preston, 395

Brown, John, slave narrative by, 178–85

Brown, John, leader of 1859 raid on Harper's Ferry, 314

Butler, General Benjamin F., 484–86, Fig. 16

Butler, Pierce M., 284–301

Buxton, Sir Thomas Fowell, 87, 88

Caldwell, Elias B., 328, 332

Calhoun, John C., 355, 370

Campbell, John, 391–95

Chambers, William, 164–73, 196–99

Chamerovzow, L. A., 178–85

Charleston, South Carolina, 57–59

Cherokees, forced migration of, 361–65

Child, David Lee, 121–31

Child, Lydia Maria, 473–83

Civil War, beginnings of, 145, 314–15, 484–94

Clarkson, Thomas, 56

Clay, Henry, 328, 336; criticized, 330–32